The Bible in Spain

THE

BIBLE IN SPAIN;

OR, THE

JOURNEYS, ADVENTURES, AND IMPRISONMENTS OF AN
ENGLISHMAN,

IN

AN ATTEMPT TO CIRCULATE THE SCRIPTURES

IN

THE PENINSULA.

BY GEORGE BORROW,

AUTHOR OF "THE GIPSIES OF SPAIN."

TWELFTH EDITION.

Philadelphia.
JAMES M. CAMPBELL, 98 CHESTNUT STREET,
SAXTON & MILES, 205 BROADWAY, NEW YORK.
STEREOTYPED BY L. JOHNSON & CO.

———

1845.

CONTENTS.

3

CONTENTS.

CONTENTS.

5

A 2

CONTENTS.

CONTENTS.

PREFACE.

It is very seldom that the preface of a work is read; indeed, of late years, most books have been sent into the world without any. I deem it, however, advisable to write a preface, and to this I humbly call the attention of the courteous reader, as its perusal will not a little tend to the proper understanding and appreciation of these volumes.

The work now offered to the public, and which is styled "The Bible in Spain," consists of a narrative of what occurred to me during a residence in that country, to which I was sent by the Bible Society, as its agent, for the purpose of printing and circulating the Scriptures. It comprehends, however, certain journeys and adventures in Portugal, and leaves me at last in "the land of the Corahai," to which region, after having undergone considerable buffeting in Spain, I found it expedient to retire for a season.

It is very probable that, had I visited Spain from mere curiosity, or with a view of passing a year or two agreeably, I should never have attempted to give any detailed account of my proceedings, or of what I heard and saw. I am no tourist, no writer of books of travels; but I went there on a somewhat remarkable errand, which necessarily led me into strange situations and positions, involved me in difficulties and perplexities, and brought me into contact with people of all descriptions and grades; so that, upon the whole, I flatter myself that a narrative of such a pilgrimage may not be wholly uninteresting to the public, more especially as the subject is not trite; for though various books have been published about Spain, I believe that the present is the only one in existence which treats of missionary labour in that country.

Many things, it is true, will be found in the following volumes which have little connection with religion or religious enterprise; I offer, however, no apology for introducing them. I was, as I may say, from first to last adrift in Spain, the land of old renown, the land of wonder and mystery, with better opportunities of becoming acquainted with its strange secrets and peculiarities than perhaps ever yet were afforded to any individual, certainly to a foreigner; and if in many instances I have introduced scenes and characters perhaps unprecedented in a work of this description, I have only to observe, that, during my sojourn in Spain, I was so unavoidably mixed up with such, that I could scarcely have given a faithful narrative of what befell me had I not brought them forward in the manner which I have done.

It is worthy of remark that, called suddenly and unexpectedly "to undertake the adventure of Spain," I was not altogether unprepared for such an enterprise. In the day-dreams of my boyhood, Spain always bore a considerable share, and I took a particular interest in her, without any presentiment that I should at a future time be called upon to take a part, however humble, in her strange dramas; which interest, at a very early period, led me to acquire her noble language, and to make myself acquainted with her literature, (scarcely worthy of the language,) her history, and traditions; so that when I entered Spain for the first time, I felt more at home than I should otherwise have done.

In Spain I passed five years, which, if not the most eventful, were, I have no hesitation in saying, the most happy years of my existence. Of Spain, at the present time, now that the day-dream has vanished, never, alas! to return, I entertain the warmest admiration: she is the most magnificent country in the world, probably the most fertile, and certainly with the finest climate. Whether her children are worthy of their mother, is another question, which I shall not attempt to answer; but content myself with observing, that, amongst much that is lamentable and reprehensible, I have found much that is noble and to be admired; much stern, heroic virtue; much savage and horrible crime; of low, vulgar vice very little, at least amongst the great body of the Spanish nation, with which my mission lay; for it will be as well here to observe, that I advance no claim to an intimate acquaintance with the Spanish nobility, from whom I kept as remote as circum-

9

stances would permit me; *en revanche*, however, I have had the honour to live on familiar terms with the peasants, shepherds, and muleteers of Spain, whose bread and bacalao I have eaten; who always treated me with kindness and courtesy, and to whom I have not unfrequently been indebted for shelter and protection.

"The generous bearing of Francisco Gonzales, and the high deeds of Ruy Diaz the Cid, are still sung amongst the fastnesses of the Sierra Morena."[*]

I believe that no stronger argument can be brought forward in proof of the natural vigour and resources of Spain, and the sterling character of her population, than the fact that, at the present day, she is still a powerful and unexhausted country, and her children still, to a certain extent, a high-minded and great people. Yes, notwithstanding the misrule of the brutal and sensual Austrian, the doting Bourbon, and, above all, the spiritual tyranny of the court of Rome, Spain can still maintain her own, fight her own combat, and Spaniards are not yet fanatic slaves and crouching beggars. This is saying much, very much; she has undergone far more than Naples had ever to bear, and yet the fate of Naples has not been hers. There is still valour in Asturia; generosity in Arragon; probity in Old Castile; and the peasant women of La Mancha can still afford to place a silver fork and a snowy napkin beside the plate of their guest. Yes, in spite of Austrian, Bourbon, and Rome, there is still a wide gulf between Spain and Naples.

Strange as it may sound, Spain is not a fanatic country. I know something about her, and declare that she is not, nor has ever been: Spain never changes. It is true that, for nearly two centuries, she was the she-butcher, *La Verduga*, of malignant Rome; the chosen instrument for carrying into effect the atrocious projects of that power; yet fanaticism was not the spring which impelled her to the work of butchery; another feeling, in her the predominant one, was worked upon—her fatal pride. It was by humouring her pride that she was induced to waste her precious blood and treasure in the Low Country wars, to launch the Armada, and to many other equally insane actions. Love of Rome had ever slight influence over her policy; but flattered by the title of Gonfaloniera of the Vicar of Jesus, and eager to prove herself not unworthy of the same, she shut her eyes and rushed upon her own destruction with the cry of "Charge, Spain!"

[*] "Om Frands Gonzales, og Rodrik Cid, End siunges i Sierra Murene!" Krönike Rüm. By Severin Grundtvig. Copenhagen, 1829.

But the arms of Spain became powerless abroad, and she retired within herself. She ceased to be the tool of the vengeance and cruelty of Rome. She was not cast aside, however. No! though she could no longer wield the sword with success against the Lutherans, she might still be turned to some account. She had still gold and silver, and she was still the land of the vine and olive. Ceasing to be the butcher, she became the banker of Rome; and the poor Spaniards, who always esteem it a privilege to pay another person's reckoning, were for a long time happy in being permitted to minister to the grasping cupidity of Rome, who, during the last century, probably extracted from Spain more treasure than from all the rest of Christendom.

But wars came into the land. Napoleon and his fierce Franks invaded Spain; plunder and devastation ensued, the effects of which will probably be felt for ages. Spain could no longer pay pence to Peter so freely as of yore, and from that period she became contemptible in the eyes of Rome, who has no respect for a nation, save so far as it can minister to her cruelty or avarice. The Spaniard was still willing to pay, as far as his means would allow; but he was soon given to understand that he was a degraded being,—a barbarian; nay, a beggar. Now, you may draw the last cuarto from a Spaniard provided you will concede to him the title of cavalier and rich man, for the old leaven still works as powerfully as in the time of the first Philip; but you must never hint that he is poor, or that his blood is inferior to your own. And the old peasant, on being informed in what slight estimation he was held, replied, "If I am a beast, a barbarian, and a beggar withal, I am sorry for it; but as there is no remedy, I shall spend these four bushels of barley, which I had reserved to alleviate the misery of the holy father, in procuring bull spectacles, and other convenient diversions, for the queen my wife, and the young princes my children. Beggar! carajo! The water of my village is better than the wine of Rome."

I see that in a late pastoral letter directed to the Spaniards, the father of Rome complains bitterly of the treatment which he has received in Spain at the hands of naughty men. "My cathedrals are let down," he says, "my priests are insulted, and the revenues of my bishops are curtailed." He consoles himself, however, with the idea that this is the effect of the malice of a few, and that the generality of the nation love him, especially the peasantry, the innocent peasantry, who shed tears when they think of the sufferings of their pope and their religion. Undeceive yourself, Batuschca, undeceive yourself! Spain was ready to fight for you so long as she could increase her own glory by doing so; but she took no pleasure in losing battle after battle on your account. She had no objection to pay money into your coffers in the shape of alms, expecting, however, that the same would be received with the gratitude and humility which become those who accept charity. Finding, however, that you were neither humble nor grateful; suspecting, moreover, that you held Austria in higher esteem than herself, even as a banker, she shrugged up her shoulders, and uttered a sentence somewhat similar to that which I have already put into the mouth of one of her children, "These four bushels of barley," &c.

It is truly surprising what little interest the great body of the Spanish nation took in the late struggle, and yet it has been called, by some who ought to know better, a war of religion and principle. It was generally supposed that Biscay was the stronghold of Carlism, and that the inhabitants were fanatically attached to their religion, which they apprehended was in danger. The truth is, that the Basques cared nothing for Carlos or Rome, but merely took up arms to defend certain rights and privileges of their own. For the dwarfish brother of Ferdinand they always exhibited supreme contempt, which his character, a compound of imbecility, cowardice, and cruelty, well merited. If they made use of his name, it was merely as a *cri de guerre*. Much the same may be said with respect to his Spanish partisans, at least those who appeared in the field for him. These, however, were of a widely different character from the Basques, who were brave soldiers and honest men. The Spanish armies of Don Carlos were composed entirely of thieves and assassins, chiefly Valencians and Manchegans, who, marshalled under two cut-throats, Cabrera and Palillos, took advantage of the distracted state of the country to plunder and massacre the honest part of the community. With respect to the Queen Regent Christina, of whom the less said the better, the reins of government fell into her hands on the decease of her husband, and with them the command of the soldiery. The respectable part of the Spanish nation, and more especially the honourable and toilworn peasantry, loathed and execrated both factions. Oft when I was sharing at nightfall the frugal fare of the villager of Old or New Castile, on hearing the distant shot of the Christino soldier or Carlist bandit, he would invoke curses on the heads of the two pretenders, not forgetting the holy father, and the goddess of Rome, Maria Santissima. Then, with the tiger energy of the Spaniard when roused, he would start up and exclaim: "Vamos, Don Jorge, to the plain, to the plain! I wish to enlist with you, and to learn the law of the English. To the plain, therefore, to the plain to-morrow, to circulate the gospel of Ingalaterra."

Amongst the peasantry of Spain I found my sturdiest supporters; and yet the holy father supposes that the Spanish labourers are friends and lovers of his. Undeceive yourself, Batuschca!

But to return to the present work: it is devoted to an account of what befell me in Spain whilst engaged in distributing the Scripture. With respect to my poor labours, I wish here to observe, that I accomplished but very little, and that I lay claim to no brilliant successes and triumphs; indeed, I was sent into Spain more to explore the country, and to ascertain how far the minds of the people were prepared to receive the truths of Christianity, than for any other object; I obtained, however, through the assistance of kind friends, permission from the Spanish government to print an edition of the sacred volume at Madrid, which I subsequently circulated in that capital and in the provinces.

During my sojourn in Spain, there were others who wrought good service in the gospel cause, and of whose efforts it were unjust to be silent in a work of this description. Base is the heart which would refuse merit its meed, and, however insignificant may be the value of any eulogium which can flow from a pen like mine, I cannot refrain from mentioning with respect and esteem a few names connected with gospel enterprise. A zealous Irish gentleman, of the name of Graydon, exerted himself with indefatigable diligence in diffusing the light of Scripture in the province of Catalonia, and along the southern shores of Spain; whilst two missionaries from Gibraltar, Messrs. Rule and Lyon, during one entire year, preached evangelic truth in a church at Cadiz. So much success attended the efforts of these two last brave disciples of the immortal Wesley, that there is every reason for supposing that, had they not been silenced and eventually banished from the country by the pseudo-liberal faction of the Moderados, not only Cadiz, but the greater part of Andalusia, would by this time have confessed the pure doctrines of the gospel, and have discarded forever the last relics of popish superstition.

More immediately connected with the Bible Society and myself, I am most happy to take this opportunity of speaking of Luis de Usoz y Rio, the scion of an ancient and honourable family of Old Castile, my coadjutor whilst editing the Spanish New Testament at Madrid. Throughout my residence in Spain, I experienced every mark of friendship from this gentleman, who, during the periods of my absence in the provinces, and my numerous and long journeys, cheerfully supplied my place at Madrid, and exerted himself to the utmost in forwarding the views of the Bible Society, influenced by no other motive than a hope that its efforts would eventually contribute to the peace, happiness, and civilization of his native land.*

In conclusion, I beg leave to state that I am fully aware of the various faults and in-

* In my account of the Spanish Gipsies, having to speak of Carlos the Third, I was indebted to Luis de Usoz for some curious facts, probably only known to himself, relative to that monarch. (See *Zincali*, p. 209–10.) Also for some interesting notices of the communeros, of which I availed myself when speaking of Maria Padilla. (*Zincali*, pp. 95–102.) Perhaps no person living is more competent to elucidate obscure portions of Spanish history than this gentleman.

accuracies of the present work. It is founded on certain journals which I kept during my stay in Spain, and numerous letters written to my friends in England, which they had subsequently the kindness to restore: the greater part, however, consisting of descriptions of scenery, sketches of character, &c., has been supplied from memory. In various instances I have omitted the names of places, which I have either forgotten, or of whose orthography I am uncertain. The work, as it at present exists, was written in a solitary hamlet in a remote part of England, where I had neither books to consult nor friends of whose opinion or advice I could occasionally avail myself, and under all the disadvantages which arise from enfeebled health; I have, however, on a recent occasion, experienced too much of the lenity and generosity of the public, both of Britain and America, to shrink from again exposing myself to its gaze, and trust that, if in the present volume it find but little to admire, it will give me credit for good spirit, and for setting down naught in malice.

November 26, 1842.

THE BIBLE IN SPAIN.

CHAPTER I.

Man overboard—The Tagus—Foreign Languages—Gesticulation—Streets of Lisbon—The Aqueduct—Bible tolerated in Portugal—Cintra—Don Sebastian—John De Castro—Conversation with a Priest—Colhares—Mafra—Its Palace—The Schoolmaster—The Portuguese—Their Ignorance of Scripture—Rural Priesthood—The Alemtejo.

On the morning of the 10th of November, 1835, I found myself off the coast of Galicia, whose lofty mountains, gilded by the rising sun, presented a magnificent appearance. I was bound for Lisbon; we passed Cape Finisterre, and standing farther out to sea, speedily lost sight of land. On the morning of the 11th the sea was very rough, and a remarkable circumstance occurred. I was on the forecastle, discoursing with two of the sailors: one of them, who had but just left his hammock, said, "I have had a strange dream, which I do not much like, for," continued he, pointing up to the mast, "I dreamt that I fell into the sea from the cross-trees." He was heard to say this by several of the crew besides myself. A moment after, the captain of the vessel perceiving that the squall was increasing, ordered the topsails to be taken in, whereupon this man with several others instantly ran aloft; the yard was in the act of being hauled down, when a sudden gust of wind whirled it round with violence, and a man was struck down from the cross-trees into the sea, which was working like yeast below. In a few moments he emerged; I saw his head on the crest of a billow, and instantly recognised in the unfortunate man the sailor who a few moments before had related his dream. I shall never forget the look of agony he cast whilst the steamer hurried past him. The alarm was given, and every thing was in confusion; it was two minutes at least before the vessel was stopped, by which time the man was a considerable way astern; I still, however, kept my eye upon him, and could see that he was struggling gallantly with the waves. A boat was at length lowered, but the rudder was unfortunately not at hand, and only two oars could be procured, with which the men could make but little progress in so rough a sea. They did their best, however, and had arrived within ten yards of the man, who still struggled for his life, when I lost sight of him, and the men on their return said that they saw him below the water, at glimpses, sinking deeper and deeper, his arms stretched out and his body apparently stiff, but that they found it impossible to save him; presently after, the sea, as if satisfied with the prey which it had acquired, became comparatively calm. The poor fellow who perished in this singular manner was a fine young man of twenty-seven, the only son of a widowed mother; he was the best sailor on board, and was beloved by all who were acquainted with him. This event occurred on the 11th of November, 1835; the vessel was the London Merchant steam ship. Truly wonderful are the ways of Providence!

That same night we entered the Tagus, and dropped anchor before the old tower of Belem; early the next morning we weighed, and, proceeding onward about a league, we again anchored at a short distance from the Caisdrea, or principal quay of Lisbon. Here we lay for some hours beside the enormous black hulk of the Reyna Nao, a man-of-war, which in old times so captivated the eye of Nelson, that he would fain have procured it for his native country. She was, long subsequently, the admiral's ship of the Miguelite squadron, and had been captured by the gallant Napier about three years previous to the time of which I am speaking.

The Reyna Nao is said to have caused him more trouble than all the other vessels of the enemy: and some assert that, had the others defended themselves with half the fury which the old vixen queen displayed, the result of the battle which decided the fate of Portugal would have been widely different.

I found disembarkation at Lisbon to be a matter of considerable vexation; the custom-house officers were exceedingly uncivil, and examined every article of my little baggage with most provoking minuteness.

My first impression on landing in the Peninsula was by no means a favourable one; and I had scarcely pressed the soil one hour before I heartily wished myself back in Russia, a country which I had quitted about one month previous, and where I had left cherished friends and warm affections.

After having submitted to much ill usage and robbery at the custom-house, I proceeded in quest of a lodging, and at last found one, but dirty and expensive. The next day I hired a servant, a Portuguese; it being my invariable custom, on arriving in a country,

B   13

to avail myself of the services of a native, chiefly with the view of perfecting myself in the language; and being already acquainted with most of the principal languages and dialects of the east and the west, I am soon able to make myself quite intelligible to the inhabitants. In about a fortnight I found myself conversing in Portuguese with considerable fluency.

Those who wish to make themselves understood by a foreigner in his own language, should speak with much noise and vociferation, opening their mouths wide. Is it surprising that the English are, in general, the worst linguists in the world, seeing that they pursue a system diametrically opposite? For example, when they attempt to speak Spanish, the most sonorous tongue in existence, they scarcely open their lips, and, putting their hands in their pockets, fumble lazily, instead of applying them to the indispensable office of gesticulation. Well may the poor Spaniards exclaim, *Estos Inglesitos hablan tan cerradamente que el mismo Demonio no es capaz de entenderlos.*

Lisbon is a huge ruinous city, still exhibiting, in almost every direction, the vestiges of that terrific visitation of God, the earthquake, which shattered it some eighty years ago. It stands on seven hills, the loftiest of which is occupied by the castle of Saint George, which is the boldest and most prominent object to the eye, whilst surveying the city from the Tagus. The most frequented and busy parts of the city are those comprised within the valley to the north of this elevation.

Here you find the Plaza of the Inquisition, the principal square in Lisbon, from which run parallel towards the river three or four streets, amongst which are those of the Gold and Silver, so designated from being inhabited by smiths cunning in the working of those metals: they are, upon the whole, very magnificent; the houses are huge, and as high as castles; immense pillars defend the causeway at intervals, producing, however, rather a cumbrous effect. These streets are quite level, and are well paved, in which respect they differ from all the others in Lisbon. The most singular street, however, of all, is that of the Alemcrin, or Rosemary, which debouches on the Casidrea. It is very precipitous, and is occupied on either side by the palaces of the principal Portuguese nobility, massive and frowning, but grand and picturesque edifices, with here and there a hanging garden, overlooking the street at a great height.

With all its ruin and desolation, Lisbon is unquestionably the most remarkable city in the Peninsula, and, perhaps, in the south of Europe. It is not my intention to enter into minute details concerning it; I shall content myself with remarking, that it is quite as much deserving the attention of the artist as even Rome itself. True it is, that though it abounds with churches, it has no gigantic cathedral, like St. Peter's to attract the eye and fill it with wonder; yet I boldly say that there is no monument of man's labour and skill,

pertaining either to ancient or modern Rome, for whatever purpose designed, which can rival the water-works of Lisbon: I mean the stupendous aqueduct whose principal arches cross the valley to the north-east of Lisbon, and which discharges its little runnel of cool and delicious water into the rocky cistern within that beautiful edifice called the Mother of the Waters, from whence all Lisbon is supplied with the crystal lymph, though the source is seven leagues distant. Let travellers devote one entire morning to inspecting the Arcos and the Mai das agoas, after which they may repair to the English church and cemetery, Pere-la-chaise in miniature, where, if they be of England, they may well be excused if they kiss the cold tomb, as I did, of the author of "Amelia," the most singular genius which their island ever produced, whose works it has long been the fashion to abuse in public and to read in secret. In the same cemetery rest the mortal remains of Doddridge, another English author of a different stamp, but justly admired and esteemed.

I had not intended, on disembarking, to remain long in Lisbon, nor, indeed, in Portugal; my destination was Spain, whither I shortly proposed to direct my steps, it being the intention of the Bible Society to attempt to commence operations in that country, the object of which should be the distribution of the word of God; for Spain had hitherto been a region barred against the admission of the Bible; not so Portugal, where, since the revolution, the Bible had been permitted both to be introduced and circulated. Little, however, had been accomplished; therefore, finding myself in the country, I determined, if possible, to effect something in the way of distribution, but, first of all, to make myself acquainted as to how far the people were disposed to receive the Bible, and whether the state of education in general would permit them to turn it to much account. I had plenty of Bibles and Testaments at my disposal, but could the people read them, or would they? A friend of the Society to whom I was recommended was absent from Lisbon at the period of my arrival; this I regretted, as he could have afforded me several useful hints. In order, however, that no time might be lost, I determined not to wait for his arrival, but at once proceed to gather the best information I could upon those points to which I have already alluded. I determined to commence my researches at some slight distance from Lisbon, being well aware of the erroneous ideas that I must form of the Portuguese in general, should I judge of their character and opinions from what I saw and heard in a city so much subjected to foreign intercourse.

My first excursion was to Cintra. If there be any place in the world entitled to the appellation of an enchanted region, it is surely Cintra: Tivoli is a beautiful and picturesque place, but it quickly fades from the mind of those who have seen the Portuguese Paradise. When speaking of Cintra, it must not for a moment be supposed that nothing more is meant than the little town or city; by Cintra must be understood the entire region, town, palace, quintas, forests, crags, Moorish ruin, which suddenly burst on the view on rounding the side of a bleak, savage, and sterile-looking mountain. Nothing is more sullen and uninviting than the south-western aspect of the stony wall which, on the side of Lisbon, seems to shield Cintra from the eye of the world, but the other side is a mingled scene of fairy beauty, artificial elegance, savage grandeur, domes, turrets, enormous trees, flowers, and waterfalls, such as is met with nowhere else beneath the sun. Oh! there are strange and wonderful objects at Cintra, and strange and wonderful recollections attached to them; the ruin on that lofty peak, and which covers part of the side of that precipitous steep, was once the principal stronghold of the Lusitanian Moors, and thither, long after they had disappeared, at a particular moon of every year, were wont to repair wild santons of Maugrabie, to pray at the tomb of a famous Sidi, who slumbers amongst the rocks. That gray palace witnessed the assemblage of the last cortes held by the boy king Sebastian; ere he departed on his romantic expedition against the Moors, who so well avenged their insulted faith and country at Alcazarquibir; and in that low shady quinta, embowered amongst those tall alcornoques, once dwelt John de Castro, the strange old viceroy of Goa, who pawned the hairs of his dead son's beard to raise money to repair the ruined wall of a fortress threatened by the heathen of Ind; those crumbling stones which stand before the portal, deeply graven, not with "runes," but things equally dark, Sanscrit rhymes from the Vedas, were brought by him from Goa, the most brilliant scene of his glory, before Portugal had become a base kingdom; and down that dingle, on an abrupt rocky promontory, stand the ruined halls of the English Millionaire, who there nursed the wayward fancies of a mind as wild, rich, and variegated as the scenes around. Yes, wonderful are the objects which meet the eye at Cintra, and wonderful are the recollections attached to them.

The town of Cintra contains about eight hundred inhabitants. The morning subsequent to my arrival, as I was about to ascend the mountain for the purpose of examining the Moorish ruins, I observed a person advancing towards me whom I judged by his dress to be an ecclesiastic; he was in fact one of the three priests of the place. I instantly accosted him, and had no reason to regret doing so; I found him affable and communicative.

After praising the beauty of the surrounding scenery, I made some inquiry as to the state of education amongst the people under his care. He answered, that he was sorry to say that they were in a state of great ignorance, very few of the common people being able either to read or write; that, with respect to schools, there was but one in the place, where four or five children were taught the alphabet, but that even 'this was at present closed; he informed me, however, that there was a school at Colhares, about a league distant. Amongst other things, he said that nothing more surprised him than to see Englishmen, the most learned and intelligent people in the world, visiting a place like Cintra, where there was no literature, science, nor any thing of utility (*coisa que presta*). I suspect that there was some covert satire in the last speech of the worthy priest; I was, however, jesuit enough to appear to receive it as a high compliment, and, taking off my hat, departed with an infinity of bows.

That same day I visited Colhares, a romantic village on the side of the mountain of Cintra, to the north-west. Seeing some peasants collected round a smithy, I inquired about the school, whereupon one of the men instantly conducted me thither. I went upstairs into a small apartment, where I found the master with about a dozen pupils standing in a row; I saw but one stool in the room, and to that, after having embraced me, he conducted me with great civility. After some discourse, he showed me the books which he used for the instruction of the children; they were spelling books, much of the same kind as those used in the village schools in England. Upon my asking him whether it was his practice to place the Scriptures in the hands of the children, he informed me that long before they had acquired sufficient intelligence to understand them they were removed by their parents, in order that they might assist in the labours of the field, and that the parents in general were by no means solicitous that their children should learn any thing, as they considered the time occupied in learning as so much squandered away. He said, that though the schools were nominally supported by the government, it was rarely that the schoolmasters could obtain their salaries, on which account many had of late resigned their employments. He told me that he had a copy of the New Testament in his possession, which I desired to see, but on examining it I discovered that it was only the epistles by Pereira, with copious notes. I asked him whether he considered that there was harm in reading the Scriptures without notes; he replied that there was certainly no harm in it, but that simple people, without the help of notes, could derive but little benefit from Scripture, as the greatest part would be unintelligible to them; whereupon I shook hands with him, and on departing said that there was no part of Scripture so difficult to understand as those very notes which were intended to elucidate it, and that it would never have been written if not calculated of itself to illume the minds of all classes of mankind.

In a day or two I made an excursion to Mafra, distant about three leagues from Cintra; the principal part of the way lay over steep hills, somewhat dangerous for horses; however, I reached the place in safety.

Mafra is a large village in the neighbourhood of an immense building, intended ʂ serve as a convent and palace, and which is built somewhat after the fashion of the Escurial. In this edifice exists the finest library in Portugal, containing books on all sciences and in all languages, and well suited to the size and grandeur of the edifice which contains it. There were no monks, however, to take care of it, as in former times; they had been driven forth, some to beg their bread, some to serve under the banners of Don Carlos, in Spain, and many, as I was informed, to prowl about as banditti. I found the place abandoned to two or three menials, and exhibiting an aspect of solitude and desolation truly appalling. Whilst I was viewing the cloisters, a fine intelligent-looking lad came up and asked (I suppose in the hope of obtaining a trifle) whether I would permit him to show me the village church, which he informed me was well worth seeing; I said no, but added, that if he would show me the village school I should feel much obliged to him. He looked at me with astonishment, and assured me that there was nothing to be seen at the school, which did not contain more than half a dozen boys, and that he himself was one of the number. On my telling him, however, that he should show me no other place, he at length unwillingly attended me. On the way I learned from him that the schoolmaster was one of the friars who had lately been expelled from the convent, that he was a very learned man, and spoke French and Greek. We passed a stone cross, and the boy bent his head and crossed himself with much devotion. I mention this circumstance as it was the first instance of the kind which I had observed amongst the Portuguese since my arrival. When near the house where the schoolmaster resided he pointed it out to me, and then hid himself behind a wall, where he awaited my return.

On stepping over the threshold I was confronted by a short stout man, between sixty and seventy years of age, dressed in a blue jerkin and gray trowsers, without shirt or waistcoat; he looked at me sternly, and inquired in the French language what was my pleasure. I apologized for intruding upon him, and stated that, being informed he occupied the situation of schoolmaster, I had come to pay my respects to him and to beg permission to ask a few questions respecting the seminary. He answered that whoever told me he was a schoolmaster lied, for that he was a friar of the convent and nothing else. "It is not then true," said I, "that all the convents have been broken up and the monks dismissed?" "Yes, yes," said he with a sigh; "it is true; it is but too true." He then was silent for a minute, and his better nature overcoming his angry feelings, he produced a snuff-box and offered it to me. The snuff-box is the olive-branch of the Portuguese, and he who wishes to be on good terms with them must never refuse to dip his finger and thumb into it when offered. I took, therefore, a huge pinch, though I detest the dust, and we were soon on the best possible terms. He was eager to obtain news, especially from Lisbon and Spain. I

told him that the officers of the troops at Lisbon had, the day before I left that place, gone in a body to the queen and insisted upon her either receiving their swords or dismissing her ministers; whereupon he rubbed his hands, and said that he was sure matters would not remain tranquil at Lisbon. On my saying, however, that I thought the affairs of Don Carlos were on the decline, (this was shortly after the death of Zumalacarreguy,) he frowned, and cried that it could not possibly be, for that God was too just to suffer it. I felt for the poor man who had been driven out of his home in the noble convent close by, and from a state of affluence and comfort reduced in his old age to indigence and misery, for his present dwelling scarcely seemed to contain an article of furniture. I tried twice or thrice to induce him to converse about the school, but he either avoided the subject or said shortly that he knew nothing about it. On my leaving him, the boy came from his hiding place and rejoined me; he said that he had hidden himself through fear of his master's knowing that he had brought me to him, for that he was unwilling that any stranger should know that he was a schoolmaster.

I asked the boy whether he or his parents were acquainted with the Scripture and ever read it; he did not, however, seem to understand me. I must here observe that the boy was fifteen years of age, that he was in many respects very intelligent, and had some knowledge of the Latin language, nevertheless he knew not the Scripture even by name, and I have no doubt, from what I subsequently observed, that at least two-thirds of his countrymen are on that important point no wiser than himself. At the doors of village inns, at the hearths of the rustics, in the fields where they labour, at the stone fountains by the way side where they water their cattle, I have questioned the lower class of the children of Portugal about the Scripture, the Bible, the Old and New Testament, and in no one instance have they known what I was alluding to, or could return me a rational answer, though on all other matters their replies were sensible enough; indeed, nothing surprised me more than the free and unembarrassed manner in which the Portuguese peasantry sustain a conversation, and the purity of the language in which they express their thoughts, and yet few of them can read or write; whereas the peasantry of England, whose education is in general much superior, are in their conversation coarse and dull almost to brutality, and absurdly ungrammatical in their language, though the English tongue is upon the whole more simple in its structure than the Portuguese.

On my return to Lisbon I found our friend ——, who received me very kindly; the next ten days were exceedingly rainy, which prevented me from making any excursions into the country. During this time I saw our friend frequently, and had long conversations with him concerning the best means of distributing the gospel. He thought we could do no better for the present than to put part of our stock into the hands of the booksellers of Lisbon, and at the same employ colporteurs to hawk the books about the streets, receiving a certain profit on every copy they sold. This plan was agreed upon, and forthwith put in practice with some success. I had thoughts of sending colporteurs into the neighbouring villages, but to this our friend objected. He thought the attempt dangerous, as it was very possible that the rural priesthood, who still possessed much influence in their own districts, and who were for the most part decided enemies to the spread of the gospel, might cause the men employed to be assassinated or ill-treated.

I determined, however, ere leaving Portugal, to establish depôts of Bibles in one or two of the provincial towns. I wished to visit the Alemtejo, which I had heard was a very benighted region. The Alemtejo means the province beyond the Tagus. This province is not beautiful and picturesque, like most other parts of Portugal; there are few hills and mountains, the greater part consists of heaths broken by knolls, and gloomy dingles, and forests of stunted pine; these places are infested with banditti. The principal city is Evora, one of the most ancient in Portugal, and formerly the seat of a branch of the Inquisition, yet more cruel and baneful than the terrible one of Lisbon. Evora lies about sixty miles from Lisbon, and to Evora I determined on going with twenty Testaments and two Bibles. How I fared there will presently be seen.

CHAPTER II.

Boatmen of the Tagus—Dangers of the Stream—Aldea Gallega—The Hostelry—Robbers—Sabocha—Adventure of a Muleteer—Estalagem de Ladroes—Don Geronimo—Vendas Novas—Royal Residence—Swine of the Alemtejo—Monte Moro—Swayne Vonved—Singular Goatherd—Children of the Fields—Infidels and Sadducees.

On the afternoon of the 6th of December I set out for Evora, accompanied by my servant. I had been informed that the tide would serve for the regular passage-boats, or felouks, as they are called, at about four o'clock, but on reaching the side of the Tagus opposite to Aldea Gallega, between which place and Lisbon the boats ply, I found that the tide would not permit them to start before eight o'clock. Had I waited for them I should have probably landed at Aldea Gallega about midnight, and I felt little inclination to make my entrée in the Alemtejo at that hour; therefore, as I saw small boats which can push off at any time lying near in abundance, I determined upon hiring one of them for the passage, though the expense would be thus considerably increased. I soon agreed with a wild-looking lad, who told me that he was in part owner of one of the boats, to take me over. I was not aware of the danger in crossing the Tagus at its broadest part, which is opposite Aldea Gallega, at any time, but especially at close of day in the winter season, or I should certainly not have ventured. The lad and his comrade, a miserable looking object, whose only clothing, notwithstanding the season, was a tattered jerkin and trousers, rowed until we had advanced about half a mile from the land; they then set up a large sail, and the lad, who seemed to direct every thing and to be the principal, took the helm and steered. The evening was now setting in; the sun was not far from its bourne in the horizon, the air was very cold, the wind was rising, and the waves of the noble Tagus began to be crested with foam. I told the boy that it was scarcely possible for the boat to carry so much sail without upsetting, upon which he laughed, and began to gabble in a most incoherent manner. He had the most harsh and rapid articulation that has ever come under my observation in any human being; it was the scream of the hyena blended with the bark of the terrier, though it was by no means an index of his disposition, which I soon found to be light, merry, and any thing but malevolent, for when I, in order to show him that I cared little about him, began to hum "Eu que sou Contrabandista," he laughed heartily and said, clapping me on the shoulder, that he would not drown us if he could help it. The other poor fellow seemed by no means averse to go to the bottom; he sat at the fore part of the boat looking the image of famine, and only smiled when the waters broke over the weather side and soaked his scanty habiliments. In a little time I had made up my mind that our last hour was come; the wind was getting higher, the short dangerous waves were more foamy; the boat was frequently on its beam, and the water came over the lee side in torrents; but still the wild lad at the helm held on laughing and chattering, and occasionally yelling out parts of the Miguelite air, "Quando el Rey chegou," the singing of which in Lisbon is imprisonment.

The stream was against us, but the wind was in our favour, and we sprang along at a wonderful rate, and I saw that our only chance of escape was in speedily passing the farther bank of the Tagus where the bight or bay at the extremity of which stands Aldea Gallega commences, for we should not then have to battle with the waves of the stream, which the adverse wind lashed into fury. It was the will of the Almighty to permit us speedily to gain this shelter, but not before the boat was nearly filled with water, and we were all wet to the skin. At about seven o'clock in the evening we reached Aldea Gallega, shivering with cold and in a most deplorable plight.

Aldea Gallega, or the Galician Village, (for the two words are Spanish, and have that signification,) is a place containing, I should think, about four thousand inhabitants. It was pitchy dark when we landed, but rockets soon began to fly about in all directions, illuming the air far and wide. As we passed along the dirty unpaved street which leads to the Largo, or square in which the inn is situated, a horrible uproar of drums and voices assailed our ears. On inquiring the cause of all this bustle, I was informed that it was the eve of the Conception of the Virgin.

As it was not the custom of the people at the inn to provide provisions for the guests, I wandered about in search of food; and at last seeing some soldiers eating and drinking in a species of wine-house, I went in and asked the people to let me have some supper, and in a short time they furnished me with a tolerable meal, for which, however, they charged three crowns.

Having engaged with a person for mules to carry us to Evora, which were to be ready at five next morning, I soon retired to bed, my servant sleeping in the same apartment, which was the only one in the house vacant. I closed not my eyes during the whole night. Beneath us was a stable, in which some almocreves, or carriers, slept with their mules; at our back, in the yard, was a pigsty. How could I sleep? The hogs grunted, the mules screamed, and the almocreves snored most horribly. I heard the village clock strike the hours until midnight, and from midnight till four in the morning, when I sprang up and began to dress, and despatched my servant to hasten the man with the mules, for I was heartily tired of the place and wanted to leave it. An old man, bony and hale, accompanied by a barefooted lad, brought the beasts, which were tolerably good. He was the proprietor of them, and intended, with the lad, who was his nephew, to accompany us to Evora.

When we started, the moon was shining brightly, and the morning was piercingly cold. We soon entered on a sandy hollow way, emerging from which we passed by a strange looking and large edifice, standing on a high bleak sand-hill on our left. We were speedily overtaken by five or six men on horseback, riding at a rapid pace, each with a long gun slung at his saddle, the muzzle depending about two feet below the horse's belly. I inquired of the old man what was the reason of this warlike array. He answered, that the roads were very bad, (meaning that they abounded with robbers,) and that they went armed in this manner for their defence; they soon turned off to the right towards Palmella.

We reached a sandy plain studded with stunted pine; the road was little more than a footpath, and as we proceeded, the trees thickened and became a wood, which extended for two leagues, with clear spaces at intervals,

in which herds of cattle and sheep were feeding; the bells attached to their necks were ringing lowly and monotonously. The sun was just beginning to show itself; but the morning was misty and dreary, which together with the aspect of desolation which the country exhibited, had an unfavourable effect on my spirits. I got down and walked, entering into conversation with the old man. He seemed to have but one theme, "the robbers," and the atrocities they were in the habit of practising in the very spots we were passing. The tales he told were truly horrible, and to avoid them I mounted again, and rode on considerably in front.

In about an hour and a half we emerged from the forest, and entered upon a savage, wild, broken ground, covered with mato, or brushwood. The mules stopped to drink at a shallow pool, and on looking to the right I saw a ruined wall. This, the guide informed me, was the remains of Vendas Velhas, or the Old Inn, formerly the haunt of the celebrated robber Sabocha. This Sabocha, it seems, had, some sixteen years ago, a band of about forty ruffians at his command, who infested these wilds, and supported themselves by plunder. For a considerable time Sabocha pursued his atrocious trade unsuspected, and many an unfortunate traveller was murdered in the dead of night at the solitary inn by the wood-side, which he kept; indeed, a more fit situation for plunder and murder I never saw. The gang were in the habit of watering their horses at the pool, and perhaps of washing therein their hands stained with the blood of their victims; the lieutenant of the troop was the brother of Sabocha, a fellow of great strength and ferocity, particularly famous for the skill he possessed in darting a long knife, with which he was in the habit of transfixing his opponents. Sabocha's connexion with the gang at length became known, and he fled, with the greater part of his associates, across the Tagus to the northern provinces. Himself and his brothers eventually lost their lives on the road to Coimbra, in an engagement with the military. His house was razed by order of the government.

The ruins are still frequently visited by banditti, who eat and drink amidst them, and look out for prey, as the place commands a view of the road. The old man assured me, that about two months previous, on returning to Aldea Gallega with his mules from accompanying some travellers, he had been knocked down, stripped naked, and all his money taken from him, by a fellow whom he believed came from this murderer's nest. He said that he was an exceedingly powerful young man, with immense mustaches and whiskers, and was armed with an espingarda, or musket. About ten days subsequently he saw the robber at Vendas Novas, where we should pass the night. The fellow on recognising him took him aside, and, with horrid imprecations, threatened that he should never be permitted to return home if he attempted to discover him; he therefore held his peace, as there was little to be gained and every thing to be risked in apprehending him, as he would have been speedily set at liberty for want of evidence to criminate him, and then he would not have failed to have had his revenge, or would have been anticipated therein by his comrades.

I dismounted and went up to the place, and saw the vestiges of a fire and a broken bottle. The sons of plunder had been there very lately. I left a New Testament and some tracts amongst the ruins, and hastened away.

The sun had dispelled the mists and was beaming very hot; we rode on for about an hour, when I heard the neighing of a horse in our rear, and our guide said there was a party of horsemen behind; our mules were good, and they did not overtake us for at least twenty minutes. The headmost rider was a gentleman in a fashionable travelling dress; a little way behind were an officer, two soldiers, and a boy in livery. I heard the principal horseman, on overtaking my servant, inquiring who I was, and whether French or English. He was told I was an English gentleman, travelling. He then asked whether I understood Portuguese; the man said I understood it, but he believed that I spoke French and Italian better. The gentleman then spurred on his horse and accosted me, not in Portuguese, nor in French or Italian, but in the purest English that I ever heard spoken by a foreigner; it had, indeed, nothing of foreign accent or pronunciation in it; and had I not known, by the countenance of the speaker, that he was no Englishman, (for there is a peculiarity in the countenance, as everybody knows, which, though it cannot be described, is sure to betray the Englishman,) I should have concluded that I was in company with a countryman. We continued discoursing until we arrived at Pegoens.

Pegoens consists of about two or three houses and an inn; there is likewise a species of barrack, where half a dozen soldiers are stationed. In the whole of Portugal there is no place of worse reputation, and the inn is nicknamed *Estalagem de Ladroes*, or the hostelry of thieves; for it is there that the banditti of the wilderness, which extends around it on every side for leagues, are in the habit of coming and spending the money, the fruits of their criminal daring; there they dance and sing, eat fricasseed rabbits and olives, and drink the muddy but strong wine of the Alemtejo. An enormous fire, fed by the trunk of a cork tree, was blazing in a niche on the left hand on entering the spacious kitchen. Close by it, seething, were several large jars, which emitted no disagreeable odour, and reminded me that I had not broken my fast, although it was now nearly one o'clock, and I had ridden five leagues. Several wild looking men, who if they were not banditti might easily be mistaken for such, were seated on .ogs about the fire. I asked them some unimportant questions, to which they replied with readiness and civility, and one of them,

who said he could read, accepted a tract which I offered him.

My new friend, who had been bespeaking dinner, or rather breakfast, now, with great civility, invited me to partake of it, and at the same time introduced me to the officer who accompanied him, and who was his brother, and also spoke English, though not so well as himself. I found I had become acquainted with Don Geronimo Joze D'Azveto, secretary to the government at Evora; his brother belonged to a regiment of hussars, whose head-quarters were at Evora, but which had outlying parties along the road,—for example, the place where we were stopping.

Rabbits at Pegoens seem to be a standard article of food, being produced in abundance on the moors around. We had one fried, the gravy of which was delicious, and afterwards a roasted one, which was brought up on a dish entire; the hostess, having first washed her hands, proceeded to tear the animal to pieces, which having accomplished, she poured over the fragments a sweet sauce. I ate heartily of both dishes, particularly of the last; owing, perhaps, to the novel and curious manner in which it was served up. Excellent figs, from the Algarves, and apples concluded our repast, which we ate in a little side room with a mud floor, which sent such a piercing chill into my system, as prevented me from deriving that pleasure from my fare and my agreeable companions that I should have otherwise experienced.

Don Geronimo had been educated in England, in which country he passed his boyhood, which in a certain degree accounted for his proficiency in the English language, the idiom and pronunciation of which can only be acquired by residing in the country at that period of one's life. He had also fled thither shortly after the usurpation of the throne of Portugal by Don Miguel, and from thence had departed to the Brazils, where he had devoted himself to the service of Don Pedro, and had followed him in the expedition which terminated in the downfall of the usurper and the establishment of the constitutional government in Portugal. Our conversation rolled chiefly on literary and political subjects, and my acquaintance with the writings of the most celebrated authors of Portugal was hailed with surprise and delight; for nothing is more gratifying to a Portuguese than to observe a foreigner taking an interest in the literature of his nation, of which, in many respects, he is justly proud.

At about two o'clock we were once more in the saddle, and pursued our way in company through a country exactly resembling that which we had previously been traversing, rugged and broken, with here and there a clump of pines. The afternoon was exceedingly fine, and the bright rays of the sun relieved the desolation of the scene. Having advanced about two leagues, we caught sight of a large edifice towering majestically in the distance, which I learnt was a royal palace standing at the farther extremity of Vendas Novas, the village in which we were to pass the night; it was considerably more than a league from us, yet, seen through the clear transparent atmosphere of Portugal, it appeared much nearer.

Before reaching it we passed by a stone cross, on the pedestal of which was an inscription commemorating a horrible murder of a native of Lisbon, which had occurred on that spot; it looked ancient, and was covered with moss, and the greater part of the inscription was illegible, at least it was to me, who could not bestow much time on its deciphering. Having arrived at Vendas Novas, and bespoken supper, my new friend and myself strolled forth to view the palace; it was built by the late king of Portugal, and presents little that is remarkable in its exterior; it is a long edifice with wings, and is only two stories high, though it can be seen afar off from being situated on elevated ground; it has fifteen windows in the upper, and twelve in the lower story, with a paltry-looking door, something like that of a barn, to which you ascend by one single step; the interior corresponds with the exterior, offering nothing which can gratify curiosity, if we except the kitchens, which are indeed magnificent, and so large that food enough might be cooked in them, at one time, to serve as a repast for all the inhabitants of the Alemtejo.

I passed the night with great comfort in a clean bed, remote from all those noises so rife in a Portuguese inn, and the next morning at six we again set out on our journey, which we hoped to terminate before sunset, as Evora is but ten leagues from Vendas Novas. The preceding morning had been cold, but the present one was far colder, so much so, that just before sunrise I could no longer support it on horseback, and therefore dismounting, ran and walked until we reached a few houses at the termination of these desolate moors. It was in one of these houses that the commissioners of Don Pedro and Miguel met, and it was there agreed that the latter should resign the crown in favour of Donna Maria, for Evora was the last stronghold of the usurper, and the moors of the Alemtejo the last area of the combats which so long agitated unhappy Portugal. I therefore gazed on the miserable huts with considerable interest, and did not fail to scatter in the neighbourhood several of the precious little tracts with which, together with a small quantity of Testaments, my carpet bag was provided.

The country began to improve; the savage heaths were left behind, and we saw hills and dales, cork trees, and azinheiras, on the last of which trees grows that kind of sweet acorn called bolotas, which is pleasant as a chestnut, and which supplies in winter the principal food on which the numerous swine of the Alemtejo subsist. Gallant swine they are, with short legs and portly bodies of a black or dark-red colour; and for the excellence of their flesh I can vouch, having frequently luxuriated upon it in the course of my wanderings in this province; the lomba, or loin, when broiled on the live embers, is delicious, especially when eaten with olives.

We were now in sight of Monte Moro, which, as the name denotes, was once a fortress of the Moors; it is a high, steep hill, on the summit and sides of which are ruined walls and towers; at its western side is a deep ravine or valley, through which a small stream rushes, traversed by a stone bridge; farther down there is a ford, over which we passed and ascended to the town, which, commencing near the northern base, passes over the lower ridge towards the north-east. The town is exceedingly picturesque, and many of the houses are very ancient, and built in the Moorish fashion. I wished much to examine the relics of Moorish sway on the upper part of the mountain, but time pressed, and the short period of our stay at this place did not permit me to gratify my inclination.

Monte Moro is the head of a range of hills which cross this part of the Alemtejo, and from hence they fork east and south-east, towards the former of which directions lies the direct road to Elvas, Badajoz, and Madrid; and towards the latter that to Evora. A beautiful mountain, covered to the top with cork trees, is the third of the chain, which skirts the way in the direction of Elvas. It is called Monte Almo; a brook brawls at its base, and as I passed it the sun was shining gloriously on the green herbage on which flocks of goats were feeding, with their bells ringing merrily, so that the tout ensemble resembled a fairy scene; and, that nothing might be wanted to complete the picture, I here met a man, a goatherd, beneath an azinheira, whose appearance recalled to my mind the Brute Carle, mentioned in the Danish ballad of Swayne Vonved:—

"A wild swine on his shoulders he kept,
And upon his bosom a black bear slept;
And about his fingers, with hair o'erhung,
The squirrel sported and weasel clung."

Upon the shoulder of the goatherd was a beast, which he told me was a lontra, or otter, which he had lately caught in the neighbouring brook; it had a string round its neck, which was attached to his arm. At his left side was a bag, from the top of which peered the heads of two or three singular-looking animals, and at his right was squatted the sullen cub of a wolf, which he was endeavouring to tame; his whole appearance was to the last degree savage and wild. After a little conversation, such as those who meet on the road frequently hold, I asked him if he could read, but he made me no answer. I then inquired if he knew any thing of God or Jesus Christ; he looked me fixedly in the face for a moment, and then turned his countenance towards the sun, which was beginning to sink in the west, nodded to it, and then again looked fixedly upon me. I believe that I understood the mute reply, which probably was, that it was God who made that glorious light which illumes and gladdens all creation; and, gratified with that belief, I left him and hastened after my companions, who were by this time a considerable way in advance.

I have always found in the disposition of the children of the fields a more determined tendency to religion and piety than amongst the inhabitants of towns and cities; and the reason is obvious, they are less acquainted with the works of man's hands than with those of God; their occupations, too, which are simple, and requiring less of ingenuity and skill than those which engage the attention of the other portion of their fellow-creatures, are less favourable to the engendering of self-conceit and sufficiency, so utterly at variance with that lowliness of spirit which constitutes the best foundation of piety. The sneerers and scoffers at religion do not spring from amongst the simple children of nature, but are the excrescences of overwrought refinement; and though their baneful influence has indeed penetrated to the country and corrupted man there, the source and fountain-head was amongst crowded houses, where nature is scarcely known. I am not one of those who look for perfection amongst the rural population of any country; perfection is not to be found amongst the children of the fall, wherever their abodes may happen to be; but, until the heart discredits the existence of a God, there is still hope for the soul of the possessor, however stained with crime he may be, for even Simon the magician was converted; but

when the heart is once steeled with infidelity, infidelity confirmed by carnal wisdom, an exuberance of the grace of God is required to melt it, which is seldom manifested; for we read in the blessed Book that the Pharisee and the wizard became receptacles of grace; but where is there mention made of the conversion of the sneering Sadducee? and is the modern infidel aught but a Sadducee of later date?

It was dark night before we reached Evora; and having taken leave of my friends, who kindly requested me to consider their house my home, I and my servant went to the Largo de San Francisco, in which the muleteer informed me was the best hostelry of the town. We rode into the kitchen, at the extreme end of which was the stable, as is customary in Portugal. The house was kept by an aged gipsy-like female and her daughter, a fine, blooming girl, about eighteen years of age. The house was large; in the upper story was a very long room, like a granary, which extended nearly the whole length of the house; the farther part was partitioned off, and formed a chamber, tolerably comfortable, but very cold, and the floor was of tiles, as was also that of the large room in which the muleteers were accustomed to sleep on the furniture of the mules. After supper I went to bed; and having offered up my devotions to Him who had protected me through a dangerous journey, I slept soundly till the morning.

CHAPTER III.

Shopkeeper at Evora—Spanish Contrabandistas—Lion and Unicorn—The Fountain—Trust in the Almighty—Distribution of Tracts—Library at Evora—Manuscript—The Bible as a Guide—The infamous Mary—The Man of Palmella—The Charm—The Monkish System—Sunday—Volney —An Auto-da-Fé—Men from Spain—Reading of a Tract—New Arrival—The Herb Rosemary.

EVORA is a small city, walled, but not regularly fortified, and could not sustain a siege of a day. It has five gates; before that to the south-west is the principal promenade of its inhabitants; the fair on St. John's Day is likewise held there; the houses are in general very ancient, and many of them unoccupied. It contains about five thousand inhabitants, though twice that number would be by no means disproportionate to its size. The two principal edifices are the See, or cathedral, and the convent of San Francisco, in the square before the latter of which was situated the posada where I had taken up my abode. A large barrack for cavalry stands on the right-hand side, on entering the south-west gate. To the south-east, at the distance of six leagues, is to be seen a blue chain of hills, the highest of which is called Serra Dorso; it is picturesquely beautiful, and contains within its recesses wolves and wild boars in numbers. About a league and a half on the other side of this hill is Estremos.

I passed the day succeeding my arrival

principally in examining the town and its environs, and as I strolled about, entered into conversation with various people that I met; several of these were of the middle class, shopkeepers and professional men; they were all Constitutionalists, or pretended to be so, but had very little to say except a few commonplace remarks on the way of living of the friars, their hypocrisy and laziness. I endeavoured to obtain some information respecting the state of instruction in the place, and from their answers was led to believe that it must be at the lowest ebb, for it seemed that there was neither bookshop nor school. When I spoke of religion, they exhibited the utmost apathy for the subject, and making their bows left me as soon as possible.

Having a letter of introduction to a person who kept a shop in the market-place, I went thither and delivered it to him as he stood behind his counter. In the course of conversation, I found that he had been much persecuted whilst the old system was in its vigour, and that he entertained a hearty aversion for it. I told him that the ignorance of the people in religious matters had served to nurse that system, and that the surest way to prevent its return was to enlighten their minds; I added, that I had brought a small stock of Bibles and Testaments to Evora, which I wished to leave for sale in the hands of some respectable merchant, and that if he were anxious to help to lay the axe to the root of superstition and tyranny, he could not do so more effectually than by undertaking the charge of these books. He declared his willingness to do so, and I went away determined to intrust to him half of my stock. I returned to the hostelry, and sat down on a log of wood on the hearth within the immense chimney in the common apartment; two surly-looking men were on their knees on the stones; before them was a large heap of pieces of old iron, brass, and copper; they were assorting it, and stowing it away in various bags. They were Spanish contrabandistas of the lowest class, and earned a miserable livelihood by smuggling such rubbish from Portugal into Spain. Not a word proceeded from their lips, and when I addressed them in their native language, they returned no other answer than a kind of growl. They looked as dirty and rusty as the iron in which they trafficked; their four miserable donkeys were in the stable in the rear.

The woman of the house and her daughter were exceedingly civil to me, and coming near crouched down, asking various questions about England. A man, dressed somewhat like an English sailor, who sat on the other side of the hearth confronting me, said, "I hate the English, for they are not baptized, and have not the law," meaning the law of God. I laughed, and told him that according to the law of England, no one who was unbaptized could be buried in consecrated ground; whereupon he said, "Then you are stricter than we." He then said, "What is meant by the lion and the unicorn which I saw the other day on the coat of arms over the door of the English Consul at St. Ubes?" I said they were the arms of England! "Yes," he replied, "but what do they represent?" I said I did not know. "Then," said he, "you do not know the secrets of your own house." I said, "Suppose I were to tell you that they represent the Lion of Bethlehem, and the horned monster of the flaming pit in combat, as to which should obtain the mastery in England, what would you say?" He replied, "I should say that you gave a fair answer." This man and myself became great friends; he came from Palmella, not far from St. Ubes; he had several mules and horses with him, and dealt in corn and barley. I again walked out and roamed in the environs of the town.

About half a mile from the southern wall is a stone fountain, where the muleteers and other people who visit the town are accustomed to water their horses. I sat down by it, and there I remained about two hours, entering into conversation with every one who halted at the fountain; and I will here observe, that during the time of my sojourn at Evora, I repeated my visit every day, and remained there the same time; and by following this plan, I believe that I spoke to at least two hundred of the children of Portugal upon matters relating to their eternal welfare. I found that very few of those whom I addressed had received any species of literary education, none of them had seen the Bible, and not more than half a dozen had the slightest inkling of what the holy book consisted. I found that most of them were bigoted Papists, and Miguelites at heart. I therefore, when they told me they were Christians, denied the possibility of their being so, as they were ignorant of Christ and his commandments, and placed their hope of salvation on outward forms and superstitious observances, which were the invention of Satan, who wished to keep them in darkness, that at last they might stumble into the pit which he had dug for them. I said repeatedly that the Pope, whom they revered, was an arch deceiver, and the head minister of Satan here on earth, and that the monks and friars, whose absence they so deplored, and to whom they had been accustomed to confess themselves, were his subordinate agents. When called upon for proofs, I invariably cited the ignorance of my auditors respecting the Scriptures, and said that if their spiritual guides had been really ministers of Christ, they would not have permitted their flocks to remain unacquainted with his word

Since this occurred, I have been frequently surprised that I experienced no insult and ill-treatment from the people, whose superstitions I was thus attacking; but I really experienced none, and am inclined to believe that the utter fearlessness which I displayed, trusting in the protection of the Almighty, may have been the cause. When threatened by danger, the best policy is to fix your eye steadily upon it, and it will in general vanish like the morning mist before the sun; whereas, if you quail before it, it is sure to become more imminent. I have fervent hope that the words of my mouth sank deep into the hearts of some of my auditors, as I observed many of them depart musing and pensive. I occasionally distributed tracts amongst them; for although they themselves were unable to turn them to much account, I thought that by their means they might become of service at some future time, and fall into the hands of others, to whom they might be of eternal interest. Many a book which is abandoned to the waters is wafted to some remote shore, and there proves a blessing and a comfort to millions, who are ignorant from whence it came.

The next day, which was Friday, I called at the house of my friend Don Geronimo Azveto. I did not find him there, but was directed to the see, or episcopal palace, in an apartment of which I found him, writing, with another gentleman, to whom he introduced me; it was the governor of Evora, who welcomed me with every mark of kindness and affability. After some discourse, we went out together to examine an ancient edifice, which was reported to have served, in by-gone times, as a temple to Diana. Part of it was evidently of Roman architecture, for there was no mistaking the beautiful light pillars which supported a dome, under which the sacrifices to the most captivating and poetical divinity of the heathen theocracy had probably been made; but the original space between the pillars had been filled up with rubbish of a modern date, and the rest of the building was apparently of the architecture of the latter end of the middle ages. It was situated at one end of the building which had once been the seat of the Inquisition, and had served, before the erection of the present see, as the residence of the bishop.

Within the see, where the governor now resides, is a superb library, occupying an immense vaulted room, like the aisle of a cathedral, and in a side apartment is a collection of paintings by Portuguese artists, chiefly portraits, amongst which is that of Don Sebastian. I sincerely hope it did not do him justice, for it represents him in the shape of an awkward lad of about eighteen, with a bloated booby face with staring eyes, and a ruff round a short apoplectic neck.

I was shown several beautifully illuminated missals and other manuscripts; but the one which most arrested my attention, I scarcely need say why, was that which bore the following title:—

"Forma sive ordinatio Capelli illustrissimi et xianissimi principis Henrici Sexti Regis Anglie et Francie am dm Hibernie descripta serenissiõ principi Alfonso Regi Portugalie illustri per humilem servitorem sm Willm. Sav. Decanū capelle supradicte."

It seemed a voice from the olden times of my dear native land! This library and picture gallery had been formed by one of the latter bishops, a person of much learning and piety.

In the evening I dined with Don Geronimo and his brother; the latter soon left us to attend to his military duties. My friend and myself had now much conversation of considerable interest; he lamented the deplorable state of ignorance in which his countrymen existed at present. He said that his friend the governor and himself were endeavouring to establish a school in the vicinity, and that they had made application to the government for the use of an empty convent, called the Espinheiro, or thorn tree, at about a league's distance, and that they had little doubt of their request being complied with. I had before told him who I was, and after expressing joy at the plan which he had in contemplation, I now urged him in the most pressing manner to use all his influence to make the knowledge of the Scripture the basis of the education which the children were to receive, and added, that half the Bibles and Testaments which I had brought with me to Evora were heartily at his service; he instantly gave me his hand, said he ac-cepted my offer with the greatest pleasure, and would do all in his power to forward my views, which were in many respects his own. I now told him that I did not come to Portugal with the view of propagating the dogmas of any particular sect, but with the hope of introducing the Bible, which is the well-head of all that is useful and conducive to the happiness of society,—that I cared not what people called themselves, provided they followed the Bible as a guide; for that where the Scriptures were read, neither priestcraft nor tyranny could long exist, and instanced the case of my own country, the cause of whose freedom and prosperity was the Bible, and that only, as the last persecutor of this book, the bloody and infamous Mary, was the last tyrant who had sat on the throne of England. We did not part till the night was considerably advanced, and the next morning I sent him the books, in the firm and confident hope that a bright and glorious morning was about to rise over the night which had so long cast its dreary shadows over the regions of the Alemtejo.

The day after this interesting event, which was Saturday, I had more conversation with the man from Palmella. I asked him if in his journeys he had never been attacked by robbers; he answered no, for that he generally travelled in company with others. "However," said he, "were I alone I should have little fear, for I am well protected." I said that I supposed he carried arms with him. "No other arms than this," said he, pulling out one of those long, desperate-looking knives, of English manufacture, with which every Portuguese peasant is usually furnished. This knife serves for many purposes, and I should consider it a far more efficient weapon than a dagger. "But," said he, "I do not place much confidence in the knife." I then inquired in what rested his hope of protection. "In this," said he; and unbuttoning his waistcoat, he showed me a small bag, attached to his neck by a silken string. "In this bag is an oracam, or prayer, written by a person of power, and as long as I carry it about with me, no ill can befall me." Curiosity is the leading feature of my character, and I instantly said, with eagerness, that I should feel great pleasure in being permitted to read the prayer. "Well," he replied, "you are my friend, and I would do for you what I would for few others, I will show it you." He then asked for my pen-knife, and having unripped the bag, took out a large piece of paper closely folded up. I hurried to my apartment and commenced the examination of it. It was scrawled over in a very illegible hand, and was moreover much stained with perspiration, so that I had considerable difficulty in making myself master of its contents; but I at last accomplished the following literal translation of the charm, which was written in bad Portuguese, but which struck me at the time as being one of the most remarkable compositions that had ever come to my knowledge.

"Just Judge and divine Son of the Virgin Maria, who wast born in Bethlehem, a Nazarene, and wast crucified in the midst of all Jewry, I beseech thee, O Lord, by thy sixth day, that the body of me be not caught, nor put to death by the hands of justice at all; peace be with you, the peace of Christ, may I receive peace, may you receive peace, said God to his disciples. If the accursed justice should distrust me, or have its eyes on me, in order to take me or to rob me, may its eyes not see me, may its mouth not speak to me, may it have ears which may not hear me, may it have hands which may not seize me, may it have feet which may not overtake me; for may I be armed with the arms of St. George, covered with the cloak of Abraham, and shipped in the ark of Noah, so that it can neither see me, nor hear me, nor draw the blood from my body. I also adjure thee, O Lord, by those three blessed crosses, by those three blessed chalices, by those three blessed clergymen, by those three consecrated hosts, that thou give me that sweet company which thou gavest to the Virgin Maria, from the gates of Bethlehem to the portals of Jerusalem, that I may go and come with pleasure and joy with Jesus Christ, the Son of the Virgin Maria, the prolific yet nevertheless the eternal virgin."

The woman of the house and her daughter had similar bags attached to their necks, containing charms, which, they said, prevented the witches having power to harm them. The belief in witchcraft is very prevalent amongst the peasantry of the Alemtejo, and I believe of other provinces of Portugal. This is one of the relics of the monkish system, the aim of which, in all countries where it has existed, seems to have been to besot the minds of the people, that they might be more easily misled. All these charms were fabrications of the monks, who had sold them to their infatuated confessants. The monks of the Greek and Syrian churches likewise deal in this ware, which they know to be poison, but which they would rather vend than the wholesome balm of the gospel, because it brings them a large price, and fosters the delusion which enables them to live a life of luxury.

The Sunday morning was fine, and the plain before the church of the convent of San Francisco was crowded with people hastening to or returning from the mass. After having performed my morning devotion, and breakfasted, I went down to the kitchen; the girl Geronima was seated by the fire. I inquired if she had heard mass? She replied in the negative, and that she did not intend to hear it. Upon my inquiring her motive for absenting herself, she replied, that since the friars had been expelled from their churches and convents she had ceased to attend mass, or to confess herself; for that the government priests had no spiritual power, and consequently she never troubled them. She said the friars were holy men and charitable; for

that every morning those of the convent over the way fed forty poor persons with the relics of the meals of the preceding day, but that now these people were allowed to starve. I replied, that the friars, who lived on the fat of the land, could well afford to bestow a few bones upon their poor, and that their doing so was merely a part of their policy, by which they hoped to secure to themselves friends in time of need. The girl then observed, that as it was Sunday, I should perhaps like to see some books, and without waiting for a reply she produced them. They consisted principally of popular stories, with lives and miracles of saints, but amongst them was a translation of Volney's Ruins of Empires. I expressed a wish to know how she became possessed of this book. She said that a young man, a great Constitutionalist, had given it to her some months previous, and had pressed her much to read it, for that it was one of the best books in the world. I replied, that the author of it was an emissary of Satan, and an enemy of Jesus Christ and the souls of mankind; that it was written with the sole aim of bringing all religion into contempt, and that it inculcated the doctrine that there was no future state, nor reward for the righteous nor punishment for the wicked. She made no reply, but going into another room, returned with her apron full of dry sticks and brushwood, all which she piled upon the fire, and produced a bright blaze. She then took the book from my hand and placed it upon the flaming pile; then sitting down, took her rosary out of her pocket and told her beads till the volume was consumed. This was an *auto-da-fé* in the best sense of the word.

On the Monday and Tuesday I paid my usual visits to the fountain, and likewise rode about the neighbourhood on a mule, for the purpose of circulating tracts. I dropped a great many in the favourite walks of the people of Evora, as I felt rather dubious of their accepting them had I proffered them with my own hand, whereas, should they be observed lying on the ground, I thought that curiosity might cause them to be picked up and examined. I likewise, on the Tuesday evening, paid a farewell visit to my friend Azveto, as it was my intention to leave Evora on the Thursday following and return to Lisbon; in which view I had engaged a calash of a man who informed me that he had served as a soldier in the grande armée of Napoleon, and been present in the Russian campaign. He looked the very image of a drunkard. His face was covered with carbuncles, and his breath impregnated with the fumes of strong waters. He wished much to converse with me in French, in the speaking of which language it seemed he prided himself, but I refused, and told him to speak the language of the country, or I would hold no discourse with him.

Wednesday was stormy, with occasional rain. On coming down, I found that my friend from Palmella had departed; but several contrabandistas had arrived from Spain. They were mostly fine fellows, and, unlike the two I had seen the preceding week, who were of much lower degree, were chatty and communicative; they spoke their native language, and no other, and seemed to hold the Portuguese in great contempt. The magnificent tones of the Spanish sounded to great advantage amidst the shrill squeaking dialect of Portugal. I was soon in deep conversation with them, and was much pleased to find that all of them could read. I presented the eldest, a man of about fifty years of age, with a tract in Spanish. He examined it for some time with great attention; he then rose from his seat, and going into the middle of the apartment, began reading it aloud, slowly and emphatically; his companions gathered around him, and every now and then expressed their approbation of what they heard. The reader occasionally called upon me to explain passages which, as they referred to particular texts of Scripture, he did not exactly understand, for not one of the party had ever seen either the Old or New Testament.

He continued reading for upwards of an hour, until he had finished the tract; and, at its conclusion, the whole party were clamorous for similar ones, with which I was happy to be able to supply them.

Most of these men spoke of priestcraft and the monkish system with the utmost abhorrence, and said that they should prefer death to submitting again to the yoke which had formerly galled their necks. I questioned them very particularly respecting the opinion of their neighbours and acquaintances on this point, and they assured me that in their part of the Spanish frontier all were of the same mind, and that they cared as little for the Pope and his monks as they did for Don Carlos; for the latter was a dwarf (*chicotito*) and a tyrant, and the others were plunderers and robbers. I told them they must beware of confounding religion with priestcraft, and that in their abhorrence of the latter they must not forget that there is a God and a Christ to whom they must look for salvation, and whose word it was incumbent upon them to study on every occasion; whereupon they all expressed a devout belief in Christ and the Virgin.

These men, though in many respects more enlightened than the surrounding peasantry, were in others as much in the dark; they believed in witchcraft and in the efficacy of particular charms. The night was very stormy, and at about nine we heard a galloping towards the door, and then a loud knocking: it was opened, and in rushed a wild-looking man, mounted on a donkey; he wore a ragged jacket of sheep skin, called in Spanish zamarra, with breeches of the same as far down as his knees; his legs were bare. Around his sombrero, or shadowy hat, was tied a large quantity of the herb which in English is called rosemary, in Spanish romero, and in the rustic language of Portugal, alecrim; which last is a word of Scandinavian origin, (*ellegren*,) signifying the elfin plant, and was probably carried into the south by the Vandals. The man seemed frantic with terror, and said that the witches had been pursuing him and hovering over his head for the last two leagues. He came from the Spanish frontier with meal and other articles; he said that his wife was following him and would soon arrive, and in about a quarter of an hour she made her appearance, dripping with rain, and also mounted on a donkey.

I asked my friends the contrabandistas why he wore the rosemary in his hat; whereupon they told me that it was good against witches and the mischances on the road. I had no time to argue against this superstition, for, as the chaise was to be ready at five the next morning, I wished to make the most of the short time which I could devote to sleep.

CHAPTER IV.

Vexatious Delays—Drunken Driver—The murdered Mule—The Lamentation—Adventure on the Heath—Fear of Darkness—Portuguese Fidalgo—The Escort—Return to Lisbon.

I ROSE at four, and after having taken some refreshment, I descended and found the strange man and his wife sleeping in the chimney corner by the fire, which was still burning; they soon awoke and began preparing their breakfast, which consisted of salt sardinhas, broiled upon the embers. In the mean time the woman sang snatches of the beautiful hymn, very common in Spain, which commences thus:—

"Once of old upon a mountain, shepherds ever-
  come with sleep,
Near to Bethlem's holy tower, kept at dead of
  night their sheep;

Round about the trunk they nodded of a huge
  ignited oak,
Whence the crackling flame ascending bright
  and clear the darkness broke."

On hearing that I was about to depart, she said, "You shall have some of my husband's rosemary, which will keep you from danger, and prevent any misfortune occurring." I was foolish enough to permit her to put some of it in my hat; and the man having by this time arrived with his mules, I bade farewell to my friendly hostesses, and entered the chaise with my servant.

I remarked, at the time, that the mules

which drew us were the finest I had ever seen; the largest could be little short of sixteen hands high; and the fellow told me in his bad French that he loved them better than his wife and children. We turned round the corner of the convent and proceeded down the street which leads to the south-western gate. The driver now stopped before the door of a large house, and having alighted, said that it was yet very early, and that he was afraid to venture forth, as it was very probable we should be robbed, and himself murdered, as the robbers who resided in the town would be apprehensive of his discovering them, but that the family who lived in this house were going to Lisbon, and would depart in about a quarter of an hour, when we might avail ourselves of an escort of soldiers which they would take with them, and in their company we should run no danger. I told him I had no fear, and commanded him to drive on; but he said he would not, and left us in the street. We waited an hour, when two carriages came to the door of the house, but it seems the family were not yet ready, whereupon the coachman likewise got down and went away. At the expiration of about half an hour the family came out, and when their luggage had been arranged they called for the coachman, but he was nowhere to be found. Search was made for him, but ineffectually, and an hour more was spent before another driver could be procured; but the escort had not yet made its appearance, and it was not before a servant had been twice despatched to the barracks that it arrived. At last every thing was ready, and they drove off.

All this time I had seen nothing of our own coachman, and I fully expected that he had abandoned us altogether. In a few minutes I saw him staggering up the street in a state of intoxication, attempting to sing the Marseillois hymn. I said nothing to him, but sat observing him. He stood for some time staring at the mules, and talking incoherent nonsense in French. At last he said, "I am not so drunk but I can ride," and proceeded to lead his mules toward the gate. When out of the town he made several ineffectual attempts to mount the smallest mule which bore the saddle; he at length succeeded, and instantly commenced spurring at a furious rate down the road. We arrived at a place where a narrow rocky path branched off, by taking which we should avoid a considerable circuit round the city wall, which otherwise it would be necessary to make before we could reach the road to Lisbon, which lay at the north-east; he now said, "I shall take this path, for by so doing we shall overtake the family in a minute;" so into the path we went; it was scarcely wide enough to admit the carriage, and exceedingly steep and broken; we proceeded ascending and descending, the wheels cracked, and the motion was so violent that we were in danger of being cast out as from a sling. I saw that if we remained in the carriage it must be broken in pieces, as our weight

must insure its destruction. I called to him in Portuguese to stop, but he flogged and spurred the beasts the more. My man now entreated me for God's sake to speak to him in French, for, if any thing would pacify him, that would. I did so, and entreated him to let us dismount and walk, till we had cleared this dangerous way. The result justified Antonio's anticipation. He instantly stopped and said, "Sir, you are master, you have only to command and I shall obey." We dismounted and walked on till we reached the great road, when we once more seated ourselves.

The family were about a quarter of a mile in advance, and we were no sooner reseated, than he lashed the mules into full gallop for the purpose of overtaking it; his cloak had fallen from his shoulder, and in endeavouring to readjust it, he dropped the string from his hand by which he guided the large mule, it became entangled in the legs of the poor animal, which fell heavily on its neck, it struggled for a moment, and then lay stretched across the way, the shafts over its body. I was pitched forward into the dirt, and the drunken driver fell upon the murdered mule.

I was in a great rage, and cried, "You drunken renegade, who are ashamed to speak the language of your own country, you have broken the staff of your existence, and may now starve." "Paciencia," said he, and began kicking the head of the mule, in order to make it rise; but I pushed him down, and taking his knife, which had fallen from his pocket, cut the bands by which it was attached to the carriage, but life had fled; and the film of death had begun to cover its eyes.

The fellow, in the recklessness of intoxication, seemed at first disposed to make light of his loss, saying, "The mule is dead, it was God's will that she should die, what more can be said? Paciencia." Meanwhile, I despatched Antonio to the town for the purpose of hiring mules, and, having taken my baggage from the chaise, waited on the road side until he should arrive.

The fumes of the liquor began now to depart from the fellow's brain; he clasped his hands, and exclaimed, "Blessed Virgin, what is to become of me? How am I to support myself? Where am I to get another mule? For my mule, my best mule, is dead, she fell upon the road, and died of a sudden! I have been in France and in other countries, and have seen beasts of all kinds, but such a mule as that I have never seen; but she is dead,—my mule is dead—she fell upon the road and died of a sudden!" He continued in this strain for a considerable time, and the burden of his lamentation was always, "My mule is dead, she fell upon the road and died of a sudden." At length he took the collar from the creature's neck, and put it upon the other, which with some difficulty he placed in the shafts.

A beautiful boy of about thirteen now came from the direction of the town, running along the road with the velocity of a hare: he stopped before the dead mule and burst into tears: it was the man's son, who had heard of the accident from Antonio. This was too much for the poor fellow; he ran up to the boy, and said, "Don't cry, our bread is gone, but it is God's will; the mule is dead!" He then flung himself on the ground, uttering fearful cries. "I could have borne my loss," said he, "but when I saw my child cry, I became a fool." I give him two or three crowns, and added some words of comfort; assuring him that I had no doubt that if he abandoned drink, the Almighty God would take compassion on him and repair his loss. At length he became more composed, and placing my baggage in the chaise, we returned to the town, where I found two excellent riding mules awaiting my arrival at the inn. I did not see the Spanish woman, or I should have told her of the little efficacy of rosemary in this instance.

I have known several drunkards amongst the Portuguese, but, without one exception, they have been individuals who, having travelled abroad, like this fellow, have returned with a contempt for their own country, and polluted with the worst vices of the lands which they have visited.

I would strongly advise any of my countrymen who may chance to read these lines, that, if their fate lead them into Spain or Portugal, they avoid hiring as domestics, or being connected with, individuals of the lower classes who speak any other language than their own, as the probability is that they are heartless thieves and drunkards. These gentry are invariably saying all they can in dispraise of their native land; and it is my opinion, grounded upon experience, that an individual who is capable of such baseness would not hesitate at the perpetration of any villany, for, next to the love of God, the love of country is the best preventive of crime. He who is proud of his country, will be particularly cautious not to do any thing which is calculated to disgrace it.

We now journeyed towards Lisbon, and reached Monte Moro about two o'clock. After taking such refreshment as the place afforded, we pursued our way till we were within a quarter of a league of the huts which stand on the edge of the savage wilderness we had before crossed. Here we were overtaken by a horseman; he was a powerful, middle-sized man, and was mounted on a noble Spanish horse. He had a broad, slouching sombrero on his head, and wore a jerkin of blue cloth, with large bosses of silver for buttons, and clasps of the same metal; he had breeches of yellow leather, and immense jack-boots: at his saddle was slung a formidable gun. He inquired if I intended to pass the night at Vendas Novas, and on my replying in the affirmative, he said that he would avail himself of our company. He now looked towards the sun, whose disk was rapidly sinking beneath the horizon, and entreated us to spur on and make the most of its light, for that the moor was a horrible place in the dusk. He placed himself at our head, and we trotted briskly on, the boy or muleteer who attended us running behind without exhibiting the slightest symptom of fatigue.

We entered upon the moor, and had advanced about a mile when dark night fell around us; we were in a wild path, with high brushwood on either side, when the rider said that he could not confront the darkness, and begged me to ride on before and he would follow after: I could hear him trembling. I asked the reason of his terror, and he replied that at one time darkness was the same thing to him as day, but that of late years he dreaded it especially in wild places. I complied with his request, but I was ignorant of the way, and as I could scarcely see my hand, was continually going wrong. This made the man impatient, and he again placed himself at our head. We proceeded so for a considerable way, when he again stopped, and said that the power of the darkness was too much for him. His horse seemed to be infected with the same panic, for it shook in every limb. I now told him to call on the name of the Lord Jesus, who was able to turn the darkness into light, but he gave a terrible shout, and, brandishing his gun aloft, discharged it in the air. His horse sprang forward at full speed, and my mule, which was one of the swiftest of its kind, took fright and followed at the heels of the charger. Antonio and the boy were left behind. On we flew like a whirlwind, the hoofs of the animals illuming the path with the sparks of fire they struck from the stones. I knew not whither we were going, but the dumb creatures were acquainted with the way, and soon brought us to Vendas Novas, where we were rejoined by our companions.

I thought this man was a coward, but I did him injustice, for during the day he was as brave as a lion, and feared no one. About five years since, he had overcome two robbers who had attacked him on the moors, and, after tying their hands behind them, had delivered them up to justice; but at night the rustling of a leaf filled him with terror. I have known similar instances of the kind in persons of otherwise extraordinary resolution. For myself, I confess I am not a person of extraordinary resolution, but the dangers of the night daunt me no more than those of mid-day. The man in question was a farmer from Évora, and a person of considerable wealth.

I found the inn at Vendas Novas thronged with people, and had some difficulty in obtaining accommodation and refreshment. It was occupied by the family of a certain Fidalgo, from Estremoz; he was on the way to Lisbon, conveying a large sum of money, as was said—probably the rents of his estates. He had with him a body-guard of four-and-twenty of his dependants, each armed with a rifle; they consisted of his swineherds, shepherds, cowherds, and hunters, and were commanded by two youths, his son, and nephew; the latter of whom was in regimentals; nevertheless, notwithstanding the number of his troop, it appeared that the Fidalgo laboured under considerable apprehension of being despoiled upon the waste which lay between Vendas Novas and Pegoens, as he had just requested a guard of four soldiers from the officer who commanded a detachment stationed here: there were many females in his company, who, I was told, were his illegitimate daughters—for he bore an infamous moral character, and was represented to me as a stanch friend of Don Miguel. It was not long before he came up to me and my new acquaintance, as we sat by the kitchen fire: he was a tall man of about sixty, but stooped much. His countenance was by no means pleasing: he had a long hooked nose, small twinkling cunning eyes, and what I liked worst of all, a continual sneering smile, which I firmly believe to be the index of a treacherous and malignant heart. He addressed me in Spanish, which, as he resided not far from the frontier, he spoke with fluency, but, contrary to my usual practice, I was reserved and silent.

On the following morning I rose at seven, and found that the party from Estremoz had started several hours previously. I breakfasted with my acquaintance of the preceding night, and we set out to accomplish what remained of our journey. The sun had now arisen; and all his fears had now left him—he breathed defiance against all the robbers of the Alemtejo. When we had advanced about a league, the boy who attended us said he saw heads of men among the brushwood. Our cavalier instantly seized his gun, and causing his horse to make two or three lofty bounds, held it in one hand, the muzzle pointed in the direction indicated, but the heads did not again make their appearance, and it was probably but a false alarm.

We resumed our way, and the conversation turned, as might be expected, upon robbers. My companion, who seemed to be acquainted with every inch of ground over which we passed, had a legend to tell of every dingle and every pine-clump. We reached a slight eminence, on the top of which grew three stately pines; about half a league farther on was another similar one; these two eminences commanded a view of the road from Pegoens and Vendas Novas, so that all people going and coming could be descried, whilst yet at a distance. My friend told me that these heights were favourite stations of robbers. Some two years since, a band of six mounted banditti remained there three days, and plundered whomsoever approached from either quarter: their horses, saddled and bridled, stood piqueted at the foot of the trees, and two scouts, one for each eminence, continually sat in the topmost branches and gave notice of the approach of travellers; when at a proper distance, the robbers below sprung upon their horses, and putting them to full gallop, made at their prey, shouting, *Rendete, Picaro! Rendete, Picaro!* (Surrender, scoundrel, surrender!) We, however, passed unmolested, and about a quarter of a mile before we reached Pegoens, overtook the family of the Fidalgo.

Had they been conveying the wealth of Ind through the deserts of Arabia, they could not have travelled with more precaution. The nephew, with drawn sabre, rode in front; pistols in his holsters, and the usual Spanish gun slung at his saddle. Behind him tramped six men in a rank, with muskets shouldered, and each of them wore at his girdle a hatchet, which was probably intended to cleave the thieves to the brisket should they venture to come to close quarters. There were six vehicles, two of them calashes, in which latter rode the Fidalgo and his daughters; the others were covered carts, and seemed to be filled with household furniture; each of these vehicles had an armed rustic on either side; and the son, a lad about sixteen, brought up the rear, with a squad equal to that of his cousin in the van. The soldiers, who by good fortune were light horse, and admirably mounted, were galloping about in all directions, for the purpose of driving the enemy from cover, should they happen to be lurking in the neighbourhood.

I could not help thinking as I passed by, that this martial array was very injudicious, for though it was calculated to awe plunderers, it was likewise calculated to allure them, as it seemed to hint that immense wealth was passing through their territories. I do not know how the soldiers and rustics would have behaved in case of an attack; but am inclined to believe that if three such men as Richard Turpin had suddenly galloped forth from behind one of the bush-covered knolls, neither the numbers nor resistance opposed to them would have prevented them from bearing away the contents of the strong box jingling in their saddle-bags.

From this moment nothing worthy of relating occurred till our arrival at Aldea Gallega, where we passed the night, and next morning at three o'clock embarked in the passage-boat for Lisbon, where we arrived at eight—and thus terminates my first wandering in the Alemtejo.

CHAPTER V.

The College—The Rector—Shibboleth—National Prejudices—Youthful Sports—Jews of Lisbon—
Bad Faith—Crime and Superstition—Strange Proposal.

ONE afternoon Antonio said to me, "It has struck me, Senhor, that your worship would like to see the college of the English * * * * *." "By all means," I replied, "pray conduct me thither." So he led me through various streets until we stopped before the gate of a large building in one of the most elevated situations in Lisbon; upon our ringing, a kind of porter presently made his appearance, and demanded our business. Antonio explained it to him. He hesitated for a moment; but presently bidding us enter, conducted us to a large gloomy-looking stone hall, where, begging us to be seated, he left us. We were soon joined by a venerable personage, seemingly about seventy, in a kind of flowing robe or surplice, with a collegiate cap upon his head; notwithstanding his age there was a ruddy tinge upon his features, which were perfectly English. Coming slowly up he addressed me in the English tongue, requesting to know how he could serve me. I informed him that I was an English traveller, and should be happy to be permitted to inspect the college, provided it were customary to show it to strangers. He informed me that there could be no objection to accede to my request, but that I came at rather an unfortunate moment, it being the hour of refection. I apologized, and was preparing to retire, but he begged me to remain, as, in a few minutes, the refection would be over. when the principals of the college would do themselves the pleasure of waiting on me.

We sat down on the stone bench, when he commenced surveying me attentively for some time, and then cast his eyes on Antonio. "Whom have we here?" said he to the latter; "surely your features are not unknown to me?" "Probably not, your reverence," replied Antonio, getting up and bowing most profoundly. "I lived in the family of the Countess * * *, at Cintra, when your venerability was her spiritual guide." "True, true," said the old gentleman, sighing, "I remember you now. Ah, Antonio, things are strangely changed since then. A new government—a new system—a new religion, I may say." Then looking again at me, he demanded whither I was journeying. "I am going to Spain," said I, "and have stopped at Lisbon by the way." "Spain, Spain!" said the old man; "surely you have chosen a strange time to visit Spain; there is much blood-shedding in Spain at present, and violent wars and tumults." "I consider the cause of Don Carlos as already crushed," I replied; "he has lost the only general capable of leading his armies to Madrid. Zumalacarregui, his Cid, has fallen." "Do not flatter yourself; I beg your pardon, but do not think, young man, that

the Lord will permit the powers of darkness to triumph so easily; the cause of Don Carlos is not lost; its success did not depend on the life of a frail worm like him whom you have mentioned." We continued in discourse some little time, when he arose, saying that by this time he believed the refection was concluded.

He had scarcely left me five minutes when three individuals entered the stone hall, and advanced slowly towards me;—the principals of the college, said I to myself; and so indeed they were. The first of those gentlemen, and to whom the other two appeared to pay considerable deference, was a thin, spare person, somewhat above the middle height; his complexion was very pale, his features emaciated but fine, his eyes dark and sparkling; he might be about fifty—the other two were men in the prime of life. One was of rather low stature; his features were dark, and wore that pinched and mortified expression so frequently to be observed in the countenance of the English * * * * *: the other was a bluff, ruddy, and rather good-looking young man; all three were dressed alike in the usual college cap and silk gown. Coming up, the eldest of the three took me by the hand and thus addressed me in clear silvery tones:—

"Welcome, Sir, to our poor house; we are always happy to see in it a countryman from our beloved native land; it will afford us extreme satisfaction to show you over it; it is true that satisfaction is considerably diminished by the reflection that it possesses nothing worthy of the attention of a traveller; there is nothing curious pertaining to it save perhaps its economy, and that, as we walk about, we will explain to you. Permit us, first of all, to introduce ourselves to you; I am rector of this poor English house of refuge; this gentleman is our professor of humanity, and this (pointing to the ruddy personage) is our professor of polite learning, Hebrew, and Syriac.

Myself.—I humbly salute you all; excuse me if I inquire who was the venerable gentleman who put himself to the inconvenience of staying with me whilst I was awaiting your leisure.

Rector.—O! a most admirable personage, our almoner, our chaplain; he came into this country before any of us were born, and here he has continued ever since. Now let us ascend that we may show you our poor house: but how is this, my dear Sir, how is it that I see you standing uncovered in our cold, damp hall?

Myself.—I can easily explain that to you; it is a custom which has become quite natural to me. I am just arrived from Russia, where

c 2

I have spent some years. A Russian invariably takes off his hat whenever he enters beneath a roof, whether it pertain to hut, shop, or palace. To omit doing so would be considered as a mark of brutality and barbarism, and for the following reason: in every apartment of a Russian house there is a small picture of the Virgin stuck up in a corner, just below the ceiling—the hat is taken off out of respect to her.

Quick glances of intelligence were exchanged by the three gentlemen. I had stumbled upon their shibboleth, and proclaimed myself an Ephraimite, and not of Gilead. I have no doubt that up to that moment they had considered me as one of themselves—a member, and perhaps a priest, of their own ancient, grand, and imposing religion, for such it is, I must confess—an error into which it was natural that they should fall. What motives could a Protestant have for intruding upon their privacy? What interest could be take in inspecting the economy of their establishment? So far, however, from relaxing in their attention after this discovery, their politeness visibly increased, though, perhaps, a scrutinizing observer might have detected a shade of less cordiality in their manner.

Rector.—Beneath the ceiling in every apartment? I think I understood you so. How delightful—how truly interesting; a picture of the *Blessed* Virgin beneath the ceiling in every apartment of a Russian house! Truly, this intelligence is as unexpected as it is delightful. I shall from this moment entertain a much higher opinion of the Russians than hitherto—most truly an example worthy of imitation. I wish sincerely that it was our own practice to place an *image* of the *Blessed* Virgin beneath the ceiling in every corner of our houses. What say you, our professor of humanity? What say you to the information so obligingly communicated to us by this excellent gentleman?

Humanity Professor.—It is, indeed, most delightful, most cheering, I may say; but I confess that I was not altogether unprepared for it. The adoration of the Blessed Virgin is becoming every day more extended in countries where it has hitherto been unknown or forgotten. Dr. W——, when he passed through Lisbon, gave me some most interesting details with respect to the labours of the propaganda in India. Even England, our own beloved country . . . .
. . . .

My obliging friends showed me all over their "poor house," it certainly did not appear a very rich one; it was spacious, and rather dilapidated. The library was small, and possessed nothing remarkable; the view, however, from the roof, over the greater part of Lisbon and the Tagus, was very grand and noble; but I did not visit this place in the hope of seeing busts, or books, or fine prospects,—I visited this strange old house to converse with its inmates, for my favourite, I might say, my only study, is man. I found these gentlemen much what I had anticipated;

for this was not the first time that I had visited an English * * * * * establishment in a foreign land. They were full of amiability and courtesy to their heretic countryman, and though the advancement of their religion was with them an object of paramount importance, I soon found that, with ludicrous inconsistency, they cherished, to a wonderful degree, national prejudices almost extinct in the mother land, even to the disparagement of those of their own darling faith. I spoke of the English * * * *, of their high respectability, and of the loyalty which they had uniformly displayed to their sovereign, though of a different religion, and by whom they had been not unfrequently subjected to much oppression and injustice.

Rector.—My dear Sir, I am rejoiced to hear you; I see that you are well acquainted with the great body of those of our faith in England. They are, as you have well described them, a most respectable and loyal body; from loyalty, indeed, they never swerved, and though they have been accused of plots and conspiracies, it is now well known that such had no real existence, but were merely calumnies invented by their religious enemies. During the civil wars the English * * * * cheerfully shed their blood and squandered their fortunes in the cause of the unfortunate martyr, notwithstanding that he never favoured them, and invariably looked upon them with suspicion. At present the English * * * * are the most devoted subjects of our gracious sovereign. I should be happy if I could say as much for our Irish brethren; but their conduct has been—oh! detestable. Yet what can you expect? The true * * * * blush for them. A certain person is a disgrace to the church of which he pretends to be the servant. Where does he find in our canons sanction for his proceedings, his undutiful expressions towards one who is his sovereign by divine right, and who can do no wrong? And above all, where does he find authority for inflaming the passions of a vile mob against a nation intended by nature and by position to command them?

Myself.—I believe there is an Irish college in this city?

Rector.—I believe there is; but it does not flourish, there are few or no pupils. Oh!

I looked through a window, at a great height, and saw about twenty or thirty fine lads sporting in a court below. "This is as it should be," said I; "those boys will not make worse priests from a little early devotion to trap-ball and cudgel playing. I dislike a staid, serious, puritanic education, as I firmly believe that it encourages vice and hypocrisy."

We then went into the Rector's room, where, above a crucifix, was hanging a small portrait.

Myself.—That was a great and portentous man, honest withal. I believe the body of which he was the founder, and which has been so much decried, has effected infinitely more good than it has caused harm.

Rector.—What do I hear! You, an Englishman and a Protestant, and yet an admirer of Ignatius Loyola!

Myself.—I will say nothing with respect to the doctrine of the Jesuits, for, as you have observed, I am a Protestant; but I am ready to assert that there are no people in the world better qualified, upon the whole, to be intrusted with the education of youth. Their moral system and discipline are truly admirable. Their pupils, in after life, are seldom vicious and licentious characters, and are in general men of learning, science, and possessed of every elegant accomplishment. I execrate the conduct of the liberals of Madrid in murdering last year the helpless fathers, by whose care and instruction two of the finest minds of Spain have been evolved—the two ornaments of the liberal cause and modern literature of Spain, for such are Toreno and Martinez de la Rosa. . . . . .

. . . .

Gathered in small clusters about the pillars at the lower extremities of the Gold and Silver streets in Lisbon, may be observed, about noon in every day, certain strange-looking men, whose appearance is neither Portuguese nor European. Their dress generally consists of a red cap, with a blue silken tassel at the top of it, a blue tunic girded at the waist with a red sash, and wide linen pantaloons or trousers. He who passes by these groups generally hears them conversing in broken Spanish or Portuguese, and occasionally in a harsh guttural language, which the oriental traveller knows to be the Arabic, or a dialect thereof. These people are the Jews of Lisbon. Into the midst of one of these groups I one day introduced myself, and pronounced a beraka, or blessing. I have lived in different parts of the world, much amongst the Hebrew race, and am well acquainted with their ways and phraseology. I was rather anxious to become acquainted with the tate of the Portuguese Jews, and I had now an opportunity. "The man is a powerful rabbi," said a voice in Arabic; "it behoves us to treat him kindly." They welcomed me. I favoured their mistake, and in a few days I knew all that related to them and their traffic in Lisbon.

I found them a vile, infamous rabble, about two hundred in number. With a few exceptions, they consist of escapados from the Barbary shore, from Tetuan, from Tangier, but principally from Mogadore; fellows who have fled to a foreign land from the punishment due to their misdeeds. Their manner of life in Lisbon is worthy of such a goodly assemblage of *amis réunis*. The generality of them pretend to work in gold and silver, and keep small peddling shops; they, however, principally depend for their livelihood on an extensive traffic in stolen goods which they carry on. It is said that there is honour amongst thieves, but this is certainly not the case with the Jews of Lisbon, for they are so greedy and avaricious, that they are constantly quarrelling about their ill-gotten gain, the re-

sult being that they frequently ruin each other. Their mutual jealousy is truly extraordinary. If one, by cheating and roguery, gains a cruzado in the presence of another, the latter instantly says, "I cry halves," and if the first refuse, he is instantly threatened with an information. The manner in which they cheat each other has, with all its infamy, occasionally something extremely droll and ludicrous. I was one day in the shop of a Swiri, or Jew of Mogadore, when a Jew from Gibraltar entered, with a Portuguese female, who held in her hand a mantle, richly embroidered with gold.

Gibraltar Jew.—(Speaking in broken Arabic.) Good-day, O Swiri; God has favoured me this day; here is a bargain by which we shall both gain. I have bought this mantle of the woman almost for nothing, for it is stolen; but I am poor, as you know; I have not a cruzado; pay her therefore the price, that we may then forthwith sell the mantle and divide the gain.

Swiri.—Willingly, brother of Gibraltar; I will pay the woman for the mantle; it does not appear a bad one.

Thereupon he flung two cruzados to the woman, who forthwith left the shop.

Gibraltar Jew.—Thanks, brother Swiri, this is very kind of you. Now let us go and sell the mantle; the gold alone is well worth a moidore: but I am poor, and have nothing to eat; give me, therefore, the half of that sum, and keep the mantle; I shall be content.

Swiri.—May Allah blot out your name, you thief! What mean you by asking me for money? I bought the mantle of the woman, and paid for it. I know nothing of you. Go out of my doors, dog of a Nazarene! if not, I will pay you with a kick.

The dispute was referred to one of the sabios, or priests; but the sabio, who was also from Mogadore, at once took the part of the Swiri, and decided that the other should have nothing. Whereupon the Gibraltar Jew cursed the sabio, his father, mother, and all his family. The sabio replied, "I put you in ndui," a kind of purgatory, or hell. "I put you in seven nduis," retorted the incensed Jew, over whom, however, superstitious fear speedily prevailed; he faltered, became pale, and, dropping his voice, retreated, trembling in every limb.

The Jews have two synagogues in Lisbon: both are small; one is, however, tolerably well furnished; it has its reading-desk, and in the middle there is a rather handsome chandelier; the other is little better than a sty, filthy to a degree, without ornament of any kind. The congregation of this last are thieves to a man; no Jew of the slightest respectability ever enters it.

How well do superstition and crime go hand in hand! These wretched beings break the eternal commandments of their Maker without scruple; but they will not partake of the beast of the uncloven foot and the fish which has no scales. They pay no regard to the denunciations of holy prophets against the children of sin, but they quake at the sound of a dark cabalistic word, pronounced by one perhaps their equal or superior in villany, as if God would delegate the exercise of his power to the workers of iniquity.

I was one day sauntering on the Casidæa, when a Jew, with whom I had previously exchanged a word or two, came up and addressed me.

Jew.—The blessing of God upon you, brother! I know you to be a wise and powerful man, and I have conceived much regard for you; it is on that account that I wish to put you in the way of gaining much money. Come with me, and I will conduct you to a place where there are forty chests of tea. It is a seréka, (a robbery,) and the thieves are willing to dispose of it for a trifle, for there is search being made, and they are in much fear. I can raise one-half of what they demand; do you supply the other: we will then divide it, each shall go his own way and dispose of his portion.

Myself.—Wherefore, O son of Arbat, do you propose this to me, who am a stranger? Surely you are mad. Have you not your own people about you, whom you know, and in whom you can confide?

Jew.—It is because I know our people here that I do not confide in them; we are in the galoot of sin. Were I to confide in my brethren, there would be a dispute, and perhaps they would rob me; and few of them have any money. Were I to apply to the sabio, he might consent, but when I ask for my portion he would put me in ndui. You I do not fear; you are good, and would do me no harm, unless I attempted to deceive you, and that I dare not do, for I know you are powerful. Come with me, master, for I wish to gain something, that I may return to Arbat, where I have children . . . .

. . . .

Such are Jews in Lisbon.

CHAPTER VI.

Cold of Portugal—Extortion prevented—Sensation of Loneliness—The Dog—The Convent—Enchanting Landscape—Moorish Fortresses—Prayer for the Sick.

ABOUT a fortnight after my return from Evora, having made the necessary preparations, I set out on my journey for Badajoz, from which town I intended to take the diligence to Madrid. Badajoz lies about a hundred miles distant from Lisbon, and is the principal frontier town of Spain in the direction of the Alemtejo. To reach this place, it was necessary to retravel the road as far as Monte Moro, which I had already passed in my excursion to Evora; I had therefore very little pleasure to anticipate from novelty of scenery. Moreover, in this journey I should be a solitary traveller, with no other companion than the muleteer, as it was my intention to take my servant no farther than Aldea Gallega, for which place I started at four in the afternoon. Warned by former experience, I did not now embark in a small boat, but in one of the regular passage felouks, in which we reached Aldea Gallega, after a voyage of six hours; for the boat was heavy, there was no wind to propel it, and the crew were obliged to ply their huge oars the whole way. In a word, this passage was the reverse of the first,—safe in every respect, but so sluggish and tiresome that I a hundred times wished myself again under the guidance of the wild lad, galloping before the hurricane over the foaming billows. From eight till ten the cold was truly terrible; and though I was closely wrapped in an excellent fur "shoob," with which I had braved the frosts of Russian winters, I shivered in every limb, and was far more rejoiced when I again set my foot on the Alemtejo, than when I landed for the first time, after having escaped the horrors of the tempest.

I took up my quarters for the night at a house to which my friend who feared the darkness had introduced me on my return from Evora, and where, though I paid mercilessly dear for every thing, the accommodation was superior to that of the common inn in the square. My first care now was to inquire for mules to convey myself and baggage to Elvas, from whence there are but three short leagues to the Spanish town of Badajoz. The people of the house informed me that they had an excellent pair at my disposal, but when I inquired the price, they were not ashamed to demand four moidores. I offered them three, which was too much, but which, however, they did not accept, for knowing me to be an Englishman, they thought they had an excellent opportunity to practice imposition, not imagining that a person so rich as an Englishman *must* be, would go out in a cold night for the sake of obtaining a reasonable bargain. They were, however, much mistaken, as I told them that rather than encourage them in their knavery I should be content to return to Lisbon; whereupon they dropped their demand to three and a half, but I made them no answer, and going out with Antonio, proceeded to the house of the old man who had accompanied us to Evora. We knocked a considerable time, for he was in bed; at length he arose and admitted us, but on hearing our object, he said that his mules were again gone to Evora, under the charge of the boy for the purpose of transporting some articles of merchandise. He, however, recommended us to a person in the neighbourhood who kept mules for hire, and there Antonio engaged two fine beasts for two moideres and a half. I say *he* engaged them, for I stood aloof and spoke not, and the proprietor, who exhibited them, and who stood half-dressed, with a lamp in his hand and shivering with cold, was not aware that they were intended for a foreigner till the agreement was made, and he had received a part of the sum in earnest. I returned to the inn well pleased, and having taken some refreshment, went to rest, paying little attention to the people, who glanced daggers at me from their small Jewish eyes.

At five the next morning the mules were at the door; a lad of some nineteen or twenty years of age attended them; he was short but exceedingly strong built, and possessed the largest head which I ever beheld upon mortal shoulders; neck he had none, at least I could discern nothing which could be entitled to that name. His features were hideously ugly, and upon addressing him I discovered that he was an idiot. Such was my intended companion in a journey of nearly a hundred miles, which would occupy four days, and which lay over the most savage and ill noted track in the whole kingdom. I took leave of my servant almost with tears, for he had always served me with the greatest fidelity, and had exhibited an assiduity and a wish to please which afforded me the utmost satisfaction.

We started, my uncouth guide sitting tailor-fashion on the sumpter mule upon the baggage. The moon had just gone down, and the morning was pitchy dark, and, as usual, piercingly cold. We soon entered the dismal wood, which I had already traversed, and through which we wended our way for some time, slowly and mournfully. Not a sound was to be heard save the trampling of the animals, not a breath of air moved the leafless branches, no animal stirred in the thickets, no bird, not even the owl, flew over our heads, all seemed desolate and dead, and during my many and far wanderings, I never experienced a greater sensation of loneliness, and a greater desire for conversation and an exchange of ideas than then. To speak to the idiot was useless, for though competent to show the road, with which he was well acquainted, he had no other answer than an uncouth laugh to any question put to him. Thus situated, like many other persons when human comfort is not at hand, I turned my heart to God, and began to commune with him, the result of which was that my mind soon became quieted and comforted.

We passed on our way uninterrupted; no thieves showed themselves, nor indeed did we see a single individual till we arrived at Pegoens, and from thence to Vendas Novas our fortune was the same. I was welcomed with great kindness by the people of the hostelry of the latter place, who were well acquainted with me, on account of my having twice passed the night under their roof. The name of the keeper of this inn is, or was, José Dias Azido, and unlike the generality of those of the same profession as himself in Portugal, he is an honest man, and a stranger and foreigner who takes up his quarters at his

inn, may rest assured that he will not be most unmercifully pillaged and cheated when the hour of reckoning shall arrive, as he will not be charged a single ré more than a native Portuguese on a similar occasion. I paid at this place exactly one half of the sum which was demanded from me at Arroyolos, where I passed the ensuing night, and where the accommodation was in every respect inferior.

At twelve next day we arrived at Monte Moro, and, as I was not pressed for time, I determined upon viewing the ruins which cover the top and middle part of the stately hill with towers above the town. Having ordered some refreshments at the inn where we dismounted, I ascended till I arrived at a large wall or rampart, which, at a certain altitude embraces the whole hill. I crossed a rude bridge of stones, which bestrides a small hollow or trench; and passing by a large tower, entered through a portal into the inclosed part of the hill. On the left hand stood a church, in good preservation, and still devoted to the purposes of religion, but which I could not enter, as the door was locked, and I saw no one at hand to open it.

I soon found that my curiosity had led me to a most extraordinary place, which quite beggars the scanty powers of description with which I am gifted. I stumbled on amongst ruined walls, and at one time found I was treading over vaults, as I suddenly started back from a yawning orifice into which my next step, as I strolled musing along, would have precipitated me. I proceeded for a considerable way by the eastern wall, till I heard a tremendous bark, and presently an immense dog, such as those which guard the flocks in the neighbourhood against the wolves, came bounding to attack me "with eyes that glowed and fangs that grinned." Had I retreated, or had recourse to any other mode of defence than that which I invariably practice under such circumstances, he would probably have worried me; but I stooped till my chin nearly touched my knee, and looked him full in the eyes, and, as John Leyden says, in the noblest ballad which the Land of Heather has produced:—

"The hound he yowled and back he fled,
  As struck with fairy charm."

It is a fact known to many people, and I believe it has been frequently stated, that no large and fierce dog or animal of any kind, with the exception of the bull, which shuts his eyes and rushes blindly forward, will venture to attack an individual who confronts it with a firm and motionless countenance. I say large and fierce, for it is much easier to repel a bloodhound or bear of Finland in this manner than a dunghill cur or a terrier, against which a stick or a stone is a much more certain defence. This will astonish no one who considers that the calm reproving glance of reason, which allays the excesses of the mighty and courageous in our own species, has seldom any other effect than to add to the insolence of the feeble and foolish, who be-

5

come placid as doves upon the infliction of chastisements, which, if attempted to be applied to the former, would only serve to render them more terrible, and, like gunpowder cast on a flame, cause them in mad desperation to scatter destruction around them.

The barking of the dog brought out from a kind of alley an elderly man, whom I supposed to be his master, and of whom I made some inquiries respecting the place. The man was civil, and informed me that he served as a soldier in the British army, under "the great lord," during the Peninsular war. He said that there was a convent of nuns a little further on, which he would show me, and thereupon led the way to the south-east part of the wall, where stood a large dilapidated edifice.

We entered a dark stone apartment, at one corner of which was a kind of window occupied by a turning table, at which articles were received into the convent or delivered out. He rang the bell, and, without saying a word, retired, leaving me rather perplexed; but presently I heard, though the speaker was invisible, a soft feminine voice demanding who I was, and what I wanted. I replied that I was an Englishman travelling into Spain, and that passing through Monte Moro I had ascended the hill for the purpose of seeing the ruins. The voice then said, "I suppose you are a military man going to fight against the king, like the rest of your countrymen." "No," said I, "I am not a military man, but a Christian, and I go not to shed blood, but to endeavour to introduce the gospel of Christ into a country where it is not known;" whereupon there was a stifled titter. I then inquired if there were any copies of the Holy Scriptures in the convent, but the friendly voice could give me no information on that point, and I scarcely believe that its possessor understood the purport of my question. It informed me, that the office of lady abbess of the house was an annual one, and that every year there was a fresh superior. On my inquiring whether the nuns did not frequently find the time exceedingly heavy on their hands, it stated that, when they had nothing better to do, they employed themselves in making cheesecakes, which were disposed of in the neighbourhood. I thanked the voice for its communications, and walked away. Whilst proceeding under the wall of the house towards the south-west, I heard a fresh and louder tittering above my head, and looking up, saw three or four windows crowded with dusky faces and black waving hair; these belonged to the nuns, anxious to obtain a view of the stranger. After kissing my hand repeatedly, I moved on, and soon arrived at the south-west end of this mountain of curiosities. There I found the remains of a large building, which seemed to have been originally erected in the shape of a cross. A tower at its eastern entrance was still entire; the western side was quite in ruins, and stood on the verge of the hill overlooking the valley at the bottom of which ran the stream I have spoken of on a former occasion.

The day was intensely hot, notwithstanding the coldness of the preceding nights; and the brilliant sun of Portugal now illumined a landscape of entrancing beauty. Groves of cork trees covered the farther side of the valley and the distant acclivities, exhibiting here and there charming vistas, where various flocks of cattle were feeding; the soft murmur of the stream, which was at intervals chafed and broken by huge stones, ascended to my ears and filled my mind with delicious feelings. I sat down on the broken wall, and remained gazing, and listening, and shedding tears of rapture; for, of all the pleasures which a bountiful God permitteth his children to enjoy, none are so dear to some hearts as the music of forests and streams, and the view of the beauties of his glorious creation. An hour elapsed, and I still maintained my seat on the wall; the past scenes of my life flitting before my eyes in airy and fantastic array, through which every now and then peeped trees and hills and other patches of the real landscape which I was confronting; the sun burned my visage, but I heeded it not; and I believe that I should have remained till night, buried in these reveries, which, I confess, only serve to enervate the mind, and steal many a minute which might be most profitably employed, had not the report of the gun of a fowler in the valley, which awakened the echoes of the woods, hills, and ruins, caused me to start on my feet, and remember that I had to proceed three leagues before I could reach the hostelry where I intended to pass the night.

I bent my steps to the inn, passing along a kind of rampart; shortly before I reached the portal, which I have already mentioned, I observed a kind of vault on my right hand, scooped out of the side of the hill; its roof was supported by three pillars, though part of it had given way towards the farther end, so that the light was admitted through a chasm in the top. It might have been intended for a chapel, a dungeon, or a cemetery, but I should rather think for the latter; one thing I am certain of, that it was not the work of Moorish hands, and indeed throughout my wandering in this place I saw nothing which reminded me of that most singular people. The hill on which the ruins stand was doubtless originally a strong fortress of the Moors, who, upon their first irruption into the peninsula, seized and fortified most of the lofty and naturally strong positions, but they had probably lost it at an early period, so that the broken walls and edifices, which at present cover the hill, are probably remains of the labours of the Christians after the place had been rescued from the hands of the terrible enemies of their faith. Monte Moro will perhaps recall Cintra to the mind of the traveller, as it exhibits a distant resemblance to that place; nevertheless, there is something in Cintra wild and savage, to which Monte Moro has no pretension: its scathed and gigantic crags are piled upon each other in a manner which seems to menace headlong destruction to whatever is in the neighbourhood; and the ruins which still cling to those crags seem more like eagles' nests than the remains of the habitations even of Moors; whereas those of Monte Moro stand comparatively at their ease on the broad back of a hill, which, though stately and commanding, has no crags nor precipices, and which can be ascended on every side without much difficulty: yet I was much gratified by my visit, and I shall wander far indeed before I forget the voice in the dilapidated convent, the ruined walls amongst which I strayed, and the rampart, where, sunk in dreamy rapture, I sat during a bright sunny hour at Monte Moro.

I returned to the inn, where I refreshed myself with tea and very sweet and delicious cheesecakes, the handiwork of the nuns in the convent above. Observing gloom and unhappiness on the countenances of the people of the house, I inquired the reason of the hostess, who sat almost motionless on the hearth by the fire; whereupon she informed me that her husband was deadly sick with a disorder which, from her description, I supposed to be a species of cholera; she added, that the surgeon who attended him entertained no hopes of his recovery. I replied that it was quite in the power of God to restore her husband in a few hours from the verge of the grave to health and vigour, and that it was her duty to pray to that Omnipotent Being with all fervency. I added, that if she did not know how to pray upon such an occasion, I was ready to pray for her, provided she would join in the spirit of the supplication. I then offered up a short prayer in Portuguese, in which I entreated the Lord to remove, if he thought proper, the burden of affliction under which the family was labouring.

The woman listened attentively, with her hands devoutly clasped, until the prayer was finished, and then gazed at me seemingly with astonishment, but uttered no word by which I could gather that she was pleased or displeased with what I had said. I now bade the family farewell, and having mounted my mule, set forward to Arroyolos.

CHAPTER VII.

The Druids' Stone—The Young Spaniard—Ruffianly Soldiers—Evils of War—Estremoz—The Brawl—Ruined Watch-Tower—Glimpse of Spain—Old Times and New.

AFTER proceeding about a league and a half, a blast came booming from the north, rolling before it immense clouds of dust; happily it did not blow in our faces, or it would have been difficult to proceed, so great was its violence. We had left the road in order to take advantage of one of those short cuts, which, though passable for a horse or a mule, are far too rough to permit any species of carriage to travel along them. We were in the midst of sands, brushwood, and huge pieces of rock, which thickly studded the ground. These are the stones which form the sierras of Spain and Portugal; those singular mountains which rise in naked horridness, like the ribs of some mighty carcass from which the flesh has been torn. Many of these stones, or rocks, grew out of the earth, and many lay on its surface unattached, perhaps wrested from their bed by the waters of the deluge. Whilst toiling along these wild wastes, I observed, a little way to my left, a pile of stones of rather a singular appearance, and rode up to it. It was a druidical altar, and the most perfect and beautiful one of the kind which I had ever seen. It was circular, and consisted of stones immensely large and heavy at the bottom, which towards the top became thinner and thinner, having been fashioned by the hand of art to something of the shape of scollop shells. These were surmounted by a very large flat stone, which slanted down towards the south, where was a door. Three or four individuals might have taken shelter within the interior, in which was growing a small thorn tree.

I gazed with reverence and awe upon the pile where the first colonists of Europe offered their worship to the unknown God. The temples of the mighty and skilful Roman, comparatively of modern date, have crumbled to dust in its neighbourhood. The churches of the Arian Goth, his successor in power, have sunk beneath the earth, and are not to be found; and the mosques of the Moor, the conqueror of the Goth, where and what are they? Upon the rock, masses of hoary and vanishing ruin. Not so the Druid's stone; there it stands on the hill of winds, as strong and as freshly new as the day, perhaps thirty centuries back, when it was first raised, by means which are a mystery. Earthquakes have heaved it, but its cope-stone has not fallen; rain floods have deluged it, but failed to sweep it from its station; the burning sun has flashed upon it, but neither split nor crumbled it; and time, stern old time, has rubbed it with his iron tooth, and with what effect let those who view it declare. There it stands, and he who wishes to study the literature, the learning, and the history of the ancient Celt and Cymbrian, may gaze on its broad covering, and glean from that blank stone the whole known amount. The Roman has left behind him his deathless writings, his history, and his songs; the Goth his liturgy, his traditions, and the germs of noble institutions; the Moor his chivalry, his discoveries in medicine, and the foundations of modern commerce; and where is the memorial of the Druidic races? Yonder: that pile of eternal stone!

We arrived at Arroyolos about seven at night. I took possession of a large two-bedded room, and, as I was preparing to sit down to supper, the hostess came to inquire whether I had any objection to receive a young Spaniard for the night. She said he had just arrived with a train of muleteers, and that she had no other room in which she could lodge him. I replied that I was willing, and in about half an hour he made his appearance, having first supped with his companions. He was a very gentlemanly, good-looking lad of seventeen. He addressed me in his native language, and, finding that I understood him, he commenced talking with astonishing volubility. In the space of five minutes he informed me that, having a desire to see the world, he had run away from his friends, who were people of opulence at Madrid, and that he did not intend to return until he had travelled through various countries. I told him that if what he said was true, he had done a very wicked and foolish action; wicked, because he must have overwhelmed those with grief whom he was bound to honour and love, and foolish, inasmuch as he was going to expose himself to inconceivable miseries and hardships, which would shortly cause him to rue the step he had taken; that he would be only welcome in foreign countries so long as he had money to spend, and when he had none, he would be repulsed as a vagabond, and would perhaps be allowed to perish of hunger. He replied that he had a considerable sum of money with him, no less than a hundred dollars, which would last him a long time,' and that when it was spent he should perhaps be able to obtain more. "Your hundred dollars," said I, "will scarcely last you three months in the country in which you are, even if it be not stolen from you; and you may as well hope to gather money on the tops of the mountains as expect to procure more by honourable means." But he had not yet sufficiently drank of the cup of experience to attend much to what I said, and I soon after changed the subject. About five next morning he came to my bed-side to take leave, as his muleteers were preparing to depart. I gave him the usual Spanish valediction, (Vaya usted con Dios,) and saw no more of him.

At nine, after having paid a most exorbitant sum for slight accommodation, I started from Arroyolos, which is a town or large village situated on very elevated ground, and discernible afar off. It can boast of the remains of a large, ancient, and seemingly Moorish castle, which stands on a hill on the left as you take the road to Estremoz.

About a mile from Arroyolos I overtook a train of carts, escorted by a number of Portuguese soldiers, conveying stores and ammunition into Spain. Six or seven of these soldiers marched a considerable way in front; they were villanous-looking ruffians, upon whose livid and ghastly countenances were written murder, and all the other crimes which the decalogue forbids. As I passed by, one of them, with a harsh, croaking voice, commenced cursing all foreigners. "There," said he, "is this Frenchman riding on horseback," (I was on a mule,) "with a man" (the idiot) "to take care of him, and all because he is rich; whilst I, who am a poor soldier, am obliged to tramp on foot. I could find it in my heart to shoot him dead, for in what respect is he better than I? But he is a foreigner, and the devil helps foreigners and hates the Portuguese." He continued shouting his remarks until I got about forty yards in advance, when I commenced laughing; but it would have been more prudent in me to have held my peace, for the next moment, with bang—bang, two bullets, well aimed, came whizzing past my ears. A small river lay just before me, though the bridge was a considerable way on my left. I spurred my animal through it, closely followed by the terrified guide, and commenced galloping along a sandy plain on the other side, and so escaped with my life.

These fellows, with the look of banditti, were in no respect better; and the traveller who should meet them in a solitary place would have little reason to bless his good fortune. One of the carriers, (all of whom were Spaniards from the neighbourhood of Badajoz, and had been despatched into Portugal for the purpose of conveying the stores,) whom I afterwards met in the aforesaid town, informed me that the whole party were equally bad, and that he and his companions had been plundered by them of various articles, and threatened with death if they attempted to complain. How frightful to figure to oneself an army of such beings in a foreign land, sent thither either to invade or defend; and yet Spain, at the time I am writing this, is looking forward to armed assistance from Portugal. May the Lord in his mercy grant that the soldiers who proceed to her assistance may be of a different stamp: and yet, from the lax state of discipline which exists in the Portuguese army, in comparison with that of England and France, I am afraid that the inoffensive population of the disturbed provinces will say that wolves have been summoned to chase away foxes from the sheepfold. O! may I live to see the day when soldiery will no longer be tolerated in any civilized, or at least Christian, country!

I pursued my route to Estremoz, passing by Monte Moro Novo, which is a tall, dusky hill, surmounted by an ancient edifice, probably Moorish. The country was dreary and deserted, but offering here and there a valley studded with cork trees and azinheiras. After mid-day the wind, which during the night and morning had much abated, again blew with such violence as nearly to deprive me of my senses, though it was still in our rear.

I was heartily glad when, on ascending a

rising ground, at about four o'clock, I saw
Estremoz on its hill at something less than a
league's distance. Here the view became
wildly interesting; the sun was sinking in the
midst of red and stormy clouds, and its rays
were reflected on the dun walls of the lofty
town to which we were wending. Not far
distant to the south-west rose Serra Dorso,
which I had seen from Evora, and which is the
most beautiful mountain in the Alemtejo. My
idiot guide turned his uncouth visage towards
it, and becoming suddenly inspired, opened
his mouth for the first time during the day, I
might almost say since we had left Aldea
Gallega, and began to tell me what rare hunting was to be obtained in that mountain. He
likewise described with great minuteness a
wonderful dog, which was kept in the neighbourhood for the purpose of catching the
wolves and wild boars, and for which the proprietor had refused twenty moidores.

At length we reached Estremoz, and took
up our quarters at the principal inn, which
looks upon a large plain or market-place occupying the centre of the town, and which is
so extensive that I should think ten thousand
soldiers at least might perform their evolutions
there with ease.

The cold was far too terrible to permit me
to remain in the chamber to which I had been
conducted; I therefore went down to a kind of
kitchen on one side of the arched passage,
which led under the house to the yard and
stable. A tremendous withering blast poured
through this passage, like the water through
the flush of a mill. A large cork tree
was blazing in the kitchen beneath a spacious chimney; and around it were gathered
a noisy crew of peasants and farmers from the
neighbourhood, and three or four Spanish
smugglers from the frontier. I with difficulty
obtained a place amongst them, as a Portuguese or a Spaniard will seldom make way
for a stranger, till called upon or pushed aside,
but prefers gazing upon him with an expression which seems to say, I know what you
want, but I prefer remaining where I am.

I now first began to observe an alteration
in the language spoken; it had become less
sibilant, and more guttural; and, when addressing each other, the speakers used the
Spanish title of courtesy *usted*, or your worth-
iness, instead of the Portuguese high flowing
vossem se, or your lordship. This is the result
of constant communication with the natives
of Spain, who never condescend to speak
Portuguese, even when in Portugal, but persist in the use of their own beautiful language, which, perhaps, at some future period,
the Portuguese will generally adopt. This
would greatly facilitate the union of the two
countries, hitherto kept asunder by the natural
waywardness of mankind.

I had not been seated long before the blazing pile, when a fellow, mounted on a fine
spirited horse, dashed from the stables through
the passage into the kitchen, where he commenced displaying his horsemanship, by
causing the animal to wheel about with the

velocity of a mill-stone, to the great danger
of everybody in the apartment. He then
galloped out upon the plain, and after half an
hour's absence returned, and having placed
his horse once more in the stable, came and
seated himself next to me, to whom he commenced talking in a gibberish of which I
understood very little, but which he intended
for French. He was half intoxicated, and
soon became three parts so, by swallowing
glass after glass of aguardiente. Finding
that I made him no answer, he directed his
discourse to one of the contrabandistas, to
whom he talked in bad Spanish. The latter
either did not or would not understand him;
but at last, losing patience, called him a
drunkard, and told him to hold his tongue.
The fellow, enraged at this contempt, flung
the glass out of which he was drinking at the
Spaniard's head, who sprang up like a tiger,
and unsheathing instantly a snick and snee
knife, made an upward cut at the fellow's
cheek, and would have infallibly laid it open;
had I not pulled his arm down just in time to
prevent worse effects than a scratch above the
lower jawbone, which, however, drew blood.
The smuggler's companions interfered, and
with much difficulty led him off to a small
apartment in the rear of the house, where
they slept, and kept the furniture of their
mules. The drunkard then commenced singing, or rather yelling, the Marseillois hymn;
and after having annoyed every one for nearly
an hour, was persuaded to mount his horse
and depart, accompanied by one of his neighbours. He was a pig merchant of the vicinity; but had formerly been a trooper in the
army of Napoleon, where, I suppose, like the
drunken coachman of Evora, he had picked
up his French and his habits of intoxication.

From Estremoz to Elvas the distance is six
leagues. I started at nine next morning; the
first part of the way lay through an enclosed
country, but we soon emerged upon wild bleak
downs, over which the wind, which still pursued us, howled most mournfully. We met
no one on the route; and the scene was desolate in the extreme; the heaven was of a dark
gray, through which no glimpse of the sun
was to be perceived. Before us, at a great
distance, on an elevated ground, rose a tower
—the only object which broke the monotony
of the waste. In about two hours from the
time when we first discovered it, we reached
a fountain, at the foot of the hill on which it
stood; the water, which gushed into a long
stone trough, was beautifully clear and transparent, and we stopped here to water the animals.

Having dismounted, I left the guide, and
proceeded to ascend the hill on which the tower
stood. Though the ascent was very gentle,
I did not accomplish it without difficulty; the
ground was covered with sharp stones, which,
in two or three instances, cut through my
boots and wounded my feet; and the distance
was much greater than I had expected. I at
last arrived at the ruin, for such it was. I
found it had been one of those watch-towers
or small fortresses called in Portuguese ata-

kiss; it was square, and surrounded by a wall, broken down in many places. The tower itself had no door, the lower part being of solid stone work; but on one side were crevices at intervals between the stones, for the purpose of placing the feet, and up this rude staircase I climbed to a small apartment, about five feet square, from which the top had fallen. It commanded an extensive view from all sides, and had evidently been built for the accommodation of those whose business it was to keep watch on the frontier, and at the appearance of an enemy to alarm the country by signals —probably by a fire. Resolute men might have defended themselves in this little fastness against many assailants, who must have been completely exposed to their arrows or musketry, in the ascent.

Being about to leave the place, I heard a strange cry behind a part of the wall which I had not visited, and hastening thither, I found a miserable object in rags, seated upon a stone. It was a maniac—a man about thirty years of age, and I believe deaf and dumb; there he sat, gibbering and mowing, and distorting his wild features into various dreadful appearances. There wanted nothing but this object to render the scene complete; banditti amongst such melancholy desolation would have been by no means so much in keeping. But the maniac, on his stone, in the rear of the wind-beaten ruin overlooking the blasted heath, above which scowled the leaden heaven, presented such a picture of gloom and misery as I believe neither painter nor poet ever conceived in the saddest of their musings. This is not the first instance in which it has been my lot to verify the wisdom of the saying, that truth is sometimes wilder than fiction.

I remounted my mule, and proceeded till, on the top of another hill, my guide suddenly exclaimed, "There is Elvas." I looked in the direction in which he pointed, and beheld a town perched on the top of a lofty hill. On the other side of a deep valley towards the left rose another hill, much higher, on the top of which is the celebrated fort of Elvas, believed to be the strongest place in Portugal. Through the opening between the fort and the town, but in the background and far in Spain, I discerned the misty sides and cloudy head of a stately mountain, which I afterwards learned was Albuquerque, one of the loftiest of Estremadura.

We now got into a cultivated country, and following the road, which wound amongst hedge-rows, we arrived at a place where the ground began gradually to shelve down. Here, on the right, was the commencement of an aqueduct by means of which the town on the opposite hill was supplied; it was at this point scarcely two feet in altitude, but, as we descended, it became higher and higher, and its proportions more colossal. Near the bottom of the valley it took a turn to the left, bestriding the road with one of its arches. I looked up, after passing under it; the water must have been flowing near a hundred feet above my head, and I was filled with wonder at the immensity of the structure which conveyed it. There was, however, one feature which was no slight drawback to its pretensions to grandeur and magnificence; the water was supported not by gigantic single arches, like those of the aqueduct of Lisbon, which stalk over the valley like legs of Titans, but by three layers of arches, which, like three distinct aqueducts, rise above each other. The expense and labour necessary for the erection of such a structure must have been enormous; and, when we reflect with what comparative ease modern art would confer the same advantage, we cannot help congratulating ourselves that we live in times when it is not necessary to exhaust the wealth of a province to supply a town on a hill with one of the first necessaries of existence.

CHAPTER VIII.

Elvas—Extraordinary Longevity—The English Nation—Portuguese Ingratitude—Illiberality—
Fortifications—Spanish Beggar—Badajoz—The Custom House.

ARRIVED at the gate of Elvas, an officer came out of a kind of guard-house, and, having asked me some questions, despatched a soldier with me to the police office, that my passport might be viséed, as upon the frontier they are much more particular with respect to passports than in other parts. This matter having been settled, I entered an hostelry near the same gate, which had been recommended to me by my host at Vendas Novas, and which was kept by a person of the name of Joze Rosado. It was the best in the town, though, for convenience and accommodation, inferior to a hedge alehouse in England. The cold still pursued me, and I was glad to take refuge in an inner kitchen, which, when the door was not open, was only lighted by a fire burning somewhat dimly on the hearth. An elderly female sat beside it in her chair, telling her beads: there was something singular and extraordinary in her look, as well as I could discern by the imperfect light of the apartment. I put a few unimportant questions to her, to which she replied, but seemed to be afflicted to a slight degree with deafness. Her hair was becoming gray, and I said that I believed she was older than myself, but that I was confident she had less snow on her head.

"How old may you be, cavalier?" said

she, giving me that title which in Spain is generally used when an extraordinary degree of respect is wished to oe exhibited. I answered that I was near thirty. "Then," said she, "your were right in supposing that I am older than yourself; I am older than your mother, or your mother's mother: it is more than a hundred years since I was a girl, and sported with the daughters of the town on the hill side." "In that case," said I, "you doubtless remember the earthquake." "Yes," she replied, "if there is any occurrence in my life that I remember, it is that; I was in the church of Elvas at the moment, hearing the mass of the king, and the priest fell on the ground, and let fall the Host from his hands. I shall never forget how the earth shook; it made us all sick; and the houses and walls reeled like drunkards. Since that happened I have seen fourscore years pass by me, yet I was older then than you are now."

I looked with wonder at this surprising female, and could scarcely believe her words. I was, however, assured that she was in fact upwards of a hundred and ten years of age, and was considered the oldest person in Portugal. She still retained the use of her faculties in as full a degree as the generality of people who have scarcely attained the half of her age. She was related to the people of the house.

As the night advanced, several persons entered for the purpose of enjoying the comfort of the fire and for the sake of conversation, for the house was a kind of newsroom, where the principal speaker was the host, a man of some shrewdness and experience, who had served as a soldier in the British army. Amongst others was the officer who commanded at the gate. After a few observations, this gentleman, who was a good-looking young man of five-and-twenty, began to burst forth in violent declamation against the English nation and government, who, he said, had at all times proved themselves selfish and deceitful, but that their present conduct in respect to Spain was particularly infamous, for though it was in their power to put an end to the war at once, by sending a large army thither, they preferred sending a handful of troops, in order that the war might be prolonged, for no other reason than that it was of advantage to them. Having paid him an ironical compliment for his politeness and urbanity, I asked whether he reckoned amongst the selfish actions of the English government and nation, their having expended hundreds of millions of pounds sterling, and an ocean of precious blood, in fighting the battles of Spain and Portugal against Napoleon. "Surely," said I, "the fort of Elvas above our heads, and still more the castle of Badajoz over the water, speak volumes respecting English selfishness, and must, every time you view them, confirm you in the opinion which you have just expressed. And then, with respect to the present combat in Spain, the gratitude which that country evinced to England after the French, by means of English armies, had been expelled,—gratitude

evinced by discouraging the trade of England on all occasions, and by offering up masses in thanksgiving when the English heretics quitted the Spanish shores,—ought now to induce England to exhaust and ruin herself, for the sake of hunting Don Carlos out of his mountains. In deference to your superior judgment," continued I to the officer, "I will endeavour to believe that it would be for the advantage of England were the war prolonged for an indefinite period; nevertheless, you would do me a particular favour by explaining by what process in chemistry blood shed in Spain will find its way into the English treasury in the shape of gold."

As he was not ready with his answer, I took up a plate of fruit which stood on a table beside me, and said, "What do you call these fruits?" "Pomegranates and bolotas," he replied. "Right," said I; "a home-bred Englishman could not have given me that answer; yet he is as much acquainted with pomegranates and bolotas as your lordship is with the line of conduct which it is incumbent upon England to pursue in her foreign and domestic policy."

This answer of mine, I confess, was not that of a Christian, and proved to me how much of the leaven of the ancient man still pervaded me; yet I must be permitted to add, that I believe no other provocation would have elicited from me a reply so full of angry feeling, but I could not command myself when I heard my own glorious land traduced in this unmerited manner. By whom? A Portuguese! a native of a country which has been twice liberated from horrid and detestable thraldom by the hands of Englishmen. But for Wellington and his heroes, Portugal would have been French at this day; but for Napier and his mariners, Miguel would now be lording it in Lisbon. To return, however, to the officer; every one laughed at him, and he presently went away.

The next day I became acquainted with a respectable tradesman of the name of Almeida, a man of talent, though rather rough in his manners. He expressed great abhorrence of the papal system, which had so long spread a darkness like that of death over his unfortunate country; and I had no sooner informed him that I had brought with me a certain quantity of Testaments, which it was my intention to leave for sale at Elvas, than he expressed a great desire to undertake the charge, and said that he would do the utmost in his power to procure a sale for them amongst his numerous customers. Upon showing him a copy, I remarked, Your name is upon the title-page; the Portuguese version of the Holy Scriptures, circulated by the Bible Society, having been executed by a Protestant of the name of Almeida, and first published in the year 1712; whereupon he smiled, and observed that he esteemed it an honour to be connected in name at least with such a man. He scoffed at the idea of receiving any remuneration. and assured me that the feeling of being permitted to co-operate in so holy and useful a cause as the circulation of the Scriptures was quite a sufficient reward.

After having accomplished this matter, I proceeded to survey the environs of the place, and strolled up the hill to the fort on the north side of the town. The lower part of the hill is planted with azinheiras, which give is a picturesque appearance, and at the bottom is a small brook, which I crossed by means of stepping-stones. Arrived at the gate of the fort, I was stopped by the sentry, who, however, civilly told me, that if I sent in my name to the commanding officer, he would make no objection to my visiting the interior. I accordingly sent in my card by a soldier who was lounging about, and, sitting down on a stone, waited his return. He presently appeared, and inquired whether I was an Englishman; to which having replied in the affirmative, he said, " In that case, sir, you cannot enter; indeed, it is not the custom to permit any foreigners to visit the fort." I answered that it was perfectly indifferent to me whether I visited it or not; and, having taken a survey of Badajoz from the eastern side of the hill, descended by the way I came.

This is one of the beneficial results of protecting a nation, and squandering blood and treasure in its defence. The English, who have never been at war with. Portugal, who have fought for its independence on land and sea, and always with success, who have forced themselves by a treaty of commerce to drink its coarse and filthy wines, which no other nation cares to taste, are the most unpopular people who visit Portugal. The French have ravaged the country with fire and sword, and shed the blood of its sons like water; the French buy not its fruits, and loathe its wines, yet there is no bad spirit in Portugal towards the French. The reason of this is no mystery; it is the nature, not of the Portuguese only, but of corrupt and unregenerate man, to dislike his benefactors, who, by conferring benefits upon him, mortify in the most generous manner his miserable vanity.

There is no country in which the English are so popular as in France; but, though the French have been frequently roughly handled by the English, and have seen their capital occupied by an English army, they have never been subjected to the supposed ignominy of receiving assistance from them.

The fortifications of Elvas are models of their kind, and, at the first view, it would seem that the town, if well garrisoned, might bid defiance to any hostile power; but it has its weak point: the western side is commanded by a hill, at the distance of half a mile, from which an experienced general would cannonade it, and probably with success. It is the last town in this part of Portugal, the distance to the Spanish frontier being barely two leagues. It was evidently built as a rival to Badajoz, upon which it looks down from its height across a sandy plain and over the sullen waters of the Guadiana; but, though a strong town, it can scarcely be called a defence to the frontier, which is open on all sides, so

that there would not be the slightest necessity for an invading army to approach within a dozen leagues of its walls, should it be disposed to avoid them. Its fortifications are so extensive, that ten thousand men at least would be required to man them, who, in the event of an invasion, might be far better employed in meeting the enemy in the open field. The French, during their occupation of Portugal, kept a small force in this place, who, at the approach of the British, retreated to the fort, where they shortly after capitulated.

Having nothing farther to detain me at Elvas, I proceeded to cross the frontier into Spain. My idiot guide was on his way back to Aldea Gallega; and, on the fifth of January, I mounted a sorry mule without bridle or stirrups, which I guided by a species of halter: and, followed by a lad who was to attend me on another, I spurred down the hill of Elvas to the plain, eager to arrive in old, chivalrous, romantic Spain. But I soon found that I had no need to quicken the beast which bore me ; for, though covered with sores, wall-eyed, and with a kind of halt in its gait, it cantered along like the wind.

In little more than half an hour we arrived at a brook, whose waters ran vigorously between steep banks. A man who was standing on the side directed me to the ford in the squeaking dialect of Portugal; but whilst I was yet splashing through the water, a voice from the other bank hailed me, in the magnificent language of Spain, in this guise: " *O Señor Caballero, que me de usted una limosna por amor de Dios, una limosnita para que io me compre un traguillo de vino tinto.*" (Charity, Sir Cavalier, for the love of God, bestow an alms upon me, that I may purchase a mouthful of red wine.) In a moment I was on Spanish ground, as the brook, which is called Acaia, is the boundary here of the two kingdoms, and having flung the beggar a small piece of silver, I cried in ecstasy, " *Santiago y cierra España!*". and scoured on my way with more speed than before, paying, as Gil Blas says, little heed to the torrent of blessings which the mendicant poured forth in my rear: yet never was charity more unwisely bestowed, for I was subsequently informed that the fellow was a confirmed drunkard, who took his station every morning at the ford, where he remained the whole day for the purpose of extorting money from the passengers, which he regularly spent every night in the wine-shops of Badajoz. To those who gave him money he returned blessings, and to those who refused, curses; being equally skilled and fluent in the use of either.

Badajoz was now in view, at the distance of little more than half a league. We soon took a turn to the left, towards a bridge of many arches across the Guadiana, which, though so famed in song and ballad, is a very unpicturesque stream, shallow and sluggish, though tolerably wide; its banks were white with linen which the washerwomen had spread out to dry in the sun, which was shining brightly; I heard their singing at a great distance, and the theme seemed to be the praises of the river where they were toiling, for as I approached I could distinguish Guadiana, Guadiana, which reverberated far and wide, pronounced by the clear and strong voices in chorus of many a dark-cheeked maid and matron. I thought there was some analogy between their employment and my own: I was about to tan my northern complexion by exposing myself to the hot sun of Spain, in the humble hope of being able to cleanse some of the foul stains of Popery from the minds of its children, with whom I had little acquaintance, whilst they were bronzing themselves on the banks of the river in order to make white the garments of strangers: the words of an Eastern poet returned forcibly to my mind:

" I'll weary myself each night and each day,
    To aid my unfortunate brothers :
As the laundress tans her own face in the ray,
    To cleanse the garments of others."

Having crossed the bridge, we arrived at the northern gate, when out rushed from a species of sentry-box a fellow wearing on his head a high-peaked Andalusian hat, with his figure wrapped up in one of those immense cloaks so well known to those who have travelled in Spain, and which none but a Spaniard can wear in a becoming manner : without saying a word, he laid hold of the halter of the mule, and began to lead it through the gate up a dirty street, crowded with long-cloaked people like himself. I asked him what he meant, but he deigned not to return an answer, the boy, however, who waited upon me said that it was one of the gate-keepers, and that he was conducting us to the Custom House or Alfandega, where the baggage would be examined. Having arrived there, the fellow, who still maintained a dogged silence, began to pull the trunks off the sumpter mule, and commenced uncording them. I was about to give him a severe reproof for his brutality, but before I could open my mouth a stout elderly personage appeared at the door, who I soon found was the principal officer. He looked at me for a moment, and then asked me, in the English language, if I was an Englishman. On my replying in the affirmative, he demanded of the fellow how he dared to have the insolence to touch the baggage without orders, and sternly bade him cord up the trunks again and place them on the mule, which he performed without uttering a word. The gentleman then asked what the trunks contained : I answered clothes and linen; when he begged pardon for the insolence of the subordinate, and informed him that I was at liberty to proceed where I thought proper. I thanked him for his exceeding politeness, and, under guidance of the boy, made the best of my way to the Inn of the Three Nations, to which I had been recommended at Elvas.

CHAPTER IX.

Badajoz—Antonio the Gipsy—Antonio's Proposal—The Proposal accepted—Gipsy Breakfast—Departure from Badajoz—The Gipsy Donkey—Merida—The ruined Wall—The Crone—The Land of the Moor—The Black Men—Life in the Desert—The Supper.

I was now at Badajoz in Spain, a country which for the next four years was destined to be the scene of my labours : but I will not anticipate. The neighbourhood of Badajoz did not prepossess me much in favour of the country which I had just entered; it consists chiefly of brown moors, which bear little but a species of brushwood, called in Spanish carrasco; blue mountains are, however, seen towering up in the far distance, which relieve the scene from the monotony which would otherwise pervade it.

It was at this town of Badajoz, the capital of Estremadura, that I first fell in with those singular people, the Zincali, Gitanos, or Spanish gipsies. It was here I met with the wild Paco, the man with the withered arm, who wielded the cachas (shears) with his left hand; his shrewd wife, Antonia, skilled in hokkano baro, or the great trick ; the fierce gipsy, Antonio Lopez, their father-in-law ; and many other almost equally singular individuals of the Errate, or gipsy blood. It was here that I first preached the gospel to the gipsy people, and commenced that translation of the New Testament in the Spanish gipsy tongue, a portion of which I subsequently printed at Madrid.

After a stay of three weeks at Badajoz, I prepared to depart for Madrid ; late one afternoon, as I was arranging my scanty baggage, the gipsy Antonio entered my apartment, dressed in his zamarra and high-peaked Andalusian hat.

Antonio.—Good evening, brother; they tell me that on the callicaste (*day after to-morrow*) you intend to set out for Madrilati.

Myself.—Such is my intention ; I can stay here no longer.

Antonio.—The way is far to Madrilati : there are, moreover, wars in the land, and many chories (*thieves*) walk about; are you not afraid to journey?

Myself.—I have no fears ; every man must accomplish his destiny : what befalls my body or soul was written in a gabicote (*book*) a thousand years before the foundation of the world.

Antonio.—I have no fears myself, brother ; the dark night is the same to me as the fair day, and the wild carrascal as the market place or the chardy (*fair*) ; I have got the bar lachi in my bosom, the precious stone to which sticks the needle.

Myself.—You mean the loadstone, I suppose. Do you believe that a lifeless stone can preserve you from the dangers which occasionally threaten your life?

Antonio.—Brother, I am fifty years old, and you see me standing before you in life and strength: how could that be unless the bar lachi had power? I have been soldier and contrabandista, and I have likewise slain and robbed the Busné. The bullets of the Gabiné (*French*) and of the jara canallis (*revenue officers*) have hissed about my ears without injuring me, for I carried the bar lachi. I have twenty times done that which by Busnée law should have brought me to the filimicha (*gallows*), yet my neck has never yet been squeezed by the cold garrote. Brother, I trust in the bar lachi, like the Caloré of old: were I in the midst of the gulf of Bombardo (*Lyons*), without a plank to float upon, I should feel no fear; for, if I carried the precious stone, it would bring me safe to shore: the bar lachi has power, brother.

Myself.—I shall not dispute the matter with you, more especially as I am about to depart from Badajoz: I must speedily bid you farewell, and we shall see each other no more.

Antonio.—Brother, do you know what brings me hither?

Myself.—I cannot tell, unless it be to wish me a happy journey: I am not gipsy enough to interpret the thoughts of other people.

Antonio.—All last night I lay awake, thinking of the affairs of Egypt; and when I arose in the morning I took the bar lachi from my bosom, and scraping it with a knife, swallowed some of the dust in aguardiente, as I am in the habit of doing when I have made up my mind; and I said to myself, I am wanted on the frontiers of Castumba (*Castile*) on a certain matter. The strange Caloro is about to proceed to Madrilati; the journey is long, and he may fall into evil hands, peradventure into those of his own blood; for let me tell you, brother, the Calés are leaving their towns and villages, and forming themselves into troops to plunder the Busné, for there is now but little law in the land, and now or never is the time for the Caloré to become once more what they were in former times; so I said, the strange Caloro may fall into the hands of his own blood and be illtreated by them, which were shame: I will therefore go with him through the Chim del Manro (*Estremadura*) as far as the frontiers of Castumba, and upon the frontiers of Castumba I will leave the London Caloro to find his own way to Madrilati, for there is less danger in Castumba, than in the Chim del Manro, and I will then betake me to the affairs of Egypt which call me from hence.

Myself.—This is a very hopeful plan of yours, my friend; and in what manner do you propose that we shall travel?

Antonio.—I will tell you, brother; I have a gras in the stall, even the one which I purchased at Olivenças, as I told you on a former occasion; it is good and fleet, and cost me, who am a gipsy, fifty chulé (*dollars*); upon that gras you shall ride. As for myself, I will journey upon the macho.

Myself.—Before I answer you, I shall wish you to inform me what business it is which renders your presence necessary in Castumba; your son-in-law, Paco, told me that it was no longer the custom of the gipsies to wander.

Antonio.—It is an affair of Egypt, brother, and I shall not acquaint you with it; peradventure it relates to a horse or an ass, or peradventure it relates to a mule or a macho; it does not relate to yourself, therefore I advise you not to inquire about it.—Dosta (*enough*). With respect to my offer, you are free to decline it; there is a drungruje (*royal road*) between here and Madrilati, and you can travel it in the birdoche (*stage-coach*) or with the dromäle (*muleteers*); but I tell you, as a brother, that there are chories upon the drun, and some of them are of the Errate.

Certainly few people in my situation would have accepted the offer of this singular gipsy. It was not, however, without its allurements for me; I was fond of adventure, and what more ready means of gratifying my love of it than by putting myself under the hands of such a guide. There are many who would have been afraid of treachery, but I had no fears on this point, as I did not believe that the fellow harboured the slightest ill intention towards me; I saw that he was fully convinced that I was one of the Errate, and his affection for his own race, and his hatred for the Busné, were his strongest characteristics. I wished, moreover, to lay hold of every opportunity of making myself acquainted with the ways of the Spanish gipsies, and an excellent one here presented itself on my first entrance into Spain. In a word I determined to accompany the gipsy. " I will go with you," I exclaimed; " as for my baggage, I will despatch it to Madrid by the birdoche." " Do so, brother," he replied, " and the gras will go lighter. Baggage, indeed!—what need of baggage have you? How the Busné on the road would laugh if they saw two Calés with baggage behind them."

During my stay at Badajoz, I had but little intercourse with the Spaniards, my time being chiefly devoted to the gipsies, with whom, from long intercourse with various sections of their race in different parts of the world, I felt myself much more at home than with the silent, reserved men of Spain, with whom a foreigner might mingle for half a century without having half a dozen words addressed to him, unless he himself made the first advances to intimacy, which, after all, might be rejected with a shrug and a *no intendo*; for, among the many deeply rooted prejudices of these people, is the strange idea that no foreigner can speak their language; an idea to which they still cling though they hear him conversing with perfect ease; for in that case the utmost that they will concede to his attainments is, *Habla quatro polabras y nada mas.*

Early one morning, before sunrise, I found myself at the house of Antonio; it was a small mean building, situated in a dirty street. The morning was quite dark; the street, however, was partially illumined by a heap of lighted straw, round which two or three men were busily engaged, apparently holding an object over the flames. Presently the gipsy's door opened, and Antonio made his appearance; and, casting his eye in the direction of the light, exclaimed, "The swine have killed their brother; would that every Busno was served as yonder hog is. Come in, brother, and we will eat the heart of that hog." I scarcely understood his words, but, following him, he led me into a low room in which was a brasero, or small pan full of lighted charcoal; beside it was a rude table, spread with a coarse linen cloth, upon which was bread and a large pipkin full of a mess which emitted no disagreeable savour. "The heart of the balichow is in that puchera," said Antonio; "eat, brother." We both sat down and ate, Antonio voraciously. When we had concluded he arose:—"Have you got your *li?*" he demanded. "Here it is," said I, showing him my passport. "Good," said he, "you may want it; I want none, my passport is the bar lachi. Now for a glass of repani, and then for the road."

We left the room, the door of which he locked, hiding the key beneath a loose brick in a corner of the passage. "Go into the street, brother, whilst I fetch the caballerias from the stable." I obeyed him. The sun had not yet risen, and the air was piercingly cold; the gray light, however, of dawn enabled me to distinguish objects with tolerable accuracy; I soon heard the clattering of the animal's feet, and Antonio presently stepped forth leading the horse by the bridle; the macho followed behind. I looked at the horse and shrugged my shoulders: as far as I could scan it, it appeared the most uncouth animal I had ever beheld. It was of a spectral white, short in the body, but with remarkably long legs. I observed that it was particularly high in the cruz or withers. "You are looking at the grasti," said Antonia; "it is eighteen years old, but it is the very best in the Chim del Manro; I have long had my eye upon it; I bought it for my own use for the affairs of Egypt. Mount, brother, mount and let us leave the foros—the gate is about being opened."

He locked the door, and deposited the key in his faja. In less than a quarter of an hour we had left the town behind us. "This does not appear to be a very good horse," said I to Antonio, as we proceeded over the plain. "It is with difficulty that I can make him move."

"He is the swiftest horse in the Chim del Manro, brother," said Antonio; "at the gallop and at the speedy trot there is no one to match him; but he is eighteen years old, and his joints are stiff, especially of a morning; but let him once become heated, and the genio del viejo (*spirit of the old man*) comes upon him and there is no holding him in with bit or bridle. I bought that horse for the affairs of Egypt, brother."

About noon we arrived at a small village in the neighbourhood of a high lumpy hill. "There is no Calo house in this place," said Antonio; "we will therefore go to the posada of the Busné, and refresh ourselves, man and beast." We entered the kitchen and sat down at the board, calling for wine and bread. There were two ill-looking fellows in the kitchen, smoking cigars; I said something to Antonio in the Calo language.

"What is that I hear?" said one of the fellows, who was distinguished by an immense pair of mustaches. "What is that I hear? is it in Calo that you are speaking before me, and I a Chalan and national? Accursed gipsy, how dare you enter this posada and speak before me in that speech? Is it not forbidden by the law of the land in which we are, even as it is forbidden for a gipsy to enter the mercado? I will tell you what, friend, if I hear another word of Calo come from your mouth, I will cudgel your bones and send you flying over the house-tops with a kick of my foot."

"You would do right," said his companion; "the insolence of these gipsies is no longer to be borne. When I am at Merida or Badajoz I go to the mercado, and there in a corner stand the accursed gipsies jabbering to each other in a speech which I understand not. 'Gipsy gentleman,' say I to one of them, 'what will you have for that donkey?' 'I will have ten dollars for it, Cabellero nacional,' says the gipsy; 'it is the best donkey in all Spain.' 'I should like to see its paces,' say I. 'That you shall, most valorous!' says the gipsy, and jumping upon its back, he puts it to its paces, first of all whispering something into its ear in Calo, and truly the paces of the donkey are most wonderful, such as I have never seen before. 'I think it will just suit me,' and after looking at it awhile, I take out the money and pay for it. 'I shall go to my house,' says the gipsy; and off he runs. 'I shall go to my village,' say I, and I mount the donkey. 'Vamonos,' say I, but the donkey won't move. I give him a switch, but I don't get on the better for that. 'How is this?' say I, and I fall to spurring him. What happens then, brother? The wizard no sooner feels the prick than he bucks down, and flings me over his head into the fango. I get up and look about me; there stands the donkey, staring at me, and there stands the whole gipsy canaille squinting at me with their filmy eyes. 'Where is the scamp who has sold me this piece of furniture?' I shout. 'He is gone to Granada, Valorous,' says one. 'He is gone to see his kindred among the Moors,' says another. 'I just saw him running over the field in the direction of ——, with the devil close behind him,' says a third. In a word, I am tricked. I wish to dispose of the donkey; no one, however, will buy him; he is a Calo donkey, and every person avoids him. At last the gipsies offer thirty rials for him; and after much chaffering I am glad to get rid of him at two dollars. It is all a trick, however; he returns to his master, and the brotherhood share the spoil amongst them. All which villany would be prevented, in my opinion, were the Calo language not spoken; for what but the word of Calo could have induced the donkey to behave in such an unaccountable manner?"

Both seemed perfectly satisfied with the justness of this conclusion, and continued smoking till their cigars were burnt to stumps, when they arose, twitched their whiskers, looked at us with fierce disdain, and dashing the tobacco-ends to the ground, strode out of the apartment.

"Those people seem no friends to the gipsies," said I to Antonio, when the two bullies had departed, "nor to the Calo language either."

"May evil glanders seize their nostrils," said Antonio; "they have been jonjabadoed by our people. However, brother, you did wrong to speak to me in Calo, in a posada like this; it is a forbidden language; for, as I have often told you, the king has destroyed the law of the Calés. Let us away, brother, or those juntunes (*sneaking scoundrels*) may set the justicia upon us."

Towards evening we drew near to a large town or village. "That is Merida," said Antonia, "formerly, as the Busné say, a mighty city of the Corohai. We shall stay here to-night, and perhaps for a day or two, for I have some business of Egypt to transact in this place. Now, brother, step aside with the horse, and wait for me beneath yonder wall. I must go before and see in what condition matters stand."

I dismounted from the horse, and sat down on a stone beneath the ruined wall to which Antonio had motioned me; the sun went down, and the air was exceedingly keen; I drew close around me an old tattered gipsy cloak with which my companion had provided me, and being somewhat fatigued, fell into a doze which lasted for nearly an hour.

"Is your worship the London Caloro?" said a strange voice close beside me.

I started, and beheld the face of a woman peering under my hat. Notwithstanding the dusk, I could see that the features were hideously ugly and almost black; they belonged, in fact, to a gipsy crone, at least seventy years of age, leaning upon a staff.

"Is your worship the London Caloro?" repeated she.

"I am he whom you seek," said I; "where is Antonio?"

"*Curelando, curelando, baribustres curelos terela*,"* said the crone: "come with me, Caloro of my garlochin, come with me to my little ker, he will be there anon."

I followed the crone, who led the way into the town, which was ruinous and seemingly

half deserted; we went up the street, from which she turned into a narrow and dark lane, and presently opened the gate of a large dilapidated house: "Come in," said she.

"And the gras?" I demanded.

"Bring the gras in too, my chabo, bring the gras in too; there is room for the gras in my little stable." We entered a large court, across which we proceeded till we came to a wide door-way. "Go in, my child of Egypt," said the hag; "go in, that is my little stable."

"The place is as dark as pitch," said I, "and may be a well, for what I know; bring a light or I will not enter."

"Give me the solabarri (*bridle*)," said the hag, "and I will lead your horse in, my chabo of Egypt, yes, and tether him to my little manger." She led the horse through the doorway, and I heard her busy in the darkness; presently the horse shook himself: "*Grasti terelamos*," said the hag, who now made her appearance with the bridle in her hand; "the horse has shaken himself, he is not harmed by his day's journey; now let us go in, my Caloro, into my little room."

We entered the house and found ourselves in a vast room, which would have been quite dark but for a faint glow which appeared at the farther end; it proceeded from a brasero, beside which were squatted two dusky figures.

"These are Callees," said the hag; "one is my daughter, and the other is her chabi; sit down, my London Caloro, and let us hear you speak."

I looked about for a chair, but could see none; at a short distance, however, I perceived the end of a broken pillar lying on the floor; this I rolled to the brasero and sat down upon it.

"This is a fine house, mother of the gipsies," said I, to the hag, willing to gratify the desire she had expressed of hearing me speak; "a fine house is this of yours, rather cold and damp, though; it appears large enough to be a barrack for hundunares."

"Plenty of houses in this foros, plenty of houses in Merida, my London Caloro, some of them just as they were left by the Corahanoes; ah, a fine people are the Corahanoes; I often wish myself in their chim once more."

"How is this, mother," said I, "have you been in the land of the Moors?"

"Twice have I been in their country, my Caloro,—twice have I been in the land of the Corahai; the first time is more than fifty years ago. I was then with the Sese (*Spaniards*), for my husband was a soldier of the Crallis of Spain, and Oran at that time belonged to Spain."

"You were not then with the real Moors," said I, "but only with the Spaniards who occupied part of their country."

"I have been with the real Moors, my London Caloro. Who knows more of the real Moors than myself? About forty years ago, I was with my ro in Ceuta, for he was still a

---

* Doing business, doing business—he has much business to do.

soldier of the king, and he said to me, one day, 'I am tired of this place, where there is no bread and less water, I will escape and turn Corahano; this night I will kill my sergeant and flee to the camp of the Moor.' 'Do so,' said I, 'my chabo, and soon as may be I will follow you and become a Corahani. That same night he killed his sergeant, who five years before had called him Calo and cursed him, then running to the wall he dropped from it, and amidst many shots he escaped to the land of the Corahai; as for myself, I remained in the presidio of Ceuta as a sutler selling wine and repani to the hundunares. Two years passed by and I neither saw nor heard from my ro; one day there came a strange man to my cachimani (*wine shop*), he was dressed like a Corahano and yet he did not look like one, he looked more like a callardo (*black*), and yet he was not a collardo either, though he was almost black, and as I looked upon him, I thought he looked something like the Errate, and he said to me, 'Zincali; chachipé!' and then he whispered to me, in queer language, which I could scarcely understand, 'your ro is waiting, come with me, my little sister, and I will take you unto him.' 'Where is he?' said I, and he pointed to the west, to the land of the Corahai, and said, 'He is yonder away; come with me, little sister, the ro is waiting.' For a moment I was afraid, but I bethought me of my husband, and I wished to be amongst the Corahai; so I took the little parné (*money*) I had, and locking up the cachimani went with the strange man; the sentinel challenged us at the gate, but I gave him repani and he let us pass; in a moment we were in the land of the Corahai. About a league from the town beneath a cerro (*hill*) we found four people, men and women, all very black like the strange man, and we joined ourselves with them, and they all saluted me and called me little sister. That was all I understood of their discourse, which was very crabbed; and they took away my dress and gave me other clothes, and I looked like a Corahani, and away we marched for many days amidst deserts and small villages, and more than once it seemed to me that I was amongst the Errate, for their ways were the same; the men would hokkawar (*cheat*) with mules and asses, and the women told baji, and after many days we came before a large town, and the black man said, 'Go in there, little sister, and there you will find your ro;' and I went to the gate, and an armed Corahano stood within the gate, and I looked in his face, and lo! it was my ro.

"O what a strange town it was that I found myself in, full of people who had once been Candoré (*Christians*), but had renegaded and become Corahai. There were Sese and Laloré (*Portuguese*), and men of other nations, and amongst them were some of the Errate from my own country; all were now soldiers of the Crallis of the Corahai and followed him to his wars; and in that town I remained with my ro a long time, occasionally going

out with him to the wars, and I often asked him about the black men who brought me thither, and he told me that he had had dealings with them, and that he believed them to be of the Errate. Well, brother, to be short, my ro was killed in the wars, before a town to which the king of the Corahai laid siege, and I became a piuli (*widow*), and I returned to the village of the renegades, as it was called, and supported myself as well as I could; and one day as I was sitting weeping, the black man, whom I had never seen since the day he brought me to my ro, again stood before me, and he said, ' Come with me, little sister, come with me, the ro is at hand;' and I went with him, and beyond the gate in the desert was the same party of black men and women which I had seen before. 'Where is my ro?' said I. 'Here he is, little sister,' said the black man, 'here he is; from this day I am the ro and you the romi: come, let us go, for there is business to be done.'

"And I went with him, and he was my ro, and we lived amongst the deserts, and hokkawar'd and choried and told baji; and I said to myself, this is good, sure I am amongst the Errate in a better chim than my own; and I often said that they were of the Errate, and then they would laugh and say that it might be so, and that they were not Corahai, but they could give no account of themselves.

"Well, things went on in this way for years, and I had three chai by the black man, two of them died, but the youngest, who is the Calli who sits by the brasero, was spared; so we roamed about and choried and told baji; and it came to pass that once in the winter time our company attempted to pass a wide and deep river, of which there are many in the Chim del Corahai, and the boat overset with the rapidity of the current and all our people were drowned, all but myself and my chabi, whom I bore in my bosom. I had now no friends amongst the Corahai, and I wandered about the desplobados howling and lamenting till I became half lili (*mad*), and in this manner I found my way to the coast, where I made friends with the captain of a ship and returned to this land of Spain. And now I am here, I often wish myself back again amongst the Corahai."

Here she commenced laughing loud and long, and when she had ceased, her daughter and grandchild took up the laugh, which they continued so long that I concluded they were all lunatics.

Hour succeeded hour, and still we sat crouching over the brasero, from which, by this time, all warmth had departed; the glow had long since disappeared, and only a few dying sparks were to be distinguished. The room or hall was now involved in darkness; the women were motionless and still; I shivered and began to feel uneasy. "Will Antonio be here to night?" at length I demanded.

"*No tenga usted cuidao*, my London Caloro," said the gipsy mother, in an unearthly tone; " Pepindorio* has been here some time."

* The Gipsy word for Antonio.

I was about to rise from my seat and attempt to escape from the house, when I felt a hand laid upon my shoulder, and in a moment I heard the voice of Antonio.

"Be not afraid, 'tis I, brother; we will have a light anon, and then supper."

The supper was rude enough, consisting of bread, cheese, and olives. Antonio, however, produced a leathern bottle of excellent wine; we despatched these viands by the light of an earthen lamp which was placed upon the floor.

"Now," said Antonio to the youngest female, "bring me the pajandi, and I will sing a gachapla."

The girl brought the guitar, which, with some difficulty, the gipsy tuned, and then, strumming it vigorously, he sang:

"I stole a plump and bonny fowl,
But ere I well had dined,

The master came with scowl and growl,
And me would captive bind.
My hat and mantle off I threw,
And scour'd across the lea,
Then cried the beng* with loud hallo,
Where does the gipsy flee?"

He continued playing and singing for a considerable time, the two younger females dancing in the meanwhile with unwearied diligence, whilst the aged mother occasionally snapped her fingers or beat time on the ground with her stick. At last Antonio suddenly laid down the instrument, exclaiming:—

"I see the London Caloro is weary; enough, enough, to-morrow more thereof—we will now to the charipé (bed)."

"With all my heart," said I; "where are we to sleep?"

"In the stable," said he, "in the manger; however cold the stable may be, we shall be warm enough in the bufa."

CHAPTER X.

The Gipsy's Grand-daughter—Proposed Marriage—The Alguazil—The Assault—Speedy Trot—Arrival at Trujillo—Night and Rain—The Forest—The Bivouac—Mount and Away—Jaraicejo—The National—The Cavalier Balmerson—Among the Thickets—Serious Discourse—What is Truth?—Unexpected Intelligence.

WE remained three days at the gipsies' house, Antonio departing early every morning, on his mule, and returning late at night. The house was large and ruinous, the only habitable part of it, with the exception of the stable, being the hall, where we had supped, and there the gipsy females slept at night, on some mats and mattrasses in a corner.

"A strange house is this," said I to Antonio, one morning, as he was on the point of saddling his mule and departing, as I supposed, on the affairs of Egypt; "a strange house and strange people; that gipsy grandmother has all the appearance of a sowanee."

"All the appearance of one," said Antonio. "And is she not really one? She knows more crabbed things and crabbed words than all the Errate betwixt here and Catalonia. She has been amongst the wild Moors, and can make more drows, poisons, and philtres than any one alive. She once made a kind of paste, and persuaded me to taste, and shortly after I had done so my soul departed from my body, and wandered through horrid forests and mountains, amidst monsters and duendes, during one entire night. She learned many things amidst the Corahai which I should be glad to know."

"Have you been long acquainted with her?" said I, "you appear to be quite at home in this house."

"Acquainted with her!" said Antonio. "Did not my own brother marry the black Calli, her daughter, who bore him the chabi, sixteen years ago, just before he was hanged by the Busné?"

In the afternoon I was seated with the gipsy mother in the hall, the two Callees were absent telling fortunes about the town and neighbourhood, which was their principal occupation. "Are you married, my London Caloro?" said the old woman to me. "Are you a ro?"

Myself.—Wherefore do you ask, O Dai de los Cales?

Gipsy Mother.—It is high time that the lacha of the chabi were taken from her, and that she had a ro. You can do no better than take her for romi, my London Caloro.

Myself.—I am a stranger in this land, O mother of the gipsies, and scarcely know how to provide for myself, much less for a romi.

Gipsy Mother.—She wants no one to provide for her, my London Caloro, she can at any time provide for herself and her ro. She can hokkawar, tell baji, and there are few to equal her at stealing á pastesas. Were she once at Madrilati, where they tell me you are going, she would make much treasure; therefore take her thither, for in this foros she is nahi (lost), as it were, for there is nothing to be gained; but in the foros baro it would be another matter; she would go dressed in lachipi and sonacai (silk and gold), whilst you would ride about on your black-tailed gra; and when you had got much treasure, you might return hither and live like a Crallis, and all the Errate of the Chim del Manro should bow down their heads to you. What say you, my London Caloro, what say you to my plan?

_____

* Devil.

Myself.—Your plan is a plausible one, mother, or at least some people would think so; but I am, as you are aware, of another chim, and have no inclination to pass my life in this country.

Gipsy Mother.—Then return to your own country, my Caloro, the chabi can cross the pani. Would she not do business in London with the rest of the Calore? Or why not go to the land of the Corahai? In which case I would accompany you; I and my daughter, the mother of the chabi.

Myself.—And what should we do in the land of the Corahai? It is a poor and wild country, I believe.

Gipsy Mother.—The London Caloro asks me what we could do in the land of the Corahai! Aromali! I almost think that I am speaking to a lilipendi (*simpleton*). Are there not horses to chore? Yes, I trow there are, and better ones than in this land, and asses and mules. In the land of the Corahai you must hokkawar and chore even as you must here, or in your own country, or else you are no Caloro. Can you not join yourselves with the black people who live in the despoblados? Yes, surely; and glad they would be to have among them the Errate from Spain and London. I am seventy years of age, but I wish not to die in this chim, but yonder, far away, where both my roms are sleeping. Take the chabi, therefore, and go to Madrilati to win the parné, and when you have got it, return, and we will give a banquet to all the Busné in Merida, and in their food I will mix drow, and they shall eat and burst like poisoned sheep . . . . . . And when they have eaten we will leave them, and away to the land of the Moor, my London Caloro.

During the whole time that I remained at Merida I stirred not once from the house; following the advice of Antonio, who informed me that it would not be convenient. My time lay rather heavily on my hands, my only source of amusement consisting in the conversation of the women, and in that of Antonio when he made his appearance at night. In these tertulias the grandmother was the principal spokeswoman, and astonished my ears with wonderful tales of the land of the Moors, prison escapes, thievish feats, and one or two poisoning adventures, in which she had been engaged, as she informed me, in her early youth.

There was occasionally something very wild in her gestures and demeanour; more than once I observed her, in the midst of much declamation, to stop short, stare in vacancy, and thrust out her palms as if endeavouring to push away some invisible substance; she goggled frightfully with her eyes, and once sank back in convulsions, of which her children took no farther notice than observing that she was only lili, and would soon come to herself.

Late in the afternoon of the third day, as the three women and myself sat conversing as usual, over the brasero, a shabby-looking fellow in an old rusty cloak, walked into the room: he came straight up to the place where we were sitting, produced a paper cigar, which he lighted at a coal, and taking a whiff or two, looked at me: "Carracho," said he, "who is this companion?"

I saw at once that the fellow was no gipsy: the women said nothing, but I could hear the grandmother growling to herself, something after the manner of an old grimalkin when disturbed.

"Carracho," reiterated the fellow, "how came this companion here?"

"*No le penela chi min chaboro,*" said the black Callee to me, in an under tone; "*sin un balicho de los chineles;*"* then looking up to the interrogator she said aloud, "he is one of our people from Portugal, come on the smuggling lay, and to see his poor sisters here."

"Then let him give me some tobacco," said the fellow, "I suppose he has brought some with him."

"He has no tobacco," said the black Callee, "he has nothing but old iron. This cigar is the only tobacco there is in the house; take it, smoke it, and go away!"

Thereupon she produced a cigar from out her shoe, which she presented to the alguazil.

"This will not do," said the fellow, taking the cigar, "I must have something better; it is now three months since I received any thing from you; the last present was a handkerchief, which was good for nothing; therefore, hand me over something worth taking, or I will carry you all to the Carcel."

"The Busno will take us to prison," said the black Callee, "ha! ha! ha!"

"The Chinel will take us to prison," giggled the young girl, "he! he! he!"

"The Bengui will carry us all to the estaripel," grunted the gipsy grandmother, "ho! ho! ho!"

The three females arose and walked slowly round the fellow, fixing their eyes steadfastly on his face; he appeared frightened, and evidently wished to get away. Suddenly the two youngest seized his hands, and whilst he struggled to release himself, the old woman exclaimed: "You want tobacco, hijo—you come to the gipsy house to frighten the Callees and the strange Caloro out of their plako—truly, hijo, we have none for you, and right sorry I am; we have, however, plenty of the dust *á su servicio.*"

Here, thrusting her hand into her pocket, she discharged a handful of some kind of dust or snuff into the fellow's eyes: he stamped and roared, but was for some time held fast by the two Callees: he extricated himself, however, and attempted to unsheath a knife which he bore at his girdle; but the two younger females flung themselves upon him like furies, while the old woman increased his disorder by thrusting her stick into his face; he was

* "Say nothing to him, my lad, he is a hog of an alguazil."

soon glad to give up the contest, and retreated, leaving behind him his hat and cloak, which the chabi gathered up and flung after him into the street.

"This is a bad business," said I, "the fellow will of course bring the rest of the justicia upon us, and we shall all be cast into the estaripel."

"Ca!" said the black Callee, biting her thumb nail, "he has more reason to fear us than we him, we could bring him to the filimicha; we have, moreover, friends in this town plenty, plenty."

"Yes," mumbled the grandmother, "the daughters of the baji have friends, my London Caloro, friends among the Busnees, baributre, baribu (*plenty, plenty*)."

Nothing farther of any account occurred in the gipsy house; the next day, Antonio and myself were again in the saddle, we travelled at least thirteen leagues before we reached the Venta, where we passed the night; we rose early in the morning, my guide informing me that we had a long day's journey to make, "Where are we bound to?" I demanded. "To Trujillo," he replied.

When the sun arose, which it did gloomily and amidst threatening rain-clouds, we found ourselves in the neighbourhood of a range of mountains which lay on our left, and which, Antonio informed me, were called the Sierra of San Selvan; our route, however, lay over wide plains, scantily clothed with brushwood, with here and there a melancholy village, with its old and dilapidated church. Throughout the greater part of the day, a drizzling rain was falling, which turned the dust of the roads into mud and mire, considerably impeding our progress. Towards evening we reached a moor, a wild place enough, strewn with enormous stones and rocks. Before us, at some distance, rose a strange conical hill, rough and shaggy, which appeared to be neither more nor less than an immense assemblage of the same kind of rocks which lay upon the moor. The rain had now ceased, but a strong wind rose and howled at our backs. Throughout the journey, I had experienced considerable difficulty in keeping up with the mule of Antonio; the walk of the horse was slow, and I could discover no vestige of the spirit which the gipsy had assured me lurked within him. We were now upon a tolerably clear spot of the moor; "I am about to see," I said, "whether this horse has any of the quality which you have described." "Do so," said Antonio, and spurred his beast onward, speedily leaving me far behind. I jerked the horse with the bit, endeavouring to arouse his dormant spirit, whereupon he stopped, reared, and refused to proceed. "Hold the bridle loose and touch him with your whip," shouted Antonio from before. I obeyed, and forthwith, the animal set off at a trot, which gradually increased in swiftness till it became a downright furious speedy trot; his limbs were now thoroughly lithy, and he brandished his fore legs in a manner perfectly wondrous; the mule of Antonio, which was a spirited animal of excellent paces, would fain have competed with him, but was passed in a twinkling. This tremendous trot endured for about a mile, when the animal, becoming yet more heated, broke suddenly into a gallop. Hurrah! no hare ever ran so wildly or blindly; it was, literally, *ventre à terre*; and I had considerable difficulty in keeping him clear of rocks, against which he would have rushed in his savage fury, and dashed himself and rider to atoms.

This race brought me to the foot of the hill, where I waited till the gipsy rejoined me: we left the hill, which seemed quite inaccessible, on our right, passing through a small and wretched village. The sun went down, and dark night presently came upon us; we proceeded on, however, for nearly three hours, until we heard the barking of dogs, and perceived a light or two in the distance. "That is Trujillo," said Antonio, who had not spoken for a long time. "I am glad of it," I replied; "I am thoroughly tired; I shall sleep soundly in Trujillo." "That is as it may be," said the gipsy, and spurred his mule to a brisker pace. We soon entered the town, which appeared dark and gloomy enough; I followed close behind the gipsy, who led the way I knew not whither, through dismal streets and dark places, where cats were squalling. "Here is the house," said he at last, dismounting before a low mean hut; he knocked, no answer was returned;— he knocked again, but still there was no reply; he shook the door and essayed to open it, but it appeared firmly locked and bolted. "Caramba!" said he, "they are out—I feared it might be so. Now what are we to do?"

"There can be no difficulty," said I, "with respect to what we have to do; if your friends are gone out, it is easy enough to go to a posada."

"You know not what you say," replied the gipsy, "I dare not go to the mesuna, nor enter any house in Trujillo save this, and this is shut; well, there is no remedy, we must move on, and, between ourselves, the sooner we leave this place the better; my own planoro (*brother*) was garroted at Trujillo."

He lighted a cigar, by means of a steel and yesca, sprang on his mule, and proceeded through streets and lanes equally dismal as those which we had already traversed till we again found ourselves out of the town.

I confess I did not much like this decision of the gipsy; I felt very slight inclination to leave the town behind, and to venture into unknown places in the dark night, amidst rain and mist, for the wind had now dropped, and the rain began again to fall briskly. I was, moreover, much fatigued, and wished for nothing better than to deposit myself in some comfortable manger, where I might sink to sleep, lulled by the pleasant sound of horses and mules despatching their provender. I had, however, put myself under the direction of the gipsy, and I was too old a traveller to quarrel with my guide under the present circomstances. I therefore followed close at his crupper; our only light being the glow emitted from the gipsy's cigar; at last he flung it from his mouth into a puddle, and we were then in darkness.

We proceeded in this manner for a long time; the gipsy was silent; I myself was equally so; the rain descended more and more. I sometimes thought I heard doleful noises, something like the hooting of owls. "This is a strange night to be wandering abroad in," I at length said to Antonio.

"It is, brother," said he, "but I would sooner be abroad in such a night, and in such places, than in the estaripel of Trujillo."

We wandered at least a league farther, and appeared now to be near a wood, for I could occasionally distinguish the trunks of immense trees. Suddenly Antonio stopped his mule: "Look, brother," said he, "to the left, and tell me if you do not see a light; your eyes are sharper than mine." I did as he commanded me. At first I could see nothing, but moving a little farther on I plainly saw a large light at some distance, seemingly amongst the trees. "Yonder cannot be a lamp or candle," said I; "it is more like the blaze of a fire." "Very likely," said Antonio. "There are no queres (houses) in this place; it is doubtless a fire made by durotunes (shepherds); let us go and join them, for, as you say, it is doleful work wandering about at night amidst rain and mire."

We dismounted and entered what I now saw was a forest, leading the animals cautiously amongst the trees and brushwood. In about five minutes we reached a small open space, at the farther side of which, at the foot of a large cork tree, a fire was burning, and by it stood or sat two or three figures; they had heard our approach, and one of them now exclaimed Quien Vive! "I know that voice," said Antonio, and leaving the horse with me, rapidly advanced towards the fire: presently I heard an Ola! and a laugh, and soon the voice of Antonio summoned me to advance. On reaching the fire, I found two dark lads, and a still darker woman of about forty; the latter seated on what appeared to be horse or mule furniture. I likewise saw a horse and two donkeys tethered to the neighbouring trees. It was in fact a gipsy bivouac . . . . "Come, forward, brother, and show yourself," said Antonio to me; "you are amongst friends; these are of the Errate, the very people whom I expected to find at Trujillo, and in whose house we should have slept."

"And what," said I, "could have induced them to leave their house in Trujillo and come into this dark forest, in the midst of wind and rain, to pass the night?"

"They come on business of Egypt, brother, doubtless," replied Antonio; "and that business is none of ours, Calla boca! It is lucky we have found them here, else we should have had no supper, and our horses no corn."

"My ro is prisoner at the village yonder," said the woman, pointing with her hand in a particular direction; "he is prisoner yonder for choring a mailla (donkey); we are come to see what we can do in his behalf; and where can we lodge better than in this forest, where there is nothing to pay? It is not the first time, I trow, that Caloré have slept at the root of a tree."

One of the striplings now gave us barley for our animals in a large bag, into which we successively introduced their heads, allowing the famished creatures to regale themselves till we conceived that they had satisfied their hunger. There was a puchero simmering at the fire, half full of bacon, garbanzos, and other provisions; this was emptied into a large wooden platter, and out of this Antonio and myself supped; the other gipsies refused to join us, giving us to understand that they had eaten before our arrival; they all, however, did justice to the leathern bottle of Antonio, which, before his departure from Merida, he had the precaution to fill.

I was by this time completely overcome with fatigue and sleep. Antonio flung me an immense horse cloth, of which he bore more than one beneath the huge cushion on which he rode; in this I wrapped myself, and placing my head upon a bundle, and my feet as near as possible to the fire, I lay down. Antonio and the other gipsies remained seated by the fire conversing. I listened for a moment to what they said, but I did not perfectly understand it, and what I did understand by no means interested me; the rain still drizzled, but I heeded it not, and was soon asleep.

The sun was just appearing as I awoke. I made several efforts before I could rise from the ground; my limbs were quite stiff, and my hair was covered with rime; for the rain had ceased and a rather severe frost set in. I looked around me, but could see neither Antonio nor the gipsies; the animals of the latter had likewise disappeared, so had the horse which I had hitherto rode; the mule, however, of Antonio still remained fastened to the tree; this latter circumstance quieted some apprehensions which were beginning to arise in my mind. "They are gone on some business of Egypt," I said to myself, "and will return anon." I gathered together the embers of the fire, and heaping upon them sticks and branches, soon succeeded in calling forth a blaze, beside which I again placed the puchero, with what remained of the provision of last night. I waited for a considerable time in expectation of the return of my companions, but as they did not appear, I sat down and breakfasted. Before I had well finished I heard the noise of a horse approaching rapidly, and presently Antonio made his appearance amongst the trees, with some agitation in his countenance. He sprang from the horse, and instantly proceeded to untie the mule. "Mount, brother, mount!" said he, pointing to the horse; "I went with the Callee and her chabés to the village where the ro is in trouble; the chinobaro, however, seized them at once with their cattle, and would have laid hands also on me, but I set spurs to the grasti, gave him the bridle, and was soon far away. Mount, brother, mount, or we shall have the whole rustic canaille upon us in a twinkling."

I did as he commanded: we were presently in the road which we had left the night before. Along this we hurried at a great rate, the horse displaying his best speedy trot; whilst the mule, with its ears pricked up, galloped gallantly at his side. "What place is that on the hill yonder?" said I to Antonio, at the expiration of an hour, as we prepared to descend a deep valley.

"That is Jaraicejo," said Antonio; "a bad place it is, and a bad place it has ever been for the Calo people."

"If it is such a bad place," said I, "I hope we shall not have to pass through it."

"We must pass through it," said Antonio, "for more reasons than one: first, forasmuch as the road lies through Jaraicejo; and second, forasmuch as it will be necessary to purchase provisions there, both for ourselves and horses. On the other side of Jaraicejo there is a wild desert, a despoblado, where we shall find nothing."

We crossed the valley, and ascended the hill, and as we drew near to the town the gipsy said, "Brother, we had best pass through that town singly. I will go in advance; follow slowly, and when there purchase bread and barley; you have nothing to fear. I will await you on the despoplado."

Without waiting for my answer he hastened forward, and was speedily out of sight.

I followed slowly behind, and entered the gate of the town; an old dilapidated place, consisting of little more than one street. Along this street I was advancing, when a man with a dirty foraging cap on his head, and holding a gun in his hand, came running up to me: "Who are you?" said he, in rather rough accents; "from whence do you come?"

"From Badajoz and Trujillo," I replied; "why do you ask?"

"I am one of the national guard," said the man, "and am placed here to inspect strangers; I am told that a gipsy fellow just now rode through the town; it is well for him that I had stepped into my house. Do you come in his company?"

"Do I look a person," said I, "likely to keep company with gipsies?"

The national measured me from top to toe, and then looked me full in the face with an expression which seemed to say, "Likely enough." In fact, my appearance was by no means calculated to prepossess people in my favour. Upon my head I wore an old Andalusian hat, which, from its condition, appeared to have been trodden under foot; a rusty cloak, which had perhaps served half a dozen generations, enwrapped my body. My nether garments were by no means of the finest description; and as far as could be seen were covered with mud, with which my face was

likewise plentifully bespattered, and upon my chin was a beard of a week's growth.

"Have you a passport?" at length demanded the national.

I remembered having read that the best way to win a Spaniard's heart is to treat him with ceremonious civility. I therefore dismounted, and taking off my hat, made a low bow to the constitutional soldier, saying, "Señor nacional, you must know that I am an English gentleman, travelling in this country for my pleasure. I bear a passport, which, on inspecting, you will find to be perfectly regular; it was given me by the great Lord Palmerston, minister of England, whom you of course have heard of here; at the bottom you will see his own handwriting; look at it and rejoice; perhaps you will never have another opportunity. As I put unbounded confidence in the honour of every gentleman, I leave the passport in your hands whilst I repair to the posada to refresh myself. When you have inspected it, you will perhaps oblige me so far as to bring it to me. Cavalier, I kiss your hands."

I then made him another low bow, which he returned with one still lower, and leaving him now staring at the passport and now looking at myself, I went into a posada, to which I was directed by a beggar whom I met.

I fed the horse, and procured some bread and barley, as the gipsy had directed me; I likewise purchased three fine partridges of a fowler, who was drinking wine in the posada. He was satisfied with the price I gave him, and offered to treat me with a copita, to which I made no objection. As we were discoursing at the table, the national entered with the passport in his hand, and sat down by us.

National.—Caballero! I return you your passport, it is quite in form. I rejoice much to have made your acquaintance; I have no doubt that you can give me some information respecting the present war.

Myself.—I shall be very happy to afford so polite and honourable a gentleman any information in my power.

National.—What is England doing,—is she about to afford any assistance to this country? If she pleased, she could put down the war in three months.

Myself.—*No tenga usted cuidao, Señor nacional;* the war will be put down, don't doubt. You have heard of the English legion, which my Lord Palmerston has sent over? Leave the matter in their hands, you will soon see the result.

National.—It appears to me that this Caballero Balmerson must be a very honest man.

Myself.—There can be no doubt of it.

National.—I have heard that he is a great general.

Myself.—There can be no doubt of it. In some things neither Napoleon nor the sawyer* would stand a chance with him for a moment. *Es mucho hombre.*

---

* El Serrador, a Carlist partisan, who about this period was much talked of in Spain.

National.—I am glad to hear it. Does he intend to head the legion himself?

Myself.—I believe not; but he has sent over, to head the fighting men, a friend of his, who is thought to be nearly as much versed in military matters as himself.

National.—*Io me alegro mucho.* I see that the war will soon be over. Caballero, I thank you for your politeness, and for the information which you have afforded me. I hope you will have a pleasant journey. I confess that I am surprised to see a gentleman of your country travelling alone, and in this manner, through such regions as these. The roads are at present very bad; there have of late been many accidents, and more than two deaths in this neighbourhood. The despoblado out yonder has a particularly evil name; be on your guard, Caballero. I am sorry that gipsy was permitted to pass; should you meet him and not like his looks, shoot him at once, stab him, or ride him down. He is a well known thief, contrabandista, and murderer, and has committed more assassinations than he has fingers on his hands. Caballero, if you please, we will allow you a guard to the other side of the pass. You do not wish it? Then, farewell. Stay, before I go I should wish to see once more the signature of the Caballero Balmerson.

I showed him the signature, which he looked upon with a profound reverence, uncovering his head for a moment; we then embraced and parted.

I mounted the horse and rode from the town, at first proceeding very slowly; I had no sooner, however, reached the moor, than I put the animal to his speedy trot, and proceeded at a tremendous rate for some time, expecting every moment to overtake the gipsy. I, however, saw nothing of him, nor did I meet with a single human being. The road along which I sped was narrow and sandy, winding amidst thickets of broom and brushwood, with which the despoblado was overgrown, and which in some places were as high as a man's head. Across the moor, in the direction in which I was proceeding, rose a lofty eminence, naked and bare. The moor extended for at least three leagues; I had nearly crossed it, and reached the foot of the ascent. I was becoming very uneasy, conceiving that I might have passed the gipsy amongst the thickets, when I suddenly heard his well known Ola! and his black savage head and staring eyes suddenly appeared from amidst a clump of broom.

"You have tarried long, brother," said he; "I almost thought you had played me false."

He bade me dismount, and then proceeded to lead the horse behind the thicket, where I found the mule picqueted to the ground. I gave him the barley and provisions, and then proceeded to relate to him my adventure with the national.

"I would I had him here," said the gipsy, on hearing the epithets which the former had lavished upon him. "I would I had him

here, then should my chulee and his carlo become better acquainted."

"And what are you doing here yourself," I demanded, "in this wild place, amidst these thickets?"

"I am expecting a messenger down yon pass," said the gipsy; "and till that messenger arrive I can neither go forward nor return. It is on business of Egypt, brother, that I am here."

As he invariably used this last expression when he wished to evade my inquiries, I held my peace, and said no more; the animals were fed, and we proceeded to make a frugal repast on bread and wine.

"Why do you not cook the game which I brought?" I demanded; "in this place there is plenty of materials for a fire."

"The smoke might discover us, brother," said Antonio. "I am desirous of escondido in this place until the arrival of the messenger."

It was now considerably past noon; the gipsy lay behind the thicket, raising himself up occasionally and looking anxiously towards the hill which lay over against us; at last, with an exclamation of disappointment and impatience, he flung himself on the ground, where he lay a considerable time, apparently ruminating; at last he lifted up his head and looked me in the face.

Antonio.—Brother, I cannot imagine what business brought you to this country.

Myself.—Perhaps the same which brings you to this moor,—business of Egypt.

Antonio.—Not so, brother; you speak the language of Egypt, it is true, but your ways and words are neither those of the Cales nor of the Busné.

Myself.—Did you not hear me speak in the foros about God and Tebleque? It was to declare his glory to the Cales and Gentiles that I came to the land of Spain.

Antonio.—And who sent you on this errand?

Myself.—You would scarcely understand me were I to inform you. Know, however, that there are many in foreign lands who lament the darkness which envelopes Spain, and the scenes of cruelty, robbery, and murder which deform it.

Antonio.—Are they Caloré or Busné?

Myself.—What matters it? Both Caloré and Busné are sons of the same God.

Antonio.—You lie, brother, they are not of one father nor of one Errate. You speak of robbery, cruelty, and murder. There are too many Busné, brother; if there were no Busné, there would be neither robbery nor murder. The Caloré neither rob nor murder each other, the Busné do; nor are they cruel to their animals, their law forbids them. When I was a child I was beating a burra, but my father stopped my hand, and chided me. "Hurt not the animal," said he; "for within it is the soul of your own sister!"

Myself.—And do you believe in this wild doctrine, O Antonio?

Antonio.—Sometimes I do, sometimes I do

not. There are some who believe in nothing; not even that they live! Long since, I knew an old Caloro, he was old, very old, upwards of a hundred years,—and I once heard him say, that all we thought we saw was a lie; that there was no world, no men nor women, no horses nor mules, no olive trees. But whither are we straying? I asked what induced you to come to this country—you tell me the glory of God and Tebleque. Disparáte! tell that to the Busné. You have good reasons for coming, no doubt, else you would not be here. Some say you are a spy of the Londoné, perhaps you are; I care not. Rise, brother, and tell me whether any one is coming down the pass.

"I see a distant object," I replied; "like a speck on the side of the hill."

The gipsy started up, and we both fixed our eyes on the object: the distance was so great that it was at first with difficulty that we could distinguish whether it moved or not. A quarter of an hour, however, dispelled all doubts, for within this time it had nearly reached the bottom of the hill, and we could descry a figure seated on an animal of some kind.

"It is a woman," said I, at length, "mounted on a gray donkey."

"Then it is my messenger," said Antonio, "for it can be no other."

The woman and the donkey were now upon the plain, and for some time were concealed from us by the copse and brushwood which intervened. They were not long, however, in making their appearance at the distance of about a hundred yards. The donkey was a beautiful creature of a silver gray, and came frisking along, swinging her tail, and moving her feet so quick that they scarcely seemed to touch the ground. The animal no sooner perceived us than she stopped short, turned round, and attempted to escape by the way she had come; her rider, however, detained her, whereupon the donkey kicked violently, and would probably have flung the former, had she not sprung nimbly to the ground. The form of the woman was entirely concealed by the large wrapping man's cloak which she wore. I ran to assist her, when she turned her face full upon me, and I instantly recognised the sharp clever features of Antonia, whom I had seen at Badajoz, the daughter of my guide. She said nothing to me, but advancing to her father, addressed something to him in a low voice, which I did not hear. He started back, and vociferated *Todos?* "Yes," said she, in a louder tone, probably repeating the words which I had not caught before, "*Todos estan presos!*"

The gipsy remained for some time like one astounded, and, unwilling to listen to their discourse, which I imagined might relate to business of Egypt, I walked away amidst the thickets. I was absent for some time, but could occasionally hear passionate expressions and oaths. In about half an hour I returned; they had left the road, but I found them behind the broom clump, where the animals stood. Both were seated on the ground; the features of the gipsy were peculiarly dark and grim; he held his unsheathed knife in his hand, which he would occasionally plunge into the earth, exclaiming: *Todos! Todos!*

"Brother," said he, at last, "I can go no farther with you; the business which carried me to Castumba is settled; you must now travel by yourself and trust to your baji (*fortune*)."

"I trust in Undevel," I replied, "who wrote my fortune long ago. But how am I to journey? I have no horse, for you doubtless want your own."

The gipsy appeared to reflect: "I want the horse, it is true, brother," he said, "and likewise the macho; but you shall not go *en pindré;* you shall purchase the burra of Antonia, which I presented her when I sent her upon this expedition."

"The burra," I replied, "appears both savage and vicious."

"She is both, brother, and on that account I bought her; a savage and vicious beast has generally four excellent legs. You are a Calo, brother, and can manage her; you shall therefore purchase the savage burra, giving my daughter Antonia a baria of gold. If you think fit, you can sell the beast at Talavera or Madrid, for Estremenian bestis are highly considered in Castumba."

In less than an hour I was on the other side of the pass, mounted on the savage burra.

CHAPTER XI.

The Pass of Mirabete—Wolves and Shepherds—Female Subtlety—Death by Wolves—The Mystery solved—The Mountains—The dark Hour—The Traveller of the Night—Abarbenel—Hoarded Treasure—Force of Gold—The Archbishop—Arrival at Madrid.

I PROCEEDED down the pass of Mirabéte, occasionally ruminating on the matter which had brought me to Spain, and occasionally admiring one of the finest prospects in the world; before me outstretched lay immense plains, bounded in the distance by huge mountains, whilst at the foot of the hill, which I was now descending, rolled the Tagus, in a deep narrow stream, between lofty banks; the whole was gilded by the rays of the setting sun; for the day, though cold and wintry, was bright and clear. In about an hour I reached the river at a place where stood the remains of what had once been a magnificent bridge, which had, however, been blown up in the Peninsular war and never since repaired.

I crossed the river in a ferry-boat; the passage was rather difficult, the current very rapid and swollen, owing to the latter rains. "Am I in New Castille?" I demanded of the ferryman, on reaching the further bank. "The raya is many leagues from hence," replied the ferryman; "you seem a stranger. Whence do you come?" "From England," I replied, and without waiting for an answer, I sprang on the burra, and proceeded on my way. The burra plied her feet most nimbly, and, shortly after nightfall, brought me to a village at about two leagues' distance from the river's bank.

I sat down in the venta where I put up; there was a huge fire, consisting of the greater part of the trunk of an olive tree; the company was rather miscellaneous: a hunter with his escopeta; a brace of shepherds with immense dogs, of that species for which Estremadura is celebrated; a broken soldier, just returned from the wars; and a beggar, who, after demanding charity por las siete llagas de Maria Santissima, took a seat amidst us, and made himself quite comfortable. The hostess was an active bustling woman, and busied herself in cooking my supper, which consisted of the game which I had purchased at Jaraicejo, and which, on my taking leave of the gipsy, he had counselled me to take with me. In the mean time, I sat by the fire listening to the conversation of the company.

"I would I were a wolf," said one of the shepherds; "or, indeed, any thing rather than what I am. A pretty life is this of ours, out in the campo, among the carascales, suffering heat and cold for a peseta a day. I would I were a wolf; he fares better and is more respected than the wretch of a shepherd."

"But he frequently fares scurvily," said I; "the shepherd and dogs fall upon him, and then he pays for his temerity with the loss of his head."

"That is not often the case, señor traveller," said the shepherd; "he watches his opportunity, and seldom runs into harm's way. And as to attacking him, it is no very pleasant task; he has both teeth and claws, and dog or man, who has once felt them, likes not to venture a second time within his reach. These dogs of mine will seize a bear singly with considerable alacrity, though he is a most powerful animal, but I have seen them run howling away from a wolf, even though there were two or three of us at hand to encourage them."

"A dangerous person is the wolf," said the other shepherd, "and cunning as dangerous; who knows more than he? He knows the vulnerable point of every animal; see, for example, how he flies at the neck of a bullock, tearing open the veins with his grim teeth and claws. But does he attack a horse in this manner? I trow not."

"Not he," said the other shepherd, "he is too good a judge; but he fastens on the haunches, and hamstrings him in a moment. O the fear of the horse when he comes near the dwelling of the wolf. My master was the other day riding in the despoblado, above the pass, on his fine Andalusian steed, which had cost him five hundred dollars; suddenly the horse stopped, and sweated and trembled like a woman in the act of fainting; my master could not conceive the reason, but presently he heard a squealing and growling in the bushes, whereupon he fired off his gun and scared the wolves, who scampered away; but he tells me, that the horse has not yet recovered from his fright."

"Yet the mares know occasionally how to balk him," replied his companion; "there is great craft and malice in mares, as there is in all females; see them feeding in the camp with their young cria about them; presently the alarm is given that the wolf is drawing near; they start wildly and run about for a moment, but it is only for a moment,—amain they gather together, forming themselves into a circle, in the centre of which they place the foals. Onward comes the wolf, hoping to make his dinner on horseflesh; he is mistaken, however, the mares have balked him, and are as cunning as himself; not a tail is to be seen—not a hind quarter—but there stand the whole troop, their fronts towards him ready to receive him, and as he runs round them barking and howling, they rise successively on their hind legs, ready to stamp him to the earth, should he attempt to hurt their cria or themselves."

"Worse than the he-wolf," said the soldier, "is the female, for, as the señor pastor has well observed, there is more malice in

E 2

women than in males; to see one of these she-demons with a troop of the males at her heels is truly surprising; where she turns they turn, and what she does that do they; for they appear bewitched, and have no power but to imitate her actions. I was once travelling with a comrade over the hills of Galicia, when we heard a howl. 'Those are wolves,' said my companion, 'let us get out of the way;' so we stepped from the path and ascended the side of the hill a little way, to a terrace, where grew vines after the manner of Galicia: presently appeared a large gray she-wolf, *deshonesta*, snapping and growling at a troop of demons, who followed close behind, their tails uplifted, and their eyes like fire-brands. What do you think the perverse brute did? Instead of keeping the path, she turned in the very direction in which we were; there was now no remedy. So we stood still. I was the first upon the terrace, and by me she passed so close that I felt her hair brush against my legs; she, however, took no notice of me, but pushed on, neither looking to the right nor left, and all the other wolves trotted by me without offering the slightest injury or even so much as looking at me. Would that I could say as much for my poor companion who stood further on, and was, I believe, less in the demon's way than I was; she had nearly passed him when suddenly she turned half round and snapped at him. I shall never forget what followed: in a moment a dozen wolves were upon him, tearing him limb from limb, with howlings like nothing in this world; in a few moments he was devoured, nothing remaining but the scull and a few bones; and then they passed on in the same manner as they came. Good reason had I to be grateful that my lady wolf took less notice of me than my poor comrade."

Listening to this and similar conversation, I fell into a doze before the fire, in which I continued for a considerable time, but was at length roused by a voice exclaiming in a loud tone, "*Todos estan presos!*" These were the exact words which, when spoken by his daughter, confounded the gipsy upon the moor. I looked around me: the company consisted of the same individuals to whose conversation I had been listening before I sank into slumber; but the beggar was now the spokesman, and he was haranguing with considerable vehemence.

"I beg your pardon, Caballero," said I, "but I did not hear the commencement of your discourse. Who are those who have been captured?"

"A band of accursed Gitános, Caballero," replied the beggar, returning the title of courtesy which I had bestowed upon him. "During more than a fortnight, they have infested the roads on the frontier of Castile, and many have been the gentleman travellers like yourself whom they have robbed and murdered. It would seem that the gipsy canaille must needs take advantage of these troublous times, and form themselves into a faction. It is said

that the fellows of whom I am speaking expected many more of their brethren to join them, which is likely enough, as all gipsies are thieves: but, praised be God, they have been put down before they became too formidable. I saw them myself conveyed to the prison at ———. Thanks be to God. *Todos estan presos!*"

"The mystery is now solved," said I to myself, and proceeded to despatch my supper, which was now ready.

The next day's journey brought me to a considerable town, the name of which I have forgotten. It is the first in New Castille, in this direction. I passed the night, as usual, in the manger of the stable, close beside the Caballeria; for, as I travelled upon a donkey, I deemed it incumbent upon me to be satisfied with a couch in keeping with my manner of journeying, being averse, by any squeamish and over-delicate airs, to generate a suspicion amongst the people with whom I mingled that I was aught higher than what my equipage and outward appearance might lead them to believe. Rising before daylight, I again proceeded on my way, hoping ere night to be able to reach Talavera, which I was informed was ten leagues distant. The way lay entirely over an unbroken level, for the most part covered with olive trees. On the left, however, at the distance of a few leagues, rose the mighty mountains which I have already mentioned. They run eastward in a seemingly interminable range, parallel with the route which I was pursuing; their tops and sides were covered with dazzling snow, and the blasts which came sweeping from them across the wide and melancholy plains were of bitter keenness.

"What mountains are those?" I inquired of a barber-surgeon who, mounted like myself on a gray burra, joined me about noon, and proceeded in my company for several leagues. "They have many names, Caballero," replied the barber; "according to the names of the neighbouring places, so are they called. Yon portion of them is styled the Serrania de Plasencia; and opposite to Madrid they are termed the Mountains of Guadarama, from a river of that name, which descends from them; they run a vast way, Caballero, and separate the two kingdoms, for on the other side is Old Castille. They are mighty mountains; and though they generate much cold, I take pleasure in looking at them, which is not to be wondered at, seeing that I was born amongst them, though at present, for my sins, I live in a village of the plain. Caballero, there is not another such range in Spain; they have their secrets too—their mysteries: strange tales are told of those hills, and of what they contain in their deep recesses, for they are a broad chain, and you may wander days and days amongst them without coming to any termino. Many have lost themselves on those hills, and have never again been heard of. Strange things are told of them: it is said that in certain places there are deep pools and lakes, in which dwell monsters, huge serpents as long as a pine tree, and horses of the flood, which sometimes come out and commit mighty damage. One thing is certain, that yonder, far away to the west, in the heart of those hills, there is a wonderful valley, so narrow that only at midday is the face of the sun to be descried from it. That valley lay undiscovered and unknown for thousands of years; no person dreamed of its existence, but at last, a long time ago, certain hunters entered it by chance, and then what do you think they found, Caballero? They found a small nation or tribe of unknown people, speaking an unknown language, who, perhaps, had lived there since the creation of the world, without intercourse with the rest of their fellow-creatures, and without knowing that other beings besides themselves existed! Caballero, did you never hear of the valley of the Batuecas? Many books have been written about that valley and those people. Caballero, I am proud of yonder hills; and were I independent, and without wife or children, I would purchase a burra like that of your own, (which I see is an excellent one, and far superior to mine,) and travel amongst them till I knew all their mysteries, and had seen all the wondrous things which they contain."

Throughout the day I pressed the burra forward, only stopping once in order to feed the animal; but, notwithstanding that she played her part very well, night came on, and I was still about two leagues from Talavera. As the sun went down, the cold become intense; I drew the old gipsy cloak, which I still wore, closer around me, but I found it quite inadequate to protect me from the inclemency of the atmosphere. The road, which lay over a plain, was not very distinctly traced, and became in the dusk rather difficult to find, more especially as cross-roads leading to different places were of frequent occurrence. I however proceeded in the best manner I could, and when I became dubious as to the course I should take, I invariably allowed the animal on which I was mounted to decide. At length the moon shone out faintly, when suddenly by its beams I beheld a figure moving before me at a slight distance. I quickened the pace of the burra, and was soon close at its side. It went on, neither altering its pace nor looking round for a moment. It was the figure of a man, the tallest and bulkiest that I had hitherto seen in Spain, dressed in a manner strange and singular for the country. On his head was a hat with a low crown and a broad brim, very much resembling that of an English wagoner; about his body was a long, loose tunic or slop, seemingly of coarse ticken, open in front, so as to allow the interior garments to be occasionally seen; these appeared to consist of a jerkin and short velveteen pantaloons. I have said that the brim of the hat was broad, but, broad as it was, it was insufficient to cover an immense bush of coal-black hair, which, thick and curly, projected on either side; over the left shoulder was flung a kind of satchel, and in the right hand was held a long staff or pole.

There was something peculiarly strange about the figure; but what struck me the most was the tranquillity with which it moved along, taking no heed of me, though of course aware of my proximity, but looking straight forward along the road, save when it occasionally raised a huge face and large eyes towards the moon, which was now shining forth in the eastern quarter.

"A cold night," said I at last. "Is this the way to Talavera?"

"It is the way to Talavera, and the night is cold."

"I am going to Talavera," said I, "as I suppose you are yourself."

"I am going thither, so are you, Bueno."

The tones of the voice which delivered these words were in their way quite as strange and singular as the figure to which the voice belonged; they were not exactly the tones of a Spanish voice, and yet there was something in them that could hardly be foreign; the pronunciation also was correct, and the language, though singular, faultless. But I was most struck with the manner in which the last word, bueno, was spoken. I had heard something like it before, but where or when I could by no means remember. A pause now ensued; the figure stalking on as before with the most perfect indifference, and seemingly with no disposition either to seek or avoid conversation.

"Are you not afraid," said I at last, "to travel these roads in the dark? It is said that there are robbers abroad."

"Are you not rather afraid," replied the figure, "to travel these roads in the dark?— you who are ignorant of the country, who are a foreigner, an Englishman?"

"How is it that you know me to be an Englishman?" demanded I, much surprised.

"That is no difficult matter," replied the figure; "the sound of your voice was enough to tell me that."

"You speak of voices," said I; "suppose the tone of your own voice were to tell me who you are?"

"That it will not do," replied my companion; "you know nothing about me—you can know nothing about me."

"Be not sure of that, my friend; I am acquainted with many things of which you have little idea."

"Por exemplo," said the figure.

"For example," said I; "you speak two languages."

The figure moved on, seemed to consider a moment, and then said slowly, bueno.

"You have two names," I continued; "one for the house and the other for the street; both are good, but the one by which you are called at home is the one which you like best."

The man walked on about ten paces, in the same manner as he had previously done; all of a sudden he turned, and taking the bridle of the burra gently in his hand, stopped her. I had now a full view of his face and figure, and those huge features and Herculean form still occasionally revisit me in my dreams. I see him standing in the moonshine, staring me in the face with his deep calm eyes. At last he said:

"*Es usted tambien de nosotros?*"

. . . .

It was late at night when we arrived at Talavera. We went to a large gloomy house, which my companion informed me was the principal posada of the town. We entered the kitchen, at the extremity of which a large fire was blazing. "Pepita," said my companion to a handsome girl, who advanced smiling towards us; "a brasero and a private apartment; this cavalier is a friend of mine, and we shall sup together." We were shown to an apartment in which were two alcoves containing beds. After supper, which consisted of the very best, by the order of my companion, we sat over the brasero and commenced talking.

Myself.—Of course you have conversed with Englishmen before, else you could not have recognised me by the tone of my voice.

Abarbenel.—I was a young lad when the war of the independence broke out, and there came to the village in which our family lived an English officer in order to teach discipline to the new levies. He was quartered in my father's house, where he conceived a great affection for me. On his departure, with the consent of my father, I attended him through both the Castilles, partly as companion, partly as domestic. I was with him nearly a year, when he was suddenly summoned to return to his own country. He would fain have taken me with him, but to that my father would by no means consent. It is now five-and-twenty years since I last saw an Englishman; but you have seen how I recognised you even in the dark night.

Myself.—And what kind of life do you pursue, and by what means do you obtain support?

Abarbenel.—I experience no difficulty. I live much in the same way as I believe my forefathers lived; certainly as my father did, for his course has been mine. At his death I took possession of the herencia, for I was his only child. It was not requisite that I should follow any business, for my wealth was great; yet, to avoid remark, I followed that of my father, who was a longanizero. I have occasionally dealt in wool; but lazily, lazily—as I had no stimulus for exertion. I was, however, successful in many instances, strangely so; much more than many others who toiled day and night, and whose whole soul was in the trade.

Myself.—Have you any children? Are you married?

Abarbenel.—I have no children though I am married. I have a wife and an amiga, or I should rather say two wives, for I am wedded to both. I however call one my amiga, for appearance sake, for I wish to live in quiet, and am unwilling to offend the prejudices of the surrounding people.

Myself.—You say you are wealthy. In what does your wealth consist?

Abarbenel.—In gold and silver, and stones of price; for I have inherited all the hoards of my forefathers. The greater part is buried under ground; indeed, I have never examined the tenth part of it. I have coins of silver and gold older than the times of Ferdinand the Accursed and Jezebel; I have also large sums employed in usury. We keep ourselves close, however, and pretend to be poor, miserably so; but on certain occasions, at our festivals, when our gates are barred, and our savage dogs are let loose in the court, we eat our food off services such as the Queen of Spain cannot boast of, and wash our feet in ewers of silver, fashioned and wrought before the Americas were discovered, though our garments are at all times coarse, and our food for the most part of the plainest description.

Myself.—Are there more of you than yourself and your two wives?

Abarbenel.—There are my two servants, who are likewise of us; the one is a youth, and is about to leave, being betrothed to one at some distance; the other is old: he is now upon the road, following me with a mule and car.

Myself.—And whither are you bound at present?

Abarbenel.—To Toledo, where I ply my trade occasionally of longanizero. I love to wander about, though I seldom stray far from home. Since I left the Englishman my feet have never once stepped beyond the bounds of New Castile. I love to visit Toledo, and to think of the times which have long since departed; I should establish myself there, were there not so many accursed ones, who look upon me with an evil eye.

Myself.—Are you known for what you are? Do the authorities molest you?

Abarbenel.—People of course suspect me to be what I am; but as I conform outwardly in most respects to their ways, they do not interfere with me. True it is that sometimes, when I enter the church to hear the mass, they glare at me over the left shoulder, as to say—"What do you here?" And sometimes they cross themselves as I pass by; but as they go no further, I do not trouble myself on that account. With respect to the authorities, they are not bad friends of mine. Many of the higher class have borrowed money from me on usury, so that I have them to a certain extent in my power, and as for the low alguazils and corchetes, they would do any thing to oblige me in consideration of a few dollars, which I occasionally give them; so that matters upon the whole go on remarkably well. Of old, indeed, it was far otherwise; yet, I know not how it was, though other families suffered much, ours always enjoyed a tolerable share of tranquillity. The truth is, that our family has always known how to guide itself wonderfully. I may say there is much of the wisdom of the snake amongst us. We have always possessed friends; and with respect to enemies, it is by no means safe to meddle with us; for it is a rule of our house never to forgive an injury, and to spare neither trouble nor expense in bringing ruin and destruction upon the heads of our evil doers.

Myself.—Do the priests interfere with you?

Abarbenel.—They let me alone, especially in our own neighbourhood. Shortly after the death of my father, one hot-headed individual endeavoured to do me an evil turn, but I soon requited him, causing him to be imprisoned on a charge of blasphemy, and in prison he remained a long time, till he went mad and died.

Myself.—Have you a head in Spain, in whom is rested the chief authority?

Abarbenel.—Not exactly. There are, however, certain holy families who enjoy much consideration; my own is one of these—the chiefest, I may say. My grandsire was a particularly holy man; and I have heard my father say, that one night an archbishop came to his house secretly, merely to have the satisfaction of kissing his head.

Myself.—How can that be; what reverence could an archbishop entertain for one like yourself or your grandsire.

Abarbenel.—More than you imagine. He was one of us, at least his father was, and he could never forget what he had learned with reverence in his infancy. He said he had tried to forget it, but he could not; that the *ruah* was continually upon him, and that even from his childhood he had borne its terrors with a troubled mind, till at last he could bear himself no longer; so he went to my grandsire, with whom he remained one whole night; he then returned to his diocese, where he shortly afterwards died, in much renown for sanctity.

Myself.—What you say surprises me. Have you reason to suppose that many of you are to be found amongst the priesthood?

Abarbenel.—Not to suppose, but to know it. There are many such as I amongst the priesthood, and not amongst the inferior priesthood

either; some of the most learned and famed of them in Spain have been of us, and of our blood at least, and many of them at this day think as I do. There is one particular festival of the year at which four dignified ecclesiastics are sure to visit me; and then, when all is made close and secure, and the fitting ceremonies have been gone through, they sit down upon the floor and curse.

Myself.—Are you numerous in the large towns?

Abarbenel.—By no means; our places of abode are seldom the large towns; we prefer the villages, and rarely enter the large towns but on business. Indeed, we are not a numerous people, and there are few provinces of Spain which contain more than twenty families. None of us are poor, and those among us who serve, do so more from choice than necessity, for by serving each other we acquire different trades. Not unfrequently the time of service is that of courtship also, and the servants eventually marry the daughters of the house.

We continued in discourse the greater part of the night; the next morning I prepared to depart. My companion, however, advised me to remain where I was for that day. "And if you respect my counsel," said he, "you will not proceed farther in this manner. To-night the diligence will arrive from Estremadura, on its way to Madrid. Deposit yourself therein; it is the safest and most speedy mode of travelling. As for your Caballeria, I will myself purchase her. My servant is here, and has informed me that she will be of service to us. Let us, therefore, pass the day together in communion, like brothers, and then proceed on our separate journeys." We did pass the day together; and when the diligence arrived I deposited myself within, and on the morning of the second day arrived at Madrid.

8

CHAPTER XII.

Lodging at Madrid—My Hostess—British Ambassador—Mendizabal—Baltasar—Duties o. a National—Young Blood—The Execution—Population of Madrid—The Higher Orders—The Lower Classes—The Bull Fighter—The Crabbed Gitano.

It was the commencement of February when I reached Madrid. After staying a few days at a posada, I removed to a lodging which I engaged at No. 3, in the Calle de la Zarza, a dark dirty street, which, however, was close to the Puerta del Sol, the most central point of Madrid, into which four or five of the principal streets debouche, and which is, at all times of the year, the great place of assemblage for the idlers of the capital, poor or rich.

It was rather a singular house in which I had taken up my abode. I occupied the front part of the first floor; my apartments consisted of an immense parlour, and a small chamber on one side in which I slept; the parlour, notwithstanding its size, contained very little furniture: a few chairs, a table, and a species of sofa, constituted the whole. It was very cold and airy, owing to the draughts which poured in from three large windows, and from sundry doors. The mistress of the house, attended by her two daughters, ushered me in. "Did you ever see a more magnificent apartment?" demanded the former; "is it not fit for a king's son! Last winter it was occupied by the great General Espartero."

The hostess was an exceedingly fat woman, a native of Valladolid, in Old Castille. "Have you any other family," I demanded, "besides these daughters?" "Two sons," she replied; "one of them an officer in the army. father of this urchin," pointing to a wicked but clever looking boy of about twelve, who at that moment bounded into the room; "the other is the most celebrated national in Madrid: he is a tailor by trade, and his name is Baltasar. He has much influence with the other nationals, on account of the liberality of his opinions, and a word from him is sufficient to bring them all out armed and furious to the Puerta del Sol. He is, however, at present confined to his bed, for he is very dissipated and fond of the company of bull-fighters and people still worse."

As my principal motive for visiting the Spanish capital was the hope of obtaining permission from the government to print the New Testament in the Castillian language, for circulation in Spain, I lost no time, upon my arrival, in taking what I considered to be the necessary steps.

I was an entire stranger at Madrid, and bore no letters of introduction to any persons of influence, who might have assisted me in this undertaking, so that notwithstanding I entertained a hope of success, relying on the assistance of the Almighty, this hope was not at all times very vivid, but was frequently overcast with the clouds of despondency.

Mendizabal was at this time prime minister of Spain, and was considered as a man of almost unbounded power, in whose hands were placed the destinies of the country. I therefore considered that if I could by any means induce him to favour my views, I should have no reason to fear interruption from other quarters, and I determined upon applying to him.

Before taking this step however, I deemed it advisable to wait upon Mr. Villiers, the British ambassador at Madrid; and with the freedom permitted to a British subject, to ask his advice in this affair. I was received with great kindness, and enjoyed a conversation with him on various subjects before I introduced the matter which I had most at heart. He said that if I wished for an interview with Mendizabal, he would endeavour to procure me one, but, at the same time, told me frankly that he could not hope that any good would arise from it, as he knew him to be violently prejudiced against the British and Foreign Bible Society, and was far more likely to discountenance than encourage any efforts which they might be disposed to make for introducing the Gospel into Spain. I, however, remained resolute in my desire to make the trial, and before I left him, obtained a letter of introduction to Mendizabal.

Early one morning I repaired to the palace, in a wing of which was the office of the Prime Minister; it was bitterly cold, and the Guadarama, of which there is a noble view from the palace-plain, was covered with snow. For at least three hours I remained shivering with cold in an ante-room, with several other aspirants for an interview with the man of power. At last his private secretary made his appearance, and after putting various questions to the others, addressed himself to me, asking who I was and what I wanted. I told him that I was an Englishman, and the bearer of a letter from the British Minister. "If you have no objection, I will myself deliver it to His Excellency," said he; whereupon I handed it to him and he withdrew. Several individuals were admitted before me; at last, however, my own turn came, and I was ushered into the presence of Mendizabal.

He stood behind a table covered with papers, on which his eyes were intently fixed. He took not the slightest notice when I entered, and I had leisure enough to survey him: he was a huge athletic man, somewhat taller than myself, who measure six feet two without my shoes; his complexion was florid, his features fine and regular, his nose quite aquiline, and his teeth splendidly white: though scarcely fifty years of age, his hair was remarkably gray; he was dressed in a rich morning gown, with a gold chain round his neck, and morocco slippers on his feet.

His secretary, a fine intellectual looking man, who, as I was subsequently informed, had acquired a name both in English and Spanish literature, stood at one end of the table with papers in his hands.

After I had been standing about a quarter of an hour, Mendizabal suddenly lifted up a pair of sharp eyes, and fixed them upon me with a peculiarly scrutinizing glance.

"I have seen a glance very similar to that amongst the Beni Israel," thought I to myself.

. . . .

My interview with him lasted nearly an hour. Some singular discourse passed between us: I found him, as I had been informed, a bitter enemy to the Bible Society, of which he spoke in terms of hatred and contempt, and by no means a friend to the Christian religion, which I could easily account for. I was not discouraged, however, and pressed upon him the matter which brought me thither, and was eventually so far successful, as to obtain a promise, that at the expiration of a few months, when he hoped the country would be in a more tranquil state, I should be allowed to print the Scriptures.

As I was going away he said, "Yours is not the first application I have had: ever since I have held the reins of government I have been pestered in this manner, by English calling themselves Evangelical Christians, who have of late come flocking over into Spain. Only last week a hunchbacked fellow found his way into my cabinet whilst I was engaged in important business, and told me that Christ was coming. . . . . .

. . . . And now you have made your appearance, and almost persuaded me to embroil myself yet more with the priesthood, as if they did not abhor me enough already. What a strange infatuation is this, which drives you over lands and waters with Bibles in your hands. My good sir, it is not Bibles we want, but rather guns and gunpowder, to put the rebels down with, and above all, money, that we may pay the troops; whenever you come with these three things you shall have a hearty welcome, if not, we really can dispense with your visits, however great the honour."

Myself.—There will be no end to the troubles of this afflicted country until the Gospel have free circulation.

Mendizabal.—I expected that answer, for I have not lived thirteen years in England without forming some acquaintance with the phraseology of you good folks. Now, now, pray go; you see how engaged I am. Come again whenever you please, but let it not be within the next three months.

"Don Jorge," said my hostess, coming into my apartment one morning, whilst I sat at breakfast with my feet upon the brasero, "here is my son Baltasarito, the national; he has risen from his bed, and hearing that

there is an Englishman in the house, he has begged me to introduce him, for he loves Englishmen on account of the liberality of their opinions; there he is, what do you think of him?"

I did not state to his mother what I thought; it appeared to me, however, that she was quite right in calling him Baltasarito, which is the diminutive of Baltasar, forasmuch as that ancient and sonorous name had certainly never been bestowed on a more diminutive personage: he might measure about five feet one inch, though he was rather corpulent for his height; his face looked yellow and sickly, he had, however, a kind of fanfaronading air, and his eyes, which were of dark brown, were both sharp and brilliant. His dress, or rather his undress, was somewhat shabby: he had a foraging cap on his head, and in lieu of a morning gown, he wore a sentinel's old great coat.

"I am glad to make your acquaintance, Señor national," said I to him, after his mother had departed, and Baltasar had taken a seat, and of course lighted a paper cigar at the brasero. "I am glad to have made your acquaintance, more especially as your lady mother has informed me that you have great influence with the nationals. I am a stranger in Spain, and may want a friend; fortune has been kind to me in procuring me one who is a member of so powerful a body."

Baltasar.—Yes, I have a great deal to say with the other nationals; there is none in Madrid better known than Baltasar, or more dreaded by the Carlists. You say you may stand in need of a friend; there is no fear of my failing you in any emergency. Both myself and any of the other nationals will be proud to go out with you as padrinos, should you have any affair of honour on your hands. But why do you not become one of us? We would gladly receive you into our body.

Myself.—Is the duty of a national particularly hard?

Baltasar.—By no means; we have to do duty about once every fifteen days, and then there is occasionally a review, which does not last long. No! the duties of a national are by no means onerous, and the privileges are great. I have seen three of my brother nationals walk up and down the Prado of a Sunday, with sticks in their hands, cudgelling all the suspicious characters, and it is our common practice to scour the streets at night; and then if we meet any person who is obnoxious to us, we fall upon him, and with a knife or a bayonet generally leave him wallowing in his blood on the pavement: no one but a national would be permitted to do that.

Myself.—Of course none but persons of liberal opinions are to be found amongst the nationals?

Baltasar.—Would it were so! there are some amongst us, Don Jorge, who are no better than they should be; they are few, however, and for the most part well known. Theirs is no pleasant life, for when they mount guard with the rest they are scouted, and not unfrequently cudgelled. The law compels all of a certain age either to serve in the army or to become national soldiers, on which account some of these Godos are to be found amongst us.

Myself.—Are there many in Madrid of the Carlist opinion?

Baltasar.—Not among the young people; the greater part of the Madrilenian Carlists capable of bearing arms departed long ago to join the ranks of the factious in the Basque provinces. Those who remain are for the most part gray-beards and priests, good for nothing but to assemble in private coffee-houses, and to prate treason together. Let them prate, Don Jorge; let them prate; the destinies of Spain do not depend on the wishes of ojalateros and pasteleros, but on the hands of stout gallant nationals like myself and friends, Don Jorge.

Myself.—I am sorry to learn from your lady mother, that you are strangely dissipated.

Baltasar.—Ho, ho, Don Jorge, she has told you that, has she; what would you have, Don Jorge? I am young, and young blood will have its course. I am called Baltasar the gay by all the other nationals, and it is on account of my gaiety and the liberality of my opinions that I am so popular among them. When I mount guard, I invariably carry my guitar with me, and then there is sure to be a funcion at the guard-house. We send for wine, Don Jorge, and the nationals become wild, Don Jorge, dancing and drinking through the night, whilst Baltasarito strums the guitar and sings them songs of Germania:

> "Una romi sin pachi
> Le peno à su chindomar," &c., &c.

That is Gitàno, Don Jorge; I learnt it from the toreros of Andalusia, who all speak Gitàno, and are mostly of Gipsy blood. I learnt it from them; they are all friends of mine, Montes Sevilla and Poquito Pan. I never miss a funcion of bulls, Don Jorge. Baltasar is sure to be there with his amiga. Don Jorge, there are no bull-funcions in the winter, or I would carry you to one, but happily to-morrow there is an execution, a funcion de la horca; and there we will go, Don Jorge.

We did go to see this execution, which I shall long remember. The criminals were two young men, brothers: they suffered for a most atrocious murder, having in the dead of night broke open the house of an aged man, whom they put to death, and whose property they stole. Criminals in Spain are not hanged as they are in England, or guillotined as in France, but strangled upon a wooden stage. They sit down on a kind of chair with a post behind, to which is affixed an iron collar with a screw; this iron collar is made to clasp the neck of the prisoner, and on a certain signal it is drawn tighter and tighter by means of the screw, until life becomes extinct. After we had waited amongst the assembled multitude a considerable time, the first of the culprits appeared; he was mounted on an ass, without saddle or stirrups, his legs being

allowed to dangle nearly to the ground. He was dressed in yellow sulphur-coloured robes, with a high peaked conical red hat on his head, which was shaven. Between his hands he held a parchment, on which was written something, I believe the confession of faith. Two priests led the animal by the bridle; two others walked on either side chanting litanies, amongst which I distinguished the words of heavenly peace and tranquillity, for the culprit had been reconciled to the church, had confessed and received absolution, and had been promised admission to heaven. He did not exhibit the least symptom of fear, but dismounted from the animal and was led, not supported, up the scaffold, where he was placed on the chair, and the fatal collar put round his neck. One of the priests then in a loud voice commenced saying the Belief, and the culprit repeated the words after him. On a sudden, the executioner, who stood behind, commenced turning the screw, which was of prodigious force, and the wretched man was almost instantly a corpse; but, as the screw went round, the priest began to shout, "*pax et misericordia et tranquillitas,*" and still as he shouted, his voice became louder and louder till the lofty walls of Madrid rang with it; then stooping down, he placed his mouth close to the culprit's ear, still shouting, just as if he would pursue the spirit through its course to eternity, cheering it on its way. The effect was tremendous. I myself was so excited that I involuntarily shouted "*misericordia,*" and so did many others. God was not thought of; Christ was not thought of; only the priest was thought of, for he seemed at that moment to be the first being in existence, and to have the power of opening and shutting the gates of heaven or of hell, just as he should think proper. A striking instance of the successful working of the Popish system, whose grand aim has ever been to keep people's minds as far as possible from God, and to centre their hopes and fears in the priesthood. The execution of the second culprit was precisely similar; he ascended the scaffold a few minutes after his brother had breathed his last.

I have visited most of the principal capitals of the world, but upon the whole none has ever so interested me as this city of Madrid, in which I now found myself. I will not dwell upon its edifices, its public squares, its fountains, though some of these are remarkable enough: but Petersburg has finer streets, Paris and Edinburgh more stately edifices, London far nobler squares, whilst Shiraz can boast of more costly fountains, though not cooler waters. But the population! Within a mud wall, scarcely one league and a half in circuit, are contained two hundred thousand human beings, certainly forming the most extraordinary vital mass to be found in the entire world; and be it always remembered that this mass is strictly Spanish. The population of Constantinople is extraordinary enough, but to form it twenty nations have contributed; Greeks, Armenians, Persians,

Poles, Jews, the latter, by the by, of Spanish origin, and speaking amongst themselves the old Spanish language; but the huge population of Madrid, with the exception of a sprinkling of foreigners, chiefly French tailors, glove makers and peruquiers, is strictly Spanish, though a considerable portion are not natives of the place. Here are no colonies of Germans, as at Saint Petersburg; no English factories, as at Lisbon; no multitudes of insolent Yankees lounging through the streets, as at the Havannah, with an air which seems to say, the land is our own whenever we choose to take it; but a population which, however strange and wild, and composed of various elements, is Spanish, and will remain so as long as the city itself shall exist. Hail, ye aguadores of Asturia! who, in your dress of coarse duffel and leathern skull-caps, are seen seated in hundreds by the fountain sides, upon your empty water casks, or staggering with them filled to the topmost stories of lofty houses. Hail, ye caleseros of Valencia! who, lolling lazily against your vehicles, rasp tobacco for your paper cigars whilst waiting for a fare. Hail to you, beggars of La Mancha! men and women, who, wrapped in coarse blankets, demand charity indifferently at the gate of the palace or the prison. Hail to you, valets from the mountains, mayordomos and secretaries from Biscay and Guipuscoa, toreros from Andalusia, riposteros from Galicia, shopkeepers from Catalonia! Hail to ye, Castilians, Estremenians and Aragonese, of whatever calling! And lastly, genuine sons of the capital, rabble of Madrid, ye twenty thousand manolos, whose terrible knives, on the second morning of May, worked such grim havoc amongst the legions of Murat!

And the higher orders—the ladies and gentlemen, the cavaliers and señoras; shall I pass them by in silence? The truth is I have little to say about them; I mingled but little in their society, and what I saw of them by no means tended to exalt them in my imagination. I am not one of those who, wherever they go, make it a constant practice to disparage the higher orders, and to exalt the populace at their expense. There are many capitals in which the high aristocracy, the lords and ladies, the sons and daughters of nobility, constitute the most remarkable and the most interesting part of the population. This is the case at Vienna, and more especially at London. Who can rival the English aristocrat in lofty stature, in dignified bearing, in strength of hand, and valour of heart? Who rides a nobler horse? Who has a firmer seat? And who more lovely than his wife, or sister, or daughter? But with respect to the Spanish aristocracy, the ladies and gentlemen, the cavaliers and señoras, I believe the less that is said of them on the points to which I have just alluded the better. I confess, however, that I know little about them; they have, perhaps, their admirers, and to the pens of such I leave their panegyric. Le Sage has described them as they were nearly two cen-

turies ago. His description is any thing but captivating, and I do not think that they have improved since the period of the sketches of the immortal Frenchman. I would sooner talk of the lower class, not only of Madrid but of all Spain. The Spaniard of the lower class has much more interest for me, whether manolo, labourer, or muleteer. He is not a common being; he is an extraordinary man. He has not, it is true, the amiability and generosity of the Russian mujik, who will give his only rouble rather than the stranger shall want; nor his placid courage, which renders him insensible to fear, and at the command of his Tsar, sends him singing to certain death.[*] There is more hardness and less self-devotion in the disposition of the Spaniard; he possesses, however, a spirit of proud independence, which it is impossible but to admire. He is ignorant, of course; but it is singular, that I have invariably found amongst the low and slightly educated classes far more liberality of sentiment than amongst the upper. It has long been the fashion to talk of the bigotry of the Spaniards, and their mean jealousy of foreigners. This is true to a certain extent; but it chiefly holds good with respect to the upper classes. If foreign valour or talent has never received its proper meed in Spain, the great body of the Spaniards are certainly not in fault. I have heard Wellington calumniated in this proud scene of his triumphs, but never by the old soldiers of Aragon and the Asturias, who assisted to vanquish the French at Salamanca and the Pyrenees. I have heard the manner of riding of an English jockey criticised, but it was by the idiotic heir of Medina Celi, and not by a picador of the Madrilenian bull ring.

Apropos of bull-fighters:—Shortly after my arrival, I one day entered a low tavern in a neigbourhood notorious for robbery and murder, and in which for the last two hours I had been wandering on a voyage of discovery. I was fatigued, and required refreshment. I found the place thronged with people, who had all the appearance of ruffians. I saluted them, upon which they made way for me to the bar, taking off their sombreros with great ceremony. I emptied a glass of val de peñas, and was about to pay for it and depart, when a horrible looking fellow, dressed in a buff jerkin, leather breeches, and jackboots, which came half way up his thighs, and having on his head a white hat, the rims of which were at least a yard and a half in circumference, pushed through the crowd, and confronting me, roared:—

"*Otra copita! vamos Inglesito: Otra copita!*"

"Thank you, my good sir, you are very kind, you appear to know me, but I have not the honour of knowing you."

"Not know me!" replied the being. "I

* At the last attack on Warsaw, when the loss of the Russians amounted to upwards of twenty thousand men, the soldiery mounted the breach repeating, in measured chant, one of their popular songs: "Come, let us cut the cabbage," &c.

F

am Sevilla, the torero. I know you well; you are the friend of Baltasarito, the national, who is a friend of mine, and a very good subject."

Then turning to the company, he said in a sonorous tone, laying a strong emphasis on the last syllable of every word, according to the custom of the gente rufianesca throughout Spain:—" Cavaliers, and strong men, this cavalier is the friend of a friend of mine. *Es mucho hombre.* There is none like him in Spain. He speaks the crabbed Gitáno though he is an Inglesito."

"We do not believe it," replied several grave voices. "It is not possible."

"It is not possible, say you? I tell you it is. Come forward, Balseiro, you who have been in prison all your life, and are always boasting that you can speak the crabbed Gitáno, though I say you know nothing of it— come forward and speak to his worship in the crabbed Gitáno."

A low, slight, but active figure stepped forward. He was in his shirt sleeves, and wore a montero cap; his features were handsome, but they were those of a demon.

He spoke a few words in the broken Gipsy slang of the prison, inquiring of me whether I had even been in the condemned cell, and whether I knew what a Gitána* was?

"Vamos Inglesito," shouted Sevilla, in a voice of thunder; "answer the monro in the crabbed Gitáno."

I answered the robber, for such he was, and one, too, whose name will live for many a year in the ruffian histories of Madrid; I answered him in a speech of some length, in the dialect of the Estremenian Gipsies.

"I believe it is the crabbed Gitáno," muttered Balseiro. "It is either that or English, for I understand not a word of it."

"Did I not say to you," cried the bull-fighter, "that you knew nothing of the crabbed Gitáno? But this Inglesito does. I understood all he said. Vaya, there is none like him for the crabbed Gitáno. He is a good ginete, too; next to myself, there is none like him, only he rides with stirrup leathers too short. Inglesito, if you have need of money, I will lend you my purse. All I have is at your service, and that is not a little; I have just gained four thousand chulés by the lottery. *Vamos Inglesito! otra copita. Io lo pagaré todo. Io Sevilla!*"

And he clapped his hand repeatedly on his breast, reiterating "*Io Sevilla! Io*"——

CHAPTER XIII.

Intrigues at Court—Quesada and Galiano—Dissolution of the Cortes—The Secretary—Aragonese Pertinacity—The Council of Trent—The Asturian—The Three Thieves—Benedict Mol—The Men of Lucerne—The Treasure.

MENDIZABAL had told me to call upon him again at the end of three months, giving me hopes that he would not then oppose himself to the publication of the New Testament; before, however, the three months had elapsed, he had fallen into disgrace, and had ceased to be prime minister.

An intrigue had been formed against him, at the head of which were two quondam friends of his, and fellow-townsmen, Gaditanians, Isturitz and Alca Galiano; both of them had been egregious liberals in their day, and indeed principal members of those cortes, which on the Angouleme invasion, had hurried Ferdinand from Madrid to Cadiz, and kept him prisoner there until that impregnable town thought proper to surrender, and both of them had been subsequently refugees in England, where they had spent a considerable number of years.

These gentlemen, however, finding themselves about this time exceedingly poor, and not seeing any immediate prospect of advantage from supporting Mendizabal; considering themselves, moreover, quite as good men as he, and as capable of governing Spain in the present emergency, determined to secede from the party of their friend, whom they had hitherto supported, and to set up for themselves.

They therefore formed an opposition to Mendizabal in the cortes: the members of this opposition assumed the name of moderados, in contradistinction to Mendizabal and his followers, who were ultra liberals. The moderados were encouraged by the Queen Regent Christina, who aimed at a little more power than the liberals were disposed to allow her, and who had a personal dislike to the minister. They were likewise encouraged by Cordova, who at that time commanded the army, and was displeased with Mendizabal, inasmuch as the latter did not supply the pecuniary demands of the general with sufficient alacrity, though it is said that the greater part of what was sent for the payment of the troops was not devoted to that purpose, but was invested in the French funds in the name and for the use and behoof of the said Cordova.

It is, however, by no means my intention to write an account of the political events which were passing around me at this period; suffice it to say, that Mendizabal, finding himself thwarted in all his projects by the regent and the general, the former of whom would adopt no measure which he recommended, whilst the latter remained inactive and refused to engage the enemy, which by this time had re-

---

* Twelve ounces of bread, small pound, as given in the prison.

novered from the check caused by the death of Zumalacarregui, and was making considerable progress, resigned and left the field for the time open to his adversaries, though he possessed an immense majority in the cortes, and had the voice of the nation, at least the liberal part of it, in his favour.

Thereupon, Isturitz became head of the cabinet, Galiano minister of marine, and a certain Duke of Rivas minister of the interior. These were the heads of the moderado government, but as they were by no means popular at Madrid, and feared the nationals, they associated with themselves one who hated the latter body and feared nothing, a man of the name of Quesada, a very stupid individual, but a great fighter, who, at one period of his life, had commanded a legion or body of men called the Army of the Faith, whose exploits both on the French and Spanish side of the Pyrenees are too well known to require recapitulation. This person was made captain general of Madrid.

By far the most clever member of this government was Galiano, whose acquaintance I had formed shortly after my arrival. He was a man of considerable literature, and particularly will versed in that of his own country. He was, moreover, a fluent, elegant, and forcible speaker, and was to the moderado party within the cortes what Quesada was without, namely, their horses and chariots. Why he was made minister of marine is difficult to say, as Spain did not possess any; perhaps, however, from his knowledge of the English language, which he spoke and wrote nearly as well as his own tongue, having indeed during his sojourn in England chiefly supported himself by writing for reviews and journals, an honourable occupation, but to which few foreign exiles in England would be qualified to devote themselves.

He was a very small and irritable man, and a bitter enemy to every person who stood in the way of his advancement. He hated Mendizabal with undisguised rancour, and never spoke of him but in terms of unmeasured contempt. "I am afraid that I shall have some difficulty in inducing Mendizabal to give me permission to print the Testament," said I to him one day. "Mendizabal is a jackass," replied Galiano. "Caligula made his horse consul, which I suppose induced Lord —— to send over this huge burro of the Stock Exchange to be our minister."

It would be very ungrateful on my part were I not to confess my great obligations to Galiano, who assisted me to the utmost of his power in the business which brought me to Spain. Shortly after the ministry was formed, I went to him and said, "that now or never was the time to make an effort in my behalf." "I will do so," said he in a waspish tone; for he always spoke waspishly whether to friend or foe; "but you must have patience for a few days, we are very much occupied at present. We have been outvoted in the cortes, and this afternoon we intend to dissolve them. It is believed that the rascals will refuse to depart, but Quesada will stand at the door ready to turn them out, should they prove refractory. Come along, and you will perhaps see a funcion." . . . .

After an hour's debate, the cortes were dissolved without it being necessary to call in the aid of the redoubtable Quesada, and Galiano forthwith gave me a letter to his colleague, the Duke of Rivas, in whose department he told me was vested the power either of giving or refusing the permission to print the book in question. The duke was a very handsome young man, of about thirty, an Andalusian by birth, like his two colleagues. He had published several works, tragedies, I believe, and enjoyed a certain kind of literary reputation. He received me with the greatest affability; and having heard what I had to say, he replied, with a most captivating bow, and a genuine Andalusian grimace, "Go to my secretary; go to my secretary—el hara por usted el gusto." So I went to the secretary, whose name was Oliban, an Aragonese, who was not handsome, and whose manners were neither elegant nor affable. "You want permission to print the Testament?" "I do," said I. "And you have come to His Excellency about it," continued Oliban. "Very true," I replied. "I suppose you intend to print it without notes." "Yes." "Then His Excellency cannot give you permission," said the Aragonese secretary: "it was determined by the Council of Trent that no part of the scripture should be printed in any Christian country without the notes of the church." "How many years was that ago?" I demanded. "I do not know how many years ago it was," said Oliban; "but such was the decree of the Council of Trent." "Is Spain at present governed according to the decrees of the Council of Trent?" I inquired. "In some points she is," answered the Aragonese, "and this is one. But tell me who are you? Are you known to the British minister?" "O yes, and he takes a great interest in the matter." "Does he?" said Oliban; "that indeed alters the case, if you can show me that His Excellency takes an interest in this business, I certainly shall not oppose myself to it."

The British minister performed all I could wish, and much more than I could expect; he had an interview with the Duke of Rivas, with whom he had much discourse upon my affair: the duke was all smiles and courtesy. He moreover wrote a private letter to the duke, which he advised me to present when I next paid him a visit, and, to crown all, he wrote a letter directed to myself, in which he did me the honour to say that he had a regard for me, and that nothing would afford him greater pleasure than to hear that I had obtained the permission which I was seeking. So I went to the duke and delivered the letter. He was ten times more kind and affable than before: he read the letter, smiled most sweetly, and then, as if seized with sudden enthusiasm, he extended his arms in a manner almost theatrical, exclaiming, "Al secretario, el hara por usted el gusto." Away I hurried to the secretary, who received me with all the coolness of an icicle. I related to him the words of his principal, and then put into his hand the letter of the British minister to myself. The secretary read it very deliberately, and then said that it was evident his excellency *did* take an interest in the matter." He then asked me my name, and taking a sheet of paper, sat down as if for the purpose of writing the permission. I was in ecstacy—all of a sudden, however, he stopped, lifted up his head, seemed to consider a moment, and then putting his pen behind his ear, he said, "Amongst the decrees of the Council of Trent is one to the effect" . . . . .

. . . .

"Oh dear!" said I.

"A singular person is this Oliban," said I to Galiano; "you cannot imagine what trouble he gives me: he is continually talking about the Council of Trent."

"I wish he was in the Trent up to the middle," said Galiano, who, as I have observed already, spoke excellent English; "I wish he was there for talking such nonsense. However," said he, "we must not offend Oliban, he is one of us, and has done us much service; he is, moreover, a very clever man, but he is an Aragonese, and when one of that nation once gets an idea into his head, it is the most difficult thing in the world to dislodge it: however, we will go to him; he is an old friend of mine, and I have no doubt but that we shall be able to make him listen to reason." So the next day I called upon Galiano, at his marine or admirality office; (what shall I call it?) and from thence we proceeded to the bureau of the interior, a magnificent edifice, which had formerly been the casa of the Inquisition, where we had an interview with Oliban, whom Galiano took aside to the window, and there held with him a long conversation, which, as they spoke in whispers, and the room was immensely large, I did not hear. At length Galiano came to me and said, "There is some difficulty with respect to this business of yours, but I have told Oliban that you are a friend of mine, and he says that that is sufficient; remain with him now, and he will do any thing to oblige you; your affair is settled—farewell;" whereupon he departed and I remained with Oliban, who proceeded forthwith to write something, which having concluded, he took out a box of cigars, and having lighted one and offered me another, which I declined as I do not smoke, he placed his feet against the table, and thus proceeded to address me, speaking in the French language.

"It is with great pleasure that I see you in this capital, and, I may say, upon this business. I consider it a disgrace to Spain that there is no edition of the Gospel in circulation, at least such a one as would be within the reach of all classes of society, the highest or poorest; one unincumbered with notes and commentaries, human devices, swelling it to an unwieldy bulk. I have no doubt that such an edition as you propose to print, would have a most beneficial influence on the minds of the people, who, between ourselves, know nothing of pure religion; how should they? seeing that the Gospel has always been sedulously kept from them, just as if civilization could exist where the light of the Gospel beameth not. The moral regeneration of Spain depends upon the free circulation of the Scriptures; to which alone England, your own happy country, is indebted for its high state of civilization, and the unmatched prosperity which it at present enjoys; all this I admit, in fact, reason compels me to do so, but"——

"Now for it," thought I.

"But"—and then he began to talk once more of the wearisome Council of Trent, and I found that his writing in the paper, the offer of the cigar, and the long and prosy harangue were—what shall I call it?—mere φλυαρία.

By this time the spring was far advanced, the sides though not the tops of the Guadarama hills had long since lost their snows; the trees of the Prado had donned their full foliage, and all the Campina in the neighbourhood of Madrid smiled and was happy: the summer heats had not commenced, and the weather was truly delicious.

Towards the west, at the foot of the hill on which stands Madrid, is a canal running parallel with the Manzanares for some leagues, from which it is separated by pleasant and fertile meadows. The banks of this canal, which was begun by Carlos Tercero, and has never been completed, are planted with beautiful trees, and form the most delightful walk in the neighbourhood of the capital. Here I would loiter for hours, looking at the shoals of gold and silver fish which basked on the surface of the green sunny waters, or listening, not to the warbling of birds—for Spain is not the land of feathered choristers—but to the prattle of the narangero or man who sold oranges and water by a little deserted watch tower, just opposite the wooden bridge that crosses the canal, which situation he had chosen as favourable for his trade, and there had placed his stall. He was an Asturian by birth, about fifty years of age, and about five feet high. As I purchased freely of his fruit, he soon conceived a great friendship for me, and told me his history: it contained, however, nothing very remarkable, the leading incident being an adventure which had befallen him amidst the mountains of Granada, where falling into the hands of certain Gipsies, they stripped him naked and then dismissed him with a sound cudgelling. "I have wandered throughout Spain," said he, "and I have come to the conclusion that there are but two places worth living in, Malaga and Madrid. At Malaga every thing is very cheap, and there is such an abundance of fish, that I have frequently seen them piled in heaps on the sea-shore; and as for Madrid, money is always stirring at the Corte, and I never go supperless to bed; my only care is to sell my oranges, and my only hope that when I die I shall be buried yonder."

And he pointed across the Manzanares, where, on the declivity of a gentle hill, at about a league's distance, shone brightly in the sunshine the white walls of the Campo Santo, or common burying ground of Madrid.

He was a fellow of infinite drollery, and, though he could scarcely read or write, by no means ignorant of the ways of the world: his knowledge of individuals was curious and extensive; few people passing his stall with whose names, character, and history he was not acquainted. "Those two gentry," said he, pointing to a magnificently dressed cavalier and lady, who had dismounted from a carriage, and arm in arm were coming across the wooden bridge, followed by two attendants; "those gentry are the Infante Francisco Paulo, and his wife the Neopolitana, sister of our Christina; he is a very good subject, but as for his wife—vaya—the veriest scold in Madrid; she can say carrajo with the most ill conditioned carrier of la Mancha, giving the true emphasis and genuine pronunciation. Don't take off your hat to her, amigo—she has neither formality nor politeness. I once saluted her, and she took no more notice of me than if I had not been what I am, an Asturian and a gentleman of better blood than herself. Good day, Señor Don Francisco.—Que tal (*how goes it*)? very fine weather this—*vaya su merced con Dios*. Those three fellows who just stopped to drink water, are great thieves, true sons of the prison; I am always civil to them, for it would not do to be on ill terms; they pay me or not, just as they think proper. I have been in some trouble on their account: about a year ago they robbed a man a little farther on beyond the second bridge. By the way, I counsel you, brother, not to go there, as I believe you often do—it is a dangerous place. They robbed a gentleman and ill treated him, but his brother, who was an escribano, was soon upon their trail, and had them arrested; but he wanted some one to identify them, and it chanced that they had stopped to drink water at my stall, just as they did now. This the escribano heard of, and forthwith had me away to the prison to confront me with them. I knew them well enough, but I had learnt in my travels when to close my eyes and when to open them; so I told the escribano that I could not say that I had ever seen them before. He was in a great rage and threatened to imprison me; I told him he might and that I cared not. Vaya, I was not going to expose myself to the resentment of those three and to that of their friends; I live too near the Hay Market for that.—Good day, my young masters—Murcian oranges, as you see; the genuine dragons' blood. Water sweet and cold. Those two boys are the children of Gabiria, comptroller of the queen's household, and the richest man in Madrid; they are nice boys, and buy much fruit. It is said their father loves them more than all his possessions. The old woman who is lying beneath yon tree is the Tia Lucilla; she has committed murders, and she owes me money, I hope one day to see her

executed. This man was of the Walloon guard;—Señor Don Benito Mol, how do you do?"

This last named personage instantly engrossed my attention: he was a bulky old man somewhat above the middle height, with white hair and ruddy features; his eyes were large and blue, and whenever he fixed them on any one's countenance, were full of an expression of great eagerness, as if he were expecting the communication of some important tidings.— He was dressed commonly enough, in a jacket and trowsers of coarse cloth of a russet colour; on his head was an immense sombrero, the brim of which had been much cut and mutilated, so as in some places to resemble the jags or denticles of a saw. He returned the salutation of the orange-man, and bowing to me, forthwith produced two scented washballs which he offered for sale in a rough dissonant jargon, intended for Spanish, but which seemed more like the Valencian or Catalan.

Upon my asking him who he was, the following conversation ensued between us:

"I am a Swiss of Lucerne, Benedict Mol by name, once a soldier in the Walloon Guard, and now a soap-boiler, *para servir usted*."

"You speak the language of Spain very imperfectly," said I; "how long have you been in the country?"

"Forty-five years," replied Benedict; "but when the guard was broken up, I went to Minorca, where I lost the Spanish language without acquiring the Catalan."

"You have been a soldier of the king of Spain," said I; "how did you like the service?"

"Not so well, but that I should have been glad to leave it forty years ago; the pay was bad, and the treatment worse. I will now speak Swiss to you, for, if I am not much mistaken, you are a German man and understand the speech of Lucerne: I should soon have deserted from the service of Spain, as I did from that of the Pope, whose soldier I was in my early youth before I came here; but I had married a woman of Minorca, by whom I had two children; it was this that detained me in these parts so long; before, however, I left Minorca, my wife died, and as for my children, one went east, the other west, and I know not what became of them; I intend shortly to return to Lucerne, and live there like a duke."

"Have you, then, realized a large capital in Spain?" said I, glancing at his hat and the rest of his apparel.

"Not a cuart, not a cuart; those two washballs are all that I possess."

"Perhaps you are the son of good parents, and have lands and money in your own country wherewith to support yourself."

"Not a heller, not a heller; my father was hangman of Lucerne, and when he died, his body was seized to pay his debts."

"Then doubtless," said I, "you intend to ply your trade of soap-boiling at Lucerne: you are quite right, my friend, I know of no occupation more honourable or useful."

"I have no thoughts of plying my trade at Lucerne," replied Bennet; "and now, as I see you are a German man, Lieber Herr, and as I like your countenance and your manner of speaking, I will tell you in confidence that I know very little of my trade, and have already been turned out of several fabriques as an evil workman; the two wash-balls that I carry in my pocket are not of my own making. *In Kurtzen,* I know little more of soap-boiling than I do of tailoring, horse-farriery, or shoe-making, all of which I have practised."

"Then I know not how you can hope to live like a hertzog in your native canton, unless you expect that the men of Lucerne, in consideration of your services to the Pope and to the king of Spain, will maintain you in splendour at the public expense."

"Lieber Herr," said Benedict, "the men of Lucerne are by no means fond of maintaining the soldiers of the Pope and the king of Spain at their own expense; many of the guard who have returned thither beg their bread in the streets, but when I go it shall be in a coach drawn by six mules with a treasure, a mighty schatz which lies in the church of Saint James of Compostella, in Galicia."

"I hope you do not intend to rob the church," said I; "if you do, however, I believe you will be disappointed. Mendizabal and the liberals have been beforehand with you. I am informed that at present no other treasure is to be found in the cathedrals of Spain than a few paltry ornaments and plated utensils."

"My good German Herr," said Benedict, "it is no church schatz, and no person living, save myself, knows of its existence: nearly thirty years ago, amongst the sick soldiers who were brought to Madrid, was one of my comrades of the Walloon Guard who had accompanied the French to Portugal; he was very sick and shortly died. Before, however, he breathed his last, he sent for me, and upon his death-bed told me that himself and two other soldiers, both of whom had since been killed, had buried in a certain church in Compostella a great booty which they had made in Portugal; it consisted of gold moidores and of a packet of huge diamonds from the Brazils; the whole was contained in a large copper kettle. I listened with greedy ears, and from that moment, I may say, I have known no rest, neither by day nor night, thinking of the schatz. It is very easy to find, for the dying man was so exact in his description of the place where it lies, that were I once at Compostella, I should have no difficulty in putting my hand upon it; several times I have been on the point of setting out on the journey, but something has always happened to stop me. When my wife died, I left Minorca with a determination to go to Saint James, but on reaching Madrid, I fell into the hands of a Basque woman, who persuaded me to live with her, which I have done for several years; she is a great hax,* and says that if I desert her she will breathe a spell which shall cling to me forever. *Dem Gott sey dank,*—she is now in the hospital, and daily expected to die. This is my history, Lieber Herr."

I have been the more careful in relating the above conversation, as I shall have frequent occasion to mention the Swiss in the course of these journals; his subsequent adventures are highly extraordinary, and the closing one caused a great sensation in Spain.

CHAPTER XIV.

State of Spain—Isturitz—Revolution of the Granja—The Disturbance—Signs of Mischief—News-paper Reporters—Quesada's Onslaught—The Closing Scene—Flight of the Moderados—The Coffee Bowl.

In the mean time the affairs of the moderados did not proceed in a very satisfactory manner; they were unpopular at Madrid, and still more so in the other large towns of Spain, in most of which juntas had been formed, which, taking the local administration into their own hands, declared themselves independent of the queen and her ministers, and refused to pay taxes; so that the government was within a short time reduced to great straits for money; the army was unpaid, and the war languished; I mean on the part of the Christinos, for the Carlists were pushing it on with considerable vigour; parties of their guerillas scouring the country in all directions, whilst a large division, under the celebrated Gomez, was making the entire circuit of Spain. To crown the whole, an insurrection was daily expected at Madrid, to prevent which the nationals were disarmed, which measure tended greatly to increase their hatred against the moderado government, and especially against Quesada, with whom it was supposed to have originated.

With respect to my own matters, I lost no opportunity of pushing forward my application; the Aragonese secretary, however, still harped upon the Council of Trent, and succeeded in baffling all my efforts. He appeared to have inoculated his principal with his own ideas upon this subject, for the duke, when he beheld me at his levees, took no farther notice of me than by a contemptuous glance; and once, when I stepped up for the pur-

---

* Witch. Ger. Hexe.

pose of addressing him, disappeared through a side door, and I never saw him again, for I was disgusted with the treatment which I had received, and forbore paying any more visits at the Casa de la Inquisicion. Poor Galiano still proved himself my unshaken friend, but candidly informed me that there was no hope of my succeeding in the above quarter. "The duke," said he, "says that your request cannot be granted; and the other day, when I myself mentioned it in the council, began to talk of the decision of Trent, and spoke of yourself as a plaguy pestilent fellow; whereupon I answered him with some acrimony, and there ensued a bit of a funcion between us, at which Isturitz laughed heartily. By the by," continued he, "what need have you of a regular permission, which it does not appear that any one has authority to grant. The best thing that you can do under all circumstances is to commit the work to the press, with an understanding that you shall not be interfered with when you attempt to distribute it. I strongly advise you to see Isturitz himself upon the matter. I will prepare him for the interview, and will answer that he receives you civilly."

In fact, a few days afterwards, I had an interview with Isturitz at the palace, and for the sake of brevity I shall content myself with saying that I found him perfectly well disposed to favour my views. "I have lived long in England," said he; "the Bible is free there, and I see no reason why it should not be free in Spain also. I am not prepared to say that England is indebted for her prosperity to the knowledge which all her children, more or less, possess of the sacred writings; but of one thing I am sure, namely, that the Bible has done no harm in that country, nor do I believe that it will effect any in Spain; print it, therefore, by all means, and circulate it as extensively as possible." I retired, highly satisfied with my interview, having obtained, if not a written permission to print the sacred volume, what, under all circumstances, I considered as almost equivalent, an understanding that my biblical pursuits would he tolerated in Spain; and I had fervent hope that whatever was the fate of the present ministry, no future one, particularly a liberal one, would venture to interfere with me, more especially as the English ambassador was my friend, and was privy to all the steps I had taken throughout the whole affair.

Two or three things connected with the above interview with Isturitz struck me as being highly remarkable. First of all, the extreme facility with which I obtained admission to the presence of the prime minister of Spain. I had not to wait, or indeed to send in my name, but was introduced at once by the door-keeper. Secondly, the air of loneliness which pervaded the place, so unlike the bustle, noise, and activity which I observed when I waited on Mendizabal. In this instance, there were no eager candidates for an interview with the great man; indeed, I did not behold a single individual, with the exception of Isturitz and the official. But that which made the most profound impression upon me, was the manner of the minister himself, who, when I entered, sat upon a sofa, with his arms folded, and his eyes directed to the ground. When he spoke, there was extreme depression in the tones of his voice, his dark features wore an air of melancholy, and he exhibited all the appearance of a person meditating to escape from the miseries of this life by the most desperate of all acts—suicide.

And a few days showed that he had, indeed, cause for much melancholy meditation: in less than a week occurred the revolution of the Granja, as it is called. The Granja or Grange, is a royal country seat, situated amongst pine forests, on the other side of the Guadarama hills, about twelve leagues distant from Madrid. To this place the queen regent Christina had retired, in order to be aloof from the discontent of the capital, and to enjoy rural air and amusements in this celebrated retreat, a monument of the taste and magnificence of the first Bourbon who ascended the throne of Spain. She was not, however, permitted to remain long in tranquillity; her own guards were disaffected, and more inclined to the principles of the constitution of 1823 than to those of absolute monarchy, which the moderados were attempting to revive again in the government of Spain. Early one morning, a party of these soldiers, headed by a certain sergeant Garcia, entered her apartment, and proposed that she should subscribe her hand to this constitution, and swear solemnly to abide by it. Christina, however, who was a woman of considerable spirit, refused to comply with this proposal, and ordered them to withdraw. A scene of violence and tumult ensued, but the regent still continuing firm, the soldiers at length led her down to one of the courts of the palace, where stood her well known paramour, Muñoz, bound and blindfolded. "Swear to the constitution, you she-rogue," vociferated the swarthy sergeant. "Never!" said the spirited daughter of the Neapolitan Bourbons. "Then your cortejo shall die!" replied the sergeant. "Ho! ho! my lads; get ready your arms, and send four bullets through the fellow's brain." Muñoz was forthwith led to the wall, and compelled to kneel down; the soldiers levelled their muskets, and another moment would have consigned the unfortunate wight to eternity, when Christina, forgetting everything but the feelings of her woman's heart, suddenly started forward with a shriek, exclaiming: "Hold, hold! I sign, I sign!"

The day after this event I entered the Puerta del Sol at about noon. There is always a crowd there about this hour, but it is generally a very quiet, motionless crowd, consisting of listless idlers calmly smoking their cigars, or listening to or retailing the—in general—very dull news of the capital; but on the day of which I am speaking the mass was no longer inert. There was much gesticulation and vociferation, and several people were running about shouting, "*Viva la constitucion!*"—a cry which, a few days previously, would have been visited on the utterer with death, the city having for some weeks past been subjected to the rigour of martial law. I occasionally heard the words, "*La Granja! La Granja!*" Which words were sure to be succeeded by the shout of "*Viva la constitucion!*" Opposite the Casa de Postas were drawn up in a line about a dozen mounted dragoons, some of whom were continually waving their caps in the air and joining the common cry, in which they were encouraged by their commander, a handsome young officer, who flourished his sword, and more than once cried out with great glee, "Long live the constitutional queen! Long live the constitution!"

The crowd was rapidly increasing, and several nationals made their appearance in their uniforms, but without their arms, of which they had been deprived, as I have already stated. "What has become of the moderado government?" said I to Baltasar, whom I suddenly observed amongst the crowd, dressed as when I had first seen him, in his old regimental great coat and foraging cap; "have the ministers been deposed and others put in their place?"

"Not yet, Don Jorge," said the little soldier-tailor; "not yet; the scoundrels still hold out, relying on the brute bull Quesada and a few infantry, who still continue true to them; but there is no fear, Don Jorge; the queen is ours, thanks to the courage of my friend Garcia, and if the brute bull should make his appearance—ho! ho! Don Jorge, you shall see something—I am prepared for him, ho! ho!" and thereupon he half opened his great coat, and showed me a small gun which he bore beneath it in a sling, and then moving away with a wink and a nod, disappeared amongst the crowd.

Presently I perceived a small body of soldiers advancing up the Calle Mayor, or principal street which runs from the Puerta del Sol in the direction of the palace; they might be about twenty in number, and an officer marched at their head with a drawn sword; the men appeared to have been collected in a hurry, many of them being in fatigue dress, with foraging caps on their heads. On they came, slowly marching; neither their officer nor themselves paying the slightest attention to the cries of the crowd which thronged about them, shouting "Long live the constitution!" save and except by an occasional surly side glance: on they marched with contracted brows and set teeth, till they came in front of the cavalry, where they halted and drew up in a rank.

"Those men mean mischief," said I to my friend D——, of the Morning Chronicle, who at this moment joined me; "and depend upon it, that if they are ordered they will commence firing, caring nothing whom they hit,—but what can those cavalry fellows behind them mean, who are evidently of the other opinion by their shouting; why don't they charge at once this handful of foot people and overturn them? Once down, the crowd would wrest from them their muskets in a moment. You are a liberal, which I am not; why do you not go to that silly young man who commands the horse, and give him a word of counsel in time?"

'D—— turned upon me his broad red good-humoured English countenance, with a peculiarly arch look, as much as to say . . . . . (whatever you think most applicable, gentle reader,) then taking me by the arm, "Let us get," said he, "out of this crowd and mount to some window, where I can write down what is about to take place, for I agree with you that mischief is meant." Just opposite the post office was a large house, in the topmost story of which we beheld a paper displayed, importing that apartments were to let; whereupon we instantly ascended the common stair, and having agreed with the mistress of the étage for the use of the front room for the day, we bolted the door, and the reporter, producing his pocket book and pencil, prepared to take notes of the coming events, which were already casting their shadow before.

What most extraordinary men are these reporters of newspapers in general, I mean English newspapers; surely if there be any class of individuals who are entitled to the appellation of cosmopolites, it is these; who pursue their avocation in all countries indifferently, and accommodate themselves at will to the manners of all classes of society: their fluency of style as writers is only surpassed by their facility of language in conversation, and their attainments in classical and polite literature only by their profound knowledge of the world, acquired by an early introduction into its bustling scenes. The activity, energy, and courage which they occasionally display in the pursuit of information, are truly remarkable. I saw them, during the three days at Paris, mingled with canaille and gamins behind the barriers, whilst the mitraille was flying in all directions, and the desperate cuirassiers were dashing their fierce horses against these seemingly feeble bulwarks. There stood they, dotting down their observations in their pocket books as unconcernedly as if reporting the proceedings of a reform meeting in Covent Garden or Finsbury Square; whilst in Spain, several of them accompanied the Carlist and Christino guerillas in some of their most desperate raids and expeditions, exposing themselves to the danger of hostile bullets, the inclemency of winter, and the fierce heat of the summer sun.

We had scarcely been five minutes at the window, when we suddenly heard the clattering of horses' feet hastening down the street called the Calle de Carretas. The house in which we had stationed ourselves was, as I have already observed, just opposite to the post office, at the left of which this street debouches from the north into the Puerta del Sol: as the sounds became louder and louder, the cries of the crowd below diminished, and a species of panic seemed to have fallen upon all: once or twice, however, I could distinguish the words, Quesada! Quesada! The foot soldiers stood calm and motionless, but I observed that the cavalry, with the young officer who commanded them, displayed both confusion and fear, exchanging with each other some hurried words; all of a sudden that part of the crowd which stood near the mouth of the Calle de Carretas fell back in great disorder, leaving a considerable space unoccupied, and the next moment Quesada, in complete general's uniform, and mounted on a bright bay thorough bred English horse, with a drawn sword in his hand, dashed at full gallop into the area, in much the same manner as I have seen a Manchegan bull rush into the amphitheatre when the gates of his pen are suddenly flung open.

He was closely followed by two mounted officers, and at a short distance by as many dragoons. In almost less time than is sufficient to relate it, several individuals in the crowd were knocked down and lay sprawling upon the ground beneath the horses of Quesada and his two friends, for as to the dragoons, they halted as soon as they had entered the Puerta del Sol. It was a fine sight to see three men, by dint of valour and good horsemanship, strike terror into at least as many thousands: I saw Quesada spur his horse repeatedly into the dense masses of the crowd, and then extricate himself in the most masterly manner. The rabble were completely awed and gave way, retiring by the Calle del Comercio and the street of Alcala. All at once, Quesada singled out two nationals, who were attempting to escape, and setting spurs to his horse, turned them in a moment and drove them in another direction, striking them in a contemptuous manner with the flat of his sabre. He was crying out, "Long live the absolute queen!" when, just beneath me, amidst a portion of the crowd which had still maintained its ground, perhaps from not having the means of escaping, I saw a small gun glitter for a moment, then there was a sharp report, and a bullet had nearly sent Quesada to his long account, passing so near to the countenance of the general as to graze his hat. I had an indistinct view for a moment of a well known foraging cap just about the spot from whence the gun had been discharged, then there was a rush of the crowd, and the shooter, whoever he was, escaped discovery amidst the confusion which arose.

As for Quesada, he seemed to treat the danger from which he had escaped with the utmost contempt. He glared about him fiercely for a moment, then leaving the two nationals, who sneaked away like whipped hounds, he went up to the young officer who commanded the cavalry, and who had been active in raising the cry of the constitution, and to him he addressed a few words with an air of stern menace; the youth evidently quailed before him, and probably in obedience to his orders, resigned the command of the party, and rode slowly away with a discomfited air; whereupon Quesada dismounted and walked slowly backwards and forwards before the Casa de Postas with a mien which seemed to bid defiance to mankind.

This was the glorious day of Quesada's existence, his glorious and last day. I call it the day of his glory, for he certainly never before appeared under such brilliant circumstances, and he never lived to see another sun set.— No action of any conqueror or hero on record, is to be compared with this closing scene of the life of Quesada, for who, by his single desperate courage and impetuosity, ever before stopped a revolution in full course?— Quesada did: he stopped the revolution at Madrid for one entire day, and brought back the uproarious and hostile mob of a huge city to perfect order and quiet. His burst into the Puerta del Sol was the most tremendous and successful piece of daring ever witnessed. I admired so much the spirit of the "brute bull" that I frequently, during his wild onset, shouted "Viva Quesada!" for I wished him well. Not that I am of any political party or system. No, no! I have lived too long with Rommany Chals and Petulengres* to be of any politics save Gipsy politics: and it is well known that, during elections, the children of Roma side with both parties so long as the event is doubtful, promising success to each; and then when the fight is done, and the battle won, invariably range themselves in the ranks of the victorious. But I repeat that I wished well to Quesada, witnessing, as I did, his stout heart and good horsemanship. Tranquillity was restored to Madrid throughout the remainder of the day; the handful of infantry bivouacked in the Puerta del Sol. No more cries of long live the constitution were heard; and the revolution in the capital seemed to have been effectually put down.— It is probable, indeed, that had the chiefs of the moderado party but continued true to themselves for forty-eight hours longer, their cause would have triumphed, and the revolutionary soldiers at the Granja would have been glad to restore the Queen Regent to liberty, and to have come to terms, as it was well known that several regiments, who still continued loyal, were marching upon Madrid. The moderados, however, were not true to themselves; that very night their hearts failed them, and they fled in various directions.— Isturitz and Galiano to France; and the Duke of Rivas to Gibraltar: the panic of his colleagues even infected Quesada, who, disguised as a civilian, took to flight. He was not, however, so successful as the rest, but was recognised at a village about three leagues from Madrid, and cast into the prison by some friends of the constitution. Intelligence of his capture was instantly transmitted to the capital, and a vast mob of the nationals, some on foot, some on horseback, and others in cabriolets, instantly set out. "The nationals are coming," said a paisano to Quesada.—

---

* A compound of the modern Greek πέταλον, and the Sanscrit kara, the literal meaning being Lord of the horse-shoe (i. e. maker); it is one of the private cognominations of "The Smiths," an English Gipsey clan.

"Then," said he, "I am lost;" and forthwith prepared himself for death.

There is a celebrated coffee-house in the Calle d'Alcala at Madrid, capable of holding several hundred individuals. On the evening of the day in question, I was seated there, sipping a cup of the brown beverage, when I heard a prodigious noise and clamour in the street; it proceeded from the nationals, who were returning from their expedition. In a few minutes I saw a body of them enter the coffee-house marching arm in arm, two by two, stamping on the ground with their feet in a kind of measure, and repeating in loud chorus as they walked round the spacious apartment, the following grisly stanza :—

> " Que es lo que abaja
> Por aquel cerro ?
> Ta ra ra ra ra.
> Son los huesos de Quesada,
> Que los trae un perro—
> Ta ra ra ra ra."

A huge bowl of coffee was then called for, which was placed upon a table, around which gathered the national soldiers; there was a silence for a moment, which was interrupted by a voice roaring out, " el panuelo ! " A blue kerchief was forthwith produced, which appeared to contain a substance of some kind : it was untied, and a gory hand and three or four dissevered fingers made their appearance, and with these the contents of the bowl were stirred up. " Cups ! cups ! " cried the nationals. . . . .

" Ho, ho, Don Jorge," cried Baltasarito, coming up to me with a cup of coffee, " pray do me the favour to drink upon this glorious occasion. This is a pleasant day for Spain, and for the gallant nationals of Madrid. I have seen many a bull funcion, but none which has given me so much pleasure as this. Yesterday the brute had it all his own way, but to-day the toreros have prevailed, as you see, Don Jorge. Pray drink; for I must now run home to fetch my pajandi to play my brethren a tune, and sing a copla. What shall it be ? Something in Gitáno ?

> ' Una noche sinava en tucue.'

You shake your head, Don Jorge. Ha, ha; I am young, and youth is the time for pleasure : well, well, out of complement to you, who are an Englishman and a monro, it shall not be that, but something liberal, something patriotic, the Hymn of Riego.—Hasta despues, Don Jorge ! ".

CHAPTER XV.

The Steamer—Cape Finisterre—The Storm—Arrival at Cadiz—The New Testament—Seville—Italica—The Amphitheatre—The Prisoners—The Encounter—Baron Taylor—The Street and Desert.

At the commencement of November, I again found myself on the salt water, on my way to Spain. I had returned to England shortly after the events which have been narrated in the last chapter, for the purpose of consulting with my friends, and for planning the opening of a biblical campaign in Spain. It was now determined by us to print the New Testament, with as little delay as possible, at Madrid; and I was to be entrusted with the somewhat arduous task of its distribution. My stay in England was very short, for time was precious, and I was eager to return to the field of action.

I embarked in the Thames, on board the M——— steamer. We had a most unpleasant passage to Falmouth; the ship was crowded with passengers, most of them were poor consumptive individuals, and other invalids, fleeing from the cold blasts of England's winter to the sunny shores of Portugal and Madeira. In a more uncomfortable vessel, especially steam ship, it has never been my fate to make a voyage. The berths were small and insupportably close, and of these wretched holes mine was amongst the worst, the rest having been bespoken before I arrived on board; so that to avoid the suffocation which seemed to threaten me should I enter it, I lay upon the floor of one of the cabins throughout the voyage. We remained at Falmouth twenty-four hours, taking in coal, and repairing the engine, which had sustained considerable damage.

On Monday, the 7th. we again started, and made for the Bay of Biscay. The sea was high, and the wind strong and contrary; nevertheless, on the morning of the fourth day, we were in sight of the rocky coast, to the north of Cape Finisterre. I must here observe, that this was the first voyage that the captain who commanded the vessel had ever made on board of her, and that he knew little or nothing of the coast towards which we were bearing. He was a person picked up in a hurry, the former captain having resigned his command on the ground that the ship was not seaworthy, and that the engines were frequently unserviceable. I was not acquainted with these circumstances at the time, or perhaps I should have felt more alarmed than I did, when I saw the vessel approaching nearer and nearer the shore, till at last we were only a few hundred yards distant. As it was, however, I felt very much surprised; for having passed it twice before, both times in steam vessels, and having seen with what care the captains endeavoured to maintain a wide offing, I could not conceive the reason of our being now so near this dangerous region. The wind was blowing hard towards the shore, if that can be called a shore which consists of steep abrupt precipices, on which the surf was breaking with the noise of thunder, tossing up clouds of spray and foam to the height of a cathedral. We coasted slowly along, rounding several tall forelands, some of them piled up by the hand of nature in the most fantastic shapes. About nightfall Cape Finisterre was not far ahead,—a bluff, brown, granite mountain, whose frowning head may be seen far away by those who traverse the ocean. The stream which poured round its breast was terrific, and though our engines plied with all their force, they made little or no way.

By about eight o'clock at night the wind had increased to a hurricane, the thunder rolled frightfully, and the only light which we had to guide us on our way was the red forked lightning, which burst at times from the bosom of the big black clouds which lowered over our heads. We were exerting ourselves to the utmost to weather the cape, which we could descry by the lightning on our lee, its brow being frequently brilliantly lighted up by the flashes which quivered around it, when suddenly, with a great crash, the engine broke, and the paddles, on which depended our lives, ceased to play.

I will not attempt to depict the scene of horror and confusion which ensued: it may be imagined, but never described. The captain, to give him his due, displayed the utmost coolness and intrepidity; he and the whole crew made the greatest exertions to repair the engine, and when they found their labour in vain, endeavoured, by hoisting the sails, and by practising all possible manœuvres, to preserve the ship from impending destruction; but all was of no avail, we were hard on a lee shore, to which the howling tempest was impelling us. About this time I was standing near the helm, and I asked the steersman if there was any hope of saving the vessel, or our lives. He replied, "Sir, it is a bad affair, no boat could live for a minute in this sea, and in less than an hour the ship will have her broadside on Finisterre, where the strongest man-of-war ever built must go to shivers instantly—none of us will see the morning." The captain, likewise, informed the other passengers in the cabin to the same effect, telling them to prepare themselves; and having done so, he ordered the door to be fastened, and none to be permitted to come on deck.— I, however, kept my station, though almost drowned with water, immense waves continually breaking over our windward side and flooding the ship. The water casks broke from their lashings, and one of them struck me down, and crushed the foot of the unfortunate man at the helm, whose place was instantly taken by the captain. We were now close to the rocks, when a horrid convulsion of the elements took place. The lightning enveloped us as with a mantle, the thunders

were louder than the roar of a million cannon, the dregs of the ocean seemed to be cast up, and in the midst of all this turmoil, the wind, without the slightest intimation, *veered right about,* and pushed us from the horrible coast faster than it had previously driven us towards it.

The oldest sailors on board acknowledged that they had never witnessed so providential an escape. I said, from the bottom of my heart, "Our Father—hallowed be thy name."

The next day we were near foundering, for the sea was exceedingly high, and our vessel, which was not intended for sailing, laboured terribly, and leaked much. The pumps were continually working. She likewise took fire, but the flames were extinguished. In the evening the steam-engine was partially repaired, and we reached Lisbon on the thirteenth, where in a few days we completed our repairs.

I found my excellent friend W——— in good health. During my absence he had been doing every thing in his power to further the sale of the sacred volume in Portuguese: his zeal and devotedness were quite admirable. The distracted state of the country, however, during the last six months, had sadly impeded his efforts. The minds of the people had been so engrossed with politics, that they found scarcely any time to think of the welfare of their souls. The political history of Portugal had of late afforded a striking parallel to that of the neighbouring country. In both a struggle for supremacy had arisen between the court and the democratic party; in both the latter had triumphed, whilst two distinguished individuals had fallen a sacrifice to the popular fury—Freire in Portugal, and Quesada in Spain. The news which reached me at Lisbon from the latter country were rather startling. The hordes of Gomez were ravaging Andalusia, which I was about to visit on my way to Madrid; Cordova had been sacked and abandoned after a three days' occupation by the Carlists. I was told that if I persisted in my attempt to enter Spain in the direction which I proposed, I should probably fall into their hands at Seville. I had, however, no fears, and had full confidence that the Lord would open the path before me to Madrid.

The vessel being repaired, we again embarked, and in two days arrived in safety at Cadiz. I found great confusion reigning there; numerous bands of the factious were reported to be hovering in the neighbourhood. An attack was not deemed improbable, and the place had just been declared in a state of siege. I took up my abode at the French hotel in the Calle de la Niveria, and was allotted a species of cockloft, or garret, to sleep in, for the house was filled with guests, being a place of much resort, on account of the excellent table d'hôte which is kept there. I dressed myself and walked about the town. I entered several coffee-houses: the din of tongues in all was deafening. In one no less than six orators were haranguing at the same time on the state of the country, and the probability of an intervention on the part of England and France. As I was listening to one of them, he suddenly called upon me for my opinion, as I was a foreigner, and seemingly just arrived. I replied that I could not venture to guess what steps the two governments would pursue under the present circumstances, but thought that it would be as well if the Spaniards would exert themselves more and call less on Jupiter. As I did not wish to engage in any political conversation, I instantly quitted the house, and sought those parts of the town where the lower classes principally reside.

I entered into discourse with several individuals, but found them very ignorant; none could read or write, and their ideas respecting religion were any thing but satisfactory,—most professing a perfect indifference. I afterwards went into a bookseller's shop and made inquiries respecting the demand for literature, which, he informed me, was small. I produced a London edition of the New Testament in Spanish, and asked the bookseller whether he thought a book of that description would sell in Cadiz. He said that both the type and paper were exceedingly beautiful, but that it was a work not sought after, and very little known. I did not pursue my inquiries in other shops, for I reflected that I was not likely to receive a very favourable opinion from booksellers respecting a publication in which they had no interest. I had, moreover, but two or three copies of the New Testament with me, and could not have supplied them had they even given me an order.

Early on the 24th, I embarked for Seville in the small Spanish steamer "The Betis:" the morning was wet, and the aspect of nature was enveloped in a dense mist, which prevented my observing surrounding objects. After proceeding about six leagues, we reached the northeastern extremity of the Bay of Cadiz, and passed by Saint Lucar, an ancient town near to the spot where the Guadalquivir disembogues itself. The mist suddenly disappeared, and the sun of Spain burst forth in full brilliancy, enlivening all around, and particularly myself, who had till then been lying on the deck in a dull melancholy stupor. We entered the mouth of "The Great River," for that is the English translation of Oued al Kiber, as the Moors designated the ancient Betis. We came to anchor for a few minutes at a little village called Bonança, at the extremity of the first reach of the river, where we received several passengers, and again proceeded. There is not much in the appearance of the Guadalquivir to interest the traveller: the banks are low and destitute of trees, the adjacent country is flat, and only in the distance is seen a range of tall blue sierras. The water is turbid and muddy, and in colour closely resembling the contents of a duck-pool; the average width of the stream is from a hundred and fifty to two hundred yards, but it is impossible to move along this river without remembering that it has borne the Roman, the Vandal, and the Arab, and

has been the witness of deeds which have resounded through the world and been the themes of immortal songs. I repeated Latin verses and fragments of old Spanish ballads till we reached Seville, at about nine o'clock of a lovely moonlight night.

Seville contains ninety thousand inhabitants, and is situated on the eastern bank of the Guadalquivir, about eighteen leagues from its mouth; it is surrounded with high Moorish walls, in a good state of preservation, and built of such durable materials that it is probable they will for many centuries still bid defiance to the encroachments of time. The most remarkable edifices are the cathedral and Alcazar, or palace of the Moorish kings; the tower of the former, called La Giralda, belongs to the period of the Moors, and formed part of the grand mosque of Seville: it is computed to be one hundred ells in height, and is ascended not by stairs or ladders but by a vaulted pathway, in the manner of an inclined plane: this path is by no means steep, so that a cavalier might ride up to the top, a feat which Ferdinand the Seventh is said to have accomplished. The view from the summit is very extensive, and on a fine clear day the mountain ridge, called the Sierra de Ronda, may be discovered, though upwards of twenty leagues distant. The cathedral itself is a noble Gothic structure, reputed the finest of the kind in Spain. In the chapels allotted to the various saints, are some of the most magnificent paintings which Spanish art has produced; indeed, the Cathedral of Seville is at the present time far more rich in splendid paintings than at any former period; possessing many very recently removed from some of the suppressed convents, particularly from the Capuchin and San Francisco.

No one should visit Seville without paying particular attention to the Alcazar, that splendid specimen of Moorish architecture. It contains many magnificent halls, particularly that of the Ambassadors, so called, which is in every respect more magnificent than the one of the same name within the Alhambra of Granada. This palace was a favourite residence of Peter the Cruel, who carefully repaired it without altering its Moorish character and appearance. It probably remains in much the same state as at the time of his death.

On the right side of the river is a large suburb, called Triana, communicating with Seville by means of a bridge of boats; for there is no permanent bridge across the Guadalquivir, owing to the violent inundations to which it is subject. This suburb is inhabited by the dregs of the populace, and abounds with Gitános or Gipsies. About a league and a half to the north-west, stands the village of Santo Ponce: at the foot and on the side of some elevated ground higher up are to be seen vestiges of ruined walls and edifices, which once formed part of Italica, the birthplace of Silius Italicus and Trajan, from which latter personage Triana derives its name.

One fine morning I walked thither, and having ascended the hill, I directed my course northward. I soon reached what had once been bagnios, and a little farther on, in a kind of valley, between two gentle declivities, the amphitheatre. This latter object is by far the most considerable relic of ancient Italica, it is oval in its form, with two gateways fronting the east and west.

On all sides are to be seen the time-worn broken granite benches, from whence myriads of human beings once gazed down on the area below, where the gladiator shouted, and the lion and the leopard yelled: all around, beneath these flights of benches, are vaulted excavations, from whence the combatants, part human, part bestial, darted forth by their several doors. I spent many hours in this singular place, forcing my way through the wild fennel and brushwood into the caverns, now the haunts of adders and other reptiles, whose hissings I heard. Having sated my curiosity, I left the ruins, and returning by another way, reached a place where lay the carcass of a horse half devoured; upon it, with lustrous eyes, stood an enormous vulture, who, as I approached, slowly soared aloft till he alighted on the eastern gate of the amphitheatre, from whence he uttered a hoarse cry, as if in anger that I had disturbed him from his feast of carrion.

Gomez had not hitherto paid a visit to Seville: when I arrived he was said to be in the neighbourhood of Ronda. The city was under watch and ward: several gates had been blocked up with masonry, trenches dug, and redoubts erected, but I am convinced that the place would not have held out six hours against a resolute attack. Gomez had proved himself to be a most extraordinary man, and with his small army of Aragonese and Basques had, within the last four months, made the tour of Spain. He had very frequently been hemmed in by forces three times the number of his own, in places whence escape appeared impossible, but he had always baffled his enemies, whom he seemed to laugh at. The most absurd accounts of victories gained over him were continually issuing from the press at Seville; amongst others it was stated that his army had been utterly defeated, himself killed, and that twelve hundred prisoners were on their way to Seville. I saw these prisoners: instead of twelve hundred desperadoes, they consisted of about twenty poor lame ragged wretches, many of them boys from fourteen to sixteen years of age. They were evidently camp followers, who, unable to keep up with the army, had been picked up straggling in the plains and amongst the hills. It subsequently appeared that no battle had occurred, and that the death of Gomez was a fiction. The grand defect of Gomez consisted in not knowing how to take advantage of circumstances: after defeating Lopez, he might have marched to Madrid and proclaimed Don Carlos there, and after sacking Cordova he might have captured Seville.

There were several booksellers' shops at Seville, in two of which I found copies of the New Testament in Spanish, which had been obtained from Gibraltar about two years before, since which time six copies had been sold in one shop and four in the other. The person who generally accompanied me in my walks about the town and the neighbourhood, was an elderly Genoese, who officiated as a kind of valet de place in the Posada del Turco, where I had taken up my residence. On learning from me that it was my intention to bring out an edition of the New Testament at Madrid, he observed that copies of the work might be extensively circulated in Andalusia. "I have been accustomed to bookselling," he continued, "and at one time possessed a small shop of my own in this place. Once having occasion to go to Gibraltar, I procured several copies of the Scriptures; some, it is true, were seized by the officers of the customs, but the rest I sold at a high price, and with considerable profit to myself."

I had returned from a walk in the country, on a glorious sunshiny morning of the Andalusian winter, and was directing my steps towards my lodging; as I was passing by the portal of a large gloomy house near the gate of Xeres, two individuals dressed in zamarras emerged from the archway, and were about to cross my path, when one, looking in my face, suddenly started back exclaiming in the purest and most melodious French: "What do I see! If my eyes do not deceive me—it is himself. Yes, the very same as I saw him first at Bayonne; then long subsequently beneath the brick wall at Novogorod; then beside the Bosphorus; and last at—at—Oh, my respectable and cherished friend, where was it that I had last the felicity of seeing your well remembered and most remarkable physiognomy?"

Myself.—It was in the south of Ireland, if I mistake not. Was it not there that I introduced you to the sorcerer who tamed the savage horses by a single whisper into their ear? But tell me what brings you to Spain and Andalusia, the last place where I should have expected to find you?

Baron Taylor.—And wherefore, my most respectable B * * * * *? Is not Spain the land of the arts; and is not Andalusia of all Spain that portion which has produced the noblest monuments of artistic excellence and inspiration. Surely you know enough of me to be aware that the arts are my passion; that I am incapable of imagining a more exalted enjoyment than to gaze in adoration on a noble picture. O come with me! for you too have a soul capable of appreciating what is lovely and exalted; a soul delicate and sensitive. Come with me and I will show you a Murillo, such as .... But first allow me to introduce you to your compatriot. My dear Monsieur W., turning to his companion, (an English gentleman from whom and from his family I subsequently experienced unbounded kindness and hospitality on various occasions, and at different periods, at Seville,) allow me to introduce to you my most cherish-

10
G

ed and respectable friend, one who is better acquainted with Gipsy ways than the Chef des Bohemiens á Triana, one who is an expert whisperer and horse-sorcerer, and who, to his honour I say it, can wield hammer and tongs, and handle a horse-shoe with the best of the smiths amongst the Alpujarras of Granada.

In the course of my travels I have formed various friendships and acquaintances, but no one has more interested me than Baron Taylor, and there is no one for whom I entertain a greater esteem and regard. To personal and mental accomplishments of the highest order he unites a kindness of heart rarely to be met with, and which is continually inducing him to seek for opportunities of doing good to his fellow creatures, and of contributing to their happiness; perhaps no person in existence has seen more of the world and life in its various phases than himself. His manners are naturally to the highest degree courtly, yet he nevertheless possesses a disposition so pliable that he finds no difficulty in accommodating himself to all kinds of company, in consequence of which he is a universal favourite. There is a mystery about him, which, wherever he goes, serves not a little to increase the sensation naturally created by his appearance and manner. Who he is, no one pretends to assert with downright positiveness: it is whispered, however, that he is a scion of royalty; and who can gaze for a moment upon that most graceful figure, that most intelligent but singularly moulded countenance, and those large and expressive eyes, without feeling as equally convinced that he is of no common lineage, so that he is no common man. Though possessed of talents and eloquence which would speedily have enabled him to attain to an illustrious position in the state, he has hitherto, and perhaps wisely, contented himself with comparative obscurity, chiefly devoting himself to the study of the arts and of literature, of both of which he is a most bounteous patron.

He has, notwithstanding, been employed by the illustrious house to which he is said to be related in more than one delicate and important mission, both in the East and the West, in which his efforts have uniformly been crowned with complete success. He was now collecting masterpieces of the Spanish school of painting, which were destined to adorn the saloons of the Tuilleries.

He has visited most portions of the earth, and it is remarkable enough that we are continually encountering each other in strange places and under singular circumstances. Whenever he descries me, whether in the street or the desert, the brilliant hall or amongst Bedouin haimas, at Novogorod or Stambul, he flings up his arms and exclaims, "O ciel! I have again the felicity of seeing my cherished and most respectable B * * * * *."

CHAPTER XVI.

Departure for Cordova—Carmona—German Colonies—Language—The Sluggish Horse—Nocturnal Welcome—Carlist Landlord—Good Advice—Gomez—The Old Genoese—The Two Opinions.

AFTER a sojourn of about fourteen days at Seville, I departed for Cordova. The diligence had for some time past ceased running, owing to the disturbed state of the province. I had therefore no resource but to proceed thither on horseback. I hired a couple of horses, and engaged the old Genoese, of whom I have already had occasion to speak, to attend me as far as Cordova, and to bring them back. Notwithstanding we were now in the depths of winter, the weather was beautiful, the days sunny and brilliant, though the nights were rather keen. We passed by the little town of Alcala, celebrated for the ruins of an immense Moorish castle, which stand on a rocky hill, overhanging a picturesque river. The first night we slept at Carmona, another Moorish town, distant about seven leagues from Seville. Early in the morning we again mounted and departed. Perhaps in the whole of Spain there is scarcely a finer Moorish monument of antiquity than the eastern side of this town of Carmona, which occupies the brow of a lofty hill, and frowns over an extensive vega or plain, which extends for leagues unplanted and uncultivated, producing nothing but brush-wood and carasco. Here rise tall and dusky walls, with square towers at short distances, of so massive a structure that they would seem to bid defiance alike to the tooth of time and the hand of man. This town, in the time of the Moors, was considered the key to Seville, and did not submit to the Christian arms till after a long and desperate siege: the capture of Seville followed speedily after. The vega upon which we now entered forms a part of the grand despoblado or desert of Andalusia, once a smiling garden, but which became what it now is on the expulsion of the Moors from Spain, when it was drained almost entirely of its population. The towns and villages from hence to the Sierra Morena, which divides Andalusia from La Mancha, are few and far between, and even of these several date from the middle of the last century, when an attempt was made by a Spanish minister to people this wilderness with the children of a foreign land.

At about midday we arrived at a place called Munclon, which consisted of a venta and a desolate looking edifice which had something of the appearance of a chateau: a solitary palm tree raised its head over the outer wall. We entered the venta, tied our horses to the manger, and having ordered barley for them, we sat down before a large fire, which burned in the middle of the venta. The host and hostess also came and sat down beside us.— " They are evil people," said the old Genoese to me in Italian, "and this is an evil house; it is a harbouring place for thieves, and murders have been committed here, if all tales be true." I looked at these two people attentively; they were both young; the man apparently about twenty-five years of age. He was a short thick made churl, evidently of prodigious strength; his features were rather handsome, but with a gloomy expression, and his eyes were full of sullen fire. His wife somewhat resembled him, but had a countenance more open and better tempered; but what struck me as most singular in connexion with these people, was the colour of their hair and complexion; the latter was fair and ruddy, and the former of a bright auburn, both in striking contrast to the black hair and swarthy visages which in general distinguish the natives of this province. " Are you an Andalusian?" said I to the hostess. " I should almost conclude you to be a German."

Hostess.—And your worship would not be very wrong. It is true that I am a Spaniard, being born in Spain, but it is equally true that I am of German blood, for my grand parents came from Germany, even like those of this gentleman, my lord and husband.

Myself.—And what chance brought your grand parents into this country?

Hostess.—Did your worship never hear of the German colonies? There are many of them in these parts. In old times the land was nearly deserted, and it was very dangerous for travellers to journey along the waste, owing to the robbers. So a long time ago, nearly a hundred years, as I am told, some potent lord sent messengers to Germany, to tell the people there what a goodly land there was in these parts uncultivated for want of hands, and to promise every labourer who would consent to come and till it, a house and a yoke of oxen, with food and provision for one year. And in consequence of this invitation a great many poor families left the German land and came hither, and settled down in certain towns and villages which had been prepared for them, which places were called German colonies, and this name they still retain.

Myself.—And how many of these colonies may there be?

Hostess.—There are several, both on this side of Cordova and the other. The nearest is Luisiana, about two leagues from hence, from which place both my husband and myself come; the next is Carlota, which is some ten leagues distant, and these are the only colonies of our people which I have seen; but there are others farther on, and some, as I have heard say, in the very heart of the Sierra Morena.

Myself.—And do the colonists still retain the language of their forefathers?

Hostess.—We speak Spanish, or rather Andalusian, and no other language. A few, indeed, amongst the very old people, retain a few words of German, which they acquired from their fathers, who were born in the other country; but the last person amongst the colonists who could understand a conversation in German, was the aunt of my mother, who came over when a girl. When I was a child I remember her conversing with a foreign traveller, a countryman of hers, in a language which I was told was German, and they understood each other, though the old woman confessed that she had lost many words : she has now been dead several years.

Myself.—Of what religion are the colonists?

Hostess.—They are Christians, like the Spaniards, and so were their fathers before them. Indeed, I have heard that they came from a part of Germany where the Christian religion is as much practised as in Spain itself.

Myself.—The Germans are the most honest people in the world; being their legitimate descendants you have of course no thieves amongst you.

The hostess glanced at me for a moment, then looked at her husband and smiled : the latter, who had hitherto been smoking without uttering a word, though with a peculiarly surly and dissatisfied countenance, now flung the remainder of his cigar amongst the embers, then springing up, he muttered " Disparate!" and " Conversacion!" and went abroad.

" You touched them in the sore place, Signor," said the Genoese, after we had left Muncloa some way behind us. "Were they honest people they would not keep that venta; and as for the colonists, I know not what kind of people they might be when they first came over, but at present their ways are not a bit better than those of the Andalusians, but rather worse, if there is any difference at all."

A certain time before sunset of the third day after our departure from Seville, we found ourselves at the Cuesta del Espinal, or hill of the thorn tree, at about two leagues from Cordova;—we could just descry the walls of the city, upon which the last beams of the descending luminary were resting. As the neighbourhood in which we were was, according to the account of my guide, generally infested with robbers, we used our best endeavours to reach the town before the night should have entirely closed in. We did not succeed, however, and before we had proceeded half the distance, pitchy darkness overtook us. Throughout the journey we had been considerably delayed by the badness of our horses, especially that of my attendant, which appeared to pay no regard to whip or spur: his rider also was no horseman, it being thirty years, as he at length confessed to me, since he last mounted in a saddle. Horses soon become aware of the powers of their riders, and the brute in question was disposed to take great advantage of the fears and weakness of the old man. There is a remedy, however, for most things in this world. I became so wearied at last of the snail's pace at which we were proceeding, that I fastened the bridle of the sluggish horse to the crupper of mine, then sparing neither spur nor cudgel, I soon forced my own horse into a kind of trot, which compelled the other to make some use of his legs. He twice attempted to fling himself down, to the great terror of his aged rider, who frequently entreated me to stop and permit him to dismount. I, however, took no notice of what he said, but continued spurring and cudgelling with unabated activity, and with such success, that in less than half an hour we saw lights close before us, and presently came to a river and a bridge, which crossing, we found ourselves at the gate of Cordova, without having broken either our horses' knees or our own necks.

We passed through the entire length of the town ere we reached the posada; the streets were dark and almost entirely deserted. The posada was a large building, the windows of which were well fenced with rejas, or iron grating: no light gleamed from them, and the silence of death not only seemed to pervade the house, but the street in which it was situated. We knocked for a long time at the gate without receiving any answer; we then raised our voices and shouted. At last some one from within inquired what we wanted. "Open the door and you will see," we replied. "I shall do no such thing," answered the individual from within, "until I know who you are." "We are travellers," said I, "from Seville." "Travellers, are you," said the voice; "why did you not tell me so before? I am not porter at this house to keep but travellers. Jesus Maria knows we have not so many of them that we need repulse any. Enter, cavalier, and welcome, you and your company."

He opened the gate and admitted us into a spacious court-yard, and then forthwith again secured the gate with various bolts and bars. "Are you afraid that the Carlists should pay you a visit," I demanded, "that you take so much precaution?" "It is not the Carlists we are afraid of," replied the porter; "they have been here already, and did us no damage whatever. It is certain scoundrels of this town that we are afraid of, who have a spite against the master of the house, and would murder both him and his family, could they but find an opportunity."

I was about to inquire the cause of this enmity, when a thick bulky man, bearing a light in his hand, came running down a stone staircase, which led into the interior of the building. Two or three females, also bearing lights, followed him. He stopped on the lowest stair. "Whom have we here?" he exclaimed; then advancing the lamp which he bore, the light fell full upon my face. "Ola!" he exclaimed; "Is it you? Only

think," said he, turning to the female who stood next him, a dark featured person, stout as himself, and about his own age, which might border upon fifty; "Only think, my dear, that at the very moment we were wishing for a guest, an Englishman should be standing before our doors; for I should know an Englishman at a mile's distance, even in the dark. Juanito," cried he to the porter; "open not the gate any more to-night, whoever may ask for admission. Should the nationals come to make any disturbance, tell them that the son of Belington (*Wellington*) is in the house, ready to attack them sword in hand unless they retire; and should other travellers arrive, which is not likely, inasmuch as we have seen none for a month past, say that we have no room, all our apartments being occupied by an English gentleman and his company."

I soon found that my friend the posadero was a most egregious Carlist. Before I had finished supper—during which, both himself and all his family were present, surrounding the little table at which I sat, and observing my every motion, particularly the manner in which I handled my knife and fork and conveyed the food to my mouth—he commenced talking politics: "I am of no particular opinion, Don Jorge," said he, for he had inquired my name in order that he might address me in a suitable manner; "I am of no particular opinion, and I hold neither for King Carlos, nor for the Chica Isabel: nevertheless I lead the life of a dog in this accursed Christino town which I would have left long ago, had it not been the place of my birth, and did I but know whither to betake myself. Ever since the troubles have commenced, I am been afraid to stir into the street, for no sooner do the canaille of the town see me turning round a corner, than they forthwith exclaim, 'Halloo, the Carlist!' and then there is a run and a rush, and stones and cudgels are in great requisition: so that, unless I can escape home, which is no easy matter, seeing that I weigh eighteen stone, my life is poured out in the street, which is neither decent nor convenient, as I think you will acknowledge, Don Jorge! You see that young man," he continued, pointing to a tall swarthy youth who stood behind my chair, officiating as waiter; "he is my fourth son, is married, and does not live in the house, but about a hundred yards down the street. He was summoned in a hurry to wait upon your worship, as is his duty: know, however, that he has come at the peril of his life; before he leaves this house, he must peep out into the street to see if the coast is clear, and then he must run like a partridge to his own door. Carlists! why should they call my family and myself Carlists? It is true that my eldest son was a friar, and when the convents were suppressed, betook himself to the royal ranks, in which he has been fighting upwards of three years; could I help that? Nor was it my fault, I trow, that my second son enlisted the other day with Gomez and the

Royalists when they entered Cordova. God prosper him, I say; but I did not bid him go! So far from being a Carlist, it was I who persuaded this very lad who is present to remain here, though he would fain have gone with his brother, for he is a brave lad and a true Christian. Stay at home, said I, for what can I do without you? Who is to wait upon the guests when it pleases God to send them. Stay at home, at least till your brother, my third son, comes back, for, to my shame be it spoken, Don Jorge, I have a son a soldier and a sergeant in the Christino armies, sorely against his own inclination, poor fellow, for he likes not the military life, and I have been soliciting his discharge for years: indeed, I have counselled him to maim himself, in order that he might procure his liberty forthwith, so I said to this lad, Stay at home, my child, till your brother comes to take your place and prevent our bread being eaten by strangers, who would perhaps sell me and betray me; so my son staid at home as you see, Don Jorge, at my request, and yet they call me a Carlist!"

"Gomez and his bands have lately been in Cordova," said I; "of course you were present at all that occurred: how did they comport themselves?"

"Bravely well," replied the innkeeper, "bravely well, and I wish they were here still. I hold with neither side, as I told you before, Don Jorge, but I confess I never felt greater pleasure in my life than when they entered the gate, and then to see the dogs of nationals flying through the streets to save their lives—that was a sight Don Jorge—those who met me then at the corner forgot to shout 'Halloo, Carlista!' and I heard not a word about cudgelling; some jumped from the wall and ran no one knows where, whilst the rest retired to the house of the Inquisition, which they had fortified, and there they shut themselves up. Now you must know, Don Jorge, that all the Carlist chiefs lodged at my house, Gomez, Cabrera, and the Sawyer; and it chanced that I was talking to my Lord Gomez in this very room in which we are now, when in came Cabrera in a mighty fury—he is a small man, Don Jorge, but he is as active as a wild cat and as fierce. 'The canaille,' said he, 'in the Casa of the Inquisition refuse to surrender; give but the order, General, and I will scale the walls with my men and put them all to the sword;' but Gomez said, 'No, we must not spill blood if we can avoid it; order a few muskets to be fired at them, that will be sufficient!' And so it proved, Don Jorge, for after a few discharges their hearts failed them, and they surrendered at discretion: whereupon their arms were taken from them and they were permitted to return to their own houses; but as soon as ever the Carlists departed, these fellows became as bold as ever, and it is now once more, 'Halloo Carlista!' when they see me turning the corner, and it is for fear of them that my son must run like a partridge to his own home, now that he has done waiting on your worship, lest

they meet him in the street and kill him with their knives!"

"You tell me that you were acquainted with Gomez: what kind of man might he be?"

"A middle sized man," replied the innkeeper; "grave and dark. But the most remarkable personage in appearance of them all was the Sawyer: he is a kind of giant, so tall, that when he entered the doorway he invariably struck his head against the lintel. The one I liked least of all was one Palillos, who is a gloomy savage ruffian whom I knew when he was a postillion. Many is the time that he has been at my house of old; he is now captain of the Manchegan thieves, for though he calls himself a royalist, he is neither more nor less than a thief: it is a disgrace to the cause that such as he should be permitted to mix with honourable and brave men; I hate that fellow, Don Jorge: it is owing to him that I have so few customers. Travellers are, at present, afraid to pass through La Mancha, lest they fall into his hands. I wish he were hanged, Don Jorge, and whether by Christinos or Royalists, I care not."

"You recognised me at once for an Englishman," said I; "do many of my countrymen visit Cordova?"

"Toma!" said the landlord, "they are my best customers; I have had Englishmen in this house of all grades, from the son of Belington to a young medico, who cured my daughter, the chica here, of the ear-ache. How should I not know an Englishman? There were two with Gomez, serving as volunteers. Vaya que gente: what noble horses they rode, and how they scattered their gold about; they brought with them a Portuguese, who was much of a gentleman but very poor; it was said that he was one of Don Miguel's people, and that these Englishmen supported him for the love they bore to royalty; he was continually singing

'El Rey chegou—El Rey chegou,
E en Belem desembarcou!'

Those were merry days, Don Jorge. By the by, I forgot to ask your worship of what opinion you are?"

The next morning, whilst I was dressing, the old Genoese entered my room: "Signore," said he, "I am come to bid you farewell. I am about to return to Seville forthwith with the horses."

"Wherefore in such a hurry," I replied; "assuredly you had better tarry till to-morrow; both the animals and yourself require rest; repose yourselves to-day, and I will defray the expense."

"Thank you, Signore, but we will depart forthwith, for there is no tarrying in this house."

"What is the matter with the house?" I inquired.

"I find no fault with the house," replied the Genoese, "it is the people who keep it of whom I complain. About an hour since, I went down to get my breakfast, and there, in the kitchen, I found the master and all his family: well, I eat down and called for chocolate, which they brought me, but ere I could despatch it, the master fell to talking politics. He commenced by telling me that he held with neither side, but he is as rank a Carlist as Carlos Quinto: for no sooner did he find that I was of the other opinion, than he glared at me like a wild beast. You must know, Signore, that in the time of the old constitution I kept a coffee-house at Seville, which was frequented by all the principal liberals, and was, indeed, the cause of my ruin: for as I admired their opinions, I gave my customers whatever credit they required, both with regard to coffee and liqueurs, so that by the time the constitution was put down and despotism re-established, I had trusted them with all I had. It is possible that many of them would have paid me, for I believe they harboured no evil intention; but the persecution came, the liberals took to flight, and, as was natural enough, thought more of providing for their own safety than of paying me for my coffee and liqueurs; nevertheless, I am a friend to their system, and never hesitate to say so. So the landlord, as I told your worship before, when he found that I was of this opinion, glared at me like a wild beast: 'Get out of my house,' said he, 'For I will have

no spies here,' and thereupon he spoke disrespectfully of the young Queen Isabel and of Christina, who, notwithstanding she is a Neapolitan, I consider as my countrywoman. Hearing this, your worship, I confess that I lost my temper and returned the compliment, by saying that Carlos was a knave and the Princess of Beira no better than she should be. I then prepared to swallow the chocolate, but ere I could bring it to my lips, the woman of the house, who is a still ranker Carlist than her husband, if that be possible, coming up to me struck the cup into the air as high as the ceiling, exclaiming, 'Begone, you dog of a negro, you shall taste nothing more in my house; may you be hanged even as a swine is hanged.' So your worship sees that it is impossible for me to remain here any longer. I forgot to say that the knave of a landlord told me that you had confessed yourself to be of the same politics as himself, or he would not have harboured you."

"My good man," said I, "I am invariably of the politics of the people at whose table I sit, or beneath whose roof I sleep; at least I never say any thing which can lead them to suspect the contrary: by pursuing which system I have more than once escaped a bloody pillow, and having the wine I drank spiced with sublimate."

CHAPTER XVII.

LITTLE can be said with respect to the town of Cordova, which is a mean dark gloomy place, full of narrow streets and alleys, without squares or public buildings worthy of attention, save and except its far-famed cathedral; its situation, however, is beautiful and picturesque. Before it runs the Guadalquivir, which, though in this part shallow and full of sandbanks, is still a delightful stream; whilst behind it rise the steep sides of the Sierra Morena, planted up to the top with olive groves. The town or city is surrounded on all sides by lofty Moorish walls, which may measure about three quarters of a league in circumference; unlike Seville, and most other towns in Spain, it has no suburbs.

I have said that Cordova has no remarkable edifices, save its cathedral; yet this is perhaps the most extraordinary place of worship in the world. It was originally, as is well

known, a mosque, built in the brightest days of Arabian dominion in Spain: in shape it was quadrangular, with a low roof, supported by an infinity of small and delicately rounded marble pillars, many of which still remain, and present at first sight the appearance of a marble grove; the greater part, however, were removed when the Christians, after the expulsion of the Moslems, essayed to convert the mosque into a cathedral, which they effected in part by the erection of a dome, and by clearing an open space for a choir. As it at present exists, the temple appears to belong partly to Mahomet, and partly to the Nazarene; and though this jombling together of massive Gothic architecture with the light and delicate style of the Arabians, produces an effect somewhat bizarre, it still remains a magnificent and glorious edifice, and well calculated to excite feelings of awe and veneration within the bosoms of those who enter it.

The Moors of Barbary seem to care but little for the exploits of their ancestors; their minds are centered in the things of the present day, and only so far as those things regard themselves individually. Disinterested enthusiasm, that truly distinguishing mark of a noble mind, and admiration for what is great, good, and grand, they appear to be totally incapable of feeling. It is astonishing with what indifference they stray amongst the relics of ancient Moorish grandeur in Spain. No feelings of exultation seem to be excited by the proof of what the Moor once was, nor of regret at the consciousness of what he now is. More interesting to them are their perfumes, their papouches, their dates, and their silks of Fez and Maraks, to dispose of which they visit Andalusia; and yet the generality of these men are far from being ignorant, and have both heard and read of what was passing in Spain in the old time. I was once conversing with a Moor at Madrid, with whom I was very intimate, about the Alhambra of Granada, which he had visited. "Did you not weep," said I, "when you passed through the courts, and thought of the Abencerrages?" "No," said he, "I did not weep; wherefore should I weep?" "And why did you visit the Alhambra?" I demanded. "I visited it," he replied, "because being at Granada on my own affairs, one of your countrymen requested me to accompany him thither, that I might explain some of the inscriptions. I should certainly not have gone of my own accord, for the hill on which it stands is steep." And yet this man could compose verses, and was by no means a contemptible poet. Once at Cordova, whilst I was in the cathedral, three Moors entered it, and proceeded slowly across its floor in the direction of a gate, which stood at the opposite side; they took no farther notice of what was around them than by slightly glancing once or twice at the pillars, one of them exclaiming, "Huaije del Mselmeen, huaije del Mselmeen;" (things of the Moors, things of the Moors;) and showed no other respect for the place where Abderrahman the Magnificent prostrated himself of old, than facing about on arriving at the farther door and making their egress backwards; yet these men were hajis and talebs, men likewise of much gold and silver, men who had read, who had travelled, who had seen Mecca, and the great city of Negroland.

I remained in Cordova much longer than I had originally intended, owing to the accounts which I was continually hearing of the unsafe state of the roads to Madrid. I soon ransacked every nook and cranny of this ancient town, formed various acquaintances amongst the populace, which is my general practice on arriving at a strange place. I more than once ascended the side of the Sierra Morena, in which excursions I was accompanied by the son of my host,—the tall lad of whom I have already spoken. The people of the house, who had imbibed the idea that I was of the same way of thinking as themselves, were exceedingly courteous; it is true that in return I was compelled to listen to a vast deal of Carlism, in other words, high treason, against the ruling powers in Spain, to which, however, I submitted with patience. "Don Jorgito," said the landlord to me one day, "I love the English; they are my best customers. It is a pity that there is not greater union between Spain and England, and that more English do not visit us. Why should there not be a marriage? The king will speedily be at Madrid. Why should there not be bodas between the son of Don Carlos and the heiress of England?"

"It would certainly tend to bring a considerable number of English to Spain," said I, "and it would not be the first time that the son of a Carlos has married a Princess of England."

The host mused for a moment, and then exclaimed, "Carracho, Don Jorgito, if this marriage could be brought about, both the king and myself should have cause to fling our caps in the air."

The house or posada in which I had taken up my abode was exceedingly spacious, containing an infinity of apartments, both large and small, the greater part of which were, however, unfurnished. The chamber in which I was lodged stood at the end of an immensely long corridor, of the kind so admirably described in the wondrous tale of Udolfo. For a day or two after my arrival I believed myself to be the only lodger in the house. One morning, however, I beheld a strange looking old man seated in the corridor, by one of the windows, reading intently in a small thick volume. He was clad in garments of coarse blue cloth, and wore a loose spencer over a waistcoat adorned with various rows of small buttons of mother of pearl; he had spectacles upon his nose. I could perceive, notwithstanding he was seated, that his stature bordered upon the gigantic. "Who is that person?" said I to the landlord, whom I presently met; "Is he also a guest of yours?" "Not exactly, Don Jorge de mi alma," replied he. "I can scarcely call him a guest, inasmuch as I gain nothing by him, though he is staying at my house. You must know, Don Jorge, that he is one of two priests who officiate at a large village at some slight distance from this place. So it came to pass, that when the soldiers of Gomez entered the village, his reverence went to meet them, dressed in full canonicals, with a book in his hand, and he, at their bidding, proclaimed Carlos Quinto in the market place. The other priest, however, was a desperate liberal, a downright negro, and upon him the royalists laid their hands, and were proceeding to hang him. His reverence, however, interfered, and obtained mercy for his colleague, on condition that he should cry Viva Carlos Quinto! which the latter did in order to save his life. Well; no sooner had the royalists departed from these parts than the black priest mounts his mule, comes to Cordova, and informs against his reverence, notwithstanding that he had saved his life. So his reverence was seized and brought hither to Cordova, and would assuredly have been thrown into the common prison as a Carlist, had I not stepped forward and offered to be surety that he should not quit the place, but should come forward at any time to answer whatever charge might be brought against him; and he is now in my house, though guest I cannot call him, for he is not of the slightest advantage to me, as his very food is daily brought from the country, and that consists only of a few eggs and a little milk and bread. As for his money, I have never seen the colour of it, notwithstanding they tell me that he has buenas pesetas. However, he is a holy man, is continually reading and praying, and is, moreover, of the right opinion. I therefore keep him in my house, and would be bail for him were he twenty times more of a skinflint than he seems to be."

The next day, as I was again passing through the corridor, I observed the old man in the same place, and saluted him. He returned my salutation with much courtesy, and closing the book, placed it upon his knee, as if willing to enter into conversation. After exchanging a word or two, I took up the book for the purpose of inspecting it.

"You will hardly derive much instruction from that book, Don Jorge," said the old man; "you cannot understand it, for it is not written in English."

"Nor in Spanish," I replied. "But with respect to understanding the book, I cannot see what difficulty there can be in a thing so simple; it is only the Roman breviary written in the Latin tongue."

"Do the English understand Latin?" exclaimed he. "Vaya! Who would have thought that it was possible for Lutherans to understand the language of the church? Vaya! the longer one lives the more one learns."

"How old may your reverence be?" I inquired.

"I am eighty years, Don Jorge; eighty years, and somewhat more."

Such was the first conversation which passed between his reverence and myself. He soon conceived no inconsiderable liking for me, and favoured me with no little of his company. Unlike our friend the landlord, I found him by no means inclined to talk politics, which the more surprised me, knowing, as I did, the decided and hazardous part which he had taken on the late Carlist irruption into the neighbourhood. He took, however, great delight in discoursing on ecclesiastical subjects and the writings of the fathers.

"I have got a small library at home, Don Jorge, which consists of all the volumes of the fathers which I have been able to pick up, and I find the perusal of them a source of great amusement and comfort. Should these dark days pass by, Don Jorge, and you should be in these parts, I hope you will look in upon me, and I will show you my little library of the fathers, and likewise my dovecote, where I rear numerous broods of pigeons, which are also a source of much solace and at the same time of profit."

"I suppose by your dovecote," said I, "you mean your parish, and by rearing broods of pigeons, you allude to the care you take of the souls of your people, instilling therein the fear of God and obedience to his revealed law, which occupation must of course afford you much solace and spiritual profit."

"I was not speaking metaphorically, Don Jorge," replied my companion; "and by rearing doves, I mean neither more nor less than that I supply the market of Cordova with pigeons, and occasionally that of Seville; for my birds are very celebrated, and plumper or fatter flesh than theirs I believe cannot be found in the whole kingdom. Should you come to my village, you will doubtless taste them, Don Jorge, at the venta where you will put up, for I suffer no dovecotes but my own within my district. With respect to the souls of my parishioners, I trust I do my duty—I trust I do, as far as in my power lies. I always took great pleasure in these spiritual matters, and it was on that account that I attached myself to the Santa Casa of Cordova, the duties of which I assisted to perform for a long period."

"Your reverence has been an inquisitor?" I exclaimed, somewhat startled.

"From my thirtieth year until the time of the suppression of the holy office in these afflicted kingdoms."

"You both surprise and delight me," I exclaimed. "Nothing could have afforded me greater pleasure than to find myself conversing with a father formerly attached to the holy house of Cordova."

The old man looked at me steadfastly; "I understand you, Don George. I have long seen that you are one of us. You are a learned and holy man; and though you think fit to call yourself a Lutheran and an Englishman, I have dived into your real condition. No Lutheran would take the interest in church matters which you do, and with respect to your being an Englishman, none of that nation can speak Castilian, much less Latin. I believe you to be one of us—a missionary priest, and I am especially confirmed in that idea by your frequent conversations and interviews with the Gitános: you appear to be labouring among them. Be, however, on your guard, Don Jorge, trust not to Egyptian faith; they are evil penitents, whom I like not. I would not advise you to trust them."

"I do not intend," I replied; "especially with money. But to return to more important matters :—of what crimes did this holy house of Cordova take cognizance?"

"You are of course aware of the matters on which the holy office exercises its functions,

I need scarcely mention sorcery, Judaism, and certain carnal misdemeanours."

"With respect to sorcery," said I, "what is your opinion of it? Is there in reality such a crime?"

"Que sé io?" said the old man shrugging up his shoulders. "How should I know? The church has power, Don Jorge, or at least it had power to punish for any thing real or unreal; and as it was necessary to punish in order to prove that it had the power of, punishing, of what consequence, whether it punished for sorcery or any other crime."

"Did many cases of sorcery occur within your own sphere of knowledge?"

"One or two, Don Jorge: they were by no means frequent. The last that I remember, was a case which occurred in a convent at Seville: a certain nun was in the habit of flying through the windows and about the garden over the tops of the orange trees; declarations of various witnesses were taken, and the process was arranged with much formality: the fact, I believe, was satisfactorily proved: of one thing I am certain, that the nun was punished."

"Were you troubled with much Judaism in these parts?"

"Wooh! Nothing gave so much trouble to the Santa Casa as this same Judaism. Its shoots and ramifications are numerous, not only in these parts but in all Spain; and it is singular enough, that, even among the priesthood, instances of Judaism of both kinds were continually coming to our knowledge, which it was of course our duty to punish."

"Is there more than one species of Judaism?" I demanded.

"I have always arranged Judaism under two heads," said the old man, "the black and the white: by the black, I mean the observance of the law of Moses in preference to the precepts of the church; then there is the white Judaism, which includes all kinds of heresy, such as Lutherism, freemasonry, and the like."

"I can easily conceive," said I, "that many of the priesthood favoured the principles of the reformation, and that the minds of not a few had been led astray by the deceitful lights of modern philosophy, but it is almost inconceivable to me that there should be Jews amongst the priesthood who follow in secret the rites and observances of the old law, though I confess that I have been assured of the fact ere now."

"Plenty of Judaism amongst the priesthood, whether of the black or white species; no lack of it, I assure you, Don Jorge; I remember once searching the house of an ecclesiastic who was accused of the black Judaism, and after much investigation, we discovered beneath the floor a wooden chest, in which was a small shrine of silver, enclosing three books in black hogskin, which on being opened, were found to be books of Jewish devotion, written in Hebrew characters, and of

great antiquity; and on being questioned, the culprit made no secret of his guilt, but rather gloried in it, saying that there was no God but one, and denouncing the adoration of Maria Santissima as rank idolatry."

"And, between ourselves, what is your own opinion of the adoration of this same Maria Santissima?"

"What is my opinion! Que sé io?" said the old man, shrugging up his shoulders still higher than on the former occasion; "but I will tell you: I think, on consideration, that it is quite right and proper; why not? Let any one pay a visit to my church, and look at her as she stands there, tan bonita, tan guapita—so well dressed and so genteel—with such pretty colours, such red and white, and he would scarcely ask me why Maria Santissima should not be adored. Moreover, Don Jorgito mio, this is a church matter and forms an important part of the church system."

"And now, with respect to carnal misdemeanours. Did you take much cognizance of them?"

"Amongst the laity, not much; we, however, kept a vigilant eye upon our own body, but, upon the whole, were rather tolerant in these matters, knowing that the infirmities of human nature are very great indeed: we rarely punished, save in cases where the glory of the church and loyalty to Maria Santissima made punishment absolutely imperative."

"And what cases might those be?" I demanded.

"I allude to the desecration of dovecotes, Don Jorge, and the introduction therein of strange flesh, for purposes neither seemly nor convenient."

"Your reverence will excuse me for not yet perfectly understanding."

"I mean, Don Jorge, certain acts of flagitiousness practised by the clergy in lone and remote palomares (dovecotes) in olive grounds and gardens; actions denounced, I believe, by the holy Pablo in his first letter to Pope Sixtus.* You understand me now, Don Jorge, for you are learned in church matters."

"I think I understand you," I replied.

After remaining several days more at Cordova, I determined to proceed on my journey to Madrid, though the roads were still said to be highly insecure. I, however, saw but little utility in tarrying and awaiting a more tranquil state of affairs, which might never arrive. I therefore consulted with the landlord respecting the best means of making the journey. "Don Jorgito," he replied, "I think I can tell you. You say you are anxious to depart, and I never wish to keep guests in my house longer than is agreeable to them; to do so, would not become a Christian innkeeper: I leave such conduct to Moors, Christinos, and Negros. I will further you on your journey, Don Jorge: I have a plan in my head, which I had resolved to propose to you before you questioned me.

---

*Qu. The Epistle to the Romans.

There is my wife's brother, who has two horses which he occasionally lets out for hire; you shall hire them, Don Jorge, and he himself shall attend you to take care of you, and to comfort you, and to talk to you, and you shall pay him forty dollars for the journey. Moreover, as there are thieves upon the route, and *malos sujetos*, such as Palillos and his family, you shall make an engagement and a covenant, Don Jorge, that provided you are robbed and stripped on the route, and the horses of my wife's brother are taken from him by the thieves, you shall, on arriving at Madrid, make good any losses to which my wife's brother may be subject in following you. This is my plan, Don Jorge, which no doubt will meet with your worship's approbation, as it is devised solely for your benefit, and not with any view of lucre or interest either to me or mine. You will find my wife's brother pleasant company on the route: he is a very respectable man, and one of the right opinion, and has likewise travelled much; for between ourselves, Don Jorge, he is something of a Contrabandista, and frequently smuggles diamonds and precious stones from Portugal, which he disposes of sometimes in Cordova and sometimes at Madrid. He is acquainted with all the short cuts, all the atajos, Don Jorge, and is much respected in all the ventas and posadas on the way; so now give me your hand upon the bargain, and I will forthwith repair to my wife's brother to tell him to get ready to set out with your worship the day after to-morrow."

CHAPTER XVIII.

Departure from Cordova—The Contrabandista—Jewish Cunning—Arrival at Madrid.

One fine morning, I departed from Cordova, in company with the Contrabandista; the latter was mounted on a handsome animal, something between a horse and a pony, which he called a jaca, of that breed for which Cordova is celebrated. It was of a bright bay colour, with a star in its forehead, with strong but elegant limbs, and a long black tail, which swept the ground. The other animal, which was destined to carry me to Madrid, was not quite so prepossessing in its appearance: in more than one respect it closely resembled a hog, particularly in the curving of its back, the shortness of its neck, and the manner in which it kept its head nearly in contact with the ground: it had also the tail of a hog, and meandered over the ground much like one. Its coat more resembled coarse bristles than hair, and with respect to size, I have seen many a Westphalian hog quite as tall. I was not altogether satisfied with the idea of exhibiting myself on the back of this most extraordinary quadruped, and looked wistfully on the respectable animal on which my guide had thought proper to place himself; he interpreted my glances, and gave me to understand that as he was destined to carry the baggage, he was entitled to the best horse; a plea too well grounded on reason for me to make any objection to it.

I found the Contrabandista by no means such pleasant company on the road as I had been led to suppose he would prove from the representation of my host at Cordova.—Throughout the day he sat sullen and silent, and rarely replied to my questions, save by a monosyllable; at night, however, after having eaten well and drank proportionably at my expense, he would occasionally become more sociable and communicative. "I have given up smuggling," said he, on one of these occasions, "owing to a trick which was played upon me the last time that I was at Lisbon: a Jew whom I had been long acquainted with palmed upon me a false brilliant for a real stone. He effected it in the most extraordinary manner, for I am not such a novice as not to know a true diamond when I see one; but the Jew appears to have had two, with which he played most adroitly, keeping the valuable one for which I bargained, and substituting therefor another which, though an excellent imitation, was not worth four dollars. I did not discover the trick until I was across the border, and upon my hurrying back, the culprit was not to be found; his priest, however, told me that he was just dead and buried, which was of course false, as I saw him laughing in the corners of his eyes. I renounced the contraband trade from that moment."

It is not my intention to describe minutely the various incidents of this journey. Leaving at our right the mountains of Jaen, we passed through Andujar and Bailen, and on the third day reached Carolina, a small but beautiful town on the skirts of the Sierra Morena, inhabited by the descendants of German colonists. Two leagues from this place, we entered the defile of Daspeña Perros, which, even in quiet times has an evil name, on account of the robberies which are continually being perpetrated within its recesses, but at the period of which I am speaking, it was said to be swarming with banditti. We of course expected to be robbed, perhaps stripped and otherwise ill treated; but Providence here manifested itself. It appeared that, the day before our arrival, the badditti of the pass had committed a dreadful robbery and murder, by which they gained forty thousand rials. This booty probably contented them for a time; certain it is that we were not interrupted: we did not even see a single individual in the pass, though we occasionally heard whistles and loud cries. We entered La Mancha, where I expected to fall into the hands of Palillos and Orejita. Providence again showed itself. It had been delicious weather, suddenly the Lord breathed forth a frozen blast, the severity of which was almost intolerable: no human being but ourselves ventured forth. We traversed snow-covered plains, and passed through villages and towns to all appearance deserted. The robbers kept close in their caves and hovels, but the cold nearly killed us. We reached Aranjuez late on Christmas Day, and I got into the house of an Englishman, where I swallowed nearly a pint of brandy: it affected me no more than warm water.

On the following day we arrived at Madrid, where we had the good fortune to find every thing tranquil and quiet. The Contrabandista continued with me for two days, at the end of which time he returned to Cordova upon the uncouth animal on which I had ridden throughout the journey. I had myself purchased the jaca, whose capabilities I had seen on the route, and which I imagined might prove useful in future journeys. The Contrabandista was so satisfied with the price which I gave him for his beast, and the general treatment which he had experienced at my hands during the time of his attendance upon me, that he would fain have persuaded me to retain him as a servant, assuring me that, in the event of my compliance, he would forget his wife and children and follow me through the world. I declined, however, to accede to his request, though I was in need of a domestic; I therefore sent him back to Cordova, where, as I subsequently learned, he died suddenly, about a week after his return.

The manner of his death was singular: one day he took out his purse, and, after counting his money, said to his wife, "I have made ninety-five dollars by this journey with the Englishman and by the sale of the jaca; this I could easily double by one successful venture in the smuggling lay. To-morrow I will depart for Lisbon to buy diamonds. I wonder if the beast requires to be shod?" He then started up and made for the door with the intention of going to the stable; ere, however, his foot had crossed the threshold, he fell dead on the floor. Such is the course of the world. Well said the wise king: Let no one boast of the morrow.

CHAPTER XIX.

Arrival at Madrid—Maria Diaz—Printing of the Testament—My Project—Andalusian Steed—Servant wanted—An Application—Antonio Buchini—General Cordova—Principles of Honour.

On my arrival at Madrid I did not repair to my former lodgings in the Calle de la Zarza, but took others in the Calle de Santiago, in the vicinity of the palace. The name of the hostess (for there was, properly speaking, no host) was Maria Diaz, of whom I shall take the present opportunity of saying something in particular.

She was a woman of about thirty-five years of age, rather good looking, and with a physiognomy every lineament of which bespoke intelligence of no common order. Her eyes were keen and penetrating, though occasionally clouded with a somewhat melancholy expression. There was a particular calmness and quiet in her general demeanour, beneath which, however, slumbered a firmness of spirit and an energy of action which were instantly displayed whenever necessary. A Spaniard and, of course, a Catholic, she was possessed of a spirit of toleration and liberality which would have done honour to individuals much her superior in station. In this woman, during the remainder of my sojourn in Spain, I found a firm and constant friend, and occasionally a most discreet adviser: she entered into all my plans, I will not say with enthusiasm, which, indeed, formed no part of her character, but with cordiality and sincerity, forwarding them to the utmost of her ability. She never shrank from me in the hour of danger and persecution, but stood my friend, notwithstanding the many inducements which were held out to her by my enemies to desert or betray me. Her motives were of the noblest kind, friendship and a proper feeling of the duties of hospitality; no prospect, no hope of self interest, however remote, influenced this admirable woman in her conduct towards me. Honour to Maria Diaz, the quiet, dauntless, clever Castilian female. I were an ingrate not to speak well of her, for richly has she deserved an eulogy in the humble pages of "The Bible in Spain."

She was a native of Villa Seca, a hamlet of new Castile, situated in what is called the Sagra, at about three leagues distance from Toledo; her father was an architect of some celebrity, particularly skilled in erecting bridges. At a very early age she married a respectable labrador of Villa Seca, Lopez by name, by whom she had three sons. On the death of her father, which occurred about five years previous to the time of which I am speaking, she removed to Madrid, partly for the purpose of educating her children, and partly in the hope of obtaining from the government a considerable sum of money for which it stood indebted to her father at the time of his decease, for various useful and ornamental works, principally in the neighbourhood of Aranjuez. The justness of her claim was at once acknowledged; but, alas! no money was forthcoming, the royal treasury being empty. Her hopes of earthly happiness were now concentrated in her children. The two youngest were still of a very tender age; but the eldest, Juan José Lopez, a lad of about sixteen, was bidding fair to realise the warmest hopes of his affectionate mother: he had devoted himself to the arts, in which he had made such progress that he had already become the favourite pupil of his celebrated namesake Lopez, the best painter of modern Spain. Such was Maria Diaz, who, according to a custom formerly universal in Spain, and still very prevalent, retained the name of her maidenhood though married. Such was Maria Diaz and her family.

One of my first cares was to wait on Mr. Villiers, who received me with his usual kindness. I asked him whether he considered that I might venture to commence printing the Scriptures without any more applications to government. His reply was satisfactory: "You obtained the permission of the government of Isturitz," said he, "which was a much less liberal one than the present. I am a witness to the promise made to you by the former ministers, which I consider sufficient. You had best commence and complete the work as soon as possible, without any fresh application; and should any one attempt to interrupt you, you have only to come to me, whom you may command at any time." So I went away with a light heart, and forthwith made preparation for the execution of the object which had brought me to Spain.

I shall not enter here into unnecessary details, which could possess but little interest for the reader; suffice it to say that, within three months from this time, an edition of the New Testament, consisting of five thousand copies, was published at Madrid. The work was printed at the establishment of Mr. Borrego, a well known writer on political economy, and proprietor and editor of an influential newspaper, called El Español. To this gentleman I had been recommended by Isturitz himself, on the day of my interview with him. That unfortunate minister had, indeed, the highest esteem for Borrego, and had intended raising him to the station of minister of finance, when the revolution of the Granja occurring, of course rendered abortive this project, with perhaps many others of a similar kind which he might have formed.

The Spanish version of the New Testament which was thus published, had been made many years before by a certain Padre Filipe Scio, confessor of Ferdinand the Seventh and had even been printed, but so encumbered by notes and commentaries as to be unfitted for general circulation, for which, indeed, it was never intended. In the present edition, the notes were of course omitted, and the inspired word, and that alone, offered to the public. It was brought out in a handsome octavo volume, and presented, upon the whole, a rather favourable specimen of Spanish typography.

The mere printing, however, of the New Testament at Madrid could be attended with no utility whatever, unless measures, and energetic ones, were taken for the circulation of the sacred volume.

In the case of the New Testament, it would not do to follow the usual plan of publication in Spain, namely, to entrust the work to the booksellers of the capital, and rest content with the sale which they and their agents in the provincial towns might be able to obtain for it, in the common routine of business; the result generally being, the circulation of a few dozen copies in the course of the year; as the demand for literature of every kind in Spain was miserably small.

The Christians of England had already made considerable sacrifices, in the hope of disseminating the word of God largely amongst the Spaniards, and it was now necessary to spare no exertion to prevent that hope becoming abortive. Before the book was ready, I had begun to make preparations for putting a plan into execution, which had occupied my thoughts occasionally during my former visit to Spain, and which I had never subsequently abandoned. I had mused on it when off Cape Finisterre in the tempest; in the cut-throat passes of the Morena; and on the the plains of La Mancha, as I jogged along a little way ahead of the Contrabandista.

I had determined, after depositing a certain number of copies in the shops of the booksellers of Madrid, to ride forth, Testament in hand, and endeavour to circulate the word of God amongst the Spaniards, not only of the towns but of the villages; amongst the children not only of the plains but of the hills and mountains. I intended to visit Old Castile, and to traverse the whole of Galicia and the Asturias,—to establish Scripture depôts in the principal towns, and to visit the people in secret and secluded spots,—to talk to them of Christ, to explain to them the nature of his book, and to place that book in the hands of those whom I should deem capable of deriving benefit from it. I was aware that such a journey would be attended with considerable danger, and very possibly the fate of St. Stephen might overtake me; but does the man deserve the name of a follower of Christ who would shrink from danger of any kind in the cause of Him whom he calls

his Master? "He who loses his life for my sake, shall find it," are words which the Lord himself uttered. These words were fraught with consolation to me, as they doubtless are to every one engaged in propagating the gospel in sincerity of heart, in savage and barbarian lands. . . . .

. . . .

I now purchased another horse; for these animals, at the time of which I am speaking, were exceedingly cheap. A royal requisition was about to be issued for five thousand, the consequence being, that an immense number were for sale, for, by virtue of this requisition, the horses of any person not a foreigner could be seized for the benefit of the service. It was probable that, when the number was made up, the price of horses would be treble what it then was, which consideration induced me to purchase this animal before I exactly wanted him. He was a black Andalusian stallion of great power and strength, and capable of performing a journey of a hundred leagues in a week's time, but he was unbroke, savage, and furious. A cargo of Bibles, however, which I hoped occasionally to put on his back, would, I had no doubt, thoroughly tame him, especially when labouring up the flinty hills of the north of Spain. I wished to have purchased a mule, but, though I offered thirty pounds for a sorry one, I could not obtain her; whereas the cost of both the horses, tall, powerful, stately animals, scarcely amounted to that sum.

The state of the surrounding country at this time was not very favourable for venturing forth: Cabrera was within nine leagues of Madrid, with an army nearly ten thousand strong; he had beaten several small detachments of the queen's troops, and had ravaged La Mancha with fire and sword, burning several towns; bands of affrighted fugitives were arriving every hour, bringing tidings of woe and disaster, and I was only surprised that the enemy did not appear, and by taking Madrid, which was almost at his mercy, put an end to the war at once. But the truth is, that the Carlist generals did not wish the war to cease, for as long as the country was involved in bloodshed and anarchy, they could plunder and exercise that lawless authority so dear to men of fierce and brutal passions. Cabrera, moreover, was a dastardly wretch, whose limited mind was incapable of harbouring a single conception approaching to grandeur; whose heroic deeds were confined to cutting down defenceless men, and to forcing and disembowelling unhappy women; and yet I have seen this wretched fellow termed by French journals (Carlist of course) the young, the heroic general. Infamy on the cowardly assassin! The shabbiest corporal of Napoleon would have laughed at his generalship, and half a battalion of Austrian grenadiers would have driven him and his rabble army headlong into the Ebro.

I now made preparations for my journey into the north. I was already provided with horses well calculated to support the fatigues

H

of the road and the burdens which I might deem necessary to impose upon them. One thing, however, was still lacking, indispensable to a person about to engage on an expedition of this description; I mean a servant to attend me. Perhaps there is no place in the world where servants more abound than at Madrid, or at least fellows eager to proffer their services in the expectation of receiving food and wages, though with respect to the actual service which they are capable of performing, not much can be said; but I was in want of a servant of no common description, a shrewd active fellow of whose advice, in cases of emergency, I could occasionally avail myself; courageous withal, for it certainly required some degree of courage to follow a master bent on exploring the greater part of Spain, and who intended to travel, not under the protection of muleteers and carmen, but on his own cabalgaduras. Such a servant, perhaps, I might have sought for years without finding; chance, however, brought one to my hand at the very time I wanted him, without it being necessary for me to make any laborious perquisitions. I was one day mentioning the subject to Mr. Borrego, at whose establishment I had printed the New Testament, and enquiring whether he thought that such an individual was to be found in Madrid, adding that I was particularly anxious to obtain a servant who, besides Spanish, could speak some other language, that occasionally we might discourse without being understood by those who might overhear us. "The very description of person," he replied, "that you appear to be in need of, quitted me about half an hour ago, and, it is singular enough, came to me in the hope that I might be able to recommend him to a master. He has been twice in my service: for his talent and courage I will answer; and I believe him to be trustworthy, at least to masters who may chime in with his humour, for I must inform you that he is a most extraordinary fellow, full of strange likes and antipathies, which he will gratify at any expense, either to himself or others. Perhaps he will attach himself to you, in which case you will find him highly valuable: for if he please he can turn his hand to any thing, and is not only acquainted with two but half a dozen languages."

"Is he a Spaniard?" I enquired.

"I will send him to you to-morrow," said Borrego, "you will best learn from his own mouth who and what he is."

The next day, as I had just sat down to my "sopa," my hostess informed me that a man wished to speak to me. Admit him, said I, and he almost instantly made his appearance. He was dressed respectably in the French fashion, and had rather a juvenile look, though I subsequently learned that he was considerably above forty. He was somewhat above the middle stature, and might have been called well made had it not been for his meagreness, which was rather remarkable. His arms were long and bony, and his whole form conveyed an idea of great activity united with no slight

degree of strength: his hair was wiry, but of jetty blackness; his forehead low; his eyes small and grey, expressive of much subtlety and no less malice, strangely relieved by a strong dash of humour; the nose was handsome, but the mouth was immensely wide, and his under jaw projected considerably. A more singular physiognomy I had never seen, and I continued staring at him for some time in silence. "Who are you?" I at last demanded.

"Domestic in search of a master," answered the man in good French, but in a strange accent. "I come recommended to you, mi Lor, by Monsieur B."

Myself.—Of what nation may you be? Are you French or Spanish?

Man.—God forbid that I should be either, mi Lor, *j'ai l'honneur d'être de la nation Grecque*, my name is Antonia Buchini, native of Pera the Belle near to Constantinople.

Myself.—And what brought you to Spain?

Buchini.—*Mi Lor, je vais vous raconter mon histoire du commencement jusqu' ici :*—my father was a native of Sceira in Greece, from whence at an early age he repaired to Pera, where he served as janitor in the hotels of various ambassadors, by whom he was much respected for his fidelity. Amongst others of these gentlemen, he served him of your own nation: this occurred at the time that there was war between England and the Porte.* Monsieur the Ambassador had to escape for his life, leaving the greater part of his valuables to the care of my father, who concealed them at his own great risk, and when the dispute was settled, restored them to Monsieur, even to the most inconsiderable trinket. I mention this circumstance to show you that I am of a family which cherishes principles of honour, and in which confidence may be placed. My father married a daughter of Pera, *et moi je suis l'unique fruit de ce mariage.* Of my mother I know nothing, as she died shortly after my birth. A family of wealthy Jews took pity on my forlorn condition and offered to bring me up, to which my father gladly consented; and with them I continued several years, until I was a *beau garçon;* they were very fond of me, and at last offered to adopt me, and at their death to bequeath me all they had, on condition of my becoming a Jew. *Mais la circoncision n'étoit guere à mon goût;* especially that of the Jews, for I am a Greek, am proud, and have principles of honour. I quitted them, therefore, saying that if ever I allowed myself to be converted, it should be to the faith of the Turks, for they are men, are proud, and have principles of honour like myself. I then returned to my father, who procured me various situations, none of which were to my liking, until I was placed in the house of Monsieur Zea.

Myself.—You mean, I suppose, Zea Bermudez, who chanced to be at Constantinople.

---

* This was possibly the period when Admiral Duckworth attempted to force the passage of the Dardanelles.

Buchini.—Just so, mi Lor, and with him I continued during his stay. He put great confidence in me, more especially as I spoke the pure Spanish language, which I acquired amongst the Jews, who, as I have heard Monsieur Zea say, speak it better than the present natives of Spain.

I shall not follow the Greek step by step throughout his history, which was rather lengthy : suffice it to say that he was brought by Zea Bermudez from Constantinople to Spain, where he continued in his service for many years, and from whose house he was expelled for marrying a Guipuscoan damsel, who was fille de chambre to Madame Zea ; since which time it appeared that he had served an infinity of masters ; sometimes as valet, sometimes as cook, but generally in the last capacity. He confessed, however, that he had seldom continued more than three days in the same service, on account of the disputes which were sure to arise in the house almost immediately after his admission, and for which he could assign no other reason than his being a Greek, and having principles of honour. Amongst other persons whom he had served was General Cordova, who he said was a bad paymaster, and was in the habit of maltreating his domestics. "But be found his match in me," said Antonio, "for I was prepared for him ; and once, when he drew his sword against me, I pulled out a pistol and pointed it in his face. He grew pale as death, and from that hour treated me with all kinds of condescension. It was only pretence, however, for the affair rankled in his mind ; he had determined upon revenge, and on being appointed to the command of the army, he was particularly anxious that I should attend him to the camp. *Mais je lui ris au nez*, made the sign of the cortamanga—asked for my wages, and left him ; and well it was that I did so, for the very domestic whom he took with him he caused to be shot upon a charge of mutiny."

"I am afraid," said I, "that you are of a turbulent disposition, and that the disputes to which you have alluded are solely to be attributed to the badness of your temper."

"What would you have, Monsieur ! *Moi je suis Grec, je suis fier et j'ai des principles d'honneur.* I expect to be treated with a certain consideration, though I confess that my temper is none of the best, and that at times I am tempted to quarrel with the pots and pans in the kitchen. I think, upon the whole, that it will be for your advantage to engage me, and I promise

you to be on my guard. There is one thing that pleases me relating to you, you are unmarried. Now, I would rather serve a young unmarried man for love and friendship than a Benedict for fifty dollars per month. Madame is sure to hate me, and so is her waiting woman ; and more particularly the latter, because I am a married man. I see that mi Lor is willing to engage me."

"But you say you are a married man," I replied ; "how can you desert your wife, for I am about to leave Madrid, and to travel into the remote and mountainous parts of Spain."

"My wife will receive the moiety of my wages, while I am absent, mi Lor, and therefore will have no reason to complain of being deserted. Complain ! did I say ; my wife is at present too well instructed to complain. She never speaks nor sits in my presence unless I give her permission. Am I not a Greek, and do I not know how to govern my own house ? Engage me, mi Lor, I am a man of many capacities : a discreet valet, an excellent cook, a good groom and light rider ; in a word, I am Ρωμαἵκός. What would you more !"

I asked him his terms, which were extravagant, notwithstanding his *principles d'honneur.* I found however, that he was willing to take one half.

I had no sooner engaged him, than seizing the tureen of soup, which had by this time become quite cold, he placed it on the top of his fore finger, or rather on the nail thereof causing it to make various circumlocutions over his head, to my great astonishment, without spilling a drop, then springing with it to the door he vanished, and in another moment made his appearance with the puchero, which, after a similar bound and flourish, he deposited on the table ; then suffering his hands to sink before him, he put one over the other and stood at his ease with half shut eyes, for all the world as if he had been in my service twenty years.

And in this manner Antonio Buchini entered upon his duties. Many was the wild spot to which he subsequently accompanied me ; many the wild adventure of which he was the sharer. His behaviour was frequently in the highest degree extraordinary, but he served me courageously and faithfully : such a valet, take him for all and all,

"His like I ne'er expect to see again."

Kesko bakh Anton

CHAPTER XX.

Illness—Nocturnal Visit—A Master Mind—The Whisper—Salamanca—Irish Hospitality—Spanish Soldiers—The Scriptures Advertised.

BUT I am anxious to enter upon the narrative of my journey, and shall therefore abstain from relating to my readers a great many circumstances which occurred previously to my leaving Madrid on this expedition. About the middle of May, I had got every thing in readiness, and I bade farewell to my friends. Salamanca was the first place which I intended to visit.

Some days previous to my departure I was very much indisposed, owing to the state of the weather, for violent and biting winds had long prevailed. I had been attacked with a severe cold, which terminated in a disagreeable cough, which the many remedies I successively tried seemed unable to subdue. I had made preparations for departing on a particular day, but owing to the state of my health, I was apprehensive that I should be compelled to defer my journey for a time. The last day of my stay in Madrid, finding myself scarcely able to stand, I was fain to submit to a somewhat desperate experiment, and by the advice of the barber-surgeon who visited me, I determined to be bled. Late on the night of that same day he took from me sixteen ounces of blood, and having received his fee left me, wishing me a pleasant journey, and assuring me, upon his reputation, that by noon the next day I should be perfectly recovered.

A few minutes after his departure, whilst I was sitting alone, meditating on the journey which I was about to undertake, and on the rickety state of my health, I heard a loud knock at the street door of the house, on the third floor of which I was lodged. In another minute Mr. ***** of the British Embassy entered my apartment. After a little conversation, he informed me that Mr. Villiers had desired him to wait upon me to communicate a resolution which he had come to. Being apprehensive that, alone and unassisted, I should experience considerable difficulty in propagating the gospel of God to any considerable extent in Spain, he was bent upon exerting to the utmost his own credit and influence to further my views, which he himself considered, if carried into proper effect, extremely well calculated to operate beneficially on the political and moral state of the country. To this end it was his intention to purchase a very considerable number of copies of the New Testament, and to despatch them forthwith to the various British consuls established in different parts of Spain, with strict and positive orders to employ all the means which their official situation should afford them to circulate the books in question, and to assure their being noticed. They

were, moreover, to be charged to afford me, whenever I should appear in their respective districts, all the protection, encouragement, and assistance which I should stand in need of.

I was of course much rejoiced on receiving this information, for though I had long been aware that Mr. Villiers was at all times willing to assist me, he having frequently given me sufficient proof, I could never expect that he would come forward in so noble, and, to say the least of it, considering his high diplomatic situation, so bold and decided a manner. I believe that this was the first instance of a British ambassador having made the cause of the Bible Society a national one, or indeed of having favoured it directly or indirectly. What renders the case of Mr. Villiers more remarkable is, that on my first arrival at Madrid, I found him by no means well disposed towards the Society. The Holy Spirit had probably illumined his mind on this point. I hoped that by his means our institution would shortly possess many agents in Spain, who, with far more power and better opportunities than I myself could ever expect to possess, would scatter abroad the seed of the gospel, and make of a barren and thirsty wilderness a green and smiling corn-field.

A word or two about the gentleman who paid me this nocturnal visit. Though he has probably long since forgotten the humble circulator of the Bible in Spain, I still bear in mind numerous acts of kindness which I experienced at his hands. Endowed with an intellect of the highest order, master of the lore of all Europe, profoundly versed in the ancient tongues, and speaking most of the modern dialects with remarkable facility,—possessed, moreover, of a thorough knowledge of mankind,—he brought with him into the diplomatic career advantages such as few, even the most highly gifted, can boast of. During his sojourn in Spain, he performed many eminent services for the government which employed him; services which, I believe, it had sufficient discernment to see, and gratitude to reward. He had to encounter, however, the full brunt of the low and stupid malignity of the party who, shortly after the time of which I am speaking, usurped the management of the affairs of Spain. This party, whose foolish manœuvres he was continually discomfiting, feared and hated him as its evil genius, taking every opportunity of showering on his head calumnies the most improbable and absurd. Amongst other things, he was accused of having acted as an agent to the English government in the affair of the Granja, bringing about that revolution by bribing the mutinous soldiers, and more particularly the notorious Sergeant Garcia. Such an accusation will of course merely extract a smile from those who are at all acquainted with the English character, and the general line of conduct pursued by the English government. It was a charge, however, universally believed in Spain, and was even preferred in print by a certain journal, the official organ of the silly Duke of Frias, one of the many prime ministers of the moderado party who followed each other in rapid succession towards the latter period of the Carlist and Christino struggle. But when did a calumnious report ever fall to the ground in Spain by the weight of its own absurdity? Unhappy land, not until the pure light of the gospel has illumined thee, wilt thou learn that the greatest of all gifts is charity.

The next day verified the prediction of the Spanish surgeon, I had to a considerable degree lost my cough and fever, though, owing to the loss of blood, I was somewhat feeble. Precisely at twelve o'clock the horses were led forth before the door of my lodging in the Calle de Santiago, and I prepared to mount; but my black entero of Andalusia would not permit me to approach his side, and whenever I made the attempt, commenced wheeling round with great rapidity.

"C'est un mauvais signe mon maître," said Antonio, who, dressed in a green jerkin, a Montero cap, and booted and spurred, stood ready to attend me, holding by the bridle the horse which I had purchased from the contrabandista. "It is a bad sign, and in my country they would defer the journey till tomorrow."

"Are there whisperers in your country?" I demanded; and taking the horse by the mane, I performed the ceremony after the most approved fashion: the animal stood still, and I mounted the saddle, exclaiming:—

"The Rommany Chal to his horse did cry,
As he placed the bit in his horse's jaw;
Kosko gry! Rommany gry!
Muk man kistur tute knaw."

We then rode forth from Madrid by the gate of San Vicente, directing our course to the lofty mountains which separate Old from New Castile. That night we rested at Guadarama, a large village at their foot, distant from Madrid about seven leagues. Rising early on the following morning, we ascended the pass and entered into Old Castile.

After crossing the mountains, the route to Salamanca lies almost entirely over sandy and arid plains, interspersed here and there with thin and scanty groves of pine. No adventure worth relating occurred during this journey. We sold a few Testaments in the villages through which we passed, more especially at Peñaranda. About noon of the third day, on reaching the brow of a hillock, we saw a huge dome before us, upon which the fierce rays of the sun striking, produced the appearance of burnished gold. It belonged to the cathedral of Salamanca, and we flattered ourselves that we were already

at our journey's end: we were deceived, however, being still four leagues distant from the town, whose churches and convents, towering up in gigantic masses, can be distinguished at an immense distance, flattering the traveller with an idea of propinquity which does not in reality exist. It was not till long after nightfall that we arrived at the city gate, which we found closed and guarded, in apprehension of a Carlist attack; and having obtained admission with some difficulty, we led our horses along dark, silent, and deserted streets, till we found an individual who directed us to a large, gloomy, and comfortless posada, that of the Bull, which we, however, subsequently found was the best which the town afforded.

A melancholy town is Salamanca; the days of its collegiate glory are long since past by never more to return: a circumstance, however, which is little to be regretted; for what benefit did the world ever derive from scholastic philosophy? And for that alone was Salamanca ever famous. Its halls are now almost silent, and grass is growing in its courts, which were once daily thronged by at least eight thousand students; a number to which, at the present day, the entire population of the city does not amount. Yet, with all its melancholy, what an interesting, nay, what a magnificent place is Salamanca. How glorious are its churches, how stupendous are its deserted convents, and with what sublime but sullen grandeur do its huge and crumbling walls, which crown the precipitous bank of the Tormes, look down upon the lovely river and its venerable bridge.

What a pity that, of the many rivers of Spain, scarcely one is navigable. The beautiful but shallow Tormes, instead of proving a source of blessing and wealth to this part of Castile, is of no farther utility than to turn the wheels of various small water mills, standing upon weirs of stone, which at certain distances traverse the river.

My sojourn at Salamanca was rendered particularly pleasant by the kind attentions and continual acts of hospitality which I experienced from the inmates of the Irish College, to the rector of which I bore a letter of recommendation from my kind and excellent friend Mr. O'Shea, the celebrated banker of Madrid. It will be long before I forget these Irish, more especially their head, Dr. Gartland, a genuine scion of the good Hibernian tree, an accomplished scholar, and a courteous and high minded gentleman. Though fully aware who I was, he held out the hand of friendship to the wandering heretic missionary, although by so doing he exposed himself to the rancorous remarks of the narrow minded native clergy, who, in their ugly shovel hats and long cloaks, glared at me askance as I passed by their whispering groups beneath the piazzas of the Plaza. But when did the fear of consequences cause an Irishman to shrink from the exercise of the duties of hospitality? However attached to his religion —and who is so attached to the Romish creed as the Irishman?—I am convinced that not all the authority of the Pope or the Cardinals would induce him to close his doors on Luther himself, were that respectable personage at present alive and in need of food and refuge.

Honour to Ireland and her "hundred thousand welcomes!" Her fields have long been the greenest in the world; her daughters the fairest; her sons the bravest and most eloquent. May they never cease to be so.

The posada where I had put up was a good specimen of the old Spanish inn, being much the same as those described in the time of Philip the Third or Fourth. The rooms were many and large, floored with either brick or stone, generally with an alcove at the end, in which stood a wretched flock bed. Behind the house was a court, and in the rear of this a stable, full of horses, ponies, mules, machos, and donkeys, for there was no lack of guests, who, however, for the most part slept in the stable with their caballerias, being either arrieros or small peddling merchants who travelled the country with coarse cloth or linen. Opposite to my room in the corridor lodged a wounded officer, who had just arrived from San Sebastian on a galled broken-kneed pony: he was an Estrimenian, and was returning to his own village to be cured. He was attended by three broken soldiers, ame or maimed, and unfit for service: they told me that they were of the same village as his worship, and on that account he permitted them to travel with him. They slept amongst the litter, and throughout the day lounged about the house smoking paper cigars. I never saw them eating, though they frequently went to a dark cool corner, where stood a bota or kind of water pitcher, which they held about six inches from their black filmy lips, permitting the liquid to trickle down their throats. They said they had no pay, and were quite destitute of money, that *su merced* the officer occasionally gave them a piece of bread, but that he himself was poor and had only a few dollars. Brave guests for an inn, thought I; yet, to the honour of Spain be it spoken, that it is one of the few countries in Europe where poverty is never insulted nor looked upon with contempt. Even at an inn, the poor man is never spurned from the door, and if not harboured, is at least dismissed with fair words, and consigned to the mercies of God and his mother. This is as it should be. I laugh at the bigotry and prejudices of Spain; I abhor the cruelty and ferocity which

have cast a stain of eternal infamy on her history; but I will say for the Spaniards, that in their social intercourse no people in the world exhibit a juster feeling of what is due to the dignity of human nature, or better understand the behaviour which it behoves a man to adopt towards his fellow beings. I have said that it is one of the few countries in Europe where poverty is not treated with contempt, and I may add, where the wealthy are not blindly idolized. In Spain the very beggar does not feel himself a degraded being, for he kisses no one's feet, and knows not what it is to be cuffed or spitten upon; and in Spain the duke or the marquis can scarcely entertain a very overweening opinion of his own consequence, as he finds no one, with perhaps the exception of his French valet, to fawn upon or flatter him.

During my stay at Salamanca, I took measures that the word of God might become generally known in this celebrated city. The principal bookseller of the town, Blanco, a man of great wealth and respectability, consented to become my agent here, and I in consequence deposited in his shop a certain number of New Testaments. He was the proprietor of a small printing press, where the official bulletin of the place was published. For this bulletin I prepared an advertisement of the work, in which, amongst other things, I said that the New Testament was the only guide to salvation; I also spoke of the Bible Society, and the great pecuniary sacrifices which it was making with the view of proclaiming Christ crucified, and of making his doctrine known. This step will perhaps be considered by some as too bold, but I was not aware that I could take any more calculated to arouse the attention of the people—a considerable point. I also ordered numbers of the same advertisement to be struck off in the shape of bills, which I caused to be stuck up in various parts of the town. I had great hope that by means of these a considerable number of New Testaments would be sold. I intended to repeat this experiment in Valladolid, Leon, St. Jago, and all the principal towns which I visited, and to distribute them likewise as I rode along: the children of Spain would thus be brought to know that such a work as the New Testament is in existence, a fact of which not five in one hundred were then aware, notwithstanding their so frequently repeated boasts of their Catholicity and Christianity.

CHAPTER XXI.

Departure from Salamanca—Reception at Pitiegua—The Dilemma—Sudden Inspiration—The good Presbyter—Combat of Quadrupeds—Irish Christians—Plains of Spain—The Catalans—The Fatal Pool—Valladolid—Circulation of the Scripture—Philippine Missions—English College—A Conversation—The Gaoleress.

ON Saturday, the 10th of June, I left Salamanca for Valladolid. As the village where we intended to rest was only five leagues distant, we did not sally forth till midday was past. There was a haze in the heavens which overcast the sun, nearly hiding his countenance from our view. My friend, Mr. Patrick Cantwell, of the Irish College, was kind enough to ride with me part of the way. He was mounted on a most sorry looking hired mule, which I expected would be unable to keep pace with the spirited horses of myself and man, for he seemed to be twin brother of the mule of Gil Perez, on which his nephew made his celebrated journey from Oviedo to Peñaflor. I was, however, very much mistaken. The creature on being mounted instantly set off at that rapid walk which I have so often admired in Spanish mules, and which no horse can emulate. Our more stately animals were speedily left in the rear, and we were continually obliged to break into a trot to follow the singular quadruped, who, ever and anon, would lift his head high in the air, curl up his lip, and show his yellow teeth, as if he were laughing at us, as perhaps he was. It chanced that none of us was well acquainted with the road; indeed, I could see nothing which was fairly entitled to that appellation. The way from Salamanca to Valladolid is amongst a medley of bridle-paths and drift-ways, where discrimination is very difficult. It was not long before we were bewildered, and travelled over more ground than was strictly necessary. However, as men and women frequently passed on donkeys and little ponies, we were not too proud to be set right by them, and by dint of diligent enquiry we at length arrived at Pitiegua, four leagues from Salamanca, a small village, containing about fifty families, consisting of mud huts, and situated in the midst of dusty plains, where corn was growing in abundance. We asked for the house of the cura, an old man whom I had seen the day before at the Irish College, and who, on being informed that I was about to depart for Valladolid, had exacted from me a promise that I would not pass through his village without paying him a visit and partaking of his hospitality.

A woman directed us to a cottage somewhat superior in appearance to those contiguous. It had a small portico, which, if I remember well, was overgrown with a vine. We knocked loud and long at the door, but received no answer; the voice of man was silent, and not even a dog barked. The truth was, that the old curate was taking his siesta, and so were his whole family, which consisted of one ancient female and a cat. The good man was at last disturbed by our noise and vociferation, for we were hungry, and consequently impatient. Leaping from his couch, he came running to the door in great hurry and confusion, and perceiving us, he made many apologies for being asleep at a period when, he said, he ought to have been on the look out for his invited guest. He embraced me very affectionately and conducted me into his parlour, an apartment of tolerable size, hung round with shelves, which were crowded with books. At one end there was a kind of table or desk covered with black leather, with a large easy chair, into which he pushed me, as I, with the true eagerness of a bibliomaniac, was about to inspect his shelves; saying, with considerable vehemence, that there was nothing there worthy of the attention of an Englishman, for that his whole stock consisted of breviaries, and dry Catholic treatises on divinity.

His care now was to furnish us with refreshments. In a twinkling, with the assistance of his old attendant, he placed on the table several plates of cakes and confectionery, and a number of large uncouth glass bottles, which I thought bore a strong resemblance to those of Schiedam, and indeed they were the very same. "There," said he, rubbing his hands; "I thank God that it is in my power to treat you in a way which will be agreeable to you. In those bottles there is Hollands, thirty years old;" and producing two large tumblers, he continued, "fill, my friends, and drink, drink it every drop if you please, for it is of little use to myself, who seldom drink aught but water. I know that you islanders love it, and cannot live without it; therefore, since it does you good, I am only sorry that there is no more."

Observing that we contented ourselves with merely tasting it, he looked at us with astonishment, and enquired the reason of our not drinking. We told him that we seldom drank ardent spirits; and I added, that as for myself, I seldom tasted even wine, but like himself, was content with the use of water. He appeared somewhat incredulous, but told us to do exactly what we pleased, and to ask for what was agreeable to us. We told him that we had not dined, and should be glad of some substantial refreshment. "I am afraid," said he, "that I have nothing in the house which will suit you; however, we will go and see." Thereupon he led us through a small yard at the back part of his house, which might have been called a garden, or orchard, if it had displayed either trees or flowers; but it produced nothing but grass, which was growing in luxuriance. At one end was a large pigeon-house, which we all entered: "for," said the curate, "if we could find some nice delicate pigeons they would afford you an excellent dinner." We were, however, disappointed; for after rummaging the nests, we only found very young ones, unfitted for our purpose. The good man became very melancholy, and said he had some misgivings that we should have to depart dinnerless. Leaving the pigeon-house, he conducted us to a place where there were several skeps of bees, round which multitudes of the busy insects were hovering, filling the air with their music. "Next to my fellow creatures," said he, "there is nothing which I love so dearly as these bees; it is one of my delights to sit watching them, and listening to their murmur." We next went to several unfurnished rooms, fronting the yard, in one of which were hanging several flitches of bacon, beneath which he stopped, and looking up, gazed intently upon them. We told him that if he had nothing better to offer, we should be very glad to eat some slices of this bacon, especially if some eggs were added. "To tell the truth," said he, "I have nothing better, and if you can content yourselves with such fare I shall be very happy; as for eggs, you can have as many as you wish, and perfectly fresh, for my hens lay every day."

So, after every thing was prepared and arranged to our satisfaction, we sat down to dine on the bacon and eggs, in a small room, not the one to which he had ushered us at first, but on the other side of the doorway. The good curate, though he ate nothing, having taken his meal long before, sat at the head of the table, and the repast was enlivened by his chat. "There, my friends," said he, "where you are now seated once sat Wellington and Crawford, after they had beat the French at Arapiles, and rescued us from the thraldom of those wicked people. I never respected my house so much as I have done since they honoured it with their presence. They were heroes, and one was a demi-god." He then burst into a most eloquent panegyric of El Gran Lord, as he termed him, which I should be very happy to translate, were my pen capable of rendering into English the robust thundering sentences of his powerful Castilian. I had till then considered him a plain uninformed old man, almost simple, and as incapable of much emotion as a tortoise within its shell; but he had become at once inspired: his eyes were replete with a bright fire, and every muscle of his face was quivering. The little silk scull-cap which he wore, according to the custom of the Catholic clergy, moved up and down with his agitation, and I soon saw that I was in the presence of one of those remarkable men who so frequently spring up in the bosom of the Romish church, and who to a child-like simplicity unite immense energy and power of mind,—equally adapted to guide a scanty flock of ignorant rustics in some ob-

scure village in Italy or Spain, as to convert millions of heathens on the shores of Japan, China, and Paraguay.

He was a thin spare man, of about sixty-five, and was dressed in a black cloak of very coarse materials, nor were his other garments of superior quality. This plainness, however, in the appearance of his outward man was by no means the result of poverty; quite the contrary. The benefice was a very plentiful one, and placed at his disposal annually a sum of at least eight hundred dollars, of which the eighth part was more than sufficient to defray the expenses of his house and himself; the rest was devoted entirely to the purest acts of charity. He fed the hungry wanderer, and despatched him singing on his way, with meat in his wallet and a peseta in his purse, and his parishioners, when in need of money, had only to repair to his study and were sure of an immediate supply. He was, indeed, the banker of the village, and what he lent he neither expected nor wished to be returned. Though under the necessity of making frequent journeys to Salamanca, he kept no mule, but contented himself with an ass, borrowed from the neighbouring miller. "I once kept a mule," said he; "but some years since it was removed without my permission by a traveller whom I had housed for the night; for in that alcove I keep two clean beds for the use of the wayfaring, and I shall be very much pleased if yourself and friend will occupy them, and tarry with me till the morning."

But I was eager to continue my journey, and my friend was no less anxious to return to Salamanca. Upon taking leave of the hospitable curate, I presented him with a copy of the New Testament. He received it without uttering a single word, and placed it on one of the shelves of his study; but I observed him nodding significantly to the Irish student, perhaps as much as to say, "Your friend loses no opportunity of propagating his book;" for he was well aware who I was. I shall not speedily forget the truly good presbyter, Anthonio Garcia de Aguilar, Cura of Pitiegua.

We reached Pedroso shortly before nightfall. It was a small village containing about thirty houses, and intersected by a rivulet, or as it is called a regata. On its banks women and maidens were washing their linen and singing couplets; the church stood lone and solitary on the farther side. We enquired for the posada, and were shown a cottage differing nothing from the rest in general appearance. We called at the door in vain, as it is not the custom of Castile for the people of these halting places to go out to welcome their visitors: at last we dismounted and entered the house, demanding of a sullen looking woman where we were to place the horses. She said there was a stable within the house, but we could not put the animals there as it contained malos machos (*savage mules*) belonging to two travellers, who would certainly fight with our horses, and then there would be a funcion, which would tear the house down. She then pointed to an outhouse across the way, saying that we could stable them there. We entered this place, which we found full of filth and swine, with a door without a lock. I thought of the fate of the cura's mule, and was unwilling to trust the horses in such a place, abandoning them to the mercy of any robber in the neighbourhood. I therefore entered the house and said resolutely, that I was resolved to place them in the stable. Two men were squatted-on the ground, with an immense bowl of stewed hare before them, on which they were supping; these were the travelling merchants, the masters of the mutes. I passed on to the stable, one of the men saying softly, "Yes, yes, go in and see what will befall." I had no sooner entered the stable than I heard a horrid discordant cry, something between a bray and a yell, and the largest of the machos, tearing his head from the manger to which he was fastened, his eyes shooting flames, and breathing a whirlwind from his nostrils, flung himself on my stallion. The horse, as savage as himself, reared on his hind legs, and after the fashion of an English pugilist, repaid the other with a pat on the forehead, which nearly felled him. A combat instantly ensued, and I thought that the words of the sullen woman would be verified by the house being torn to pieces. It ended by my seizing the mute by the halter, at the risk of my limbs, and hanging upon him with all my weight, whilst Antonio, with much difficulty, removed the horse. The man who had been standing at the entrance now came forward, saying, "This would not have happened if you had taken good advice." Upon my stating to him the unreasonableness of expecting that I would risk horses in a place where they would probably be stolen before the morning, he replied, "True, true, you have perhaps done right." He then refastened his macho, adding for additional security a piece of whipcord, which he said rendered escape impossible.

After supper, I roamed about the village. I addressed two or three labourers whom I found standing at their doors; they appeared, however, exceedingly reserved, and with a gruff "*buenas noches*" turned into their houses without inviting me to enter. I at last found my way to the church porch, where I continued some time in meditation. At last I bethought myself of retiring to rest; before departing, however, I took out and affixed to the porch of the church an advertisement to the effect that the New Testament was to be purchased at Salamanca. On returning to the house, I found the two travelling merchants enjoying profound slumber on various mantas or mule-cloths stretched on the floor. "You are a French merchant, I suppose, Caballero," said a man, who it seemed was the master of the house, and whom I had not before seen. "You are a French merchant, I suppose, and are on the way to the fair of Medina." "I am neither Frenchman nor merchant," I replied, "and though I purpose passing through Medina, it is not with the view of attending the fair." "Then you are

one of the Irish Christians from Salamanca, Caballero," said the man; "I hear you come from that town." "Why do you call them *Irish Christians?*" I replied. "Are there pagans in their country?" "We call them Christians," said the man, "to distinguish them from the Irish English, who are worse than pagans, who are Jews and heretics." I made no answer, but passed on to the room which had been prepared for me, and from which, the door being ajar, I heard the following short conversation passing between the innkeeper and his wife:—

Innkeeper.—Muger, it appears to me that we have evil guests in the house.

Wife.—You mean the last comers, the Caballero and his servant. Yes, I never saw worse countenances in my life.

Innkeeper.—I do not like the servant, and still less the master. He has neither formality nor politeness: he tells me that he is not French, and when I spoke to him of the Irish Christians, he did nor seem to belong to them. I more than suspect that he is a heretic or a Jew at least.

Wife.—Perhaps they are both. Maria Santissima! what shall we do to purify the house when they are gone?

Innkeeper.—O, as for that matter, we must of course charge it in the cuenta.

I slept soundly, and rather late in the morning arose and breakfasted, and paid the bill, in which by its extravagance, I found the purification had not been forgotten. The travelling merchants had departed at daybreak. We now led forth the horses and mounted; there were several people at the door staring at us. "What is the meaning of this?" said I to Antonio.

"It is whispered that we are no Christians," said Antonio; "they have come to cross themselves at our departure."

In effect, the moment that we rode forward a dozen hands at least were busied in this evil-averting ceremony. Antonio instantly turned and crossed himself in the Greek fashion,—much more complex and difficult than the Catholic.

"*Mirad que Santiguo! que Santiguo de los demonios!*" exclaimed many voices, whilst for fear of consequences we hastened away.

The day was exceedingly hot, and we wended our way slowly along the plains of Old Castile. With all that pertains to Spain, vastness and sublimity are associated: grand are its mountains, and no less grand are its plains, which seem of boundless extent, but which are not tame unbroken flats, like the steppes of Russia. Rough and uneven ground is continually occurring: here a deep ravine and gully worn by the wintry torrent; yonder an eminence not unfrequently craggy and savage, at whose top appears the lone solitary village. There is little that is blithesome and cheerful, but much that is melancholy. A few solitary rustics are occasionally seen toiling in the fields—fields without limit or boundary, where the green oak, the elm or the ash are unknown; where only the sad and desolate pine displays its pyramid-like form, and where no grass is to be found. And who are the travellers of these districts? For the most part arrieros, with their long trains of mules hung with monotonous tinkling bells. Behold them with their brown faces, brown dresses, and broad slouched hats;—the arrieros, the true lords of the roads of Spain, and to whom more respect is paid in these dusty ways than to dukes and condes;—the arrieros, sullen, proud, and rarely courteous, whose deep voices may be sometimes heard at the distance of a mile, either cheering the sluggish animals or shortening the dreary way with savage and dissonant songs.

Late in the afternoon, we reached Medina Del Campo, formerly one of the principal cities of Spain, though at present an inconsiderable place. Immense ruins surround it in every direction, attesting the former grandeur of this "city of the plain." The great square or market place is a remarkable spot, surrounded by a heavy massive piazza, over which rise black buildings of great antiquity. We found the town crowded with people awaiting the fair, which was to be held in a day or two. We experienced some difficulty in obtaining admission into the posada, which was chiefly occupied by Catalans from Valladolid. These people not only brought with them their merchandize but their wives and children. Some of them appeared to be people of the worst description: there was one in particular, a burly savage looking fellow, of about forty, whose conduct was atrocious; he sat with his wife, or perhaps concubine, at the door of a room which opened upon the court: he was continually venting horrible and obscene oaths, both in Spanish and Catalan. The woman was remarkably handsome, but robust and seemingly as savage as himself; her conversation likewise was as frightful as his own. Both seemed to be under the influence of an incomprehensible fury. At last, upon some observation from the woman, he started up, and drawing a long knife from his girdle, stabbed at her naked bosom; she, however, interposed the palm of her hand, which was much cut. He stood for a moment viewing the blood trickling upon the ground, whilst she held up her wounded hand, then with an astounding oath he hurried up the court to the Plaza. I went up to the woman and said, "What is the cause of this? I hope the ruffian has not seriously injured you." She turned her countenance upon me with the glance of a demon, and at last with a sneer of contempt exclaimed, "Carâls, que es eso? Cannot a Catalan gentleman be conversing with his lady upon their own private affairs without being interrupted by you?" She then bound up her hand with a handkerchief, and going into the room brought a small table to the door, on which she placed several things as if for the evening's repast, and then sat down on a stool: presently returned the Catalan, and without a word took his seat on the threshold; then, as if nothing had oc-

curred, the extraordinary couple commenced eating and drinking, interlarding their meal with oaths and jests.

We spent the night at Medina, and departing early next morning, passed through much the same country as the day before, until about noon we reached a small venta, distant half a league from the Duero; here we reposed ourselves during the heat of the day, and then remounting, crossed the river by a handsome stone bridge, and directed our course to Valladolid. The banks of the Duero in this place have much beauty: they abound with trees and brushwood, amongst which, as we passed along, various birds were singing melodiously. A delicious coolness proceeded from the water, which in some parts brawled over stones or rippled fleetly over white sand, and in others glided softly over blue pools of considerable depth. By the side of one of these last, sat a woman of about thirty, neatly dressed as a peasant: she was gazing upon the water into which she occasionally flung flowers and twigs of trees. I stopped for a moment to ask a question; she, however, neither looked up nor answered, but continued gazing at the water as if lost to consciousness of all beside. "Who is that woman?" said I to a shepherd, whom I met the moment after. "She is mad, la pobrecita," said he; "she lost her child about a month ago in that pool, and she has been mad ever since; they are going to send her to Valladolid, to the Casa de los Locos. There are many who perish every year in the eddies of the Duero; it is a bad river; vaya usted con la Virgen, Caballero." So I rode on through the pinares, or thin scanty pine forests, which skirt the way to Valladolid in this direction.

Valladolid is seated in the midst of an immense valley, or rather hollow, which seems to have been scooped by some mighty convulsion out of the plain ground of Castile. The eminences which appear in the neighbourhood are not properly high grounds, but are rather the sides of this hollow. They are jagged and precipitous, and exhibit a strange and uncouth appearance. Volcanic force seems at some distant period to have been busy in these districts. Valladolid abounds with convents, at present deserted, which afford some of the finest specimens of architecture in Spain. The principal church, though rather ancient, is unfinished: it was intended to be a building of vast size, but the means of the founders were insufficient to carry out their plan: it is built of rough granite. Valladolid is a manufacturing town, but the commerce is chiefly in the hands of the Catalans, of whom there is a colony of nearly three hundred established here. It possesses a beautiful alameda or public walk, through which flows the river Escurva. The population is said to amount to sixty thousand souls.

We put up at the Posada de las Diligencias, a very magnificent edifice: this posada, however, we were glad to quit on the second day after our arrival, the accommodation being of the most wretched description, and the incivility of the people great; the master of the house, an immense tall fellow, with huge moustachios and an assumed military air, being far too high a cavalier to attend to the wants of his guests, with whom, it is true, he did not appear to be overburdened, as I saw no one but Antonio and myself. He was a leading man amongst the national guards of Valladolid, and delighted in parading about the city on a clumsy steed, which he kept in a subterranean stable.

Our next quarters were at the Trojan Horse, an ancient posada, kept by a native of the Basque provinces, who at least was not above his business. We found every thing in confusion at Valladolid, a visit from the factious being speedily expected. All the gates were blockaded, and various forts had been built to cover the approaches to the city. Shortly after our departure the Carlists actually did arrive, under the command of the Biscayan chief, Zariategui. They experienced no opposition; the staunchest nationals retiring to the principal fort, which they, however, speedily surrendered, not a gun being fired throughout the affair. As for my friend the hero of the inn, on the first rumour of the approach of the enemy, he mounted his horse and rode off, and was never subsequently heard of. On our return to Valladolid, we found the inn in other and better hands, those of a Frenchman from Bayonne, from whom we received as much civility as we had experienced rudeness from his predecessor.

In a few days I formed the acquaintance of the bookseller of the place, a kind-hearted simple man, who willingly undertook the charge of vending the Testaments which I brought.

I found literature of every description at the lowest ebb at Valladolid. My newly acquired friend merely carried on bookselling in connexion with other business; it being, as he assured me, in itself quite insufficient to afford him a livelihood. During the week, however, that I continued in this city, a considerable number of copies were disposed of, and a fair prospect opened that many more would be demanded. To call attention to my books, I had recourse to the same plan which I had adopted at Salamanca, the affixing of advertisements to the walls. Before leaving the city, I gave orders that these should be renewed every week; from pursuing which course I expected that much and manifold good would accrue, as the people would have continual opportunities of learning that a book which contains the living word was in existence, and within their reach, which might induce them to secure it and consult it even unto salvation.

In Valladolid I found both an English and Scotch College. From my obliging friends, the Irish at Salamanca, I bore a letter of introduction to the rector of the latter. I found this college an old gloomy edifice, situated in a retired street. The rector was dressed in the habiliments of a Spanish ecclesiastic, a character which he was evidently ambitious of assuming. There was something dry and cold in his manner, and nothing of that generous warmth and eager hospitality which had so captivated me in the fine Irish rector of Salamanca; he was, however, civil and polite, and offered to shew me the curiosities of the place. He evidently knew who I was, and on that account was, perhaps, more reserved than he otherwise would have been: not a word passed between us on religious matters, which we seemed to avoid by common consent. Under the auspices of this gentleman, I visited the college of the Philippine Missions, which stands beyond the gate of the city, where I was introduced to the superior, a fine old man of seventy, very stout, in the habiliments of a friar. There was an air of placid benignity on his countenance which highly interested me: his words were few and simple, and he seemed to have bid adieu to all worldly passions. One little weakness was, however, still clinging to him.

Myself.—This is a noble edifice in which you dwell, Father; I should think it would contain at least two hundred students.

Rector.—More, my son: it is intended for more hundreds than it now contains single individuals.

Myself.—I observe that some rude attempts have been made to fortify it; the walls are pierced with loopholes in every direction.

Rector.—The nationals of Valladolid visited us a few days ago, and committed much useless damage; they were rather rude, and threatened me with their clubs: poor men, poor men.

Myself.—I suppose that even these missions, which are certainly intended for a noble end, experience the sad effects of the present convulsed state of Spain?

Rector.—But too true: we at present receive no assistance from the government, and are left to the Lord and ourselves.

Myself.—How many aspirants for the mission are you at present instructing?

Rector.—Not one, my son; not one. They are all fled. The flock is scattered and the shepherd left alone.

Myself.—Your reverence has doubtless taken an active part in the mission abroad?

Rector.—I was forty years in the Philippines, my son; forty years amongst the Indians. Ah me! how I love those Indians of the Philippines.

Myself.—Can your reverence discourse in the language of the Indians?

Rector.—No, my son. We teach the Indians Castilian. There is no better language, I believe. We teach them Castilian, and the adoration of the Virgin. What more need they know?

Myself.—And what did your reverence think of the Philippines as a country?

Rector.—I was forty years in the Philippines, but I know little of the country. I do not like the country. I love the Indians. The country is not very bad; it is, however, not worth Castile.

Myself.—Is your reverence a Castilian?

Rector.—I am an *Old* Castilian, my son.

From the house of the Philippine Missions my friend conducted me to the English College: this establishment seemed in every respect to be on a more magnificent scale than its Scottish sister. In the latter there were few pupils, scarcely six or seven, I believe, whilst, in the English seminary, I was informed that between thirty and forty were receiving their education. It is a beautiful building, with a small but splendid church, and a handsome library. The situation is light and airy: it stands by itself in an unfrequented part of the city, and, with genuine English exclusiveness, is surrounded by a high wall, which incloses a delicious garden. This is by far the most remarkable establishment of the kind in the Peninsula, and I believe the most prosperous. From the cursory view which I enjoyed of its interior, I of course cannot be expected to know much of its economy. I could not, however, fail to be struck with the order, neatness, and system which pervaded it. There was, however, an air of severe monastic discipline, though I am far from asserting that such actually existed. We were attended throughout by the sub-rector, the principal being absent. Of all the curiosities of this college, the most remarkable is the picture gallery, which contains neither more nor less than the portraits of a variety of scholars of this house who eventually suffered martyrdom in England, in the exercise of their vocation, in the angry times of the Sixth Edward and fierce Elizabeth. Yes, in this very house were many of those pale smiling half-foreign priests educated, who, like stealthy grimalkins, traversed green England in all directions; crept into old halls beneath umbrageous rookeries, fanning the dying embers of Popery, with no other hope nor perhaps wish than to perish disembowelled by the bloody hands of the executioner, amongst the yells of a rabble as bigoted as themselves: priests like Bedingfield and Garnet, and many others who have left a name in English story. Doubtless many a history, only the more wonderful for being true, could be wrought out of the archives of the English Popish seminary at Valladolid.

There was no lack of guests at the Trojan Horse, where we had taken up our abode at Valladolid. Amongst others who arrived during my sojourn was a robust buxom dame, exceedingly well dressed in black silk, with a costly mantilla. She was accompanied by a very handsome, but sullen and malicious looking urchin of about fifteen, who appeared to be her son. She came from Toro, a place about a day's journey from Valladolid, and celebrated for its wine. One night, as we were seated in the court of the inn enjoying the fresco, the following conversation ensued between us.

Lady.—Vaya, vaya, what a tiresome place is Valladolid! How different from Toro!

Myself.—I should have thought that it is at least as agreeable as Toro, which is not a third part so large.

Lady.—As agreeable as Toro! Vaya, vaya! Were you ever in the prison of Toro, Sir Cavalier?

Myself.—I have never had that honour: the prison is generally the last place which I think of visiting.

Lady.—See the difference of tastes: I have been to see the prison of Valladolid, and i seems as tiresome as the town.

Myself.—Of course, if grief and tediousness exist anywhere, you will find them in the prison.

Lady.—Not in that of Toro.

Myself.—What does that of Toro possess to distinguish it from all others?

Lady.—What does it possess? Vaya! Am I not the carcelera? Is not my husband the alcayde? Is not that son of mine a child of the prison?

Myself.—I beg your pardon, I was not aware of that circumstance; it of course makes much difference.

Lady.—I believe you. I am a daughter of that prison: my father was alcayde, and my son might hope to be so, were he not a fool.

Myself.—His countenance then belies him strangely: I should be loth to purchase that youngster for a fool.

Gaoleress.—You would have a fine bargain if you did; he has more picardias than any Calabozero in Toro. What I mean is, that he does not take to the prison as he ought to do, considering what his fathers were before him. He has too much pride—too many fancies; and he has at length persuaded me to bring him to Valladolid, where I have arranged with a merchant who lives in the Plaza to take him on trial. I wish he may not find his way to the prison: if he do, he will find that being a prisoner is a very different thing from being a son of the prison.

Myself.—As there is so much merriment at Toro, you of course attend to the comfort of your prisoners.

Gaoleress.—Yes, we are very kind to them; I mean to those who are caballeros; but as for those with vermin and miseria, what can we do? It is a merry prison that of Toro; we allow as much wine to enter as the prisoners can purchase and pay duty for. This of Valladolid is not half so gay: there is no prison like Toro. I learned there to play on the guitar. An Andalusian cavalier taught me to touch the guitar and to sing à la Gitána. Poor fellow, he was my first novio. Juanito, bring me the guitar, that I may play this gentleman a tune of Andalusia.

The carcelera had a fine voice, and touched the favourite instrument of the Spaniards in a truly masterly manner. I remained listening to her performance for nearly an hour, when I retired to my apartment and my repose. I believe that she continued playing and singing during the greater part of the night, for as I occasionally awoke I could still hear her; and, even in my slumbers, the strings were ringing in my ears.

CHAPTER XXII.

Duenas—Children of Egypt—Jockeyism—The Baggage Pony—The Fall—Palencia—Carlist Priests—The Look Out—Priestly Sincerity—Leon—Antonio Alarmed—Heat and Dust.

AFTER a sojourn of about ten days at Valladolid, we directed our course towards Leon. We arrived about noon at Duenas, a town at the distance of six short leagues from Valladolid. It is in every respect a singular place: it stands on a rising ground, and directly above it towers a steep conical mountain of calcareous earth, crowned by a ruined castle. Around Duenas are seen a multitude of caves scooped in the high banks and secured with strong doors. These are cellars, in which is deposited the wine, of which abundance is grown in the neighbourhood, and which is chiefly sold to the Navarrese and the mountaineers of Santander, who arrive in cars drawn by oxen, and convey it away in large quantities. We put up at a mean posada in the suburb for the purpose of refreshing our horses. Several cavalry soldiers were quartered there, who instantly came forth, and began, with the eyes of connoisseurs, to inspect my Andalusian entero. " A capital horse that would be for our troop," said the corporal; what a chest he has. By what right do you travel with that horse, Sñeor, when so many are wanted for the Queen's service ? He belongs to the requiso." " I travel with him by right of purchase, and being an Englishman," I replied. " Oh, your worship is an Englishman," answered the corporal; "that, indeed, alters the matter; the English in Spain are allowed to do what they please with their own. which is more than the Spaniards are. Cavalier, I have seen your countrymen in the Basque provinces; Vaya, what riders! what horses ! They do not fight badly either. But their chief skill is in riding: I have seen them dash over barrancos to get at the factious, who thought themselves quite secure, and then they would fall upon them on a sudden and kill them to a man. In truth, your worship, this is a fine horse, I must look at his teeth."

I looked at the corporal—his nose and eyes were in the horse's mouth : the rest of the party, who might amount to six or seven, were not less busily engaged. One was examining his fore feet, another his hind ; one fellow was pulling at his tail with all his might, while another pinched the windpipe, for the purpose of discovering whether the animal was at all touched there. At last, perceiving that the corporal was about to remove the saddle that he might examine the back of the animal, I exclaimed :—

"Stay, ye chabés of Egypt, ye forget that ye are hundunares, and are no longer paruguing grastes in the chardy."

The corporal at these words turned his face full upon me, and so did all the rest.

Yes, sure enough, there were the countenances of Egypt, and the fixed filmy stare of eye. We continued looking at each other for a minute at least, when the corporal, a villanous looking fellow, at last said, in the richest gipsy whine imaginable, "the erray knows us, the poor Caloré! And he. an Englishman! Bullati! I should not have thought that there was e'er a Busno would know us in these parts, where Gitános are never seen. Yes, your worship is right; we are all here of the. blood of the Caloré: we are from Melegrana (Granada,) your worship; they took us from thence and sent us to the wars. Your worship is right, the sight of that horse made us believe we were at home again in the mercado. of Granada; he is a countryman of ours, a real Andalou. Por dios, your worship, sell us that horse : we are poor Caloré, but we can buy him."

" You forgot that you are soldiers," said I. " How should you buy my horse ?"

" We are soldiers, your worship," said the corporal, "but we are still Caloré; we buy and sell beasts ; the captain of our troop is in league with us. We have been to the wars, but not to fight; we left that to the Busné. We have kept together, and, like true Caloré, have stood back to back. We have made money in the wars, your worship. No tenga usted cuidao. We can buy your horse."

Here he pulled out a purse, which contained at least ten ounces of gold.

" If I were willing to sell," I replied, " what would you give me for that horse ?"

" Then your worship wishes to sell your horse—that alters the matter. We will give ten dollars for your worship's horse. He is good for nothing."

" How is this ?" said I. " You this moment told me that he was a fine horse, an Andalusian, and a countryman of yours."

" No, Sñeor ! we did not say that he was an Andalou. We said he was an Estremou, and the worst of his kind. He is eighteen years old, your worship, short winded and galled."

" I do not wish to sell my horse," said I; "quite the contrary; I had rather buy than sell."

" Your worship does not wish to sell his horse," said the gipsy. " Stay, your worship, we will give sixty dollars for your worship's horse."

" I would not sell him for two hundred and sixty. Meclis ! Meclis ! say no more. I know your gipsy tricks. I will have no dealings with you."

" Did I not hear your worship say that you wished to buy a horse ?" said the gipsy.

"I do not want to buy a horse," said I; "if I need any thing, it is a pony to carry our baggage; but it is getting late. Antonio, pay the reckoning."

"Stay, your worship, do not be in a hurry," said the gipsy; "I have got the very pony which will suit you."

Without waiting for my answer, he hurried into the stable, from whence he presently returned, leading an animal by a halter. It was a pony of about thirteen hands high, of a dark red colour; it was very much galled all over, the marks of ropes and thongs being visible on its hide. The figure, however, was good, and there was an extraordinary brightness in its eye.

"There, your worship," said the gipsy; "there is the best pony in all Spain."

"What do you mean by showing me this wretched creature?" said I.

"This wretched creature," said the gipsy, "is a better horse than your Andalou!"

"Perhaps you would not exchange," said I, smiling.

"Señor, what I say is, that he shall run with your Andalou and beat him!"

"He looks feeble," said I; "his work is well nigh done."

"Feeble as he is, Señor, you could not manage him; no, nor any Englishman in Spain."

I looked at the creature again, and was still more struck with its figure. I was in need of a pony to relieve occasionally the horse of Antonio in carrying the baggage which we had brought from Madrid, and though the condition of this was wretched, I thought that by kind treatment I might possibly soon bring him round.

"May I mount this animal?" I demanded.

"He is a baggage pony, Señor, and is ill to mount. He will suffer none but myself to mount him, who am his master. When he once commences running, nothing will stop him but the sea. He springs over hills and mountains, and leaves them behind in a moment. If you will mount him, Señor, suffer me to fetch a bridle, for you can never hold him in with the halter."

"This is nonsense," said I. "You pretend that he is spirited in order to enhance the price. I tell you his work is done."

I took the halter in my hand and mounted. I was no sooner on his back than the creature, who had before stood stone still, without displaying the slightest inclination to move, and who in fact gave no farther indication of existence than occasionally rolling his eyes and pricking up an ear, sprang forward like a racehorse, at a most desperate gallop. I had expected that he might kick or fling himself down on the ground, in order to get rid of his burden, but for this escapade I was quite unprepared. I had no difficulty, however, in keeping on his back, having been accustomed from my childhood to ride without a saddle. To stop him, however, baffled all my endeavours, and I almost began to pay credit to the words of the gipsy, who had said that he would run on until he reached the sea. I had, however, a strong arm, and I tugged at the halter until I compelled him to turn slightly his neck, which from its stiffness might almost have been of wood; he, however, did not abate his speed for a moment. On the left side of the road down which he was dashing was a deep trench, just where the road took a turn towards the right, and over this he sprang in a sideward direction; the halter broke with the effort, the pony shot forward like an arrow, whilst I fell back into the dust.

"Señor!" said the gipsy, coming up with the most serious countenance in the world, "I told you not to mount that animal unless well bridled and bitted. He is a baggage pony, and will suffer none to mount his back, with the exception of myself, who feed him." (Here he whistled, and the animal, who was scurrying over the field, and occasionally kicking up his heels, instantly returned with a gentle neigh.) "Now, your worship, see how gentle he is. He is a capital baggage pony, and will carry all you have over the hills of Galicia."

"What do you ask for him?" said I.

"Señor, as your worship is an Englishman, and a good ginete, and, moreover, understands the ways of the Caloré, and their tricks and their language also, I will sell him to you a bargain. I will take two hundred and sixty dollars for him, and no less."

"That is a large sum," said I.

"No, Señor, not at all, considering that he is a baggage pony, and belongs to the troop, and is not mine to sell."

Two hours' ride brought us to Palencia, a fine old town, beautifully situated on the Carrion, and famous for its trade in wool. We put up at the best posada which the place afforded, and I forthwith proceeded to visit one of the principal merchants of the town, to whom I was recommended by my banker in Madrid. I was told, however, that he was taking his siesta. "Then I had better take my own," said I, and returned to the posada. In the evening I went again, when I saw him. He was a short bulky man, about thirty, and received me at first with some degree of bluntness; his manner, however, presently became more kind, at last he scarcely appeared to know how to show me sufficient civility. His brother had just arrived from Santander, and to him he introduced me. This last was a highly intelligent person, and had passed many years of his life in England. They both insisted upon showing me the town, and, indeed, led me all over it, and about the neighbourhood. I particularly admired the cathedral, a light, elegant, but ancient Gothic edifice. Whilst we walked about the aisles, the evening sun pouring its mellow rays through the arched windows, illumined some beautiful paintings of Murillo, with which the sacred edifice is adorned. From the church my friends conducted me to a fulling mill in the neighbourhood, by a picturesque walk. There was no lack either of trees or water, and I remarked, that the environs of Palencia were amongst the most pleasant places that I had ever seen.

Tired at last with rambling, we repaired to a coffee-house, where they regaled me with chocolate and sweetmeats. Such was their hospitality; and of hospitality of this simple and agreeable kind there is much in Spain.

On the next day we pursued our journey, a dreary one, for the most part, over bleak and barren plains, interspersed with silent and cheerless towns and villages, which stood at the distance of two or three leagues from each other. About midday we obtained a dim and distant view of an immense range of mountains, which are in fact those which bound Castile on the north. The day, however, became dim and obscure, and we speedly lost sight of them. A hollow wind now arose and blew over these desolate plains with violence, wafting clouds of dust into our faces; the rays of the sun were few, and those red and angry. I was tired of my journey, and when about four we reached * * * * *, a large village, half way between Palencia and Leon, I declared my intention of stopping for the night. I scarcely ever saw a more desolate place than this same town or village of * * * * *. The houses were for the most part large, but the walls were of mud, like those of barns. We saw no person in the long winding street to direct us to the venta, or posada, till at last, at the farther end of the place, we descried two black figures standing at a door, of whom, on making enquiry, we learned that the door at which they stood was that of the house we were in quest of. There was something strange in the appearance of these two beings, who seemed the genii of the place. One was a small slim man, about fifty, with sharp ill-natured features. He was dressed in coarse black worsted stockings, black breeches, and an ample black coat with long trailing skirts. I should at once have taken him for an ecclesiastic, but for his hat, which had nothing clerical about it, being a pinched diminutive beaver. His companion was of low stature, and a much younger man. He was dressed in similar fashion, save that he wore a dark blue cloak. Both carried walking-sticks in their hands, and kept hovering about the door, now within and now without, occasionally looking up the road, as if they expected some one.

"Trust me, mon maître," said Antonio to me, in French, "those two fellows are Carlist priests, and are awaiting the arrival of the Pretender. Les imbecilles!"

We conducted our horses to the stable, to which we were shown by the woman of the house. "Who are those men?" said I to her.

"The eldest is head curate to our pueblo," said she; "the other is brother to my husband. Pobrecito! he was a friar in our convent before it was shut up and the brethren driven forth."

We returned to the door. "I suppose, gentlemen," said the curate, "that you are Cata-

lans. Do you bring any news from that kingdom?"

"Why do you suppose we are Catalans?" I demanded.

"Because I heard you this moment conversing in that language."

"I bring no news from Catalonia," said I. "I believe, however, that the greater part of that principality is in the hands of the Carlists."

"Ahem, brother Pedro! This gentleman says that the greater part of Catalonia is in the hands of the royalists. Pray sir, where may Don Carlos be at present with his army?"

"He may be coming down the road this moment," said I, "for what I know;" and, stepping out, I looked up the way.

The two figures were at my side in a moment; Antonio followed, and we all four looked intently up the road.

"Do you see any thing?" said I at last to Antonio.

"Non, mon maître."

"Do you see anything, sir?" said I to the curate.

"I see nothing," said the curate, stretching out his neck.

"I see nothing," said Pedro, the ex-friar; "I see nothing but the dust, which is becoming every moment more blinding."

"I shall go in, then," said I. "Indeed, it is scarcely prudent to be standing here looking out for the Pretender: should the nationals of the town hear of it, they might perhaps shoot us."

"Ahem," said the curate, following me; "there are no nationals in this place: I would fain see what inhabitant would dare become a national. When the vecinos of this place were ordered to take up arms as nationals, they refused to a man, and on that account we had to pay a mulct; therefore, friend, you may speak out if you have anything to communicate; we are all of your opinion here."

"I am of no opinion at all," said I, "save that I want my supper. I am neither for Rey nor Roque. You say that I am a Catalan, and you know that Catalans think only of their own affairs."

In the evening I strolled by myself about the village, which I found still more forlorn and melancholy than it at first appeared; perhaps, however, it had been a place of consequence in its time. In one corner of it I found the ruins of a large clumsy castle, chiefly built of flint stones: into these ruins I attempted to penetrate, but the entrance was secured by a gate. From the castle I found my way to the convent, a sad desolate place, formerly the residence of mendicant brothers of the order of St. Francis. I was about to return to the inn, when I heard a loud buzz of voices, and, following the sound, presently reached a kind of meadow, where, upon a small knoll, sat a priest in full canonicals, reading in a loud voice a newspaper, while around him, either erect or seated on the grass, were assembled about fifty vecinos, for the most part dressed in long cloaks, amongst whom I discovered my two friends the curate and friar. A fine knot of Carlist quidnuncs, said I to myself, and turned away to another part of the meadow, where the cattle of the village were grazing. The curate, on observing me, detached himself instantly from the group and followed. "I am told you want a pony," said he; "there now is mine feeding amongst those horses, the best in all the kingdom of Leon." He then began with all the volubility of a chalan to descant on the points of the animal. Presently the friar joined us, who, observing his opportunity, pulled me by the sleeve and whispered, "Have nothing to do with the curate, master, he is the greatest thief in the neighbourhood: if you want a pony, my brother has a much better, which he will dispose of cheaper." "I shall wait till I arrive at Leon," I exclaimed, and walked away, musing on priestly friendship and sincerity.

From * * * * * to Leon, a distance of eight leagues, the country rapidly improved: we passed over several small streams, and occasionally found ourselves amongst meadows in which grass was growing in the richest luxuriance. The sun shone out brightly, and I hailed his re-appearance with joy, though the heat of his beams was oppressive. On arriving within two leagues of Leon, we passed numerous cars and wagons, and bands of people with horses and mules, all hastening to the celebrated fair which is held in the city on St. John's or Midsummer day, and which took place within three days after our arrival. This fair, though principally intended for the sale of horses, is frequented by merchants from many parts of Spain, who attend with goods of various kinds, and amongst them I remarked many of the Catalans whom I had previously seen at Medina and Valladolid.

There is nothing remarkable in Leon, which is an old gloomy town, with the exception of its cathedral, in many respects a counterpart of the church of Palencia, exhibiting the same light and elegant architecture, but, unlike its beautiful sister, unadorned with splendid paintings. The situation of Leon is highly pleasant, in the midst of a blooming country abounding with trees, and watered by many streams, which have their source in the mighty mountains in the neighbourhood. It is, however, by no means a healthy place, especially in summer, when the heats raise noxious exhalations from the waters, generating many kinds of disorders, especially fevers.

I had scarcely been at Leon three days when I was seized with a fever, against which I thought the strength even of my constitution would have yielded, for it wore me almost to a skeleton, and when it departed, at the end of about a week, left me in such a deplorable state of weakness that I was scarcely able to make the slightest exertion. I had, however, previously persuaded a bookseller to undertake the charge of vending the Testaments, and had published my advertisements as usual, though without very sanguine hope of success, as Leon is a place where the inhabitants, with

very few exceptions, are furious Carlists, and ignorant and blinded followers of the old papal church. It is, moreover, a bishop's see, which was once enjoyed by the prime counsellor of Don Carlos, whose fierce and bigoted spirit still seems to pervade the place. Scarcely had the advertisements appeared, when the clergy were in motion. They went from house to house, banning and cursing, and denouncing misery to whomsoever should either purchase or read "the accursed books," which had been sent into the country by heretics for the purpose of perverting the innocent minds of the population. They did more; they commenced a process against the bookseller in the ecclesiastical court. Fortunately this court is not at present in the possession of much authority; and the bookseller, a bold and determined man, set them at defiance, and went so far as to affix an advertisement to the gate of the very cathedral. Notwithstanding the cry raised against the book, several copies were sold at Leon: two were purchased by ex-friars, and the same number by parochial priests from neighbouring villages. I believe the whole number disposed of during my stay amounted to fifteen; so that my visit to this dark corner was not altogether in vain, as the seed of the Gospel has been sown, though sparingly. But the palpable darkness which envelopes Leon is truly lamentable, and the ignorance of the people is so great, that printed charms and incantations against Satan and his host, and against every kind of misfortune, are publicly sold in the shops, and are in great demand. Such are the results of Popery, a delusion which, more than any other, has tended to debase and brutalize the human mind.

I had scarcely risen from the bed where the fever had cast me, when I found that Antonio had become alarmed. He informed me that he had seen several soldiers in the uniform of Don Carlos lurking at the door of the posada, and that they had been making inquiries concerning me.

It was indeed a singular fact connected with Leon, that upwards of fifty of these fellows, who had on various accounts left the ranks of the Pretender, were walking about the streets dressed in his livery, and with all the confidence which the certainty of protection from the local authorities could afford them should any one be disposed to interrupt them.

I learned moreover from Antonio, that the person in whose house we were living was a notorious "alcahuete," or spy to the robbers in the neighbourhood, and that unless we took our departure speedily and unexpectedly, we should to a certainty be plundered on the road. I did not pay much attention to these hints, but my desire to quit Leon was great, as I was convinced that as long as I continued there I should be unable to regain my health and vigour.

Accordingly, at three in the morning, we departed for Galicia. We had scarcely proceeded half a league when we were overtaken by a thunder-storm of tremendous violence. We were at that time in the midst of a wood which extends to some distance in the direction in which we were going. The trees were bowed almost to the ground by the wind or torn up by the roots, whilst the earth was ploughed up by the lightning, which burst all around and nearly blinded us. The spirited Andalusian on which I rode became furious, and bounded into the air as if possessed. Owing to my state of weakness, I had the greatest difficulty in maintaining my seat, and avoiding a fall which might have been fatal. A tremen-

dous discharge of rain followed the storm, which swelled the brooks and streams and flooded the surrounding country, causing much damage amongst the corn. After riding about five leagues, we began to enter the mountainous district which surrounds Astorga: the heat now became almost suffocating; swarms of flies began to make their appearance, and settling down upon the horses, stung them almost to madness, whilst the road was very flinty and trying. It was with great difficulty that we reached Astorga, covered with mud and dust, our tongues cleaving to our palates with thirst.

CHAPTER XXIII.

Astorga—The Inn—The Maragatos—Habits of the Maragatos—The Statue.

WE went to a posada in the suburbs, the only one, indeed, which the place afforded. The court-yard was full of arrieros and carriers, brawling loudly; the master of the house was fighting with two of his customers, and universal confusion reigned around. As I dismounted I received the contents of a wine-glass in my face, of which greeting, as it was probably intended for another, I took no notice. Antonio, however, was not so patient, for on being struck with a cudgel, he instantly returned the salute with his whip, scarifying the countenance of a carman. In my endeavours to separate these two antagonists, my horse broke loose, and rushing amongst the promiscuous crowd, overturned several individuals and committed no little damage. It was a long time before peace was restored: at last we were shown to a tolerably decent chamber. We had, however, no sooner taken possession of it, than the waggon from Madrid arrived on its way to Coruña, filled with dusty travellers, consisting of women, children, invalid officers, and the like. We were now forthwith dislodged, and our baggage flung into the yard. On our complaining of this treatment, we were told that we were two vagabonds whom nobody knew; who had come without an arriero, and had already set the whole house in confusion. As a great favour, however, we were at length permitted to take up our abode in a ruinous building down the yard, adjoining the stable, and filled with rats and vermin. Here there was an old bed with a tester, and with this wretched accommodation we were glad to content ourselves, for I could proceed no farther, and was burnt with fever. The heat of the place was intolerable, and I sat on the staircase with my head between my hands, gasping for breath: soon appeared

Antonio with vinegar and water, which I drank and felt relieved.

We continued in this suburb three days, during the greatest part of which time I was stretched on the tester bed. I once or twice contrived to make my way into the town, but found no bookseller, nor any person willing to undertake the charge of disposing of my Testaments. The people were brutal, stupid, and uncivil, and I returned to my tester bed fatigued and dispirited. Here I lay listening from time to time to the sweet chimes which rang from the clock of the old cathedral. The master of the house never came near me, nor, indeed, once enquired about me. Beneath the care of Antonio, however, I speedily waxed stronger. *"Mon maître,"* said he to me one evening, "I see you are better; let us quit this bad town and worse posada to-morrow morning. *Allons, mon maître! Il est temps de nous mettre en chemin pour Lugo et Galice."*

Before proceeding, however, to narrate what befel us in this journey to Lugo and Galicia, it will, perhaps, not be amiss to say a few words concerning Astorga and its vicinity. It is a walled town, containing about five or six thousand inhabitants, with a cathedral and college, which last is, however, at present deserted. It is situated on the confines, and may be called the capital of a tract of land called the country of the Maragatos, which occupies about three square leagues, and has for its north-western boundary a mountain called Telleno, the loftiest of a chain of hills which have their origin near the mouth of the river Minho, and are connected with the immense range which constitutes the frontier of the Asturias and Guipuscoa.

The land is ungrateful and barren, and niggardly repays the toil of the cultivator, being for the most part rocky, with a slight sprinkling of red brick earth.

The Maragatos are perhaps the most singular caste to be found amongst the chequered population of Spain. They have their own peculiar customs and dress, and never intermarry with the Spaniards. Their name is a clue to their origin, as it signifies "Moorish Goths," and at the present day their garb differs but little from that of the Moors of Barbary, as it consists of a long tight jacket, secured at the waist by a broad girdle, loose short trousers which terminate at the knee, and boots and gaiters. Their heads are shaven, a slight fringe of hair being only left at the lower part. If they wore the turban or barret, they could scarcely be distinguished from the Moors in dress, but in lieu thereof they wear the sombrero, or broad slouching hat of Spain. There can be little doubt that they are a remnant of those Goths who sided with the Moors on their invasion of Spain, and who adopted their religion, customs, and manner of dress, which, with the exception of the first, are still to a considerable degree retained by them. It is, however, evident that their blood has at no time mingled with that of the wild children of the desert, for scarcely amongst the hills of Norway would you find figures and faces more essentially Gothic than those of the Maragatos. They are strong athletic men, but loutish and heavy, and their features, though for the most part well formed, are vacant and devoid of expression. They are slow and plain of speech, and those eloquent and imaginative sallies so common in the conversation of other Spaniards, seldom or never escape them; they have, moreover, a coarse thick pronunciation, and when you hear them speak, you almost imagine that it is some German or English peasant attempting to express himself in the language of the Peninsula. They are constitutionally phlegmatic, and it is very difficult to arouse their anger; but they are dangerous and desperate when once incensed; and a person who knew them well, told me that he would rather face ten Valencians, people infamous for their ferocity and blood-thirstiness, than confront one angry Maragato, sluggish and stupid though he be on other occasions.

The men scarcely ever occupy themselves in husbandry, which they abandon to the women, who plough the flinty fields and gather in the scanty harvests. Their husbands and sons are far differently employed: for they are a nation of arrieros or carriers, and almost esteem it a disgrace to follow any other profession. On every road of Spain, particularly those north of the mountains which divide the two Castiles, may be seen gangs of fives and sixes of these people, lolling or sleeping beneath the broiling sun, on gigantic and heavily laden mules and mules. In a word, almost the entire commerce of nearly one half of Spain passes through the hands of the Maragatos, whose fidelity to their trust is such, that no one accustomed to employ them would hesitate to confide to them the transport of a ton of treasure from the sea of Biscay to Madrid: knowing well that it would not be their fault were it not delivered safe and undiminished, even of a grain, and that bold must be the thieves who would seek to wrest it from the far feared Maragatos, who would cling to it whilst they could stand, and would cover it with their bodies when they fell in the act of loading or discharging their long carbines.

But they are far from being disinterested, and if they are the most trustworthy of all the arrieros of Spain, they in general demand for the transport of articles, a sum at least double to what others of the trade would esteem a reasonable recompense: by this means they accumulate large sums of money, notwithstanding that they indulge themselves in far superior fare to that which contents in general the parsimonious Spaniard;—another argument in favour of their pure Gothic descent: for the Maragatos, like true men of the north, delight in swilling liquors and battening upon gross and luscious meats, which help to swell out their tall and goodly figures. Many of them have died possessed of considerable riches, part of which they have not unfrequently bequeathed to the erection or embellishment of religious houses.

On the east end of the Cathedral of Astorga, which towers over the lofty and precipitous wall, a colossal figure of lead may be seen on the roof. It is the statue of a Maragato carrier who endowed the cathedral with a large sum. He is in his national dress, but his head is averted from the land of his fathers, and whilst he waves in his hand a species of flag, he seems to be summoning his race from their unfruitful region to other climes, where a richer field is open to their industry and enterprise.

I spoke to several of these men respecting the all-important subject of religion; but "I found their hearts gross, and their ears dull of hearing, and their eyes closed." There was one in particular to whom I showed the New Testament, and whom I addressed for a considerable time. He listened or seemed to listen patiently, taking occasionally copious draughts from an immense jug of whitish wine which stood between his knees. After I had concluded he said, "To-morrow I set out for Lugo, whither, I am told, yourself are going. If you wish to send your chest, I have no objection to take it at so much (naming an extravagant price.) As for what you have told me, I understand little of it, and believe not a word of it; but in respect to the books which you have shown me, I will take three or four. I shall not read them, it is true, but I have no doubt that I can sell them at a higher price than you demand."

So much for the Maragatos.

CHAPTER XXIV.

Departure from Astorga—The Venta—The By-Path—Narrow Escape—The Cup of Water—Sun and Shade—Bembibre—Convent of the Rocks—Sunset—Cacabelos—Midnight Adventure—Villafranca.

It was four o'clock of a beautiful morning when we sallied from Astorga, or rather from its suburbs, in which we had been lodged: we directed our course to the north, in the direction of Galicia. Leaving the mountain Telleno on our left, we passed along the eastern skirts of the land of the Maragatos, over broken uneven ground, enlivened here and there by small green valleys and runnels of water. Several of the Maragatan women, mounted on donkeys, passed us on their way to Astorga, whither they were carrying vegetables. We saw others in the fields handling their rude ploughs, drawn by lean oxen. We likewise passed through a small village, in which we, however, saw no living soul. Near this village we entered the high road which leads direct from Madrid to Coruna, and at last, having travelled near four leagues, we came to a species of pass, formed on our left by a huge lumpish hill, (one of those which descend from the great mountain Telleno,) and on our right by one of much less altitude. In the middle of this pass, which was of considerable breadth, a noble view opened itself to us. Before us, at the distance of about a league and a half, rose the mighty frontier chain, of which I have spoken before; its blue sides and broken and picturesque peaks still wearing a thin veil of the morning mist, which the fierce rays of the sun were fast dispelling. It seemed an enormous barrier, threatening to oppose our farther progress, and it reminded me of the fables respecting the children of Magog, who are said to reside in remotest Tartary, behind a gigantic wall of rocks, which can only be passed by a gate of steel a thousand cubits in height.

We shortly after arrived at Manzanal, a village consisting of wretched huts, and exhibiting every sign of poverty and misery. It was now time to refresh ourselves and horses, and we accordingly put up at a venta, the last habitation in the village, where, though we found barley for the animals, we had much difficulty in procuring any thing for ourselves. I was at length fortunate enough to obtain a large jug of milk, for there was plenty of cows in the neighbourhood, feeding in a picturesque valley which we had passed by, where was abundance of grass and trees, and a rivulet broken by tiny cascades. The jug might contain about half a gallon, but I emptied it in a few minutes, for the thirst of fever was still burning within me, though I was destitute of appetite. The venta had something the appearance of a German baiting-house. It con-

sisted of an immense stable, from which was partitioned a kind of kitchen, and a place where the family slept. The master, a robust young man, lolled on a large solid stone bench, which stood within the door. He was very inquisitive respecting news, but I could afford him none; whereupon he became communicative, and gave me the history of his life, the sum of which was, that he had been a courier in the Basque provinces, but about a year since had been despatched to this village, where he kept the post-house. He was an enthusiastic liberal, and spoke in bitter terms of the surrounding population, who, he said, were all Carlists and friends of the friars. I paid little attention to his discourse, for I was looking at a Maragato lad of about fourteen, who served in the house as a kind of hostler. I asked the master if we were still in the land of the Maragatos; but he told me that we had left it behind nearly a league, and that the lad was an orphan and was serving until he could rake up a sufficient capital to become an arriero. I addressed several questions to the boy, but the urchin looked sullenly in my face, and either answered by monosyllables or was doggedly silent. I asked him if he could read. "Yes," said he, "as much as that brute of yours who is tearing down the manger."

Quitting Manzanal, we continued our course. We soon arrived at the verge of a deep valley amongst mountains, not those of the chain which we had seen before us, and which we now left to the right, but those of the Telleno range, just before they unite with that chain. Round the sides of this valley, which exhibited something of the appearance of a horse-shoe, wound the road in a circuitous manner; just before us, however, and diverging from the road, lay a footpath which seemed, by a gradual descent, to lead across the valley and to rejoin the road on the other side, at the distance of about a furlong; and into this we struck in order to avoid the circuit.

We had not gone far before we met two Galicians, on their way to cut the harvests of Castile. One of them shouted, "Cavalier, turn back: in a moment you will be amongst precipices, where your horses will break their necks, for we ourselves could scarcely climb them on foot." The other cried, "Cavalier, proceed, but be careful, and your horses, if sure-footed, will run no great danger; my comrade is a fool." A violent dispute instantly ensued between the two mountaineers, each supporting his opinion with loud oaths and curses; but without stopping to see the result, I passed on, but the path was now filled with stones and huge slaty rocks, on which my horse was continually slipping. I likewise heard the sound of water in a deep gorge, which I had hitherto not perceived, and I soon saw that it would be worse than madness to proceed. I turned my horse, and was hastening to regain the path which I had left, when Antonio, my faithful Greek, pointed out to me a meadow by which, he said, we might regain the high road much lower down than if we returned on our steps. The meadow was brilliant with short green grass, and in the middle .there was a small rivulet of water. I spurred my horse on, expecting to be in the high road in a moment; the horse, however, snorted and stared wildly, and was evidently unwilling to cross the seemingly inviting spot. I thought that the scent of a wolf or some other wild animal might have disturbed him, but was soon undeceived by his sinking up to the knees in a bog. The animal uttered a shrill sharp neigh, and exhibited every sign of the greatest terror, making at the same time great efforts to extricate himself, and plunging forward, but every moment sinking deeper. At last he arrived where a small vein of rock showed itself: on this he placed his fore feet, and with one tremendous exertion freed himself from the deceitful soil, springing over the rivulet, and alighting on comparatively firm ground, where he stood panting, his heaving sides covered with a foamy sweat. Antonio, who had observed the whole scene, afraid to venture forward, returned by the path by which we came, and shortly afterwards rejoined me. This adventure brought to my recollection the meadow with its footpath which tempted Christian from the straight road to heaven, and finally conducted him to the dominions of the giant Despair.

We now began to descend the valley by a broad and excellent carretera or carriage road, which was cut out of the steep side of the mountain on our right. On our left was the gorge, down which tumbled the runnel of of water which I have before mentioned. The road was tortuous, and at every turn the scene became more picturesque. The gorge gradually widened, and the brook at its bottom, fed by a multitude of springs, increased in volume and in sound, but it was soon far beneath us, pursuing its headlong course till it reached level ground, where it flowed in the midst of a beautiful but confined prairie. There was something sylvan and savage in the mountains on the farther side, clad from foot to pinnacle with trees so closely growing that the eye was unable to obtain a glimpse of the hill sides, which were uneven with ravines and gulleys, the haunts of the wolf, the wild boar, and the corso or mountain-stag; the latter of which, as I was informed by a peasant who was driving a car of oxen, frequently descended to feed in the prairie, and were there shot for the sake of their skins, for the flesh, being strong and disagreeable, is held in no account. But notwithstanding the wildness of these

regions, the handiworks of man were visible. The sides of the gorge, though precipitous, were yellow with little fields of barley, and we saw a hamlet and church down in the prairie below, whilst merry songs ascended to our ears from where the mowers were toiling with their scythes, cutting the luxuriant and abundant grass. I could scarcely believe that I was in Spain, in general so brown, so arid and cheerless, and I almost fancied myself in Greece, in that land of ancient glory, whose mountain and forest scenery Theocritus has so well described.

At the bottom of the valley we entered a small village, washed by the brook, which had now swelled almost to a stream. A more romantic situation I had never witnessed. It was surrounded, and almost overhung, by mountains, and embowered in trees of various kinds; waters sounded, nightingales sang, and the cuckoo's full note boomed from the distant branches, but the village was miserable. The huts were built of slate stones, of which the neighbouring hills seemed to be principally composed, and roofed with the same, but not in the neat tidy manner of English houses, for the slates were of all sizes, and seemed to be flung on in confusion. We were spent with heat and thirst, and sitting down on a stone bench, I entreated the woman to give me a little water. The woman said she would, but added that she expected to be paid for it. Antonio, on hearing this, became highly incensed, and speaking Greek, Turkish, and Spanish, invoked the vengeance of the Panhagia on the heartless woman, saying, "If I were to offer a Mahometan gold for a draught of water he would dash it in my face; and you are a Catholic, with the stream running at your door." I told him to be silent, and giving the woman two cuartos, repeated my request, whereupon she took a pitcher, and going to the stream filled it with water. It tasted muddy and disagreeable, but it drowned the fever which was devouring me.

We again remounted and proceeded on our way, which, for a considerable distance, lay along the margin of the stream, which now fell in small cataracts, now brawled over stones, and at other times ran dark and silent through deep pools overhung with tall willows, —pools which seemed to abound with the finny tribe, for large trout frequently sprang from the water, catching the brilliant fly which skimmed along its deceitful surface. The scene was deceitful. The sun was rolling high in the firmament, casting from its orb of fire the most glorious rays, so that the atmosphere was flickering with their splendour, but their fierceness was either warded off by the shadow of the trees or rendered innocuous by the refreshing coolness which rose from the waters, or by the gentle breezes which murmured at intervals over the meadows, "fanning the cheek or raising the hair" of the wanderer. The hills gradually receded, till at last we entered a plain where tall grass was waving, and mighty chestnut trees, in full blossom, spread out their giant and umbrageous boughs.

Beneath many stood cars, the tired oxen prostrate on the ground, the crossbar of the pole which they support pressing heavily on their heads, whilst their drivers were either employed in cooking or were enjoying a delicious siesta in the grass and shade. I went up to one of the largest of these groups and demanded of the individuals whether they were in need of the Testament of Jesus Christ. They stared at one another, and then at me, till at last a young man, who was dandling a long gun in his hands as he reclined, demanded of me what it was, at the same time enquiring whether I was a Catalan, "for you speak hoarse," said he, "and are tall and fair like that family." I sat down amongst them and said that I was no Catalan, but that I came from a spot in the Western Sea, many leagues distant, to sell that book at half the price it cost: and that their souls' welfare depended on their being acquainted with it. I then explained to them the nature of the New Testament, and read to them the parable of the Sower. They stared at each other again, but said that they were poor and could not buy books. I rose, mounted, and was going away, saying to them: "Peace bide with you." Whereupon the young man with the gun rose, and saying, "Caspita! this is odd," snatched the book from my hand, and gave me the price I had demanded.

Perhaps the whole world might be searched in vain for a spot whose natural charms could rival those of this plain or valley of Bembibre, as it is called, with its wall of mighty mountains, its spreading chestnut trees, and its groves of oaks and willows, which clothe the banks of its stream, a tributary to the Minho. True it is, that when I passed through it, the candle of heaven was blazing in full splendour, and every thing lighted by its rays looked gay, glad, and blessed. Whether it would have filled me with the same feelings of admiration if viewed beneath another sky, I will not pretend to determine; but it certainly possesses advantages which at no time could fail to delight, for it exhibits all the peaceful beauties of an English landscape blended with something wild and grand, and I thought within myself, that he must be a restless dissatisfied man, who, born amongst those scenes, would wish to quit them. At the time, I would have desired no better fate than that of a shepherd on the prairies, or a hunter on the hills of Bembibre.

Three hours passed away, and we were in another situation. We had halted and refreshed ourselves and horses at Bembibre, a village of mud and slate, and which possessed little to attract attention: we were now ascending, for the road was over one of the extreme ledges of those frontier hills which I have before so often mentioned; but the aspect of heaven had blackened, clouds were rolling rapidly from the west over the mountains, and a cold wind was moaning dismally. "There is a storm travelling through the air," said a peasant, whom we overtook, mounted on a wretched mule; "and the Aus-

trians had better be on the look out, for it is speeding in their direction." He had scarce spoken, when a light, so vivid and dazzling that it seemed as if the whole lustre of the fiery element were concentrated in it, broke around us, filling the whole atmosphere, and covering rock, tree and mountain with a glare not to be described. The mule of the peasant tumbled prostrate, while the horse I rode reared himself perpendicularly, and turning round, dashed down the hill at headlong speed, which for some time it was impossible to check. The lightning was followed by a peal almost as terrible, but distant, for it sounded hollow and deep; the hills, however, caught up its voice, seemingly repeating it from summit to summit, till it was lost in interminable space. Other flashes and peals succeeded, but slight in comparison, and a few drops of rain descended. The body of the tempest seemed to be over another region. "A hundred families are weeping where that bolt fell," said the peasant when I rejoined him, "for its blaze has blinded my mule at six leagues' distance." He was leading the animal by the bridle, as its sight was evidently affected. "Were the friars still in their nest above there," he continued, "I should say that this was their doing, for they are the cause of all the miseries of the land."

I raised my eyes in the direction in which he pointed. Half way up the mountain, over whose foot we were wending, jutted forth a black frightful crag, which at an immense altitude overhung the road, and seemed to threaten destruction. It resembled one of those ledges of the rocky mountains in the picture of the Deluge, up to which the terrified fugitives have scrambled from the eager pursuit of the savage and tremendous billows, and from whence they gaze down in horror, whilst above them rise still higher and giddier heights, to which they seem unable to climb. Built on the very edge of this crag, stood an edifice, seemingly devoted to the purposes of religion, as I could discern the spire of a church rearing itself high over wall and roof. "That is the house of the Virgin of the Rocks," said the peasant, "and it was lately full of friars, but they have been thrust out, and the only inmates now are owls and ravens." I replied, that their life in such a bleak exposed abode could not have been very enviable, as in winter they must have incurred great risk of perishing with cold. "By no means," said he; "they had the best of wood for their braseros and chimneys, and the best of wine to warm them at their meals, which were not the most sparing. Moreover, they had another convent down in the vale yonder, to which they could retire at their pleasure." On my asking him the reason of his antipathy to the friars, he replied, that he had been their vassal, and that they had deprived him every year of the flower of what he possessed. Discoursing in this manner, we reached a village just below the convent, where he left me, having first pointed out to me a house of stone, with an image over the door, which, he said,

14

once also belonged to the canalla (rabble) above.

The sun was setting fast, and eager to reach Villafranca, where I had determined on resting, and which was still distant three leagues and a half, I made no halt at this place. The road was now down a rapid and crooked descent, which terminated in a valley, at the bottom of which was a long and narrow bridge; beneath it rolled a river, descending from a wide pass between two mountains, for the chain was here cleft, probably by some convulsion of nature. I looked up the pass, and on the hills on both sides. Far above, on my right, but standing forth bold and clear, and catching the last rays of the sun, was the Convent of the Precipices, whilst directly over against it, on the farther side of the valley, rose the perpendicular side of the rival hill, which, to a considerable extent intercepting the light, flung its black shadow over the upper end of the pass, involving it in mysterious darkness. Emerging from the centre of this gloom, with thundering sound, dashed a river, white with foam, and bearing along with it huge stones and branches of trees, for it was the wild Sil hurrying to the ocean from its cradle in the heart of the Austrian hills, and probably swollen by the recent rains.

Hours again passed away. It was now night, and we were in the midst of woodlands, feeling our way, for the darkness was so great that I could scarcely see the length of a yard before my horse's head. The animal seemed uneasy, and would frequently stop short, prick up his ears, and utter a low mournful whine. Flashes of sheet lightning frequently illumined the black sky, and flung a momentary glare over our path. No sound interrupted the stillness of the night, except the slow tramp of the horses hoofs, and occasionally the croaking of frogs from some pool or morass. I now bethought me that I was in Spain, the chosen land of the two fiends, assassination and plunder, and how easily two tired and unarmed wanderers might become their victims.

We at last cleared the woodlands, and after proceeding a short distance, the horse gave a joyous neigh, and broke into a smart trot. A barking of dogs speedily reached my ears, and we seemed to be approaching some town or village. In effect, we were close to Cacabelos, a town about five miles distant from Villafranca.

It was near eleven at night, and I reflected that it would be far more expedient to tarry in this place till the morning than to attempt at present to reach Villafranca, exposing ourselves to all the horrors of darkness in a lonely and unknown road. My mind was soon made up on this point; but I reckoned without my hosts, for at the first posada which I attempted to enter, I was told that we could not be accommodated, and still less our horses, as the stable was full of water. At the second, and here were but two, I was answered from the window by a gruff voice, nearly in the words of Scripture: "Trouble me not: the door is now shut, and my children are with me in bed; I cannot arise to let you in." Indeed, we had no particular desire to enter, as it appeared a wretched hovel, though the poor horses pawed piteously against the door, and seemed to crave admittance.

We had now no choice but to resume our doleful way to Villafranca, which, we were told, was a short league distant, though it proved a league and a half. We found it no easy matter to quit the town, for we were bewildered amongst its labyrinths, and could not find the outlet. A lad about eighteen was, however, persuaded, by the promise of a peseta, to guide us; whereupon he led us by many turnings to a bridge, which he told us to cross, and to follow the road, which was that of Villafranca; he then, having received his fee, hastened from us.

We followed his directions, not, however, without a suspicion that he might be deceiving us. The night had settled darker down upon us, so that it was impossible to distinguish any object, however nigh. The lightning had become more faint and rare. We heard the rustling of trees, and occasionally the barking of the dogs, which last sound, however, soon ceased, and we were in the midst of night and silence. My horse, either from weariness, or the badness of the road, frequently stumbled; whereupon I dismounted, and leading him by the bridle, soon left Antonio far in the rear.

I had proceeded in this manner a considerable way, when a circumstance occurred of a character well suited to the time and place.

I was again amidst trees and bushes, when the horse stopping short, nearly pulled me back. I know not how it was, but fear suddenly came over me, which, though in darkness and in solitude, I had not felt before. I was about to urge the animal forward, when I heard a noise at my right hand, and listened attentively. It seemed to be that of a person or persons forcing their way through branches and brushwood. It soon ceased, and I heard feet on the road. It was the short staggering kind of tread of people carrying a very heavy substance, nearly too much for their strength, and I thought I heard the hurried breathing of men over-fatigued. There was a short pause, during which I conceived they were resting in the middle of the road; then the stamping recommenced, until it reached the other side, when I again heard a simila rustling amidst branches; it continued fo some time and died gradually away.

I continued my road, musing on what had just occurred, and forming conjectures as to the cause. The lighting resumed its flashing, and I saw that I was approaching tall black mountains.

This nocturnal journey endured so long that I almost lost all hope of reaching the town, and had closed my eyes in a doze, though I still trudged on mechanically, leading the horse. Suddenly a voice at a slight distance before me roared out, "*Quien vive?*"

for I had at last found my way to Villafranca. It proceeded from the sentry in the suburb, one of those singular half soldiers half guerillas, called Miguelets, who are in general employed by the Spanish government to clear the roads of robbers. I gave the usual answer, " Espana," and went up to the place where he stood. After a little conversation, I sat down on a stone, awaiting the arrival of Antonio, who was long in making his appearance. On his arrival, I asked if any one had passed him on the road, but he replied that he had seen nothing. The night, or rather the morning, was still very dark, though a small corner of the moon was occasionally visible. On our enquiring the way to the gate, the Miguelet directed us down a street to the left, which we followed. The street was steep, we could see no gate, and our progress was soon stopped by houses and wall. We knocked at the gates of two or three of these houses, (in the upper stories of which lights were burning,) for the purposes of being set right, but we were either disregarded or not heard. A horrid squalling of cats, from the tops of the houses and dark corners, saluted our ears, and I thought of the night arrival of Don Quixote and his squire at Toboso, and their vain search amongst the deserted streets for the palace of Dulcinea. At length we saw light and heard voices in a cottage at the other side of a kind of ditch. Leading the horses over, we called at the door, which was opened by an aged

man, who appeared by his dress to be a baker, as indeed he proved, which accounted for his being up at so late an hour. On begging him to show us the way into the town, he led us up a very narrow alley at the end of his cottage, saying that he would likewise conduct us to the posada.

The alley led directly to what appeared to be the market-place, at a corner house of which our guide stopped and knocked. After a long pause an upper window was opened, and a female voice demanded who we were. The old man replied, that two travellers had arrived who were in need of lodging. "I cannot be disturbed at this time of night," said the woman; " they will be wanting supper, and there is nothing in the house; they must go elsewhere." She was going to shut the window, but I cried that we wanted no supper, but merely a resting place for ourselves and horses—that we had come that day from Astoiga, and were dying with fatigue. "Who is that speaking?" cried the woman. "Surely that is the voice of Gil, the German clock-maker from Pontevedra. Welcome, old companion; you are come at the right time, for my own is out of order. I am sorry I have kept you waiting, but I will admit you in a moment."

The window was slammed to, presently a light shone through the crevices of the door, a key turned in the lock, and we were admitted.

CHAPTER XXV.

Villafranca—The Pass—Gallegan Simplicity—The Frontier Guard—The Horse-Shoe—Gallegan Peculiarities—A Word on Language—The Courier—Wretched Cabins—Host and Guests— Andalusians.

"Ave Maria," said the woman; " whom have we here? This is not Gil the clock-maker." "Whether it be Gil or Juan," said I, " we are in need of your hospitality, and can pay for it." Our first care was to stable the horses, who were much exhausted. We then went in search of some accommodation for ourselves. The house was large and commodious, and having tasted a little water, I stretched myself on the floor of one of the rooms on some matrasses which the woman produced, and in less than a minute was sound asleep.

The sun was shining bright when I awoke. I walked forth into the market-place, which was crowded with people. I looked up and could see the peaks of tall black mountains peeping over the tops of the houses. The town lay in a deep hollow, and appeared to be surrounded by hills on almost every side. " Quel pays babare !" said Antonio, who now joined me, " the farther we go, my master, the wilder every thing looks. I am half

afraid to venture into Galicia; they tell me that to get to it we must clamber up those hills; the horses will founder." Leaving the market-place I ascended the wall of the town and endeavoured to discover the gate by which we should have entered the preceding night; but I was not more successful in the bright sunshine than in the darkness. The town in the direction of Astorga appeared to be hermetically sealed.

I was eager to enter Galicia, and finding that horses were to a certain extent recovered from the fatigue of the journey of the preceding day, we again mounted and proceeded on our way. Crossing a bridge, we presently found ourselves in a deep gorge amongst the mountains, down which rushed an impetuous rivulet, overhung by the high road which leads into Galicia. We were in the far-famed pass of Fuencebadon.

It is impossible to describe this pass or the circumjacent region, which contains some of the most extraordinary scenery in all Spain;

a feeble and imperfect outline is all that I can hope to effect. The traveller who ascends it follows for nearly a league the course of the torrent, whose banks are in some places precipitous, and in others slope down to the waters, and are covered with lofty trees, oaks, poplars, and chestnuts. Small villages are at first continually seen, with low walls, and roofs formed of immense slates, the eaves nearly touching the ground; these hamlets, however, gradually become less frequent as the path grows more steep and narrow, until they finally cease at a short distance before the spot is attained where the rivulet is abandoned and is no more seen, though its tributaries may yet be heard in many a gully, or described in tiny rills dashing down the steeps. Every thing here is wild, strange, and beautiful the hill up which winds the path towers above on the right, whilst on the farther side of a profound ravine rises an immense mountain, to whose extreme altitudes the eye is scarcely able to attain, but the most singular feature of this pass are hanging fields or meadows which cover its sides. In these, as I passed, the grass was growing luxuriantly, and in many the mowers were plying their scythes, though it seemed scarcely possible that their feet could find support on ground so precipitous: above and below were driftways so small as to seem threads along the mountain side. A car, drawn by oxen, is creeping round yon airy eminence; the nearer wheel is actually hanging over the horrid descent; giddiness seizes the brain, and the eye is rapidly withdrawn. A cloud intervenes, and when again you turn to watch their progress, the objects of your anxiety have disappeared. Still more narrow becomes the path along which you yourself are toiling, and its turns more frequent. You have already come a distance of two leagues, and still one third of the ascent remains unsurmounted. You are not yet in Galicia; and you still hear Castilian, coarse and unpolished, it is true, spoken in the miserable cabins placed in the sequestered nooks which you pass by in your route.

Shortly before we reached the summit of the pass thick mists began to envelope the tops of the hills, and a drizzling rain descended. "These mists," said Antonio, "are what the Gallegans call bretima; and it is said there is never any lack of them in their country." "Have you ever visited the country before?" I demanded. "Non, mon maître; but I have frequently lived in houses where the domestics were in part Gallegans, on which account I know not a little of their ways, and even something of their language." "Is the opinion which you have formed of them at all in their favour?" I enquired. "By no means, mon maître; the men in general seem clownish and simple, yet they are capable of deceiving the most clever filou of Paris; and as for the women, it is impossible to live in the same house with them, more especially if they are Camareras, and wait upon the Señora; they are continually breeding dissensions and disputes in the house, and telling tales of the other domestics. I have already lost two or three excellent situations in Madrid, solely owing to these Gallegan chambermaids. We have now come to the frontier, mon maître, for such I conceive this village to be."

We entered the village, which stood on the summit of the mountain, and as our horses and ourselves were by this time much fatigued, we looked round for a place in which to obtain refreshment. Close by the gate stood a building which, from the circumstance of a mule or two and a wretched pony standing before it, we concluded was the posada, as in effect it proved to be. We entered: several soldiers were lolling on heaps of coarse hay, with which the place, which much resembled a stable, was half filled. All were exceedingly ill looking fellows, and very dirty. They were conversing with each other in a strange sounding dialect, which I supposed to be Gallegan. Scarcely did they perceive us when two or three of them, starting from their couch, ran up to Antonio, whom they welcomed with much affection, calling him *companhiero*. "How came you to know these men?" I demanded in French. "*Ces messieurs sont presque tous de ma connoissance*," he replied, "*et, éntre nous, ce sont, des véritables vauriens;* they are almost all robbers and assassins. That fellow with one eye, who is the corporal, escaped a little time ago from Madrid, more than suspected of being concerned in an affair of poisoning; but he is safe enough here in his own country, and is placed to guard the frontier, as you see; but we must treat them civilly, mon maître; we must give them wine, or they will be offended. I know them, mon maître—I know them. Here, hostess, bring an arrobe of wine."

Whilst Antonio was engaged in treating his friends, I led the horses to the stable; this was through the house, inn, or whatever it might be called. The stable was a wretched shed, in which the horses sank to their fetlocks in mud and puddle. On enquiring for barley, I was told that I was now in Galicia, where barley was not used for provender, and was very rare. I was offered in lieu of it Indian corn, which, however, the horses ate without hesitation. There was no straw to be had: coarse hay, half green, being the substitute. By trampling about in the mud of the stable my horse soon lost a shoe, for which I searched in vain. "Is there a blacksmith in the village?" I demanded of a shock-headed fellow who officiated as ostler.

Ostler.—Si, Senhor; but I suppose you have brought horse-shoes with you, or that large beast of yours cannot be shod in this village.

Myself.—What do you mean? Is the black-smith unequal to his trade? Cannot he put on a horse-shoe?

Ostler.—Si, Senhor; he can put on a horse-shoe if you give it him; but there are no horse-shoes in Galicia, at least in these parts.

Myself.—Is it not customary then to shoe the horses in Galicia.

Ostler.—Senhor, there are no horses in Galicia, there are only ponies; and those who bring horses to Galicia, and none but madmen ever do, must bring shoes to fit them; only shoes of ponies are to be found here.

Myself.—What do you mean by saying that only madmen bring horses to Galicia?

Ostler.—Senhor, no horse can stand the food of Galicia and the mountains of Galicia long, without falling sick; and then if he does not die at once, he will cost you in farriers more than he is worth; besides, a horse is of no use here, and cannot perform amongst the broken ground the tenth part of the service which a little pony mare can. By the by, Senhor, I perceive that yours is an entire horse; now out of twenty ponies that you see on the roads of Galicia, nineteen are mares; the males are sent down into Castile to be sold. Senhor, your horse will become heated on our roads, and will catch the bad glanders, for which there is no remedy. Senhor, a man must be mad to bring any horse to Galicia, but twice mad to bring an entero, as you have done."

"A strange country this of Galicia," said I, and went to consult with Antonio.

It appeared that the information of the ostler was literally true with regard to the horse-shoe; at least the blacksmith of the village, to whom we conducted the animal, confessed his inability to shoe him, having none that would fit his hoof: he said it was very probable that we should be obliged to lead the animal to Lugo, which, being a cavalry station, we might perhaps find there what we wanted. He added, however, that the greater part of the cavalry soldiers were mounted on the ponies of the country, the mortality amongst the horses brought from the level ground into Galicia being frightful. Lugo was ten leagues distant: there seemed, however, to be no remedy at hand but patience, and, having refreshed ourselves, we proceeded, leading our horses by the bridle.

We were now on level ground, being upon the very top of one of the highest mountains in Galicia. This level continued for about a league, when we began to descend. Before we had crossed the plain, which was overgrown with furze and brushwood, we came suddenly upon half a dozen fellows armed with muskets and wearing a tattered uniform. We at first supposed them to be banditti: they were, however, only a party of soldiers who had been detached from the station we had just quitted to escort one of the provincial posts or couriers. They were clamorous for cigars, but offered us no farther incivility. Having no cigars to bestow, I gave them in lieu thereof a small piece of silver. Two of the worst looking were very eager to be permitted to escort us to Nogales, the village where we proposed to spend the night. "By no means permit them, mon maître," said Antonio, "they are two famous assassins of

K

my acquaintance, I have known them at Madrid: in the first ravine they will shoot and plunder us." I therefore civilly declined their offer and departed. "You seem to be acquainted with all the cut-throats in Galicia," said I to Antonio, as we descended the hill.

"With respect to those two fellows," he replied, "I knew them when I lived as cook in the family of General Q——, who is a Gallegan: they were sworn friends of the repostero. All the Gallegans in Madrid know each other, whether high or low makes no difference; there, at least, they are all good friends, and assist each other on all imaginable occasions; and if there be a Gallegan domestic in a house, the kitchen is sure to be filled with his countrymen, as the cook frequently knows to his cost, for they generally contrive to eat up any little perquisites which he may have reserved for himself and family."

Somewhat less than half way down the mountain we reached a small village. On observing a blacksmith's shop, we stopped, in the faint hope of finding a shoe for the horse, who for want of one was rapidly becoming lame. To our great joy we found that the smith was in possession of one single horseshoe, which some time previously he had found upon the way. This, after undergoing much hammering and alteration, was pronounced by the Gallegan vulcan to be capable of serving in lieu of a better; whereupon we again mounted, and slowly continued our descent.

Shortly ere sunset we arrived at Nogales, a hamlet situate in a narrow valley at the foot of the mountain in traversing which we had spent the day. Nothing could be more picturesque than the appearance of this spot: steep hills, thickly clad with groves and forests of chestnuts, surrounded it on every side; the village itself was almost embowered in trees, and close beside it ran a purling brook. Here we found a tolerably large and commodious posada.

I was languid and fatigued, but felt little desire to sleep. Antonio cooked our supper, or rather his own, for I had no appetite. I sat by the door, gazing at the wood-covered heights above me, or on the waters of the rivulet, occasionally listening to the people who lounged about the house, conversing in the country dialect. What a strange tongue is the Gallegan, with its half singing half whining accent, and with its confused jumble of words from many languages, but chiefly from the Spanish and Portuguese. "Can you understand this conversation?" I demanded of Antonio, who had by this time rejoined me. "I cannot, mon maître," he replied; "I have acquired at various times a great many words amongst the Gallegan domestics in the kitchens where I have officiated as cook, but am quite unable to understand any long conversation. I have heard the Gallegans say that in no two villages is it spoken in one and the same manner, and that very frequently they do not understand each éther. The worst of this language is, that every body on first hearing it thinks that nothing is more easy than to understand it, as words are continually occurring which he has heard before; but these merely serve to bewilder and puzzle him, causing him to misunderstand every thing that is said; whereas, if he were totally ignorant of the tongue, he would occasionally give a shrewd guess at what was meant, as I myself frequently do when I hear Basque spoken, though the only word which I know of that language is *jaunguicoa*."

As the night closed in I retired to bed, where I remained four or five hours, restless and tossing about; the fever of Leon still clinging to my system. It was considerably past midnight when, just as I was sinking into a slumber, I was aroused by a confused noise in the village, and the glare of lights through the lattice of the window of the room where I lay; presently entered Antonio, half dressed, "Mon maître," said he, "the grand post from Madrid to Coruña has just arrived in the village, attended by a considerable escort, and an immense number of travellers. The road, they say, between here and Lugo, is infested with robbers and Carlists, who are committing all kinds of atrocities; let us, therefore, avail ourselves of the opportunity, and by midday to-morrow we shall find ourselves safe in Lugo." On hearing these words, I instantly sprang out of bed and dressed myself, telling Antonio to prepare the horses with all speed.

We were soon mounted and in the street, amidst a confused throng of men and quadrupeds. The light of a couple of flambeaus, which were borne before the courier, shone on the arms of several soldiers, seemingly drawn up on either side of the road; the darkness, however, prevented me from distinguishing objects very clearly. The courier himself was mounted on a little shaggy pony; before and behind him were two immense portmanteaus or leather sacks, the ends of which nearly touched the ground. For about a quarter of an hour there was much hubbub, shouting, and trampling, at the end of which period, the order was given to proceed. Scarcely had we left the village, when the flambeaus were extinguished, and we were left in almost total darkness; for some time we were amongst woods and trees, as was evident from the rustling of leaves on every side. My horse was very uneasy and neighed fearfully, occasionally raising himself bolt upright. "If your horse is not more quiet, cavalier, we shall be obliged to shoot him," said a voice in an Andalusian accent; "he disturbs the whole cavalcade." "That would be a pity, sergeant," I replied, "for he is a Cordovese by the four sides; he is not used to the ways of this barbarous country." "Oh, he is a Cordovese," said the voice, "vaya, I did not know that; I am from Cordova myself. Pobrecito! let me pat him—yes, I know by his coat that he is my countryman—shoot him, indeed! vaya, I would fain see the

Gallegan devil who would dare to harm him. Barbarous country, *io lo creo:* neither oil nor olives, bread nor barley. You have been at Cordova. Vaya; oblige me, cavalier, by taking this cigar."

In this manner we proceeded for several hours, up hill and down dale, but generally at a very slow pace. The soldiers who escorted us from time to time sang patriotic songs, breathing love and attachment to the young Queen Isabel, and detestation of the grim tyrant Carlos. One of the stanzas which reached my ears, ran something in the following style:—

"Don Carlos is a hoary churl,
    Of cruel heart, and cold;
But Isabel's a harmless girl,
    Of only six years old."

At last the day began to break, and I found myself amidst a train of two or three hundred people, some on foot, but the greater part mounted, either on mules or the pony mares: I could not distinguish a single horse except my own and Antonio's. A few soldiers were thinly scattered along the road. The country was hilly, but less mountainous and picturesque than the one which we had traversed the preceding day; it was for the most part partitioned into small fields which were planted with maize. At the distance of every two or three leagues we changed our escort, at some village where was stationed a detachment. The villages were mostly an assemblage of wretched cabins; the roofs were thatched, dank, and moist, and not unfrequently covered with rank vegetation. There were dunghills before the doors, and no lack of pools and puddles. Immense swine were stalking about, intermingled with naked children. The interior of the cabins corresponded with their external appearance: they were filled with filth and misery.

We reached Lugo about two hours past noon: during the last two or three leagues, I became so overpowered with weariness, the result of want of sleep and my late illness, that I was continually dozing in my saddle, so that I took but little notice of what was passing. We put up at a large posada without the wall of the town, built upon a steep bank, and commanding an extensive view of the country towards the East. Shortly after our arrival, the rain began to descend in torrents, and continued without intermission during the next two days, which was, however, to me but a slight source of regret, as I passed the entire time in bed, and I may almost say in slumber. On the evening of the third day I arose.

There was much bustle in the house, caused by the arrival of a family from Coruña; they came in a large jaunting car, escorted by four carabineers. The family was rather numerous, consisting of a father, son, and eleven daughters, the eldest of whom might be about eighteen. A shabby looking fellow, dressed in a jerkin and wearing a high crowned hat, attended as domestic. They arrived very wet and shivering, and all seemed very disconsolate, especially the father, who was a well-looking middle-aged man. "Can we be accommodated?" he demanded in a gentle voice of the man of the house; "can we be accommodated in this fonda?"

"Certainly, your worship," replied the other; "our house is large. How many apartments does your worship require for your family?"

"One will be sufficient," replied the stranger.

The host, who was a gouty personage and leaned upon a stick, looked for a moment at the traveller, then at every member of his family, not forgetting the domestic, and, without any farther comment than a slight shrug, led the way to the door of an apartment containing two or three flock beds, and which on my arrival I had objected to as being small, dark, and incommodious; this he flung open and demanded whether it would serve.

"It is rather small," replied the gentleman; "I think, however, that it will do."

"I am glad of it," replied the host. "Shall we make any preparations for the supper of your worship and family?"

"No, I thank you," replied the stranger, "my own domestic will prepare the slight refreshment we are in need of."

The key was delivered to the domestic, and the whole family ensconsed themselves in their apartment; before, however, this was effected, the escort were dismissed, the principal carabineer being presented with a peseta. The man stood surveying the gratuity for about half a minute, as it glittered in the palm of his hand; then with an abrupt *Vamos!* he turned upon his heel, and without a word of salutation to any person, departed with the men under his command.

"Who can these strangers be?" said I to the host, as we sat together in a large corridor open on one side, and which occupied the entire front of the house.

"I know not," he replied; "but by their escort I suppose they are people holding some official situation. They are not of this province, however, and I more than suspect them to be Andalusians."

In a few minutes the door of the apartment occupied by the strangers was opened, and the domestic appeared, bearing a cruise in his hand. "Pray, Senor Patron," demanded he, "where can I buy some oil?"

"There is oil in the house," replied the host, "if you want to purchase any; but if as is probable, you suppose that we shall gain a cuarto by selling it you will find some over the way. It is as I suspected," continued the host, when the man departed on his errand, "they are Andalusians, and are about to make what they call gaspacho, on which they will all sup. Oh, the meanness of these Andalusians! they are come here to suck the vitals of Galicia, and yet envy the poor inn-keeper the gain of a cuarto in the oil which they require for their gaspaco. I tell you one thing, master, when that fellow returns, and demands bread and garlic to mix with the oil, I will tell him there is none in the house: as he has bought the oil abroad, so he may the bread and garlic; ay, and the water too, for that matter."

CHAPTER XXVI.

Lugo—The Baths—A Family History—Miguelets—The Three Heads—A Farrier—English Squadron—Sale of Testaments—Coruna—The Recognition—Luigi Piozzi—The Speculation—A Blank Prospect—John Moore.

At Lugo I found a wealthy bookseller to whom I brought a letter of recommendation from Madrid. He willingly undertook the sale of my books. The Lord deigned to favour my feeble exertions in his cause at Lugo. I brought thither thirty Testaments, all of which were disposed of in one day; the Bishop of the place for Lugo is an episcopal see, purchasing two copies for himself, whilst several priests and ex-friars, instead of following the example of their brethren at Leon, by persecuting the work, spoke well of it and recommended its perusal. I was much grieved that my stock of these holy books was exhausted, there being a great demand; and had I been able to supply them, quadruple the quantity might have been sold during the few days that I continued at Lugo.

Lugo contains about six thousand inhabitants. It is situate on lofty ground, and is defended by ancient walls. It possesses no very remarkable edifice, and the cathedral church itself is a small mean building. In the centre of the town is the principal square, a light cheerful place, not surrounded by those heavy cumbrous buildings with which the Spaniards, both in ancient and modern times, have encircled their plazas. It is singular enough that Lugo, at present a place of very little importance, should at one period have been the capital of Spain: yet such it was in the time of the Romans, who, as they were a people not much guided by caprice, had doubtless very excellent reasons for the preference which they gave to the locality.

There are many Roman remains in the vicinity of this place, the most remarkable of which are the ruins of the ancient medicinal baths, which stand on the southern side of the river Minho, which creeps through the valley beneath the town. The Minho in this place is a dark and sullen stream, with high precipitous and thickly wooded banks.

One evening I visited the baths, accompanied by my friend the bookseller. They had been built over warm springs which flow into the river. Notwithstanding their ruinous condition, they were crowded with sick, hoping to derive benefit from the waters, which are still famed for their sanative power. These patients exhibited a strange spectacle as, wrapped in flannel gowns much resembling shrouds, they lay immersed in the tepid waters amongst disjointed stones, and overhung with steam and reek.

Three or four days after my arrival I was seated in the corridor which, as I have already observed, occupied the entire front of the house. The sky was unclouded, and the sun shone most gloriously, enlivening every object around. Presently the door of the apartment in which the strangers were lodged opened, and forth walked the whole family, with the exception of the father, who, I presumed, was absent on business. The shabby domestic brought up the rear, and, on leaving the apartment, carefully locked the door, and secured the key in his pocket. The one son and the eleven daughters were all dressed remarkably well: the boy something after the English fashion, in jacket and trousers, the young ladies in spotless white: they were, upon the whole, a very good looking family, with dark eyes and olive complexions, but the eldest daughter was remarkably handsome. They arranged themselves upon the benches of the corridor, the shabby domestic sitting down amongst them without any ceremony whatever. They continued for some time in silence, gazing with disconsolate looks upon the houses of the suburb, and the dark walls of the town, until the eldest daughter, or señorita as she was called, broke silence with an "*Ay Dios mio!*"

Domestic.—*Ay Dios mio!* we have found our way to a pretty country.

Myself.—I really can see nothing so very bad in the country, which is by nature the richest in all Spain, and the most abundant. True it is that the generality of the inhabitants are wretchedly poor, but they themselves are to blame, and not the country.

Domestic.—Cavalier, the country is a horrible one, say nothing to the contrary. We are all frightened, the young ladies, the young gentleman, and myself; even his worship is frightened, and says that we are come to this country for our sins. It rains every day, and this is almost the first time that we have seen the sun since our arrival. It rains continually, and one cannot step out without being up to the ancles in fango; and then, again, there is not a house to be found.

Myself.—I scarcely understand you. There

appears to be no lack of houses in this neighbourhood.

Domestic.—Excuse me, sir. His worship hired yesterday a house, for which he engaged to pay fourteen pence daily; but when the senorita saw it, she wept, and said it was no house but a hog-sty, so his worship paid one day's rent and renounced his bargain. Fourteen pence a day! why, in our country, we can have a palace for that money.

Myself.—From what country do you come?

Domestic.—Cavalier, you appear to be a decent gentleman, and I will tell you our history. We are from Andalusia, and his worship was last year receiver-general for Granada: his salary was fourteen thousand rials, with which we contrived to live very commodiously—attending the bull funcions regularly, or if there were no bulls, we went to see the novillos, and now and then to the opera. In a word, sir, we had our diversions and felt at our ease; so much so, that his worship was actually thinking of purchasing a pony for the young gentleman, who is fourteen, and must learn to ride now or never. Cavalier, the ministry was changed, and the new comers, who were no friends to his worship, deprived him of his situation. Cavalier, they removed us from that blessed country of Granada, where our salary was fourteen thousand rials, and sent us to Galicia, to this fatal town of Lugo, where his worship is compelled to serve for ten thousand, which is quite insufficient to maintain us in our former comforts. Good bye, I trow, to bull funcions, and novillos, and the opera. Good bye to the hope of a horse for the young gentleman. Cavalier, I grow desperate: hold your tongue, for God's sake! for I can talk no more.

On hearing this history I no longer wondered that the receiver-general was eager to save a cuarto in the purchase of the oil for the gaspacho of himself and family of eleven daughters, one son, and a domestic.

We stayed one week at Lugo, and then directed our steps to Coruña, about twelve leagues distant. We arose before daybreak in order to avail ourselves of the escort of the general post, in whose company we travelled upwards of six leagues. There was much talk of robbers, and flying parties of the factious, on which account our escort was considerable. At the distance of five or six leagues from Lugo, our guard, in lieu of regular soldiers, consisted of a body of about fifty Miguelets. They had all the appearance of banditti, but a finer body of ferocious fellows I never saw. They were all men in the prime of life, mostly of tall stature and of Herculean brawn and limbs. They wore huge whiskers, and walked with a fanfaronading air, as if they courted danger and despised it. In every respect they stood in contrast to the soldiers who had hitherto escorted us, who were mere feeble boys from sixteen to eighteen years of age, and possessed of neither energy nor activity. The proper dress of the Miguelet, if it resembles any thing military, is something akin to that anciently used by the English marines. They wear a peculiar kind of hat, and generally leggings, or gaiters, and their arms are the gun and bayonet. The colour of their dress is mostly dark brown. They observe little or no discipline, whether on a march or in the field of action. They are excellent irregular troops, and when on actual service, are particularly useful as skirmishers. Their proper duty, however, is to officiate as a species of police, and to clear the roads of robbers, for which duty they are in one respect admirably calculated, having been generally robbers themselves at one period of their lives. Why these people are called Miguelets is not easy to say, but it is probable that they have derived this appellation from the name of their original leader. I regret that the paucity of my own information will not allow me to enter into farther particulars with respect to this corps, concerning which I have little doubt that many remarkable things might be said.

Becoming weary of the slow travelling of the post, I determined to brave all risk, and to push forward. In this, however, I was guilty of no slight imprudence, as by so doing I was near falling into the hands of robbers. Two fellows suddenly confronted me with presented carbines, which they probably intended to discharge into my body, but they took fright at the noise of Antonio's horse, who was following a little way behind. This affair occurred at the bridge of Castellanos, a spot notorious for robbery and murder, and well adapted for both, for it stands at the bottom of a deep dell surrounded by wild desolate hills. Only a quarter of an hour previous, I had passed three ghastly heads stuck on poles standing by the way side; they were those of a captain of banditti and two of his accomplices, who had been seized and executed about two months before. Their principal haunt was the vicinity of the bridge, and it was their practice to cast the bodies of the murdered into the deep black water which runs rapidly beneath. Those three heads will always live in my remembrance, particularly that of the captain, which stood on a higher pole than the other two: the long hair was waving in the wind, and the blackened, distorted features were grinning in the sun. The fellows whom I met were the relics of the band.

We arrived at Betanzos late in the afternoon. This town stands on a creek at some distance from the sea, and about three leagues from Coruna. It is surrounded on three sides by lofty hills. The weather during the greater part of the day had been dull and lowering, and we found the atmosphere of Betanzos insupportably close and heavy. Sour and disagreeable odours assailed our olfactory organs from all sides. The streets were filthy, so

were the houses, and especially the posada. We entered the stable; it was strewed with rotton sea-weeds and other rubbish, in which pigs were wallowing; huge and loathsome flies were buzzing around. " What a pesthouse!" I exclaimed. But we could find no other stable, and were therefore obliged to tether the unhappy animals to the filthy mangers. The only provender that could be obtained was Indian corn. At nightfall I led them to drink at a small river which passes through Betanzos. My entero swallowed the water greedily; but as we returned towards the inn, I observed that he was sad, and that his head drooped. He had scarcely reached the stall, when a deep hoarse cough assailed him. I remembered the words of the ostler in the mountains, "The man must be mad who brings a horse to Galicia, and doubly so he who brings an entero." During the greater part of the day the animal had been much heated, walking amidst a throng of at least a hundred pony mares. He now began to shiver violently. I procured a quart of anise brandy, with which, assisted by Antonio, I rubbed his body for nearly an hour, till his coat was covered with a white foam; but his cough increased perceptibly, his eyes were becoming fixed, and his members rigid. "There is no remedy but bleeding," said I. "Run for a farrier." The farrier came. "You must bleed the horse," I shouted; "take from him an azumbre of blood." The farrier looked at the animal, and made for the door. "Where are you going?" I demanded. "Home," he replied. "But we want you here." "I know you do," was his answer; "and on that account I am going." "But you must bleed the horse, or he will die." "I know he will," said the farrier, "but I will not bleed him." "Why?" I demanded. "I will not bleed him, but under one condition." "What is that?" "What is it!—that you pay me an ounce of gold." "Run up stairs for the red morocco case," said I to Antonio. The case was brought; I took out a large fleam, and with the assistance of a stone, drove it into the principal artery of the horse's leg. The blood at first refused to flow, at last, with much rubbing it began to trickle, and then to stream; it continued so for half an hour. "The horse is fainting, mon maître," said Antonio. "Hold him up," said I, "and in another ten minutes we will stop the vein."

I closed the vein, and whilst doing so I looked up into the farrier's face, arching my eyebrows.

"Carracho! what an evil wizard," muttered the farrier, as he walked away. "If I had my knife here I would stick him." We bled the horse again during the night, which second bleeding I believe saved him. Towards morning he began to eat his food.

The next day we departed for Coruña leading our horses by the bridle: the day was magnificent, and our walk delightful. We passed along beneath tall umbrageous trees, which skirted the road from Betanzos to within a short distance of Coruña. Nothing could be more smiling and cheerful than the appearance of the country around. Vines were growing in abundance in the vicinity of the villages through which we passed, whilst millions of maize plants upreared their tall stalks and displayed their broad green leaves in the fields. After walking about three hours, we obtained a view of the bay of Coruna, in which, even at the distance of a league, we could distinguish three or four immense ships riding at anchor. "Can these vessels belong to Spain?" I demanded of myself. In the very next village, however, we were informed, that the preceding evening an English squadron had arrived, for what reason nobody could say. "However," continued our informant, "they have doubtless some design upon Galicia. These foreigners are the ruin of Spain."

We put up in what is called the Calle Real, in an excellent fonda, or posada, kept by a short, thick, comical looking person, a Genoese by birth. He was married to a tall, ugly, but good tempered Basque woman, by whom he had been blessed with a son and daughter. His wife, however, had it seems of late summoned all her female relations from Guipuscoa, who now filled the house to the number of nine, officiating as chambermaids, cooks, and scullions: they were all very ugly, but good natured, and of immense volubility of tongue. Throughout the whole day the house resounded with their excellent Basque and very bad Castilian. The Genoese, on the contrary, spoke little, for which he might have assigned a good reason; he had lived thirty years in Spain, and had forgotten his own language without acquiring Spanish, which he spoke very imperfectly.

We found Coruña full of bustle and life, owing to the arrival of the English squadron. On the following day, however, it departed, being bound for the Mediterranean on a short cruize, whereupon matters instantly returned to their usual course.

I had a depôt of five hundred Testaments at Coruña, from which it was my intention to supply the principal towns of Galicia. Immediately on my arrival I published advertisements, according to my usual practice, and the book obtained a tolerable sale—seven or eight copies per day, on the average. Some people, perhaps, on perusing these details, will be tempted to exclaim: "These are small matters, and scarcely worthy of being mentioned." But let such bethink them, that till within a few months previous to the time of which I am speaking, the very existence of the gospel was almost unknown in Spain, and that it must necessarily be a difficult task to induce a people like the Spaniards, who read very little, to purchase a work like the New Testament, which, though of paramount importance to the soul, affords but slight prospect of amusement to the frivolous and carnally minded. I hoped that the present was the dawning of better and more enlightened times, and rejoiced in the idea that Testaments,

though but few in number, were being sold in unfortunate benighted Spain, from Madrid to the furthermost parts of Galicia, a distance of nearly four hundred miles.

Coruña stands on a peninsula, having on one side the sea, and on the other the celebrated bay, generally called the Groyne. It is divided into the old and new town, the latter of which was at one time probably a mere suburb. The old town is a desolate ruinous place, separated from the new by a wide moat. The modern town is a much more agreeable spot, and contains one magnificent street, the Calle Real, where the principal merchants reside. One singular feature of this street is, that it is laid entirely with flags of marble, along which troop ponies and cars as if it were a common pavement.

It is a saying amongst the inhabitants of Coruña, that in their town there is a street so clean, that puchera may be eaten of it without the slightest inconvenience. This may certainly be the fact after one of those rains which are so frequently drench Galicia, when the appearance of the pavement of the street is particularly brilliant. Coruña was at one time a place of considerable commerce, the greater part of which has latterly departed to Santander, a town which stands a considerable distance down the Bay of Biscay.

"Are you going to Saint James, Giorgio? If so, you will perhaps convey a message to my poor countryman," said a voice to me one morning in broken English, as I was standing at the door of my posada, in the royal street of Coruña.

I looked round and perceived a man standing near me at the door of a shop contiguous to the inn. He appeared to be about sixty-five, with a pale face and remarkably red nose. He was dressed in a loose green great coat, in his mouth was a long clay pipe, in his hand a long painted stick.

"Who are you, and who is your countryman?" I demanded; "I do not know you."

"I know you, however," replied the man; "you purchased the first knife that I ever sold in the market place of N******."

Myself.—Ah, I remember you now, Luigi Piozzi; and well do I remember also, how, when a boy, twenty years ago, I used to repair to your stall, and listen to you and your countrymen discoursing in Milanese.

Luigi.—Ah, those were happy times to me. Oh, how they rushed back on my remembrance when I saw you ride up to the door of the posada. I instantly went in, closed my shop, lay down upon my bed and wept.

Myself.—I see no reason why you should so much regret those times. I knew you formerly in England as an itinerant pedlar, and occasionally as master of a stall in the market-place of a country town. I now find you in a sea-port of Spain, the proprietor, seemingly, of a considerable shop. I cannot see why you should regret the difference.

Luigi (dashing his pipe on the ground.)—Regret the difference! Do you know one thing? England is the heaven of the Piedmontese and Milanese, and especially those of Como. We never lie down to rest but we dream of it, whether we are in our own country or in a foreign land, as I am now. Regret the difference, Giorgio! Do I hear such words from your lips, and you an Englishman! I would rather be the poorest tramper on the roads of England, than lord of all within ten leagues of the shore of the lake of Como, and much the same say all my countrymen who have visited England, wherever they now be. Regret the difference! I have ten letters, from as many countrymen in America, who say they are rich and thriving, and principal men and merchants; but every night, when their heads are reposing on their pillows, their souls *auslandra*, hurrying away to England, and its green lanes and farm-yards. And there they are with their boxes on the ground, displaying their looking glasses and other goods to the honest rustics and their dames and their daughters, and selling away and chaffering and laughing just as of old. And there they are again at nightfall in the hedge alehouses, eating their toasted cheese and their bread, and drinking the Suffolk ale, and listening to the roaring song and merry jests of the labourers. Now, if they regret England so who are in America, which they own to be a happy country, and good for those of Piedmont and of Como, how much more must I regret it, when, after the lapse of so many years, I find myself in Spain, in this frightful town of Coruña, driving a ruinous trade, and where months pass by without my seeing a single English face, or hearing a word of the blessed English tongue.

Myself.—With such a predilection for England, what could have induced you to leave it and come to Spain?

Luigi.—I will tell you: about sixteen years ago a universal desire seized our people in England to become something more than they had hitherto been, pedlars and trampers; they wished, moreover, for mankind are never satisfied, to see other countries: so the greater part forsook England. Where formerly there had been ten, at present scarcely lingers one. Almost all went to America, which, as I told you before, is a happy country, and especially good for us men of Como. Well, all my comrades and relations passed over the sea to the West. I, too, was bent on travelling: but whither? Instead of going towards the West with the rest, to a country where they have all thriven, I must needs come by myself to this land of Spain: a country in which no foreigner settles without dying of a broken heart sooner or later. I had an idea in my head that I could make a fortune at once, by bringing a cargo of common English goods, like those which I had been in the habit of selling amongst the villagers of England. So I freighted half a ship with such goods, for I had been successful in England in my little speculations, and I arrived at Coruña. Here at once my vexations began: disappointment followed disappointment. It was with the utmost difficulty that I could obtain permis-

sion to land my goods, and this only at a considerable sacrifice in bribes and the like; and when I had established myself here, I found that the place was one of no trade, and that my goods went off very slowly, and scarcely at prime cost. I wished to remove to another place, but was informed that, in that case, I must leave my goods behind, unless I offered fresh bribes, which would have ruined me; and in this way I have gone on for fourteen years, selling scarcely enough to pay for my shop and to support myself. And so I shall doubtless continue till I die, or my goods are exhausted. In an evil day I left England and came to Spain.

Myself.—Did you not say that you had a countryman at St. James?

Luigi.—Yes, a poor honest fellow, who, like myself, by some strange chance found his way to Galicia. I sometimes contrive to send him a few goods, which he sells at St. James at a greater profit than I can here. He is a happy fellow, for he has never been in England and knows not the difference between the two countries. Oh, the green English hedge rows! and the alehouses! and, what is much more, the fair dealing and security. I have travelled all over England and never met with ill usage, except once down in the north amongst the Papists, upon my telling them to leave all their mummeries and go to the parish church as I did, and as all my countrymen in England did; for know one thing, Signor Giorgio, not one of us who have lived in England, whether Piedmontese or men of Como, but wished well to the Protestant religion, if he had not actually become a member of it.

Myself.—What do you propose to do at present, Luigi? What are your prospects?

Luigi.—My prospects are a blank, Giorgio; my prospects are a blank. I propose nothing but to die in Coruña, perhaps in the hospital, if they will admit me. Years ago I thought of fleeing, even if I left all behind me, and either returning to England, or betaking myself to America; but is too late now, Giorgio, it is too late. When I first lost all hope, I took to drinking, to which I was never before inclined, and I am now what I suppose you see.

"There is hope in the Gospel," said I, "even for you. I will send you one."

There is a small battery of the old town which fronts the east, and whose wall is washed by the waters of the bay. It is a sweet spot, and the prospect which opens from it is extensive. The battery itself may be about eighty yards square; some young trees are springing up about it, and it is rather a favourite resort of the people of Coruña.

In the centre of this battery stands the tomb of Moore, built by the chivalrous French, in commemoration of the fall of their heroic antagonist. It is oblong and surmounted by a slab, and on either side bears one of the simple and sublime epitaphs for which our rivals are celebrated, and which stand in such powerful contrast with the bloated and bombastic inscriptions which deform the walls of Westminster Abbey;—

"JOHN MOORE,
LEADER OF THE ENGLISH ARMIES,
SLAIN IN BATTLE,
1809."

The tomb itself is of marble, and around it is a quadrangular wall, breast high, of rough Gallegan granite; close to each corner rises from the earth the breech of an immense brass cannon, intended to keep the wall compact and close. These outer erections are, however, not the work of the French, but of the English government.

Yes, there lies the hero, almost within sight of the glorious hill where he turned upon his pursuers like a lion at bay and terminated his career. Many acquire immortality without seeking it, and die before its first ray has gilded their name; of these was Moore. The harassed general, flying through Castile with his dispirited troops before a fierce and terrible enemy, little dreamed that he was on the point of attaining that for which many a better, greater, though certainly not braver man, had sighed in vain. His very misfortunes were the means which secured him immortal fame; his disastrous route, bloody death, and finally, his tomb on a foreign strand, far from kin and friends. There is scarcely a Spaniard but has heard of this tomb, and speaks of it with a strange kind of awe. Immense treasures are said to have been buried with the heretic general, though for what purpose no one pretends to guess. The demons of the clouds, if we may trust the Gallegans, followed the English in their flight, and assailed them with water-spouts as they toiled up the steep winding paths of Fuencebadon; whilst legends the most wild are related of the manner in which the stout soldier fell. Yes, even in Spain, immortality has already crowned the head of Moore;—Spain, the land of oblivion, where the Guadalete* flows

---

CHAPTER XXVII.

Compostella—Rey Romero—The Treasure-Seeker—Hopeful Project—The Church of Refuge—Hidden Riches—The Canon Spirit of Localism—The Leaper—Bones of Saint James.

AT the commencement of August, I found myself at St. James of Compostella. To this place I travelled from Coruña with the courier or weekly post, who was escorted by a strong party of soldiers, in consequence of the distracted state of the country, which was overrun with banditti. From Coruña to Saint James, the distance is but ten leagues; the journey, however, endured for a day and a half. It was a pleasant one, through a most beautiful country, with a rich variety of hill and dale; the road was in many places shaded with various kinds of trees clad in a most luxuriant foliage. Hundred of travellers, both on foot and on horseback, availed themselves of the security which the escort afforded: the dread of banditti was strong. During the journey two or three alarms were given; we, however, reached Saint James without having been attacked.

Saint James stands on a pleasant level amidst mountains: the most extraordinary of these is a conical hill, called the Pico Sacro, or Sacred Peak, connected with which are many wonderful legends. A beautiful old town is Saint James, containing about twenty thousand inhabitants. Time has been when, with the single exception of Rome, it was the most celebrated resort of pilgrims in the world; its cathedral being said to contain the bones of Saint James the elder, the child of the thunder, who, according to the legend of the Romish church, first preached the Gospel in Spain. Its glory, however, as a place of pilgrimage is rapidly passing away.

The cathedral, though a work of various periods and exhibiting various styles of architecture, is a majestic venerable pile, in every respect calculated to excite awe and admiration; indeed, it is almost impossible to walk its long dusky aisles, and hear the solemn music and the noble chanting, and inhale the incense of the mighty censers, which are at times swung so high by machinery as to smite the vaulted roof, whilst gigantic tapers glitter here and there amongst the gloom, from the shrine of many a saint, before which the worshippers are kneeling, breathing forth their prayers and petitions for help, love, and mercy and entertain a doubt that we are treading the floor of a house where God delighteth to dwell. Yet the Lord is distant from that house; he hears not, he sees not, or if he do, it is anger. What availeth that solemn music, that noble chanting, that incense of sweet savour? What availeth kneeling before that grand altar of silver, surmounted by that figure with its silver hat and breast-plate, the emblem of one who, though an apostle and confessor, was at best an unprofitable servant? What availeth hoping for remission of sin by trusting in the merits of one who possessed none, or by paying homage to others

---

* The ancient Lethe.

who were born and nurtured in sin, and who alone, by the exercise of a lively faith granted from above, could hope to preserve themselves from the wrath of the Almighty?

Rise from your knees, ye children of Compostella, or if ye bend, let it be to the Almighty alone, and no longer on the eve of your patron's day address him in the following strain, however sublime it may sound:

" Thou shield of that faith which in Spain we
    revere,
Thou scourge of each foeman who dares to
    draw near ;
Whom the Son of that God who the elements
    tames,
Called child of the thunder, immortal Saint
    James !

" From the blessed asylum of glory intense,
Upon us thy sovereign influence dispense ;
And list to the praises our gratitude aims
To offer up worthily, mighty Saint James.

" To thee fervent thanks Spain shall ever outpour ;
In thy name though she glory, she glories yet
    more
In thy thrice-hallowed corse, which the sanc-
    tuary claims
Of high Compostella, O, blessed Saint James.

" When heathen impiety, loathsome and dread,
With a chaos of darkness our Spain overspread,
Thou wast the first light which dispell'd with
    its flames
The hell-born obscurity, glorious Saint James !

" And when terrible wars had nigh wasted our
    force,
All bright 'midst the battle we saw thee on horse,
Fierce scatt'ring the hosts, whom their fury
    proclaims
To be warriors of Islam, victorious Saint James.

' Beneath thy direction, stretch'd prone at thy
    feet,
With hearts low and humble, this day we intreat
Thou wilt strengthen the hope which enlivens
    our frames,
The hope of thy favour and presence, Saint
    James.

" Then praise to the Son and the Father above,
And to that Holy Spirit which springs from their
    love ,
To that bright emanation whose vividness shames
The sun's burst of splendour, and praise to
    Saint James."

At Saint James I met with a kind and cordial coadjutor in my biblical labours in the bookseller of the place, Rey Romero, a man of about sixty. This excellent individual, who was both wealthy and respected, took up the matter with an enthusiasm which doubtless emanated from on high, losing no opportunity of recommending my book to those who entered his shop, which was in the Azabacheria, and was a very splendid and commodious establishment. In many instances, when the peasants of the neighbourhood came with an intention of purchasing some of the foolish popular story-books of Spain, he persuaded them to carry home Testaments instead, assuring them that the sacred volume was a better, more instructive,

and even far more entertaining book than those they came in quest of. He speedily conceived a great fancy for me, and regularly came to visit me every evening at my posada, and accompanied me in my walks about the town and the environs. He was a man of considerable information, and though of much simplicity, possessed a kind of good-natured humour which was frequently highly diverting.

I was walking late one night alone in the Alameda of Saint James, considering in what direction I should next bend my course, for I had been already ten days in this place ; the moon was shining gloriously, and illumined every object around to a considerable distance. The Alameda was quite deserted ; every body, with the exception of myself, having for some time retired. I sat down on a bench and continued my reflections, which were suddenly interrupted by a heavy stumping sound. Turning my eyes in the direction from which it proceeded, I perceived what at first appeared a shapeless bulk slowly advancing : nearer and nearer it drew, and I could now distinguish the outline of a man dressed in coarse brown garments, a kind of Andalusian hat, and using as a staff the long peeled branch of a tree. He had now arrived opposite the bench where I was seated, when, stopping, he took off his hat and demanded charity in uncouth tones and in a strange jargon, which had some resemblance to the Catalan. The moon shone on gray locks and on a ruddy weather-beaten countenance which I at once recognized : " Benedict Mol," said I, " is it possible that I see you at Compostella?"

" Och, mein Got, es ist der Herr !" replied Benedict. " Och, what good fortune, that the Herr is the first person I meet at Compostella."

Myself.—I can scarcely believe my eyes. Do you mean to say that you have just arrived at this place?

Benedict.—Ow yes, I am this moment arrived. I have walked all the long way from Madrid.

Myself.—What motive could possibly bring you such a distance?

Benedict.—Ow, I am come for the schatz— the treasure. I told you at Madrid that I was coming ; and now I have met you here, I have no doubt that I shall find it, the schatz.

Myself.—In what manner did you support yourself by the way?

Benedict.—Ow, I begged, I betteled, and so contrived to pick up some cuartos ; and when I reached Toro, I worked at my trade of soap-making for a time, till the people said I knew nothing about it and drove me out of the town. So I went on and begged and betteled till I arrived at Orense, which is in this country of Galicia. Ow, I do not like this country of Galicia at all.

Myself.—Why not?

Benedict.—Why ! because here they all beg and bettel, and have scarce any thing for themselves, much less for me whom they know to be a foreign man. O the misery of

Galicia. When I arrive at night at one of their pigsties, which they call posadas, and ask for bread to eat in the name of God, and straw to lie down in, they curse me, and say there is neither bread nor straw in Galicia; and sure enough, since I have been here I have seen neither, only something that they call broa, and a kind of reedy rubbish with which they litter the horses; all my bones are sore since I entered Galicia.

Myself.—And yet you have come to this country, which you call so miserable, in search of treasure?

Benedict.—Ow yaw, but the schatz is buried; it is not above ground; there is no money above ground in Galicia. I must dig it up; and when I have dug it up I will purchase a coach with six mules, and ride out of Galicia to Lucerne; and if the Herr pleases to go with me, he shall be welcome to go with me and the schatz.

Myself.—I am afraid that you have come on a desperate errand. What do you propose to do? Have you any money?

Benedict.—Not a cuart; but I do not care now I have arrived at Saint James. The schatz is nigh; and I have, moreover, seen you, which is a good sign; it tells me that the schatz is still here. I shall go to the best posada in the place and live like a duke till I have an opportunity of digging up the schatz, when I will pay all scores.

"Do nothing of the kind," I replied; "find out some place in which to sleep, and endeavour to seek some employment. In the mean time, here is a trifle with which to support yourself; but as for the treasure which you have come to seek, I believe it only exists in your own imagination." I gave him a dollar and departed.

I have never enjoyed more charming walks than in the neighbourhood of Saint James. In these I was almost invariably accompanied by my friend the good old bookseller. The streams are numerous, and along their wooded banks we were in the habit of straying and enjoying the delicious summer evenings of this part of Spain. Religion generally formed the topic of our conversation, but we not unfrequently talked of the foreign lands which I had visited, and at other times of matters which related particularly to my companion. "We booksellers of Spain," said he, "are all liberals; we are no friends to the monkish system. How indeed should we be friends to it? It fosters darkness, whilst we live by disseminating light. We love our profession, and have all more or less suffered for it; many of us in the times of terror were hanged for selling an innocent translation from the French or English. Shortly after the Constitution was put down by Angoulême and the French bayonets, I was obliged to flee from Saint James and take refuge in the wildest part of Galicia, near Corcubion. Had I not possessed good friends, I should not have been alive now; as it was, it cost me a considera-

ble sum of money to arrange matters. Whilst I was away, my shop was in charge of the ecclesiastical officers. They frequently told my wife that I ought to be burnt for the books which I had sold. Thanks be to God, those times are past, and I hope they will never return."

Once as we were walking through the streets of Saint James, he stopped before a church and looked at it attentively. As there was nothing remarkable in the appearance of this edifice, I asked him what motive he had for taking such notice of it. "In the days of the Friars," said he, "this church was one of refuge, to which if the worst criminals escaped, they were safe. All were protected there save the negros, as they called us liberals." "Even murderers, I suppose?" said I. "Murderers!" he answered, "far worse criminals than they. By the by, I have heard that you English entertain the utmost abhorrence of murder. Do you in reality consider it a crime of very great magnitude?" "How should we not," I replied; "for every other crime some reparation can be made; but if we take away life, we take away all. A ray of hope with respect to this world may occasionally enliven the bosom of any other criminal, but how can the murderer hope?" "The friars were of another way of thinking," replied the old man; "they always looked upon murder as a friolera; but not so the crime of marrying your first cousin without dispensation, for which, if we believe them, there is scarcely any atonement either in this world or the next."

Two or three days after this, as we were seated in my apartment at the posada, engaged in conversation, the door was opened by Antonio, who, with a smile on his countenance, said that there was a foreign *gentleman* below who desired to speak with me. "Show him up," I replied; whereupon almost instantly appeared Benedict Mol.

"This is a most extraordinary person," said I to the bookseller. "You Galicians, in general, leave your country in quest of money; he, on the contrary, is come hither to find some."

Rey Romero.—And he is right. Galicia is by nature the richest province of Spain, but the inhabitants are very stupid, and know not how to turn the blessings which surround them to any account; but as a proof of what may be made out of Galicia, see how rich the Catalans become who have settled down here and formed establishments. There are riches all around us, upon the earth and in the earth.

Benedict.—Ow yaw, in the earth, that is what I say. There is much more treasure below the earth than above it.

Myself.—Since I last saw you, have you discovered the place in which you say the treasure is deposited?

Benedict.—O yes, I know all about it now.

It is buried 'neath the sacristy in the church of San Roque.

Myself.—How have you been able to make that discovery?

Benedict.—I will tell you: the day after my arrival I walked about all the city in quest of the church, but could find none which at all answered to the signs which my comrade who died in the hospital gave me. I entered several and looked about, but all in vain; I could not find the place which I had in my mind's eye. At last the people with whom I lodge, and to whom I told my business, advised me to send for a meiga.

Myself.—A meiga! What is that?

Benedict.—Ow! a haxweib, a witch; the Gallegos call them so in their jargon, of which I can scarcely understand a word. So I consented, and they sent for the meiga! Och! what a weib is that meiga! I never saw such a woman; she is as large as myself, and has a face as round and red as the sun. She asked me a great many questions in her Gallegan, and when I had told her all she wanted to know, she pulled out a pack of cards and laid them on the table in a particular manner, and then she said that the treasure was in the church of San Roque; and sure enough, when I went to that church, it answered in every respect to the signs of my comrade who died in the hospital. O she is a powerful hax, that meiga; she is well known in the neighbourhood, and has done much harm to the cattle. I gave her half the dollar I had from you for her trouble.

Myself.—Then you acted like a simpleton; she has grossly deceived you. But even suppose that the treasure is really deposited in the church you mention, it is not probable that you will be permitted to remove the floor of the sacristy to search for it.

Benedict.—Ow, the matter is already well advanced. Yesterday I went to one of the canons to confess myself and receive absolution and benediction; not that I regard these things much, but I thought this would be the best means of broaching the matter, so I confessed myself, and then I spoke of my travels to the canon, and at last I told him of the treasure, and proposed that if he assisted me we should share it between us. Ow, I wish you had seen him; he entered at once into the affair, and said that it might turn out a very profitable speculation: and he shook me by the hand, and said that I was an honest Swiss and a good Catholic. And I then proposed that he should take me into his house and keep me there till we had an opportunity of digging up the treasure together. This he refused to do.

Rey Romero.—Of that I have no doubt: trust one of our canons for not committing himself so far until he sees very good reason. These tales of treasure are at present rather too stale: we have heard of them ever since the time of the Moors.

Benedict.—He advised me to go to the Captain General and obtain permission to make excavations, in which case he promised to assist me to the utmost of his power.

Thereupon the Swiss departed, and I neither saw nor heard any thing farther of him during the time that I continued at Saint James.

The bookseller was never weary of showing me about his native town, of which he was enthusiastically fond. Indeed, I have never seen the spirit of localism, which is so prevalent throughout Spain, more strong than at Saint James. If their town did but flourish, the Santiagians seemed to care but little if all others in Galicia perished. Their antipathy to the town of Coruña was unbounded, and this feeling had of late been not a little increased from the circumstance that the seat of the provincial government had been removed from Saint James to Coruña. Whether this change was advisable or not, it is not for me who am a foreigner to say; my private opinion, however, is by no means favourable to the alteration. Saint James is one of the most central towns in Galicia, with large and populous communities on every side of it, whereas Coruña stands in a corner, at a considerable distance from the rest. "It is a pity that the vecinos of Coruña cannot contrive to steal away from us our cathedral, even as they have done our government," said a Santiagian; "then, indeed, they would be able to cut some figure. As it is, they have not a church fit to say mass in." "A great pity too, that they cannot remove our hospital," would another exclaim; "as it is, they are obliged to send us their sick, poor wretches. I always think that the sick of Coruña have more ill-favoured countenances than those from other places; but what good can come from Coruña?"

Accompanied by the bookseller, I visited this hospital, in which, however, I did not remain long; the wretchedness and uncleanliness which I observed speedily driving me away. Saint James, indeed, is the grand lazar-house for all the rest of Galicia, which accounts for the prodigious number of horrible objects to be seen in its streets, who have for the most part arrived in the hope of procuring medical assistance, which, from what I could learn, is very scantily and inefficiently administered. Amongst these unhappy wretches I occasionally observed the terrible leper, and instantly fled from him with a "God help thee," as if I had been a Jew of old. Galicia is the only province of Spain where cases of leprosy are still frequent; a convincing proof this that the disease is the result of foul feeding, and an inattention to cleanliness, as the Gallegans, with regard to the comforts of life and civilized habits, are confessedly far behind all the other natives of Spain.

"Besides a general hospital we have likewise a leper-house," said the bookseller. "Shall I show it you? We have every thing at Saint James. There is nothing

lacking; the very leper finds an inn here."
"I have no objection to your showing me
the house," I replied, "but it must be at a
distance, for enter it I will not." Thereupon
he conducted me down the road which leads
towards Padron and Vigo, and pointing to
two or three huts, exclaimed, "That is our
leper-house." "It appears a miserable
place," I replied: "what accommodation
may there be for the patients, and who attends
to their wants?" "They are left to themselves," answered the bookseller, "and probably sometimes perish from neglect: the
place at one time was endowed and had rents
which were appropriated to its support, but
even these have been sequestered during the
late troubles. At present, the least unclean of
the lepers generally takes his station by the
road side, and begs for the rest. See there
he is now."

And sure enough the leper in his shining
scales, and half naked, was seated beneath a
ruined wall. We dropped money into the
hat of the unhappy being, and passed on.

"A bad disorder that," said my friend.
"I confess that I, who have seen so many
of them, am by no means fond of the company of lepers. Indeed, I wish that they
would never enter my shop, as they occasionally do to beg. Nothing is more infec-
tious, as I have heard, than leprosy: there is
one very virulent species, however, which is
particularly dreaded here, the elephantine:
those who die of it should, according to law,
be burnt, and their ashes scattered to the
winds; for if the body of such a leper be
interred in the field of the dead, the disorder
is forthwith communicated to all the corses
even below the earth. Such, at least, is our
idea in these parts. Lawsuits are at present
pending from the circumstance of elephan-
tides having been buried with the other dead.
Sad is leprosy in all its forms, but most so
when elephantine."

"Talking of corses," said I, "do you believe that the bones of St. James are verita-
bly interred at Compostella?"

"What can I say," replied the old man;
"you know as much of the matter as myself. Beneath the high altar is a large stone
slab or lid, which is said to cover the mouth
of a profound well, at the bottom of which
it is believed that the bones of the saint are
interred; though why they should be placed
at the bottom of a well, is a mystery which
I cannot fathom. One of the officers of the
church told me that at one time he and
another kept watch in the church during the
night, one of the chapels having shortly before been broken open and a sacrilege committed. At the dead of night, finding the
time hang heavy on their hands, they took a
crowbar and removed the slab and looked
down into the abyss below; it was dark as
the grave; whereupon they affixed a weight
to the end of a long rope and lowered it
down. At a very great depth it seemed to
strike against something dull and solid like
lead; they supposed it might be a coffin;
perhaps it was, but whose is the question.

CHAPTER XXVIII.

Skippers of Padron—Caldas de los Reyes—Pontevedra—The Notary Public—Insane Barber—An Introduction—Gallegan Language—Afternoon Ride—Vigo—The Stranger—Jews of the Desert—Bay of Vigo—Sudden Interruption—The Governor.

AFTER a stay of about a fortnight at Saint James, we again mounted our horses and proceeded in the direction of Vigo. As we did not leave Saint James till late in the afternoon, we travelled that day no farther than Padron, a distance of only three leagues. This place is a small port, situate at the extremity of a frith which communicates with the sea. It is called for brevity's sake Padron, but its proper appellation is Villa del Padron, or the town of the patron saint; it having been, according to the legend, the principal residence of Saint James during his stay in Galicia. By the Romans it was termed Ira Flavia. It is a flourishing little town, and carries on rather an extensive commerce, some of its tiny barks occasionally finding their way across the Bay of Biscay, and even so far as the Thames and London.

There is a curious anecdote connected with the skippers of Padron, which can scarcely be considered as out of place here, as it relates to the circulation of the Scriptures. I was one day in the shop of my friend the bookseller at Saint James, when a stout, good-humoured-looking priest entered. He took up one of my Testaments, and forthwith burst into a violent fit of laughter. "What is the matter?" demanded the bookseller. "The sight of this book reminds me of a circumstance," replied the other: "about twenty years ago, when the English first took it into their heads to be very zealous in converting us Spaniards to their own way of thinking, they distributed a great number of books of this kind amongst the Spaniards who chanced to be in London; some of them fell into the hands of certain skippers of Padron, and these good folks, on their return to Galicia, were observed to have become on a sudden exceedingly opinionated and fond of dispute. It was scarcely possible to make an assertion in their hearing without receiving a flat contradiction, especially when religious subjects were brought on the carpet. 'It is false,' they would say; 'Saint Paul, in such a chapter and in such a verse, says exactly the contrary.' 'What can you know concerning what Saint Paul or any other saint has written?' the priests would ask them. 'Much more than you think,' they replied; 'we are no longer to be kept in darkness and ignorance respecting these matters;' and then they would produce their books and read paragraphs, making such comments that every person was scandalized: they cared nothing about the Pope, and even spoke with irreverence of the bones of Saint James. However, the matter was soon bruited about, and a commission was despatched from our see to collect the books and burn them. This

was effected, and the skippers were either punished or reprimanded, since which I have heard nothing more of them. I could not forbear laughing when I saw these books; they instantly brought to my mind the skippers of Padron and their religious disputations."

Our next day's journey brought us to Pontevedra. As there was no talk of robbers in these parts, we travelled without any escort and alone. The road was beautiful and picturesque, though somewhat solitary, especially after we had left behind us the small town of Caldas. There is more than one place of this name in Spain; the one of which I am speaking is distinguished from the rest by being called Caldas de los Reyes, or the warm baths of the kings. It will not be amiss to observe, that the Spanish *Caldas* is synonymous with the Moorish *Alhama*, a word of frequent occurrence both in Spanish and African topography. Caldas seemed by no means undeserving of its name: it stands on a confluence of springs, and the place when we arrived was crowded with people who had come to enjoy the benefit of the waters. In the course of my travels I have observed that wherever warm springs are found, vestiges of volcanoes are sure to be nigh; the smooth black precipice, the divided mountain, or huge rocks standing by themselves on the plain or on the hill-side, as if Titans had been playing at bowls. This last feature occurs near Caldas de los Reyes, the side of the mountain which overhangs it in the direction of the south being covered with immense granite stones, apparently at some ancient period eructed from the bowels of the earth. From Caldas to Pontevedra the route was hilly and fatiguing, the heat was intense, and those clouds of flies, which constitute one of the pests of Galicia, annoyed our horses to such a degree that we were obliged to cut down branches from the trees to protect their heads and necks from the tormenting stings of these blood-thirsty insects. Whilst travelling in Galicia at this period of the year on horseback, it is always advisable to carry a fine net for the protection of the animal, a sure and commodious means of defence, which appears, however, to be utterly unknown in Galicia, where, perhaps, it is more wanted than in any other part of the world.

Pontevedra, upon the whole, is certainly entitled to the appellation of a magnificent town, some of its public edifices, especially the convents, being such as are nowhere to be found but in Spain and Italy. It is surrounded by a wall of hewn stone, and stands at the end of a creek into which the river Levroz disembogues. It is said to have been founded

16

L

by a colony of Greeks, whose captain was no less a personage than Teucer the Telemonian. It was in former times a place of considerable commerce; and near its port are to be seen the ruins of a farol, or lighthouse, said to be of great antiquity. The port, however, is at a considerable distance from the town, and is shallow and incommodious. The whole country in the neighbourhood of Pontevedra is inconceivably delicious, abounding with fruits of every description, especially grapes, which in the proper season are seen hanging from the "parras" in luscious luxuriance. An old Andalusian author has said that it produces as many orange and citron trees as the neighbourhood of Cordova. Its oranges are, however, by no means good, and cannot compete with those of Andalusia. The Pontevedrians boast that their land produces two crops every year, and that whilst they are gathering in one they may be seen ploughing and sowing another. They may well be proud of their country, which is certainly a highly favoured spot.

The town itself is in a state of great decay, and notwithstanding the magnificence of its public edifices, we found more than the usual amount of Galician filth and misery. The posada was one of the most wretched description, and to mend the matter, the hostess was a most intolerable scold and shrew. Antonio having found fault with the quality of some provision which she produced, she cursed him most immoderately in the country language, which was the only one she spoke, and threatened that if he attempted to breed any disturbance in her house, to turn the horses, himself, and his master forthwith out of doors. Socrates himself, however, could not have conducted himself on this occasion with greater forbearance than Antonio, who shrugged his shoulders, muttered something in Greek, and then was silent.

"Where does the notary public live?" I demanded. Now, the notary public vended books, and to this personage I was recommended by my friend at Saint James. A boy conducted me to the house of Señor Garcia, for such was his name. I found him a brisk, active, talkative little man of forty. He undertook with great alacrity the sale of my Testaments, and in a twinkling sold two to a client who was waiting in the office and appeared to be from the country. He was an enthusiastic patriot, but of course in a local sense, for he cared for no other country than Pontevedra.

"Those fellows of Vigo," said he, "say their town is a better one than ours, and that it is more deserving to be the capital of this part of Galicia. Did you ever hear such folly? I tell you what, friend, I should not care if Vigo were burnt, and all the fools and rascals within it. Would you ever think of comparing Vigo with Pontevedra?"

"I don't know," I replied; "I have never been at Vigo, but I have heard say that the bay of Vigo is the finest in the world."

"Bay! my good sir. Bay! yes, the rascals have a bay, and it is that bay of theirs which has robbed us of all our commerce. But what needs the capital of a district with a bay? It is public edifices that it wants, where the provincial deputies can meet to transact their business; now, so far from there being a commodious public edifice, there is not a decent house in all Vigo. Bay! yes, they have a bay, but have they water fit to drink? Have they a fountain? Yes, they have, and the water is so brackish that it would burst the stomach of a horse. I hope, my dear sir, that you have not come all this distance to take the part of such a gang of pirates as those of Vigo."

"I am not come to take their part," I replied; "indeed, I was not aware that they wanted my assistance in this dispute. I am merely carrying to them the New Testament, of which they evidently stand in much need, if they are such knaves and scoundrels as you represent them."

"Represent them, my dear sir. Does not the matter speak for itself? Do they not say that their town is better than ours, more fit to be the capital of a district, *que disparate! que briboneria!*"

"Is there a bookseller's shop at Vigo?" I inquired.

"There was one," he replied, "kept by an insane barber. I am glad, for your sake, that it is broken up, and the fellow vanished; he would have played you one of two tricks: he would either have cut your throat with his razor, under pretence of shaving you, or have taken your books and never have accounted to you for the proceeds. Bay! I never could see what right such an owl's nest as Vigo has to a bay."

No person could exhibit greater kindness to another, than did the notary public to myself, as soon as I had convinced him that I had no intention of siding with the men of Vigo against Pontevedra. It was now six o'clock in the evening, and he forthwith conducted me to a confectioner's shop, where he treated me with an iced cream and a small cup of chocolate. From hence, we walked about the city, the notary showing the various edifices, especially the Convent of the Jesuits: "See that front," said he, "what do you think of it?"

I expressed to him the admiration which I really felt, and by so doing entirely won the good notary's heart: "I suppose there is nothing like that at Vigo?" said I. He looked at me for a moment, winked, gave a short triumphant chuckle, and then proceeded on his way, walking at a tremendous rate. The Señor Garcia was dressed in all respects as any English notary might be: he wore a white hat, brown frock coat, drab breeches buttoned at the knees, white stockings, and well blacked shoes. But I never saw an English notary walk so fast: it could scarcely be called walking: it seemed more like a succession of galvanic leaps and bounds. I found it impossible to keep up with him; "Where are you conducting me?" I at last demanded, quite breathless.

"To the house of the cleverest man in Spain," he replied, "to whom I intend to introduce you; for you must not think that Pontevedra has nothing to boast of but its splendid edifices and its beautiful country; it produces more illustrious minds than any other town in Spain. Did you ever hear of the grand Tamerlane?"

"Oh, yes," said I, "but he did not come from Pontevedra or its neighbourhood: he came from the steppes of Tartary, near the river Oxus."

"I know he did," replied the notary, "but what I mean to say is, that when Enrique the Third wanted an ambassador to send to that African, the only man he could find suited to the enterprise, was a knight of Pontevedra, Don * * * * * by name. Let the men of Vigo contradict that fact if they can."

We entered a large portal and ascended a splendid staircase, at the top of which the notary knocked at a small door: "Who is the gentleman to whom you are about to introduce me?" demanded I.

"It is the Advocate * * * *," replied Garcia; "he is the cleverest man in Spain, and understands all languages and sciences."

We were admitted by a respectable-looking female, to all appearance a housekeeper, who, on being questioned, informed us that the Advocate was at home, and forthwith conducted us to an immense room, or rather library, the walls being covered with books, except in two or three places, where hung some fine pictures of the ancient Spanish school. There was a rich mellow light in the apartment, streaming through a window of stained glass, which looked to the west. Behind the table sat the Advocate, on whom I looked with no little interest: his forehead was high and wrinkled, and there was much gravity on his features, which were quite Spanish. He was dressed in a long robe, and might be about sixty; he sat reading behind a large table, and on our entrance half raised himself and bowed slightly.

The notary public saluted him most profoundly, and, in an under voice, hoped that he might be permitted to introduce a friend of his, an English gentleman, who was travelling through Galicia.

"I am very glad to see him," said the Advocate, "but I hope he speaks Castilian, else we can have but little communication; for, although I can read both French and Latin, I cannot speak them."

"He speaks, sir, almost as good Spanish," said the notary, "as a native of Pontevedra."

"The natives of Pontevedra," I replied, "appear to be better versed in Gallegan than in Castilian, for the greater part of the conversation which I hear in the streets is carried on in the former dialect."

"The last gentleman which my friend Garcia introduced to me," said the Advocate, "was a Portuguese, who spoke little or no Spanish. It is said that the Gallegan and Portuguese are very similar, but when we attempted to converse in the two languages, we found it impossible. I understood little of what he said, whilst my Gallegan was quite unintelligible to him. Can you understand our country dialect?" he continued.

"Very little of it," I replied; "which I believe chiefly proceeds from the peculiar accent and uncouth enunciation of the Gallegans, for their language is certainly almost entirely composed of Spanish and Portuguese words."

"So you are an Englishman," said the Advocate. "Your countrymen have committed much damage in times past in these regions, if we may trust our histories."

"Yes," said I, "they sank your galleons and burned your finest men-of-war in Vigo Bay, and under old Cobham, levied a contribution of forty thousand pounds sterling on this very town of Pontevedra."

"Any foreign power," interrupted the notary public, "has a clear right to attack Vigo, but I cannot conceive what plea your countryman could urge for distressing Pontevedra, which is a respectable town, and could never have offended them."

"Señor Cavalier," said the Advocate, "I will show you my library. Here is a curious work, a collection of poems, written mostly in Gallegan, by the Curate of Fruime. He is our national poet, and we are very proud of him."

We stopped upwards of an hour with the Advocate, whose conversation, if it did not convince me that he was the cleverest man in Spain, was, upon the whole, highly interesting, and who certainly possessed an extensive store of general information, though he was by no means the profound philologist which the notary had represented him to be.

When I was about to depart from Pontevedra, in the afternoon of the next day, the Señor Garcia stood by the side of my horse, and having embraced me, thrust a small pamphlet into my hand: "This book," said he, "contains a description of Pontevedra. Wherever you go, speak well of Pontevedra." I nodded. "Stay," said he, "my dear friend, I have heard of your society, and will do my best to further its views. I am quite disinterested, but if at any future time you should have an opportunity in speaking in print of Señor Garcia, the notary public of Pontevedra,—you understand me,—I wish you would do so."

"I will," said I.

It was a pleasant afternoon's ride from Pontevedra to Vigo, the distance being only four leagues. As we approached the latter town, the country became exceedingly mountainous, though scarcely any thing could exceed the beauty of the surrounding scenery. The sides of the hills were for the most part clothed with luxuriant forests, even to the very summits, though occasionally a flinty and naked peak would present itself, rising to the clouds. As the evening came on, the route along which we advanced became very gloomy, the hills and forests enwrapping it in deep shade. It appeared, however, to be well frequented: numerous cars were creaking along it, and both horsemen and pedestrians were continually passing us. The villages were frequent. Vines, supported on parras, were growing, if possible, in still greater abundance than in the neighbourhood of Pontevedra. Life and activity seemed to pervade every thing. The hum of insects, the cheerful bark of dogs, the rude songs of Galicia, were blended together in pleasant symphony. So delicious was my ride, that I almost regretted when we entered the gate of Vigo.

The town occupies the lower part of a lofty hill, which, as it ascends, becomes extremely steep and precipitous, and the top of which is crowned with a strong fort or castle. It is a small, compact place, surrounded with low walls; the streets are narrow, steep, and winding, and in the middle of the town is a small square.

There is rather an extensive faubourg extending along the shore of the bay. We found an excellent posada, kept by a man and woman from the Basque provinces, who were both civil and intelligent. The town seemed to be crowded, and resounded with noise and merriment. The people were making a wretched attempt at an illumination, in consequence of some victory lately gained, or pretended to have been gained, over the forces of the Pretender. Military uniforms were glancing about in every direction. To increase the bustle, a troop of Portuguese players had lately arrived from Oporto, and their first representation was to take place this evening. "Is the play to be performed in Spanish?" I demanded. "No," was the reply; "and on that account every person is so eager to go; which would not be the case if it were in a language which they could understand."

On the morning of the next day I was seated at breakfast in a large apartment which looked out upon the Plaza Mayor, or great square of the good town of Vigo. The sun was shining very brilliantly, and all around looked lively and gay. Presently a stranger entered, and bowing profoundly, stationed himself at the window, where he remained a considerable time in silence. He was a man of very remarkable appearance, of about thirty-five. His features were of perfect symmetry, and I may almost say, of perfect beauty. His hair was the darkest I had ever seen, glossy and shining; his eyes large, black, and melancholy; but that which most struck me was his complexion. It might be called olive, it is true, but it was a livid olive. He was dressed in the very first style of French fashion. Around his neck was a massive gold chain, while upon his fingers were large rings, in one of which was set a magnificent ruby. Who can that man be? thought I;— Spaniard or Portuguese, perhaps a Creole. I asked him an indifferent question in Spanish, to which he forthwith replied in that language, but his accent convinced me that he was neither Spaniard nor Portuguese.

"I presume I am speaking to an English man, Sir?" said he, in as good English as was possible for one not an Englishman to speak.

Myself.—You know me to be an Englishman; but I should find some difficulty in guessing to what country you belong.

Stranger.—May I take a seat?

Myself.—A singular question. Have you not as much right to sit in the public apartment of an inn as myself?

Stranger.—I am not certain of that. The people here are not in general very gratified at seeing me seated by their side.

Myself.—Perhaps owing to your political opinions, or to some crime which it may have been your misfortune to commit?

Stranger.—I have no political opinions, and I am not aware that I ever committed any particular crime,—I am hated for my country and my religion.

Myself.—Perhaps I am speaking to a Protestant, like myself?

Stranger.—I am no Protestant. If I were, they would be cautious here of showing their dislike, for I should then have a government and a consul to protect me. I am a Jew—a Barbary Jew, a subject of Abderrahman.

Myself.—If that be the case, you can scarcely complain of being looked upon with dislike in this country, since in Barbary the Jews are slaves.

Stranger.—In most parts, I grant you, but not where I was born, which was far up the country, near the deserts. There the Jews are free, and are feared, and are as valiant men as the Moslems themselves; as able to tame the steed, or to fire the gun. The Jews of our tribe are not slaves, and I like not to be treated as a slave either by Christian or Moor.

Myself.—Your history must be a curious one, I would fain hear it.

Stranger.—My history I shall tell to no one. I have travelled much, I have been in commerce and have thriven. I am at present established in Portugal, but I love not the people of Catholic countries, and least of all these of Spain. I have lately experienced the most shameful injustice in the Aduana of this town, and when I complained, they laughed at me and called me Jew. Wherever he turns the Jew is reviled, save in your country, and on that account my blood always warms when I see an Englishman. You are a stranger here. Can I do aught for you? You may command me.

Myself.—I thank you heartily, but I am in need of no assistance.

Stranger.—Have you any bills? I will accept them if you have.

Myself.—I have no need of assistance; but you may do me a favour by accepting of a book.

Stranger.—I will receive it with thanks. I know what it is. What a singular people! The same dress, the same look, the same book. Pelham gave me one in Egypt. Farewell! Your Jesus was a good man, perhaps a prophet; but . . . farewell!

Well may the people of Pontevedra envy the natives of Vigo their bay, with which, in many respects, none other in the world can compare. On every side it is defended by steep and sublime hills, save on the part of the west, where is the outlet to the Atlantic; but in the midst of this outlet, up towers a huge rocky wall, or island, which breaks the swell, and prevents the billows of the western sea from pouring through in full violence. On either side of this island is a passage, so broad that navies might pass through at all times in safety. The bay itself is oblong, running far into the land, and so capacious, that a thousand sail of the line might ride in it uncrowded. The waters are dark, still, and deep, without quicksands or shallows, so that the proudest man-of-war might lie within a stone's throw of the town ramparts without any fear of injuring her keel.

Of many a strange event, and of many a mighty preparation has this bay been the scene. It was here that the bulky dragons of the grand armada were mustered, and it was from hence that, fraught with the pomp, power, and terror of Old Spain, the monster fleet, spreading its enormous sails to the wind, and bent on the ruin of the Lutheran isle, proudly steered;—that fleet, to build and man which half the forests of Galicia had been felled, and all the mariners impressed from the thousand bays and creeks of the stern Cantabrian shore. It was here that the united flags of Holland and England triumphed over the pride of Spain and France; when the burning timbers of exploded war-ships soared above the tops of the Gallegan hills, and blazing galleons sank with their treasure-chests whilst drifting in the direction of Sampayo. It was on the shores of this bay that the English guards first emptied Spanish bodegas, whilst the bombs of Cobham were crushing the roofs of the castle of Castro, and the vecinos of Pontevedra buried their doubloons in cellars, and flying posts were conveying to Lugo and Orensee the news of the heretic invasion and the disaster of Vigo. All these events occurred to my mind as I stood far up the hill, at a short distance from the fort, surveying the bay.

"What are you doing there, Cavalier?" roared several voices. "Stay, Carracho! if you attempt to run we will shoot you!" I looked around and saw three or four fellows in dirty uniforms, to all appearance soldiers, just above me, on a winding path which led up the hill. Their muskets were pointed at me. "What am I doing? Nothing, as you see," said I, "save looking at the bay; and as for running, this is by no means ground for a course." "You are our prisoner," said they, "and you must come with us to the fort." "I was just thinking of going there," I replied, "before you thus kindly invited me. The fort is the very spot I was desirous of seeing." I thereupon climbed up to the place where they stood, when they instantly surrounded me, and with this escort I was marched into the fort, which might have been a strong place in its time, but was now rather ruinous. "You are suspected of being a spy," said the corporal, who walked in front. "Indeed," said I. "Yes," replied the corporal, "and several spies have lately been taken and shot."

Upon one of the parapets of the fort stood a young man, dressed as a subaltern officer, and to this personage I was introduced. "We have been watching you this half hour," said he, "as you were taking observations." "Then you gave yourselves much useless trouble," said I. "I am an Englishman, and was merely looking at the bay. Have the kindness now to show me the fort." . . . .

After some conversation, he said, "I wish to be civil to people of your nation, you may therefore consider yourself at liberty." I bowed, made my exit, and proceeded down the hill. Just before I entered the town, however, the corporal, who had followed me unperceived, tapped me on the shoulder. "You must go with me to the governor," said he. "With all my heart," I replied. The governor was shaving when we were shown up to him. He was in his shirt sleeves, and held a razor in his hand. He looked very ill-natured, which was perhaps owing to his being thus interrupted in his toilet. He asked me two or three questions, and on learning that I had a passport, and was the bearer of a letter to the English consul, he told me that I was at liberty to depart. So I bowed to the governor of the town, as I had done to the governor of the fort, and making my exit proceeded to my inn.

At Vigo I accomplished but little in the way of distribution, and after a sojourn of a few days, I returned in the direction of Saint James.

CHAPTER XXIX.

Arrival at Padron—Projected Enterprise.—The Alquilador—Breach of Promise—An odd Companion—A plain Story—Rugged Paths—The Desertion—The Pony—A Dialogue—Unpleasant Situation—The Estadea—Benighted—The Hut—The Traveller's Pillow.

I ARRIVED at Padron late in the evening, on my return from Pontevedra and Vigo. It was my intention at this place to send my servant and horses forward to Santiago, and to hire a guide to Cape Finisterra. It would be difficult to assign any plausible reason for the ardent desire which I entertained to visit this place; but I remembered that last year I had escaped almost by a miracle from shipwreck and death on the rocky sides of this extreme point of the Old World, and I thought that to convey the Gospel to a place so wild and remote, might perhaps be considered an acceptable pilgrimage in the eyes of my Maker. True it is that but one copy remained of those which I had brought with me on this last journey; but this reflection, far from discouraging me in my projected enterprise, produced the contrary effect, as I called to mind that ever since the Lord revealed himself to man it has seemed good to him to accomplish the greatest ends by apparently the most insufficient means; and I reflected that this one copy might serve as an instrument for more good than the four thousand nine hundred and ninety-nine copies of the edition of Madrid.

I was aware that my own horses were quite incompetent to reach Finisterra, as the roads or paths lie through stony ravines, and over rough and shaggy hills, and therefore determined to leave them behind with Antonio, whom I was unwilling to expose to the fatigues of such a journey. I lost no time in sending for an alquilador, or person who lets out horses, and informing him of my intention. He said he had an excellent mountain pony at my disposal, and that he himself would accompany me, but at the same time observed, that it was a terrible journey for man and horse, and that he expected to be paid accordingly. I consented to give him what he demanded, but on the express condition that he would perform his promise of attending me himself, as I was unwilling to trust myself four or five days amongst the hills with any low fellow of the town whom he might select, and who it was very possible might play me some evil turn. He replied by the term invariably used by the Spaniards when they see doubt or distrust exhibited, "No tengo usted cuidado," I will go myself. Having thus arranged the matter perfectly satisfactorily, as I thought, I partook of a slight supper, and shortly afterwards retired to repose.

I had requested the alquilador to call me the next morning at three o'clock; he however did not make his appearance till five, having, I suppose, overslept himself, which was indeed my own case. I arose in a hurry, dressed, put a few things in a bag, not forgetting the Testament which I had resolved to present to the inhabitants of Finisterra. I then sallied forth and saw my friend the alquilador, who was holding by the bridle the pony or jaca which was destined to carry me in my expedition. It was a beautiful little animal, apparently strong and full of life, without one single white hair in its whole body, which was black as the plumage of the crow.

Behind it stood a strange-looking figure of the biped species, to whom, however, at the moment, I paid little attention, but of whom I shall have plenty to say in the sequel.

Having asked the horse-lender whether he was ready to proceed, and being answered in the affirmative, I bade adieu to Antonio, and putting the pony in motion, we hastened out of the town, taking at first the road which leads towards Santiago. Observing that the figure which I have previously alluded to was following close at our heels, I asked the alquilador who it was, and the reason of its following us; to which he replied, that it was a servant of his, who would proceed a little way with us and then return. So on we went at a rapid rate, till we were within a quarter of a mile of the Convent of the Esclavitud, a little beyond which, he had informed me, that we should have to turn off from the high road; but here he suddenly stopped short, and in a moment we were all at a standstill. I questioned the guide as to the reason of this, but I received no answer. The fellow's eyes were directed to the ground, and he seemed to be counting with the most intense solicitude the prints of the hoofs of the oxen, mules, and horses in the dust of the road. I repeated my demand in a louder voice; when, after a considerable pause, he somewhat elevated his eyes, without however looking me in the face, and said that he believed that I entertained the idea that he himself was to guide me to Finisterra, which, if I did, he was very sorry for it, the thing being quite impossible, as he was perfectly ignorant of the way, and, moreover, incapable of performing such a journey over rough and difficult ground, as he was no longer the man he had been, and over and above all that, he was engaged that day to accompany a gentleman over to Pontevedra, who was at that moment expecting him. "But," continued he, "as I am always desirous of behaving like a caballero to every body, I have taken measures to prevent your being disappointed. This person," pointing to the figure, "I have engaged to accompany you. He is a most trustworthy person, and is well acquainted with the route to Finisterra, having been thither several times with this very jaca on which you are mounted. He will, besides, be an agreeable companion to you on the way, as he speaks French and English very well, and has been all over the world." The fellow ceased speaking at last; and I was so struck with his craft, impudence, and villany, that some time elapsed before I could find an answer. I then reproached him in the bitterest terms for his breach of promise, and said that I was much tempted to return to the town instantly, complain of him to the alcalde, and have him punished at any expense. To which he replied, " Sir cavalier, by so doing you will be nothing nearer Finisterra, to which you seem so eager to get. Take my advice, spur on the jaca, for you see it is getting late, and it is twelve long leagues from hence to Corcuvion, where you must pass the night; and from thence to Finisterra is no trifle. As for the man, *no tenga usted cuidado*, he is the best guide in all Galicia, speaks English and French, and will bear you pleasant company."

By this time I had reflected that by returning to Padron I should indeed be only wasting time, and that by endeavouring to have the fellow punished, no benefit would accrue to me; moreover, as he seemed to be a scoundrel in every sense of the word, I might as well proceed in the company of any person as in his. I therefore signified my intention of proceeding, and told him to go back in the Lord's name, and repent of his sins. But having gained one point, he thought he had best attempt another; so placing himself about a yard before the jaca, he said that the price which I had agreed to pay him for the loan of his horse (which by-the-by was the full sum he had demanded) was by no means sufficient, and that before I proceeded I must promise him two dollars more, adding that he was either drunk or mad when he had made such a bargain. I was now thoroughly incensed, and, without a moment's reflection, spurred the jaca which flung him down in the dust, and passed over him. Looking back at the distance of a hundred yards, I saw him standing in the same place, his hat on the ground, gazing after us, and crossing himself most devoutly. His servant, or whatever he was, far from offering any assistance to his principal, no sooner saw the jaca in motion than he ran on by its side, without word or comment, farther than striking himself lustily on the thigh with his right palm. We soon passed the Esclavitud, and presently afterwards turned to the left into a stony broken path leading to fields of maize. We passed by several farm-houses, and at last arrived at a dingle, the sides of which were plentifully overgrown with dwarf oaks, and which slanted down to a small dark river shaded with trees, which we crossed by a rude bridge. By this time I had had sufficient time to scan my odd companion from head to foot. His utmost height, had he made the most of himself, might perhaps have amounted to five feet one inch; but he seemed somewhat inclined to stoop. Nature had gifted him with an immense head, and placed

it clean upon his shoulders, for amongst the items of his composition it did not appear that a neck had been included. Arms long and brawny swung at his sides, and the whole of his frame was as strong built and powerful as a wrestler's; his body was supported by a pair of short but very nimble legs. His face was very long, and would have borne some slight resemblance to a human countenance had the nose been more visible, for its place seemed to have been entirely occupied by a wry mouth and large staring eyes. His dress consisted of three articles: an old and tattered hat of the Portuguese kind, broad at the crown and narrow at the eaves, something which appeared to be a shirt, and dirty canvas trousers. Willing to enter into conversation with him, and remembering that the alquilador had informed me that he spoke languages, I asked him, in English, if he had always acted in the capacity of guide? Whereupon he turned his eyes with a singular expression upon my face, gave a loud laugh, a long leap, and clapped his hands thrice above his head. Perceiving that he did not understand me, I repeated my demand in French, and was again answered by the laugh, leap, and clapping. At last he said in broken Spanish, " Master mine, speak Spanish in God's name, and I can understand you, and still better if you speak Gallegan, but I can promise no more. I heard what the alquilador told you, but he is the greatest embustero in the whole land, and deceived you then as he did when he promised to accompany you. I serve him for my sins; but it was an evil hour when I left the deep sea and turned guide." He then informed me that he was a native of Padron, and a mariner by profession, having spent the greater part of his life in the Spanish navy, in which service he had visited Cuba and many parts of the Spanish Americas, adding, " when my master told you that I should bear you pleasant company by the way, it was the only word of truth that has come from his mouth for a month; and long before you reach Finisterra you will have rejoiced that the servant, and not the master, went with you: he is dull and heavy, but I am what you see." He then gave two or three first-rate summersets, again laughed loudly, and clapped his hands. " You would scarcely think," he continued, " that I drove that little pony yesterday heavily laden all the way from Coruña. We arrived at Padron at two o'clock this morning; but we are nevertheless both willing and able to undertake a fresh journey. *No tenga usted cuidado*, as my master said, no one ever complains of that pony or of me." In this kind of discourse we proceeded a considerable way through a very picturesque country, until we reached a beautiful village at the skirt of a mountain. "This village," said my guide, "is called Los Angeles, because its church was built long since by the angels; they placed a beam of gold beneath it, which they brought down from heaven, and which was once a rafter of God's own house. It runs all the way under the ground from hence to the cathedral of Compostella."

Passing through the village, which he likewise informed me possessed baths, and was much visited by the people of Santiago, we shaped our course to the north-west, and by so doing doubled a mountain which rose majestically over our heads, its top crowned with bare and broken rocks, whilst on our right, on the other side of a spacious valley, was a high range, connected with the mountains to the northward of St. James. On the summit of this range rose high embattled towers, which my guide informed me were those of Altamira, an ancient and ruined castle, formerly the principal residence in this province of the counts of that name. Turning now due west, we were soon at the bottom of a steep and rugged pass, which led to more elevated regions. The ascent cost us nearly half an hour, and the difficulties of the ground were such, that I more than once congratulated myself on having left my own horses behind, and being mounted on the gallant little pony, which, accustomed to such paths, scrambled bravely forward, and eventually brought us in safety to the top of the ascent.

Here we entered a Gallegan cabin, or choza, for the purpose of refreshing the animal and ourselves. The quadruped ate some maize, whilst we two bipeds regaled ourselves on some broa and aguardiente, which a woman whom we found in the hut placed before us. I walked out for a few minutes to observe the aspect of the country, and on my return found my guide fast asleep on the bench where I had left him. He sat bolt upright, his back supported against the wall, and his legs pendulous, within three inches of the ground, being too short to reach it. I remained gazing upon him for at least five minutes, whilst he enjoyed slumbers seemingly as quiet and profound as those of death itself. His face brought powerfully to my mind some of those uncouth visages of saints and abbots which are occasionally seen in the niches of the walls of ruined convents. There was not the slightest gleam of vitality in his countenance, which for colour and rigidity might have been of stone, and which was as rude and battered as one of the stone heads at Icolmkill, which have braved the winds of twelve hundred years. I continued gazing on his face till I became almost alarmed, concluding that life might have departed from its harassed and fatigued tenement. On my shaking him rather roughly by the shoulder, he slowly awoke, opening his eyes with a stare and then closing them again. For a few moments he was evidently unconscious of where he was. On my shouting to him, however, and inquiring whether he intended to sleep all day, instead of conducting me to Finisterra, he dropped upon his legs, snatched up his hat, which lay on the table, and instantly ran out of the door, exclaiming, "Yes, yes, I remember: follow me, captain, and I will lead you to Finisterra in no time." I looked after him, and perceived

that he was hurrying at a considerable pace in the direction in which we had hitherto been proceeding. "Stop!" said I, "stop! Will you leave me here with the pony? Stop! we have not paid the reckoning. Stop!" He, however, never turned his head for a moment, and in less than a minute was out of sight. The pony, which was tied to a crib at one end of the cabin, began now to neigh terrifically, to plunge, and to erect its tail and mane in a most singular manner. It tore and strained at the halter till I was apprehensive that strangulation would ensue. "Woman," I exclaimed, "where are you, and what is the meaning of all this?" But the hostess had likewise disappeared, and though I ran about the choza, shouting myself hoarse, no answer was returned. The pony still continued to scream and to strain at the halter more violently than ever. "Am I beset with lunatics?" I cried, and, flinging down a peseta on the table, unloosed the halter, and attempted to introduce the bit into the mouth of the animal. This, however, I found impossible to effect. Released from the halter, the pony made at once for the door, in spite of all the efforts which I could make to detain it. "If you abandon me," said I, "I am in a pretty situation; but there is a remedy for everything!" with which words I sprang into the saddle, and in a moment more the creature was bearing me at a rapid gallop in the direction, as I supposed, of Finisterra. My position, however diverting to the reader, was rather critical to myself. I was on the back of a spirited animal, over which I had no control, dashing along a dangerous and unknown path. I could not discover the slightest vestige of my guide, nor did I pass any one from whom I could derive any information. Indeed, the speed of the animal was so great, that even in the event of my meeting or overtaking a passenger, I could scarcely have hoped to have exchanged a word with him. "Is the pony trained to this work?" said I mentally. "Is he carrying me to some den of banditti, where my throat will be cut, or does he follow his master by instinct?" Both of these suspicions I however soon abandoned; the pony's speed relaxed, he appeared to have lost the road. He looked about uneasily: at last, coming to a sandy spot, he put his nostrils to the ground, and then suddenly flung himself down, and wallowed in true pony fashion. I was not hurt, and instantly made use of this opportunity to slip the bit into his mouth, which previously had been dangling beneath his neck; I then remounted in quest of the road.

This I soon found, and continued my way for a considerable time. The path lay over a moor, patched with heath and furze, and here and there strewn with large stones, or rather rocks. The sun had risen high in the firmament, and burned fiercely. I passed several people, men and women, who gazed at me with surprise, wondering, probably, what a person of my appearance could be about without a guide in so strange a place. I inquired of two females whom I met whether they had seen my guide; but they either did not or would not understand me, and exchanging a few words with each other, in one of the hundred dialects of the Gallegan, passed on. Having crossed the moor, I came rather abruptly upon a convent, overhanging a deep ravine, at the bottom of which brawled a rapid stream.

It was a beautiful and picturesque spot: the sides of the ravine were thickly clothed with wood, and on the other side a tall, black hill uplifted itself. The edifice was large, and apparently deserted. Passing by it, I presently reached a small village, as deserted, to all appearance, as the convent, for I saw not a single individual, nor so much as a dog to welcome me with his bark. I proceeded, however, until I reached a fountain, the waters of which gushed from a stone pillar into a trough. Seated upon this last, his arms folded, and his eyes fixed upon the neighbouring mountain, I beheld a figure which still frequently recurs to my thoughts, especially when asleep and oppressed by the nightmare. This figure was my runaway guide.

Myself.—Good-day to you, my gentleman. The weather is hot, and yonder water appears delicious. I am almost tempted to dismount and regale myself with a slight draught.

Guide.—Your worship can do no better. The day is, as you say, hot; you can do no better than drink a little of this water. I have myself just drunk. I would not, however, advise you to give that pony any, it appears heated and blown.

Myself.—It may well be so. I have been galloping at least two leagues in pursuit of a fellow who engaged to guide me to Finisterra, but who deserted me in a most singular manner, so much so, that I almost believe him to be a thief, and no true man. You do not happen to have seen him?

Guide.—What kind of a man might he be?

Myself.—A short, thick fellow, very much like yourself, with a hump upon his back, and, excuse me, of a very ill-favoured countenance.

Guide.—Ha, ha! I know him. He ran with me to this fountain, where he has just left me. That man, Sir Cavalier, is no thief. If he is any thing at all, he is a Nuveiro,—a fellow who rides upon the clouds, and is occasionally whisked away by a gust of wind. Should you ever travel with that man again, never allow him more than one glass of anise at a time, or he will infallibly mount into the clouds and leave you, and then he will ride and run till he comes to a water brook, or knocks his head against a fountain—then one draught, and he is himself again. So you are going to Finisterra, Sir Cavalier. Now, it is singular enough, that a cavalier much of your appearance engaged me to conduct him there this morning, I however lost him on the way. So it appears to me our best plan is to travel together until you find your own guide and I find my own master.

It might be about two o'clock in the after-

noon, that we reached a long and ruinous bridge, seemingly of great antiquity, and which, as I was informed by my guide, was called the bridge of Don Alonzo. It crossed a species of creek, or rather frith, for the sea was at no considerable distance, and the small town of Noyo lay at our right. "When we have crossed that bridge, captain," said my guide, "we shall be in an unknown country, for I have never been farther than Noyo, and as for Finisterra, so far from having been there, I never heard of such a place; and though I have inquired of two or three people since we have been upon this expedition, they know as little about it as I do. Taking all things, however, into consideration, it appears to me, that the best thing we can do is to push forward to Corcuvion, which is five mad leagues from hence, and which we may perhaps reach ere nightfall, if we can find the way or get any one to direct us; for as I told you before, I know nothing about it." "To fine hands have I confided myself," said I; "however, we had best, as you say, push forward to Corcuvion, where, peradventure, we may hear something of Finisterra, and find a guide to conduct us." Whereupon, with a hop, skip, and a jump, he again set forward at a rapid pace, stopping occasionally at a choza, for the purpose, I suppose, of making inquiries, though I understood scarcely any thing of the jargon in which he addressed the people, and in which they answered him.

We were soon in an extremely wild and hilly country, scrambling up and down ravines, wading brooks, and scratching our hands and faces with brambles, on which grew a plentiful crop of wild mulberries, to gather some of which we occasionally made a stop. Owing to the roughness of the way we made no great progress. The pony followed close at the back of the guide, so near, indeed, that its nose almost touched his shoulder. The country grew wilder and wilder, and since we had passed a water-mill, we had lost all trace of human habitation. The mill stood at the bottom of a valley shaded by large trees, and its wheels were turning with a dismal and monotonous noise. "Do you think we shall reach Corcuvion to-night?" said I to the guide, as we emerged from this valley to a savage moor, which appeared of almost boundless extent.

Guide.—I do not, I do not. We shall in no manner reach Corcuvion to-night, and I by no means like the appearance of this moor. The sun is rapidly sinking, and then, if there come on a haze, we shall meet the Estadéa.

Myself.—What do you mean by the Estadéa?

Guide.—What do I mean by the Estadéa! My master asks me what I mean by the Estadinha.* I have met the Estadinha but once, and it was upon a moor something like this. I was in company with several women, and a thick haze came on, and suddenly a thousand

* *Inha,* when affixed to words, serves as a diminutive. It is much in use amongst the Gallegans.

lights shone above our heads in the haze, and there was a wild cry, and the women fell to the ground screaming Estadéa! Estadéa! and I myself fell to the ground crying out Estadinha! The Estadea are the spirits of the dead which ride upon the haze, bearing candles in their hands. I tell you frankly, my master, that if we meet the assembly of the souls, I shall leave you at once, and then I shall run and run till I drown myself in the sea somewhere about Muros. We shall not reach Corcuvion this night; my only hope is that we may find some choza upon these moors, where we may hide our heads from the Estadinha."

The night overtook us ere we had traversed the moor; there was, however, no haze, to the great joy of my guide, and a corner of the moon partially illumined our steps. Our situation, however, was dreary enough: we were upon the wildest heath of the wildest province of Spain, ignorant of our way, and directing our course we scarcely knew whither, for my guide repeatedly declared to me, that he did not believe that such a place as Finisterra existed, or if it did exist, it was some bleak mountain pointed out in a map. When I reflected on the character of this guide I derived but little comfort or encouragement: he was at best evidently half-witted, and was by his own confession occasionally seized with paroxysms which differed from madness in no essential respect; his wild escapade in the morning of nearly three leagues, without any apparent cause, and lastly, his superstitious and frantic fears of meeting the souls of the dead upon this heath, in which event he intended, as he himself said, to desert me and make for the sea, operated rather powerfully upon my nerves. I likewise considered that it was quite possible that we might be in the route neither of Finisterra nor Corcuvion, and I therefore determined to enter the first cabin at which we should arrive, in preference to running the risk of breaking our necks by tumbling down some pit or precipice. No cabin, however, appeared in sight: the moor seemed interminable, and we wandered on until the moon disappeared, and we were left in almost total darkness.

At length we arrived at the foot of a steep ascent, up which a rough and broken pathway appeared to lead. "Can this be our way?" said I to the guide.

"There appears to be no other for us, captain," replied the man; "let us ascend it by all means, and when we are at the top, if the sea be in the neighbourhood we shall see it."

I then dismounted, for to ride up such a pass in such darkness would have been madness.

We clambered up in a line, first the guide, next the pony, with his nose as usual on his master's shoulder, of whom he seemed passionately fond, and I bringing up the rear, with my left hand grasping the animal's tail. We had many a stumble, and more than one fall: once, indeed, we were all rolling down the side of the hill together. In about twenty minutes we reached the summit, and looked

around us, but no sea was visible: a black moor, indistinctly seen, seemed to spread on every side.

"We shall have to take up our quarters here till morning," said I.

Suddenly my guide seized me by the hand: "There is lúme, Senhor," said he, "there is lúme." I looked in the direction in which he pointed, and, after straining my eyes for some time, imagined that I perceived, far below and at some distance, a faint glow. "That is lúme," shouted the guide, "and it proceeds from the chimney of a choza."

On descending the eminence, we roamed about for a considerable time, until we at last found ourselves in the midst of about six or eight black huts. "Knock at the door of one of these," said I to the guide, "and inquire of the people whether they can shelter us for the night." He did so, and a man presently made his appearance, bearing in his hand a lighted firebrand.

"Can you shelter a Cavalheiro from the night and the Estadéa?" said my guide.

"From both, I thank God," said the man, who was an athletic figure, without shoes and stockings, and who, upon the whole, put me much in mind of a Munster peasant from the bogs. "Pray enter, gentlemen, we can accommodate you both and your cavalgadura besides."

We entered the choza, which consisted of three compartments; in the first we found straw, in the second cattle and ponies, and in the third the family, consisting of the father and mother of the man who admitted us, and his wife and children.

"You are a Catalan, Sir Cavalier, and are going to your countrymen at Corcuvion," said the man in tolerable Spanish. "Ah, you are brave people, you Catalans, and fine establishments you have on the Gallegan shores; pity that you take all the money out of the country."

Now, under all circumstances, I had not the slightest objection to pass for a Catalan; and I rather rejoiced that these wild people should suppose that I had powerful friends and countrymen in the neighbourhood who were, perhaps, expecting me. I therefore favoured their mistake, and began with a harsh Catalan accent to talk of the fish of Galicia, and the high duties on salt. The eye of my guide was upon me for an instant, with a singular expression, half serious half droll; he, however, said nothing, but slapped his thigh as usual, and with a spring nearly touched the roof of the cabin with his grotesque head. Upon inquiry, I discovered that we were still two long leagues distant from Corcuvion, and that the road lay over moor and hill, and was hard to find. Our host now demanded whether we were hungry, and upon being answered in the affirmative, produced about a dozen eggs and some bacon. Whilst our supper was cooking, a long conversation ensued between my guide and the family, but as it was carried on in Gallegan, I tried in vain to understand it. I believe, however, that it principally related to witches and witchcraft, as the Estadéa was frequently mentioned. After supper I demanded where I could rest: whereupon the host pointed to a trap-door in the roof, saying that above there was a loft where I could sleep by myself, and have clean straw. For curiosity's sake, I asked whether there was such a thing as a bed in the cabin.

"No," replied the man; "nor nearer than Corcuvion. I never entered one in my life, nor any one of my family: we sleep around the hearth, or among the straw with the cattle."

I was too old a traveller to complain, but forthwith ascended by a ladder into a species of loft, tolerably large and nearly empty, where I placed my cloak beneath my head, and lay down on the boards, which I preferred to the straw for more reasons than one. I heard the people below talking in Gallegan for a considerable time, and could see the gleams of the fire through the interstices of the floor. The voices, however, gradually died away, the fire sank low and could no longer be distinguished. I dozed, started, dozed again, and dropped finally into a profound sleep, from which I was only roused by the crowing of the second cock.

CHAPTER XXX.

Autumnal Morning—The World's End—Corcuvion—Duyo—The Cape—A Whale—The Outer Bay —The Arrest—The Fisher-Magistrate—Calros Rey—Hard of Belief—Where is your Passport? —The Beach—A Mighty Liberal—The Handmaid—The Grand Baintham—Eccentric Book— Hospitality.

It was a beautiful autumnal morning when we left the choza and pursued our way to Corcuvion. I satisfied our host by presenting him with a couple of pesetas, and he requested as a favour, that if on our return we passed that way, and were overtaken by the night, we would again take up our abode beneath his roof. This I promised, at the same time determining to do my best to guard against the contingency; as sleeping in the loft of a Gallegan hut, though preferable to passing the night on a moor or mountain, is any thing but desirable.

So we again started at a rapid pace along rough bridle-ways and foot-paths, amidst furze and brushwood. In about an hour we obtained a view of the sea, and directed by a lad, whom we found on the moor employed in tending a few miserable sheep, we bent our course to the north-west, and at length reached the brow of an eminence, where we stopped for some time to survey the prospect which opened before us.

It was not without reason that the Latins gave the name of Finisterræ to this district. We had arrived exactly at such a place as in my boyhood I had pictured to myself as the termination of the world, beyond which there was a wild sea, or abyss, or chaos. I now saw far before me an immense ocean, and below me a long and irregular line of lofty and precipitous coast. Certainly in the whole world there is no bolder coast than the Gallegan shore, from the debouchement of the Minho to Cape Finisterra. It consists of a granite wall of savage mountains, for the most part serrated at the top, and occasionally broken, where bays and friths like those of Vigo and Pontevedra intervene, running deep into the land. These bays and friths are invariably of an immense depth, and sufficiently capacious to shelter the navies of the proudest maritime nations.

There is an air of stern and savage grandeur in every thing around, which strongly captivates the imagination. This savage coast is the first glimpse of Spain which the voyager from the north catches, or he who has ploughed his way across the wide Atlantic: and well does it seem to realize all his visions of this strange land. "Yes," he exclaims, "this is indeed Spain—stern, flinty Spain—land emblematic of those spirits to which she has given birth. From what land but that before me could have proceeded those portentous beings who astounded the Old World and filled the New with horror and blood: Alba, and Philip, Cortez, and Pizarro: stern colossal spectres, looming through the gloom of bygone years, like yonder granite mountains through the haze, upon the eye of the mariner. Yes, yonder is indeed Spain; flinty, indomitable Spain; land emblematic of its sons!"

As for myself, when I viewed that wide ocean and its savage shore, I cried, "Such is the grave, and such are its terrific sides; those moors and wilds, over which I have passed, are the rough and dreary journey of life. Cheered with hope, we struggle along through all the difficulties of moor, bog, and mountain, to arrive at—what? The grave and its dreary sides. Oh, may hope not desert us in the last hour: hope in the Redeemer and in God!"

We descended from the eminence, and again lost sight of the sea amidst ravines and dingles, amongst which patches of pine were occasionally seen. Continuing to descend, we at last came, not to the sea, but to the extremity of a long narrow frith, where stood a village or hamlet; whilst at a small distance, on the western side of the frith, appeared one considerably larger, which was indeed almost entitled to the appellation of town. This last was Corcuvion; the first, if I forget not, was called Ria de Silla. We hastened on to Corcuvion, where I bade my guide make inquiries respecting Finisterra. He entered the door of a wine-house, from which proceeded much noise and vociferation, and presently returned, informing me that the village of Finisterra was distant about a league and a half. A man, evidently in a state of intoxication, followed him to the door: "Are you bound for Finisterra, Cavalheiros?" he shouted.

"Yes, my friend," I replied, "we are going thither."

"Then you are going amongst a flock of drunkards (*fato de borrachos*)," he answered. "Take care they do not play you a trick."

We passed on, and striking across a sandy peninsula at the back of the town, soon reached the shore of an immense bay, the north-westernmost end of which was formed by the far-famed cape of Finisterra, which we now saw before us stretching far into the sea.

Along a beach of dazzling white sand, we advanced towards the cape, the bourn of our journey. The sun was shining brightly, and every object was illumined by his beams. The sea lay before us like a vast mirror, and the waves which broke upon the shore were so tiny as scarcely to produce a murmur. On we sped along the deep winding bay, overhung by gigantic hills and mountains. Strange recollections began to throng upon my mind. It was upon this beach that, according to the tradition of all ancient Christendom, Saint James, the patron saint of Spain, preached the Gospel to the heathen Spaniards. Upon this beach had once stood an immense commercial city, the proudest in all Spain. This now desolate bay had once resounded with the voices of myriads, when the keels and commerce of all the then known world were wafted to Duyo.

"What is the name of this village?" said I to a woman, as we passed by five or six ruinous houses at the bend of the bay, ere we entered upon the peninsula of Finisterra.

"This is no village," said the Gallegan, "this is no village, Sir Cavalier, this is a city, this is Duyo."

So much for the glory of the world! These huts were all that the roaring sea and the tooth of time had left of Duyo, the great city! Onward now to Finisterra.

It was midday when we reached the village of Finisterra, consisting of about one hundred houses, and built on the southern side of the peninsula, just before it rises into the huge bluff head which is called the Cape. We sought in vain for an inn or venta, where we might stable our beast; at one moment we thought that we had found one, and had even tied the animal to the manger. Upon our going out, however, he was instantly untied and driven forth into the street. The few people whom we saw appeared to gaze upon us in a singular manner. We, however, took little notice of these circumstances, and proceeded along the straggling street, until we found shelter in the house of a Castilian shopkeeper, whom some chance had brought to this corner of Galicia,—this end of the world. Our first care was to feed the animal, who now began to exhibit considerable symptoms of fatigue. We then requested some refreshment for ourselves; and in about an hour, a tolerably savoury fish, weighing about three pounds, and fresh from the bay, was prepared for us by an old woman who appeared to officiate as housekeeper. Having finished our meal, I and my uncouth companion went forth and prepared to ascend the mountain.

We stopped to examine a small dismantled fort or battery facing the bay: and whilst engaged in this examination, it more than once occurred to me that we were ourselves the objects of scrutiny and investigation: indeed I caught a glimpse of more than one countenance peering upon us through the holes and chasms of the walls. We now commenced ascending Finisterra; and making numerous and long detours, we wound our way up its flinty sides. The sun had reached the top of heaven, whence he showered upon us perpendicularly his brightest and fiercest rays. My boots were torn, my feet cut, and the perspiration streamed from my brow. To my guide, however, the ascent appeared to be neither toilsome nor difficult. The heat of the day for him had no terrors, no moisture was wrung from his taned countenance: he drew not one short breath; and hopped upon the stones and rocks with all the provoking agility of a mountain goat. Before we had accomplished one half of the ascent, I felt myself quite exhausted. I reeled and staggered. "Cheer up, master mine, be of good cheer, and have no care," said the guide. "Yonder I see a wall of stones; lie down beneath it in the shade." He put his long and strong arm round my waist, and though his stature compared with mine was that of a dwarf, he supported me, as if I had been a child, to a rude wall which seemed to traverse the greatest part of the hill, and served probably as a kind of boundary. It was difficult to find a shady spot: at last he perceived a small chasm, perhaps scooped by some shepherd as a couch in which to enjoy his siesta. In this he laid me gently down, and taking off his enormous hat, commenced fanning me with great assiduity. By degrees I revived, and after having rested for a considerable time, I again attempted the ascent, which, with the assistance of my guide, I at length accomplished.

We were now standing at a great altitude between two bays; the wilderness of waters before us. Of all the ten thousand barks which annually plough those seas in sight of that old cape, not one was to be descried. It was a blue shiny waste, broken by no object save the black head of a spermaceti whale, which would occasionally show itself on the top, casting up thin jets of brine. The principal bay, that of Finisterra, as far as the entrance was beautifully variegated by an immense shoal of sardinhas, on whose extreme skirts the monster was probably feasting. From the northern side of the cape we looked down upon a smaller bay, the shore of which was overhung by rocks of various and grotesque shapes; this is called the outer bay, or, in the language of the country, *Prai do mas de fora*; a fearful place in seasons of wind and tempest, when the long swell of the Atlantic pouring in, is broken into surf and foam by the sunken rocks with which it abounds. Even in the calmest day there is a rumbling and a hollow roar in that bay which fill the heart with uneasy sensations.

On all sides there was grandeur and sublimity. After gazing from the summit of the cape for nearly an hour, we descended.

On reaching the house where we had taken up our temporary habitation, we perceived that the portal was occupied by several men, some of whom were reclining on the floor drinking wine out of small earthen pans, which are much used in this part of Galicia. With a civil salutation I passed on, and ascended the staircase to the room in which we had taken our repast. Here there was a rude and dirty bed, on which I flung myself, exhausted with fatigue. I determined to take a little repose, and in the evening to call the people of the place together, to read a few chapters of the Scripture, and then to address them with a little Christian exhortation. I was soon asleep, but my slumbers were by no means tranquil. I thought I was surrounded with difficulties of various kinds amongst rocks and ravines, vainly endeavouring to extricate myself; uncouth visages showed themselves amidst the trees and in the hollows, thrusting out cloven tongues and uttering angry cries. I looked around for my guide, but could not find him; methought, however, that I heard his voice down a deep dingle. He appeared to be talking of me. How long I might have continued in these wild dreams I know not. I was suddenly, however, seized roughly by the shoulder and nearly dragged from the bed. I looked up in amazement, and by the light of the descending sun I beheld hanging over me a wild and uncouth figure; it was that of an elderly man, built as strong as a giant, with much beard and whisker, and huge bushy eyebrows, dressed in the habiliments of a fisherman: in his hand was a rusty musket.

Myself.—Who are you, and what do you want?

Figure.—Who I am matters but little. Get up and follow me; it is you I want.

Myself.—By what authority do you thus presume to interfere with me?

Figure.—By the authority of the justicia of Finisterra. Follow me peaceably, Calros, or it will be the worse for you.

"Calros," said I, "what does the person mean?" I thought it, however, most prudent to obey his command, and followed him down the staircase. The shop and the portal were now thronged with the inhabitants of Finisterra, men, women, and children; the latter for the most part in a state of nudity, and with bodies wet and dripping, having been probably summoned in haste from their gambols in the brine. Through this crowd the figure whom I have attempted to describe pushed his way with an air of authority.

On arriving in the street, he laid his heavy hand upon my arm, not roughly however. "It is Calros! it is Calros!" said a hundred voices; "he has come to Finisterra at last, and the justicia has now got hold of him." Wondering what all this could mean, I attended my strange conductor down the street. As we proceeded, the crowd increased every moment, following and vociferating. Even the sick were brought to the doors to obtain a view of what was going forward and a glance at the redoutable Calros. I was particularly struck by the eagerness displayed by one man, a cripple, who, in spite of the entreaties of his wife, mixed with the crowd, and having lost his crutch hopped forward on one leg, exclaiming,—"*Carracho! tambien voy yo!*"

We at last reached a house of rather larger size than the rest, my guide having led me into a long low room, placed me in the middle of the floor, and then hurrying to the door, he endeavoured to repulse the crowd who strove to enter with us. This he effected, though not without considerable difficulty, being once or twice compelled to have recourse to the butt of his musket, to drive back unauthorized intruders. I now looked round the room. It was rather scantily furnished: I could see nothing but some tubs and barrels, the mast of a boat, and a sail or two. Seated upon the tubs were three or four men coarsely dressed, like fishermen or shipwrights. The principal personage was a surly ill-tempered-looking fellow of about thirty-five, whom eventually I discovered to be the alcalde of Finisterra, and lord of the house in which we now were. In a corner I caught a glimpse of my guide, who was evidently in durance, two stout fishermen standing before him, one with a musket and the other with a boat-hook. After I had looked about me for a minute, the alcalde, giving his whiskers a twist, thus addressed me:—

"Who are you, where is your passport, and what brings you to Finisterra?"

Myself.—I am an Englishman. Here is my passport, and I came to see Finisterra.

This reply seemed to discomfit them for a moment. They looked at each other, then at my passport. At length the alcalde, striking it with his finger, bellowed forth:

"This is no Spanish passport; it appears to be written in French."

Myself.—I have already told you that I am a foreigner. I of course carry a foreign passport.

Alcalde.—Then you mean to assert that you are not Calros Rey.

Myself.—I never heard before of such a king, nor indeed of such a name.

Alcalde.—Hark to the fellow: he has the audacity to say that he has never heard of Calros the pretender, who calls himself king.

Myself.—If you mean by Calros, the pretender Don Carlos, all I can reply is that you can scarcely be serious. You might as well assert that yonder poor fellow, my guide, whom I see you have made prisoner, is his nephew, the infante, Don Sebastian.

M

Alcalde.—See, you have betrayed yourself; that is the very person we suppose him to be.

Myself.—It is true that they are both hunch-backs. But how can I be like Don Carlos? I have nothing of the appearance of a Spaniard, and am nearly a foot taller than the pretender.

Alcalde.—That makes no difference; you of course carry many waistcoats about you, by means of which you disguise yourself, and appear tall or low according to your pleasure.

This last was so conclusive an argument that I had of course nothing to reply to it. The alcalde looked around him in triumph, as if he had made some notable discovery. "Yes, it is Calros; it is Calros," said the crowd at the door. "It will be as well to have these men shot instantly," continued the alcalde; "if they are not the two pretenders, they are at any rate two of the factious."

"I am by no means certain that they are either one or the other," said a gruff voice.

The justicia of Finisterra turned their eyes in the direction from which these words proceeded, and so did I. Our glances rested upon the figure who held the watch at the door. He had planted the barrel of his musket on the floor, and was now leaning his chin against the butt.

"I am by no means certain that they are either one or the other," repeated he, advancing forward. "I have been examining this man," pointing to myself, "and listening whilst he spoke, and it appears to me that after all he may prove an Englishman; he has their very look and voice. Who knows the English better than Antonio de la Trava, and who has a better right? Has he not sailed in their ships; has he not eaten their biscuit; and did he not stand by Nelson when he was shot dead?"

Here the alcalde became violently incensed. "He is no more an Englishman than yourself," he exclaimed; "if he were an Englishman, would he have come in this manner, skulking across the land? Not so, I trow. He would have come in a ship, recommended to some of us, or to the Catalans. He would have come to trade; to buy; but nobody knows him in Finisterra, nor does he know anybody: and the first thing, moreover, that he does when he reaches this place is to inspect the fort, and to ascend the mountain, where, no doubt, he has been marking out a camp. What brings him to Finisterra, if he is neither Calros nor a bribon of a faccioso?"

I felt that there was a good deal of justice in some of these remarks; and I was aware, for the first time, that I had, indeed, committed a great imprudence in coming to this wild place, and among these barbarous people, without being able to assign any motive which could appear at all valid in their eyes. I endeavoured to convince the alcalde that I had come across the country for the purpose of making myself acquainted with the many remarkable objects which it contained, and of obtaining information respecting the cha-

racter and condition of the inhabitants. He could understand no such motives. "What did you ascend the mountain for?" "To see prospects." "Disparate! I have lived at Finisterra forty years, and never ascended that mountain. I would not do it in a day like this for two ounces of gold. You went to take altitudes, and to mark out a camp."

I had, however, a stanch friend in old Antonio, who insisted, from his knowledge of the English, that all I had said might very possibly be true. "The English," said he, "have more money than they know what to do with, and on that account they wander all over the world, paying dearly for what no other people care a groat for." He then proceeded, notwithstanding the frowns of the alcalde, to examine me in the English language. His own entire knowledge of this tongue was confined to two words—*knife* and *fork*, which words I rendered into Spanish by their equivalents, and was forthwith pronounced an Englishman by the old fellow, who, brandishing his musket, exclaimed:—

"This man is not Calros; he is what he declares himself to be, an Englishman, and whoever seeks to injure him, shall have to do with Antonio de la Trava el valiente de Finisterra." No person sought to impugn this verdict, and it was at length determined that I should be sent to Corcuvion, to be examined by the alcalde mayor of the district. "But," said the alcalde of Finisterra, "what is to be done with the other fellow? He at least is no Englishman. Bring him forward, and let us hear what he has to say for himself. Now, fellow, who are you, and what is your master?"

Guide.—I am Sebastianillo, a poor broken mariner of Padron, and my master for the present is this gentleman whom you see, the most valiant and wealthy of all the English. He has two ships at Vigo, laden with riches. I told you so when you first seized me up there in our posada.

Alcalde.—Where is your passport?

Guide.—I have no passport. Who would think of bringing a passport to such a place as this, where I don't suppose there are two individuals who can read? I have no passport; my master's passport of course includes me.

Alcalde.—It does not. And since you have no passport, and have confessed that your name is Sebastian, you shall be shot. Antonio de la Trava, do you and the musketeer lead this Sebastianillo forth, and shoot him before the door.

Antonio de la Trava.—With much pleasure, Señor Alcalde, since you order it. With respect to this fellow, I shall not trouble myself to interfere. He at least is no Englishman. He has more the look of a wizard or nuveiro; one of those devils who raise storms and sink launches. Moreover, he says he is from Padron; and those of that place are all thieves and drunkards. They once played me a trick, and I would gladly be at the shooting of the whole pueblo.

I now interfered, and said that if they shot the guide they must shoot me too; expatiating at the same time on the cruelty and barbarity of taking away the life of a poor unfortunate fellow who, as might be seen at the first glance, was only half-witted; adding, moreover, that if any person was guilty in this case, it was myself, as the other could only be considered in the light of a servant acting under my orders.

"The safest plan after all," said the alcalde, "appears to be, to send you both prisoners to Corcuvion, where the head alcalde can dispose of you as he thinks proper. You must, however, pay for your escort; for it is not to be supposed that the housekeepers of Finisterra have nothing else to do than to ramble about the country with every chance fellow who finds his way to this town." "As for that matter," said Antonio, "I will take charge of them both. I am the valiente of Finisterra, and fear no two men living. Moreover, I am sure that the captain here will make it worth my while, else he is no Englishman. Therefore let us be quick, and set out for Corcuvion at once, as it is getting late. First of all, however, captain, I must search you and your baggage. You have no arms of course? But it is best to make all sure."

Long ere it was dark I found myself again on the pony, in company with my guide, wending our way along the beach in the direction of Corcuvion. Antonio de la Trava tramped heavily on before, his musket on his shoulder.

Myself.—Are you not afraid, Antonio, to be thus alone with two prisoners, one of whom is on horseback? If we were to try, I think we could overpower you.

Antonio de la Trava.—I am the valiente de Finisterra, and I fear no odds.

Myself.—Why do you call yourself the valiente of Finisterra?

Antonio de la Trava.—The whole district call me so. When the French came to Finisterra, and demolished the fort, three perished by my hand. I stood on the mountain, up where I saw you scrambling to-day. I continued firing at the enemy, until three detached themselves in pursuit of me. The fools! two perished amongst the rocks by the fire of this musket, and as for the third, I beat his head to pieces with the stock. It is on that account that they call me the valiente of Finisterra.

Myself.—How came you to serve with the English fleet? I think I heard you say that you were present when Nelson fell.

Antonio de la Trava.—I was captured by your countrymen, captain, and as I had been a sailor from my childhood, they were glad of my services. I was nine months with them, and assisted at Trafalgar. I saw the English admiral die. You have something of his face, and your voice, when you spoke, sounded in my ears like his own. I love the English, and on that account I saved you. Think not that I would toil along these sands

with you if you were one of my own countrymen. Here we are at Duyo, captain. Shall we refresh?

We did refresh, or rather Antonio de la Trava refreshed, swallowing pan after pan of wine, with a thirst which seemed unquenchable. "That man was a greater wizard than myself," whispered Sebastian, my guide, "who told us that the drunkards of Finisterra would play us a trick." At length the old hero of the Cape slowly rose, saying, that we must hasten on to Corcuvion, or the night would overtake us by the way.

"What kind of person is the alcalde to whom you are conducting me?" said I.

"Oh, very different from him of Finisterra," replied Antonio. "This is a young Senorito, lately arrived from Madrid. He is not even a Gallegan. He is a mighty liberal, and it is owing chiefly to his orders that we have lately been so much on the alert. It is said that the Carlists are meditating a descent on these parts of Galicia. Let them only come to Finisterra, we are liberals there to a man, and the old valiente is ready to play the same part as in the time of the French. But, as I was telling you before, the alcalde to whom I am conducting you is a young man, and very learned, and if he thinks proper, he can speak English to you, even better than myself, notwithstanding I was a friend of Nelson, and fought by his side at Trafalgar."

It was dark night before we reached Corcuvion. Antonio again stopped to refresh at a wine-shop, after which he conducted us to the house of the alcalde. His steps were by this time not particularly steady, and on arriving at the gate of the house, he stumbled over the threshold and fell. He got up with an oath, and instantly commenced thundering at the door with the stock of his musket. "Who is it?" at length demanded a soft female voice in Gallegan. "The valiente of Finisterra," replied Antonio; whereupon the gate was unlocked, and we beheld before us a very pretty female with a candle in her hand. "What brings you here so late, Antonio?" she inquired. "I bring two prisoners, mi pulida," replied Antonio. "Ave Maria!" she exclaimed. "I hope they will do no harm." "I will answer for one," replied the old man; "but as for the other, he is a nuveiro, and has sunk more ships than all his brethren in Galicia. But be not afraid, my beauty," he continued, as the female made the sign of the cross; "first lock the gate, and then show me the way to the alcalde. I have much to tell him." The gate was locked, and bidding us stay below in the courtyard, Antonio followed the young woman up a stone stair, whilst we remained in darkness below.

After the lapse of about a quarter of an hour, we again saw the candle gleam upon the staircase, and the young female appeared. Coming up to me, she advanced the candle to my features, on which she gazed very intently. After a long scrutiny she went to my guide; and having surveyed him still more fixedly, she turned to me, and said, in her best Spa-

nish, "Senhor Cavalier, I congratulate you on
your servant. He is the best-looking mozo
in all Galicia. Vaya! if he had but a coat to
his back, and did not go barefoot, I would
accept him at once as a novio; but I have unfortunately made a vow never to marry a poor
man, but only one who has got a heavy purse
and can buy me fine clothes. So you are a
Carlist, I suppose? Vaya! I do not like you
the worse for that. But, being so, how went
you to Finisterra, where they are all Christinos and negros? Why did you not go to
my village? None would have meddled with
you there. Those of my village are of a different stamp to the drunkards of Finisterra.
Those of my village never interfere with honest people. Vaya! how I hate that drunkard of Finisterra who brought you, he is so
old and ugly! Were it not for the love which
I bear to the Senhor Alcalde, I would at once
unlock the gate and bid you go forth, you and
your servant, the buen mozo."

Antonio now descended. "Follow me,"
said he; "his worship the alcalde will be
ready to receive you in a moment." Sebastian and myself followed him up stairs to a
room where, seated behind a table, we beheld
a young man of low stature, but handsome
features, and very fashionably dressed. He
appeared to be inditing a letter, which, when
he had concluded, he delivered to a secretary
to be transcribed. He then looked at me for
a moment fixedly, and the following conversation ensued between us :—

Alcalde.—I see that you are an Englishman,
and my friend Antonio here informs me that
you have been arrested at Finisterra.

Myself.—He tells you true; and but for him
I believe that I should have fallen by the hands
of those savage fishermen.

Alcalde.—The inhabitants of Finisterra are
brave, and are all liberals. Allow me to look
at your passport. Yes, all in form. Truly it
was very ridiculous that they should have arrested you as a Carlist.

Myself.—Not only as a Carlist, but as Don
Carlos himself.

Alcalde.—Oh, most ridiculous! mistake a
countryman of the grand Baintham for such a
Goth!

Myself.—Excuse me, Sir, you speak of the
grand somebody.

Alcalde.—The grand Baintham; he who
has invented laws for all the world. I hope
shortly to see them adopted in this unhappy
country of ours.

Myself.—Oh, you mean Jeremy Bentham.
Yes—a very remarkable man in his way.

Alcalde.—In his way!—in all ways. The
most universal genius which the world ever
produced:—a Solon, a Plato, and a Lope de
Vega.

Myself.—I have never read his writings. I
have no doubt that he was a Solon, and, as
you say, a Plato. I should scarcely have
thought, however, that he could be ranked as
a poet with Lope de Vega.

Alcalde.—How surprising! I see, indeed,
that you know nothing of his writings, though
an Englishman. Now here am I, a simple
alcalde of Galicia, yet I possess all the writings of Baintham on that shelf, and I study
them day and night.

Myself.—You doubtless, Sir, possess the
English language.

Alcalde.—I do—I mean that part of it which
is contained in the writings of Baintham. I
am most truly glad to see a countryman of his
in these Gothic wildernesses. I understand
and appreciate your motives for visiting them:
excuse the incivility and rudeness which you
have experienced. But we will endeavour to
make you reparation. You are this moment
free: but it is late; I must find you a lodging
for the night. I know one close by which will
just suit you. Let us repair thither this moment. Stay, I think I see a book in your hand.

Myself.—The New Testament.

Alcalde.—What book is that?

Myself.—A portion of the sacred writings,
the Bible.

Alcalde.—Why do you carry such a book
with you?

Myself.—One of my principal motives in
visiting Finisterra was to carry this book to
that wild place.

Alcalde.—Ha, ha! how very singular. Yes,
I remember. I have heard that the English
highly prize this eccentric book. How very
singular that the countrymen of the grand
Baintham should set any value upon that old
monkish book!

It was now late at night, and my new
friend attended me to the lodging which he
had destined for me, and which was at the
house of a respectable old female, where I
found a clean and comfortable room. On the
way I slipped a gratuity into the hand of Antonio, and on my arrival, formally, and in the
presence of the alcalde, presented him with
the Testament, which I requested he would
carry back to Finisterra, and keep in remembrance of the Englishman in whose behalf he
had so effectually interposed.

Antonio.—I will do so, your worship; and
when the winds blow from the north-west,
preventing our launches from putting to sea,
I will read your present. Farewell, my captain; and when you next come to Finisterra,
I hope it will be in a valiant English bark,
with plenty of contrabando on board, and not
across the country on a pony, in company
with nuveiros and men of Padron.

Presently arrived the handmaid of the alcalde with a basket, which she took into the
kitchen, where she prepared an excellent supper for her master's friend. On its being
served up the alcalde bade me farewell, having first demanded whether he could in any
way forward my plans.

"I return to St. James to-morrow," I replied, "and I sincerely hope that some occasion will occur which will enable me to
acquaint the world with the hospitality which
I have experienced from so accomplished a
scholar as the Alcalde of Corcuvion."

CHAPTER XXXI.

Coruna—Crossing the Bay—Ferrol—The Dock-yard—Where are we Now?—Greek Ambassador —Lantern-Light—The Ravine—Viveiro—Evening—Marsh and Quagmire—Fair Words and Fair Money—The Leathern Girth—Eyes of Lynx—The Knavish Guide.

FROM Corcuvion I returned to Saint James and Coruña, and now began to make preparation for directing my course to the Asturias. In the first place I parted with my Andalusian horse, which I considered unfit for the long and mountainous journey I was about to undertake; his constitution having become much debilitated from his Gallegan travels. Owing to horses being exceedingly scarce at Coruña, I had no difficulty in disposing of him at a far higher price than he originally cost me. A young and wealthy merchant of Coruña, who was a national guardsman, became enamoured of his glossy skin and long mane and tail. For my own part, I was glad to part with him for more reasons than one; he was both vicious and savage, and was continually getting me into scrapes in the stables of the posadas where we slept or baited. An old Castilian peasant, whose pony he had maltreated, once said to me, "Sir Cavalier, if you have any love or respect for yourself, get rid I beseech you of that beast, who is capable of proving the ruin of a kingdom." So I left him behind at Coruña, where I subsequently learned that he became glandered and died. Peace to his memory!

From Coruña I crossed the bay to Ferrol, whilst Antonio with our remaining horse followed by land, a rather toilsome and circuitous journey, although the distance by water is scarcely three leagues. I was very sea-sick during the passage, and lay almost senseless at the bottom of the small launch in which I had embarked, and which was crowded with people. The wind was adverse, and the water rough. We could make no sail, but were impelled along by the oars of five or six stout mariners, who sang all the while Gallegan ditties. Suddenly the sea appeared to have become quite smooth, and my sickness at once deserted me. I rose upon my feet and looked around. We were in one of the strangest places imaginable. A long and narrow passage overhung on either side by a stupendous barrier of black and threatening rocks. The line of the coast was here divided by a natural cleft, yet so straight and regular that it seemed not the work of chance but design. The water was dark and sullen, and of immense depth. This passage, which is about a mile in length, is the entrance to a broad basin, at whose farther extremity stands the town of Ferrol. Sadness came upon me as soon as I entered this place. Grass was growing in the streets, and misery and distress stared me in the face on every side. Ferrol is the grand naval arsenal of Spain, and has shared in the ruin of the once splendid Spanish navy: it is no longer thronged with those thousand shipwrights who prepared for sea the tremendous three-deckers and long frigates, the greater part of which were destroyed at Trafalgar. Only a few ill-paid and half-starved workmen still linger about, scarcely sufficient to repair any guarda costa which may put in dismantled by the fire of some English smuggling schooner from Gibraltar. Half the inhabitants of Ferrol beg their bread; and amongst these, as it is said, are not unfrequently found retired naval officers, many of them maimed or otherwise wounded, who are left to pine in indigence; their pensions or salaries having been allowed to run three or four years in arrear, owing to the exigencies of the times. A crowd of importunate beggars followed me to the posada, and even attempted to penetrate to the apartment to which I was conducted. "Who are you?" said I to a woman who flung herself at my feet, and who bore in her countenance evident marks of former gentility. "A widow, sir," she replied, in very good French; "a widow of a brave officer, once admiral of this port." The misery and degradation of modern Spain are nowhere so strikingly manifested as at Ferrol.

Yet even here there is still much to admire. Notwithstanding its present state of desolation, it contains some good streets, and abounds with handsome houses. The alameda is planted with nearly a thousand elms, of which almost all are magnificent trees, and the poor Ferrolese, with the genuine spirit of localism so prevalent in Spain, boast their town contains a better public walk than Madrid, of whose prado, when they compare the two, they speak in terms of unmitigated contempt. At one end of this alameda stands the church, the only one in Ferrol. To this church I repaired the day after my arrival, which was Sunday. I found it quite insufficient to contain the number of worshippers who, chiefly from the country, not only crowded the interior, but, bare-headed, were upon their knees before the door to a considerable distance down the walk.

Parallel with the alameda extends the wall of the naval arsenal and dock. I spent several hours in walking about these places, to visit which it is necessary to procure a written permission from the captain-general of Ferrol. They filled me with astonishment. I have seen the royal dock-yards of Russia and England, but for grandeur of design and costliness of execution, they cannot for a moment compare with these wonderful monuments of the bygone naval pomp of Spain. I shall not attempt to describe them, but content myself with observing, that the oblong basin, which is surrounded with a granite mole, is capacious enough to permit a hundred first-rates to lie conveniently in ordinary : but instead of such a force, I saw only a sixty gun frigate and two brigs lying in this basin, and to this inconsiderable number of vessels is the present war marine of Spain reduced.

I waited for the arrival of Antonio two or three days at Ferrol, and still he came not : late one evening, however, as I was looking down the street, I perceived him advancing, leading our only horse by the bridle. He informed me that at about three leagues from Coruna, the heat of the weather and the flies had so distressed the animal that it had fallen down in a kind of fit, from which it had been only relieved by copious bleeding, on which account he had been compelled to halt for a day upon the road. The horse was evidently in a very feeble state; and had a strange rattling in its throat, which alarmed me at first. I however administered some remedies, and in a few days deemed him sufficiently recovered to proceed.

We accordingly started from Ferrol; having first hired a pony for myself, and a guide who was to attend us as far as Rivadeo, twenty leagues from Ferrol, and on the confines of the Asturias. The day at first was fine, but ere we reached Novales, a distance of three leagues, the sky became overcast, and a mist descended, accompanied by a drizzling rain. The country through which we passed was very picturesque. At about two in the afternoon, we could descry through the mist the small fishing town of Santa Marta on our left, with its beautiful bay. Travelling along the summit of a line of hills, we presently entered a chestnut forest, which appeared to be without limit: the rain still descended and kept up a ceaseless pattering among the broad green leaves. "This is the commencement of the autumnal rains," said the guide. "Many is the wetting that you will get, my masters, before you reach Oviedo." "Have you ever been as far as Oviedo?" I demanded. "No," he replied, "and once only to Rivadeo, the place to which I am now conducting you, and I tell you frankly that we shall soon be in the wildernesses where the way is hard to find, especially at night, and amidst rain and waters. I wish I were fairly back to Ferrol, for I like not this route, which is the worst in Galicia, in more respects than one : but where my master's pony goes, there must I go too; such is the life of us guides." I shrugged my shoulders at this intelligence, which was by no means cheering, but made no answer. At length, about nightfall, we emerged from the forest, and presently descended into a deep valley at the foot of lofty hills.

"Where are we now?" I demanded of the guide, as we crossed a rude bridge at the bottom of the valley, down which a rivulet swollen by the rain foamed and roared. "In the valley of Coisa doiro," he replied; "and it is my advice that we stay here for the night, and do not venture among those hills,

through which lies the path to Viveiro; for as soon as we get there, adios ! I shall be bewildered, which will prove the destruction of us all." "Is there a village nigh?" "Yes, the village is right before us, and we shall be there in a moment." We soon reached the village, which stood amongst some tall trees at the entrance of a pass which led up amongst the hills. Antonia dismounted and entered two or three of the cabins, but presently came to me, saying, "We cannot stay here, mon maître, without being devoured by vermin; we had better be amongst the hills than in this place; there is neither fire nor light in these cabins, and the rain is streaming through the roofs." The guide, however, refused to proceed : "I could scarcely find my way amongst those hills by daylight," he cried, surlily, "much less at night, midst storm and bretima." We procured some wine and maize bread from one of the cottages. Whilst we were partaking of these, Antonio said, "Mon maître, the best thing we can do in our present situation, is to hire some fellow of this village to conduct us through the hills to Viveiro. There are no beds in this place, and if we lie down in the litter in our damp clothes we shall catch a tertian of Galicia. Our present guide is of no service, we must therefore find another to do his duty." Without waiting for a reply, he flung down the crust of bread which he was munching and disappeared. I subsequently learned that he went to the cottage of the alcalde, and demanded, in the Queen's name, a guide for the Greek ambassador, who was benighted on his way to the Asturias. In about ten minutes I again saw him, attended by the local functionary, who, to my surprise, made me a profound bow, and stood bareheaded in the rain. "His excellency," shouted Antonio, "is in need of a guide to Viveiro. People of our description are not compelled to pay for any service which they may require; however, as his excellency has bowels of compassion, he is willing to give three pesetas to any competent person who will accompany him to Viveiro, and as much bread and wine as he can eat and drink on his arrival." "His excellency shall be served," said the alcalde; "however, as the way is long and the path is bad, and there is much bretima amongst the hills, it appears to me that, besides the bread and wine, his excellency can do no less than offer four pesetas to the guide who may be willing to accompany him to Viveiro; and I know no better one than my own son-in-law, Juanito." "Content, señor alcalde," I replied ; "produce the guide, and the extra peseta shall be forthcoming in due season."

Soon appeared Juanito with a lantern in his hand. We instantly set forward. The two guides began conversing in Gallegan. "Mon maître," said Antonio, "this new scoundrel is asking the old what he thinks we have got in our portmanteaus." Then without awaiting my answer, he shouted, "Pistols, ye barbarians ! Pistols, as you shall learn to your cost, if you do not cease speaking in that gibberish and converse in Castilian." The Gallegans were silent, and presently the first guide dropped behind, whilst the other with the lantern moved before. "Keep in the rear," said Antonio to the former, "and at a distance: know one thing, moreover, that I can see behind as well as before. Mon maître," said he to me, "I don't suppose these fellows will attempt to do us any harm, more especially as they do not know each other; it is well, however, to separate them, for this is a time and place which might tempt any one to commit robbery and murder too."

The rain still continued to fall uninterruptedly, the path was rugged and precipitous, and the night was so dark that we could only see indistinctly the hills which surrounded us. Once or twice our guide seemed to have lost his way: he stopped, muttered to himself, raised his lantern on high, and would then walk slowly and hesitatingly forward. In this manner we proceeded for three or four hours, when I asked the guide how far we were from Viveiro. "I do not know exactly where we are, your worship," he replied, "though I believe we are in the route. We can scarcely, however, be less than two mad leagues from Viveiro." "Then we shall not arrive there before morning," interrupted Antonio, "for a mad league of Galicia means at least two of Castile; and perhaps we are doomed never to arrive there, if the way thither leads down this precipice." As he spoke, the guide seemed to descend into the bowels of the earth. "Stop," said I, "where are you going?" "To Viveiro, Senhor," replied the fellow: "this is the way to Viveiro, there is no other; I now know where we are." The light of the lantern shone upon the dark red features of the guide, who had turned round to reply, as he stood some yards down the side of a dingle or ravine overgrown with thick trees, beneath whose leafy branches a frightfully steep path descended. I dismounted from the pony, and delivering the bridle to the other guide, said, "Here is your master's horse, if you please you may lead him down that abyss, but as for myself I wash my hands of the matter." The fellow, without a word of reply, vaulted into the saddle, and with a vamos, Perico! to the poney, impelled the creature to the descent. "Come, Senhor," said he with the lantern, "there is no time to be lost, my light will be presently extinguished, and this is the worst bit in the whole road." I thought it very probable that he was about to lead us to some den of cut-throats, where we might be sacrificed; but, taking courage, I seized our own horse by the bridle, and followed the fellow down the ravine amidst rocks and brambles. The descent lasted nearly ten minutes, and ere we had entirely accomplished it, the light in the lantern went out, and we remained in nearly total darkness.

Encouraged, however, by the guide, who assured us there was no danger, we at length reached the bottom of the ravine; here we encountered a rill of water, through which we were compelled to wade as high as the knee. In the midst of the water I looked up and caught a glimpse of the heavens through the branches of the trees, which all around clothed the shelving sides of the ravine and completely embowered the channel of the stream: to a place more strange and replete with gloom and horror no benighted traveller ever found his way. After a short pause, we commenced scaling the opposite bank, which we did not find so steep as the other, and a few minutes' exertion brought us to the top.

Shortly afterwards the rain abated, and the moon arising cast a dim light through the watery mists: the way had become less precipitous, and in about two hours we descended to the shore of an extensive creek, along which we proceeded till we reached a spot where many boats and barges lay with their keels upward upon the sand. Presently we beheld before us the walls of Viveiro, upon which the moon was shedding its sickly lustre. We entered by a lofty and seemingly ruinous archway, and the guide conducted us at once to the posada.

Every person in Viveiro appeared to be buried in profound slumber; not so much as a dog saluted us with his bark. After much knocking, we were admitted into the posada, a large and dilapidated edifice. We had scarcely housed ourselves and horses when the rain began to fall with yet more violence than before, attended with much thunder and lightning. Antonio and I, exhausted with fatigue, betook ourselves to flock beds in a ruinous chamber, into which the rain penetrated through many a cranny, whilst the guides ate bread and drank wine till the morning.

When I arose, I was gladdened by the sight of a fine day. Antonio forthwith prepared a savoury breakfast of stewed fowl, of which we stood in much need after the ten league journey of the preceding day over the ways which I have attempted to describe. I then walked out to view the town, which consists of little more than one long street on the side of a steep mountain thickly clad with forest and fruit trees. At about ten we continued our journey, accompanied by our first guide, the other having returned to Coisa doiro some hours previously.

Our route throughout this day was almost constantly within sight of the shores of the Cantabrian sea, whose windings we followed. The country was barren, and in many parts covered with huge stones: cultivated spots, however, were to be seen, where vines were growing. We met with but few human habitations. We, however, journeyed on cheerfully, for the sun was once more shining in full brightness, gilding the wild moors, and shining upon the waters of the distant sea, which lay in unruffled calmness.

At evening fall we were in the neighbourhood of the shore, with a range of wood-covered hills on our right. Our guide led us towards a creek bordered by a marsh, but he soon stopped and declared that he did not know whither he was conducting us.

"Mon maître," said Antonio, "let us be our own guides; it is, as you see, of no use to depend upon this fellow, whose whole science consists in leading people into quagmires."

We therefore turned aside and proceeded along the marsh for a considerable distance, till we reached a narrow path which led us into a thick wood, where we soon became completely bewildered. On a sudden, after wandering about a considerable time, we heard the noise of water, and presently the clack of a wheel. Following the sound, we arrived at a low stone mill, built over a brook; here we stopped and shouted, but no answer was returned. "The place is deserted," said Antonio; "here, however, is a path, which, if we follow it, will doubtless lead us to some human habitation." So we went along the path, which, in about ten minutes, brought us to the door of a cabin in which we saw lights. Antonio dismounted and opened the door: "Is there any one here who can conduct us to Rivadeo?" he demanded.

"Senhor," answered a voice, "Rivadeo is more than five leagues from here, and, moreover, there is a river to cross!"

"Then to the next village," continued Antonio.

"I am a vecino of the next village, which is on the way to Rivadeo," said another voice, "and I will lead you thither if you will give me fair words, and what is better, fair money."

A man now came forth, holding in his hand a large stick. He strode sturdily before us, and in less than half an hour led us out of the wood. In another half hour he brought us to a group of cabins situated near the sea; he pointed to one of these, and having received a peseta, bade us farewell.

The people of the cottage willingly consented to receive us for the night: it was much more cleanly and commodious than the wretched huts of the Gallegan peasantry in general. The ground floor consisted of a keeping room and stable, whilst above us was a long loft, in which were some neat and comfortable flock beds. I observed several masts and sails of boats. The family consisted of two brothers with their wives and families; one was a fisherman, but the other, who appeared to be the principal person, informed me that he had resided for many years in service at Madrid, and having amassed a small sum, he had at length returned to his native village, where he had purchased some land which he farmed. All the family used the Castilian language in their common discourse, and on inquiry I learned that the Gallegan was not much spoken in that neighbourhood. I have forgotten the name of this village, which is situated on the estuary of the Foz, which rolls down from Mondonedo. In the morning we crossed this estuary in a large boat with our horses, and about noon arrived at Rivadeo.

"Now, your worship," said the guide who had accompanied us from Ferrol, "I have brought you as far as I bargained, and a hard journey it has been: I therefore hope you will suffer Perico and myself to remain here to-night at your expense, and to-morrow we will go back; at present we are both sorely tired."

"I never mounted a better pony than Perico," said I, "and never met with a worse guide than yourself. You appear to be perfectly ignorant of the country, and have done nothing but bring us into difficulties. You may, however, stay here for the night, as you say you are tired, and to-morrow you may return to Ferrol, where I counsel you to adopt some other trade." This was said at the door of the posada of Rivadeo.

"Shall I lead the horses to a stable?" said the fellow.

"As you please," said I.

Antonio looked after him for a moment, as he was leading the animals away, and then shaking his head, followed slowly after. In about a quarter of an hour he returned, laden with the furniture of our own horse, and with a smile upon his countenance: "Mon maître," said he, "I have throughout the journey had a bad opinion of this fellow, and now I have detected him: his motive in requesting permission to stay, was a desire to purloin something from us. He was very officious in the stable about our horse, and I now miss the new leathern girth which secured the saddle, and which I observed him looking at frequently on the road. He has by this time doubtless hid it somewhere; we are quite secure of him, however, for he has not yet received the hire for the pony, nor the gratuity for himself."

The guide returned just as he had concluded speaking. Dishonesty is always suspicious. The fellow cast a glance upon us, and probably beholding in our countenances something which he did not like, he suddenly said, "Give me the horse-hire and my own propina, for Perico and I wish to be off instantly."

"How is this," said I; "I thought you and Perico were both fatigued, and wished to rest here for the night; you have soon recovered from your weariness."

"I have thought over the matter," said the fellow, "and my master will be angry if I loiter here: pay us, therefore, and let us go."

"Certainly," said I, "if you wish it. Is the horse-furniture all right?"

"Quite so," said he; "I delivered it all to your servant."

"It is all here," said Antonio, "with the exception of the leathern girth."

"I have not got it," said the guide.

"Of course not," said I. "Let us proceed to the stable, we shall perhaps find it there."

To the stable we went, which we searched through; no girth, however, was forthcoming. "He has got it buckled round his middle beneath his pantaloons, mon maître," said Antonio, whose eyes were moving about like those of a lynx; "I saw the protuberance as he stooped down. However, let us take no notice: he is here surrounded by his countrymen, who, if we were to seize him, might perhaps take his part. As I said before, he is in our power, as we have not paid him."

The fellow now began to talk in Gallegan to the bystanders, (several persons having collected,) wishing the Denho to take him if he knew any thing of the missing property. Nobody, however, seemed inclined to take his part; and those who listened, only shrugged their shoulders. We returned to the portal of the posada, the fellow following us, clamouring for the horse-hire and propina. We made him no answer, and at length he went away, threatening to apply to the justicia; in about ten minutes, however, he came running back with the girth in his hand: "I have just found it," said he, "in the street; your servant dropped it."

I took the leather and proceeded very deliberately to count out the sum to which the horse-hire amounted, and having delivered it to him in the presence of witnesses, I said: "During the whole journey you have been of no service to us whatever; nevertheless, you have fared like ourselves, and have had all you could desire to eat and drink. I had intended, on your leaving us, to have presented you, moreover, with a propina of two dollars; but since, notwithstanding our kind treatment, you endeavoured to pillage us, I will not give you a cuarto: go, therefore, about your business."

All the audience expressed their satisfaction at this sentence, and told him that he had been rightly served, and that he was a disgrace to Galicia. Two or three women crossed themselves, and asked him if he was not afraid that the Denho, whom he had invoked, would take him away. At last, a respectable-looking man said to him: "Are you not ashamed to have attempted to rob two innocent strangers?"

"Strangers!" roared the fellow, who was by this time foaming with rage; "innocent strangers, carracho! they know more of Spain and Galicia too, than the whole of us. Oh, Denho, that servant is no man but a wizard, a nuveiro.—Where is Perico?"

He mounted Perico, and proceeded forthwith to another posada. The tale, however, of his dishonesty had gone before him, and no person would house him; whereupon he returned on his steps, and seeing me looking out of the window of the house, he gave a savage shout, and shaking his fist at me, galloped out of the town; the people pursuing him with hootings and revilings.

CHAPTER XXXII.

Martin of Rivadeo—The factious Mare—Asturians—Luarca—The seven Bellotas—Hermits—The Asturian's Tale—Strange Guests—The big Servant—Batuschca.

"WHAT may your business be?" said I to a short, thick, merry-faced fellow in a velveteen jerkin and canvas pantaloons, who made his way into my apartment, in the dusk of the evening.

"I am Martin of Rivadeo, your worship," replied the man, "an esquilador by profession; I am told that you want a horse for your journey into the Asturias to-morrow, and of course a guide: now if that be the case, I counsel you to hire myself and mare."

"I am become tired of guides," I replied; "so much so that I was thinking of purchasing a pony, and proceeding without any guide at all. The last which we had was an infamous character."

"So I have been told, your worship, and it was well for the bribon that I was not in Rivadeo when the affair to which you allude occurred. But he was gone with the pony Perico before I came back, or I would have bled the fellow to a certainty with my knife. He is a disgrace to the profession, which is one of the most honourable and ancient in the world. Perico himself must have been ashamed of him, for Perico, though a pony, is a gentleman, one of many capacities, and well known upon the roads. He is only inferior to my mare."

"Are you well acquainted with the road to Oviedo?" I demanded.

"I am not, your worship; that is, no farther than Luarca, which is the first day's journey. I do not wish to deceive you, therefore let me go with you no farther than that place; though perhaps I might serve for the whole journey, for though I am unacquainted with the country, I have a tongue in my head, and nimble feet to run and ask questions. I will, however, answer for myself no farther than Luarca, where you can please yourselves. Your being strangers is what makes me wish to accompany you, for I like the conversation of strangers, from whom I am sure to gain information both entertaining and profitable. I wish, moreover, to convince you that we guides of Galicia are not all thieves, which I am sure you will not suppose if you will only permit me to accompany you as far as Luarca."

I was so much struck with the fellow's good humour and frankness, and more especially by the originality of character displayed in almost every sentence which he uttered, that I readily engaged him to guide us to Luarca; whereupon he left me, promising to be ready with his mare at eight next morning.

Rivadeo is one of the principal sea-ports of

Galicia, and is admirably situated for commerce, on a deep frith, into which the river Mirando debouches. It contains many magnificent buildings, and an extensive square or plaza, which is planted with trees. I observed several vessels in the harbour; and the population, which is rather numerous, exhibited none of those marks of misery and dejection which I had lately observed among the Ferrolese.

On the morrow Martin of Rivadeo made his appearance at the appointed hour with his mare. It was a lean haggard animal, not much larger than a pony; it had good points, however, and was very clean in its hinder legs, and Martin insisted that it was the best animal of its kind in all Spain. "It is a factious mare," said he, "and I believe an Alavese. When the Carlists came here it fell lame, and they left it behind, and I purchased it for a dollar. It is not lame now, however, as you shall soon see."

We had now reached the frith which divides Galicia from the Asturias. A kind of barge was lying about two yards from the side of the quay, waiting to take us over. Towards this Martin led his mare, and giving an encouraging shout, the creature without any hesitation sprang over the intervening space into the barge. "I told you she was a facciosa," said Martin; "none but a factious animal would have taken such a leap."

"We all embarked in the barge and crossed over the frith, which is in this place nearly a mile broad, to Castro Pol, the first town in the Asturias. I now mounted the factious mare, whilst Antonio followed on my own horse. Martin led the way, exchanging jests with every person whom he met on the road, and occasionally enlivening the way with an extemporaneous song.

We were now in the Austurias, and about noon we reached Navias, a small fishing town, situate on a ria or frith: in the neighbourhood are ragged mountains, called the Sierra de Buron, which stands in the shape of a semicircle. We saw a small vessel in the harbour, which we subsequently learned was from the Basque provinces, come for a cargo of cider or sagadua, the beverage so dearly loved by the Basques. As we passed along the narrow street, Antonio was hailed with an "Ola" from a species of shop in which three men, apparently shoemakers, were seated. He stopped for some time to converse with them, and when he joined us at the posada where we halted, I asked him who they were: "Mon maître," said he, "ce sont des messieurs de ma connoissance. I have been fellow servant at different times with all three; and I tell you beforehand, that we shall scarcely pass through a village in this country where I shall not find an acquaintance. All the Asturians, at some period of their lives, make a journey to Madrid, where, if they can obtain a situation, they remain until they have scraped up sufficient to turn to advantage in their own country; and as I have served in all the great houses in Madrid,

I am acquainted with the greatest part of them. I have nothing to say against the Asturians, save that they are close and penurious whilst at service; but they are not thieves, neither at home nor abroad, and though we must have our wits about us in their country, I have heard we may travel from one end of it to the other without the slightest fear of being either robbed or ill-treated, which is not the case in Galicia, where we were always in danger of having our throats cut."

Leaving Navias, we proceeded through a wild desolate country, till we reached the pass of Baralla, which lies up the side of a huge wall of rocks, which at a distance appear of a light green colour, though perfectly bare of herbage or plants of any description.

"This pass," said Martin of Rivadeo, "bears a very evil reputation, and I should not like to travel it after sunset. It is not infested by robbers, but by things much worse, the duendes of two friars of Saint Francis. It is said that in the old time, long before the convents were suppressed, two friars of the order of Saint Francis left their convent to beg; it chanced that they were very successful, but as they were returning at nightfall by this pass, they had a quarrel about what they had collected, each insisting that he had done his duty better than the other; at last, from high words they fell to abuse, and from abuse to blows. What do you think these demons of friars did? They took off their cloaks, and at the end of each they made a knot, in which they placed a large stone, and with these they thrashed and belaboured each other till both fell dead. Master, I know not which are the worst plagues, friars, curates, or sparrows:

'May the Lord God preserve us from evil birds three:
From all friars and curates and sparrows that be;
For the sparrows eat up all the corn that we sow,
The friars drink down all the wine that we grow.
Whilst the curates have all the fair dames at their nod;
From these three evil curses preserve us, Lord God.'"

In about two hours from this time, we reached Luarca, the situation of which is most singular. It stands in a deep hollow, whose sides are so precipitous that it is impossible to descry the town until you stand just above it. At the northern extremity of this hollow is a small harbour, the sea entering by a narrow cleft. We found a large and comfortable posada, and by the advice of Martin, made inquiry for a fresh guide and horse; we were informed, however, that all the horses of the place were absent, and that if we waited for their return, we must tarry for two days. "I had a presentiment," said Martin, "when we entered Luarca, that we were not doomed to part at present. You must now hire my mare and me as far as Giyon, from whence there is a conveyance to Oviedo. To tell you the truth, I am by no means sorry that the guides are absent, for I am pleased with your company, as I make no doubt you are with mine. I will now go and

write a letter to my wife at Rivadeo, informing her that she must not expect to see me
back for several days." He then went out
of the room singing the following stanza :

> "A handless man a letter did write,
> A dumb dictated it word for word :
> The person who read it had lost his sight,
> And deaf was he who listened and heard."

Early the next morning we emerged from
the hollow of Luarca : about an hour's riding
brought us to Caneiro, a deep and romantic
valley of rocks, shaded by tall chestnut trees.
Through the midst of this valley rushes a
rapid stream, which we crossed in a boat.
"There is not such a stream for trout in all
the Asturias," said the ferryman ; "look
down into the waters, and observe the large
stones over which it flows ; now in the proper season, and in fine weather, you cannot
see those stones for the multitudes of fish
which cover them."

Leaving the valley behind us, we entered
into a wild and dreary country, stony and
mountainous. The day was dull and gloomy,
and all around looked sad and melancholy.
"Are we in the way for Giyon and Oviedo ?"
demanded Martin of an ancient female, who
stood at the door of a cottage.

"For Giyon and Oviedo !" replied the
crone ; "many is the weary step you will
have to make before you reach Giyon and
Oviedo. You must first of all crack the bellotas ; you are just below them."

"What does she mean by cracking the bellotas ?" demanded I, of Martin of Rivadeo.

"Did your worship never hear of the seven
bellotas ?" replied our guide. "I can scarcely
tell you what they are, as I have never seen
them ; I believe they are seven hills which
we have to cross, and are called bellotas from
some resemblance to acorns which it is fancied
they bear. I have often heard of these acorns,
and am not sorry that I have now an opportunity of seeing them, though it is said that
they are rather hard things for horses to di-
gest."

The Asturian mountains in this part rise to
a considerable altitude. They consist for the
most part of dark granite, covered here and
there with a thin layer of earth. They approach very near to the sea, to which they
slope down in broken ridges, between which
are deep and precipitous defiles, each with its
rivulet, the tribute of the hills to the salt flood.
The road traverses these defiles. There are
seven of them, which are called, in the language of the country, Las siete bellotas. Of
all these, the most terrible is the midmost,
down which rolls an impetuous torrent. At
the upper end of it rises a precipitous wall of
rock, black as soot, to the height of several
hundred yards ; its top, as we passed, was
enveloped with a veil of bretima. From this
gorge branch off, on either side, small dingles
or glens, some of them so overgrown with
trees and copsewood, that the eye is unable
to penetrate the obscurity beyond a few yards.

"Fine places would some of those dingles
prove for hermitages," said I, to Martin of

Rivadeo. "Holy men might lead a happy
life there on roots and water, and pass many
years absorbed in heavenly contemplation,
without ever being disturbed by the noise and
turmoil of the world."

"True," your worship, replied Martin ;
"and perhaps on that very account there are
no hermitages in the barrancos of the seven
bellotas. Our hermits had little inclination
for roots and water, and had no kind of objection to be occasionally disturbed in their
meditations. Vaya ! I never yet saw a her-
mitage that was not hard by some rich town
or village, or was not a regular resort for all
the idle people in the neighbourhood. Hermits are not fond of living in dingles, amongst
wolves and foxes ; for how in that case could
they dispose of their poultry ? A hermit of
my acquaintance left, when he died, a fortune
of seven hundred dollars to his niece, the
greatest part of which he scraped up by fat-
tening turkeys."

At the top of this bellota we found a wretched venta, where we refreshed ourselves, and
then continued our journey. Late in the afternoon we cleared the last of these difficult
passes. The wind began now to rise, bearing on its wings a drizzling rain. We passed
by Soto Luino, and shaping our course through
a wild but picturesque country, we found ourselves about nightfall at the foot of a steep
hill, up which led a narrow bridle-way, amidst
a grove of lofty trees. Long before we had
reached the top it had become quite dark, and
the rain had increased considerably. We
stumbled along in the obscurity, leading our
horses, which were occasionally down on
their knees, owing to the slipperiness of the
path. At last we accomplished the ascent in
safety, and pushing briskly forward, we found
ourselves, in about half an hour, at the entrance of Muros, a large village situated just
on the declivity of the farther side of the hill.

A blazing fire in the posada soon dried our
wet garments, and in some degree recompensed us for the fatigues which we had undergone in scrambling up the bellotas. A
rather singular place was this same posada
of Muros. It was a large rambling house,
with a spacious kitchen, or common room, on
the ground floor. Above stairs was a large
dining apartment, with an immense oak table,
and furnished with cumbrous leathern chairs
with high backs, apparently three centuries
old at least. Communicating with this apartment was a wooden gallery, open to the air,
which led to a small chamber, in which I was
destined to sleep, and which contained an old-
fashioned tester-bed with curtains. It was
just one of those inns which romance writers
are so fond of introducing in their descriptions,
especially when the scene of adventure lies in
Spain. The host was a talkative Asturian.

The wind still howled, and the rain descended in torrents. I sat before the fire in a
very drowsy state, from which I was presently aroused by the conversation of the
host. "Senor," said he, "it is now three
years since I beheld foreigners in my house.

I remember it was about this time of the year, and just such a night as this, that two men on horseback arrived here. What was singular, they came without any guide. Two more strange looking individuals I never yet beheld with eye-sight. I shall never forget them. The one was as tall as a giant, with much tawny moustache, like the coat of a badger, growing about his mouth. He had a huge ruddy face, and looked dull and stupid, as he no doubt was; for when I spoke to him, he did not seem to understand, and answered in a jabber, valgame Dios! so wild and strange that I remained staring at him with mouth and eyes open. The other was neither tall nor red-faced, nor had he hair about his mouth, and, indeed, he had very little upon his head. He was very diminutive, and looked like a jorobado; but, valgame Dios! such eyes, like wild cat's, so sharp and full of malice. He spoke as good Spanish as I myself do, and yet he was no Spaniard. A Spaniard never looked like that man. He was dressed in a zamarra, with much silver and embroidery, and wore an Andalusian hat, and I soon found that he was master, and that the other was servant.

"Valgame Dios! what an evil disposition had that same foreign jorobado; and yet he had much grace, much humour, and said occasionally to me such comical things, that I was fit to die of laughter. So he sat down to supper in the room above—and I may as well tell you here, that he slept in the same chamber where your worship will sleep to-night—and his servant waited behind his chair. Well, I had curiosity, so I sat myself down at the table too, without asking leave. Why should I? I was in my own house, and an Asturian is fit company for a king, and is often of better blood. Oh, what a strange supper was that! If the servant made the slightest mistake in helping him, up would start the jorobado, jump upon his chair, and seizing the big giant by the hair, would cuff him on both sides of his face, till I was afraid his teeth would have fallen out. The giant, however, did not seem to care about it much. He was used to it, I suppose. Valgame Dios! if he had been a Spaniard, he would not have submitted to it so patiently. But what surprised me most was, that after beating his servant, the master would sit down, and the next moment would begin conversing and laughing with him, as if nothing had happened, and the giant also would laugh and converse with his master for all the world as if he had not been beaten.

"You may well suppose, Señor, that I understood nothing of their discourse, for it was all in that strange unchristian tongue in which the giant answered me when I spoke to him; the sound of it is still ringing in my ears. It was nothing like other languages. Not like Bascuen, not like the language in which your worship speaks to my namesake Signor Antonio here. Valgame Dios! I can compare it to nothing but the sound a person makes when he rinses his mouth with water. There is one word which I think I still remember, for it was continually proceeding from the giant's lips, but his master never used it.

"But the strangest part of the story is yet to be told. The supper was ended, and the night was rather advanced, the rain still beat against the windows, even as it does this moment. Suddenly the jorobado pulled out his watch. Valgame Dios, such a watch! I will tell you one thing, Señor, that I could purchase all the Asturias, and Muros besides, with the brilliants which shone about the sides of that same watch: the room wanted no lamp, I trow, so great was the splendour which they cast. So the jorobado looked at his watch, and then said to me, I shall go to rest. He then took the lamp and went through the gallery to his room, followed by his big servant. Well, Señor, I cleared away the things, and then waited below for the servant, for whom I had prepared a comfortable bed, close to my own. Señor, I waited patiently for an hour, till at last my patience was exhausted, and I ascended to the supper apartment, and passed through the gallery till I came to the door of the strange guest. Señor, what do you think I saw at the door?"

"How should I know?" I replied. "His riding boots, perhaps."

"No, Señor, I did not see his riding boots; but, stretched on the floor with his head against the door, so that it was impossible to open it without disturbing him, lay the big servant fast asleep, his immense legs reaching nearly the whole length of the gallery. I crossed myself, as well I might, for the wind was howling even as it is now, and the rain was rushing down into the gallery in torrents; yet there lay the big servant fast asleep, without any covering, without any pillow, not even a log, stretched out before his master's door.

"Señor, I got little rest that night, for I said to myself, I have evil wizards in my house, folks who are not human. Once or twice I went up and peeped into the gallery, but there still lay the big servant fast asleep, so I crossed myself and returned to my bed again."

"Well," said I, "and what occurred next day?"

"Nothing particular occurred next day: the jorobado came down and said comical things to me in good Spanish; and the big servant came down, but whatever he said, and he did not say much, I understood not, for it was in that disastrous jabber. They stayed with me throughout the day till after supper-time, and then the jorobado gave me a gold ounce, and mounting their horses, they both departed as strangely as they had come, in the dark night, I know not whither."

"Is that all?" I demanded.

"No, Señor, it is not all; for I was right in supposing them evil brujos: the very next day an express arrived, and a great search was made after them, and I was arrested for having harboured them. This occurred just after the present wars had commenced. It was said they were spies and emissaries of I don't know what nation, and that they had been in all parts of the Asturias, holding conferences with some of the disaffected. They escaped, however, and were never heard of more, though the animals which they rode were found without their riders, wandering amongst the hills; they were common ponies, and were of no value. As for the brujos, it is believed that they embarked in some small vessel which was lying concealed in one of the rias of the coast."

Myself.—What was the word which you continually heard proceeding from the lips of the big servant, and which you think you can remember?

Host.—Señor, it is now three years since I heard it, and at times I can remember it and at others not; sometimes I have started up from my sleep repeating it. Stay, Señor, I have it now at the point of my tongue: it was Patusca.

Myself.—Batuschca, you mean; the men were Russians.

CHAPTER XXXIII.

Oviedo—The ten Gentlemen—The Swiss again—Modest Request—The Robbers—Episcopal Benevolence—The Cathedral—Portrait of Feijoo.

I must now take a considerable stride in my journey, no less than from Muros to Oviedo, contenting myself with observing, that we proceeded from Muros to Velez, and from thence to Giyon, where our guide Martin bade us farewell, and returned with his mare to Rivadeo. The honest fellow did not part without many expressions of regret, indeed he even expressed a desire that I should take him and his mare into my service; "for," said he, "I have a great desire to run through all Spain, and even the world: and I am sure I shall never have a better opportunity than by attaching myself to your worship's skirts." On my reminding him, however, of his wife and family, for he had both, he said, "True, true, I had forgotten them: happy the guide whose only wife and family are a mare and foal."

Oviedo is about three leagues from Giyon. Antonio rode the horse, whilst I proceeded thither in a kind of diligence, which runs daily between the two towns. The road is good, but mountainous. I arrived safely at the capital of the Asturias, although at a rather unpropitious season, for the din of war was at the gate, and there was the cry of the captains and the shouting. Castile, at the time of which I am writing, was in the hands of the Carlists, who had captured and plundered Valladolid in much the same manner as they had Segovia some time before. They were every day expected to march on Oviedo, in which case they might perhaps have experienced some resistance, a considerable body of troops being stationed there, who had erected some redoubts, and strongly fortified several of the convents, especially that of Santa Clara de la Vega. All minds were in a state of feverish anxiety and suspense, more especially as no intelligence arrived from Madrid, which, by the last accounts, was said to be occupied by the bands of Cabrera and Palillos.

So it came to pass that one night I found myself in the ancient town of Oviedo, in a very large, scantily furnished, and remote room in an ancient posada, formerly a palace of the counts of Santa Cruz. It was past ten, and the rain was descending in torrents. I was writing, but suddenly ceased on hearing numerous footsteps ascending the creaking stairs which led to my apartment. The door was flung open, and in walked nine men of tall stature, marshalled by a little hunchbacked personage. They were all muffled in the long cloaks of Spain, but I instantly knew by their demeanour that they were caballeros, or gentlemen. They placed themselves in a rank before the table where I was sitting. Suddenly and simultaneously they all flung back their cloaks, and I perceived that every one bore a book in his hand; a book which I knew full well. After a pause, which I was unable to break, for I sat lost in astonishment, and almost conceived myself to be visited by apparitions, the hunchback, advancing somewhat before the rest, said in soft, silvery tones, "Señor Cavalier, was it you who brought this book to the Asturias?" I now supposed that they were the civil authorities of the place come to take me into custody, and rising from my seat, I exclaimed, "It certainly was I, and it is my glory to have done so; the book is the New Testament of God: I wish it was in my power to bring a million." "I heartily wish so too," said the little personage with a sigh. "Be under no apprehension, Sir Cavalier, these gentlemen are my friends; we have just purchased these books in the shop where you placed them for sale, and have taken the liberty of calling upon you to return you our thanks for the treasure you have brought us. I hope you can furnish us with the Old Testament also." I replied that I was sorry to inform him that at present it was entirely out of my power to comply with his wish, as I had no Old Testaments in my possession, but did not despair of procuring some speedily from England. He then asked me a great many questions concerning my biblical travels in Spain, and my success, and the views entertained by the society with respect to Spain, adding that he hoped we should pay particular attention to the Asturias, which he assured me was the best ground in the peninsula for our labour. After about half an hour's conversation, he suddenly said, in the English language, "Good night, sir," wrapped his cloak around him, and walked out as he had come. His companions, who had hitherto not uttered a word, all repeated, "Good night, sir," and, adjusting their cloaks, followed him.

In order to explain this strange scene, I must state that in the morning I had visited the petty bookseller of the place, Longoria, and having arranged preliminaries with him, I sent him in the evening a package of forty Testaments, all I possessed, with some advertisements. At the time, he assured me that, though he was willing to undertake the sale, there was, nevertheless, not a prospect of success, as a whole month had elapsed since he had sold a book of any description, on account of the uncertainty of the times, and the poverty which pervaded the land; I therefore felt much dispirited. This incident, however, admonished me not to be cast down when things look gloomiest, as the hand of the Lord is generally then most busy; that men may learn to perceive, that whatever good is accomplished is not their work but His.

Two or three days after this adventure, I was once more seated in my large scantily furnished room, it was about ten of a dark melancholy morning, and the autumnal rain was again falling. I had just breakfasted, and was about to sit down to my journal, when the door was flung open and in bounded Antonio.

"Mon maître," said he, quite breathless, "who do you think has arrived!"

"The pretender, I suppose," said I, in some trepidation; "if so, we are prisoners."

"Bah, bah!" said Antonio, "it is not the pretender, but one worth twenty of him; it is the Swiss of Saint James."

"Benedict Mol, the Swiss!" said I. "What! has he found the treasure! But how did he come! How is he dressed!"

"Mon maître," said Antonio, "he came on foot, if we may judge by his shoes, through which his toes are sticking; and as for his dress, he is in most villanous apparel."

"There must be some mystery in this," said I; "where is he at present!"

"Below, mon maître," replied Antonio; "he came in quest of us. But I no sooner saw him, than I hurried away to let you know."

In a few minutes Benedict Mol found his way up stairs; he was, as Antonio had remarked, in most villanous apparel, and nearly barefooted; his old Andalusian hat was dripping with rain.

"Och, lieber herr," said Benedict, "how rejoiced I am to see you again. Oh, the sight of your countenance almost repays me for all the miseries I have undergone since I parted with you at Saint James."

Myself.—I can scarcely believe that I really see you here at Oviedo. What motive can have induced you to come to such an out-of-the-way place from such an immense distance!

Benedict.—Lieber herr, I will sit down and tell you all that has befallen me. Some few days after I saw you last, the canonigo persuaded me to go to the captain-general to apply for permission to disinter the schatz, and also to crave assistance. So I saw the captain-general, who at first received me very kindly, asked me several questions, and told me to come again. So I continued visiting him till he would see me no longer, and do what I could not obtain a glance of him. The canon now became impatient, more especially as he had given me a few pesetas out of the charities of the church. He frequently called me a bribon and impostor. At last, one morning I went to him, and said that I proposed to return to Madrid, in order to lay the matter before the government, and requested that he would give me a certificate to the effect that I had performed a pilgrimage to Saint James, which I imagined would be of assistance to me upon the way, as it would enable me to beg with some colour of authority. He no sooner heard this request, than, without saying a word or allowing me a moment to put myself on my defence, he sprang upon me like a tiger, grasping my throat so hard that I thought he would have strangled me. I am a Swiss, however, and a man of Lucerne, and when I had recovered myself a little, I had no difficulty in flinging him off; I then threatened him with my staff and went away. He followed me to the gate with the most horrid curses, saying that if I presumed to return again, he would have me thrown at once into prison as a thief and a heretic. So I went in quest of yourself, lieber herr, but they told me that you were departed for Coruña; I then set out for Coruña after you.

Myself.—And what befell you on the road!

Benedict.—I will tell you: about half-way between Saint James and Coruña, as I was walking along thinking of the schatz, I heard a loud galloping, and looking around me I saw two men on horseback coming across the field with the swiftness of the wind, and making directly for me. Lieber Gott, said I, these are thieves, these are factious, and so they were. They came up to me in a moment and bade me stand, so I flung down my staff, took off my hat and saluted them. "Good day, caballeros," said I to them. "Good day, countryman," said they to me, and then we stood staring at each other for more than a minute. Lieber himmel, I never saw such robbers; so finely dressed, so well armed, and mounted so bravely on two fiery little hakkas, that looked as if they could have taken wing and flown up into the clouds! So we continued staring at each other, till at last one asked me who I was, whence I came, and where I was going. "Gentlemen," said I, "I am a Swiss, I have been to Saint James to perform a religious vow, and am now returning to my own country." I said not a word about the treasure, for I was afraid that they would have shot me at once, conceiving that I carried part of it about me. "Have you any money?" they demanded. "Gentlemen," I replied, "you see how I travel on foot, with my shoes torn to pieces; I should not do so if I had money. I will not deceive you, however, I have a peseta and a few cuartos," and thereupon I took out what I had and offered it to them. "Fellow," said they, we are caballeros of Galicia, and do not take pesetas, much less cuartos. Of what opinion are you? Are you for the queen?" "No, gentlemen," said I, "I am not for the queen, but, at the same time, allow me to tell you that I am not for the king either; I know nothing about the matter; I am a Swiss, and fight neither for nor against anybody unless I am paid." This made them laugh, and then they questioned me about Saint James, and the troops there, and the captain-general; and not to disoblige them, I told them all I knew and much more. Then one of them, who looked the fiercest and most determined, took his trombone in his hand, and pointing it at me, said, "Had you been a Spaniard, we would have blown your head to shivers, for we should have thought you a spy, but we see you are a foreigner, and believe what you have said; take, therefore, this peseta and go your way, but beware that you tell nobody any thing about us, for if you do, carracho!" he then discharged his trombone just over my head, so that for a moment I thought myself shot, and then with an awful shout, they both galloped away, their horses leaping over the barrancos, as if possessed with many devils.

Myself.—And what happened to you on your arrival at Coruña?

Benedict.—When I arrived at Coruña, I inquired after yourself, lieber herr, and they informed me that, only the day before my arrival, you had departed for Oviedo: and when I heard that my heart died within me, for I was now at the far end of Galicia, without a friend to help me. For a day or two I knew not what to do; at last I determined to make for the frontier of France, passing through Oviedo in the way, where I hoped to see you and ask counsel of you. So I begged and bettled among the Germans of Coruña. I, however, got very little from them, only a few cuarts, less than the thieves had given me on the road from Saint James, and with these I departed for the Asturias by the way of Mondonedo. Och, what a town is that, full of canons, priests, and pfaffen, all of them more Carlist than Carlos himself.

One day I went to the bishop's palace and spoke to him, telling him I was a pilgrim from Saint James, and requesting assistance. He told me, however, that he could not relieve me, and as for my being a pilgrim from Saint James, he was glad of it, and hoped that it would be of service to my soul. So I left Mondonedo, and got amongst the wild mountains, begging and bettling at the door of every choza that I passed, telling all I saw that I was a pilgrim from Saint James, and

showing my passport in proof that I had been there. Lieber herr, no person gave me a cuart nor even a piece of broa, and both Gallegans and Asturians laughed at Saint James and told me that his name was no longer a passport in Spain. I should have starved if I had not sometimes plucked an ear or two out of the maize fields; I likewise gathered grapes from the parras and berries from the brambles, and in this manner I subsisted till I arrived at the bellotas, where I slaughtered a stray kid, which I met, and devoured part of the flesh raw, so great was my hunger. It made me, however, very ill, and for two days I lay in a barranco half dead and unable to help myself; it was a mercy that I was not devoured by the wolves. I then struck across the country for Oviedo: how I reached it I do not know; I was like one walking in a dream. Last night I slept in an empty hogsty about two leagues from here, and ere I left it, I fell down on my knees and prayed to God that I might find you, lieber herr, for you were my last hope.

Myself.—And what do you propose to do at present?

Benedict.—What can I say, lieber herr? I know not what to do. I will be guided in every thing by your counsel.

Myself.—I shall remain at Oviedo a few days longer, during which time you can lodge at this posada, and endeavour to recover from the fatigue of your disastrous journeys; perhaps, before I depart, we may hit on some plan to extricate you from your present difficulties.

Oviedo contains about fifteen thousand inhabitants. It is picturesquely situated between two mountains, Morcin and Naranco; the former is very high and ragged, and during the greater part of the year is covered with snow; the sides of the latter are cultivated and planted with vines. The principal ornament of the town is the cathedral, the tower of which is exceedingly lofty, and is perhaps one of the purest specimens of Gothic architecture at present in existence. The interior of the cathedral is neat and appropriate, but simple and unadorned. I observed but one picture, the Conversion of Saint Paul. One of the chapels is a cemetery, in which rest the bones of eleven Gothic kings; to whose souls be peace.

I bore a letter of recommendation from Coruña to a merchant of Oviedo. This person received me very courteously, and generally devoted some portion of every day to showing me the remarkable things of Oviedo.

One morning he thus addressed me: "You have doubtless heard of Feijoo, the celebrated philosophic monk of the order of Saint Benedict, whose writings have so much tended to remove the popular fallacies and superstitions so long cherished in Spain; he is buried in one of our convents, where he passed a considerable portion of his life. Come with me and I will show you his portrait. Carlos Tercero, our great king, sent his own painter from Madrid to execute it. It is now in the possession of a friend of mine, Don Ramon Valdez, an advocate."

Thereupon, he led me to the house of Don Ramon Valdez, who very politely exhibited the portrait of Feijoo. It was circular in shape, about a foot in diameter, and was surrounded by a little brass frame, something like the rim of a barber's basin. The countenance was large and massive but fine, the eyebrows knit, the eyes sharp and penetrating, nose aquiline. On the head was a silken scull-cap; the collar of the coat or vest was just perceptible. The painting was decidedly good, and struck me as being one of the very best specimens of modern Spanish art which I had hitherto seen.

A day or two after this, I said to Benedict Mol, "to-morrow I start from hence for Santander. It is therefore high time that you decide upon some course, whether to return to Madrid or to make the best of your way to France, and from thence proceed to your own country."

"Lieber herr," said Benedict, "I will follow you to Santander by short journeys, for I am unable to make long ones amongst these hills; and when I am there, peradventure I may find some means of passing into France. It is a great comfort, in my horrible journeys, to think that I am travelling over the ground which yourself have trodden, and to hope that I am proceeding to rejoin you once more. This hope kept me alive in the bellotas, and without it I should never have reached Oviedo. I will quit Spain as soon as possible, and betake me to Lucerne, though it is a hard thing to leave the schatz behind me in the land of the Gallegans."

Thereupon I presented him with a few dollars.

"A strange man is this Benedict," said Antonio to me next morning, as, accompanied by a guide, we sallied forth from Oviedo; "a strange man, mon maître, is this same Benedict. A strange life has he led, and a strange death he will die,—it is written on his countenance. That he will leave Spain I do not believe, or if he leave it, it will be only to return, for he is bewitched about this treasure. Last night he sent for a sorciere, whom he consulted in my presence; and she told him that he was doomed to possess it, but that first of all he must cross water. She cautioned him likewise against an enemy, which he supposes must be the canon of Saint James. I have often heard people speak of the avidity of the Swiss for money, and here is a proof of it. I would not undergo what Benedict has suffered in these last journeys of his, to possess all the treasures in Spain."

CHAPTER XXXIV.

Departure from Oviedo—Villa Viciosa—The Young Man of the Inn—Antonio's Tale—The General and his Family—Woful Tidings—To-morrow we die—San Vincente—Santander—An Harangue —Flinter the Irishman.

So we left Oviedo and directed our course towards Santander. The man who accompanied us as guide, and from whom I hired the pony on which I rode, had been recommended to me by my friend the merchant of Oviedo. He proved, however, a lazy, indolent fellow; he was generally loitering two or three hundred yards in our rear, and instead of enlivening the way with song and tale, like our late guide, Martin of Rivadeo, he scarcely ever opened his lips, save to tell us not to go so fast, or that I should burst his pony if I spurred him so. He was thievish withal, and though he had engaged to make the journey seco, that is, to defray the charges of himself and beast, he contrived throughout to keep both at our expense. When journeying in Spain, it is invariably the cheapest plan to agree to maintain the guide and his horse or mule, for by so doing the hire is diminished at least one-third, and the bills upon the road are seldom increased; whereas, in the other case, he pockets the difference, and yet goes shot-free, and at the expense of the traveller, through the connivance of the innkeepers, who have a kind of fellow-feeling with the guides.

Late in the afternoon we reached Villa Viciosa, a small dirty town, at the distance of eight leagues from Oviedo: it stands beside a creek which communicates with the bay of Biscay. It is sometimes called La Capital de las Avellanas, or the capital of the Filberts, from the immense quantity of this fruit which is grown in the neighbourhood, and the greatest part of which is exported to England. As we drew nigh, we overtook numerous cars laden with avellanas proceeding in the direction of the town. I was informed that several small English vessels were lying in the harbour. Singular as it may seem, however, notwithstanding we were in the capital of the Avellanas, it was with the utmost difficulty that I procured a scanty handful for my dessert, and of these more than one-half were decayed. The people of the house informed me that the nuts were intended for exportation, and that they never dreamed either of partaking of them themselves or of offering them to their guests.

At an early hour on the following day we reached Colunga, a beautiful village on a rising ground, thickly planted with chestnut trees. It is celebrated, at least in the Asturias, as being the birth-place of Arguelles, the father of the Spanish constitution.

As we dismounted at the door of the posada,

where we intended to refresh ourselves, a person who was leaning out of an upper window uttered an exclamation and disappeared. We were yet at the door, when the same individual came running forth and cast himself on the neck of Antonio. He was a good-looking young man, apparently about five-and-twenty, genteelly dressed, with a Montero cap on his head. Antonio looked at him for a moment, and then, with a *Ah, Monsieur, est ce bien vous?* shook him affectionately by the hand. The stranger then motioned him to follow him, and they forthwith proceeded to the room above.

Wondering what this could mean, I sat down to my morning repast. Nearly an hour elapsed, and still Antonio did not make his appearance; through the boards, however, which composed the ceiling of the kitchen where I sat, I could hear the voices of himself and his acquaintance, and thought that I could occasionally distinguish the sound of broken sobs and groans: at last there was a long pause. I became impatient, and was about to summon Antonio, when he made his appearance, but unaccompanied by the stranger. "What, in the name of all that is singular," I demanded, "have you been about? Who is that man?" "Mon maître," said Antonio, "*c'est un monsieur de ma connoissance*. With your permission I will now take a mouthful, and as we journey along I will tell you all that I know of him."

"Monsieur," said Antonio as we rode out of Colunga, "you are anxious to know the history of the gentleman whom you saw embrace me at the inn. Know, mon maître, that these Carlist and Christino wars have been the cause of much misery and misfortune in this country; but a being so thoroughly unfortunate as that poor young gentleman of the inn, I do not believe is to be found in Spain; and his misfortunes proceed entirely from the spirit of party and faction which for some time past has been so prevalent.

"Mon maître, as I have often told you, I have lived in many houses and served many masters; and it chanced that about ten years ago I served the father of this gentleman, who was then a mere boy. It was a very high family, for Monsieur the father was a general in the army, and a man of large possessions. The family consisted of the general, his lady, and two sons, the youngest of whom is the person you have just seen; the other was several years older. Pardieu! I felt myself very comfortable in that house, and every individual of the family had all kind of complaisance for me. It is singular enough, that though I have been turned out of so many families, I was never turned out of that; and though I left it thrice, it was of my own free will. I became dissatisfied with the other servants, or with the dog or the cat. The last time I left was on account of the quail which was nung out of the window of madame, and which waked me in the morning with its call. *Eh bien, mon maître*, things went on in this way during the three years that I continued in the family, out and in; at the end of which

time it was determined that the young gentleman should travel, and it was proposed that I should attend him as valet; this I wished very much to do. However, par malheur, I was at this time very much dissatisfied with madame his mother about the quail, and I insisted that before I accompanied him the bird should be slaughtered for the kitchen. To this madame would by no means consent; and even the young gentleman, who had always taken my part on other occasions, said that I was unreasonable; so I left the house in a huff, and never entered it again.

"*Eh bien, mon maître*, the young gentleman went upon his travels, and continued abroad several years; and from the time of his departure, until we met him at Colunga, I have not set eye upon, nor indeed heard of him. I have heard enough, however, of his family; of monsieur the father, of madame, and of the brother, who was an officer of cavalry. A short time before the troubles, I mean before the death of Ferdinand, monsieur the father was appointed captain-general of Coruña. Now monsieur, though a good master, was rather a proud man, and fond of discipline, and all that kind of thing, and of obedience. He was, moreover, no friend to the populace, to the canaille, and he had a particular aversion to the nationals. So when Ferdinand died, it was whispered about at Coruña, that the general was no liberal, and that he was a better friend to Carlos than Christina. *Eh bien*, it chanced that there was a grand fête, or festival at Coruna, on the water; and the nationals were there, and the soldiers. And I know not how it befell, but there was an emeute, and the nationals laid hands on monsieur the general, and tying a rope round his neck, flung him overboard from the barge in which he was, and then dragged him astern about the harbour until he was drowned. They then went to his house and pillaged it, and so ill-treated madame, who at that time happened to be enceinte, that in a few hours she expired.

"I tell you what, mon maître, when I heard of the misfortune of madame and the general, you would scarcely believe it, but I actually shed tears, and was sorry that I had parted with them in unkindness on account of that pernicious quail.

"*Eh bien, mon maître, nous poursuivrons notre histoire*. The eldest son, as I told you before, was a cavalry officer, and a man of resolution, and when he heard of the death of his father and mother, he vowed revenge. Poor fellow! So what does he do but desert, with two or three discontented spirits of his troop, and going to the frontier of Galicia, he raised a small faction, and proclaimed Don Carlos. For some little time he did considerable damage to the liberals, burning and destroying their possessions, and putting to death several nationals that fell into his hands. However, this did not last long, his faction was soon dispersed, and he himself taken and hanged, and his head stuck on a pole.

"*Nous sommes déjà presque au bout.* When

N 2

we arrived at the inn, the young man took me above, as you saw, and there for some time he could do nothing but weep and sob. His story is soon told :—he returned from his travels, and the first intelligence which awaited him on his arrival in Spain was, that his father was drowned, his mother dead, and his brother hanged, and, moreover, all the possessions of his family confiscated. This was not all ; wherever he went, he found himself considered in the light of a factious and discontented person, and was frequently assailed by the nationals with blows of sabres and cudgels. He applied to his relations, and some of these, who were of the Carlist persuasion, advised him* to betake himself to the army of Don Carlos, and the Pretender himself, who was a friend of his father, and remembered the services of his brother, offered to give him a command in his army. But, mon maître, as I told you before, he was a pacific young gentleman, and as mild as a lamb, and hated the idea of shedding blood. He was, moreover, not of the Carlist opinion, for during his studies he had read books written a long time ago by countrymen of mine, all about republics and liberties, and the rights of man, so that he was much more inclined to the liberal than the Carlist system ; he therefore declined the offer of Don Carlos, whereupon all his relations deserted him, whilst the liberals hunted him from one place to another like a wild beast. At last, he sold some little property which still remained to him, and with the proceeds he came to this remote place of Colunga, where no one knew him, and where he has been residing for several months, in a most melancholy manner, with no other amusement than that which he derives from a book or two, or occasionally hunting a leveret with his spaniel.

"He asked me for counsel, but I had none to give him, and could only weep with him. At last he said, 'Dear Antonio, I see there is no remedy. You say your master is below, beg him, I pray to stay till to-morrow, and we will send for the maidens of the neighbourhood, and for a violin and a bagpipe, and we will dance and cast away care for a moment.' And then he said something in old Greek, which I scarcely understood, but which I think was equivalent to, 'Let us eat, and drink, and be merry, for to-morrow we die !'

"Eh bien, mon maître, I told him that you were a serious gentleman who never took any amusement, and that you were in a hurry. Whereupon he wept again, and embraced me, and bade me farewell. And now, mon maître, I have told you the history of the young man of the inn."

We slept at Ribida de Sella, and the next day, at noon, arrived at Llanes. Our route lay between the coast and an immense range of mountains, which rose up like huge ramparts at about a league's distance from the sea. The ground over which we passed was tolerably level, and seemingly well cultivated. There was no lack of vines and trees, whilst at short intervals rose the cortijos of the pro-

prietors,—square stone buildings surrounded with an outer wall. Llanes is an old town, formerly of considerable strength. In its neighbourhood is the convent of San Cilorio, one of the largest monastic edifices in all Spain. It is now deserted, and stands lone and desolate upon one of the peninsulas of the Cantabrian shore. Leaving Llanes, we soon entered one of the most dreary and barren regions imaginable, a region of rock and stone, where neither grass nor trees were to be seen. Night overtook us in these places. We wandered on, however, until we reached a small village, termed Santo Colombo. Here we passed the night, in the house of a carabineer of the revenue, a tall athletic figure who met us at the gate armed with a gun. He was a Castilian, and with all that ceremonious formality and grave politeness for which his countrymen were at one time so celebrated. He chid his wife for conversing with her handmaid about the concerns of the house before us. "Barbara," said he, "this is not conversation calculated to interest the strange cavaliers; hold your peace, or go aside with the muchacha." In the morning he refused any remuneration for his hospitality. "I am a caballero," said he, "even as yourselves. It is not my custom to admit people into my house for the sake of lucre. I received you because you were benighted and the posada distant."

Rising early in the morning, we pursued our way through a country equally stony and dreary as that which we had entered, upon the preceding day. In about four hours we reached San Vincente, a large dilapidated town, chiefly inhabited by miserable fishermen. It retains, however, many remarkable relics of former magnificence : the bridge, which bestrides the broad and deep frith, on which stands the town, has no less than thirty-two arches, and is built of gray granite. It is very ancient, and in some part in so ruinous a condition as to be dangerous.

Leaving San Vincente behind us, we travelled for some leagues on the sea-shore, crossing occasionally a narrow inlet or frith. The country at last began to improve, and in the neighbourhood of Santillana was both beautiful and fertile. About a league before we reached the country of Gil Blas, we passed through an extensive wood, in which were rocks and precipices; it was exactly such a place as that in which the cave of Rolando was situated, as described in the novel. This wood has an evil name, and our guide informed us that robberies were occasionally committed in it. No adventure, however, befell us, and we reached Santillana at about six in the evening.

We did not enter the town, but halted at a large venta or posada at the entrance, before which stood an immense ash tree. We had scarcely housed ourselves when a tremendous storm of rain and wind commenced, accompanied with thunder and lightning, which continued without much interruption for several hours, and the effects of which were visible in our journey of the following day, the streams over which we passed being much swollen, and several trees lying uptorn by the wayside. Santillana contains four thousand inhabitants, and is six short leagues distance from Santander, where we arrived early the next day.

Nothing could exhibit a stronger contrast to the desolate tracts and the half ruined towns through which we had lately passed, than the bustle and activity of Santander, which, though it stands on the confines of the Basque provinces, the stronghold of the Pretender, is almost the only city in Spain which has not suffered by the Carlist wars. Till the close of the last century it was little better than an obscure fishing town, but it has of late years almost entirely engrossed the commerce of the Spanish transatlantic possessions, especially of the Havannah. The consequence of which has been, that whilst Santander has rapidly increased in wealth and magnificence, both Coruna and Cadiz have been as rapidly hastening to decay. At present it possesses a noble quay, on which stands a line of stately edifices, far exceeding in splendour the palaces of the aristocracy at Madrid. These are built in the French style, and are chiefly occupied by the merchants. The population of Santander is estimated at sixty thousand souls.

On the day of my arrival I dined at the table d'hôte of the principal inn, kept by a Genoese. The company was very miscellaneous, French, Germans, and Spaniards, all speaking in their respective languages, whilst at the ends of the table, confronting each other, sat two Catalan merchants, one of whom weighed nearly twenty stone, grunting across the board in their harsh dialect. Long, however, before dinner was concluded, the conversation was entirely engrossed, and the attention of all present directed to an individual who sat on one side of the bulky Catalan. He was a thin man of about the middle height, with a remarkable red face, and something in his eyes which, if not a squint, bore a striking resemblance to it. He was dressed in a blue military frock, and seemed to take much more pleasure in haranguing than in the fare which was set before him. He spoke perfectly good Spanish, yet his voice betrayed something of a foreign accent. For a long time he descanted with immense volubility on war and all its circumstances, freely criticizing the conduct of the generals, both Carlist and Christinos, in the present struggle, till at last he exclaimed, "Had I but twenty thousand men allowed me by the government, I would bring the war to a conclusion in six months."

"Pardon me, sir," said a Spaniard who sat at the table, "the curiosity which induces me to request the favour of your distinguished name."

"I am Flinter," replied the individual in the military frock; "a name which is in the mouth of every man, woman, and child in Spain. I am Flinter the Irishman, just escaped from the Basque provinces and the claws of Don Carlos. On the decease of Ferdinand I declared for Isabella, esteeming it the duty of every good cavalier and Irishman in the Spanish service to do so. You have all heard of my exploits, and permit me to tell you they would have been yet more glorious had not jealousy been at work and cramped my means. Two years ago I was despatched to Estremadura, to organize the militias. The bands of Gomez and Cabrera entered the province and spread devastation around. They found me, however, at my post; and had I been properly seconded by those under my command, the two rebels would never have returned to their master to boast of their success. I stood behind my intrenchments. A man advanced and summoned us to surrender. 'Who are you?' I demanded. 'I am Cabrera,' he replied; 'and I am Flinter,' I retorted, flourishing my sabre; 'retire to your battalions or you will forthwith die the death.' He was awed and did as I commanded. In an hour we surrendered. I was led a prisoner to the Basque provinces; and the Carlists rejoiced in the capture they had made, for the name of Flinter had long sounded amongst the Carlist ranks. I was flung into a loathsome dungeon, where I remained twenty months. I was cold; I was naked; but I did not on that account despond, my spirit was too indomitable for such weakness. My keeper at last pitied my misfortunes. 'He said that it grieved him to see so valiant a man perish in inglorious confinement.' We laid a plan to escape together; disguises were provided, and we made the attempt. We passed unobserved till we arrived at the Carlist lines above Bilbao; there we were stopped. My presence of mind, however, did not desert me. I was disguised as a carman, as a Catalan, and the coolness of my answers deceived my interrogators. We were permitted to pass, and soon were safe within the walls of Bilbao. There was an illumination that night in the town, for the lion had burst his toils, Flinter had escaped, and was once more returned to reanimate a drooping cause. I have just arrived at Santander on my way to Madrid, where I intend to ask of the government a command, with twenty thousand men."

Poor Flinter! a braver heart, and a more gasconading mouth were surely never united in the same body. He proceeded to Madrid, and through the influence of the British ambassador, who was his friend, he obtained the command of a small division, with which he contrived to surprise and defeat, in the neighbourhood of Toledo, a body of the Carlists, commanded by Orejita, whose numbers more than trebled his own. In reward for this exploit he was persecuted by the government, which, at that time, was the moderado or juste milieu, with the most relentless animosity; the prime minister, Ofalia, supporting with all his influence numerous and ridiculous accusations of plunder and robbery brought against the too successful general by the Carlist canons of Toledo. He was likewise charged with a dereliction of duty, in having permitted, after the battle of Valdepeñas, which he likewise won in the most gallant manner, the Carlist force to take possession of the mines of Almaden, although the government, who were bent on his ruin, had done all in their power to prevent him from following up his successes by denying him the slightest supplies and reinforcements. The fruits of victory thus wrested from him, his hopes blighted, a morbid melancholy seized upon the Irishman; he resigned his command, and in less than ten months from the period when I saw him at Santander, afforded his dastardly and malignant enemies a triumph which satisfied even them, by cutting his own throat with a razor.

Ardent spirits of foreign climes who hope to distinguish yourselves in the service of Spain, and to earn honours and rewards, remember the fate of Columbus, and of another as brave and as ardent—Flinter!

CHAPTER XXXV.

Departure from Santander—The Night-alarm—The Black Pass.

I HAD ordered two hundred Testaments to be sent to Santander from Madrid: I found, however, to my great sorrow that they had not arrived, and I supposed that they had either been seized on the way by the Carlists, or that my letter had miscarried. I then thought of applying to England for a supply, but I abandoned the idea for two reasons. In the first place, I should have to remain idly loitering, at least a month before I could receive them, at a place where every article was excessively dear; and, secondly, I was very unwell, and unable to procure medical advice at Santander. Ever since I left Coruña I had been afflicted with a terrible dysentery, and latterly with an ophthalmia, the result of the other malady. I therefore determined on returning to Madrid. To effect this, however, seemed no very easy task. Parties of the army of Don Carlos, which, in a partial degree, had been routed in Castile, were hovering about the country through which I should have to pass, more especially in that part called "The Mountains," so that all communication had ceased between Santander and the southern districts. Nevertheless, I determined to trust as usual in the Almighty, and to risk the danger. I purchased, therefore, a small horse, and sallied forth with Antonio.

Before departing, however, I entered into conference with the booksellers as to what they should do in the event of my finding an opportunity of sending them a stock of Testaments from Madrid; and, having arranged matters to my satisfaction, I committed myself to Providence. I will not dwell long on this journey of three hundred miles. We were in the midst of the fire, yet, strange to say, escaped without a hair of our heads being singed. Robberies, murders, and all kinds of atrocities were perpetrated before, behind, and on both sides of us, but not so much as a dog barked at us, though in one instance a plan had been laid to intercept us. About four leagues from Santander, whilst we were baiting our horses at a village hostelry, I saw a fellow run off after having held a whispering conversation with a boy who was dealing out barley to us. I instantly inquired of the latter what the man had said to him, but only obtained an evasive answer. It appeared afterwards that the conversation was about ourselves. Two or three leagues farther there was an inn and village where we had proposed staying, and indeed had expressed our intention of doing so; but on arriving there, finding that the sun was still far from its bourn, I determined to proceed farther, expecting to meet with a resting-place at the distance of a league; though I was mistaken, as we found none until we reached Montaneda, nine leagues and a half from Santander, where was stationed a small detachment of soldiers. At the dead of night, we were aroused from our sleep by a cry that the factious were not far off. A messenger had arrived from the alcalde of the village where we had previously intended staying, who stated that a party of Carlists had just surprised that place, and were searching for an English spy, whom they supposed to be at the inn. The officer commanding the soldiers, upon hearing this, not deeming his own situation a safe one, instantly drew off his men, falling back on a stronger party stationed in a fortified village near at hand. As for ourselves, we saddled our horses and continued our way in the dark. Had the Carlists succeeded in apprehending me, I should instantly have been shot, and my body cast on the rocks to feed the vultures and wolves. But "it was not so written," said Antonio, who, like many of his countrymen, was a fatalist. The next night we had another singular escape: we had arrived near the entrance of a horrible pass called "El puerto de la puente de las tablas," or the pass of the bridge of planks, which wound through a black and frightful mountain, on the farther side of which was the town of Oñas, where we meant to tarry for the night. The sun had set about a quarter of an hour. Suddenly a man, with his face covered with blood, rushed out of the pass. "Turn back, sir," he said, "in the name of God; there are murderers in that pass; they have just robbed me of my mule and all I possess, and I have hardly escaped with life from their hands." I scarcely know why, but I made him no answer and proceeded; indeed I was so weary and unwell that I cared not what became of me.

We entered; the rocks rose perpendicularly, right and left, entirely intercepting the scanty twilight, so that the darkness of the grave, or rather the blackness of the valley of the shadow of death reigned around us, and we knew not where we went, but trusted to the instinct of the horses, who moved on with their heads close to the ground. The only sound which we heard was the splash of a stream which tumbled down the pass. I expected every moment to feel a knife at my throat, but "*it was not so written.*" We threaded the pass without meeting a human being, and within three quarters of an hour after the time we entered it, we found ourselves within the posada of the town of Onas, which was filled with troops and armed peasants expecting an attack from the grand Carlist army, which was near at hand.

Well, we reached Burgos in safety; we reached Valladolid in safety; we passed the Guadarama in safety; and were at length safely housed in Madrid. People said we had been very lucky; Antonio said, "It was so written;" but I say, Glory be to the Lord for his mercies vouchsafed to us.

CHAPTER XXXVI.

State of affairs at Madrid—The New Ministry—Pope of Rome—The Bookseller of Toledo—Sword Blades—Houses of Toledo—The Forlorn Gipsy—Proceedings at Madrid—Another Servant.

DURING my journey in the northern provinces of Spain, which occupied a considerable portion of the year 1837, I had accomplished but a slight portion of what I proposed to myself to effect in the outset. Insignificant are the results of man's labours, compared with the swelling ideas of his presumption; something, however, had been effected by the journey, which I had just concluded. The New Testament of Christ was now enjoying a quiet sale in the principal towns of the north; and I had secured the friendly interest and co-operation of the booksellers of those parts, particularly of him the most considerable of them all, old Rey of Compostella. I had, moreover, disposed of a considerable number of Testaments with my own hands, to private individuals, entirely of the lower classes, namely, muleteers, carmen, contrabandistas, &c., so that upon the whole I had abundant cause for gratitude and thanksgiving.

I did not find our affairs in a very prosperous state at Madrid, few copies having been sold in the booksellers' shops, yet what could be rationally expected during these latter times? Don Carlos, with a large army had been at the gates; plunder and massacre had been expected; so that people were too much occupied in forming plans to secure their lives and property, to give much attention to reading of any description.

The enemy, however, had now retired to his strongholds in Alava and Guipuscoa. I hoped that brighter days were dawning, and that the work, under my own superintendence, would, with God's blessing, prosper in the capital of Spain. How far the result corresponded with my expectations will be seen in the sequel.

During my absence in the north, a total change of ministers had occurred. The liberal party had been ousted from the cabinet, and in their place had entered individuals attached to the moderado or court party: unfortunately, however, for my prospects, they consisted of persons with whom I had no acquaintance whatever, and with whom my former friends, Galiano and Isturitz, had little or no influence. These gentlemen were now regularly laid on the shelf, and their political career appeared to be terminated forever.

From the present ministry I could expect but little; they consisted of men, the greater part of whom had been either courtiers or employés of the deceased King Ferdinand, who were friends to absolutism, and by no means inclined to do or to favour any thing calculated to give offence to the court of Rome, which they were anxious to conciliate, hoping that eventually it might be induced to recognise the young queen, not as the constitutional but as the absolute Queen Isabella the Second.

Such was the party which continued in power throughout the remainder of my sojourn in Spain, and which persecuted me less from rancour and malice than from policy. It was not until the conclusion of the war of the succession that it lost the ascendancy, when it sank to the ground with its patroness the queen-mother, before the dictatorship of Espartero.

The first step which I took after my return to Madrid, towards circulating the Scriptures, was a very bold one. It was neither more nor less than the establishment of a shop for the sale of Testaments. This shop was situated in the Calle del Principe, a respectable and well frequented street in the neighbourhood of the Square of Cervantes. I furnished it handsomely with glass cases, and chandeliers, and procured an acute Gallegan of the name of Pepe Calzado, to superintend the business, who gave me weekly a faithful account of the copies sold.

"How strangely times alter," said I, the second day subsequent to the opening of my establishment, as I stood on the opposite side of the street, leaning against the wall with folded arms, surveying my shop, on the windows of which were painted in large yellow characters, *Despacho de la Sociedad Biblica y Estrangero;* " how strangely times alter; here have I been during the last eight months running about old Popish Spain, distributing Testaments, as agent of what the Papists call an heretical society, and have neither been stoned nor burnt; and here am I now in the capital, doing that which one would think were enough to cause all the dead inquisitors and officials buried within the circuit of the walls to rise from their graves and cry abomination; and yet no one interferes with me. Pope of Rome! Pope of Rome! look to thyself. That shop may be closed, but oh! what a sign of the times, that it has been permitted to exist for one day. It appears to me, my Father, that the days of your sway are numbered in Spain; that you will not be permitted much longer to plunder her, to scoff at her, and to scourge her with scorpions, as in bygone periods. See I not the hand on the wall? See I not in yonder letters a ' Mene, mene, Tekel Upharsin'? Look to thyself, Batuschca.''

And I remained for two hours, leaning against the wall, staring at the shop.

A short time after the establishment of the despacho at Madrid, I once more mounted the saddle, and, attended by Antonio, rode over to Toledo, for the purpose of circulating the Scriptures, sending beforehand by a muleteer a cargo of one hundred Testaments. I instantly addressed myself to the principal bookseller of the place, whom, from the circumstance of his living in a town so abounding with canons, priests, and ex-friars, as Toledo, I expected to find a Carlist, or a *servile* at least. I was never more mistaken in my life: on entering the shop, which was very large and commodious, I beheld a stout athletic man, dressed in a kind of cavalry uniform, with a helmet on his head and an immense sabre in his hand: this was the bookseller himself, who I soon found was an officer in the national cavalry. Upon learning who I was, he shook me heartily by the hand, and said that nothing would give him greater pleasure than taking charge of the books, which he would endeavour to circulate to the utmost of his ability.

" Will not your doing so bring you into odium with the clergy?''

" Ca!'' said he; " who cares? I am rich, and so was my father before me. I do not depend on them, they cannot hate me more than they do already, for I make no secret of my opinions. I have just returned from an expedition,'' said he; " my brother nationals and myself have, for the last three days, been occupied in hunting down the factious and thieves of the neighbourhood; we have killed three and brought in several prisoners. Who cares for the cowardly priests? I am a liberal, Don Jorge, and a friend of your countryman, Flinter. Many is the Carlist guerilla-curate and robber friar whom I have assisted him to catch. I am rejoiced to hear that he has just been appointed captain-general of Toledo;

there will be fine doings here when he arrives, Don Jorge. We will make the clergy shake between us, I assure you.''

Toledo was formerly the capital of Spain. Its population at present is barely fifteen thousand souls, though in the time of the Romans, and also during the middle ages, it is said to have amounted to between two and three hundred thousand. It is situated about twelve leagues (forty miles) westward of Madrid, and is built upon a steep rocky hill, round which flows the Tagus, on all sides but the north. It still possesses a great many remarkable edifices, notwithstanding that it has long since fallen into decay. Its cathedral is the most magnificent of Spain, and is the see of the primate. In the tower of this cathedral is the famous bell of Toledo, the largest in the world with the exception of the monster bell of Moscow, which I have also seen. It weighs 1543 arrobes, or 37,032 pounds. It has, however, a disagreeable sound, owing to a cleft in its side. Toledo could once boast the finest pictures in Spain, but many were stolen or destroyed by the French during the Peninsular war, and still more have lately been removed by order of the government. Perhaps the most remarkable one still remains; I allude to that which represents the burial of the Count of Orgaz, the masterpiece of Domenico, the Greek, a most extraordinary genius, some of whose productions possess merit of a very high order. The picture in question is in the little parish church of San Tome, at the bottom of the aisle, on the left side of the altar. Could it be purchased, I should say it would be cheap at five thousand pounds.

Amongst the many remarkable things which meet the eye of the curious observer at Toledo, is the manufactory of arms, where are wrought the swords, spears, and other weapons intended for the army, with the exception of fire-arms, which mostly come from abroad.

In old times, as is well known, the sword-blades of Toledo were held in great estimation, and were transmitted as merchandise throughout Christendom. The present manufactory, or fabrica, as it is called, is a handsome modern edifice, situated without the wall of the city, on a plain contiguous to the river, with which it communicates by a small canal. It is said that the water and the sand of the Tagus are essential for the proper tempering of the swords. I asked some of the principal workmen whether, at the present day, they could manufacture weapons of equal value to those of former days, and whether the secret had been lost.

" Ca!'' said they, " the swords of Toledo were never so good as those which we are daily making. It is ridiculous enough to see strangers coming here to purchase old swords, the greater part of which are mere rubbish, and never made at Toledo, yet for such they will give a large price, whilst they would grudge two dollars for this jewel which was made but yesterday;'' thereupon putting into my hand a middle-sized rapier. " Your worship," said they, "seems to have a strong arm, prove its temper against the stone wall; —thrust boldly and fear not."

I *have* a strong arm and dashed the point with my utmost force against the solid granite: my arm was numbed to the shoulder from the violence of the concussion, and continued so for nearly a week, but the sword appeared not to be at all blunted, or to have suffered in any respect.

"A better sword than that," said an ancient workman, a native of Old Castile, "never transfixed Moor out yonder on the sagra."

During my stay at Toledo, I lodged at the Posada de los Caballeros, which signifies the inn of the gentlemen, which name, in some respects, it certainly well deserved, for there are many palaces far less magnificent than this inn of Toledo. By magnificence it must not be supposed, however, that I allude to costliness of furniture, or any kind of luxury which pervaded the culinary department. The rooms were as empty as those of Spanish inns generally are, and the fare, though good in its kind, was plain and homely; but I have seldom seen a more imposing edifice. It was of immense size, consisting of several stories, and was built something in the Moorish taste, with a quadrangular court in the centre, beneath which was an immense algibe or tank, serving as a reservoir for rain-water. All the houses in Toledo are supplied with tanks of this description, into which the waters in the rainy season flow from the roofs through pipes. No other water is used for drinking: that of the Tagus not being considered salubrious, is only used for purposes of cleanliness, being conveyed up the steep narrow streets on donkeys, in large stone jars. The city standing on a rocky mountain, has no wells. As for the rain-water, it deposits a sediment in the tank, and becomes very sweet and potable: these tanks are cleaned out twice every year. During the summer, at which time the heat in this part of Spain is intense, the families spend the greater part of the day in the courts, which are overhung with a linen awning, the heat of the atmosphere being tempered by the coolness arising from the tank below, which answers the same purpose as the fountain in the southern provinces of Spain.

I spent about a week at Toledo, during which time several copies of the Testament were disposed of in the shop of my friend, the bookseller. Several priests took it up from the mostrador on which it lay, examined it, but made no remarks; none of them purchased it. My friend showed me through his house, almost every apartment of which was lined from roof to floor with books, many of which were highly valuable. He told me that he possessed the best collection in Spain of the ancient literature of the country. He was, however, less proud of his library than his stud: finding that I had some acquaintance with horses, his liking for me and also his respect considerably increased. "All I have," said he, "is at your service; I see you are a

man after my own heart. When you are disposed to ride out upon the sagra, you have only to apply to my groom, who will forthwith saddle you my famed Cordovese entero; I purchased him from the stables at Aranjuez, when the royal stud was broken up. There is but one other man to whom I would lend him, and that man is Flinter."

At Toledo I met with a forlorn gipsy woman and her son, a lad of about fourteen years of age; she was not a native of the place, but had come from La Mancha, her husband having been cast into the prison of Toledo on a charge of mule-stealing; the crime had been proved against him, and in a few days he was to depart for Malaga, with the chain of galley slaves. He was quite destitute of money, and his wife was now in Toledo, earning a few cuartos by telling fortunes about the streets, to support him in prison. She told me that it was her intention to follow him to Malaga, where she hoped to be able to effect his escape. What an instance of conjugal affection; and yet the affection here was all on one side, as is too frequently the case! Her husband was a worthless scoundrel, who had previously abandoned her and betaken himself to Madrid, where he had long lived in concubinage with the notorious she-thug Aurora, at whose instigation he had committed the robbery for which he was now held in durance. "Should your husband escape from Malaga, in what direction will he fly?" I demanded.

"To the chim of the Corohai, my son; to the land of the Moors, to be a soldier of the Moorish king."

"And what will become of yourself?" I inquired; "think you that he will take you with him?"

"He will leave me on the shore, my son, and as soon as he has crossed the black pawnee, he will forget me and never think of me more."

"And knowing his ingratitude, why should you give yourself so much trouble about him?"

"Am I not his romi, my son, and am I not bound by the law of the Cales to assist him to the last? Should he return from the land of the Corohai at the end of a hundred years, and should find me alive, and should say, I am hungry, little wife, go forth and steal or tell bahi, I must do it, for he is the rom and I the romi."

On my return to Madrid, I found the despacho still open: various Testaments had been sold, though the number was by no means considerable: the work had to labour under great disadvantage, from the ignorance of the people at large with respect to its tenor and contents. It was no wonder, then, that little interest was felt respecting it. To call, however, public attention to the despacho, I printed three thousand advertisements on paper, yellow, blue, and crimson, with which I almost covered the sides of the streets, and besides this, inserted an account of it in all the journals and periodicals; the consequence was, that in a short time almost every person in Madrid was aware of its existence. Such exertions in London or Paris would probably have ensured the sale of the entire edition of the New Testament within a few days. In Madrid, however, the result was not quite so flattering; for after the establishment had been open an entire month, the copies disposed of barely amounted to one hundred.

These proceedings of mine did not fail to cause a great sensation : the priests and their partisans were teeming with malice and fury, which, for some time, however, they thought proper to exhibit only in words; it being their opinion that I was favoured by the ambassador and by the British government; but there was no attempt, however atrocious, that might not be expected from their malignity; and were it right and seemly for me, the most insignificant of worms, to make such a comparison, I might say, like Paul at Ephesus, I was fighting with wild beasts.

On the last day of the year 1837, my servant Antonio thus addressed me : "Mon maître, it is necessary that I leave you for a time. Ever since we have returned from our journeys, I have become unsettled and dissatisfied with the house, the furniture, and with Donna Marequita. I have therefore engaged myself as cook in the house of the Count of * * * * *, where I am to receive four dollars per month less than what your worship gives me. I am fond of change, though it be for the worse. Adieu, mon maître, may you be as well served as you deserve; should you chance, however, to have any pressing need de mes soins, send for me without hesitation, and I will at once give my new master warning, if I am still with him, and come to you."

Thus was I deprived for a time of the services of Antonio. I continued for a few days without a domestic, at the end of which time I hired a certain Cantabrian or Basque, a native of the village of Hernani, in Guipuscoa, who was strongly recommended to me.

CHAPTER XXXVII.

Euscarra—Basque not Irish—Sanscrit and Tartar Dialects—A vowel Language—Popular Poetry—The Basques—Their Persons—Basque Women.

I now entered upon the year 1838, perhaps the most eventful of all those which I passed in Spain. The despacho still continued open, with a somewhat increasing sale. Having at this time little of particular moment with which to occupy myself, I committed to the press two works, which for some time past had been in the course of preparation. These were the Gospel of Saint Luke in the Spanish gipsy and the Euscarra languages.

With respect to the gipsy Gospel, I have little to say, having already spoken of it in a former work, (The Zincali :) it was translated by myself, together with the greater part of the New Testament, during my long intercourse with the Spanish gipsies. Concerning the Luke in Euscarra, however, it will be as well to be more particular, and to avail myself of the present opportunity to say a few words concerning the language in which it was written, and the people for whom it was intended.

The Euscarra, then, is the proper term for a certain speech or language, supposed to have been at one time prevalent throughout Spain, but which is at present confined to certain districts, both on the French and Spanish side of the Pyrenees, which are laved by the waters of the Cantabrian Gulf or Bay of Biscay. This language is commonly known as the Basque or Biscayan, which words are mere modifications of the word Euscarra, the consonant B having been prefixed for the sake of euphony. Much that is vague, erroneous, and hypothetical, has been said and written concerning this tongue. The Basques assert that it was not only the original language of Spain, but also of the world, and that from it all other languages are derived; but the Basques are a very ignorant people, and know nothing of the philosophy of language. Very little importance, therefore, need be attached to any opinion of theirs on such a subject. A few amongst them, however, who affect some degree of learning, contend that it is neither more nor less than a dialect of the Phenician, and that the Basques are the descendants of a Phenician colony, established at the foot of the Pyrenees at a very remote period. Of this theory, or rather conjecture, as it is unsubstantiated by the slightest proof, it is needless to take further notice than to observe that, provided the Phenician language, as many of the truly learned have supposed and almost proved, was a dialect of the Hebrew, or closely allied to it, it were as unreasonable to suppose that the Basque is derived from it, as that the Kamschatdale and Cherokee are dialects of the Greek and Latin.

There is, however, another opinion with respect to the Basque which deserves more especial notice, from the circumstance of its being extensively entertained amongst the literati of various countries of Europe, more especially England. I allude to the Celtic origin of this tongue, and its close connexion with the most cultivated of all the Celtic dialects, the Irish. People who pretend to be well conversant with the subject, have even gone so far as to assert, that so little difference exists between the Basque and Irish tongues, that individuals of the two nations, when they meet together, find no difficulty in understanding each other, with no other means of communication than their respective languages; in a word, that there is scarcely a greater difference between the two, than between the French and the Spanish Basque. Such similarity, however, though so strongly insisted upon, by no means exists in fact, and perhaps in the whole of Europe it would be difficult to discover two languages which exhibit fewer points of mutual resemblance than the Basque and Irish.

The Irish, like most other European languages, is a dialect of the Sanscrit, a *remote* one, as may well be supposed. The corner of the western world in which it is still preserved being, of all countries in Europe, the most distant from the proper home of the parent tongue. It is still, however, a dialect of that venerable and most original speech, not so closely resembling it, it is true, as the English, Danish, and those which belong to what is called the Gothic family, and far less than those of the Sclavonian; for the nearer we approach to the east, in equal degree the assimilation of languages to this parent stock becomes more clear and distinct; but still a dialect, agreeing with the Sanscrit in structure, in the arrangement of words, and in many instances in the words themselves, which, however modified, may still be recognised as Sanscrit. But what is the Basque, and to what family does it properly pertain?

To two great Asiatic languages, all the dialects spoken at present in Europe may be traced. These two, if not now spoken, still exist in books, and are, moreover, the languages of two of the principal religions of the east. I allude to the Tibetian and Sanscrit—the sacred languages of the followers of Buddh and Bramah. These tongues, though they possess many words in common, which is easily to be accounted for by their close proximity, are properly distinct, being widely different in structure. In what this difference consists, I have neither time nor inclination to state; suffice it to say, that the Celtic, Gothic, and Sclavonian dialects in Europe belong to the Sanscrit family, even as in the east the Persian, and to a less degree the Arabic, Hebrew, &c.; whilst to the Tibetian or Tartar family in Asia pertain the Mandchou and Mongolian, the Calmuc and the Turkish of the Caspian Sea; and in Europe, the Hungarian and the Basque *partially.*

Indeed this latter language is a strange anomaly, so that upon the whole it is less difficult to say what it is not than what it is. It abounds with Sanscrit words to such a degree that its surface seems strewn with them. Yet would it be wrong to term it a Sanscrit dialect, for in the collocation of these words the Tartar form is most decidedly observable. A considerable proportion of Tartar words is likewise to be found in this language, though perhaps not in equal number to the terms derived from the Sanscrit. Of these Tartar etymons I shall at present content myself with citing one, though, if necessary, it were easy to adduce hundreds. This word is *Jauna,* or as it is pronounced *Khauna,* a word in constant use amongst the Basques, and which is the *Khan* of the Mongols and Mandchous, and of the same signification—*Lord.*

Having closely examined the subject in all its various bearings, and having weighed what is to be said on one side against what is to be advanced on the other, I am inclined to rank the Basque rather amongst the Tartar than the Sanscrit dialects. Whoever should have an opportunity of comparing the enunciation of the Basques and Tartars would, from that alone, even if he understood them not, come to the conclusion that their respective languages were formed on the same principles. In both occur periods seemingly interminable, during which the voice gradually ascends to a climax, and then gradually sinks down.

I have spoken of the surprising number of Sanscrit words contained in the Basque language, specimens of some of which will be found below. It is remarkable enough, that in the greater part of the derivations from the Sanscrit, the Basque has dropped the initial consonant so that the word commences with a vowel. The Basque, indeed, may be said to be almost a vowel language; the number of consonants employed being comparatively few: perhaps eight words out of ten commence and terminate with a vowel, owing to which it is a language to the highest degree soft and melodious, far excelling in this respect any other language in Europe, not even excepting the Italian.

Here follow a few specimens of Basque words, with the Sanscrit roots in juxtaposition;—

BASQUE.	SANSCRIT.	
Ardoa	Sandhána	*Wine.*
Arratsa	Ratri	*Night.*
Beguia	Akshi	*Eye.*
Choria	Chiria	*Bird.*
Chacurra	Cucura	*Dog.*
Erreguina	Rani	*Queen.*
Icusi	Iksha	*To see.*
Iru	Treya	*Three.*
Jan (Khan)	Khana	*To eat.*
Uria	Puri	*City.*
Urruti	Dura	*Far.*

Such is the tongue in which I brought out Saint Luke's Gospel at Madrid. The translation I procured originally from a Basque physician of the name of Oteiza. Previous to being sent to the press, the version had lain nearly two years in my possession, during which time, and particularly during my travels, I lost no opportunity of submitting it to the inspection of those who were considered competent scholars in the Euscarra. It did not entirely please me; but it was in vain to seek for a better translation.

In my early youth I had obtained a slight acquaintance with the Euscarra, as it exists in books. This acquaintance I considerably increased during my stay in Spain; and by occasionally mingling with Basques, was

O

enabled to understand the spoken language to a certain extent, and even to speak it, but always with considerable hesitation; for to speak Basque, even tolerably, it is necessary to have lived in the country from a very early period. So great are the difficulties attending it, and so strange are its peculiarities, that it is very rare to find a foreigner possessed of any considerable skill in the oral language; and the Spaniards consider the obstacles so formidable, that they have a proverb to the effect that Satan once lived seven years in Biscay, and then departed, finding himself unable either to understand or to make himself understood.

There are few inducements to the study of this language. In the first place, the acquisition of it is by no means necessary even to those who reside in the countries where it is spoken; the Spanish being generally understood throughout the Basque provinces pertaining to Spain, and the French in those pertaining to France.

In the second place, neither dialect is in possession of any peculiar literature capable of repaying the toil of the student. There are various books extant both in French and Spanish Basque, but these consist entirely of Popish devotion, and are for the most part translations.

It will, perhaps, here be asked whether the Basques do not possess popular poetry like most other nations, however small and inconsiderable. They have certainly no lack of songs, ballads, and stanzas, but of a character by no means entitled to the appellation of poetry. I have noted down from recitation a considerable portion of what they call their poetry, but the only tolerable specimen of verse which I ever discovered amongst them was the following stanza, which, after all, is not entitled to very high praise:—

> "Ichasoa urac aundi,
> Estu ondoric agueri—
> Pasaco ninsaqueni andic
> Maitea icusten gatic."

i. e. "The waters of the sea are vast, and their bottom cannot be seen; but over them I will pass, that I may behold my love."

The Basques are a singing rather than a poetical people. Notwithstanding the facility with which their tongue lends itself to the composition of verse, they have never produced among them a poet with the slightest pretensions to reputation; but their voices are singularly sweet, and they are known to excel in musical composition. It is the opinion of a certain author, the Abbé D'Ilharce, who has written about them, that they derived the name *Cantabri*, by which they were known to the Romans, from *Khantor-ber*, signifying sweet singers. They possess much music of their own, some of which is said to be exceedingly ancient. Of this music specimens were published at Donostian (San Sebastian) in the year 1826, edited by a certain Juan Ignacio Iztueta. These consist of wild and thrilling marches, to the sound of which it is believed that the ancient Basques were in the habit of

descending from their mountains to combat with the Romans, and subsequently with the Moors. Whilst listening to them, it is easy to suppose oneself in the close vicinity of some desperate encounter. We seem to hear the charge of cavalry on the sounding plain, the clash of swords, and the rushing of men down the gorges of hills. This music is accompanied with words, but such words! Nothing can be imagined more stupid, commonplace, and uninteresting. So far from being martial, they relate to every-day incidents, and appear to have no connection whatever with the music. They are evidently of modern date.

In person the Basques are of the middle size, and are active and athletic. They are in general of fair complexion and handsome features, and in appearance bear no slight resemblance to certain Tartar tribes of the Caucasus. Their bravery is unquestionable, and they are considered as the best soldiery belonging to the Spanish crown; a fact highly corroborative of the supposition that they are of Tartar origin, the Tartars being of all races the most warlike, and amongst whom the most remarkable conquerors have been produced. They are faithful and honest, and capable of much disinterested attachment, kind and hospitable to strangers; all of which points are far from being at variance with the Tartar character. But they are somewhat dull, and their capacities are by no means of a high order, and in these respects they again resemble the Tartars.

No people on earth are prouder than the Basques, but theirs is a kind of republican pride. They have no nobility amongst them, and no one will acknowledge a superior. The poorest carman is as proud as the governor of Tolosa. "He is more powerful than I," he will say, "but I am of as good blood; perhaps hereafter I may become a governor myself." They abhor servitude, at least out of their own country; and though circumstances frequently oblige them to seek masters, it is very rare to find them filling the places of common domestics; they are stewards, secretaries, accountants, &c. True it is, that it was my own fortune to obtain a Basque domestic; but then he always treated me more as an equal than a master, would sit down in my presence, give me his advice unasked, and enter into conversation with me at all times and occasions. Did I check him? Certainly not! for in that case he would have left me, and a more faithful creature I never knew. His fate was a mournful one, as will appear in the sequel.

I have said that the Basques abhor servitude, and are rarely to be found serving as domestics amongst the Spaniards. I allude, however, merely to the males. The females, on the contrary, have no objection whatever to enter houses as servants. Women, indeed, amongst the Basques are not looked upon with all the esteem which they deserve, and are considered as fitted for little else than to perform menial offices, even as in the East, where they are viewed in the light of servants and slaves. The Basque females differ widely in character from the men; they are quick and vivacious, and have in general much more talent. They are famous for their skill as cooks, and in most respectable houses of Madrid a Biscayan female may be found in the kitchen, queen supreme of the culinary department.

CHAPTER XXXVIII.

The Prohibition—Gospel Persecuted—Charge of Sorcery—Ofalia.

ABOUT the middle of January a swoop was made upon me by my enemies, in the shape of a peremptory prohibition from the political governor of Madrid to sell any more New Testaments. This measure by no means took me by surprise, as I had for some time previously been expecting something of the kind, on account of the political sentiments of the ministers then in power. I forthwith paid a visit to Sir George Villiers, informing him of what had occurred. He promised to do all he could to cause the prohibition to be withdrawn. Unfortunately at this time he had not much influence, having opposed with all his might the entrance of the moderado ministry to power, and the nomination of Ofalia to the presidency of the cabinet. I, however, never lost confidence in the Almighty, in whose cause I was engaged.

Matters were going on very well before this check. The demand for Testaments was becoming considerable, so much so, that the clergy were alarmed, and this step was the consequence. But they had previously recourse to another, well worthy of them, they attempted to act upon my fears. One of the ruffians of Madrid, called Manolos, came up to me one night, in a dark street, and told me that unless I discontinued selling my "Jewish books," I should have a knife "*nailed in my heart*;" but I told him to go home, say his prayers, and tell his employers that I pitied them; whereupon he turned away with an oath. A few days after, I received an order to send two copies of the Testament to the office of the political governor, with which I complied, and in less than twenty-four hours an alguazil arrived at the shop with a notice prohibiting the farther sale of the work.

One circumstance rejoiced me. Singular as it may appear, the authorities took no measures to cause my little despacho to be closed, and I received no prohibition respecting the sale of any work but the New Testament, and as the Gospel of Saint Luke, in Rommany and Basque, would within a short time be ready for delivery, I hoped to carry on matters in a small way till better times should arrive.

I was advised to erase from the shop windows the words, "Despacho of the British and Foreign Bible Society." This, however, I refused to do. Those words had tended very much to call attention, which was my grand object. Had I attempted to conduct things in an underhand manner, I should, at the time of which I am speaking, scarcely have sold thirty copies in Madrid, instead of nearly three hundred. People who know me not, may be disposed to call me rash; but I am far from being so, as I never adopt a venturous course when any other is open to me. I am not, however, a person to be terrified by any danger, when I see that braving it is the only way to achieve an object.

The booksellers were unwilling to sell my work, so I was compelled to establish a shop of my own. Every shop in Madrid has a name. What name could I give it but the true one? I was not ashamed of my cause or my colours. I hoisted them, and fought beneath them not without success.

The priestly party in Madrid, in the mean time, spared no effort to vilify me. They started a publication, called "The Friend of the Christian Religion," in which a stupid but furious attack upon me appeared, which I, however, treated with the contempt it deserved. But not satisfied with this, they endeavoured to incite the populace against me, by telling them that I was a sorcerer, and a companion of gipsies and witches, and their agents even called me so in the streets. That I was an associate of gipsies and fortune-tellers I do not deny. Why should I be ashamed of their company when my Master mingled with publicans and thieves? Many of the gipsy race came frequently to visit me; received instruction, and heard parts of the Gospel read to them in their own language, and when they were hungry and faint, I gave them to eat and drink. This might be deemed sorcery in Spain, but I am not without hope that it will be otherwise estimated in England, and had I perished at this period, I think there are some who would have been disposed to acknowledge that I had not lived altogether in vain, (always as an instrument of the "Most Highest,") having been permitted to turn one of the most valuable books of God into the speech of the most degraded of his creatures.

In the mean time I endeavoured to enter into negotiations with the ministry, for the purpose of obtaining permission to sell the New Testament in Madrid, and the nullification of the prohibition. I experienced, however, great opposition, which I was unable to surmount. Several of the ultra-popish bishops, then resident in Madrid, had denounced the Bible, the Bible Society, and myself. Nevertheless, notwithstanding their powerful and united efforts, they were unable to effect their principal object, namely, my expulsion from Madrid and Spain. The Count Ofalia, notwithstanding he had permitted himself to be made the instrument, to a certain extent, of these people, would not consent to be pushed to such a length. Throughout this affair, I cannot find words sufficiently strong to do justice to the zeal and interest which Sir George Villiers displayed in the cause of the Testament. He had various interviews with Ofalia on the subject, and in these he expressed to him his sense of the injustice and tyranny which had been practised in this instance towards his countryman.

Ofalia had been moved by these remonstrances, and more than once promised to do all in his power to oblige Sir George; but then the bishops again beset him, and playing upon his political if not religious fears, prevented him from acting a just, honest, and honourable part. At the desire of Sir George Villiers, I drew up a brief account of the Bible Society, and an exposition of its views, especially in respect to Spain, which he presented with his own hand to the Count. I shall not trouble the reader by inserting this memorial, but content myself with observing, that I made no attempts to flatter and cajole, but expressed myself honestly and frankly, as a Christian ought. Ofalia, on reading it, said, " What a pity that this is a Protestant society, and that all its members are not Catholics."

A few days subsequently, to my great astonishment, he sent a message to me by a friend, requesting that I would send him a copy of my gipsy Gospel. I may as well here state, that the fame of this work, though not yet published, had already spread like wildfire through Madrid, and every person was passionately eager to possess a copy; indeed, several grandees of Spain sent messages with similar requests, all of which I however denied. I instantly resolved to take advantage of this overture on the part of Count Ofalia, and to call on him myself. I therefore caused a copy of the Gospel to be handsomely bound, and proceeding to the palace, was instantly admitted to him. He was a dusky, diminutive person, between fifty and sixty years of age, with false hair and teeth, but exceedingly gentlemanly manners. He received me with great affability, and thanked me for my present; but on my proceeding to speak of the New Testament, he told me that the subject was surrounded with difficulties, and that the great body of the clergy had taken up the matter against me; he conjured me, however, to be patient and peaceable, in which case he said he would endeavour to devise some plan to satisfy me. Amongst other things, he observed that the bishops hated a sectarian more than an Atheist. Whereupon I replied, that like the Pharisees of old, they cared more for the gold of the temple than the temple itself. Throughout the whole of our interview, he evidently laboured under great fear, and was continually looking behind and around him, seemingly in dread of being overheard, which brought to my mind an expression of a friend of mine, that if there be any truth in metempsychosis, the soul of Count Ofalia must have originally belonged to a mouse. We parted in kindness, and I went away, wondering by what strange chance this poor man had become prime minister of a country like Spain.

CHAPTER XXXIX.

The Two Gospels—The Alguazil—The Warrant—The Good Maria—The Arrest—Sent to Prison —Reflections—The Reception—The Prison Room—Redress Demanded.

AT length the Gospel of Saint Luke in the gipsy language was in a state of readiness. I therefore deposited a certain number of copies in the despacho, and announced them for sale. The Basque, which was by this time also printed, was likewise advertised. For this last work there was little demand. Not so, however, for the gipsy Luke, of which I could have easily disposed of the whole edition in less than a fortnight. Long, however, before this period had expired, the clergy were up in arms. "Sorcery!" said one bishop. "There is more in this than we can dive into," exclaimed a second. "He will convert all Spain by means of the gipsy language," cried a third. And then came the usual chorus on such occasions, of *Que infamia! Que picardia!* At last, having consulted together, away they hurried to their tool the corregidor, or, according to the modern term, the gefe politico of Madrid. I have forgotten the name of this worthy, of whom I had myself no personal knowledge whatever. Judging from his actions, however, and from common report, I should say that he was a stupid wrong-headed creature, savage withal—a melange of borrico, mule, and wolf. Having an inveterate antipathy to all foreigners, he lent a willing ear to the complaint of my accusers, and forthwith gave orders to make a seizure of all the copies of the gipsy Gospel which could be found in the despacho. The consequence was, that a numerous body of alguazils directed their steps to the Calle del principe; some thirty copies of the book in question were pounced upon, and about the same number of Saint Luke in Basque. With this spoil these satellites returned in triumph to the gefatura politica, where they divided the copies of the gipsy volume amongst themselves, selling subsequently the greater number at a large price, the book being in the greatest demand, and thus becoming unintentionally agents of an heretical society. But every one must live by his trade, say these people, and they lose no opportunity of making their words good, by disposing to the best advantage of any booty which falls into their hands. As no person cared about the Basque Gospel, it was safely stowed away, with other unmarketable captures, in the warehouses of the office.

The gipsy Gospels had now been seized, at least as many as were exposed for sale in the despacho. The corregidor and his friends, however, were of opinion that many more might be obtained by means of a little management. Fellows, therefore, hangers-on of the police office, were daily despatched to the shop in all kinds of disguises, inquiring, with great seeming anxiety, for "gipsy books," and offering high prices for copies. They, however, returned to their employers empty-handed. My Gallegan was on his guard, informing all who made inquiries that books of no description would be sold at the establishment for the present. Which was in truth the case, as I had given him particular orders to sell no more under any pretence whatever.

I got no credit, however, for my frank dealing. The corregidor and his confederates could not persuade themselves but that by some means mysterious and unknown to them, I was daily selling hundreds of these gipsy books, which were to revolutionize the country, and annihilate the power of the Father of Rome. A plan was therefore resolved upon, by means of which they hoped to have an opportunity of placing me in a position which would incapacitate me for some time from taking any active measures to circulate the Scriptures, either in gipsy or in any other language.

It was on the morning of the first of May, if I forget not, that an unknown individual made his appearance in my apartment as I was seated at breakfast; he was a mean-looking fellow, about the middle stature, with a countenance on which knave was written in legible characters. The hostess ushered him in, and then withdrew. I did not like the appearance of my visitor, but assuming some degree of courtesy, I requested him to sit down, and demanded his business. "I come from his excellency the political chief of Madrid," he replied, "and my business is to inform you that his excellency is perfectly aware of your proceedings, and is at any time able to prove that you are still disposing of in secret those evil books which you have been forbidden to sell." "Is he so," I replied; "pray let him do so forthwith, but what need of giving me information?" "Perhaps," continued the fellow, "you think his worship

has no witnesses; know, however, that he has many, and respectable ones too." "Doubtless," I replied, "and from the respectability of your own appearance, you are perhaps one of them. But you are occupying my time unprofitably; begone, therefore, and tell whoever sent you that I have by no means a high opinion of his wisdom." "I shall go when I please," retorted the fellow; "do you know to whom you are speaking? Are you aware that if I think fit I can search your apartment, yes even below your bed? What have we here," he continued, and commenced with his stick poking a heap of papers which lay upon a chair; "what have we here; are these also papers of the gipsies?" I instantly determined upon submitting no longer to this behaviour, and taking the fellow by the arm, led him out of the apartment, and then still holding him, conducted him down stairs from the third floor in which I lived, into the street, looking him steadfastly in the face the whole while.

The fellow had left his sombrero on the table, which I despatched to him by the landlady, who delivered it into his hand as he stood in the street staring with distended eyes at the balcony of my apartment.

"A trampa has been laid for you, Don Jorge," said Maria Diaz, when she had reascended from the street; "that corchete came here with no other intention than to have a dispute with you; out of every word you have said he will make a long history, as is the custom with these people: indeed he said, as I handed him his hat, that ere twenty-four hours were over, you should see the inside of the prison of Madrid."

In effect, during the course of the morning, I was told that a warrant had been issued for my apprehension. The prospect of incarceration, however, did not fill me with much dismay. An adventurous life and inveterate habits of wandering having long familiarized me to situations of every kind, so much so as to feel myself quite as comfortable in a prison as in the gilded chambers of palaces; indeed more so, as in the former place I can always add to my store of useful information, whereas in the latter ennui frequently assails me. I had, moreover, been thinking for some time past of paying a visit to the prison, partly in the hope of being able to say a few words of Christian instruction to the criminals, and partly with the view of making certain investigations in the robber language of Spain, a subject about which I had long felt much curiosity; indeed, I had already made application for admittance into the Carcel de la Corte, but had found the matter surrounded with difficulties, as my friend Ofalia would have said. I rather rejoiced then in the opportunity which was now about to present itself of entering the prison, not in the character of a visitor for an hour, but as a martyr, and as one suffering in the holy cause of religion. I was determined, however, to disappoint my enemies for that day at least, and to render null the threat of the alguazil, that

I should be imprisoned within twenty-four hours. I therefore took up my abode for the rest of the day in a celebrated French tavern in the Calle del Caballero de Gracia, which, as it was one of the most fashionable and public places in Madrid, I naturally concluded was one of the last where the corregidor would think of seeking me.

About ten at night, Maria Diaz, to whom I had communicated the place of my retreat, arrived with her son, Juan Lopez. "O senor," said she on seeing me, "they are already in quest of you; the alcalde of the barrio, with a large comitiva of alguazils and such like people, have just been at our house, with a warrant for your imprisonment from the corregidor. They searched the whole house, and were much disappointed at not finding you. Wo is me, what will they do when they catch you?" "Be under no apprehensions, good Maria," said I; "you forget that I am an Englishman, and so it seems does the corregidor. Whenever he catches me, depend upon it, he will be glad enough to let me go. For the present, however, we will permit him to follow his own course, for the spirit of folly seems to have seized him."

I slept at the tavern, and in the forenoon of the following day repaired to the embassy, where I had an interview with Sir George, to whom I related every circumstance of the affair. He said that he could scarcely believe that the corregidor entertained any serious intentions of imprisoning me: in the first place, because I had committed no offence; and in the second, because I was not under the jurisdiction of that functionary, but under that of the captain-general, who was alone empowered to decide upon matters which relate to foreigners, and before whom I must be brought in the presence of the consul of my nation. "However," said he, "there is no knowing to what lengths these jacks in office may go. I therefore advise you, if you are under any apprehension, to remain as my guest at the embassy for a few days, for here you will be quite safe." I assured him that I was under no apprehension whatever, having long been accustomed to adventures of this kind. From the apartment of Sir George I proceeded to that of the first secretary of embassy, Mr. Southern, with whom I entered into conversation. I had scarcely been there a minute when my servant Francisco rushed in much out of breath, and in violent agitation, exclaiming in Basque, "Niri jauna (master mine), the alguaziloac and the corchetoac, and all the other lapurrac (thieves) are again at the house. They seem half mad, and not being able to find you, are searching your papers, thinking, I suppose, that you are hid among them." Mr. Southern, here interrupting him, inquired of me what all this meant. Whereupon I told him, saying, at the same time, that it was my intention to proceed at once to my lodgings. "But perhaps these fellows will arrest you," said Mr. S., "before we can interfere." "I

must take my chance as to that," I replied, and presently afterwards departed.

Ere, however, I had reached the middle of the street of Alcala, two fellows came up to me, and telling me that I was their prisoner, commanded me to follow them to the office of the corregidor. They were in fact alguazils, who, suspecting that I might enter or come out of the embassy, had stationed themselves in the neighbourhood. I instantly turned round to Francisco, and told him in Basque to return to the embassy, and to relate there to the secretary what had just occurred. The poor fellow set off like lightning, turning half round, however, to shake his fist, and to vent a Basque execration at the two lapurrac, as he called the alguazils.

They conducted me to the gefatura or office of the corregidor, where they ushered me into a large room, and motioned me to sit down on a wooden bench. They then stationed themselves on each side of me: there were at least twenty people in the apartment besides ourselves, evidently from their appearance officials of the establishment. They were all well dressed, for the most part in the French fashion, in round hats, coats, and pantaloons; and yet they looked what in reality they were, Spanish alguazils, spies, and informers; and Gil Blas, could he have waked from his sleep of two centuries, would, notwithstanding the change of fashion, have had no difficulty in recognising them. They glanced at me as they stood lounging about the room; then gathered themselves together in a circle and began conversing in whispers. I heard one of them say, "he understands the seven gipsy jargons." Then presently another, evidently from his language an Andalusian, said "Es muy diestro, and can ride a horse and dart a knife full as well as if he came from my own country." Thereupon they all turned round and regarded me with a species of interest, evidently mingled with respect, which most assuredly they would not have exhibited had they conceived that I was merely an honest man bearing witness in a righteous cause.

I waited patiently on the bench at least one hour, expecting every moment to be summoned before my lord the corregidor. I suppose, however, that I was not deemed worthy of being permitted to see so exalted a personage; for at the end of that time, an elderly man, one however evidently of the alguazil genus, came into the room and advanced directly towards me. "Stand up," said he. I obeyed. "What is your name?" he demanded. I told him. "Then," he replied, exhibiting a paper which he held in his hand, "Señor, it is the will of his excellency the corregidor that you be forthwith sent to prison."

He looked at me steadfastly as he spoke, perhaps expecting that I should sink into the earth at the formidable name of prison; I however only smiled. He then delivered the paper, which I suppose was the warrant for my committal, into the hand of one of my two captors, and obeying a sign which they made, I followed them.

I subsequently learned that the secretary of legation, Mr. Southern, had been despatched by Sir George, as soon as the latter had obtained information of my arrest, and had been waiting at the office during the greater part of the time that I was there. He had demanded an audience of the corregidor, in which he had intended to have remonstrated with him, and pointed out to him the danger to which he was subjecting himself by the rash step which he was taking. The sullen functionary, however, had refused to see him, thinking, perhaps, that to listen to reason would be a dereliction of dignity: by this conduct, however, he most effectually served me, as no person, after such a specimen of uncalled-for insolence, felt disposed to question the violence and injustice which had been practised towards me.

The alguazils conducted me across the Plaza Mayor to the Carcel de la Corte, or prison of the court, as it is called. Whilst going across the square, I remembered that this was the place where, in "the good old times," the Inquisition of Spain was in the habit of holding its solemn *Autos da fé*, and I cast my eye to the balcony of the city hall, where at the most solemn of them all, the last of the Austrian line in Spain sat, and after some thirty heretics, of both sexes, had been burnt by fours and by fives, wiped his face, perspiring with heat, and black with smoke, and calmly inquired, "No hay mas?" for which exemplary proof of patience he was much applauded by his priests and confessors, who subsequently poisoned him.. "And here am I," thought I, "who have done more to wound Popery than all the poor Christian martyrs that ever suffered in this accursed square, merely sent to prison, from which I am sure to be liberated in a few days, with credit and applause. Pope of Rome! I believe you to be as malicious as ever, but you are sadly deficient in power. You are become paralytic, Batuschca, and your club has degenerated to a crutch."

We arrived at the prison, which stands in a narrow street not far from the great square. We entered a dusky passage, at the end of which was a wicket door. My conductors knocked, a fierce visage peered through the wicket; there was an exchange of words, and in a few moments I found myself within the prison of Madrid, in a kind of corridor which overlooked at a considerable altitude what appeared to be a court, from which arose a hubbub of voices, and occasionally wild shouts and cries. Within the corridor, which served as a kind of office, were several people; one of them sat behind a desk, and to him the alguazils went up, and after discoursing with him for some time in low tones, delivered the warrant into his hands. He perused it with attention, then rising he advanced to me. What a figure! He was about forty years of age, and his height might have amounted to some six feet two inches, had he not been

curved much after the fashion of the letter S. No weasel ever appeared lanker, and he looked as if a breath of air would have been sufficient to blow him away; his face might certainly have been called handsome, had it not been for its extraordinary and portentous meagreness; his nose was like an eagle's bill, his teeth white as ivory, his eyes black, (Oh how black!) and fraught with a strange expression, his skin was dark, and the hair of his head like the plumage of the raven. A deep quiet smile dwelt continually on his features; but with all the quiet it was a cruel smile, such a one as would have graced the countenance of a Nero. "*Mais en revanche personne n'etoit plus honnête.*" "Caballero," said he, "allow me to introduce myself to you as the alcayde of this prison. I perceive by this paper that I am to have the honour of your company for a time, a short time, doubtless, beneath this roof; I hope you will banish every apprehension from your mind. I am charged to treat you with all the respect which is due to the illustrious nation to which you belong, and which a cavalier of such exalted category as yourself is entitled to expect. A needless charge, it is true, as I should only have been too happy of my own accord to have afforded you every comfort and attention. Caballero, you will rather consider yourself here as a guest than a prisoner; you will be permitted to roam over every part of this house whenever you think proper. You will find matters here not altogether below the attention of a philosophic mind. Pray issue whatever commands you may think fit to the turnkeys and officials, even as if they were your own servants. I will now have the honour of conducting you to your apartment—the only one at present unoccupied. We invariably reserve it for cavaliers of distinction. I am happy to say that my orders are again in consonance with my inclination. No charge whatever will be made for it to you, though the daily hire of it is not unfrequently an ounce of gold. I entreat you, therefore, to follow me, cavalier, who am at all times and seasons the most obedient and devoted of your servants." Here he took off his hat and bowed profoundly.

Such was the speech of the alcayde of the prison of Madrid; a speech delivered in pure sonorous Castilian, with calmness, gravity, and almost with dignity; a speech which would have done honour to a gentleman of high birth, to Monsieur Bassompierre, of the Old Bastile, receiving an Italian prince, or the high constable of the Tower an English duke attainted of high treason. Now, who in the name of wonder was this alcayde?

One of the greatest rascals in all Spain. A fellow who had more than once by his grasping cupidity, and by his curtailment of the miserable rations of the prisoners, caused an insurrection in the court below only to be repressed by bloodshed, and by summoning military aid; a fellow of low birth, who, only five years previous, had been *drummer* to a band of royalist volunteers!

But Spain is the land of extraordinary characters.

I followed the alcayde to the end of the corridor, where was a massive grated door, on each side of which sat a grim fellow of a turnkey. The door was opened, and turning to the right, we proceeded down another corridor, in which were many people walking about, whom I subsequently discovered to be prisoners like myself, but for political offences. At the end of this corridor, which extended the whole length of the patio, we turned into another, and the first apartment in this was the one destined for myself. It was large and lofty, but totally destitute of every species of furniture, with the exception of a huge wooden pitcher, intended to hold my daily allowance of water. "Caballero," said the alcayde, "the apartment is without furniture, as you see. It is already the third hour of the tarde, I therefore advise you to lose no time in sending to your lodgings for a bed and whatever you may stand in need of, the llavero here shall do your bidding. Caballero, adieu, till I see you again."

I followed his advice, and writing a note in pencil to Maria Diaz, I despatched it by the llavero, and then sitting down on the wooden pitcher, I fell into a revery, which continued for a considerable time.

Night arrived, and so did Maria Diaz, attended by two porters and Francisco, all loaded with furniture. A lamp was lighted, charcoal was kindled in the brasero, and the prison gloom was to a certain degree dispelled.

I now left my seat on the pitcher, and sitting down on a chair, proceeded to despatch some wine and viands, which my good hostess had not forgotten to bring with her. Suddenly Mr. Southern entered. He laughed heartily at finding me engaged in the manner I have described. "B * * * * *," said he, "you are the man to get through the world, for you appear to take all things coolly, and as matters of course. That, however, which most surprises me with respect to you is, your having so many friends ; here you are in prison, surrounded by people ministering to your comforts. Your very servant is your friend, instead of being your worst enemy, as is usually the case. That Basque of yours is a noble fellow. I shall never forget how he spoke for you, when he came running to the embassy to inform us of your arrest. He interested both Sir George and myself in the highest degree : should you ever wish to part with him, I hope you will give me the refusal of his services. But now to other matters." He then informed me that Sir George had already sent in an official note to Ofalia, demanding redress for such a wanton outrage on the person of a British subject. "You must remain in prison," said he to-night, "but depend upon it that to-morrow, if you are disposed, you may quit in triumph." "I am by no means disposed for any such thing," I replied. "They have put me in prison for their pleasure, and I intend to remain here for my own." "If the confinement is not irksome to you," said Mr. Southern, "I think, indeed, it will be your wisest plan; the government have committed themselves sadly with regard to you; and, to speak plainly, we are by no means sorry for it. They have on more than one occasion treated ourselves very cavalierly, and we have now, if you continue firm, an excellent opportunity of humbling their insolence. I will instantly acquaint Sir George with your determination, and you shall hear from us early on the morrow." He then bade me farewell ; and flinging myself on my bed, I was soon asleep in the prison of Madrid.

CHAPTER XL.

Ofalia—The Juez—Carcel de la Corte—Sunday in Prison—Robber Dress—Father and Son—Characteristic Behaviour—The Frenchman—Prison Allowance—Valley of the Shadow—Pure Castilian—Balseiro—The Cave—Robber Glory.

Ofalia quickly perceived that the imprisonment of a British subject in a manner so illegal as that which had attended my own, was likely to be followed by rather serious consequences. Whether he himself had at all encouraged the corregidor in his behaviour towards me, it is impossible to say ; the probability is that he had not: the latter, however, was an officer of his own appointing, for whose actions himself and the government were to a certain extent responsible. Sir George had already made a very strong remonstrance upon the subject, and had even gone so far as to state in an official note that he should desist from all farther communication with the Spanish government until full and ample reparation had been afforded me for the violence to which I had been subjected. Ofalia's reply was, that immediate measures should be taken for my liberation, and that it would be my own fault if I remained in prison. He forthwith ordered a juez de la primera instancia, a kind of solicitor-general, to wait upon me, who was instructed to hear my account of the affair, and then to dismiss me with an admonition to be cautious for the future. My friends of the embassy, however, had advised me how to act in such a case. Accordingly, when the juez on the second night of my imprisonment made his appearance at the prison, and summoned me before him, I went, but on his proceeding to question me, I absolutely refused to answer. "I deny your right to put any questions to me," said

I; "I entertain, however, no feelings of disrespect to the government or to yourself, Caballero Juez; but I have been illegally imprisoned. So accomplished a jurist as yourself cannot fail to be aware that, according to the laws of Spain, I, as a foreigner, could not be committed to prison for the offence with which I had been charged, without previously being conducted before the captain-general of this royal city, whose duty it is to protect foreigners, and see that the laws of hospitality are not violated in their persons."

Juez.—Come, come, Don Jorge, I see what you are aiming at; but listen to reason: I will not now speak to you as a juez but as a friend who wishes you well, and who entertains a profound reverence for the British nation. This is a foolish affair altogether; I will not deny that the political chief acted somewhat hastily on the information of a person not perhaps altogether worthy of credit. No great damage, however, has been done to you, and to a man of the world like yourself, a little adventure of this kind is rather calculated to afford amusement than any thing else. Now be advised, forget what has happened; you know that it is the part and duty of a Christian to forgive; so, Don Jorge, I advise you to leave this place forthwith, I dare say you are getting tired of it. You are this moment free to depart; repair at once to your lodgings, where, I promise you, that no one shall be permitted to interrupt you for the future. It is getting late, and the prison doors will speedily be closed for the night. *Vamos, Don Jorge, a la casa, a la posada!*

Myself.—"But Paul said unto them, they have beaten us openly uncondemned, being Romans, and have cast us into prison; and now do they thrust us out privily? Nay, verily: but let them come themselves and fetch us out."

I then bowed to the juez, who shrugged his shoulders and took snuff. On leaving the apartment I turned to the alcayde, who stood at the door: "Take notice," said I, "that I will not quit this prison till I have received full satisfaction for being sent hither uncondemned. You may expel me, if you please, but any attempt to do so shall be resisted with all the bodily strength of which I am possessed."

"*Usted hace bien,*" said the alcayde with a bow, but in a low voice.

Sir George, on hearing of this affair, sent me a letter, in which he highly commended my resolution not to leave the prison for the present, at the same time begging me to let him know if there were any thing that he could send me from the embassy to render my situation more tolerable. I will now leave for the present my own immediate affairs and proceed to give some account of the prison of Madrid and its inmates.

The Carcel de la Corte, where I now was, though the principal prison of Madrid, is one which certainly in no respect does credit to the capital of Spain. Whether it was originally intended for the purpose to which it is at present applied, I have no opportunity of knowing. The chances, however, are, that it was not; indeed it was not till of late years that the practice of building edifices expressly intended and suited for the incarceration of culprits came at all into vogue. Castles, convents, and deserted palaces, have in all countries, at different times, been converted into prisons, which practice still holds good upon the greater part of the continent, and more particularly in Spain and Italy, which accounts, to a certain extent, for the insecurity of the prisons, and the misery, want of cleanliness, and unhealthiness which in general pervade them.

I shall not attempt to enter into a particular description of the prison of Madrid, indeed it would be quite impossible to describe so irregular and rambling an edifice. Its principal features consisted of two courts, the one behind the other: intended for the great body of the prisoners to take air and recreation in. Three large vaulted dungeons or calabozos occupied three sides of this court, immediately below the corridors of which I have already spoken. These dungeons were roomy enough to contain respectively from one hundred to one hundred and fifty prisoners, who were at night secured therein with lock and bar, but during the day were permitted to roam about the courts as they thought fit. The second court was considerably larger than the first, though it contained but two dungeons; horribly filthy and disgusting places; this second court being used for the reception of the lower grades of thieves. Of the two dungeons one was, if possible, yet more horrible than the other; it was called the gallineria, or chicken coop, and within it every night were pent up the young fry of the prison, wretched boys from seven to fifteen years of age, the greater part almost in a state of nudity. The common bed of all the inmates of these dungeons was the ground, between which and their bodies nothing intervened, save occasionally a manta or horse-cloth, or perhaps a small mattress; this latter luxury was, however, of exceedingly rare occurrence.

Besides the calabozos connected with the courts, were other dungeons in various parts of the prison; some of them quite dark, intended for the reception of those whom it might be deemed expedient to treat with peculiar severity. There was likewise a ward set apart for females. Connected with the principal corridor were many small apartments, where resided prisoners confined for debt or for political offences. And, lastly, there was a small capilla or chapel, in which prisoners cast for death passed the last three days of their existence in the company of their ghostly advisers.

I shall not soon forget my first Sunday in prison. Sunday is the gala day of the prison, at least of that of Madrid, and whatever robber finery is to be found within it, is sure to be exhibited on that day of holiness. There is not a set of people in the world more vain than robbers in general, more fond of cutting a figure whenever they have an opportunity of attracting the eyes of their fellow-creatures by the gallantry of their appearance. The famous Sheppard of olden times delighted in sporting a suit of Genoese velvet, and when he appeared in public generally wore a silver-hilted sword at his side; whilst Vaux and Hayward, heroes of a later day, were the best dressed men on the pavé of London. Many of the Italian bandits go splendidly decorated, and the very gipsy robber has a feeling for the charms of dress; the cap alone of the Haram Pasha, or leader of the cannibal gipsy band which infested Hungary towards the conclusion of the last century, was adorned with gold and jewels to the value of four thousand guilders. Observe, ye vain and frivolous, how vanity and crime harmonize. The Spanish robbers are as fond of this species of display as their brethren of other lands, and, whether in prison or out of it, are never so happy as when, decked out in a profusion of white linen, they can loll in the sun, or walk jauntily up and down.

Snow white linen, indeed, constitutes the principal feature in the robber foppery of Spain. Neither coat nor jacket is worn over the shirt, the sleeves of which are wide and flowing, only a waistcoat of green or blue silk with an abundance of silver buttons, which are intended more for show than use, as the vest is seldom buttoned. Then there are wide trousers, something after the Turkish fashion; around the waist is a crimson faja or girdle, and about the head is tied a gaudily coloured handkerchief from the loom of Barcelona; light pumps and silk stockings complete the robber's array. This dress is picturesque enough, and well adapted to the fine sunshiny weather of the Peninsula; there is a dash of effeminacy about it, however, hardly in keeping with the robber's desperate trade. It must not, however, be supposed that it is every robber who can indulge in all this luxury; there are various grades of thieves, some poor enough, with scarcely a rag to cover them. Perhaps in the crowded prison of Madrid, there were not more than twenty who exhibited the dress which I have attempted to describe above; these were *jente de reputacion*, tip-top thieves, mostly young-fellows, who, though they had no money of their own, were supported in prison by their majas and amigas, females of a certain class, who form friendships with robbers, and whose delight it is to administer to the vanity of these fellows with the wages of their own shame and abasement. These females supplied their cortejos with the snowy linen, washed, perhaps, by their own hands in the waters of the Manzanares, for the display of the Sunday, when they would themselves make their appearance dressed à la maja, and from the corridors would gaze with admiring eyes upon the robbers vapouring about in the court below.

Amongst those of the snowy linen who most particularly attracted my attention, were

a father and son; the former was a tall athletic figure of about thirty, by profession a house-breaker, and celebrated throughout Madrid for the peculiar dexterity which he exhibited in his calling. He was now in prison for a rather atrocious murder committed in the dead of night, in a house at Caraman-chel in which his only accomplice was his son, a child under seven years of age. "The apple," as the Danes say, "had not fallen far from the tree;" the imp was in every respect the counterpart of the father, though in miniature. He, too, wore the robber shirt sleeves, the robber waistcoat with the silver buttons, the robber kerchief round his brow, and, ridiculous enough, a long Manchegan knife in the crimson faja. He was evidently the pride of the ruffian father, who took all imaginable care of this chick of the gallows, would dandle him on his knee, and would occasionally take the cigar from his own moustached lips and insert it into the urchin's mouth. The boy was the pet of the court, for the father was one of the valientes of the prison, and those who feared his prowess, and wished to pay their court to him were always fondling the child. What an enigma is this world of ours! How dark and mysterious are the sources of what is called crime and virtue! If that infant wretch become eventually a murderer like his father, is he to blame? Fondled by robbers, already dressed as a robber, born of a robber, whose own history was perhaps similar. Is it right? . . . .

O, man, man, seek not to dive into the mystery of moral good and evil; confess thyself a worm, cast thyself on the earth, and murmur with thy lips in the dust, Jesus, Jesus!

What most surprised me, with respect to the prisoners, was their good behaviour; I call it good when all things are taken into consideration, and when I compare it with that of the general class of prisoners in foreign lands. They had their occasional bursts of wild gaiety, their occasional quarrels, which they were in the habit of settling in a corner of the interior court with their long knives; the result not unfrequently being death, or a dreadful gash in the face or the abdomen; but, upon the whole, their conduct was infinitely superior to what might have been expected from the inmates of such a place. Yet this was not the result of coercion, or any particular care which was exercised over them; for perhaps in no part of the world are prisoners so left to themselves and so utterly neglected as in Spain: the authorities having no farther anxiety about them than to prevent their escape; not the slightest attention being paid to their moral conduct, and not a thought bestowed upon their health, comfort, or mental improvement, whilst within the walls. Yet in this prison of Madrid, and I may say in Spanish prisons in general, for I have been an inmate of more than one, the ears of the visitor are never shocked with horrid blasphemy and obscenity, as in those of some other countries, and more particularly in civilized France; nor are his eyes outraged and him self insulted, as he would assuredly be, were he to look down upon the courts from the galleries of the Bicêtre. And yet in this prison of Madrid were some of the most desperate characters in Spain: ruffians who had committed acts of cruelty and atrocity sufficient to made the flesh shudder. But gravity and sedateness are the leading characteristics of the Spaniards, and the very robber, except in those moments when he is engaged in his occupation, and then no one is more sanguinary, pitiless, and wolfishly eager for booty, is a being who can be courteous and affable, and who takes pleasure in conducting himself with sobriety and decorum.

Happily, perhaps, for me, that my acquaintance with the ruffians of Spain commenced and ended in the towns about which I wandered, and in the prisons into which I was cast for the Gospel's sake, and that, notwithstanding my long and frequent journeys, I never came in contact with them on the road or in the despoblado.

The most ill-conditioned being in the prison was a Frenchman, though probably the most remarkable. He was about sixty years of age, of the middle stature, but thin and meagre, like most of his countrymen; he had a villanously formed head, according to all the rules of craniology, and his features were full of evil expression. He wore no hat, and his clothes, though in appearance nearly new, were of the coarsest description. He generally kept aloof from the rest, and would stand for hours together leaning against the walls with his arms folded, glaring sullenly on what was passing before him. He was not one of the professed valientes, for his age prevented his assuming so distinguished a character, and yet all the rest appeared to hold him in a certain awe: perhaps they feared his tongue, which he occasionally exerted in pouring forth withering curses on those who incurred his displeasure. He spoke perfectly good Spanish, and to my great surprise excellent Basque, in which he was in the habit of conversing with Francisco, who, lolling from the window of my apartment, would exchange jests and witticisms with the prisoners in the court below, with whom he was a great favourite.

One day when I was in the patio, to which I had free admission whenever I pleased, by permission of the alcayde, I went up to the Frenchman, who stood in his usual posture, leaning against the wall, and offered him a cigar. I do not smoke myself, but it will never do to mix among the lower classes of Spain unless you have a cigar to present occasionally. The man glared at me ferociously for a moment, and appeared to be on the point of refusing my offer with perhaps a hideous execration. I repeated it, however, pressing my hand against my heart, whereupon suddenly the grim feature relaxed, and with a genuine French grimace, and a low bow, he accepted the cigar, exclaiming, "Ah Monsieur, pardon, mais c'est faire trop d'honneur à un pauvre diable comme moi."

"Not at all," said I, "we are both fellow-prisoners in a foreign land, and being so we ought to countenance each other. I hope that whenever I have need of your co-operation in this prison you will afford it me."

"Ah, Monsieur," exclaimed the Frenchman in rapture, "vous avez bien raison; il faut que les étrangers se donnent la main dans ce . . . pays de barbares. Tenez," he added in a whisper, "if you have any plan for escaping, and require my assistance, I have an arm and a knife at your service: you may trust me, and that is more than you could any of these sacres gens ici," glancing fiercely round at his fellow-prisoners.

"You appear to be no friend to Spain and the Spaniards," said I. "I conclude that you have experienced injustice at their hands. For what have they immured you in this place?"

"Pour rien du tout, c'est à dire pour une bagatelle; but what can you expect from such animals. For what are you imprisoned? Did I not hear say for gipsyism and sorcery?"

"Perhaps you are here for your opinions?"

"Ah, mon Dieu, non; je ne suis pas homme à semblable betise. I have no opinions. Je faisois . . . . . mais ce n'importe; je me trouve ici, où je crève de faim."

"I am sorry to see a brave man in such a distressed condition," said I; "have you nothing to subsist on beyond the prison allowance? Have you no friends?"

"Friends in this country! you mock me; here one has no friends, unless one buy them. I am bursting with hunger: since I have been here, I have sold the clothes off my back, that I might eat, for the prison allowance will not support nature, and of half of that we are robbed by the Batu, as they called the barbarian of a governor. Les haillons which now cover me were given by two or three devotees who sometimes visit here. I would sell them if they would fetch aught. I have not a sou, and for want of a few crowns I shall be garroted within a month unless I can escape, though, as I told you before, I have done nothing, a mere bagatelle; but the worst crimes in Spain are poverty and misery."

"I have heard you speak Basque; are you from French Biscay?"

"I am from Bordeaux, Monsieur; but I have lived much on the Landes and in Biscay, travaillant à mon metier. I see by your look that you wish to know my history. I shall not tell it you. It contains nothing that is remarkable. See, I have smoked out your cigar; you may give me another, and add a dollar if you please, nous sommes crevés ici de faim. I would not say as much to a Spaniard, but I have a respect for your countrymen; I know much of them; I have met them at Maida and the other place."*

"Nothing remarkable in his history!" Why, or I greatly err, one chapter of his life, had it been written, would have unfolded more of the wild and wonderful than fifty volumes of what are in general called adventures and hair-breadth escapes by land and

---

* Perhaps Waterloo.

sea. A soldier! what a tale could that man have told of marches and retreats, of battles lost and won, towns sacked, convents plundered; perhaps he had seen the flames of Moscow ascending to the clouds, and had "tried his strength with nature in the wintry desert," pelted by the snow-storm, and bitten by the tremendous cold of Russia: and what could he mean by plying his trade in Biscay and the Landes, but that he had been a robber in those wild regions, of which the latter is more infamous for brigandage and crime than any other part of the French territory. Nothing remarkable in his history! then what history in the world contains aught that is remarkable?

I gave him the cigar and dollar: he received them, and then once more folding his arms, leaned back against the wall and appeared to sink gradually into one of his reveries. I looked him in the face and spoke to him, but he did not seem either to hear or see me. His mind was perhaps wandering in that dreadful valley of the shadow, into which the children of earth, whilst living, occasionally find their way; that dreadful region where there is no water, where hope dwelleth not, where nothing lives but the undying worm. This valley is the fac-simile of hell, and he who has entered it, has experienced here on earth for a time what the spirits of the condemned are doomed to suffer through ages without end.

He was executed about a month from this time. The bagatelle for which he was confined was robbery and murder by the following strange device. In concert with two others, he hired a large house in an unfrequented part of the town, to which place he would order tradesmen to convey valuable articles, which were to be paid for on delivery; those who attended paid for their credulity with the loss of their lives and property. Two or three had fallen into the snare. I wished much to have had some private conversation with this desperate man, and in consequence begged of the alcayde to allow him to dine with me in my own apartment; whereupon Monsieur Basompierre, for so I will take the liberty of calling the governor, his real name having escaped my memory, took off his hat, and, with his usual smile and bow, replied in purest Castilian, "English Cavalier, and I hope I may add friend, pardon me, that it is quite out of my power to gratify your request, founded, I have no doubt, on the most admirable sentiments of philosophy. Any of the other gentleman beneath my care shall, at any time you desire it, be permitted to wait upon you in your apartment. I will even go so far as to cause their irons, if irons they wear, to be knocked off in order that they may partake of your refection with that comfort which is seemly and convenient: but to the gentlemen in question I must object; he is the most evil disposed of the whole of this family, and would most assuredly breed a funcion either in your apartment or in the corridor, by an attempt to escape. Cavalier, *me pesa*, but I

cannot accede to your request. But with respect to any other gentlemen, I shall be most happy, even Balseiro, who, though strange things are told of him, still knows how to comport himself, and in whose behaviour there is something both of formality and politeness, shall this day share your hospitality if you desire it, Cavalier."

Of Balseiro I have already had occasion to speak in the former part of this narrative. He was now confined in an upper story of the prison, in a strong room, with several other malefactors. He had been found guilty of aiding and assisting one Pepe Candelas, a thief of no inconsiderable renown, in a desperate robbery perpetrated in open daylight upon no less a personage than the queen's milliner, a Frenchwoman, whom they bound in her own shop, from which they took goods and money to the amount of five or six thousand dollars. Candelas had already expiated his crime on the scaffold, but Balseiro, who was said to be by far the worst ruffian of the two, had by dint of money, an ally which his comrade did not possess, contrived to save his own life; the punishment of death, to which he was originally sentenced, having been commuted to twenty years' hard labour in the presidio of Malaga. I visited this worthy, and conversed with him for some time through the wicket of the dungeon. He recognised me, and reminded me of the victory which I had once obtained over him, in the trial of our respective skill in the crabbed Gitáno, at which Sevilla the bullfighter was umpire.

Upon my telling him that I was sorry to see him in such a situation, he replied that it was an affair of no matter of consequence, as within six weeks he should be conducted to the presidio, from which, with the assistance of a few ounces distributed amongst the guards, he could at any time escape. "But whither would you flee?" I demanded. "Can I not flee to the land of the Moors," replied Balseiro, "or to the English in the camp of Gibraltar; or, if I prefer it, cannot I return to this foro (*city*), and live as I have hitherto done, choring the gachos (*robbing the natives*); what is to hinder me? Madrid is large, and Balseiro has plenty of friends, especially among the lumias (*women*)," he added with a smile. I spoke to him of his ill-fated accomplice Candelas; whereupon his face assumed a horrible expression. "I hope he is in torment," exclaimed the robber. The friendship of the unrighteous is never of long duration; the two worthies had it seems quarrelled in prison; Candelas having accused the other of bad faith and an undue appropriation to his own use of the *corpus delicti* in various robberies which they had committed in company.

I cannot refrain from relating the subsequent history of this Balseiro. Shortly after my own liberation, too impatient to wait until the presidio should afford him a chance of regaining his liberty, he in company with some other convicts broke through the roof of the prison and escaped. He instantly resumed his former habits, committing several dashing robberies both within and without the walls of Madrid. I now come to his last, I may call it his master crime, a singular piece of atrocious villany. Dissatisfied with the proceeds of street robbery and house-breaking, he determined upon a bold stroke, by which he hoped to acquire money sufficient to support him in some foreign land in luxury and splendour.

There was a certain comptroller of the queen's household, by name Gabiria, a Basque by birth, and a man of immense possessions: this individual had two sons, handsome boys, between twelve and fourteen years of age, whom I had frequently seen, and indeed conversed with, in my walks on the bank of the Manzanares, which was their favourite promenade. These children, at the time of which I am speaking, were receiving their education at a certain seminary in Madrid. Balseiro, being well acquainted with the father's affection for his children, determined to make it subservient to his own rapacity. He formed a plan which was neither more nor less than to steal the children, and not to restore them to their parent until he had received an enormous ransom. This plan was partly carried into execution: two associates of Balseiro, well dressed, drove up to the door of the seminary, where the children were, and, by means of a forged letter, purporting to be written by the father, induced the schoolmaster to permit the boys to accompany them for a country jaunt, as they pretended. About five leagues from Madrid, Balseiro had a cave in a wild unfrequented spot between the Escurial and a village called Torre Lodones: to this cave the children were conducted, where they remained in durance under the custody of the two accomplices; Balseiro in the mean time remaining in Madrid for the purpose of conducting negotiations with the father. The father, however, was a man of considerable energy, and instead of acceding to the terms of the ruffian, communicated in a letter, instantly took the most vigorous measures for the recovery of his children. Horse and foot were sent out to scour the country, and in less than a week the children were found near the cave, having been abandoned by their keepers, who had taken fright on hearing of the decided measures which had been resorted to; they were, however, speedily arrested and identified by the boys as their ravishers. Balseiro, perceiving that Madrid was becoming too hot to hold him, attempted to escape, but whether to the camp of Gibraltar or to the land of the Moor, I know not; he was recognised, however, at a village in the neighbourhood of Madrid, and being apprehended, was forthwith conducted to the capital, where he shortly after terminated his existence on the scaffold, with his two associates; Gabiria and his children being present at the ghastly scene, which they surveyed from a chariot at their ease.

Such was the end of Balseiro, of whom I should certainly not have said so much, but for the affair of the crabbed Gitáno. Poor wretch! he acquired that species of immortality which is the object of the aspirations of many a Spanish thief, whilst vapouring about in the patio, dressed in the snowy linen; the rape of the children of Gabiria made him at once the pet of the fraternity. A celebrated robber, with whom I was subsequently imprisoned at Seville, spoke his eulogy in the following manner.

"Balseiro was a very good subject, and an honest man. He was the head of our family, Don Jorge; *nunca se ha visto su igual;* pity that he did not sack the parné (*money*), and escape to the camp of the Moor, Don Jorge."

CHAPTER XLI.

Maria Diaz—Priestly Vituperation—Antonio's Visit—Antonio at Service—A Scene—Benedict Mol —Wandering in Spain—The Four Evangiles.

"WELL," said I to Maria Diaz, on the third morning after my imprisonment, "what do the people of Madrid say to this affair of mine?"

"I do not know what the people of Madrid in general say about it, probably they do not take much interest in it; indeed, imprisonments at the present time are such common matters that people seem to be quite indifferent to them: the priests, however, are in no slight commotion, and confess that they have committed an imprudent thing in causing you to be arrested by their friend the corregidor of Madrid."

"How is that?" I inquired. "Are they afraid that their friend will be punished?"

"Not so, Señor," replied Maria; "slight grief indeed would it cause them, however great the trouble in which he had involved himself on their account, for this description of people have no affection, and would not care if all their friends were hanged, provided they themselves escaped. But they say that they have acted imprudently in sending you to prison, inasmuch as by so doing they have given you an opportunity of carrying a plan of yours into execution. 'This fellow is a bribon,' say they, 'and has commenced tampering with the prisoners; they have taught him their language, which he already speaks as well as if he were a son of the prison. As soon as he comes out he will

P

publish a thieves' gospel, which will be a still more dangerous affair than the gipsy one, for the gipsies are few, but the thieves! wo is us; we shall all be Lutheranized. What infamy, what rascality! It was a trick of his own. He was always eager to get into prison, and now, in an evil hour, we have sent him there, *el bribonazo:* there will be no safety for Spain until he is hanged; he ought to be sent *à los cuatro infiernos*, where at his leisure he might translate his fatal gospels into the language of the demons.'"

"I but said three words to the alcayde of the prison," said I, "relative to the jargon used by the children of the prison."

"Three words, Don Jorge; and what may not be made out of three words? You have lived amongst us to little purpose if you think we require more than three words to build a system with: those three words about the thieves and their tongue were quite sufficient to cause it to be reported throughout Madrid that you had tampered with the thieves, had learned their language, and had written a book which was to overturn Spain, open to the English the gates of Cadiz, give Mendizabal all the church plate and jewels, and to Don Martin Luther the archiepiscopal palace of Toledo."

Late in the afternoon of rather a gloomy day, as I was sitting in the apartment which the alcayde had allotted me, I heard a rap at the door. "Who is that?" I exclaimed. "*C'est moi*, mon maître," cried a well known voice, and presently in walked Antonio Buchini, dressed in the same style as when I first introduced him to the reader, namely, in a handsome but rather faded French surtout, vest and pantaloons, with a diminutive hat in one hand, and holding in the other a long and slender cane.

"*Bon jour, mon maître*," said the Greek; then glancing around the apartment, he continued, "I am glad to find you so well lodged. If I remember right, mon maître, we have slept in worse places during our wanderings in Galicia and Castile."

"You are quite right, Antonio," I replied; "I am very comfortable. Well, this is kind of you to visit your ancient master, more especially now he is in the toils; I hope, however, that by so doing you will not offend your present employer. His dinner hour must be at hand; why are not you in the kitchen!"

"Of what employer are you speaking, mon maître?" demanded Antonio.

"Of whom should I speak but Count * * *, to serve whom you abandoned me, being tempted by an offer of a monthly salary less by four dollars than that which I was giving you."

"Your worship brings an affair to my remembrance which I had long since forgotten. I have at present no other master than yourself, Monsieur Georges, for I shall always consider you as my master, though I may not enjoy the felicity of waiting upon you."

"You have left the Count, then," said I,

"after remaining three days in the house, according to your usual practice."

"Not three hours, mon maître," replied Antonio; "but I will tell you the circumstances. Soon after I left you I repaired to the house of Monsieur le Comte; I entered the kitchen, and looked about me. I cannot say that I had much reason to be dissatisfied with what I saw: the kitchen was large and commodious, and every thing appeared neat and in its proper place, and the domestics civil and courteous; yet I know not how it was, the idea at once rushed into my mind that the house was by no means suited to me, and that I was not destined to stay there long; so hanging my haversac upon a nail, and sitting down on the dresser, I commenced singing a Greek song, as I am in the habit of doing when dissatisfied. The domestics came about me asking questions; I made them no answer, however, and continued singing till the hour for preparing the dinner drew nigh, when I suddenly sprang on the floor and was not long in thrusting them all out of the kitchen, telling them that they had no business there at such a season: I then at once entered upon my functions, I exerted myself, mon maître, I exerted myself, and was preparing a repast which would have done me honour; there was, indeed, some company expected that day, and I therefore determined to show my employer that nothing was beyond the capacity of his Greek cook. *Eh bien*, mon maître, all was going on remarkably well, and I felt almost reconciled to my new situation, when who should rush into the kitchen but *le fils de la maison*, my young master, an ugly urchin of thirteen years or thereabouts; he bore in his hand a manchet of bread, which, after prying about for a moment, he proceeded to dip in a pan where some delicate woodcocks were in the course of preparation. You know, mon maître, how sensitive I am on certain points, for I am no Spaniard, but a Greek, and have principles of honour. Without a moment's hesitation I took my young master by the shoulders, and hurrying him to the door, dismissed him in the manner which he deserved: squalling loudly, he hurried away to the upper part of the house. I continued my labours, but ere three minutes had elapsed, I heard a dreadful confusion above stairs, *on faisoit une horrible tintamarre*, and I could occasionally distinguish oaths and execrations: presently doors were flung open, and there was an awful rushing down stairs, a galopade. It was my lord, the count, his lady, and my young master, followed by a regular bevy of women and filles de chambre. Far in advance of all, however, was my lord with a drawn sword in his hand, shouting, "Where is the wretch who has dishonoured my son?— where is he? He shall die forthwith." I know not how it was, mon maître, but I just then chanced to spill a large bowl of garbanzos, which were intended for the puchera of the following day. They were uncooked, and were as hard as marbles; these I dashed upon the floor, and the greater part of them fell just about the doorway. *Eh bien,* mon maître, in another moment in bounded the count, his eyes sparkling like coals, and, as I have already said, with a rapier in his hand. '*Tenez, gueux enragé,*' he screamed, making a desperate lunge at me; but ere the words were out of his mouth, his foot slipping on the peas, he fell forward with great violence at his full length, and his weapon flew out of his hand, *comme une flèche.* You should have heard the outcry which ensued! There was a terrible confusion: the count lay upon the floor, to all appearance stunned; I took no notice, however, continuing busily employed. They at last raised him up, and assisted him till he came to himself, though very pale and much shaken. He asked for his sword: all eyes were now turned upon me, and I saw that a general attack was meditated. Suddenly I took a large caserolle from the fire, in which various eggs were frying; this I held out at arm's length, peering at it along my arm, as if I were curiously inspecting it; my right foot advanced and the other thrown back as far as possible. All stood still, imagining, doubtless, that I was about to perform some grand operation, and so I was: for suddenly the sinister leg advancing, with one rapid *coup de pied,* I sent the caserolle and its contents flying over my head, so that they struck the wall far behind me. This was to let them know that I had broken my staff, and had shaken the dust off my feet: so, casting upon the count the peculiar glance of the Sceirote cooks when they feel themselves insulted, and extending my mouth on either side nearly as far as the ears, I took down my haversac and departed, singing as I went the song of the ancient Demos, who, when dying, asked for his supper, and water wherewith to lave his hands:

'Ο ἥλιος ἐβασίλευε, κί ὁ Δῆμος διατάζει.
Σύρτε, παιδιά μου, 'ς τὸ νερὸν ψωμί νὰ φάτ' ἀπόψα.

And in this manner, mon maître, I left the house of the Count of * * * * *."

Myself.—And a fine account you have given of yourself; by your own confession, your behaviour was most atrocious. Were it not for the many marks of courage and fidelity which you have exhibited in my service, I would from this moment hold no farther communication with you.

Antonio.—*Mais qu'est ce que vous voudriez,* mon maître? Am I not a Greek, full of honour and sensibility? Would you have the cooks of Sceira and Stambul submit to be insulted here in Spain by the sons of counts rushing into the temple with manchets of bread? Non, non, mon maître, you are too too noble to require that, and, what is more, *too just.* But we will talk of other things. Mon maître, I come not alone; there is one now waiting in the corridor anxious to speak to you.

Myself.—Who is it?

Antonio.—One whom you have met, mon maître, in various and strange places.

Myself.—But who is it?

Antonio.—One who will come to a strange end, *for so it is written.* The most extraordinary of all the Swiss, he of Saint James,—*Der schatz gräber.*

Myself.—Not Benedict Mol?

"Yaw, mein lieber herr," said Benedict, pushing open the door, which stood ajar; "it is myself. I met Herr Anton in the street, and hearing that you were in this place, I came with him to visit you."

Myself.—And, in the name of all that is singular, how is it that I see you in Madrid again? I thought that by this time you were returned to your own country.

Benedict.—Fear not, lieber herr; I shall return thither in good time; but not on foot, but with mules and coach. The schatz is still yonder, waiting to be dug up, and now I have better hope than ever; plenty of friends, plenty of money. See you not how I am dressed, lieber herr?

And verily his habiliments were of a much more respectable appearance than any which he had sported on former occasions. His coat and pantaloons, which were of light green, were nearly new. On his head he still wore an Andalusian hat, but the present one was neither old nor shabby, but fresh and glossy, and of immense altitude of cone; whilst in his hand, instead of the ragged staff which I had observed at St. James and Oviedo, he now carried a huge bamboo ratan, surmounted by the grim head of either a bear or lion, curiously cut out of pewter.

"You have all the appearance of a treasure-seeker returned from a successful expedition," I exclaimed.

"Or rather," interrupted Antonio, "of one who has ceased to trade on his own bottom, and now goes seeking treasures at the cost and expense of others."

I questioned the Swiss minutely concerning his adventures since I last saw him, when I left him at Oviedo to pursue my route to Santander. From his answers I gathered that he had followed me to the latter place; he was, however, a long time in performing the journey, being weak from hunger and privation. At Santander he could hear no tidings of me, and by this time the trifle which he had received from me was completely exhausted. He now thought of making his way into France, but was afraid to venture through the disturbed provinces, lest he should fall into the hands of the Carlists, who he conceived might shoot him as a spy. No one relieving him at Santander, he departed and begged his way till he found himself in some part of Aragon, but where he scarcely knew. "My misery was so great," said Bennet, "that I nearly lost my senses. Oh, the horror of wandering about the savage hills and wide plains of Spain, without money and without hope! Sometimes I became desperate, when I found myself amongst rocks and barrancos, perhaps after having tasted no food from sunrise to sunset, and then I would raise my staff towards the sky and shake it, crying, Lieber herr Gott, ach lieber herr Gott, you must help me now or never; if you tarry, I am lost; you must help me now, now! And once, when I was raving in this manner, methought I heard a voice, nay, I am sure I heard it, sounding from the hollow of a rock, clear and strong; and it cried, 'Der schatz, der schatz, it is not yet dug up; to Madrid, to Madrid! The way to the schatz is through Madrid.' And then the thought of the schatz once more rushed into my mind, and I reflected how happy I might be, could I but dig up the schatz. No more begging then, no more wandering amidst horrid mountains and deserts; so I brandished my staff, and my body and my limbs became full of new and surprising strength, and I strode forward, and was not long before I reached the high road; and then I begged and bettled as I best could, until I reached Madrid."

"And what has befallen you since you reached Madrid?" I inquired. "Did you find the treasure in the streets?"

On a sudden Bennet became reserved and taciturn, which the more surprised me, as, up to the present moment, he had at all times been remarkably communicative with respect to his affairs and prospects. From what I could learn from his broken hints and inuendoes, it appeared that, since his arrival at Madrid, he had fallen into the hands of certain people who had treated him with kindness, and provided him both with money and clothes; not from disinterested motives, however, but having an eye to the treasure. "They expect great things from me," said the Swiss; "and perhaps, after all, it would have been more profitable to have dug up the treasure without their assistance, always provided that were possible." Who his new friends were, he either knew not or would not tell me, save that they were people in power. He said something about Queen Christina, and an oath which he had taken in the presence of a bishop on the crucifix and "the four Evangiles." I thought that his head was turned, and forbore questioning. Just before taking his departure, he observed, "Lieber herr, pardon me for not being quite frank towards you, to whom I owe so much, but I dare not; I am not now my own man. It is, moreover, an evil thing at all times to say a word about treasure before you have secured it. There was once a man in my own country, who dug deep into the earth until he arrived at a copper vessel which contained a schatz. Seizing it by the handle, he merely exclaimed, in his transport, 'I have it!' that was enough, however: down sank the kettle, though the handle remained in his grasp. That was all he ever got for his trouble and digging. Farewell, lieber herr; I shall speedily be sent back to Saint James to dig up the schatz; but I will visit you ere I go—Farewell."

CHAPTER XLII.

Liberation from Prison—The Apology—Human Nature—The Greek's Return—Church of Rome —Light of Scripture—Archbishop of Toledo—An Interview—Stones of Price—A Resolution— The Foreign Language—Benedict's Farewell—Treasure Hunt at Compostella—Truth and Fiction.

I REMAINED about three weeks in the prison of Madrid, and then left it. If I had possessed any pride, or harboured any rancour against the party who had consigned me to durance, the manner in which I was restored to liberty would no doubt have been highly gratifying to those evil passions; the government having acknowledged, by a document transmitted to Sir George, that I had been incarcerated on insufficient grounds, and that no stigma attached itself to me from the imprisonment I had undergone; at the same time agreeing to defray all the expenses to which I had been subjected throughout the progress of this affair.

It moreover expressed its willingness to dismiss the individual owing to whose information I had been first arrested, namely, the corchete or police officer who had visited me in my apartments in the Calle de Santiago, and behaved himself in the manner which I have described in a former chapter. I declined, however, to avail myself of this condescension of the government, more especially as I was informed that the individual in question had a wife and family, who, if he were disgraced, would be at once reduced to want. I moreover considered that in what he had done and said he had probably only obeyed some private orders which he had received; I therefore freely forgave him, and if he does not retain his situation at the present moment, it is certainly no fault of mine.

I likewise refused to accept any compensation for my expenses, which were considerable. It is probable that many persons in my situation would have acted very differently in this respect, and I am far from saying that herein I acted discreetly or laudably; but I was averse to receive money from people such as those of which the Spanish government was composed, people whom I confess I heartily despised, and I was unwilling to afford them an opportunity of saying that after they had imprisoned an Englishman unjustly, and without a cause, he condescended to receive money at their hands. In a word, I confess my own weakness; I was willing that they should continue my debtors, and have little doubt that they had not the slightest objection to remain so: they kept their money and probably laughed in their sleeves at my want of common sense.

The heaviest loss which resulted from my confinement, and for which no indemnification could be either offered or received, was in the death of my affectionate and faithful Basque Francisco, who having attended me during the whole time of my imprisonment, caught the pestilential typhus or jail fever, which was then raging in the Carcel de la Corte, of which he expired within a few days subsequent to my liberation. His death occurred late one evening; the next morning as I was lying in bed ruminating on my loss, and wondering of what nation my next servant would be, I heard a noise which seemed to be that of a person employed vigorously in cleaning boots or shoes, and at intervals a strange discordant voice singing snatches of a song in some unknown language: wondering who it could be, I rang the bell.

" Did you ring, mon maître?" said Antonio, appearing at the door with one of his arms deeply buried in a boot.

"I certainly did ring," said I, "but I scarcely expected that you would have answered the summons."

" *Mais pourquoi non, mon maître?*" cried Antonio. " Who should serve you now but myself? *N'est pas que le sieur Francois est mort?* And did I not say, as soon as I heard of his departure, I shall return to my functions *chez mon maître*, Monsieur Georges?"

"I suppose you had no other employment, and on that account you came."

"*Au contraire*, mon maître," replied the Greek, "I had just engaged myself at the house of the Duke of Frias, from whom I was to receive ten dollars per month more than I shall accept from your worship; but on hearing that you were without a domestic, I forthwith told the Duke, though it was late at night, that he would not suit me, and here I am."

"I shall not receive you in this manner," said I; "return to the duke, apologize for your behaviour, request your dismission in a regular way; and then if his grace is willing to part with you, as will most probably be the case, I shall be happy to avail myself of your services."

It was reasonable to expect that after having been subjected to an imprisonment which my enemies themselves admitted to be unjust, I should in future experience more liberal treatment at their hands than that which they had hitherto adopted towards me. The sole object of my ambition at this time was to procure toleration for the sale of the gospel in this unhappy and distracted kingdom, and to have attained this end I would not only have consented to twenty such imprisonments in succession, as that which I had undergone, but would gladly have sacrificed life itself. I soon perceived, however, that I was likely to gain nothing by my incarceration; on the contrary, I had become an object of personal dislike to the government since the termination of this affair,

which, it was probable, I had never been before: their pride and vanity were humbled by the concessions which they had been obliged to make in order to avoid a rupture with England. This dislike they were now determined to gratify, by thwarting my views as much as possible. I had an interview with Ofalia on the subject uppermost in my mind; I found him morose and snappish. "It will be for your interest to be still," said he; "beware! you have already thrown the whole corte into confusion; beware, I repeat; another time you may not escape so easily." "Perhaps not," I replied, "and perhaps I do not wish it; it is a pleasant thing to be persecuted for the gospel's sake. I now take the liberty of inquiring whether, if I attempt to circulate the word of God, I am to be interrupted." "Of course;" exclaimed Ofalia; "the church forbids such circulation." "I shall make the attempt, however," I exclaimed. "Do you mean what you say?" demanded Ofalia, arching his eyebrows and elongating his mouth. "Yes," I continued, "I shall make the attempt in every village in Spain to which I can penetrate."

Throughout my residence in Spain the clergy were the party from which I experienced the strongest opposition; and it was at their instigation that the government originally adopted those measures which prevented any extensive circulation of the sacred volume through the land. I shall not detain the course of my narrative with reflections as to the state of a church, which, though it pretends to be founded on Scripture, would yet keep the light of Scripture from all mankind, if possible. But Rome is fully aware that she is not a Christian church, and having no desire to become so, she acts prudently in keeping from the eyes of her followers the page which would reveal to them the truths of Christianity. Her agents and minions throughout Spain exerted themselves to the utmost to render my humble labours abortive, and to vilify the work which I was attempting to disseminate. All the ignorant and fanatical clergy (the great majority) were opposed to it, and all those who were anxious to keep on good terms with the court of Rome were loud in their cry against it. There was, however, one section of the clergy, a small one, it is true, rather favourably disposed towards the circulation of the Gospel, though by no means inclined to make any particular sacrifice for the accomplishment of such an end: these were such as professed liberalism, which is supposed to mean a disposition to adopt any reform both in civil and church matters, which may be deemed conducive to the weal of the country. Not a few amongst the Spanish clergy were supporters of this principle, or at least declared themselves so, some doubtless for their own advancement, hoping to turn the spirit of the times to their own personal profit; others, it is to be hoped, from conviction, and a pure love of the principle itself. Amongst these were to be found, at the time of which I am speaking, several

THE BIBLE IN SPAIN.

bishops. It is worthy of remark, however, that of all these not one but owed his office, not to the Pope, who disowned them one and all, but to the Queen Regent, the professed head of liberalism throughout all Spain. It is not, therefore, surprising that men thus circumstanced should feel rather disposed than not to countenance any measure or scheme at all calculated to favour the advancement of liberalism; and surely such an one was the circulation of the Scriptures. I derived but little assistance from their good will however, supposing that they entertained some, as they never took any decided stand nor lifted up their voices in a bold and positive manner, denouncing the conduct of those who would withhold the light of Scripture from the world. At one time I hoped by their instrumentality to accomplish much in Spain in the Gospel cause; but I was soon undeceived, and became convinced that reliance on what they would effect, was like placing the hand on a staff of reed which will only lacerate the flesh. More than once some of them sent messages to me, expressive of their esteem, and assuring me how much the cause of the Gospel was dear to their hearts. I even received an intimation that a visit from me would be agreeable to the Archbishop of Toledo, the Primate of Spain.

Of this personage I can say but little, his early history being entirely unknown to me. At the death of Ferdinand, I believe, he was Bishop of Mallorca, a small insignificant see, of very scanty revenues, which perhaps he had no objection to exchange for one more wealthy; it is probable, however, that had he proved a devoted servant of the Pope, and consequently a supporter of legitimacy, he would have continued to the day of his death to fill the episcopal chair of Mallorca; but he was said to be a liberal, and the Queen Regent thought fit to bestow upon him the dignity of Archbishop of Toledo, by which he became the head of the Spanish church. The Pope, it is true, had refused to ratify the nomination, on which account all good Catholics were still bound to consider him as Bishop of Mallorca, and not as Primate of Spain. He however received the revenues belonging to the see, which, though only a shadow of what they originally were, were still considerable, and lived in the primate's palace at Madrid, so that if he were not archbishop de jure, he was what many people would have considered much better, archbishop de facto.

Hearing that this personage was a personal friend of Ofalia, who was said to entertain a very high regard for him, I determined upon paying him a visit, and accordingly one morning, betook myself to the palace in which he resided. I experienced no difficulty in obtaining an interview, being forthwith conducted to his presence by a common kind of footman, an Asturian, I believe, whom I found seated on a stone bench in the entrance hall. When I was introduced, the Archbishop was alone, seated behind a table in a large apartment, a kind of drawing-room; he was plainly dressed, in a black cassock and silken cap; on his finger, however, glittered a superb amethyst, the lustre of which was truly dazzling. He rose for a moment as I advanced, and motioned me to a chair with his hand. He might be about sixty years of age; his figure was very tall, but he stooped considerably, evidently from feebleness, and the pallid hue of ill-health overspread his emaciated features. When he had reseated himself, he dropped his head, and appeared to be looking on the table before him.

"I suppose your lordship knows who I am?" said I, at last breaking silence.

The Archbishop bent his head towards the right shoulder, in a somewhat equivocal manner, but said nothing.

"I am he whom the Manolos of Madrid call Don Jorgito el Ingles; I am just come out of prison, whither I was sent for circulating my Lord's Gospel in this kingdom of Spain."

The Archbishop made the same equivocal motion with his head, but still said nothing.

"I was informed that your lordship was desirous of seeing me, and on that account I have paid you this visit."

"I did not send for you," said the Archbishop, suddenly raising his head with a startled look.

"Perhaps not: I was, however, given to understand that my presence would be agreeable: but as that does not seem to be the case, I will leave."

"Since you have come, I am very glad to see you."

"*Io me alegro mucho*," said I, reseating myself; "and since I am here, we may as well talk of an all-important matter, the circulation of the Scripture. Does your lordship see any way by which an end so desirable might be brought about?"

"No," said the Archbishop faintly.

"Does not your lordship think that a knowledge of the Scripture would work inestimable benefit in these realms?"

"*No sé.*"

"Is it probable that the government may be induced to consent to the circulation?"

"*Que sé io?*" and the archbishop looked me in the face.

I looked in the face of the Archbishop; there was an expression of helplessness in it, which almost amounted to dotage. "Dear me," thought I, "whom have I come to on an errand like mine? Poor man, you are not fitted to play the part of Martin Luther, and least of all in Spain. I wonder why your friends selected you to be Archbishop of Toledo; they thought perhaps that you would do neither good nor harm, and made choice of you, as they sometimes do primates in my own country, for your incapacity. You do not seem very happy in your present situation; no very easy stall this of yours. You were more comfortable, I trow, when you were the poor Bishop of Mallorca; could enjoy your puchera then without fear that the salt would turn out sublimate. No fear then of being smothered in your bed. A siesta is a pleasant thing when one is not subject to be disturbed by ' the sudden fear.' I wonder whether they have poisoned you already," I continued, half aloud, as I kept my eyes fixed on his countenance, which methought was becoming ghastly.

"Did you speak, Don Jorge?" demanded the Archbishop.

"That is a fine brilliant on your lordship's hand," said I.

"You are fond of brilliants, Don Jorge," said the Archbishop, his features brightening up; "vaya! so am I; they are pretty things. Do you understand them?"

"I do," said I, "and I never saw a finer brilliant than your own, one excepted; it belonged to an acquaintance of mine, a Tartar Khan. He did not bear it on his finger, however; it stood in the frontlet of his horse, where it shone like a star. He called it Daoud Scharr, which, being interpreted, meaneth *light of war*."

"Vaya!" said the Archbishop, "how very extraordinary; I am glad you are fond of brilliants, Don Jorge. Speaking of horses, reminds me that I have frequently seen you on horseback. Vaya! how you ride; it is dangerous to be in your way."

"Is your lordship fond of equestrian exercise?"

"By no means, Don Jorge; I do not like horses; it is not the practice of the church to ride on horseback. We prefer mules: they are the quieter animals; I fear horses, they kick so violently."

"The kick of a horse is death," said I, "if it touches a vital part. I am not, however, of your lordship's opinion with respect to mules; a good ginete may retain his seat on a horse however, but a mule—vaya! when a false mule *tira por detras*, I do not believe that the Father of the Church himself could keep the saddle a moment, however sharp his bit."

As I was going away, I said, "And with respect to the Gospel, your lordship; what am I to understand?"

"*No sé*," said the Archbishop, again bending his head towards the right shoulder, whilst his features resumed their former vacant expression. And thus terminated my interview with the Archbishop of Toledo.

"It appears to me," said I to Maria Diaz, on returning home; "it appears to me, Marequita mia, that if the Gospel in Spain is to wait for toleration until these liberal bishops and archbishops come forward boldly in its behalf, it will have to tarry a considerable time."

"I am much of your worship's opinion," answered Maria; "a fine thing truly, it would be to wait till they exerted themselves in its behalf. Ca! the idea makes me smile: was your worship ever innocent enough to suppose that they cared one tittle about the Gospel or its cause? Vaya! they are true priests, and had only self-interest in view in their advances to you. The Holy Father disowns them, and

they would now fain, by awaking his fears and jealousy, bring him to some terms; but let him once acknowledge them, and see whether they would admit you to their palaces or hold any intercourse with you : ' Forth with the fellow,' they would say ; ' vaya! is he not a Lutheran ? Is he not an enemy to the church ? *A la horca, á la horca!*' I know this family better than you do, Don Jorge."

"It is useless tarrying," said I; "nothing, however, can be done in Madrid. I cannot sell the work at the despacho, and I have just received intelligence that all the copies exposed for sale in the libraries in the different parts of Spain which I visited, have been sequestrated by order of the government. My resolution is taken: I shall mount my horses, which are neighing in the stable, and betake myself to the villages and plains of dusty Spain. *Al campo, al campo:* 'Ride forth because of the word of righteousness, and thy right hand shall show thee terrible things.' I will ride forth, Maria."

"Your worship can do no better; and allow me here to tell you, that for every single book you might sell in a despacho in the city, you may dispose of one hundred amongst the villages, always provided you offer them cheap : for in the country money is rather scant. Vaya! should I not know ? Am I not a villager myself, a villana from the Sagra? Ride forth, therefore ; your horses are neighing in the stall, as your worship says, and you might almost have added that the Señor Antonio is neighing in the house. He says he has nothing to do, on which account he is once more dissatisfied and unsettled. He finds fault with every thing, but more particularly with myself. This morning I saluted him, and he made me no reply, but twisted his mouth in a manner very uncommon in this land of Spain."

"A thought strikes me," said I; "you have mentioned the Sagra; why should not I commence my labours amongst the villages of that district ?"

"Your worship can do no better," replied Maria; "the harvest is just over there, you will find the people comparatively unemployed, with leisure to attend and listen to you; and if you follow my advice, you will establish yourself at the Villa Seca, in the house of my fathers, where at present lives my lord and husband. Go, therefore, to Villa Seca in the first place, and from thence you can sally forth with the Señor Antonio upon your excursions. Peradventure, my husband will accompany you; and if so, you will find him highly useful. The people of Villa Seca are civil and courteous, your worship; when they address a foreigner, they speak to him at the top of their voice and in Gallegan."

"In Gallegan!" I exclaimed.

"They all understand a few words of Gallegan, which they have acquired from the mountaineers, who occasionally assist them in cutting the harvest; and as Gallegan is the only foreign language they know, they deem it but polite to address a foreigner in that tongue. Vaya! it is not a bad village, that of Villa Seca, nor are the people; the only ill-conditioned person living there is his reverence the curate."

I was not long in making preparations for my enterprise. A considerable stock of Testaments were sent forward by an arriero, I myself followed the next day. Before my departure, however, I received a visit from Benedict Mol.

"I am come to bid you farewell, lieber herr; to-morrow I return to Compostella."

"On what errand?"

"To dig up the schatz, lieber herr. For what else should I go? For what have I lived until now, but that I may dig up the schatz in the end?"

"You might have lived for something better," I exclaimed. "I wish you success, however. But on what grounds do you hope? Have you obtained permission to dig? Surely you remember your former trials in Galicia?"

"I have not forgotten them lieber herr, nor the journey to Oviedo, nor 'the seven acorns,' nor the fight with death in the barranco. But I must accomplish my destiny. I go now to Galicia, as is becoming a Swiss, at the expense of the government, with coach and mule; I mean in the galera. I am to have all the help I require, so that I can dig down to the earth's centre if I think fit. I—but I must not tell your worship, for I am sworn on 'the four Evangiles,' not to tell."

"Well, Benedict, I have nothing to say, save that I hope you will succeed in your digging."

"Thank you, lieber herr, thank you; and now farewell. Succeed! I shall succeed!" Here he stopped short, started, and looking upon me with an expression of countenance almost wild, he exclaimed: "Heiliger Gott! I forgot one thing. Suppose I should not find the treasure after all."

"Very rationally said; pity, though, that you did not think of that contingency till now. I tell you, my friend, that you have engaged in a most desperate undertaking. It is true that you may find a treasure. The chances are, however, a hundred to one that you do not; and in that event, what will be your situation? You will be looked upon as an impostor, and the consequences may be horrible to you. Remember where you are, and amongst whom you are. The Spaniards are a credulous people, but let them once suspect that they have been imposed upon, and above all laughed at, and their thirst for vengeance knows no limit. Think not that your innocence will avail you. That you are no impostor I feel convinced; but they would never believe it. It is not too late. Return your fine clothes and magic rattan to those from whom you had them. Put on your old garments, grasp your ragged staff, and come with me to the Sagra, to assist in circulating the illustrious Gospel amongst the rustics on the Tagus' bank."

Benedict mused for a moment, then shaking his head, he cried, "No, no, I must accomplish my destiny. The schatz is not yet dug up. So said the voice in the barranco. To-morrow to Compostella. I shall find it—the schatz—it is still there—it must be there."

He went, and I never saw him more. What I heard, however, was extraordinary enough. It appeared that the government had listened to his tale, and had been so struck with Bennet's exaggerated description of the buried treasure, that they imagined that, by a little trouble and outlay, gold and diamonds might be dug up at Saint James sufficient to enrich themselves and to pay off the national debt of Spain. The Swiss returned to Compostella "like a duke," to use his own words. The affair, which had at first been kept a profound secret, was speedily divulged. It was, indeed, resolved tha the investigation, which involved consequences of so much importance, should take place in a manner the most public and imposing. A solemn festival was drawing nigh, and it was deemed expedient that the search should take place upon that day. The day arrived. All the bells in Compostella pealed. The whole populace thronged from their houses; a thousand troops were drawn up in the square; the expectation of all was wound up to the highest pitch. A procession directed its course to the church of San Roque; at its head was the captain-general and the Swiss, brandishing in his hand the magic rattan, close behind walked the *meiga*, the Gallegan witch-wife, by whom the treasure-seeker had been originally guided in the search; numerous masons brought up the rear, bearing implements to break up the ground. The procession enters the church, they pass through it in solemn march, they find themselves in a vaulted passage. The Swiss looks around. "Dig here," said he suddenly. "Yes, dig here," said the meiga. The masons labour, the floor is broken up,— a horrible and fetid odour arises. . . .

Enough; no treasure was found, and my warning to the unfortunate Swiss turned out but too prophetic. He was forthwith seized and flung into the horrid prison of Saint James, amidst the execrations of thousands, who would have gladly torn him limb from limb.

The affair did not terminate here. The political opponents of the government did not allow so favourable an opportunity to escape for launching the shafts of ridicule. The Moderados were taunted in the cortes for their avarice and credulity, whilst the liberal press wafted on its wings through Spain the story of the treasure-hunt at Saint James.

"After all, it was a *trampa* of Don Jorge's," said one of my enemies. "That fellow is at the bottom of half the picardias which happen in Spain."

Eager to learn the fate of the Swiss, I wrote to my old friend Rey Romero, at Compostella. In his answer he states: "I saw the Swiss in prison, to which place he sent for me, craving my assistance, for the sake of the friendship which I bore to you. But how could I help him? He was speedily after removed from Saint James, I know not whither. It is said that he disappeared on the road."

Truth is sometimes stranger than fiction. Where in the whole cycle of romance shall we find any thing more wild, grotesque, and sad, than the easily authenticated history of Benedict Mol, the treasure-digger of Saint James?

CHAPTER XLIII.

Villa Seca—Moorish House—The Puchera—The Rustic Council—Polite Ceremonial—The Flower of Spain—The Bridge of Azeca—The Ruined Castle—Taking the Field—Demand for the Word—The old Peasant—The Curate and Blacksmith—Cheapness of the Scriptures.

It was one of the most fiercely hot days in which I ever braved the sun, when I arrived at Villa Seca. The heat in the shade must have amounted at least to one hundred degrees, and the entire atmosphere seemed to consist of flickering flame. At a place called Leganez, six leagues from Madrid, and about half-way to Toledo, we diverged from the highway, bending our course seemingly towards the southeast. We rode over what are called plains in Spain, but which, in any other part of the world, would be called undulating and broken ground. The crops of corn and barley had already disappeared. The last vestiges discoverable being here and there a few sheaves, which the labourers were occupied in removing to their garners in the villages. The country could scarcely be called beautiful, being perfectly naked, exhibiting neither trees nor verdure. It was not, however, without its pretensions to grandeur and magnificence, like every part of Spain. The most prominent objects were two huge calcareous hills, or rather one cleft in twain, which towered up on high; the summit of the nearest being surmounted by the ruins of an ancient castle, that of Villaluenga. About an hour past noon we reached Villa Seca.

We found it a large village, containing about seven hundred inhabitants, and surrounded by a mud wall. A plaza or marketplace, stood in the midst, one side of which is occupied by what is called a palace, a clumsy quadrangular building of two stories, belonging to some noble family, the lords of the neighbouring soil. It was deserted, however, being only occupied by a kind of steward, who stored up in its chambers the grain which he received as rent from the tenants and villanos who farmed the surrounding district.

The village stands at the distance of about a quarter of a league from the bank of the Tagus, which even here, in the heart of Spain, is a beautiful stream, not navigable however, on account of the sand-banks, which in many places assume the appearance of small islands, and are covered with trees and brushwood. The village derives its supply of water entirely from the river, having none of its own, such at least as is potable, the water of its wells being all brackish, on which account it is probably termed Villa Seca, which signifies "the dry hamlet." The inhabitants are said to have been originally Moors; certain it is, that various customs are observable here highly favourable to such a supposition. Amongst others a very curious one: it is deemed infamous for a woman of Villa Seca to go across the market-place, or to be seen there, though they have no hesitation in showing themselves in the streets and lanes. A deep-rooted hostility exists between the inhabitants of this place and those of a neighbouring village, called Vargas; they rarely speak when they meet, and never intermarry. There is a vague tradition that the people of the latter place are old Christians, and it is highly probable that these neighbours were originally of widely different blood; those of Villa Seca being of particularly dark complexions, whilst the indwellers of Vargas are light and fair. Thus the old feud between Moor and Christian is still kept up in the nineteenth century in Spain.

Drenched in perspiration, which fell from our brows like rain, we arrived at the door of Juan Lopez, the husband of Maria Diaz. Having heard of our intention to pay him a visit, he was expecting us, and cordially welcomed us to his habitation, which, like a genuine Moorish house, consisted only of one story. It was amply large, however, with a court and stable. All the apartments were deliciously cool. The floors were of brick or stone, and the narrow and trellissed windows, which were without glass, scarcely permitted a ray of sun to penetrate into the interior.

A puchera had been prepared in expectation of our arrival; the heat had not taken away my appetite, and it was not long before I did full justice to this the standard dish of Spain. Whilst I ate, Lopez played upon the guitar, singing occasionally snatches of Andalusian songs. He was a short, merry-faced, active fellow, whom I had frequently seen at Madrid, and was a good specimen of the Spanish labrador or yeoman. Though far from possessing the ability and intellect of his wife, Maria Diaz, he was by no means deficient in shrewdness and understanding. He was, moreover, honest and disinterested, and performed good service in the Gospel cause, as will presently appear.

When the repast was concluded, Lopez thus

23

addressed me :—"Señor Don Jorge, your arrival in our village has already caused a sensation, more especially as these are times of war and tumult, and every person is afraid of another, and we dwell here close to the confines of the factious country ; for, as you well know, the greater part of La Mancha is in the hands of the Carlinos and thieves, parties of whom frequently show themselves on the other side of the river : on which account the alcalde of this city, with the other grave and notable people thereof, are desirous of seeing your worship, and conversing with you, and of examining your passport." "It is well," said I; "let us forthwith pay a visit to these worthy people." Whereupon he conducted me across the plaza, to the house of the alcalde, where I found the rustic dignitary seated in the passage, enjoying the refreshing coolness of a draught of air which rushed through. He was an elderly man, of about sixty, with nothing remarkable in his appearance or his features, which latter were placid and good-humoured. There were several people with him, amongst whom was the surgeon of the place, a tall and immensely bulky man, an Alavese by birth, from the town of Vitoria. There was also a red, fiery-faced individual, with a nose very much turned on one side, who was the blacksmith of the village, and was called in general, El Tuerto, from the circumstance of his having but one eye. Making the assembly a low bow, I pulled out my passport, and thus addressed them :—

"Grave men and cavaliers of this city of Villa Seca, as I am a stranger, of whom it is not possible that you should know any thing, I have deemed it my duty to present myself before you, and to tell you who I am. Know, then, that I am an Englishman of good blood and fathers, travelling in these countries for my own profit and diversion, and for that of other people also. I have now found my way to Villa Seca, where I propose to stay some time, doing that which may be deemed convenient ; sometimes riding across the plain, and sometimes bathing myself in the waters of the river, which are reported to be of advantage in times of heat. I therefore beg that, during my sojourn in this capital, I may enjoy such countenance and protection from its governors as they are in the habit of affording to those who are of quiet and well-ordered life, and are disposed to be buxom and obedient to the customs and laws of the republic."

"He speaks well," said the alcalde, glancing around.

"Yes, he speaks well," said the bulky Alavese; "there is no denying it."

"I never heard any one speak better," cried the blacksmith, starting up from a stool on which he was seated. "Vaya! he is a big man and a fair complexioned, like myself. I like him, and have a horse that will just suit him ; one that is the flower of Spain, and is eight inches above the mark."

I then, with another bow, presented my passport to the alcalde, who, with a gentle motion of his hand, appeared to decline taking it, at the same time saying, "It is not necessary." "Oh, not at all," exclaimed the surgeon. "The housekeepers of Villa Seca know how to comport themselves with formality," observed the blacksmith. "They would be very loth to harbour any suspicion against a cavalier so courteous and well spoken." Knowing, however, that this refusal amounted to nothing, and that it merely formed part of a polite ceremonial, I proffered the passport a second time, whereupon it was instantly taken, and in a moment the eyes of all present were bent upon it with intense curiosity. It was examined from top to bottom, and turned round repeatedly, and though it is not probable that an individual present understood a word of it, it being written in French, it gave nevertheless universal satisfaction ; and when the alcalde, carefully folding it up, returned it to me, they all observed that they had never seen a better passport in their lives, or one which spake in higher terms of the bearer.

Who was it said that "Cervantes sneered Spain's chivalry away?" I know not; and the author of such a line scarcely deserves to be remembered. How the rage for scribbling tempts people at the present day to write about lands and nations of which they know nothing, or worse than nothing. Vaya! it is not from having seen a bull-fight at Seville or Madrid, or having spent a handful of ounces at a pasada in either of those places, kept perhaps by a Genoese or a Frenchman, that you are competent to write about such a people as the Spaniards, and to tell the world how they think, how they speak, and how they act. Spain's chivalry sneered away! Why there is every probability that the great body of the Spanish nation speak, think, and live precisely as their forefathers did six centuries ago.

In the evening the blacksmith, or, as he would be called in Spanish, El Herrador, made his appearance at the door of Lopez on horseback. "Vamos, Don Jorge," he shouted. "Come with me, if your worship is disposed for a ride. I am going to bathe my horse in the Tagus, by the bridge of Azeca." I instantly saddled my jaca Cordovesa, and joining him, we rode out of the village, directing our course across the plain towards the river. "Did you ever see such a horse as this of mine, Don Jorge?" he demanded. "Is he not a jewel—an alaja?" And in truth the horse was a noble and gallant creature, in height at least sixteen hands, broad chested, but of clean and elegant limbs. His neck was superbly arched, and his head towered on high, like that of a swan. In colour he was a bright chestnut, save his flowing mane and tail, which were almost black. I expressed my admiration, whereupon the herrador, in high spirits, pressed his heels to the creature's sides, and flinging the bridle on its neck, speeded over the plain with prodigious swiftness, shouting the old Spanish cry, Cierra! I attempted to keep up with him, but had not a chance. "I call him the flower of Spain," said the herrador, rejoining me. "Purchase him, Don Jorge, his price is but three thousand reals.* I would not sell him for double that sum, but the Carlist thieves have their eyes upon him, and I am apprehensive that they will some day make a dash across the river and break into Villa Seca, all to get possession of my horse, 'The Flower of Spain.'"

It may be as well to observe here, that within a month of this period, my friend the herrador, not being able to find a regular purchaser for his steed, entered into negotiations with the aforesaid thieves respecting him, and finally disposed of the animal to their leader, receiving not the three thousand reals he demanded, but an entire herd of horned cattle, probably driven from the plains of La Mancha. For this transaction, which was neither more nor less than high treason, he was cast into the prison of Toledo, where, however, he did not continue long: for during a short visit to Villa Seca, which I made in the spring of the following year, I found him alcalde of that "republic."

We arrived at the bridge of Azeca, which is about half a league from Villa Seca; close beside it is a large water-mill, standing upon a dam which crosses the river. Dismounting from his steed, the herrador proceeded to divest it of the saddle, then causing it to enter the mill-pool he led it by means of a cord to a particular spot, where the water reached half way up its neck, then fastening the cord to a post on the bank, he left the animal standing in the pool. I thought I could do no better than follow his example, and accordingly, procuring a rope from the mill, I led my own horse into the water. "It will refresh their blood, Don Jorge," said the herrador; "let us leave them there for an hour, whilst we go and divert ourselves."

Near the bridge, on the side of the river on which we were, was a kind of guard-house, where were three carbineers of the revenue, who collected the tolls of the bridge; we entered into conversation with them: "Is not this a dangerous position of yours," said I to one of them, who was a Catalan; "close beside the factious country? Surely it would not be difficult for a body of the Carlinos or bandits to dash across the bridge and make prisoners of you all."

"It would be easy enough at any moment, Cavalier," replied the Catalan; "we are, however, all in the hands of God, and he has preserved us hitherto, and perhaps still will. True it is that one of our number, for there were four of us originally, fell the other day into the hands of the canaille : he had wandered across the bridge amongst the thickets with his gun in search of a hare or rabbit, when three or four of them fell upon him and put him to death in a manner too horrible to relate. But patience! every man who lives must die. I shall not sleep the worse to-night

because I may chance to be hacked by the knives of these malvados to-morrow. Cavalier, I am from Barcelona, and have seen there mariners of your nation ; this is not so good a country as Barcelona. Paciencia ! Cavalier, if you will step into our house, I will give you a glass of water; we have some that is cool, for we dug a deep hole in the earth and buried there our pitcher ; it is cool, as I told you, but the water of Castile is not like that of Catalonia."

The moon had arisen when we mounted our horses to return to the village, and the rays of the beauteous luminary danced merrily on the rushing waters of the Tagus, silvered the plain over which we were passing, and bathed in a flood of brightness the bold sides of the calcareous hill of Villaluenga and the antique ruins which crowned its brow. "Why is that place called the Castle of Villaluenga?" I demanded.

"From a village of that name, which stands on the other side of the hill, Don Jorge," replied the herrador. "Vaya! it is a strange place, that castle: some say it was built by the Moors in the olden times, and some by the Christians when they first laid siege to Toledo. It is not inhabited now, save by rabbits, which breed there in abundance amongst the long grass and broken stones, and by eagles and vultures, which build on the tops of the towers ; I occasionally go there with my gun to shoot a rabbit. On a fine day, you may descry both Toledo and Madrid from its walls. I cannot say I like the place, it is so dreary and melancholy. The hill on which it stands is all of chalk, and is very difficult of ascent. I heard my grandame say that once, when she was a girl, a cloud of smoke burst from that hill, and that flames of fire were seen, just as if it contained a volcano, as perhaps it does, Don Jorge."

The grand work of Scripture circulation soon commenced in the Sagra. Notwithstanding the heat of the weather, I rode about in all directions. It was well that heat agrees with my constitution, otherwise it would have been impossible to effect any thing in this season, when the very arrieros frequently fall dead from their mules, smitten by a sun-stroke. I had an excellent assistant in Antonio, who, disregarding the heat like myself, and afraid of nothing, visited several villages with remarkable success. "Mon maître," said he, "I wish to show you that nothing is beyond my capacity." But he who put the labours of us both to shame, was my host, Juan Lopez, whom it had pleased the Lord to render favourable to the cause. "Don Jorge," said he, "io quiero engancharme con usted (I wish to enlist with you); I am a liberal, and a foe to superstition ; I will take the field, and, if necessary, will follow you to the end of the world: Viva Ingalaterra; viva el Evangelio." Thus saying, he put a large bundle of Testaments into a satchel, and springing upon the crupper of his gray donkey, he cried " Arrhe burra," and hastened away. I sat down to my journal.

---

* About thirty pounds.

Ere I had finished writing, I heard the voice of the burra in the court-yard, and going out I found my host returned. He had disposed of his whole cargo of twenty Testaments at the village of Vargas, distant from Villa Seca about a league. Eight poor harvest men, who were refreshing themselves at the door of a wine-house, purchased each a copy, whilst the village school-master secured the rest for the little ones beneath his care, lamenting, at the same time, the great difficulty he had long experienced in obtaining religious books, owing to their scarcity and extravagant price. Many other persons were also anxious to purchase Testaments, but Lopez was unable to supply them: at his departure, they requested him to return within a few days.

I was aware that I was playing rather a daring game, and that it was very possible that when I least expected it, I might be seized, tied to the tail of a mule, and dragged either to the prison of Toledo or Madrid. Yet such a prospect did not discourage me in the least, but rather urged me to persevere; for at this time, without the slightest wish to magnify myself, I could say that I was eager to lay down my life for the cause, and whether a bandit's bullet or the gaol fever brought my career to a close, was a matter of indifference to me; I was not then a stricken man: "Ride on because of the word of righteousness," was my cry.

The news of the arrival of the book of life soon spread like wild-fire through the villages of the Sagra of Toledo, and wherever my people and myself directed our course we found the inhabitants disposed to receive our merchandise; it was even called for where not exhibited. One night as I was bathing myself and horse in the Tagus, a knot of people gathered on the bank, crying, "Come out of the water, Englishman, and give us books; we have got our money in our hands." The poor creatures then held out their hands, filled with cuartos, a copper coin of the value of a farthing, but unfortunately I had no Testaments to give them. Antonio, however, who was at a short distance, having exhibited one, it was instantly torn from his hands by the people, and a scuffle ensued to obtain possession of it. It very frequently occurred, that the poor labourers in the neighbourhood, being eager to obtain Testaments, and having no money to offer us in exchange, brought various articles to our habitation as equivalents; for example, rabbits, fruit, and barley, and I made a point never to disappoint them, as such articles were of utility either for our own consumption or that of the horses.

In Villa Seca there was a school in which fifty-seven children were taught the first rudiments of education. One morning the schoolmaster, a tall slim figure of about sixty, bearing on his head one of the peaked hats of Andalusia, and wrapped, notwithstanding the excessive heat of the weather, in a long cloak, made his appearance, and having seated himself, requested to be shown one of our books. Having delivered it to him, he remained examining it for nearly half an hour, without uttering a word. At last he laid it down with a sigh, and said that he should be very happy to purchase some of these books for his school, but from their appearance, especially from the quality of the paper and binding, he was apprehensive that to pay for them would exceed the means of the parents of his pupils, as they were almost destitute of money, being poor labourers. He then commenced blaming the government, which he said established schools without affording the necessary books, adding that in his school there were but two books for the use of all his pupils, and these he confessed contained but little good. I asked him what he considered the Testaments worth? He said "Señor, Cavalier, to speak frankly, I have in other times paid twelve reals for books inferior to yours in every respect, but I assure you that my poor pupils would be utterly unable to pay the half of that sum." I replied, "I will sell you as many as you please for three reals each. I am acquainted with the poverty of the land, and my friends and myself, in affording the people the means of spiritual instruction have no wish to curtail their scanty bread." He replied: "Bendito sea Dios," (*blessed be God,*) and could scarcely believe his ears. He instantly purchased a dozen, expending, as he said, all the money he possessed, with the exception of a few cuartos. The introduction of the word of God into the country schools of Spain is therefore begun, and I humbly hope that it will prove one of those events which the Bible Society, after the lapse of years, will have most reason to remember with joy and gratitude to the Almighty.

An old peasant is reading in the portico. Eighty-four years have passed over his head, and he is almost entirely deaf; nevertheless, he is reading aloud the second of Matthew: three days since he bespoke a Testament, but not being able to raise the money, he has not redeemed it until the present moment. He has just brought thirty farthings; as I survey the silvery hair which overshadows his sunburnt countenance, the words of the song occurred to me, "Lord, now lettest thou thy servant depart in peace according to thy word, for mine eyes have seen thy salvation."

I experienced much grave kindness and simple hospitality from the good people of Villa Seca during my sojourn amongst them. I had at this time so won their hearts by the "formality" of my behaviour and language, that I firmly believe they would have resisted to the knife any attempt which might have been made to arrest or otherwise maltreat me. He who wishes to become acquainted with the genuine Spaniard, must seek him not in sea-ports and large towns, but in lone and remote villages, like those of the Sagra. There he will find all that gravity of deportment and chivalry of disposition which Cervantes is said to have sneered away: and there he will hear, in every day conversation, those grandiose expressions, which, when met with in the romances of chivalry, are scoffed at as ridiculous exaggerations.

I had one enemy in the village—it was the curate.

"The fellow is a heretic and a scoundrel," said he one day in the conclave. "He never enters the church, and is poisoning the minds of the people with his Lutheran books. Let him be bound and sent to Toledo, or turned out of the village at least."

"I will have nothing of the kind," said the alcalde, who was said to be a Carlist. "If he has his opinions, I have mine too. He has conducted himself with politeness. Why should I interfere with him? He has been courteous to my daughter, and has presented her with a volume. Que viva! and with respect to his being a Lutheran, I have heard say that among the Lutherans there are sons of as good fathers as here. He appears to me a caballero. He speaks well."

"There is no denying it," said the surgeon.

"Who speaks so well?" shouted the herrador. "And who has more formality? Vaya! did he not praise my horse, 'The Flower of Spain?' Did he not say that in the whole of Ingalaterra there was not a better? Did he not assure me, moreover, that if he were to remain in Spain he would purchase it, giving me my own price? Turn him out, indeed! Is he not of my own blood, is he not fair-complexioned? Who shall say turn him out when I, 'the one-eyed,' say no?"

In connexion with the circulation of the Scriptures I will now relate an anecdote not altogether divested of singularity. I have already spoken of the water-mill by the bridge of Azeca. I had formed acquaintance with the tenant of this mill, who was known in the neighbourhood by the name of Don Antero. One day, taking me into a retired place, he asked me, to my great astonishment, whether I would sell him a thousand Testaments at the price at which I was disposing of them to the peasantry; saying, if I would

consent he would pay me immediately. In fact, he put his hand into his pocket, and pulled it out filled with gold ounces. I asked him what was his reason for wishing to make so considerable a purchase. Whereupon he informed me, that he had a relation in Toledo whom he wished to establish, and that he was of opinion that his best plan would be to hire him a shop there and furnish it with Testaments. I told him that he must think of nothing of the kind, as probably the books would be seized on the first attempt to introduce them into Toledo, as the priests and canons were much averse to their distribution.

He was not disconcerted, however, and said his relation could travel, as I myself was doing, and dispose of them to the peasants with profit to himself. I confess I was inclined at first to accept his offer, but at length declined, as I did not wish to expose a poor man to the risk of losing money, goods, and perhaps liberty and life. I was likewise averse to the books being offered to the peasantry at an advanced price, being aware that they could not afford it, and the books, by such an attempt, would lose a considerable part of that influence which they then enjoyed; for their cheapness struck the minds of the people, and they considered it almost as much in the light of a miracle as the Jews the manna which dropped from heaven at the time they were famishing, or the spring which suddenly gushed from the flinty rock to assuage their thirst in the wilderness.

At this time a peasant was continually passing and repassing between Villa Seca and Madrid, bringing us cargoes of Testaments on a burrico. We continued our labours until the greater part of the villages of the Sagra were well supplied with books, more especially those of Vargas, Coveja, Mocejon, Villaluenga, Villa Seca, and Yungler. Hearing at last that our proceedings were known at Toledo, and were causing considerable alarm, we returned to Madrid.

Q

CHAPTER XLIV.

Aranjuez—A Warning—A Night Adventure—A Fresh Expedition—Segovia—Abades—Factious Curas—Lopez in Prison—Rescue of Lopez.

THE success which had attended our efforts in the Sagra of Toledo speedily urged me on to a new enterprise. I now determined to direct my course to La Mancha, and to distribute the word amongst the villages of that province. Lopez, who had already performed such important services in the Sagra, had accompanied us to Madrid, and was eager to take part in this new expedition. We determined in the first place to proceed to Aranjuez, where we hoped to obtain some information which might prove of utility in the further regulation of our movements; Aranjuez being but a slight distance from the frontier of La Mancha, and the high road into that province passing directly through it. We accordingly sallied forth from Madrid, selling from twenty to forty Testaments in every village which lay in our way, until we arrived at Aranjuez, to which place we had forwarded a large supply of books.

A lovely spot is Aranjuez, though in desolation: here the Tagus flows through a delicious valley, perhaps the most fertile in Spain; and here upsprang, in Spain's better days, a little city, with a small but beautiful palace shaded by enormous trees, where royalty delighted to forget its cares. Here Ferdinand the Seventh spent his latter days, surrounded by lovely señoras and Andalusian bull-fighters; but as the German Schiller has it in one of his tragedies,—

"The happy days of fair Aranjuez
Are past and gone."

When the sensual king went to his dread account, royalty deserted it, and it soon fell into decay. Intriguing courtiers no longer crowd its halls; its spacious circus, where Manchegan bulls once roared in rage and agony, is now closed; and the light tinkling of guitars is no longer heard amidst its groves and gardens.

At Aranjuez I made a sojourn of three days, during which time Antonio, Lopez, and myself visited every house in the town. We found a vast deal of poverty and ignorance amongst the inhabitants, and experienced some opposition: nevertheless it pleased the Almighty to permit us to dispose of about eighty Testaments, which were purchased entirely by the very poor people; those in easier circumstances paying no attention to the word of God, but rather turning it to scoff and ridicule.

One circumstance was very gratifying and cheering to me, namely, the ocular proof which I possessed that the books which I disposed of were read, and with attention, by those to whom I sold them; and that many others participated in their benefit. In the streets of Aranjuez, and beneath the mighty cedars and gigantic elms and plantains which compose its noble woods, I have frequently seen groups assembled, listening to individuals who, with the New Testament in their hands, were reading aloud the comfortable words of salvation.

It is probable that, had I remained a longer period at Aranjuez, I might have sold many more of these divine books, but I was eager to gain La Mancha and its sandy plains, and to conceal myself for a season amongst its solitary villages, for I was apprehensive that a storm was gathering around me; but when once through Ocaña, the frontier town, I knew well that I should have nothing to fear from the Spanish authorities, as their power ceased there, the rest of La Mancha being almost entirely in the hands of the Carlists, and overrun by small parties of banditti, from whom, however, I trusted that the Lord would preserve me. I therefore departed for Ocaña, distant three leagues from Aranjuez.

I started with Antonio at six in the evening, having early in the morning sent forward Lopez with between two and three hundred Testaments. We left the high road, and proceeded by a shorter way through wild hills and over very broken and precipitous ground: being well mounted, we found ourselves just after sunset opposite Ocaña, which stands on a steep hill. A deep valley lay between us and the town: we descended, and came to a small bridge, which traverses a rivulet at the bottom of the valley, at a very small distance from a kind of suburb. We crossed the bridge, and were passing by a deserted house on our left hand, when a man appeared from under the porch.

What I am about to state will seem incomprehensible, but a singular history and a singular people are connected with it: the man placed himself before my horse so as to bar the way, and said " *Schophon*," which, in the Hebrew tongue, signifies a rabbit. I knew this word to be one of the Jewish countersigns, and asked the man if he had any thing to communicate. He said, " You must not enter the town, for a net is prepared for you. The corregidor of Toledo, on whom may all evil light, in order to give pleasure to the priests of Maria, in whose face I spit, has ordered all the alcaldes of these parts and the escribanos and the corchetes to lay hands on you wherever they may find you, and to send you and your books, and all that pertains to you to Toledo. Your servant was seized this morning in the town above, as he was selling the writings in the streets, and they are now awaiting your arrival in the posada;

but I knew you from the accounts of my brethren, and I have been waiting here four hours to give you warning in order that your horse may turn his tail to your enemies, and neigh in derision of them. Fear nothing for your servant, for he is known to the alcalde, and will be set at liberty, but do you flee, and may God attend you." Having said this, he hurried towards the town.

I hesitated not a moment to take his advice, knowing full well that, as my books had been taken possession of, I could do no more in that quarter. We turned back in the direction of Aranjuez, the horses, notwithstanding the nature of the ground, galloping at full speed; but our adventures were not over. Midway, and about half a league from the village of Antigola, we saw close to us on our left hand three men on a low bank. As far as the darkness would permit us to distinguish, they were naked, but each bore in his hand a long gun. These were rateros, or the common assassins and robbers of the roads. We halted and cried out, "Who goes there?" They replied, "What's that to you? pass by." Their drift was to fire at us from a position from which it would be impossible to miss. We shouted, "If you do not instantly pass to the right side of the road, we will tread you down beneath the horses' hoofs." They hesitated and then obeyed, for all assassins are dastards, and the least show of resolution daunts them. As we galloped past, one cried, with an obscene oath, "Shall we fire?" But another said, "No! hay peligro." We reached Aranjuez, where early next morning Lopez rejoined us, and we returned to Madrid.

I am sorry to state that two hundred Testaments were seized at Ocaña, from whence, after being sealed up, they were despatched to Toledo. Lopez informed me, that in two hours he could have sold them all, the demand was so great. As it was, twenty-seven were disposed of in less than ten minutes.

"Ride on because of the word of righteousness." Notwithstanding the check which we had experienced at Ocaña, we were far from being discouraged, and forthwith prepared ourselves for another expedition. As we returned from Aranjuez to Madrid, my eyes had frequently glanced towards the mighty wall of mountains dividing the two Castiles, and I said to myself, "Would it not be well to cross those hills, and commence operations on the other side, even in Old Castile? There I am unknown, and intelligence of my proceedings can scarcely have been transmitted thither. Peradventure the enemy is asleep, and before he has roused himself, I may have sown much of the precious seed amongst the villages of the Old Castilians. To Castile, therefore, to Castilla la Vieja!" Accordingly, on the day after my arrival, I despatched several cargoes of books to various places which I proposed to visit, and sent forward Lopez and his donkey, well laden, with directions to meet me on a parti-

cular day beneath a particular arch of the aqueduct of Segovia. I likewise gave him orders to engage any persons willing to cooperate with us in the circulation of the Scriptures, and who might be likely to prove of utility in the enterprise. A more useful assistant than Lopez in an expedition of this kind it was impossible to have. He was not only well acquainted with the country, but had friends, and even connexions, on the other side of the hills, in whose houses he assured me that we should at all times find a hearty welcome. He departed in high spirits, exclaiming, "Be of good cheer, Don Jorge; before we return we will have disposed of every copy of your evangelic library. Down with the friars! Down with superstition! Viva Ingalaterra, viva el Evangelio!"

In a few days I followed with Antonio. We ascended the mountains by the pass called Peña Cerrada, which lies about three leagues to the eastward of that of Guadarama. It is very unfrequented, the high road between the two Castiles passing through Guadarama. It has, moreover, an evil name, being, according to common report, infested with banditti. The sun was just setting when we reached the top of the hills, and entered a thick and gloomy pine forest, which entirely covers the mountains on the side of Old Castile. The descent soon became so rapid and precipitous, that we were fain to dismount from our horses and to drive them before us. Into the woods we plunged deeper and deeper still; night-birds soon began to hoot and cry, and millions of crickets commenced their shrill chirping above, below, and around us. Occasionally, amidst the trees at a distance, we could see blazes, as if from immense fires. "They are those of the charcoal-burners, mon maitre," said Antonio; "we will not go near them, however, for they are savage people, and half bandits. Many is the traveller whom they have robbed and murdered in these horrid wildernesses."

It was blackest night when we arrived at the foot of the mountains; we were still, however, amidst woods and pine forests, which extended for leagues in every direction. "We shall scarcely reach Segovia tonight, mon maitre," said Antonio. And so indeed it proved, for we became bewildered, and at last arriving where two roads branched off in different directions, we took not the left hand road, which would have conducted us to Segovia, but turned to the right, in the direction of La Granja, where we arrived at midnight.

We found the desolation of La Granja far greater than that of Aranjuez; both had suffered from the absence of royalty, but the former to a degree which was truly appalling. Nine-tenths of the inhabitants had left this place, which, until the late military revolution, had been the favourite residence of Christiana. So great is the solitude of La Granja, that wild boars from the neighbouring forests, and especially from the beautiful pine-covered mountain which rises like a cone directly behind the palace, frequently find their way into the streets and squares, and whet their tusks against the pillars of the porticos.

"Ride on because of the word of righteousness." After a stay of twenty-four hours at La Granja, we proceeded to Segovia. The day had arrived on which I had appointed to meet Lopez. I repaired to the aqueduct, and sat down beneath the hundred and seventh arch, where I waited the greater part of the day, but he came not, whereupon I arose and went into the city.

At Segovia I tarried two days in the house of a friend, still I could hear nothing of Lopez. At last, by the greatest chance in the world, I heard from a peasant that there were men in the neighbourhood of Abades selling books.

Abades is about three leagues distant from Segovia, and upon receiving this intelligence, I instantly departed for the former place, with three donkeys laden with Testaments. I reached Abades at nightfall, and found Lopez, with two peasants whom he had engaged, in the house of the surgeon of the place, where I also took up my residence. He had already disposed of a considerable number of Testaments in the neighbourhood, and had that day commenced selling at Abades itself; he had, however, been interrupted by two of the three curas of the village, who, with horrid curses, denounced the work, threatening eternal condemnation to Lopez for selling it, and to any person who should purchase it; whereupon Lopez, terrified, forbore until I should arrive. The third cura, however, exerted himself to the utmost to persuade the people to provide themselves with Testaments, telling them that his brethren were hypocrites and false guides, who, by keeping them in ignorance of the word and will of Christ, were leading them to the abyss. Upon receiving this information, I instantly sallied forth to the market-place, and that same night succeeded in disposing of upwards of thirty Testaments. The next morning the house was entered by the two factious curas, but upon my rising to confront them, they retreated, and I heard no more of them, except that they publicly cursed me in the church more than once, an event which, as no ill resulted from it, gave me little concern.

I will not detail the events of the next week, suffice it to say that, arranging my forces in the most advantageous way, I succeeded, by God's assistance, in disposing of from five to six hundred Testaments amongst the villages from one to seven leagues distance from Abades. At the expiration of that period I received information that my proceedings were known in Segovia, in which province Abades is situated, and that an order was about to be sent to the alcalde to seize all books in my possession. Whereupon, notwithstanding that it was late in the evening, I decamped with all my people, and upwards of three hundred Testaments, having a few hours previously received a fresh supply from Madrid. That night we passed in the fields, and next morning proceeded to Labajos, a village on the high road from Madrid to Valladolid. In this place we offered no books for sale but contented ourselves with supplying the neighbouring villages with the word of God: we likewise sold it in the highways.

We had not been at Labajos a week, during which time we were remarkably successful, when the Carlist chieftain, Balmaseda, at the head of his cavalry, made his desperate inroad into the southern part of Old Castile, dashing down like an avalanche from the pine-woods of Soria. I was present at all the horrors which ensued,—the sack of Arrevalo, and the forcible entry into Martin Muñoz. Amidst these terrible scenes we continued our labours. Suddenly I lost Lopez for three days, and suffered dreadful anxiety on his account, imagining that he had been shot by the Carlists; at last I heard that he was in prison at Villallos, three leagues distant. The steps which I took to rescue him will be found detailed in a communication, which I deemed it my duty to transmit to Lord William Hervey, who, in the absence of Sir George Villiers, now become Earl of Clarendon, fulfilled the duties of minister at Madrid:—

Labajos, Province of Segovia,
August 23d, 1838.

My Lord,

I beg leave to call your attention to the following facts. On the 21st inst. I received information that a person in my employ, of the name of Juan Lopez, had been thrown into the prison of Villallos, in the province of Avila, by order of the cura of that place. The crime with which he was charged was selling the New Testament. I was at that time at Labajos, in the province of Segovia, and the division of the factious chieftain Balmaseda was in the immediate neighbourhood. On the 22d, I mounted my horse and rode to Villallos, a distance of three leagues. On my arrival there, I found that Lopez had been removed from the prison to a private house. An order had arrived from the Corregidor of Avila, commanding that the person of Lopez should be set at liberty, and that the books which had been found in his possession should be alone detained. Nevertheless, in direct opposition to this order, (a copy of which I herewith transmit,) the alcalde of Villallos, at the instigation of the cura, refused to permit the said Lopez to quit the place, either to proceed to Avila or in any other direction. It had been hinted to Lopez that as the factious were expected, it was intended on their arrival to denounce him to them as a liberal, and to cause him to be sacrificed. Taking these circumstances into consideration, I deemed it my duty, as a Christian and a gentleman, to rescue my unfortunate servant from such lawless hands, and in consequence, defying opposition, I bore him off, though entirely unarmed, through a crowd of at least one hundred peasants. On leaving the place I shouted, "*Viva Isabel Segunda.*"

As it is my belief that the cura of Villallos is a person capable of any infamy, I beg leave humbly to entreat your lordship to cause a copy of the above narration to be forwarded to the Spanish government.

I have the honour to remain,
My Lord,
Your Lordship's most obedient,
GEORGE BORROW.

To the Right Honourable
LORD WILLIAM HERVEY.

After the rescue of Lopez we proceeded in the work of distribution. Suddenly, however, the symptoms of an approaching illness came over me, which compelled us to return in all haste to Madrid. Arrived there, I was attacked by a fever which confined me to my bed for several weeks: occasional fits of delirium came over me, during one of which, I imagined myself in the market-place of Martin Muñoz, engaged in deadly struggle with the chieftain Balmaseda.

The fever had scarcely departed, when a profound melancholy took possession of me, which entirely disqualified me for active exertion. Change of scene and air was recommended; I therefore returned to England.

CHAPTER XLV.

Return to Spain—Seville—A hoary Persecutor—Manchegan Prophetess—Antonio's Dream.

On the thirty-first of December, 1838, I again visited Spain for the third time. After staying a day or two at Cadiz, I repaired to Seville, from which place I proposed starting for Madrid with the mail post. Here I tarried about a fortnight, enjoying the delicious climate of this terrestrial paradise, and the balmy breezes of the Andalusian winter, even as I had done two years previously. Before leaving Seville I visited the bookseller, my correspondent, who informed me that seventy-six copies of the hundred Testaments intrusted to his care had been placed in embargo by the government last summer, and that they were at the present time in the possession of the ecclesiastical governor, whereupon I determined to visit this functionary also, with the view of making inquiries concerning the property.

He lived in a large house in the Pajaria, or strawmarket. He was a very old man, between seventy and eighty, and, like the generality of those who wear the sacerdotal habit in this city, was a fierce, persecuting papist. I imagine that he scarcely believed his ears when his two grand-nephews, beautiful black-haired boys who were playing in the court-yard, ran to inform him that an Englishman was waiting to speak with him, as it is probable that I was the first heretic who ever ventured into his habitation. I found him in a vaulted room, seated on a lofty chair, with two sinister-looking secretaries, also in sacerdotal habits, employed in writing at a table before him. He brought powerfully to my mind the grim old inquisitor who persuaded Philip the Second to slay his own son as an enemy to the church.

He rose as I entered, and gazed upon me with a countenance dark with suspicion and dissatisfaction. He at last condescended to point me to a sofa, and I proceeded to state to

him my business. He became much agitated when I mentioned the Testaments to him; but I no sooner spoke of the Bible Society and told him who I was, than he could contain himself no longer: with a stammering tongue and with eyes flashing fire like hot coals, he proceeded to rail against the society and myself, saying that the aims of the first were atrocious, and that, as to myself, he was surprised that, being once lodged in the prison of Madrid, I had ever been permitted to quit it; adding, that it was disgraceful in the government to allow a person of my character to roam about an innocent and peaceful country corrupting the minds of the ignorant and unsuspicious. Far from allowing myself to be disconcerted by his rude behaviour, I replied to him with all possible politeness, and assured him that in this instance he had no reason to alarm himself, as my sole motive in claiming the books in question, was to avail myself of an opportunity which at present presented itself, of sending them out of the country, which, indeed, I had been commanded to do by an official notice. But nothing would sooth him, and he informed me that he should not deliver up the books on any condition, save by a positive order of the government. As the matter was by no means an affair of consequence, I thought it wise not to persist, and also prudent to take my leave before he requested me. I was followed even down into the street by his niece and grand-nephews, who, during the whole of the conversation, had listened at the door of the apartment and heard every word.

In passing through La Mancha, we stayed for four hours at Manzanares, a large village. I was standing in the market-place conversing with a curate, when a frightful ragged object presented itself; it was a girl about eighteen or nineteen, perfectly blind, a white film being spread over her huge staring eyes. Her countenance was as yellow as that of a mulatto. I thought at first that she was a gipsy, and addressing myself to her, inquired in Gitáno if she were of that race; she understood me, but shaking her head, replied, that she was something better than a Gitána, and could speak something better than that jargon of witches; whereupon she commenced asking me several questions in exceedingly good Latin. I was of course very much surprised, but, summoning all my Latinity, I called her Manchegan Prophetess, and expressing my admiration for her learning, begged to be informed by what means she became possessed of it. I must here observe that a crowd instantly gathered around us, who, though they understood not one word of our discourse, at every sentence of the girl shouted applause, proud in the possession of a prophetess who could answer the Englishman.

She informed me that she was born blind, and that a Jesuit priest had taken compassion on her when she was a child, and had taught her the holy language, in order that the attention and hearts of Christians might be more easily turned towards her. I soon discovered that he had taught her something more than Latin; for upon telling her that I was an Englishman, she said that she had always loved Britain, which was once the nursery of saints and sages, for example Bede and Alcuin, Columbus and Thomas of Canterbury; but, she added, those times had gone by since the reappearance of Semiramis (Elizabeth). Her Latin was truly excellent, and when I, like a genuine Goth, spoke of Anglia and Terra Vandalica (Andalusia), she corrected me by saying, that in her language those places were called Britannia and Terra Betica. When we had finished our discourse, a gathering was made for the prophetess, the very poorest contributing something.

After travelling four days and nights, we arrived at Madrid, without having experienced the slightest accident, though it is but just to observe, and always with gratitude to the Almighty, that the next mail was stopped. A singular incident befell me immediately after my arrival: on entering the arch of the posada called La Reyna, where I intended to put up, I found myself encircled in a person's arms, and on turning round in amazement, beheld my Greek servant, Antonio. He was haggard and ill-dressed, and his eyes seemed starting from their sockets.

As soon as we were alone, he informed me that since my departure he had undergone great misery and destitution, having, during the whole period, been unable to find a master in need of his services, so that he was brought nearly to the verge of desperation; but that on the night immediately preceding my arrival he had a dream, in which he saw me, mounted on a black horse, ride up to the gate of the posada, and that on that account he had been waiting there during the greater part of the day. I do not pretend to offer an opinion concerning this narrative, which is beyond the reach of my philosophy, and shall content myself with observing that only two individuals in Madrid were aware of my arrival in Spain. I was very glad to receive him again into my service, as, notwithstanding his faults, he had in many instances proved of no slight assistance to me in my wanderings and biblical labours.

I was soon settled in my former lodgings, when one of my first cares was to pay a visit to Lord Clarendon. Amongst other things, he informed me that he had received an official notice from the government, stating the seizure of the New Testaments at Ocaña, the circumstances relating to which I have described on a former occasion, and informing him that unless steps were instantly taken to remove them from the country, they would be destroyed at Toledo, to which place they had been conveyed. I replied that I should give myself no trouble about the matter; and that if the authorities of Toledo, civil or ecclesiastic, determined upon burning these books, my only hope was that they would commit them to the flames with all possible publicity, as by so doing they would but manifest their own hellish rancour and their hostility to the word of God.

Being eager to resume my labours, I had no sooner arrived at Madrid than I wrote to Lopez at Villa Seca, for the purpose of learning whether he was inclined to co-operate in the work, as on former occasions. In reply, he informed me that he was busily employed in his agricultural pursuits: to supply his place, however, he sent over an elderly villager, Victoriano Lopez by name, a distant relation of his own.

What is a missionary in the heart of Spain without a horse? Which consideration induced me now to purchase an Arabian of high caste, which had been brought from Algiers by an officer of the French legion. The name of this steed, the best I believe that ever issued from the desert, was Sidi Habismilk.

CHAPTER XLVI.

Work of Distribution resumed—Adventure at Cobenna—Power of the Clergy—Rural Authorities—Fuente la Higuera—Victoriano's Mishap—Village Prison—The Rope—Antonio's Errand—Antonio at Mass.

IN my last chapter, I stated that, immediately after my arrival at Madrid, I proceeded to get every thing in readiness for commencing operations in the neighbourhood; and I soon entered upon my labours in reality. Considerable success attended my feeble efforts in the good cause, for which, at present, after the lapse of some years, I still look back with gratitude to the Almighty. .

All the villages within the distance of four leagues to the east of Madrid were visited in less than a fortnight, and Testaments to the number of nearly two hundred disposed of. These villages for the most part are very small, some of them consisting of not more than a dozen houses, or I should rather say miserable cabins. I left Antonio, my Greek, to superintend matters in Madrid, and proceeded with Victoriano, the peasant from Villa Seca, in the direction which I have already mentioned. We, however, soon parted company, and pursued different routes.

The first village at which I made an attempt was Cobenna, about three leagues from Madrid. I was dressed in the fashion of the peasants in the neighbourhood of Segovia, in Old Castile; namely, I had on my head a species of leather helmet or montera, with a jacket and trousers of the same material. I had the appearance of a person between sixty and seventy years of age, and drove before me a borrico with a sack of Testaments lying across its back. On nearing the village, I met a genteel-looking young woman leading a little boy by the hand: as I was about to pass her with the customary salutation of *vaya usted con Dios*, she stopped, and after looking at me for a moment, she said: "Uncle (*Tio*), what is that you have got on your borrico? Is it soap?"

"Yes," I replied; "it is soap to wash souls clean."

She demanded what I meant; whereupon I told her that I carried cheap and godly books for sale. On her requesting to see one, I produced a copy from my pocket, and handed it to her. She instantly commenced reading with a loud voice, and continued so for at least ten minutes, occasionally exclaiming: "*Que lectura tan bonita, que lectura tan linda!* What beautiful, what charming reading!" At last, on my informing her that I was in a hurry and could not wait any longer, she said, "true, true," and asked me the price of the book: I told her "but three reals," whereupon she said, that though what I asked was very little, it was more than she could afford to give, as there was little or no money in those parts. I said I was sorry for it, but that I could not dispose of the books for less than I had demanded, and accordingly, resuming it, wished her farewell, and left her. I had not, however, proceeded thirty yards, when the boy came running behind me, shouting, out of breath: "Stop, uncle, the book!" Upon overtaking me, he delivered the three reals in copper, and seizing the Testament, ran back to her, who I suppose was his sister, flourishing the book over his head with great glee.

On arriving at the village, I directed my steps to a house around the door of which I saw several people gathered, chiefly women. On my displaying my books, their curiosity was instantly aroused, and every person had speedily one in his hand, many reading aloud; however, after waiting nearly an hour, I had disposed of but one copy, all complaining bitterly of the distress of the times, and the almost total want of money, though at the same time, they acknowledged that the books were wonderfully cheap, and appeared to be very good and Christian-like. I was about to gather up my merchandise and depart, when on a sudden the curate of the place made his appearance. After having examined the books for some time with considerable attention, he asked me the price of a copy, and upon my informing him that it was three reals, he replied that the binding was worth more, and that he was much afraid that I had stolen the books, and that it was perhaps his duty to send me to prison as a suspicious character; but added, that the books were good books, however they might be obtained, and concluded by purchasing two copies. The poor people no sooner heard their curate recommend the volumes, than all were eager to secure one, and hurried here and there for the purpose of procuring money, so that between twenty and thirty copies were sold almost in an instant. This adventure not only affords an instance of the power still possessed by the Spanish clergy over the minds of the people, but proves that such influence is not always exerted in a manner favourable to the maintenance of ignorance and superstition.

In another village, on my showing a Testament to a woman, she said that she had a child at school for whom she should like to purchase one, but that she must know first whether the book was calculated to be of service to him. She then went away, and presently returned with the schoolmaster, followed by all the children under his care; she then, showing the schoolmaster a book, inquired if it would answer for her son. The schoolmaster called her a simpleton for asking such a question, and said that he knew the book well, and there was not its equal in the world (*no hay otro en el mundo*). He instantly purchased five copies for his pupils, regretting that he had no more money, "for if I had," said he, "I would buy the whole cargo." Upon hearing this, the woman purchased four copies, namely, one for her living son, another for her *deceased husband*, a third for herself, and a fourth for her brother, whom she said she was expecting home that night from Madrid.

In this manner we proceeded, not, however, with uniform success. In some villages the people were so poor and needy that they literally had no money; even in these, however, we managed to dispose of a few copies in exchange for barley or refreshments. On entering one very small hamlet, Victoriano was stopped by the curate, who, on learning what he carried, told him that unless he instantly departed, he would cause him to be imprisoned, and would write to Madrid in order to give information of what was going on. The excursion lasted about eight days. Immediately after my return, I despatched Victoriano to Caramanchel, a village at a short distance from Madrid, the only one towards the west which had not been visited last year. He stayed there about an hour, and disposed of twelve copies, and then returned, as he was exceedingly timid, and was afraid of being met by the thieves who swarm on that road in the evening.

Shortly after these events, a circumstance occurred which will perhaps cause the English reader to smile, whilst, at the same time, it will not fail to prove interesting, as affording an example of the feeling prevalent in some of the lone villages of Spain with respect to innovation and all that savours thereof, and the strange acts which are sometimes committed by the rural authorities and the priests, without the slightest fear of being called to account; for as they live quite apart* from the rest of the world, they know no people greater than themselves, and scarcely dream of a higher power than their own.

I was about to make an excursion to Guadalajara, and the villages of Alcarria, about seven leagues distant from Madrid; indeed I merely awaited the return of Victoriano to sally forth; I having despatched him in that direction with a few Testaments, as a kind of explorer, in order that, from his report as to the disposition manifested by the people for purchasing, I might form a tolerably accurate opinion as to the number of copies which it might be necessary to carry with me. However, I heard nothing of him for a fortnight, at the end of which period a letter was brought to me by a peasant, dated from the prison of Fuente la Higuera, a village eight leagues from Madrid, in the Campiña of Alcala; this letter, written by Victoriano, gave me to understand that he had been already eight days imprisoned, and that unless I could find some means to extricate him, there was every probability of his remaining in durance until he should perish with hunger, which he had no doubt would occur as soon as his money was exhausted. From what I afterwards learned,

* Κατὰ τὸν τόπον καὶ ὁ τρόπος, as Antonio said.

it appeared that, after passing the town of Alcala, he had commenced distributing, and with considerable success. His entire stock consisted of sixty-one Testaments, twenty-five of which he sold without the slightest difficulty or interruption in the single village of Arganza; the poor labourers showering blessings on his head for providing them with such good books at an easy price.

Not more than eighteen of his books remained, when he turned off the high road towards Fuente la Higuera. This place was already tolerably well known to him, he having visited it of old, when he travelled the country in the capacity of a vender of cacharras or earthen pans. He subsequently stated that he felt some misgiving whilst on the way, as the village had invariably borne a bad reputation. On his arrival, after having put up his cavallejo or little pony at a posada, he proceeded to the alcalde for the purpose of asking permission to sell the books, which that dignitary immediately granted. He now entered a house and sold a copy, and likewise a second. Emboldened by success, he entered a third, which, it appeared, belonged to the barber-surgeon of the village. This personage having just completed his dinner, was seated in an arm-chair within his doorway, when Victoriano made his appearance. He was a man about thirty-five, of a savage truculent countenance. On Victoriano's offering him a Testament, he took it in his hand to examine it, but no sooner did his eyes glance over the title-page than he burst out into a loud laugh, exclaiming:—"Ha, ha, Don Jorge Borrow, the English heretic, we have encountered you at last. Glory to the Virgin and the Saints! We have long been expecting you here, and at length you are arrived." He then inquired the price of the book, and on being told three reals, he flung down two, and rushed out of the house with the Testament in his hand.

Victoriano now became alarmed, and determined upon leaving the place as soon as possible. He therefore hurried back to the posada, and having paid for the barley which his pony had consumed, went into the stable, and placing the packsaddle on the animal's back, was about to lead it forth, when the alcalde of the village, the surgeon, and twelve other men, some of whom were armed with muskets, suddenly presented themselves. They instantly made Victoriano prisoner, and after seizing the books and laying an embargo on the pony, proceeded amidst much abuse to drag the captive to what they denominated their prison, a low damp apartment with a little grated window, where they locked him up and left him. At the expiration of three quarters of an hour, they again appeared, and conducted him to the house of the curate, where they sat down in conclave; the curate, who was a man stone-blind, presiding, whilst the sacristan officiated as secretary. The surgeon having stated his accusation against the prisoner, namely, that he had detected him in the fact of selling a version of the Scriptures in the vulgar tongue, the curate proceeded to examine Victoriano, asking him his name and place of residence, to which he replied that his name was Victoriano Lopez, and that he was a native of Villa Seca, in the Sagra of Toledo. The curate then demanded what religion he professed? and whether he was a Mahometan, or freemason? and received for answer that he was a Roman Catholic. I must here state, that Victoriano, though sufficiently shrewd in his way, was a poor old labourer of sixty-four; and until that moment had never heard either of Mahometans or freemasons. The curate becoming now incensed, called him a *tunante* or scoundrel, and added, you have sold your soul to a heretic; we have long been aware of your proceedings, and those of your master. You are the same Lopez, whom he last year rescued from the prison of Villallos, in the province of Avila; I sincerely hope that he will attempt to do the same thing here. "Yes, yes," shouted the rest of the conclave, "let him but venture here, and we will shed his heart's blood on our stones." In this manner they went on for nearly half an hour. At last they broke up the meeting, and conducted Victoriano once more to his prison.

During his confinement he lived tolerably well, being in possession of money. His meals were sent him twice a day from the posada, where his pony remained in embargo. Once or twice he asked permission of the alcalde, who visited him every night and morning with his armed guard, to purchase pen and paper, in order that he might write to Madrid; but this favour was peremptorily refused him, and all the inhabitants of the village were forbidden under terrible penalties to afford him the means of writing, or to convey any message from him beyond the precincts of the place, and two boys were stationed before the window of his cell for the purpose of watching every thing which might be conveyed to him.

It happened one day that Victoriano, being in need of a pillow, sent word to the people of the posada to send him his alforjas or saddlebags, which they did. In these bags there chanced to be a kind of rope, or, as it is called in Spanish, *soga*, with which he was in the habit of fastening his satchel to the pony's back. The urchins seeing an end of this rope, hanging from the alforjas, instantly ran to the alcalde to give him information. Late at evening, the alcalde again visited the prisoner at the head of his twelve men as usual. "*Buenas noches*," said the alcalde. "*Buenas noches tenga usted*," replied Victoriano. "For what purpose did you send for the soga this afternoon?" demanded the functionary. "I sent for no soga," said the prisoner, "I sent for my alforjas to serve as a pillow, and it was sent in them by chance." "You are a false malicious knave," retorted the alcalde; "you intend to hang yourself, and by so doing ruin us all, as your death would be laid at our door. Give me the soga." No greater insult can be offered to a Spaniard than to tax

him with an intention of committing suicide. Poor Victoriano flew into a violent rage, and after calling the alcalde several very uncivil names, he pulled the soga from his bags, flung it at his head: and told him to take it home and use it for his own neck.

At length the people of the posada took pity on the prisoner, perceiving that he was very harshly treated for no crime at all; they therefore determined to afford him an opportunity of informing his friends of his situation, and accordingly sent him a pen and inkhorn, concealed in a loaf of bread, and a piece of writing paper, pretending that the latter was intended for cigars. So Victoriano wrote the letter; but now ensued the difficulty of sending it to its destination, as no person in the village dare have carried it for any reward. The good people, however, persuaded a disbanded soldier from another village, who chanced to be at Fuente la Higuera in quest of work, to charge himself with it, assuring him that I would pay him well for his trouble. The man, watching his opportunity, received the letter from Victoriano at the window: and it was he who, after travelling on foot all night, delivered it to me in safety at Madrid.

I was now relieved from my anxiety, and had no fears for the result. I instantly went to a friend who is in possession of large estates about Guadalajara, in which province Fuente la Higuera is situated, who furnished me with letters to the civil governor of Guadalajara and all the principal authorities; these I delivered to Antonio, whom, at his own request, I despatched on the errand of the prisoner's liberation. He first directed his course to Fuente la Higuera, where, entering the alcalde's house, he boldly told him what he had come about. The alcalde expecting that I was at hand, with an army of Englishmen, for the purpose of rescuing the prisoner, became greatly alarmed, and instantly despatched his wife to summon his twelve men; however, on Antonio's assuring him that there was no intention of having recourse to violence, he became more tranquil. In a short time Antonio was summoned before the conclave and its blind sacerdotal president. They at first attempted to frighten him by assuming a loud bullying tone, and talking of the necessity of killing all strangers, and especially the detested Don Jorge and his dependents. Antonio, however, who was not a person apt to allow himself to be easily terrified, scoffed at their threats, and showing them his letters to the authorities of Guadalajara, said that he should proceed there on the morrow and denounce their lawless conduct, adding that he was a Turkish subject, and that should they dare to offer him the slightest incivility, he would write to the Sublime Porte, in comparison with whom the best kings in the world were but worms, and who would not fail to avenge the wrongs of any of his children, however distant, in a manner too terrible to be mentioned. He then returned to his posada. The conclave now proceeded to deliberate amongst themselves, and at last determined to send their prisoner on the morrow to Guadalajara, and deliver him into the hands of the civil governor.

Nevertheless, in order to keep up a semblance of authority, they that night placed two men armed at the door of the posada where Antonio was lodged, as if he himself were a prisoner. These men, as often as the clock struck the hour, shouted "Ave Maria! Death to the heretics." Early in the morning the alcalde presented himself at the posada, but before entering he made an oration at the door to the people in the street, saying, amongst other things, " Brethren, these are the fellows who have come to rob us of our religion." He then went in to Antonio's apartment, and after saluting him with great politeness, said, that as a royal or high mass was about to be celebrated that morning, he had come to invite him to go to church with him. Whereupon Antonio, though by no means a mass-goer, rose and accompanied him, and remained two hours, as he told me, on his knees on the cold stones, to his great discomfort; the eyes of the whole congregation being fixed upon him during the time.

After mass and breakfast, he departed for Guadalajara, Victoriano having been already despatched under a guard. On his arrival, he presented his letters to the individuals for whom they were intended. The civil governor was convulsed with merriment on hearing Antonio's account of the adventure. Victoriano was set at liberty, and the books were placed in embargo at Guadalajara; the governor stating, however, that though it was his duty to detain them at present, they should be sent to me whenever I chose to claim them: he moreover said that he would do his best to cause the authorities of Fuente la Higuera to be severely punished, as in the whole affair they had acted in the most cruel, tyrannical manner, for which they had no authority. Thus terminated this affair, one of those little accidents which chequer missionary life in Spain.

CHAPTER XLVII

Termination of our rural Labours—Alarm of the Clergy—A new Experiment—Success at Madrid—Goblin-Alguazil—Staff of Office—The Corregidor—An Explanation—The Pope in England—New Testament Expounded—Works of Luther.

WE proceeded in our task of distributing the Scriptures with various success, until the middle of March, when I determined upon starting for Talavera, for the purpose of seeing what it was possible to accomplish in that town and the neighbourhood. I accordingly bent my course in that direction, accompanied by Antonio and Victoriano. On our way thither we stopped at Naval Carnero, a large village five leagues to the west of Madrid, where I remained three days, sending forth Victoriano to the circumjacent hamlets with small cargoes of Testaments. Providence, however, which had hitherto so remarkably favoured us in these rural excursions, now withdrew from us its support, and brought them to a sudden termination; for in whatever place the sacred writings were offered for sale, they were forthwith seized by persons who appeared to be upon the watch; which events compelled me to alter my intention of proceeding to Talavera and to return forthwith to Madrid.

I subsequently learned that our proceedings on the other side of Madrid having caused alarm amongst the heads of the clergy, they had made a formal complaint to the government, who immediately sent orders to all the alcaldes of the villages, great and small, in New Castile, to seize the New Testament wherever it might be exposed for sale; but at the same time enjoining them to be particularly careful not to detain or maltreat the person or persons who might be attempting to vend it.

An exact description of myself accompanied these orders, and the authorities both civil and military were exhorted to be on their guard against me and my arts and machinations; for, as the document stated, I was to-day in in one place, and to-morrow at twenty leagues' distance.

I was not much discouraged by this blow, which indeed did not come entirely unexpected. I, however, determined to change the sphere of action, and not expose the sacred volume to seizure at every step which I should take to circulate it. In my late attempts, I had directed my attention exclusively to the villages and small towns, in which it was quite easy for the government to baffle my efforts by means of circulars to the local authorities, who would of course be on the alert, and whose vigilance it would be impossible to baffle, as every novelty which occurs in a small place is forthwith bruited about. But the case would be widely different amongst the crowds of the capital, where I could pursue my labours with comparative secrecy. My present plan was to abandon the rural districts, and to offer the sacred volume at Madrid, from house to house, at the same low price as in the country. This plan I forthwith put into execution.

Having an extensive acquaintance amongst the lower orders, I selected eight intelligent individuals to co-operate with me, amongst whom were five women. All these I supplied with Testaments, and then sent them forth to all the parishes in Madrid. The result of their efforts more than answered my expectations. In less than fifteen days after my return from Naval Carnero, nearly six hundred copies of the life and words of Him of Nazareth had been sold in the streets and alleys of Madrid: a fact which I hope I may be permitted to mention with gladness and with decent triumph in the Lord.

One of the richest streets is the Calle Montera, where reside the principal merchants and shopkeepers of Madrid. It is, in fact, the street of commerce, in which respect, and in being a favourite promenade, it corresponds with the far-famed "Nefsky" of St. Petersburg. Every house in this street was supplied with its Testament, and the same might be said with respect to the Puerto del Sol. Nay, in some instances, every individual in the house, man and child, man-servant and maid-servant, was furnished with a copy. My Greek, Antonio, made wonderful exertions in this quarter; and it is but justice to say that, but for his instrumentality, on many occasions, I might have been by no means able to give so favourable an account of the spread of "the Bible in Spain." There was a time when I was in the habit of saying "dark Madrid," an expression which, I thank God, I could now drop. It were scarcely just to call a city "dark," in which thirteen hundred Testaments at least were in circulation, and in daily use.

It was now that I turned to account a supply of Bibles which I had received from Barcelona, in sheets, at the commencement of the preceding year. The demand for the entire Scriptures was great; indeed far greater than I could answer, as the books were disposed of faster than they could be bound by the man whom I employed for that purpose. Eight-and-twenty copies were bespoken and paid for before delivery. Many of these Bibles found their way into the best houses in Madrid. The Marquis of * * * * * had a large family, but every individual of it, old and young, was in possession of a Bible, and likewise a Testament, which, strange to say, were recommended by the chaplain of the house. One of my most zealous agents in the propagation of the Bible was an ecclesiastic. He never walked out without carrying one beneath his gown, which he offered to the first person he met whom he thought likely to purchase. Another excellent assistant was an elderly gentleman of Navarre, enormously rich, who was continually purchasing copies on his own account, which he, as I was told, sent into his native province, for distribution amongst his friends and the poor.

On a certain night I had retired to rest rather more early than usual, being slightly indisposed. I soon fell asleep, and had continued so for some hours, when I was suddenly aroused by the opening of the door of the small apartment in which I lay. I started up, and beheld Maria Diaz, with a lamp in her hand, enter the room. I observed that her features, which were in general peculiarly calm and placid, bore a somewhat startled expression. "What is the hour, and what brings you here?" I demanded.

"Señor," said she, closing the door, and coming up to the bed-side. "It is close upon midnight; but a messenger belonging to the police has just entered the house, and demanded to see you. I told him that it was impossible, for that your worship was in bed. Whereupon he sneezed in my face, and said that he would see you if you were in your coffin. He has all the look of a goblin, and has thrown me into a tremor. I am far from being a timid person, as you are aware, Don Jorge; but I confess that I never cast my eyes on these wretches of the police, but my heart dies away within me! I know them but too well, and what they are capable of."

"Pooh," said I, "be under no apprehension, let him come in, I fear him not, whether he be alguazil or hobgoblin. Stand, however, at the doorway, that you may be a witness of what takes place, as it is more than probable that he comes at this unseasonable hour to create a disturbance, that he may have an opportunity of making an unfavourable report to his principals, like the fellow on the former occasion."

The hostess left the apartment, and I heard her say a word or two to some one in the passage, whereupon there was a loud sneeze, and in a moment after a singular figure appeared at the doorway. It was that of a very old man, with long white hair, which escaped from beneath the eaves of an exceedingly high-peaked hat. He stooped considerably, and moved along with a shambling gait. I could not see much of his face, which, as the landlady stood behind him with the lamp, was consequently in deep shadow. I could observe, however, that his eyes sparkled like those of a ferret. He advanced to the foot of the bed, in which I was still lying, wondering what this strange visit could mean; and there he stood gazing at me for a minute, at least, without uttering a syllable. Suddenly, however, he protruded a spare skinny hand from the cloak in which it had hitherto been enveloped, and pointed with a short staff, tipped with metal, in the direction of my face, as if he were commencing an exorcism. He appeared to be about to speak, but his words, if he intended any, were stifled in their birth by a sudden sternutation which escaped him, and which was so violent that the hostess started back, exclaiming, "Ave Maria, purisima!" and nearly dropped the lamp in her alarm.

"My good person," said I, "what do you mean by this foolish hobgoblinary? If you have any thing to communicate do so at once, and go about your business. I am unwell, and you are depriving me of my repose."

"By the virtue of this staff," said the old man, "and the authority which it gives me to do and say that which is convenient, I do command, order, and summon you to appear to-morrow, at the eleventh hour, at the office of my lord the corregidor of this village of Madrid; in order that, standing before him humbly, and with befitting reverence, you may listen to whatever he may have to say, or if necessary, may yield yourself up to receive the castigation of any crimes which you may have committed, whether trivial or enormous. *Tenez, compère,*" he added in most villanous French, "*voilà mon affaire; voilà ce que je viens vous dire.*"

Thereupon he glared at me for a moment, nodded his head twice, and replacing his staff beneath his cloak, shambled out of the room, and, with a valedictory sneeze in the passage, left the house.

Precisely at eleven on the following day, I attended at the office of the corregidor. He was not the individual whose anger I had incurred on a former occasion, and who had thought proper to imprison me, but another person, I believe a Catalan, whose name I have also forgotten. Indeed, these civil employments were at this period given to-day and taken away to-morrow, so that the person who held one of them for a month might consider himself a functionary of long standing. I was not kept waiting a moment, but as soon as I had announced myself, was forthwith ushered into the presence of the corregidor, a good-looking, portly, and well-dressed personage, seemingly about fifty. He was writing at a desk when I entered, but almost immediately arose and came towards me. He looked me full in the face, and I, nothing abashed, kept my eyes fixed upon his. He had, perhaps, expected a less independent bearing, and that I should have quaked and crouched before him; but now, conceiving himself bearded in his own den, his old Spanish leaven was forthwith stirred up. He plucked his whiskers fiercely. " Escuchad," said he, casting upon me a ferocious glance, "I wish to ask you a question."

" Before I answer any question of your excellency," said I, "I shall take the liberty of putting one myself. What law or reason is there that I, a peaceable individual and a foreigner, should have my rest disturbed by *duendes* and hobgoblins sent at midnight to summon me to appear at public offices like a criminal?"

" *Usted falta á la verdad,*" shouted the corregidor; " the person sent to summon you was neither duende nor hobgoblin, but one of the most ancient and respectable officers of this casa, and so far from being despatched at midnight, it wanted twenty-five minutes to that hour by my own watch when he left this office, and as your lodging is not distant, he must have arrived there at least ten minutes before midnight, so that you are by no means accurate, and are found wanting in regard to truth."

" A distinction without a difference," I replied. " For my own part, if I am to be disturbed in my sleep, it is of little consequence whether at midnight or ten minutes before that time; and with respect to your messenger, although he might not be a hobgoblin, he had all the appearance of one, and assuredly answered the purpose, by frightening the wo-

man of the house almost into fits by his hideous grimaces and sneezing convulsions."

Corregidor.—You are a—*yo no sé que.* Do you know that I have the power to imprison you?

Myself.—You have twenty alguazils at your beck and call, and have of course the power, and so had your predecessor, who nearly lost his situation by imprisoning me; but you know full well that you have not the right, as I am not under your jurisdiction, but that of the Captain-general. If I have obeyed your summons, it was simply because I had a curiosity to know what you wanted with me, and from no other motive whatever. As for imprisoning me, I beg leave to assure you, that you have my full consent to do so; the most polite society in Madrid is to be found in the prison, and as I am at present compiling a vocabulary of the language of the Madrilenian thieves, I should have, in being imprisoned, an excellent opportunity of completing it. There is much to be learnt even in the prison, for, as the gipsies say, "The dog that trots about finds a bone."

Corregidor.—Your words are not those of a Caballero. Do you forget where you are, and in whose presence? Is this a fitting place to talk of thieves and gipsies in?

Myself.—Really I know of no place more fitting, unless it be the prison. But we are wasting time, and I am anxious to know for what I have been summoned; whether for crimes trivial or enormous, as the messenger said.

It was a long time before I could obtain the required information from the incensed Corregidor; at last, however, it came. It appeared that a box of Testaments, which I had despatched to Naval Carnero, had been seized by the local authorities, and having been detained there for some time, was at last sent back to Madrid, intended, as it now appeared, for the hands of the Corregidor. One day as it was lying at the wagon-office, Antonio chanced to enter on some business of his own and recognised the box, which he instantly claimed as my property, and having paid the carriage, removed it to my warehouse. He had considered the matter as of so little importance, that he had not as yet mentioned it to me. The poor Corregidor, however, had no doubt that it was a deep-laid scheme to plunder and insult him. And now, working himself up into almost a frenzy of excitement, he stamped on the ground, exclaiming, " *Que picardia! Que infamia!*"

The old system, thought I, of prejudging people and imputing to them motives and actions of which they never dreamed. I then told him frankly, that I was entirely ignorant of the circumstance by which he had felt himself aggrieved; but that if upon inquiry I found that the chest had actually been removed by my servant from the office to which it had been forwarded, I would cause it forthwith to be restored, although it was my own property. "I have plenty more Testaments," said I, "and can afford to lose fifty or a hundred. I am a man of peace, and wish not to have any dispute with the authorities for the sake of an old chest and a cargo of books, whose united value would scarcely amount to forty dollars."

He looked at me for a moment, as if in doubt of my sincerity, then, again plucking his whiskers, he forthwith proceeded to attack me in another quarter: "*Pero que infamia, que picardia!* to come into Spain for the purpose of overturning the religion of the country. What would you say if the Spaniards were to go to England and attempt to overturn the Lutheranism established there?"

"They would be most heartily welcome," I replied; "more especially if they would attempt to do so by circulating the Bible, the book of Christians, even as the English are doing in Spain. But your excellency is not perhaps aware that the Pope has a fair field and fair play in England, and is permitted to make as many converts from Lutheranism every day in the week as are disposed to go over to him. He cannot boast, however, of much success; the people are too fond of light to embrace darkness, and would smile at the idea of exchanging their gospel privileges for the superstitious ceremonies and observances of the church of Rome."

On my repeating my promise that the books and chest should be forthwith restored, the Corregidor declared himself satisfied, and all of a sudden became excessively polite and condescending: he even went so far as to say that he left it entirely with myself, whether to return the books or not; "and," continued he, "before you go, I wish to tell you that my private opinion is, that it is highly advisable in all countries to allow full and perfect tolerance in religious matters, and to permit every religious system to stand or fall according to its own merits."

Such were the concluding words of the Corregidor of Madrid, which, whether they expressed his private opinion or not, were certainly grounded on sense and reason. I saluted him respectfully and retired, and forthwith performed my promise with regard to the books; and thus terminated this affair.

It almost appeared to me at this time, that a religious reform was commencing in Spain; indeed, matters had of late come to my knowledge, which, had they been prophesied only a year before, I should have experienced much difficulty in believing.

The reader will be surprised when I state that in two churches of Madrid, the New Testament was regularly expounded every Sunday evening by the respective curates, to about twenty children who attended, and who were all provided with copies of the Society's

edition of Madrid, 1837. The churches which I allude to were those of San Gines and Santa Cruz. Now I humbly conceive that this fact alone is more than equivalent to all the expense which the society had incurred in the efforts which it had been making to introduce the Gospel into Spain; but be this as it may, I am certain that it amply recompensed me for all the anxiety and unhappiness which I had undergone. I now felt that whenever I should be compelled to discontinue my labours in the Peninsula, I should retire without the slightest murmur, my heart being filled with gratitude to the Lord for having permitted me, useless vessel as I was, to see at least some of the seed springing up, which during two years I had been casting on the stony ground of the interior of Spain.

When I recollected the difficulties which had encompassed our path, I could sometimes hardly credit all that the Almighty had permitted us to accomplish within the last year. A large edition of the New Testament had been almost entirely disposed of in the very centre of Spain, in spite of the opposition and the furious cry of the sanguinary priesthood and the edicts of a deceitful government, and a spirit of religious inquiry excited, which I had fervent hope would sooner or later lead to blessed and most important results. Till of late the name most abhorred and dreaded in these parts of Spain was that of Martin Luther, who was in general considered as a species of demon, a cousin-german to Belial and Beelzebub, who, under the disguise of a man, wrote and preached blasphemy against the Highest; yet now, strange to say, this once abominated personage was spoken of with no slight degree of respect. People with Bibles in their hands not unfrequently visited me, inquiring with much earnestness, and with no slight degree of simplicity, for the writings of the great Doctor Martin, whom, indeed, some supposed to be still alive.

It will be as well here to observe, that of all the names connected with the reformation, that of Luther is the only one known in Spain; and let me add, that no controversial writings but his are likely to be esteemed as possessing the slightest weight or authority, however great their intrinsic merit may be.

The common description of tracts, written with the view of exposing the errors of popery, are therefore not calculated to prove of much benefit in Spain, though it is probable that much good might be accomplished by well-executed translations of judicious selections from the works of Luther

CHAPTER XLVIII.

Protected Journey—A Scene of Blood—The Friar—Seville—Beauties of Seville—Orange Trees and Flowers—Murillo—The Guardian Angel—Dionysius—My Coadjutors—Demand for the Bible.

By the middle of April I had sold as many Testaments as I thought Madrid would bear: I therefore called in my people, for I was afraid to overstock the market, and to bring the book into contempt by making it too common. I had, indeed, by this time, barely a thousand copies remaining of the edition which I had printed two years previously; and with respect to Bibles, every copy was by this time disposed of, though there was still a great demand for them, which, of course, I was unable to satisfy.

With the remaining copies of the Testament, I now determined to betake myself to Seville, where little had hitherto been effected in the way of circulation: my preparations were soon made. The roads were at this time in a highly dangerous state, on which account I thought to go along with a convoy, which was about to start for Andalusia. Two days, however, before its departure, understanding that the number of people who likewise proposed to avail themselves of it was likely to be very great, and reflecting on the slowness of this way of travelling, and moreover the insults to which civilians were frequently subjected from the soldiers and petty officers, I determined to risk the journey with the mail. This resolution I carried into effect. Antonio, whom I had resolved to take with me, and my two horses, departed with the convoy, whilst in a few days I followed with the mail courier.

We travelled all the way without the slightest accident, my usual wonderful good fortune accompanying us. I might well call it wonderful, for I was running into the den of the lion; the whole of La Mancha, with the exception of a few fortified places, being once more in the hands of Palillos and his banditti, who, whenever it pleased them, stopped the courier, burnt the vehicle and letters, murdered the paltry escort, and carried away any chance passenger to the mountains, where an enormous ransom was demanded, the alternative being four shots through the head, as the Spaniards say.

The upper part of Andalusia was becoming rapidly nearly as bad as La Mancha. The last time the mail had passed, it was attacked at the defile of La Rumblar by six mounted robbers; it was guarded by an escort of as many soldiers, but the former suddenly galloped from behind a solitary venta, and dashed the soldiers to the ground, who were taken quite by surprise, the hoofs of the robbers' horses making no noise on account of the sandy nature of the ground. The soldiers were instantly disarmed and bound to olive trees, with the exception of two, who escaped amongst the rocks; they were then mocked and tormented by the robbers, or rather fiends, for nearly half an hour, when they were shot; the head of the corporal who commanded being blown to fragments with a blunderbuss. The robbers then burned the coach, which they accomplished by igniting the letters by means of the tow with which they light their cigars. The life of the courier was saved by one of them, who had formerly been his postillion; he was, however, robbed and stripped. As we passed by the scene of the butchery the poor fellow wept, and, though a Spaniard, cursed Spain and the Spaniards, saying that he intended shortly to pass over to the Moreria, to confess Mahomet, and to learn the law of the Moors, for that any country and religion were better than his own. He pointed to the tree where the corporal had been tied; though much rain had fallen since, the ground around was still saturated with blood, and a dog was gnawing a piece of the unfortunate wretch's skull. A friar travelled with us the whole way from Madrid to Seville; he was of the missionaries, and was going to the Philippine islands, to conquer (para conquistar), for such was his word, by which I suppose he meant preaching to the Indians. During the whole journey he exhibited every symptom of the most abject fear, which operated upon him so that he became deadly sick, and we were obliged to stop twice in the road and lay him amongst the green corn. He said that if he fell into the hands of the factious, he was a lost priest, for that they would first make him say mass, and then blow him up with gunpowder. He had been a professor of philosophy, as he told me, in one of the convents (I think it was San Tomas) of Madrid before their suppression, but appeared to be grossly ignorant of the Scriptures, which he confounded with the works of Virgil.

We stopped at Manzanares as usual; it was Sunday morning, and the market-place was crowded with people. I was recognised in a moment, and twenty pair of legs instantly hurried away in quest of the prophetess, who presently made her appearance in the house to which we had retired to breakfast. After many greetings on both sides, she proceeded, in her Latin, to give me an account of all that had occurred in the village since I had last been there, and of the atrocities of the factious in the neighbourhood. I asked her to breakfast, and introduced her to the friar, whom she addressed in this manner: "Anne Domine Reverendissime facis adhuc sacrificium?" But the friar did not understand her, and waxing angry, anathematized her for a witch, and bade her begone. She was, however, not to be disconcerted, and commenced singing, in extemporary Castilian verse the praises of friars and religious houses in general. On departing, I gave her a peseta, upon which she burst into tears, and entreated that I would write to her if I reached Seville in safety.

We did arrive at Seville in safety, and I took leave of the friar, telling him that I hoped to meet him again at Philippi. As it was my intention to remain at Seville for some months, I determined to hire a house, in which I conceived I could live with more privacy, and at the same time more economically than in a posada. It was not long before I found one in every respect suited to me. It was situated in the Plazuela de la Pila Seca, a retired part of the city, in the neighbourhood of the cathedral, and at a short distance from the gate of Xeres; and in this house, on the arrival of Antonio and the horses, which occurred within a few days, I took up my abode.

I was now once more in beautiful Seville, and had soon ample time and leisure to enjoy its delights and those of the surrounding country; unfortunately, at the time of my arrival, and indeed for the next ensuing fortnight, the heaven of Andalusia, in general so glorious, was overcast with black clouds, which discharged tremendous showers of rain, such as few of the Sevillians, according to their own account, had ever seen before. This extraordinary weather had wrought no little damage in the neighbourhood, causing the Guadalquivir, which, during the rainy season, is a rapid and furious stream, to overflow its banks and to threaten an inundation. It is true that intervals were occurring when the sun made his appearance from his cloudy tabernacle, and with his golden rays caused every thing around to smile, enticing the butterfly forth from the bush, and the lizard from the hollow tree, and I invariably availed myself of these intervals to take a hasty promenade.

O how pleasant it is, especially in springtide, to stray along the shores of the Guadalquivir. Not far from the city, down the river, lies a grove called Las Delicias, or the Delights. It consists of trees of various kinds, but more especially of poplars and elms, and is traversed by long shady walks. This grove is the favourite promenade of the Sevillians, and there one occasionally sees assembled whatever the town produces of beauty or gallantry. There wander the black-eyed Andalusian dames and damsels, clad in their graceful silken mantillas; and there gallops the Andalusian cavalier on his long-tailed thick-maned steed of Moorish ancestry. As the sun is descending, it is enchanting to glance back from this place in the direction of the city: the prospect is inexpressibly beautiful. Yonder, in the distance, high and enormous, stands the Golden Tower, now used as a toll-house, but the principal bulwark of the city in the time of the Moors. It stands on the shore of the river, like a giant keeping watch, and is the first edifice which attracts the eye of the voyager as he moves up the stream to Seville. On the other side, opposite the tower, stands the noble Augustine convent, the ornament of the faubourg of Triana, whilst between the two edifices rolls the broad Guadalquivir, bearing on its bosom a flotilla of barks from Catalonia and Valencia. Farther up is seen the bridge of boats which traverses the water. The principal object of this prospect, however, is the Golden Tower, where the beams of the setting sun seem to be concentrated as in a focus, so that it appears built of pure gold, and probably from that circumstance received the name which it now bears. Cold, cold must the heart be which can remain insensible to the beauties of this magic scene, to do justice to which the pencil of Claude himself were barely equal. Often have I shed tears of rapture whilst I beheld it, and listened to the thrush and the nightingale piping forth their melodious songs in the woods, and inhaled the breeze laden with the perfume of the thousand orange gardens of Seville:

"Kennst du das land wo die citronen bluhen?"

The interior of Seville scarcely corresponds with the exterior: the streets are narrow, badly paved, and full of misery and beggary. The houses are for the most part built in the Moorish fashion, with a quadrangular patio or court in the centre, where stands a marble fountain, constantly distilling limpid water. These courts, during the time of the summer heats, are covered over with a canvas awning, and beneath this the family sit during the greater part of the day. In many, especially those belonging to the houses of the wealthy, are to be found shrubs, orange trees, and all kinds of flowers, and perhaps a small aviary, so that no situation can be conceived more delicious than to lie here in the shade, hearkening to the song of the birds and the voice of the fountain.

Nothing is more calculated to interest the stranger as he wanders through Seville, than a view of these courts obtained from the street, through the iron-grated door. Oft have I stopped to observe them, and as often sighed that my fate did not permit me to reside in such an Eden for the remainder of my days. On a former occasion, I have spoken of the cathedral of Seville, but only in a brief and cursory manner. It is perhaps the most magnificent cathedral in all Spain, and though not so regular in its architecture as those of Toledo and Burgos, is far more worthy of admiration when considered as a whole. It is utterly impossible to wander through the long aisles, and to raise one's eyes to the richly inlaid roof, supported by colossal pillars, without experiencing sensations of sacred awe, and deep astonishment. It is true that the interior, like those of the generality of the Spanish cathedrals, is somewhat dark and gloomy; yet it loses nothing by this gloom, which, on the contrary, rather increases the solemnity of the effect. Nôtre Dame of

Paris is a noble building, yet to him who has seen the Spanish cathedrals, and particularly this of Seville, it almost appears trivial and mean, and more like a town-hall than a temple of the Eternal. The Parisian cathedral is entirely destitute of that solemn darkness and gloomy pomp which so abound in the Sevillian, and is thus destitute of the principal requisite to the cathedral.

In most of the chapels are to be found some of the very best pictures of the Spanish school; and in particular many of the masterpieces of Murillo, a native of Seville. Of all the pictures of this extraordinary man, one of the least celebrated is that which has always wrought on me the most profound impression. I allude to the Guardian Angel, (*Angel de la Guardia*,) a small picture which stands at the bottom of the church, and looks up the principal aisle. The angel, holding a flaming sword in his right hand, is conducting the child. This child is, in my opinion, the most wonderful of all the creations of Murillo; the form is that of an infant about five years of age, and the expression of the countenance is quite infantine, but the tread—it is the tread of a conqueror, of a God, of the Creator of the universe; and the earthly globe appears to tremble beneath its majesty.

The service of the cathedral is in general well attended, especially when it is known that a sermon is to be preached. All these sermons are extemporaneous; some of them are edifying and faithful to the Scriptures. I have often listened to them with pleasure, though I was much surprised to remark, that when the preachers quoted from the Bible, their quotations were almost invariably taken from the apocryphal writings. There is in general no lack of worshippers at the principal shrines—women for the most part—many of whom appear to be animated with the most fervent devotion.

I had flattered myself, previous to my departure from Madrid, that I should have experienced but little difficulty in the circulation of the Gospel in Andalusia, at least for a time, as the field was new, and myself and the object of my mission less known and dreaded than in New Castile. It appeared, however, that the government at Madrid had fulfilled its threat, transmitting orders throughout Spain for the seizure of my books wherever found. The Testaments that arrived from Madrid were seized at the custom-house, to which place all goods on their arrival, even from the interior, are carried, in order that a duty be imposed upon them. Through the management of Antonio, however, I procured one of the two chests, whilst the other was sent down to San Lucar, to be embarked for a foreign land as soon as I could make arrangements for that purpose.

I did not permit myself to be discouraged by this slight *contretemps*, although I heartily regretted the loss of the books which had been seized, and which I could no longer hope to circulate in these parts, where they were so much wanted; but I consoled myself with the reflection, that I had still several hundred at my disposal, from the distribution of which, if it pleased the Lord, a blessed harvest might still proceed.

I did not commence operations for some time, for I was in a strange place, and scarcely knew what course to pursue. I had no one to assist me but poor Antonio, who was as ignorant of the place as myself. Providence, however, soon sent me a coadjutor, in rather a singular manner. I was standing in the court-yard of the Reyna Posada, where I occasionally dined, when a man, singularly dressed and gigantically tall, entered. My curiosity was excited, and I inquired of the master of the house who he was. He informed me that he was a foreigner, who had resided a considerable time in Seville, and he believed a Greek. Upon hearing this, I instantly went up to the stranger, and accosted him in the Greek language, in which, though I speak it very ill, I can make myself understood. He replied in the same idiom, and flattered by the interest which I, a foreigner, expressed for his nation, was not slow in communicating to me his history. He told me that his name was Dionysius, that he was a native of Cephalonia, and had been educated for the church, which, not suiting his temper, he had abandoned, in order to follow the profession of the sea, for which he had an early inclination. That after many adventures and changes of fortune, he found himself one morning on the coast of Spain, a shipwrecked mariner, and that, ashamed to return to his own country in poverty and distress, he had remained in the Peninsula, residing chiefly at Seville, where he now carried on a small trade in books. He said that he was of the Greek religion, to which he professed strong attachment, and soon discovering that I was a Protestant, spoke with unbounded abhorrence of the papal system; nay, of its followers in general, whom he called Latins, and whom he charged with the ruin of his own country, inasmuch as they sold it to the Turk. It instantly struck me, that this individual would be an excellent assistant in the work which had brought me to Seville, namely, the propagation of the eternal Gospel, and accordingly, after some more conversation, in which he exhibited considerable learning, I explained myself to him. He entered into my views with eagerness, and in the sequel I had no reason to regret my confidence, he having disposed of a considerable number of New Testaments, and even contrived to send a certain number of copies to two small towns at some distance from Seville.

Another helper in the circulation of the Gospel I found in an aged professor of music, who, with much stiffness and ceremoniousness, united much that was excellent and admirable. This venerable individual, only three days after I had made his acquaintance, brought me the price of six Testaments and a gipsy Gospel, which he had sold under the heat of an Andalusian sun. What was his motive? A Christian one truly. He said that his unfortunate countrymen, who were then robbing and murdering each other, might probably be rendered better by the reading of the Gospel, but could never be injured. Adding, that many a man had been reformed by the Scriptures, but that no one ever yet became a thief or assassin from its perusal.

But my most extraordinary agent was one whom I occasionally employed in circulating the Scriptures amongst the lower classes. I might have turned the services of this individual to far greater account had the quantity of books at my disposal been greater; but they were now diminishing rapidly, and as I had no hopes of a fresh supply, I was almost tempted to be niggard of the few which remained. This agent was a Greek bricklayer, by name Johannes Chrysostom, who had been introduced to me by Dionysius. He was a native of the Morea, but had been upwards of thirty-five years in Spain, so that he had almost entirely lost his native language. Nevertheless, his attachment to his own country was so strong, that he considered whatever was not Greek as utterly barbarous and bad. Though entirely destitute of education, he had, by his strength of character, and by a kind of rude eloquence which he possessed, obtained such a mastery over the minds of the labouring classes of Seville, that they assented to almost every thing he said, notwithstanding the shocks which their prejudices were continually receiving. So that, although he was a foreigner, he could at any time have become the Massaniello of Seville. A more honest creature I never saw; and I soon found that if I employed him, notwithstanding his eccentricities, I might entertain perfect confidence that his actions would be no disparagement to the book he vended.

We were continually pressed for Bibles, which of course we could not supply. Testaments were held in comparatively little esteem. I had by this time made the discovery of a fact which it would have been well had I been aware of three years before; but we live and learn. I mean the inexpediency of printing Testaments, and Testaments *alone*, for Catholic countries. The reason is plain : the Catholic, unused to Scripture reading, finds a thousand things which he cannot possibly understand in the New Testament, the foundation of which is the Old. "Search the Scriptures, for they bear witness of me," may well be applied to this point. It may be replied, that New Testaments separate are in great demand, and of infinite utility in England; but England, thanks be to the Lord, is not a papal country; and though an English labourer may read a Testament, and derive from it the most blessed fruit, it does not follow that a Spanish or Italian peasant will enjoy similar success, as he will find many dark things with which the other is well acquainted, and competent to understand, being versed in the Bible history from his childhood. I confess, however, that in my summer campaign of the preceding year, I could not have accomplished with Bibles what Providence permitted me to effect with Testaments, the former being far too bulky for rural journeys.

CHAPTER XLIX.

The Solitary House—The Dehesa—Johannes Chrysostom—Manuel—Bookselling at Seville—Dionysius and the Priests—Athens and Rome—Proselytism—Seizure of Testaments—Departure from Seville.

I HAVE already stated, that I had hired an empty house in Seville, wherein I purposed to reside for some months. It stood in a solitary situation, occupying one side of a small square. It was built quite in the beautiful taste of Andalusia, with a court paved with small slabs of white and blue marble. In the middle of this court was a fountain well supplied with the crystal lymph, the murmur of which, as it fell from its slender pillar into an octangular basin, might be heard in every apartment. The house itself was large and spacious, consisting of two stories, and containing room sufficient for at least ten times the number of inmates which now occupied it. I generally kept during the day in the lower apartments, on account of the refreshing coolness which pervaded them. In one of these was an immense stone water-trough, over overflowing with water from the fountain, in which I immersed myself every morning. Such were the premises to which, after having provided myself with a few indispensable articles of furniture, I now retreated with Antonio and my two horses.

I was fortunate in the possession of these quadrupeds, inasmuch as it afforded me an opportunity of enjoying to a greater extent the beauties of the surrounding country. I know of few things in this life more delicious than a ride in the spring or summer season in the neighbourhood of Seville. My favourite one was in the direction of Xerez, over the wide Dehesa, as it is called, which extends from Seville to the gates of the former town, a distance of nearly fifty miles, with scarcely a town or village intervening. The ground is irregular and broken, and is for the most part covered with that species of brushwood called carrasco, amongst which winds a bridle-path, by no means well defined, chiefly trodden by the arrieros, with their long trains of mules and borricos. It is here that the balmy air of beautiful Andalusia is to be inhaled in full perfection. Aromatic herbs and flowers are growing in abundance, diffusing their perfume around. Here dark and gloomy cares are dispelled as if by magic from the bosom, as the eyes wander over the prospect, lighted by unequalled sunshine, in which gaily painted butterflies wanton, and green and golden Salamanquesas lie extended, enjoying the luxurious warmth, and occasionally startling the traveller, by springing up and making off with portentous speed to the nearest coverts, whence they stare upon him with their sharp and lustrous eyes. I repeat, that it is impossible to continue melancholy in regions like these, and the ancient Greeks and Romans were right in making them the site of their Elysian fields. Most beautiful they are, even in their present desolation, for the hand of man has not cultivated them since the fatal era of the expulsion of the Moors, which drained Andalusia of at least two thirds of its population.

Every evening it was my custom to ride along the Dehesa, until the topmost towers of Seville were no longer in sight. I then turned about, and pressing my knees against the sides of Sidi Habismilk, my Arabian, the fleet creature, to whom spur or lash had never been applied, would set off in the direction of the town with the speed of a whirlwind, seeming in his headlong course to devour the ground of the waste, until he had left it behind, then dashing through the elm-covered road of the Delicias, his thundering hoofs were soon heard beneath the vaulted archway of the Puerta de Xerez, and in another moment he would stand stone still before the door of my solitary house in the little silent square of the Pila Seca.

It is eight o'clock at night, I am returned from the Dehesa, and am standing on the sotea, or flat roof of my house, enjoying the cool breeze. Johannes Chrysostom has just arrived from his labour. I have not spoken to him, but I hear him below in the court-yard, detailing to Antonio the progress he has made in the last two days. He speaks barbarous Greek, plentifully interlarded with Spanish words; but I gather from his discourse, that he has already sold twelve Testaments among his fellow labourers. I hear copper coin falling on the pavement, and Antonio, who is not of a very Christian temper, reproving him for not having brought the proceeds of the sale in silver. He now asks for fifteen more, as he says the demand is becoming great, and that he shall have no difficulty in disposing of them in the course of the morrow, whilst pursuing his occupations. Antonio goes to fetch them, and he now stands alone by the marble fountain, singing a wild song, which I believe to be a hymn of his beloved Greek church. Behold one of the helpers which the Lord has sent me in my Gospel labours on the shores of the Guadalquivir.

I lived in the greatest retirement during the whole time that I passed at Seville, spending the greater part of each day in study, or in that half dreamy state of inactivity which is the natural effect of the influence of a warm climate. There was little in the character of the people around to induce me to enter much into society. The higher class of the Andalusians are probably upon the whole the most vain and foolish of human beings, with a taste for nothing but sensual amusements, foppery in dress, and ribald discourse. Their insolence is only equalled by their meanness, and their prodigality by their avarice. The lower classes are a shade or two better than their superiors in station: little, it is true, can be said for the tone of their morality; they are over-reaching, quarrelsome, and revengeful, but they are upon the whole more courteous, and certainly not more ignorant.

The Andalusians are in general held in the lowest estimation by the rest of the Spaniards, even those in opulent circumstances finding some difficulty at Madrid in procuring admission into respectable society, where, if they find their way, they are invariably the objects of ridicule, from the absurd airs and grimaces in which they indulge,—their tendency to boasting and exaggeration, their curious accent, and the incorrect manner in which they speak and pronounce the Castilian language.

In a word, the Andalusians, in all estimable traits of character, are as far below the other Spaniards as the country which they inhabit is superior in beauty and fertility to the other provinces of Spain.

Yet let it not for a moment be supposed that I have any intention of asserting, that excellent and estimable individuals are not to be found amongst the Andalusians; it was amongst *them* that I myself discovered one, whom I have no hesitation in asserting to be the most extraordinary character that has ever come within the sphere of my knowledge; but this was no scion of a noble or knightly house, " no wearer of soft clothing," no sleek highly perfumed personage, none of the romanticos who walk in languishing attitudes about the streets of Seville, with long black hair hanging upon their shoulders in luxuriant curls; but one of those whom the proud and unfeeling style the dregs of the populace, a haggard, houseless, penniless man, in rags and tatters: I allude to Manuel, the—what shall I call him ?—seller of lottery tickets, driver of death carts, or poet laureate in gipsy songs ? I wonder whether thou art still living, my friend Manuel; thou gentleman of Nature's forming —honest, pure-minded, humble, yet dignified being ! Art thou still wandering through the courts of beautiful Safacoro, or on the banks of the Lea Baro, thine eyes fixed in vacancy, and thy mind striving to recall some half-forgotten couplet of Luis Lobo; or art thou gone to thy long rest, out beyond the Xerez gate within the wall of the Campo Santo, to which in times of pest and sickness thou wast wont to carry so many, Gipsy and Gentile, in thy cart of the tinkling bell ? Oft in the *reunions* of the lettered and learned in this land of universal literature, when weary of the display of pedantry and egotism, have I recurred with yearning to our gipsy recitations at the old house in the Pila Seca. Oft, when sickened by the high-wrought professions of those who bear the cross in gilded chariots, have I thought on thee, thy calm faith, without pretence,— thy patience in poverty, and fortitude in affliction; and as oft, when thinking of my speedily approaching end, have I wished that I

might meet thee once again, and that thy hands might help to bear me to " the dead man's acre" yonder on the sunny plain, O Manuel !

My principal visiter was Dionysius, who seldom failed to make his appearance every forenoon: the poor fellow came for sympathy and conversation. It is difficult to imagine a situation more forlorn and isolated than that of this man,—a Greek at Seville, with scarcely a single acquaintance, and depending for subsistence on the miserable pittance to be derived from selling a few books, for the most part hawked about from door to door. " What could have first induced you to commence bookselling in Seville ?" said I to him, as he arrived one sultry day, heated and fatigued, with a small bundle of books secured together by a leather strap.

Dionysius.—For want of a better employment, Kyrie, I have adopted this most unprofitable and despised one. Oft have I regretted not having been bred up as a shoemaker, or having learnt in my youth some other useful handicraft, for gladly would I follow it now. Such, at least, would procure me the respect of my fellow-creatures, inasmuch as they needed me; but now all avoid me and look upon me with contempt; for what have I to offer in this place that any one cares about ? Books in Seville ! where no one reads, or at least nothing but new romances, translated from the French, and obscenity. Books ! Would I were a gipsy and could trim donkeys, for then I were at least independent and were more respected than I am at present.

Myself.—Of what kind of books does your stock in trade consist ?

Dionysius.—Of those not likely to suit the Seville market, Kyrie; books of sterling and intrinsic value; many of them in ancient Greek, which I picked up upon the dissolution of the convents, when the contents of the libraries were hurled into the court-yards, and there sold by the arrobe. I thought at first that I was about to make a fortune, and in fact my books would be so in any other place; but here I have offered an Elzevir for half a dollar in vain. I should starve were it not for the strangers, who occasionally purchase of me.

Myself.—Seville is a large cathedral city, abounding with priests and canons; surely some of these occasionally visit you to make purchases of classic works, and books connected with ecclesiastical literature.

Dionysius.—If you think so, Kyrie, you know little respecting the ecclesiastics of Seville. I am acquainted with many of them and can assure you that a tribe of beings can scarcely be found with a more confirmed aversion to intellectual pursuits of every kind. Their reading is confined to newspapers, which they take up in the hope of seeing that their friend Don Carlos is at length reinstated at Madrid; but they prefer their chocolate and biscuits, and nap before dinner, to the wisdom of Plato and the eloquence of Tully. They occasionally visit me, but it is only to pass away a heavy hour in chattering nonsense.

Once on a time, three of them came, in the hope of making me a convert to their Latin superstition. "Signior Donatio," said they, (for so they called me,) "how is it that an unprejudiced person like yourself, a man really with some pretension to knowledge, can still cling to this absurd religion of yours? Surely, after having resided so many years in a civilized country like this of Spain, it is high time to abandon your half-pagan form of worship, and to enter the bosom of the church: now pray be advised, and you shall be none the worse for it." "Thank you, gentlemen," I replied, "for the interest you take in my welfare; I am always open to conviction; let us proceed to discuss the subject. What are the points of my religion which do not meet your approbation? You are of course well acquainted with all our dogmas and ceremonies." "We know nothing about your religion, Signior Dognatio, save that it is a very absurd one, and therefore it is incumbent upon you, as an unprejudiced and well informed man, to renounce it." "But, gentlemen, if you know nothing of my religion, why call it absurd? Surely it is not the part of unprejudiced people to disparage that of which they are ignorant." "But, Signior Donatio, it is not the Catholic Apostolic Roman religion, is it?" "It may be, gentlemen, for what you appear to know of it; for your information, however, I will tell you that it is not; it is the Greek Apostolic religion. I do not call it catholic, for it is absurd to call that catholic which is not universally acknowledged." "But, Signior Donatia, does not the matter speak for itself? What can a set of ignorant Greek barbarians know about religion? If they set aside the authority of Rome, whence should they derive any rational ideas of religion? whence should they get the Gospel?" "The Gospel, gentlemen? Allow me to show you a book, here it is, what is your opinion of it?" "Signior Donatio, what does this mean? What characters of the devil are these, are they Moorish? Who is able to understand them?" "I suppose your worships, being Roman priests, know something of Latin; if you inspect the title-page to the bottom, you will find, in the language of your own church, "the Gospel of our Lord and Saviour Jesus Christ," in the original Greek, of which your vulgate is merely a translation, and not a very correct one. With respect to the barbarism of Greece, it appears that you are not aware that Athens was a city, and a famed one, centuries before the first mud cabin of Rome was thatched, and the gipsy vagabonds who first peopled it, had escaped from the hands of justice." "Signior Donatio, you are an ignorant heretic and insolent withal, *what nonsense is this!....*". But I will not weary your ears, Kyrie, with all the absurdities which the poor Latin *Papas* poured into mine; the burden of their song being invariably, *what nonsense is this!* which was certainly applicable enough to what they themselves were saying. Seeing, however, that I was more than their match in religious controversy, they fell foul

of my country. "Spain is a better country than Greece," said one; "You never tasted bread before you came to Spain," cried another. "And little enough since," thought I. "You never before saw such a city as Seville," said the third. But then ensued the best part of the comedy: my visitors chanced to be natives of three different places; one was of Seville, another of Utrera, and the third of Miguel Turra, a miserable village in La Mancha. At the mention of Seville, the other two instantly began to sing the praises of their respective places of birth; this brought on comparisons, and a violent dispute was the consequence. Much abuse passed between them, whilst I stood by, shrugged my shoulders, and said *tipotas*. At last, as they were leaving the house, I said, "Who would have thought, gentlemen, that the polemics of the Greek and Latin churches were so closely connected with the comparative merits of Seville, Utrera, and Miguel Turra?"

Myself.—Is the spirit of proselytism very prevalent here? Of what description of people do their converts generally consist?

Dionysius.—I will tell you, Kyrie: the generality of their converts consist of German or English Protestant adventurers, who come here to settle, and in course of time take to themselves wives from amongst the Spanish, prior to which it is necessary to become members of the Latin church. A few are vagabond Jews, from Gibraltar or Tangier, who have fled for their crimes into Spain, and who renounce their faith to escape from starvation. These gentry, however, it is necessary to pay, on which account the priests procure for them padrinos or godfathers; these generally consist of rich devotees over whom the priests have influence, and who esteem it a glory and a meritorious act to assist in bringing back lost souls to the church. The neophyte allows himself to be convinced on the promise of a peseta a day, which is generally paid by the godfathers for the first year, but seldom for a longer period. About forty years ago, however, they made a somewhat notable convert. A civil war arose in Morocco, caused by the separate pretensions of two brothers to the throne. One of these being worsted, fled over to Spain, imploring the protection of Charles the Fourth. He soon became an object of particular attention to the priests, who were not slow in converting him, and induced Charles to settle upon him a pension of a dollar per day. He died some few years since in Seville, a despised vagabond. He left behind him a son, who is at present a notary, and outwardly very devout, but a greater hypocrite and picaroon does not exist. I would you could see his face, Kyrie, it is that of Judas Iscariot. I think you would say so, for you are a physiognomist. He lives next door to me, and notwithstanding his pretensions to religion, is permitted to remain in a state of great poverty.

And now nothing farther for the present about Dionysius.

About the middle of July our work was

concluded at Seville, and for the very efficient reason, that I had no more Testaments to sell; somewhat more than two hundred having been circulated since my arrival.

About ten days before the time of which I am speaking, I was visited by various alguazils, accompanied by a kind of headborough, who made a small seizure of Testaments and Gipsy Gospels, which happened to be lying about. This visit was far from being disagreeable to me, as I considered it to be a very satisfactory proof of the effect of our exertions in Seville. I cannot help here relating an anecdote :—A day or two subsequent, having occasion to call at the house of the headborough respecting my passport, I found him lying on his bed, for it was the hour of siesta, reading intently one of the Testaments which he had taken away, all of which, if he had obeyed his orders, would have been deposited in the office of the civil governor. So intently, indeed, was he engaged in reading, that he did not at first observe my entrance; when he did, however, he sprang up in great confusion, and locked the book up in his cabinet, whereupon I smiled, and told him to be under no alarm, as I was glad to see him so usefully employed. Recovering himself, he said that he had read the book nearly through, and that he had found

no harm in it, but on the contrary, every thing to praise. Adding, he believed that the clergy must be possessed with devils (*endemoniados*) to persecute it in the manner they did.

It was Sunday when the seizure was made, and I happened to be reading the Liturgy. One of the alguazils, when going away, made an observation respecting the very different manner in which the Protestants and Catholics keep the sabbath; the former being in their own houses reading good books, and the latter abroad in the bull-ring, seeing the wild bulls tear out the gory bowels of the poor horses. The bull amphitheatre at Seville is the finest in all Spain, and is invariably on a Sunday (the only day on which it is open) filled with applauding multitudes.

I now made preparations for leaving Seville for a few months, my destination being the coast of Barbary. Antonio, who did not wish to leave Spain, in which were his wife and children, returned to Madrid, rejoicing in a handsome gratuity with which I presented him. As it was my intention to return to Seville, I left my house and horses in the charge of a friend in whom I could confide, and departed.

The reasons which induced me to visit Barbary will be seen in the following chapters.

CHAPTER L.

Night on the Guadalquivir—Gospel Light—Bonanza—Strand of San Lucar—Andalusian scenery—History of a Chest—Cosas de Los Ingleses—The two Gipsies—The Driver—The Red Nightcap—The Steam-boat—Christian Language.

On the night of the 31st of July I departed from Seville upon my expedition, going on board one of the steamers which ply on the Guadalquivir between Seville and Cadiz.

It was my intention to stop at San Lucar, for the purpose of recovering the chest of Testaments which had been placed in embargo there, until such time as they could be removed from the kingdom of Spain. These Testaments I intended for distribution amongst the Christians whom I hoped to meet on the shores of Barbary. San Lucar is about fifteen leagues distant from Seville, at the entrance of the bay of Cadiz, where the yellow waters of the Guadalquivir unite with the brine. The steamer shot from the little quay, or wharf, at about half-past nine, and then arose a loud cry,—it was the voices of those on board and on shore wishing farewell to their friends. Amongst the tumult I thought I could distinguish the accents of some friends of my own who had accompanied me to the bank, and I instantly raised my own voice louder than all. The night was very dark, so much so, indeed, that as we passed along we could scarcely distinguish the trees which cover the eastern shore of the river until it takes its first turn. A calmazo had reigned during the day at Seville, by which is meant, exceedingly sultry

weather, unenlivened by the slightest breeze. The night likewise was calm and sultry. As I had frequently made the voyage of the Guadalquivir, ascending and descending this celebrated river, I felt nothing of that restlessness and curiosity which people experience in a strange place, whether in light or darkness, and being acquainted with none of the other passengers, who were talking on the deck, I thought my best plan would be to retire to the cabin and enjoy some rest, if possible. The cabin was solitary and tolerably cool, all its windows on either side being open for the admission of air. Flinging myself on one of the cushioned benches, I was soon asleep, in which state I continued for about two hours, when I was aroused by the furious biting of a thousand bugs, which compelled me to seek the deck, where, wrapping myself in my cloak, I again fell asleep. It was near daybreak when I awoke; we were then about two leagues from San Lucar. I arose and looked towards the east, watching the gradual progress of dawn, first the dull light, then the streak, then the tinge, then the bright blush, till at last the golden disk of that orb which giveth day emerged from the abyss of immensity, and in a moment the whole prospect was covered with brightness and glory. The land smiled, the waters sparkled, the birds sang, and men arose from their resting places and rejoiced; for it was day, and the sun was gone forth on the errand of its creator, the diffusion of light and gladness, and the dispelling of darkness and sorrow.

"Behold the morning sun
　　Begins his glorious way;
His beams through all the nations run,
　　And life and light convey.

"But where the Gospel comes,
　　It spreads diviner light;
It calls dead sinners from their tombs,
　　And gives the blind their sight."

We now stopped before Bonanza: this is properly speaking the port of San Lucar, although it is half a league distant from the latter place. It is called Bonanza on account of its good anchorage, and its being secured from the boisterous winds of the ocean; its literal meaning is " fair weather." It consists of several large white buildings, principally government store-houses, and is inhabited by the coast-guard, dependents on the custom-house, and a few fishermen. A boat came off to receive those passengers whose destination was San Lucar, and to bring on board about half a dozen who were bound for Cadiz: I entered with the rest. A young Spaniard of very diminutive stature addressed some questions to me in French as to what I thought of the scenery and climate of Andalusia. I replied that I admired both, which evidently gave him great pleasure. The boatman now came demanding two reals for conveying me on shore. I had no small money, and offered him a dollar to change. He said that it was impossible. I asked him what was to be done; whereupon he replied uncivilly that he knew not, but could not lose time, and expected to be paid instantly. The young Spaniard, observing my embarrassment, took out two reals and paid the fellow. I thanked him heartily for this act of civility, for which I felt really grateful; as there are few situations more unpleasant than to be in a crowd in want of change, whilst you are importuned by people for payment. A loose character once told me that it was far preferable to be without money at all, as you then knew what course to take. I subsequently met the young Spaniard at Cadiz, and repaid him with thanks.

A few cabriolets were waiting near the wharf, in order to convey us to San Lucar. I ascended one, and we proceeded slowly along the Playa or strand. This place is famous in the ancient novels of Spain, of that class called Picaresque, or those devoted to the adventures of notorious scoundrels, the father of which, as also of all others of the same kind, in whatever language, is Lazarillo de Tormes. Cervantes himself has immortalized this strand in the most amusing of his smaller tales, La Ilustre Fregona. In a word, the strand of San Lucar in ancient times, if not in modern, was a rendezvous for ruffians, contrabandistas, and vagabonds of every description, who nested

there in wooden sheds, which have now vanished. San Lucar itself was always noted for the thievish propensities of its inhabitants —the worst in all Andalusia. The roguish innkeeper in Don Quixote perfected his education at San Lucar. All these recollections crowded into my mind as we proceeded along the strand, which was beautifully gilded by the Andalusian sun. We at last arrived nearly opposite to San Lucar, which stands at some distance from the water-side. Here a lively spectacle presented itself to us: the shore was covered with a multitude of females either dressing or undressing themselves, while (I speak within bounds) hundreds were in the water sporting and playing: some were close by the beach, stretched at their full length on the sand and pebbles, allowing the little billows to dash over their heads and bosoms; whilst others were swimming boldly out into the firth. There was a confused hubbub of female cries, thin shrieks, and shrill laughter; couplets likewise were being sung, on what subject it is easy to guess, for we were in sunny Andalusia, and what can its black-eyed daughters think, speak, or sing of but *amór*, *amór*, which now sounded from the land and the waters. Farther on along the beach we perceived likewise a crowd of men bathing; we passed not by them, but turned to the left up an alley or avenue which leads to San Lucar, and which may be a quarter of a mile long. The view from hence was truly magnificent; before us lay the town, occupying the side and top of a tolerably high hill, extending from east to west. It appeared to be of considerable size, and I was subsequently informed that it contained at least twenty thousand inhabitants. Several immense edifices and walls towered up in a style of grandeur which can be but feebly described by words; but the principal object was an ancient castle towards the left. The houses were all white, and would have shone brilliantly in the sun had it been higher, but at this early hour they lay comparatively in shade. The *tout ensemble* was very Moorish and oriental, and indeed in ancient times San Lucar was a celebrated stronghold of the Moors, and, next to Almeria, the most frequented of their commercial places in Spain. Every thing, indeed, in these parts of Andalusia, is perfectly oriental. Behold the heavens, as cloudless and as brightly azure as those of Ind; the fiery sun which tans the fairest cheek in a moment, and which fills the air with flickering flame; and O remark the scenery and the vegetable productions. The alley up which we were moving was planted on each side with that remarkable tree or plant, for I know not which to call it, the giant aloe, which is called in Spanish, *pita*, and in Moorish, *gurséan*. It rises here to a height almost as magnificent as on the African shore. Need I say that the stem, which springs up from the middle of the bush of green blades, which shoot out from the root on all sides, is as high as a palm-tree; and need I say that those blades, which are of an immense thickness at the root, are at the tip sharper than the point of a spear, and would inflict a terrible wound on any animal which might inadvertently rush against them?

One of the first houses at San Lucar was the posada at which we stopped. It confronted, with some others, the avenue up which we had come. As it was still early, I betook myself to rest for a few hours, at the end of which time I went out to visit Mr. Phillippi, the British vice-consul, who was already acquainted with me by name, as I had been recommended to him by in a letter from a relation of his at Seville. Mr. Phillippi was at home in his counting-house, and received me with much kindness and civility. I told him the motive of my visit to San Lucar, and requested his assistance towards obtaining the books from the custom-house, in order to transport them out of the country, as I was very well acquainted with the difficulties which every one has to encounter in Spain, who has any business to transact with the government authorities. He assured me that he should be most happy to assist me, and accordingly despatched with me to the custom-house his head clerk, a person well known and much respected at San Lucar.

It may be as well here at once to give the history of these books, which might otherwise tend to embarrass the narrative. They consisted of a chest of Testaments in Spanish, and a small box of Saint Luke's Gospel in the Gitano or language of the Spanish Gipsies. I obtained them from the custom-house at San Lucar, with a pass for that of Cadiz. At Cadiz I was occupied two days, and also a person whom I employed, in going through all the formalities, and in procuring the necessary papers. The expense was great, as money was demanded at every step I had to take, though I was simply complying in this instance with the orders of the Spanish government in removing prohibited books from Spain. The farce did not end until my arrival at Gibraltar, where I paid the Spanish consul a dollar for certifying on the back of the pass, which I had to return to Cadiz, that the books were arrived at the former place. It is true that he never saw the books nor inquired about them, but he received the money, for which he alone seemed to be anxious.

Whilst at the custom-house of San Lucar I was asked one or two questions respecting the books contained in the chests: this afforded me some opportunity of speaking of the New Testament, and the Bible Society. What I said excited attention, and presently all the officers and dependents of the house, great and small, were gathered around me, from the governor to the porter. As it was necessary to open the boxes to inspect their contents, we all proceeded to the court-yard, where, holding a Testament in my hand, I recommenced my discourse. I scarcely know what I said; for I was much agitated, and hurried away by my feelings, when I bethought me of the manner in which the word of God was persecuted in this unhappy kingdom. My words evidently made impression, and to my astonishment every person present pressed me for a copy. I sold several within the walls of the custom-house. The object, however, of most attention was the gipsy Gospel, which was minutely examined amidst smiles and exclamations of surprise; an individual every now and then crying, "Cosas de los Ingleses." A bystander asked me whether I could speak the Gitano language. I replied that I could not only speak it, but write it, and instantly made a speech of about five minutes in the gipsy tongue, which I had no sooner concluded than all clapped their hands and simultaneously shouted, "Cosas de Inglaterra," "Cosas de los Ingleses." I disposed of several copies of the gipsy Gospel likewise, and having now settled the business which had brought me to the custom-house, I saluted my new friends and departed with my books.

I now revisited Mr. Phillippi, who, upon learning that it was my intention to proceed to Cadiz next morning by the steamer, which would touch at Bonanza at four o'clock, despatched the chests and my little luggage to the latter place, where he likewise advised me to sleep, in order that I might be in readiness to embark at that early hour. He then introduced me to his family, his wife an English woman, and his daughter an amiable and beautiful girl of about eighteen years of age, whom I had previously seen at Seville; three or four other ladies from Seville were likewise there on a visit, and for the purpose of sea-bathing. After a few words in English between the lady of the house and myself, we all commenced chatting in Spanish, which seemed to be the only language understood or cared for by the rest of the company; indeed, who would be so unreasonable as to expect Spanish females to speak any language but their own, which, flexible and harmonious as it is, (far more so I think than any other,) seems at times quite inadequate to express the wild sallies of their luxuriant imagination. Two hours fled rapidly away in discourse, interrupted occasionally by music and song, when I bade farewell to this delightful society, and strolled out to view the town.

It was now past noon, and the heat was exceedingly fierce: I saw scarcely a living being in the streets, the stones of which burnt my feet through the soles of my boots. I passed through the square of the Constitution, which presents nothing particular to the eye of the stranger, and ascended the hill to obtain a nearer view of the castle. It is a strong heavy edifice of stone, with round towers, and, though deserted, appears to be still in a tolerable state of preservation. I became tired of gazing, and was retracing my steps, when I was accosted by two gipsies, who by some means had heard of my arrival. We exchanged some words in Gitano, but they appeared to be very ignorant of the dialect, and utterly unable to maintain a conversation in it. They were clamorous for a gabicote, or book in the gipsy tongue. I refused it them, saying that they could turn it to no profitable account; but finding that they could read, I promised them each a Testament in Spanish. This offer, however, they refused with disdain, saying that they cared for nothing written in the language of the Busne or Gentiles. They then persisted in their demand, to which I at last yielded, being unable to resist their importunity; whereupon they accompanied me to the inn, and received what they so ardently desired.

In the evening I was visited by Mr. Phillipi, who informed me that he had ordered a cabriolet to call for me at the inn at eleven at night, for the purpose of conveying me to Bonanza, and that a person there who kept a small wine-house, and to whom the chests and other things had been forwarded, would receive me for the night, though it was probable that I should have to sleep on the floor. We then walked to the beach, where there were a great number of bathers, all men. Amongst them were some good swimmers; two, in particular, were out at a great distance in the firth of the Guadalquivir, I should say at least a mile; their heads could just be descried with the telescope. I was told that they were friars. I wondered at what period of their lives they had acquired their dexterity at natation. I hoped it was not at a time when, according to their vows, they should have lived for prayer, fasting, and mortification alone. Swimming is a noble exercise, but it certainly does not tend to mortify either the flesh or the spirit. As it was becoming dusk, we returned to the town, when my friend bade me a kind farewell. I then retired to my apartment, and passed some hours in meditation.

It was night, ten o'clock;—eleven o'clock, and the cabriolet was at the door. I got in, and we proceeded down the avenue and along the shore, which was quite deserted. The waves sounded mournfully; every thing seemed to have changed since the morning. I even thought that the horse's feet sounded differently as it trotted slowly over the moist firm sand. The driver, however, was by no means mournful, nor inclined to be silent long: he soon commenced asking me an infinity of questions as to whence I came and whither I was bound. Having given him what answers I thought most proper, I, in return, asked him whether he was not afraid to drive along that beach, which had always borne so had a character, at so unseasonable an hour. Whereupon, he looked around him, and seeing no person, he raised a shout of derision, and said that a fellow with his whiskers feared not all the thieves that ever walked the playa, and that no dozen men in San Lucar dare to waylay any traveller whom they knew to be beneath his protection. He was a good specimen of the Andalusian braggart. We soon saw a light or two shining dimly before us; they proceeded from a few barks and small vessels stranded on the sand close below Bonanza: amongst them I distinguished two or three dusky figures. We were now at our journey's end, and stopped before the door of the place where I was to lodge for the night. The driver, dismounting, knocked loud and long,

until the door was opened by an exceedingly stout man of about sixty years of age; he held a dim light in his hand, and was dressed in a red night-cap and dirty striped shirt. He admitted us, without a word, into a very large long room with a clay floor. A species of counter stood on one side near the door; behind it stood a barrel or two, and against the wall, or shelves, many bottles of various sizes. The smell of liquors and wine was very powerful. I settled with the driver and gave him a gratuity, whereupon he asked me for something to drink to my safe journey. I told him he could call for whatever he pleased; whereupon he demanded a glass of aguardiente, which the master of the house, who had stationed himself behind the counter, handed him without saying a word. The fellow drank it off at once, but made a great many wry faces after having swallowed it, and, coughing, said that he made no doubt it was good liquor, as it burnt his throat terribly. He then embraced me, went out, mounted his cabriolet, and drove off.

The old man with the red night-cap now moved slowly to the door, which he bolted and otherwise secured; he then drew forward two benches, which he placed together, and pointed to them as if to intimate to me that there was my bed: he then blew out the candle and retired deeper into the apartment, where I heard him lay himself down sighing and snorting. There was now no farther light than what proceeded from a small earthen pan on the floor, filled with water and oil, on which floated a small piece of card with a lighted wick in the middle, which simple species of lamp is called "mariposa." I now laid my carpet bag on the bench as a pillow, and flung myself down. I should have been asleep instantly, but he of the red night-cap now commenced snoring awfully, which brought to my mind that I had not yet commended myself to my friend and Redeemer: I therefore prayed, and then sank to repose.

I was awakened more than once during the night by cats, and I believe rats, leaping upon my body. At the last of these interruptions I arose, and, approaching the mariposa, looked at my watch; it was half past three o'clock. opened the door and looked out; whereupon some fishermen entered, clamouring for their morning draught; the old man was soon on his feet serving them. One of the men said to me that, if I was going by the steamer, I had better order my things to the wharf without delay, as he had heard the vessel coming down the river. I despatched my luggage, and then demanded of the red nightcap what I owed him. He replied, "One real." These were the only two words which I heard proceed from his mouth: he was certainly addicted to silence, and perhaps to philosophy, neither of which are much practised in Andalusia. I now hurried to the wharf; the steamer was not yet arrived, but I heard its thunder up the river every moment becoming more distinct: there was mist and darkness upon the face of the waters, and I felt awe as I listened to the approach of the invisible monster booming through the stillness of the night. It came at last in sight, plashed its way forward, stopped, and I was soon on board. It was the Peninsula, the best boat on the Guadalquivir.

What a wonderful production of art is a steamboat; and yet why should we call it wonderful, if we consider its history? More than five hundred years have elapsed since the idea of making one first originated; but it was not until the close of the last century that the first, worthy of the name, made its appearance on a Scottish river.

During this long period of time, acute minds and skilful hands were occasionally busied in attempting to remove those imperfections in the machinery, which alone prevented a vessel being made capable of propelling itself against wind and tide. All these attempts were successively abandoned in despair, yet scarcely one was made which was perfectly fruitless; each inventor leaving behind him some monument of his labour, of which those who succeeded him took advantage, until at last a fortunate thought or two, and a few more perfect arrangements, were all that were wanting. The time arrived, and now, at length, the very Atlantic is crossed by haughty steamers. Much has been said of the utility of steam in spreading abroad civilization, and I think justly. When the first steam vessels were seen on the Guadalquivir, about ten years ago, the Sevillians ran to the banks of the river, crying "sorcery, sorcery," which idea was not a little favoured by the speculation being an English one, and the boats, which were English built, being provided with English engineers, as, indeed, they still are; no Spaniard having

been found capable of understanding the machinery. They soon, however, became accustomed to them, and the boats are in general crowded with passengers. Fanatic and vain as the Sevillians still are, and bigoted as they remain to their own customs, they know that good, in one instance at least, can proceed from a foreign land, and that land a land of heretics; inveterate prejudice has been shaken, and we will hope that this is the dawn of their civilization.

Whilst passing over the bay of Cadiz, I was reclining on one of the benches on the deck, when the captain walked by in company with another man; they stopped a short distance from me, and I heard the captain ask the other, in a low voice, how many languages he spoke; he replied "only one." "That one," said the captain, "is of course the Christian; by which name the Spaniards style their own language in contradistinction to all others. "That fellow," continued the captain, "who is lying on the deck, can speak Christian too when it serves his purpose, but he speaks others, which are by no means Christian: he can talk English, and I myself have heard him chatter in Gitano with the gipsies of Triana; he is now going amongst the Moors, and when he arrives in their country, you will hear him, should you be there, converse as fluently in their gibberish as in Christiano, nay, better, for he is no Christian himself. He has been several times on board my vessel already, but I do not like him, as I consider that he carries something about with him which is not good."

This worthy person, on my coming aboard the boat, had shaken me by the hand and expressed his joy at seeing me again.

S

CHAPTER LI.

Cadiz—The Fortifications—The Consul-General—Characteristic Anecdote—Catalan Steamer—Trafalgar—Alonzo Guzman—Gibil Muza—Orestes Frigate—The Hostile Lion—Works of the Creator—Lizard of the Rock—The Concourse—Queen of the Waters—Broken Prayer.

CADIZ stands, as is well known, upon a long narrow neck of land stretching out into the ocean, from whose bosom the town appears to rise, the salt waters laving its walls on all sides save the east, where a sandy isthmus connects it with the coast of Spain. The town, as it exists at the present day, is of modern construction, and very unlike any other town which is to be found in the Peninsula, being built with great regularity and symmetry. The streets are numerous, and intersect each other, for the most part, at right angles. They are very narrow in comparison to the height of the houses, so that they are almost impervious to the rays of the sun, except when at its midday altitude. The principal street, however, is an exception, it being of some width. This street, in which stands the Bolsa or Exchange, and which contains the houses of the chief merchants and nobility, is the grand resort of loungers as well as men of business during the early part of the day, and in that respect resembles the Puerta del Sol at Madrid. It is connected with the great square, which, though not of very considerable extent, has many pretensions to magnificence, it being surrounded with large imposing houses, and planted with fine trees, with marble seats below them for the accommodation of the public. There are few public edifices worthy of much attention: the chief church, indeed, might be considered a fine monument of labour in some other countries, but in Spain, the land of noble and gigantic cathedrals, it can be styled nothing more than a decent place of worship; it is still in an unfinished state. There is a public walk or alameda on the northern ramparts, which is generally thronged in summer evenings: the green of its trees, when viewed from the bay, affords an agreeable relief to the eye, dazzled with the glare of the white buildings, for Cadiz is also a bright city. It was once the wealthiest place in all Spain, but its prosperity has of late years sadly diminished, and its inhabitants are continually lamenting its ruined trade; on which account many are daily abandoning it for Seville, where living at least is cheaper. There is still, however, much life and bustle in the streets, which are adorned with many splendid shops, several of which are in the style of Paris and London. The present population is said to amount to eighty thousand souls.

It is not without reason that Cadiz has been called a strong town: the fortifications on the land side, which were partly the work of the French during the sway of Napoleon, are perfectly admirable, and seem impregnable: towards the sea it is defended as much by nature as by art, water and sunken rocks being no contemptible bulwarks. The defences of the town, however, except the landward ones, afford melancholy proofs of Spanish apathy and neglect, even when allowance is made for the present peculiarly unhappy circumstances of the country. Scarcely a gun, except a few dismounted ones, is to be seen on the fortifications, which are rapidly falling to decay, so that this insulated stronghold is at present almost at the mercy of any foreign nation which, upon any pretence, or none at all, should seek to tear it from the grasp of its present legitimate possessors, and convert it into a foreign colony.

A few hours after my arrival, I waited upon Mr. B., the British consul-general at Cadiz. His house, which is the corner one at the entrance of the alameda, commands a noble prospect of the bay, and is very large and magnificent. I had of course long been acquainted with Mr. B. by reputation; I knew that for several years he had filled, with advantage to his native country and with honour to himself, the distinguished and highly responsible situation which he holds in Spain. I knew, likewise, that he was a good and pious Christian, and, moreover, the firm and enlightened friend of the Bible Society. Of all this I was aware, but I had never yet enjoyed the advantage of being personally acquainted with him. I saw him now for the first time, and was much struck with his appearance. He is a tall, athletic, finely built man, seemingly about forty-five or fifty; there is much dignity in his countenance, which is, however softened by an expression of good humour truly engaging. His manner is frank and affable in the extreme. I am not going to enter into minute details of our interview, which was to me a very interesting one. He knew already the leading parts of my history since my arrival in Spain, and made several comments upon it, which displayed his intimate knowledge of the situation of the country as regards ecclesiastical matters, and the state of opinion respecting religious innovation.

I was pleased to find that his ideas in many points accorded with my own, and we were both decidedly of opinion that, notwithstanding the great persecution and outcry which had lately been raised against the gospel, the battle was by no means lost, and that the holy cause might yet triumph in Spain, if zeal united with discretion and Christian humility were displayed by those called upon to uphold it.

During the greater part of this and the following day, I was much occupied at the custom-house, endeavouring to obtain the documents necessary for the exportation of the Testaments. On the afternoon of Saturday, I dined with Mr. B. and his family, an interesting group,—his lady, his beautiful daughters, and his son, a fine intelligent young man. Early the next morning, a steamer, the Balear, was to quit Cadiz for Marseilles, touching on the way at Algeziras, Gibraltar, and various other ports of Spain. I had engaged my passage on board her as far as Gibraltar, having nothing farther to detain me at Cadiz; my business with the custom-house having been brought at last to a termination, though I believe I should never have got through it but for the kind assistance of Mr. B. I quitted this excellent man and my other charming friends at a late hour with regret. I believe that I carried with me their very best wishes; and, in whatever part of the world I, a poor wanderer in the Gospel's cause, may chance to be, I shall not unfrequently offer up sincere prayers for their happiness and well-being.

Before taking leave of Cadiz, I shall relate an anecdote of the British consul, characteristic of him and the happy manner in which he contrives to execute the most disagreeable duties of his situation. I was in conversation with him in a parlour of his house, when we were interrupted by the entrance of two very unexpected visitors: they were the captain of a Liverpool merchant vessel and one of the crew. The latter was a rough sailor, a Welshman, who could only express himself in very imperfect English. They looked unutterable dislike and defiance at each other. It appeared that the latter had refused to work, and insisted on leaving the ship, and his master had in consequence brought him before the consul, in order that, if he persisted, the consequences might be detailed to him, which would be the forfeiture of his wages and clothes. This was done; but the fellow became more and more dogged, refusing ever to tread the same deck again with his captain, who, he said, had called him " Greek, lazy lubberly Greek," which he would not bear. The word Greek rankled in the sailor's mind, and stung him to the very core. Mr. B., who seemed to be perfectly acquainted with the character of Welshmen in general, who are proverbially obstinate when opposition is offered to them, and who saw at once that the dispute had arisen on foolish and trivial grounds, now told the man, with a smile, that he would inform him of a way by which he might gain the weather-gage of every one of them, consul and captain and all, and secure his wages and clothes; which was by merely going on board a brig of war of her Majesty, which was then lying in the bay. The fellow said he was aware of this, and intended to do so. His grim features, however, instantly relaxed in some degree, and he looked more humanely upon his captain. Mr. B. then,

addressing himself to the latter, made some observations on the impropriety of using the word Greek to a British sailor; not forgetting, at the same time, to speak of the absolute necessity of obedience and discipline on board every ship. His words produced such an effect, that in a very little time the sailor held out his hand towards his captain, and expressed his willingness to go on board with him and perform his duty, adding, that the captain, upon the whole, was the best man in the world. So they departed mutually pleased; the consul making both of them promise to attend divine service at his house on the following day.

Sunday morning came, and I was on board the steamer by six o'clock. As I ascended the side, the harsh sound of the Catalan dialect assailed my ears. In fact, the vessel was Catalan built, and the captain and crew were of that nation; the greater part of the passengers already on board, or who subsequently arrived, appeared to be Catalans, and seemed to vie with each other in producing disagreeable sounds. A burly merchant, however, with a red face, peaked chin, sharp eyes, and hooked nose, clearly bore off the palm; he conversed with astonishing eagerness on seemingly the most indifferent subjects, or rather on no subject at all; his voice would have sounded exactly like a coffee-mill but for a vile nasal twang: he poured forth his Catalan incessantly till we arrived at Gibraltar. Such people are never sea-sick, though they frequently produce or aggravate the malady in others. We did not get under way until past eight o'clock, for we waited for the Governor of Algeziras, and started instantly on his coming on board. He was a tall, thin, rigid figure of about seventy, with a long, grave, wrinkled countenance; in a word, the very image of an old Spanish grandee. We stood out of the bay, rounding the lofty lighthouse, which stands on a ledge of rocks, and then bent our course to the south, in the direction of the Straits. It was a glorious morning, a blue sunny sky and blue sunny ocean; or, rather, as my friend Oehlenschläger has observed on a similar occasion, there appeared two skies and two suns, one above and one below.

Our progress was rather slow, notwithstanding the fineness of the weather, probably owing to the tide being against us. In about two hours we passed the Castle of Santa Petra, and at noon were in sight of Trafalgar. The wind now freshened and was dead ahead; on which account we hugged closely to the coast, in order to avoid as much as possible the strong heavy sea which was pouring down from the Straits. We passed within a very short distance of the Cape, a bold bluff foreland, but not of any considerable height.

It is impossible for an Englishman to pass by this place—the scene of the most celebrated naval action on record—without emotion. Here it was that the united navies of France and Spain were annihilated by a far inferior force; but that force was British, and was directed by one of the most remarkable men of the age, and perhaps the greatest hero of any time. Huge fragments of wreck still frequently emerge from the watery gulf whose billows chafe the rocky sides of Trafalgar: they are relics of the enormous ships which were burnt and sunk on that terrible day, when the heroic champion of Britain concluded his work and died. I never heard but one individual venture to say a word in disparagement of Nelson's glory: it was a pert American, who observed, that the British admiral was much overrated. "Can that individual be overrated," replied a stranger, "whose every thought was bent on his country's honour, who scarcely ever fought without leaving a piece of his body in the fray, and who, not to speak of minor triumphs, was victorious in two such actions as Aboukir and Trafalgar?"

We were now soon in sight of the Moorish coast, Cape Spartel appearing dimly through mist and vapour on our right. A regular Levanter had now come on, and the vessel pitched and tossed to a very considerable degree. Most of the passengers were sea-sick; the governor, however, and myself held out manfully: we sat on a bench together, and entered into conversation respecting the Moors and their country. Torquemada himself could not have spoken of both with more abhorrence. He informed me that he had been frequently in several of the principal Moorish towns of the coast, which he described as heaps of ruins: the Moors themselves he called Caffres and wild beasts. He observed that he had never been even at Tangier, where the people were most civilized, without experiencing some insult, so great was the abhorrence of the Moors to any thing in the shape of a Christian. He added, however, that they treated the English with comparative civility, and that they had a saying among them to the effect that Englishman and Mahometan were one and the same: he then looked particularly grave for a moment, and, crossing himself, was silent. I guessed what was passing in his mind:

"From heretic boors,
And Turkish Moors,
Star of the sea,
Gentle Marie,
Deliver me!"

At about three we were passing Tarifa, so frequently mentioned in the history of Moors and Christians. Who has not heard of Alonzo Guzman the faithful, who allowed his only son to be crucified before the walls of the town rather than submit to the ignominy of delivering up the keys to the Moorish monarch, who, with a host which is said to have amounted to nearly half a million of men, had landed on the shores of Andalusia, and threatened to bring all Spain once more beneath the Moslem yoke? Certainly if there be a land and a spot where the name of that good patriot is not sometimes mentioned and sung, that land, that spot is modern Spain and modern Tarifa. I have heard the ballad of Alonzo Guzman chanted in Danish, by a hind in the wilds of Jutland;

but once speaking of "the Faithful" to some inhabitants of Tarifa, they replied that they had never heard of Guzman the faithful of Tarifa, but were acquainted with Alonzo Guzman, "the one-eyed," (el tuerto,) and that he was one of the most villainous arrieros on the Cadiz road.

The voyage of these narrow seas can scarcely fail to be interesting to the most apathetic individual, from the nature of the scenery which presents itself to the eye on either side. The coasts are exceedingly high and bold, especially that of Spain, which seems to overcrow the Moorish; but opposite to Tarifa the African continent, rounding towards the south-west, assumes an air of sublimity and grandeur. A hoary mountain is seen uplifting its summits above the clouds: it is mount Abyla, or as it is called in the Moorish tongue, Gibil Muza, or the hill of Muza, from the circumstance of its containing the sepulchre of a prophet of that name. This is one of the two excrescences of nature on which the Old World bestowed the title of the Pillars of Hercules. Its skirts and sides occupy the Moorish coast for many leagues in more than one direction, but the broad aspect of its steep and stupendous front is turned full towards that part of the European continent where Gibraltar lies like a huge monster stretching far into the brine. Of the two hills or pillars, the most remarkable, when viewed from afar, is the African one, Gibil Muza. It is the tallest and bulkiest, and is visible at a greater distance; but scan them both from near, and you feel that all your wonder is engrossed by the European column. Gibil Muza is an immense shapeless mass, a wilderness of rocks, with here and there a few trees and shrubs nodding from the clefts of its precipices; it is uninhabited, save by wolves, wild swine, and chattering monkeys, on which last account it is called by the Spaniards, Montana de las Monas (the hill of the baboons;) whilst, on the contrary, Gibraltar, not to speak of the strange city which covers part of it, a city inhabited by men of all nations and tongues, its batteries and excavations, all of them miracles of art, is the most singular looking mountain in the world—a mountain which can neither be described by pen nor pencil, and at which the eye is never satiated with gazing.

It was near sunset, and we were crossing the bay of Gibraltar. We had stopped at Algeziras, on the Spanish side, for the purpose of landing the old governor and his suite, and delivering and receiving letters.

Algeziras is an ancient Moorish town, as the name denotes, which is an Arabic word, and signifies "the place of the islands." It is situated at the water's edge, with a lofty range of mountains in the rear. It seemed a sad deserted place, as far as I could judge at the distance of half a mile. In the harbour, however, lay a Spanish frigate and French war brig. As we passed the former, some of the Spaniards on board our steamer became boastful at the expense of the English. It appeared that, a few weeks before, an English vessel, suspected to be a contraband trader, was seen by this frigate hovering about a bay on the Andalusian coast, in company with an English frigate, the Orestes. The Spaniard dodged them for some time, till one morning observing that the Orestes had disappeared, he hoisted English colours, and made a signal to the trader to bear down; the latter, deceived by the British ensign, and supposing that the Spaniard was the friendly Orestes, instantly drew near, was fired at and boarded, and proving in effect to be a contraband trader, she was carried into port and delivered over to the Spanish authorities. In a few days, the captain of the Orestes hearing of this, and incensed at the unwarrantable use made of the British flag, sent a boat on board the frigate, demanding that the vessel should be instantly restored, as, if she was not, he would retake her by force; adding, that he had forty cannons on board. The captain of the Spanish frigate returned for answer, that the trader was in the hands of the officers of the customs, and was no longer at his disposal; that the captain of the Orestes, however, could do what he pleased, and that if he had forty guns, he himself had forty-four: whereupon the Orestes thought proper to bear away. Such at least was the Spanish account, as related by the journals. Observing the Spaniards to be in great glee at the idea of one of their nation having frightened away the Englishman, I exclaimed, "Gentlemen, all of you who suppose that an English sea captain has been deterred from attacking a Spaniard, from an apprehension of a superior force of four guns, remember, if you please, the fate of the Santissima Trinidad, and be pleased also not to forget that we are almost within cannon sound of Trafalgar."

It was near sunset, I repeat, and we were crossing the bay of Gibraltar. I stood on the prow of the vessel, with my eyes intently fixed on the mountain fortress, which, though I had seen it several times before, filled my mind with admiration and interest. Viewed from this situation, it certainly, if it resembles any animate object in nature, has something of the appearance of a terrible couchant lion, whose stupendous head menaces Spain. Had I been dreaming, I should almost have concluded it to be the genius of Africa, in the shape of its most puissant monster, who had bounded over the sea from the clime of sand and sun, bent on the destruction of the rival continent, more especially as the hue of its stony sides, its crest and chine, is tawny even as that of the hide of the desert king. A hostile lion has it almost invariably proved to Spain, at least since it first began to play a part in history, which was at the time when Tarik seized and fortified it. It has for the most part been in the hands of foreigners: first the swarthy and turbaned Moor possessed it, and it is now tenanted by a fair haired race from a distant isle. Though a part of Spain, it seems to disavow the connexion, and at the end of a long narrow sandy isthmus, almost level with the sea, raising its blasted and perpendicular brow to denounce the crimes which deform the history of that fair and majestic land.

It was near sunset, I say it for the third time, and we were crossing the bay of Gibraltar. Bay! it seemed no bay, but an inland sea, surrounded on all sides by enchanted barriers, so strange, so wonderful was the aspect of its coasts. Before us lay the impregnable hill; on our right, the African continent, with its gray Gibil Muza, and the crag of Ceuta, to which last a solitary bark seemed steering its way; behind us the town we had just quitted, with its mountain wall; on our left the coast of Spain. The surface of the water was unruffled by a wave, and as we rapidly glided on, the strange object which we were approaching became momentarily more distinct and visible. There, at the base of the mountain, and covering a small portion of its side, lay the city with its ramparts garnished with black guns pointing significantly at its moles and harbours; above, seemingly on every crag which could be made available for the purpose of defence or destruction, peered batteries, pale and sepulchral-looking, as if ominous of the fate which awaited any intrusive foe; whilst east and west, towards Africa and Spain, on the extreme points, rose castles, towers, or atalias which overcrowed the whole, and all the circumjacent region, whether land or sea. Mighty and threatening appeared the fortifications, and doubtless, viewed in any other situation, would have alone occupied the mind and engrossed its wonder; but the hill, the wondrous hill, was everywhere about them, beneath them or above them, overpowering their effect as a spectacle. Who, when he beholds the enormous elephant, with his brandished trunk, dashing impetuously to the war, sees the castle which he bears, or fears the javelins of those whom he carries, however skilful and warlike they may be? Never does God appear so great and powerful as when the works of his hands stand in contrast with the labours of man. Survey the Escurial, it is a proud work, but wonder if you can when you see the mountain mocking it behind; survey that boast of Moorish kings, survey Granada from its plain, and wonder if you can, for you see the Alpujarra mocking it from behind. O what are the works of man compared with those of the Lord? Even as man is compared with his Creator. Man builds pyramids, and God builds pyramids: the pyramids of man are heaps of shingles, tiny hillocks on a sandy plain; the pyramids of the Lord are Andes and Indian hills. Man builds walls and so does his master; but the walls of God are the black precipices of Gibraltar and Horneel, eternal, indestructible, and not to be scaled; whilst those of man can be climbed, can be broken by the wave or shattered by the lightning or the powder blast.

Would man display his power and grandeur to advantage, let him flee far from the hills; for the broad pennants of God, even his clouds, float upon the tops of the hills, and the majesty of God is most manifest among the hills. Call Gibraltar the hill of Tarik or Hercules if you will, but gaze upon it for a moment and you will call it the hill of God. Tarik and the old giant may have built upon it; but not all the dark race of whom Tarik was one, nor all the giants of old renown of whom the other was one, could have built up its crags or chiseled the enormous mass to its present shape.

We dropped anchor not far from the mole. As we expected every moment to hear the evening gun, after which no person is permitted to enter the town, I was in trepidation lest I should be obliged to pass the night on board the dirty Catalan steamer, which, as I had no occasion to proceed farther in her, I was in great haste to quit. A boat now drew nigh, with two individuals at the stern, one of whom, standing up, demanded, in an authoritative voice, the name of the vessel, her destination and cargo. Upon being answered, they came on board. After some conversation with the captain, they were about to depart, when I inquired whether I could accompany them on shore. The person I addressed was a tall young man, with a fustian frock coat. He had a long face, long nose, and wide mouth, with large restless eyes. There was a grin on his countenance which seemed permanent, and had it not been for his bronzed complexion, I should have declared him to be a cockney, and nothing else. He was, however, no such thing, but what is called a rock lizard, that is, a person born at Gibraltar of English parents. Upon hearing my question, which was in Spanish, he grinned more than ever, and enquired, in a strange accent, whether I was a son of Gibraltar. I replied that I had not that honour, but that I was a British subject. Whereupon he said that he should make no difficulty in taking me ashore. We entered the boat, which was rapidly rowed toward the land by four Genoese sailors. My two companions chattered in their strange Spanish, he of the fustian occasionally turning his countenance full upon me, the last grin appearing ever more hideous than the preceding ones. We soon reached the quay, where my name was noted down by a person who demanded my passport, and I was then permitted to advance.

It was now dusk, and I lost no time in crossing the drawbridge and entering the long low archway which, passing under the rampart, communicates with the town. Beneath this archway paced with measured tread, tall red-coated sentinels with shouldered guns. There was no stopping, no sauntering in these men. There was no laughter, no exchange of light conversation with the passers by, but their bearing was that of British soldiers, conscious of the duties of their station. What a difference between them and the listless loiterers who stand at guard at the gate of a Spanish garrisoned town.

I now proceeded up the principal street, which runs with a gentle ascent along the base of the hill. Accustomed for some months past to the melancholy silence of Seville, I was almost deafened by the noise and bustle which reigned around. It was Sunday night, and of course no business was going on, but there were throngs of people passing up and down. Here was a military guard proceeding along; here walked a group of officers, there a knot of soldiers stood talking and laughing. The greater part of the civilians appeared to be Spaniards, but there was a large sprinkling of Jews in the dress of those of Barbary, and here and there a turbaned Moor. There were gangs of sailors likewise, Genoese, judging from the patois which they were speaking, though I occasionally distinguished the sound of "tou logou sas," by which I knew there were Greeks at hand, and twice or thrice caught a glimpse of the red cap and blue silken petticoats of the mariner from the Romaic isles. On still I hurried, till I arrived at a well known hostelry, close by a kind of square, in which stands the little exchange of Gibraltar. Into this I ran and demanded lodging, receiving a cheerful welcome from the genius of the place, who stood behind the bar, and whom I shall perhaps have occasion subsequently to describe. All the lower rooms were filled with men of the rock, burly men in general, with swarthy complexions and English features, with white hats, white jean jerkins, and white jean pantaloons. They were smoking pipes and cigars, and drinking porter, wine, and various other fluids, and conversing in the rock Spanish, or rock English, as the fit took them. Dense was the smoke of tobacco, and great the din of voices, and I was glad to hasten up stairs to an unoccupied apartment, where I was served with some refreshment, of which I stood much in need.

I was soon disturbed by the sound of martial music close below my windows. I went down and stood at the door. A military band was marshalled upon the little square before the exchange. It was preparing to beat the retreat. After the prelude, which was admirably executed, the tall leader gave a flourish with his stick, and strode forward up the street, followed by the whole company of noble looking fellows and a crowd of admiring listeners. The cymbals clashed, the horns screamed, and the kettle-drum emitted its deep awful note, till the old rock echoed again, and the hanging terraces of the town rang with the stirring noise:

"Dub-a-dub, dub-a-dub—thus go the drums,
Tantara, tantara, the Englishman comes."

O England! long, long may it be ere the sun of thy glory sink beneath the wave of darkness! Though gloomy and portentous clouds are now gathering rapidly around thee, still, still may it please the Almighty to disperse them, and to grant thee a futurity longer in duration and still brighter in renown than thy past! Or if thy doom be at hand, may that doom be a noble one, and worthy of her who has been styled the Old Queen of the waters! May thou sink, if thou dost sink, amidst blood and flame, with a mighty noise, causing more than one nation to participate in thy downfall! Of all fates, may it please the Lord to preserve thee from a disgraceful and a slow decay; becoming, ere extinct, a scorn and a mockery for those selfsame foes who now, though they envy and abhor thee, still fear thee, nay, even against their will, honour and respect thee.

Arouse thee, whilst yet there is time, and prepare thee for the combat of life and death! Cast from thee the foul scurf which now encrusts thy robust limbs, which deadens their force, and makes them heavy and powerless! Cast from thee thy false philosophers, who would fain decry what, next to the love of God, has hitherto been deemed most sacred, the love of the mother land! Cast from thee thy false patriots, who, under the pretext of redressing the wrongs of the poor and weak, seek to promote internal discord, so that thou mayest become only terrible to thyself! And remove from thee the false prophets, who have seen vanity and divined lies; who have daubed thy wall with untempered mortar, that it may fall; who see visions of peace where there is no peace; who have strengthened the hands of the wicked, and made the heart of the righteous sad. O, do this, and fear not the result, for either shall thy end be a majestic and an enviable one, or God shall perpetuate thy reign upon the waters, thou Old Queen!

The above was part of a broken prayer for my native land, which, after my usual thanksgiving, I breathed to the Almighty ere retiring to rest that Sunday night at Gibraltar.

CHAPTER LII.

The Jolly Hostler—Aspirants for Glory—A Portrait—Hamálos—Solomons—An Expedition—The Yeoman Soldier—The Excavations—The Pull by the Skirt—Judah and his Father—Judah's Pilgrimage—The Bushy Beard—The False Moors—Judah and the King's Son—Premature Old Age.

PERHAPS it would have been impossible to have chosen a situation more adapted for studying at my ease Gibraltar and its inhabitants, than that which I found myself occupying about ten o'clock on the following morning. Seated on a small bench just opposite the bar, close by the door, in the passage of the hostelry at which I had taken up my temporary abode, I enjoyed a view of the square of the exchange and all that was going on there, and by merely raising my eyes, could gaze at my leisure on the stupendous hill which towers above the town to an altitude of some thousand feet. I could likewise observe every person who entered or left the house, which is one of great resort, being situated in the most frequented place of the principal thoroughfare of the town. My eyes were busy and so were my ears. Close beside me stood my excellent friend Griffiths, the jolly hostler, of whom I take the present opportunity of saying a few words, though I dare say he has been frequently described before, and by far better pens. Let those who know him not figure to themselves a man of about fifty, at least six feet in height, and weighing some eighteen stone, an exceedingly florid countenance and good features, eyes full of quickness and shrewdness, but at the same time beaming with good nature. He wears white pantaloons, white frock, and white hat, and is, indeed, all white, with the exception of his polished Wellingtons and rubicund face. He carries a whip beneath his arm, which adds wonderfully to the knowingness of his appearance, which is rather more that of a gentleman who keeps an inn on the Newmarket road, "purely for the love of travellers, and the money which they carry about them," than of a native of the rock. Nevertheless, he will tell you himself that he is a rock lizard; and you will scarcely doubt it when, beside his English, which is broad and vernacular, you hear him speak Spanish, ay, and Genoese too, when necessary, and it is no child's play to speak the latter, which I myself could never master. He is a good judge of horse-flesh, and occasionally sells "a bit of a blood," or a Barbary steed, to a young hand, though he has no objection to do business with an old one; for there is not a thin, crouching, livid faced, lynx-eyed Jew of Fez capable of outwitting him in a bargain, or cheating him out of one single pound of the fifty thousand sterling which he possesses; and yet ever bear in mind that he is a good natured fellow to those who are disposed to behave honourably to him, and know likewise that he will lend you money, if you are a gentleman, and are in need of it; but depend upon it, if he refuse you, there is something not altogether right about you, for Griffiths knows *his world*, and is not to be made a fool of

There was a prodigious quantity of porter consumed in my presence during the short hour that I sat on the bench of that hostelry of the rock. The passage before the bar was frequently filled with officers, who lounged in for a refreshment which the sultry heat of the weather rendered necessary, or at least inviting; whilst not a few came galloping up to the door on small Barbary horses, which are to be found in great abundance at Gibraltar. All seemed to be on the best terms with the host, with whom they occasionally discussed the merits of particular steeds, and whose jokes they invariably received with unbounded approbation. There was much in the demeanour and appearance of these young men, for the greater part were quite young, which was highly interesting and agreeable. Indeed, I believe it may be said of English officers in general, that in personal appearance, and in polished manners, they bear the palm from those of the same class over the world. True it is, that the officers of the royal guard of Russia, especially of the three noble regiments styled the Priberjensky, Simeonsky, and Finlansky polks, might fearlessly enter in competition in almost all points with the flower of the British army; but it must be remembered, that those regiments are officered by the choicest specimens of the Sclavonian nobility, young men selected expressly for the splendour of their persons, and for the superiority of their mental endowments; whilst, probably, amongst all the fair-haired Anglo-Saxon youths whom I now saw gathered near me, there was not a single one of noble ancestry, nor of proud and haughty name; and certainly, so far from having been selected to flatter the pride and add to the pomp of a despot, they had been taken indiscriminately from a mass of ardent aspirants for military glory, and sent on their country's service to a remote and unhealthy colony. Nevertheless, they were such as their country might be proud of, for gallant boys they looked, with courage on their brows, beauty and health on their cheeks, and intelligence in their hazel eyes.

Who is he who now stops before the door without entering, and addresses a question to my host, who advances with a respectful salute? He is no common man, or his appearance belies him strangely. His dress is simple enough; a Spanish hat, with a peaked crown and broad shadowy brim—the veritable sombrero—jean pantaloons and blue hussar jacket; but how well that dress becomes one of the most noble-looking figures I ever beheld. I gazed upon him with strange respect and admiration as he stood benignantly smiling and joking in good Spanish with an impudent rock rascal, who held in his hand a huge bogamante, or coarse carrion lobster, which he would fain have persuaded him to purchase. He was almost gigantically tall, towering nearly three inches above the burly host himself, yet athletically symmetrical, and straight as a pine tree of Dovrefeld. He must have counted eleven lustres, which cast an air of mature dignity over a countenance which seemed to have been chiseled by some Grecian sculptor, and yet his hair was black as the plume of the Norwegian raven, and so was the moustache which curled above his well formed lip. In the garb of Greece, and in the camp before Troy, I should have taken him for Agamemnon. "Is that man a general?" said I to a short queer looking personage, who sat by my side, intently studying a newspaper. "That gentleman," he whispered in a lisping accent, "is, Sir, the Lieutenant-Governor of Gibraltar."

On either side outside the door, squatting on the ground, or leaning indolently against the walls, were some half dozen men of very singular appearance. Their principal garment was a kind of blue gown, something resembling the blouse worn by the peasants of the north of France, but not so long; it was compressed around their waists by a leathern girdle, and depended about half way down their thighs. Their legs were bare, so that I had an opportunity of observing the calves, which appeared unnaturally large. Upon the head they wore small scull-caps of black wool. I asked the most athletic of these men, a dark-visaged fellow of forty, who they were. He answered, "hamalos." This word I knew to be Arabic, in which tongue it signifies a porter; and, indeed, the next moment, I saw a similar fellow staggering across the square under an immense burden, almost sufficient to have broken the back of a camel. On again addressing my swarthy friend, and enquiring whence he came, he replied, that he was born at Mogadore, in Barbary, but had passed the the greatest part of his life at Gibraltar. He added, that he was the "capitaz," or head man of the "hamálos" near the door. I now addressed him in the Arabic of the East, though with scarcely the hope of being understood, more especially as he had been so long from his own country. He however answered very pertinently, his lips quivering with eagerness, and his eyes sparkling with joy, though it was easy to perceive that the Arabic, or rather the Moorish, was not the language in which he was accustomed either to think or speak. His companions all gathered around and listened with avidity, occasionally exclaiming, when any thing was said which they approved of: "Wakhud rajil shereef hada, min beled del scharki." (A holy man this, from the kingdoms of the East.) At last I produced the shekel, which I invariably carry about me as a pocket-piece, and asked the capataz whether he had ever seen that money before. He surveyed the censer and olive-branch for a considerable time, and evidently knew not what to make of it. At length he fell to inspecting the characters round about it on both sides, and giving a cry, exclaimed to the other hamálos: "Brothers, brothers, these are the letters of Solomon. This silver is blessed. We must kiss this money." He then put it upon his head, pressed it to his eyes, and finally kissed it with enthusiasm, as did successively all his brethren. Then regaining it, he returned it to me, with a low reverence. Griffiths subsequently informed me, that the fellow refused to work during all the rest of the day, and did nothing but smile, laugh, and talk to himself.

"Allow me to offer you a glass of bitters, sir," said the queer looking personage before mentioned; he was a corpulent man, very short, and his legs particularly so. His dress consisted of a greasy snuff-coloured coat, dirty white trousers, and dirtier stockings. On his head he wore a rusty silk hat, the eaves of which had a tendency to turn up before and behind. I had observed that, during my conversation with the hamálos, he had several times uplifted his eyes from the newspaper, and the production of the shekel had grinned very significantly, and had inspected it when in the hand of the capataz. "Allow me to offer you a glass of bitters," said he; "I guessed you was one of our people before you spoke to the hamálos. Sir, it does my heart good to see a gentleman of your appearance not above speaking to his poor brethren. It is what I do myself not unfrequently, and I hope God will blot out my name, and that is Solomons, when I despise them. I do not pretend to much Arabic myself, yet I understood you tolerably well, and I liked your discourse much. You must have a great deal of shillam eidri, nevertheless you startled me when you asked the hamalo if he ever read the Torah; of course you meant with the meforshim; poor as he is, I do not believe him becoresh enough to read the Torah without the commentators. So help me, sir, I believe you to be a Salamancan Jew; I am told there are still some of the old families to be found there. Ever at Tudela, sir? not very far from Salamanca, I believe; one of my own kindred once lived there: a great traveller, sir, like yourself; went over all the world to look for the Jews,—went to the top of Sinai. Any thing that I can do for you at at Gibraltar, sir? Any commission? will execute it as reasonably, and more expeditiously than any one else. My name is Solomons. I am tolerably well known at Gibraltar; yes, sir, and in the Crooked Friars, and, for that matter, in the Neuen SteinSteg, at Hamburgh; so help me, sir, I think I once saw your face at the fair at Bremen. Speak German, sir? though of course you do. Allow me, sir, to offer you a glass of bitters. I wish, sir, they were mayim, hayim for your sake, I do indeed, sir, I wish they were living waters. Now, sir, do give me your opinion as to this matter (lowering his voice and striking the newspaper.) Do you not think it is very hard that one Yudken should betray the other? When I put my little secret beyad peluni,—you understand me, sir? when I entrust my poor secret to the custody of an individual, and that individual a Jew, a Yudken, sir, I do not wish to be blown, indeed, I do not expect it. In a word what do you think of *the gold dust robbery*, and what will be done to those unfortunate people, who I see are convicted?"

That same day I made inquiry respecting

the means of transferring myself to Tangier, having no wish to prolong my stay at Gibraltar, where, though it is an exceedingly interesting place to an observant traveller, I had no particular business to detain me. In the evening I was visited by a Jew, a native of Barbary, who informed me that he was secretary to the master of a small Genoese bark which plied between Tangier and Gibraltar. Upon his assuring me that the vessel would infallibly start for the former place on the following evening, I agreed with him for my passage. He said that as the wind was blowing from the Levant quarter, the voyage would be a speedy one. Being desirous how of disposing to the most advantage of the short time which I expected to remain at Gibraltar, I determined upon visiting the excavations, which I had as yet never seen, on the following morning, and accordingly sent for and easily obtained the necessary permission.

About six on Tuesday morning, I started on this expedition, attended by a very intelligent good-looking lad of the Jewish persuasion, one of two brothers who officiated at the inn in the capacity of valets de place.

The morning was dim and hazy, yet sultry to a degree. We ascended a precipitous street, and proceeding in an easterly direction, soon, arrived in the vicinity of what is generally known by the name of the Moorish Castle, a large tower, but so battered by the cannon balls discharged against it in the famous siege, that it is at present little better than a ruin; hundreds of round holes are to be seen in its sides, in which, as it is said, the shot are still imbedded; here, at a species of hut, we were joined by an artillery sergeant, who was to be our guide. After saluting us, he led the way to a huge rock, where he unlocked a gate at the entrance of a dark vaulted passage which passed under it, emerging from which passage we found ourselves in a steep path, or rather staircase, with walls on either side.

We proceeded very leisurely, for hurry in such a situation would have been of little avail, as we should have lost our breath in a minute's time. The soldier, perfectly well acquainted with the locality, stalked along with measured steps, his eyes turned to the ground.

I looked fully as much at that man as at the strange place where we now were, and which was every moment becoming stranger. He was a fine specimen of the yeoman turned soldier; indeed, the corps to which he belonged consists almost entirely of that class. There he paces along, tall, strong, ruddy, and chestnut-haired, an Englishman every inch; be hold him pacing along, sober, silent, and civil, a genuine English soldier. I prize the sturdy Scot; I love the daring and impetuous Irishman; I admire all the various races which constitute the population of the British isles; yet I must say that, upon the whole, none are so well adapted to ply the soldier's hardy trade as the rural sons of old England, so strong, so cool, yet, at the same time, animated with so much hidden fire. Turn to the history of England and you will at once perceive of what such men are capable: even at Hastings, in the gray old time, under almost every disadvantage, weakened by a recent and terrible conflict, without discipline, comparatively speaking, and uncouthly armed, they all but vanquished the Norman chivalry. Trace their deeds in France, which they twice subdued; and even follow them to Spain, where they twanged the yew and raised the battle-axe, and left behind them a name of glory at Inglis Mendi, a name that shall last till fire consumes the Cantabrian hills. And, oh, in modern times, trace the deeds of these gallant men all over the world, and especially in France and Spain, and admire them, even as I did that sober, silent, soldier-like man who was showing me the wonders of a foreign mountain fortress, wrested by his countrymen from a powerful and proud nation more than a century before, and of which he was now a trusty and efficient guardian.

We arrived close to the stupendous precipice, which rises abruptly above the isthmus called the neutral ground, staring gauntly and horridly at Spain, and immediately entered the excavations. They consist of galleries scooped in the living rock at the distance of some twelve feet from the outside, behind which they run the whole breadth of the hill in this direction. In these galleries, at short distances, are ragged yawning apertures, all formed by the hand of man, where stand the cannon upon neat slightly raised pavements of small flint stones, each with its pyramid of bullets on one side, and on the other a box, in which is stowed the gear which the gunner requires in the exercise of his craft. Every thing was in its place, every thing in the nicest English order, every thing ready to scathe and overwhelm in a few moments the proudest and most numerous host which might appear marching in hostile array against this singular fortress on the land side.

There is not much variety in these places, one cavern and one gun resembling the other. As for the guns, they are not of large calibre, indeed, such are not needed here, where a pebble discharged from so great an altitude would be fraught with death. On descending a shaft, however, I observed, in one cave of special importance, two enormous carronades looking with peculiar wickedness and malignity down a shelving rock, which perhaps, although not without tremendous difficulty, might be scaled. The mere wind of one of these huge guns would be sufficient to topple over a thousand men. What sensations of dread and horror must be awakened in the breast of a foe when this hollow rock, in the day of siege, emits its flame, smoke, and thundering wind from a thousand yawning holes; horror not inferior to that felt by the peasant of the neighbourhood when Mongibello belches forth from all its orifices its sulphureous fires.

Emerging from the excavations, we proceeded to view various batteries. I asked the sergeant whether his companions and himself were dexterous at the use of the guns. He replied that these cannons were to them what the fowling-piece is to the fowler, that they handled them as easily, and, he believed, pointed them with more precision, as they seldom or never missed an object within range of the shot. This man never spoke until he was addressed, and then the answers which he gave were replete with good sense, and in general well worded. After our excursion, which lasted at least two hours, I made him a small present, and took leave with a hearty shake of the hand.

In the evening I prepared to go on board the vessel bound for Tangier, trusting in what the Jewish secretary had told me as to its sailing. Meeting him, however, accidentally in the street, he informed me that it would not start until the following morning, advising me at the same time to be on board at an early hour. I now roamed about the streets until night was beginning to set in, and becoming weary, I was just about to direct my steps to the inn, when I felt myself gently pulled by the skirt. I was amidst a concourse of people who were gathered around some Irish soldiers who were disputing, and I paid no attention; but I was pulled again more forcibly than before, and I heard myself addressed in a language which I had half forgotten, and which I scarcely expected ever to hear again. I looked round, and lo! a tall figure stood close to me and gazed in my face with anxious inquiring eyes. On its head was the kauk or furred cap of Jerusalem; depending from its shoulders, and almost trailing on the ground, was a broad blue mantle, whilst kandrisa or Turkish trousers enveloped its nether limbs. I gazed on the figure as wistfully as it gazed upon me. At first the features appeared perfectly strange, and I was about to exclaim, I know you not, when one or two lineaments struck me, and I cried, though somewhat hesitatingly, "Surely this is Judah Lib."

I was in a steamer in the Baltic in the year '34, if I mistake not. There was a drizzling rain and a high sea, when I observed a young man of about two and twenty leaning in a melancholy attitude against the side of the vessel. By his countenance I knew him to be one of the Hebrew race, nevertheless there was something very singular in his appearance, something which is rarely found amongst that people, a certain air of nobleness which highly interested me. I approached him, and in a few minutes we were in earnest conversation. He spoke Polish and Jewish German indiscriminately. The story which he related to me was highly extraordinary, yet I yielded implicit credit to all his words, which came from his mouth with an air of sincerity which precluded doubt; and, moreover, he could have no motive for deceiving me. One idea, one object, engrossed him entirely: "My father," said he, in language which strongly marked his race, "was a native of Galatia, a Jew of high caste, a learned man, for he knew Zohar,* and he was likewise skilled in medicine. When I was a child of some eight years, he left Galatia, and taking his wife, who was my mother, and myself with him, he bent his way unto the East, even to Jerusalem; there he established himself as a merchant, for he was acquainted with trade and the arts of getting money. He was much respected by the Rabbins of Jerusalem, for he was a Polish man, and he knew more Zohar and more secrets than the wisest of them. He made frequent journeys, and was absent for weeks and for months, but he never exceeded six moons. My father loved me, and he taught me part of what he knew in the moments of his leisure. I assisted him in his trade, but he took me not with him in his journeys. We had a shop at Jerusalem, even a shop of commerce, where we sold the goods of the Nazarene, and my mother and myself, and even a little sister who was born shortly after our arrival at Jerusalem, all assisted my father in his commerce. At length it came to pass, that on a particular time he told us that he was going on a journey, and he embraced us and bade us farewell, and he departed, whilst we continued at Jerusalem attending to the business. We awaited his return, but months passed, even six months, and he came not, and we wondered; and months passed, even other six passed, but still he came not, nor did we hear any tidings of him, and our hearts were filled with heaviness and sorrow. But when years, even two years, were expired, I said to my mother, 'I will go and seek my father;' and she said, 'Do so,' and she gave me her blessing, and I kissed my little sister, and I went forth as far as Egypt, and there I heard tidings of my father, for people told me he had been there, and they named the time, and they said that he had passed from thence to the land of the Turk; so I myself followed to the land of the Turk, even unto Constantinople. And when I arrived there I again heard of my father, for he was well known amongst the Jews, and they told me the time of his being there, and they added that he had speculated and prospered, and departed from Constantinople, but whither he went they knew not. So I reasoned within myself and said, perhaps he may have gone to the land of his fathers, even unto Galatia, to visit his kindred; so I determined to go there myself, and I went, and I found our kindred, and I made myself known to them, and they rejoiced to see me: but when I asked them for my father, they shook their heads and could give me no intelligence; and they would fain have had me tarry with them, but I would not, for the thought of my father was working strong within me,

and I could not rest. So I departed and went to another country, even unto Russia, and I went deep into that country, even as far as Kazan, and of all I met, whether Jew, or Russ, or Tartar, I enquired for my father: but no one knew him, nor had heard of him. So I turned back and here thou seest me; and I now purpose going through all Germany and France, nay, through all the world, until I have received intelligence of my father, for I cannot rest until I know what is become of my father, for the thought of him burneth in my brain like fire, even like the fire of Jehinnim.

Such was the individual whom I now saw again, after a lapse of five years, in the street of Gibraltar, in the dusk of the evening. "Yes," he replied, "I am Judah, surnamed the Lib. Thou didst not recognise me, but I knew thee at once. I should have known thee amongst a million, and not a day has passed since I last saw thee, but I have thought on thee." I was about to reply, but he pulled me out of the crowd, and led me into a shop where, squatted on the floor, sat six or seven Jews cutting leather; he said something to them which I did not understand, whereupon they bowed their heads and followed their occupation without taking any notice of us. A singular figure had followed us to the door; it was a man dressed in exceedingly shabby European garments, which exhibited nevertheless the cut of a fashionable tailor. He seemed about fifty; his face, which was very broad, was of a deep bronze colour; the features were rugged but exceedingly manly, and, notwithstanding they were those of a Jew, exhibited no marks of cunning, but on the contrary, much simplicity and good nature. His form was above the middle height and tremendously athletic, the arms and back were literally those of a Hercules squeezed into a modern surtout; the lower part of his face was covered with a bushy beard, which depended half way down his breast. This figure remained at the door, his eyes fixed upon myself and Judah.

The first enquiry which I now addressed was, "Have you heard of your father?"

"I have," he replied. "When we parted, I proceeded through many lands, and wherever I went I inquired of the people respecting my father, but still they shook their heads, until I arrived at the land of Tunis; and there I went to the head rabbi, and he told me that he knew my father well, and that he had been there, even at Tunis, and he named the time, and he said that from thence he departed for the land of Fez; and he spoke much of my father and of his learning, and he mentioned the Zohar, even that dark book which my father loved so well; and he spoke yet more of my father's wealth and his speculations, in all of which it seems he had thriven. So I departed and I mounted a ship, and I went into the land of Barbary, even unto Fez, and when I arrived there I heard much intelligence of my father, but it was intelligence which per-

---

* A Rabbinical book, very difficult to be understood, though written avowedly for the purpose of elucidating many points connected with the religious ceremonies of the Hebrews.

haps was worse than ignorance. For the Jews told me that my father had been there, and had speculated and had thriven, and that from thence he departed for Tafilaltz, which is the country of which the Emperor, even Muley Abderrahman, is a native; and there he was still prosperous, and his wealth in gold and silver was very great; and he wished to go to a not far distant town, and he engaged certain Moors, two in number, to accompany him and defend him and his treasures; and the Moors were strong men, even makhasniah or soldiers; and they made a covenant with my father, and they gave him their right hands, and they swore to spill their blood rather than his should be shed. And my father was encouraged, and he waxed bold, and he departed with them, even with the two false Moors. And when they arrived in the uninhabited place, they smote my father, and they prevailed against him, and they poured out his blood in the way, and they robbed him of all he had, of his silks and his merchandize, and of the gold and silver which he had made in his speculations, and they went to their own village, and there they sat themselves down and bought lands and houses, and they rejoiced and they triumphed, and they made a merit of their deed, saying : ' We have killed an infidel, even an accursed Jew ;' and these things were notorious in Fez. And when I heard these tidings my heart was sad, and I became like a child, and I wept; but the fire of Jehinnim burned no longer in my brain, for I now knew what was become of my father. At last I took comfort and I reasoned with myself, saying, ' Would it not be wise to go unto the Moorish king and demand of him vengeance for my father's death, and that the spoilers be despoiled, and the treasure, even my father's treasure, be wrested from their hands and delivered up to me who am his son?' And the king of the Moors was not at that time in Fez, but was absent in his wars; and I arose and followed him, even unto Arbat, which is a seaport, and when I arrived there, lo! I found him not, but his son was there, and men said unto me, that to speak unto the son was to speak unto the king, even Muley Abderrahman; so I went in unto the king's son, and I kneeled before him, and I lifted up my voice and I said unto him what I had to say, and he looked courteously upon me and said, ' Truly thy tale is a sorrowful one, and it maketh me sad : and what thou askest that will I grant, and thy father's death shall be avenged, and the spoilers shall be despoiled; and I will write thee a letter with my own hand unto the Pasha, even the Pasha of Tafilaltz, and I will enjoin him to make inquiry into thy matter, and the letter thou shalt thyself carry and deliver unto him.' And when I heard these words, my heart died within my bosom for very fear, and I replied, ' Not so, my lord ; it is good that thou write a letter unto the Pasha, even unto the Pasha of Tafilaltz, but that letter will I not take,

neither will I go to Tafilaltz, for no sooner should I arrive there and my errand be known, than the Moors would arise and put me to death, either privily or publicly, for are not the murderers of my father Moors; and am I aught but a Jew, though I be a Polish man ?' And he looked benignantly, and he said, ' Truly, thou speakest wisely; I will write the letter, but thou shalt not take it, for I will send it by other hands; therefore set thy heart at rest, and doubt not that, if thy tale be true, thy father's death shall be avenged, and the treasure, or the value thereof, be recovered and given up to thee; tell me, therefore, where wilt thou abide till then?' And I said unto him, ' My lord, I will go into the land of Suz and will tarry there.' And he replied : ' Do so, and thou shalt hear speedily from me.' So I arose and departed and went into the land of Suz, even unto Sweerah, which the Nazarenes call Mogadore; and I waited with a troubled heart for intelligence from the son of the Moorish king, but no intelligence came, and never since that day have I heard from him, and it is now three years since I was in his presence. And I sat me down at Mogadore, and I married a wife, a daughter of our nation, and I wrote to my mother, even to Jerusalem, and she sent me money, and with that I entered into commerce, even as my father had done, and I speculated, and I was not successful in my speculations, and I speedily lost all I had. And now I am come to Gibraltar to speculate on the account of another, a merchant of Mogadore, but I like not my occupation, he has deceived me; I am going back, when I shall again seek the presence of the Moorish king and demand that the treasure of my father be taken from the spoilers and delivered up to me, even to me his son."

I listened with mute attention to the singular tale of this singular man, and when he had concluded I remained a considerable time without saying a word; at last he inquired what had brought me to Gibraltar. I told him I was merely a passer through on my way to Tangier, for which place I expected to sail the following morning. Whereupon he observed, that in the course of a week-or two he expected to be there also, when he hoped that we should meet, as he had much more to tell me. "And peradventure," he added, " you can afford me counsel which will be profitable, for you are a person of experience, versed in the ways of many nations; and when I look in your countenance, heaven seems to open to me, for I think I see the countenance of a friend, even of a brother." He then bade me farewell, and departed; the strange bearded man, who during our conversation had remained patiently waiting at the door, followed him. I remarked that there was less wildness in his look than on the former occasion, but, at the same time, more melancholy, and his features were wrinkled like those of an aged man, though he had not yet passed the prime of youth.

CHAPTER LIII.

Genoese Mariners—Saint Michael's Cave—Midnight Abysses—Young American—A Slave Proprietor—The Fairy Man—Infidelity.

THROUGHOUT the whole of that night it blew very hard, but as the wind was in the Levant quarter, I had no apprehension of being detained longer at Gibraltar on that account. I went on board the vessel at an early hour, when I found the crew engaged in hauling the anchor close, and making other preparations for sailing. They informed me that we should probably start in an hour. That time however passed, and we still remained where we were, and the captain continued on shore. We formed one of a small flotilla of Genoese barks, the crew of which seemed in their leisure moments to have no better means of amusing themselves than the exchange of abusive language: a furious fusillade of this kind presently commenced, in which the mate of our vessel particularly distinguished himself; he was a grey-haired Genoese of sixty. Though not able to speak their patois, I understood much of what was said; it was truly shocking, and as they shouted it forth, judging from their violent gestures and distorted features, you would have concluded them to be bitter enemies; they were, however, nothing of the kind, but excellent friends all the time, and indeed very good-humoured fellows at bottom. Oh, the infirmities of human nature! When will man learn to become truly Christian?

I am upon the whole very fond of the Genoese; they have, it is true, much ribaldry and many vices, but they are a brave and chivalrous people, and have ever been so, and from them I have never experienced aught but kindness and hospitality.

After the lapse of another two hours, the Jew secretary arrived and said something to the old mate, who grumbled much; then coming up to me, he took off his hat and informed me that we were not to start that day, saying at the same time that it was a shame to lose such a noble wind, which would carry us to Tangier in three hours. "Patience" said I, and went on shore.

I now strolled towards Saint Michael's cave, in company with the Jewish lad whom I have before mentioned.

The way thither does not lie in the same direction as that which leads to the excavations; these confront Spain, whilst the cave yawns in the face of Africa. It lies nearly at the top of the mountain, several hundred yards above the sea. We passed by the public walks, where there are noble trees, and also by many small houses, situated delightfully in gardens, and occupied by the officers of the garrison. It is wrong to suppose Gibraltar a mere naked barren rock; it is not without its beautiful spots—spots such as these, looking cool and refreshing, with bright green foliage. The path soon became very steep, and we left behind us the dwellings of man. The gale of the preceding night had entirely ceased, and not a breath of air was stirring; the midday sun shone in all its fierce glory, and the crags up which we clambered were not unfrequently watered with the perspiration drops which rained from our temples: at length we arrived at the cavern.

The mouth is a yawning cleft in the side of the mountain, about twelve feet high and as many wide; within there is a very rapid precipitous descent for some fifty yards, where the cavern terminates in an abyss which leads to unknown depths. The most remarkable object is a natural column, which rises up something like the trunk of an enormous oak, as if for the purpose of supporting the roof; it stands at a short distance from the entrance, and gives a certain air of wildness and singularity to that part of the cavern which is visible which it would otherwise not possess. The floor is exceedingly slippery, consisting of soil which the continual drippings from the roof have saturated, so that no slight precaution is necessary for him who treads it. It is very dangerous to enter this place without a guide well acquainted with it, as, besides the black pit at the extremity, holes which have never been fathomed present themselves here and there, falling into which the adventurer would be dashed to pieces. Whatever men may please to say of this cave, one thing it seems to tell to all who approach it, namely, that the hand of man has never been busy about it; there is many a cave of nature's forming, old as the earth on which we exist, which nevertheless exhibits indications that man has turned it to some account, and that it has been subjected more or less to his modifying power; not so this cave of Gibraltar, for, judging from its appearance, there is not the slightest reason for supposing that it ever served for aught else than a den for foul night birds, reptiles, and beasts of prey. It has been stated by some to have been used in the days of paganism as a temple to the god Hercules, who, according to the ancient tradition, raised the singular mass of crags now called Gibraltar, and the mountain which confronts it on the African shores, as columns which should say to all succeeding times that he had been there, and had advanced no farther. Sufficient to observe, that there is nothing within the cave which would authorize the adoption of such an opinion, not even a platform on which an altar could have stood, whilst a narrow path passes before it, leading to the summit of the mountain. As I have myself never penetrated into its depths, I can of course, not pretend to describe them. Numerous have been the individuals who, instigated by curiosity, have ventured down to immense depths, hoping to discover an end, and indeed scarcely a week passes without similar attempts being made either by the officers or soldiers of the garrison, all of which have proved perfectly abortive. No termination has ever been reached, nor any discoveries made to repay the labour and frightful danger incurred; precipice succeeds precipice, and abyss succeeds abyss, in apparently endless succession, with ledges at intervals, which afford the adventurers opportunities for resting themselves and affixing their rope-ladders for the purpose of descending yet farther. What is, however, most mortifying and perplexing, is to observe that these abysses are not only before, but behind you, and on every side; indeed, close within the entrance of the cave, on the right, there is a gulf almost equally dark and full as threatening as that which exists at the nether end, and perhaps contains within itself as many gulfs and horrid caverns branching off in all directions. Indeed, from what I have heard, I have come to the opinion that the whole hill of Gibraltar is honeycombed, and I have little doubt that, were it cleft asunder, its interior would be found full of such abysses of Erebus as those to which Saint Michael's cave conducts. Many valuable lives are lost every year in these horrible places; and only a few weeks before my visit, two sergeants, brothers, had perished in the gulf on the right hand side of the cave, having, when at a great depth, slipped down a precipice. The body of one of these adventurous men is even now rotting in the bowels of the mountain, preyed upon by its blind and noisome worms; that of his brother was extricated. Immediately after this horrible accident, a gate was placed before the mouth of the cave, to prevent individuals, and especially the reckless soldiers, from indulging in their extravagant curiosity. The lock, however, was speedily forced, and at the period of my arrival the gate swung idly upon its hinges.

As I left the place, I thought that perhaps similar to this was the cave of Horeb, where dwelt Elijah, when he heard the still small voice, after the great and strong wind which rent the mountains and brake in pieces the rocks before the Lord; the cave to the entrance of which he went out and stood with his face wrapped in his mantle, when he heard the voice say unto him, "What doest thou here Elijah?" [1 Kings, xix. 11—13.] And what am I doing here, I inquired of myself as, vexed at my detention, I descended into the town.

That afternoon I dined in the company of a young American, a native of South Carolina. I had frequently seen him before as he had been staying for some time at the inn previous to my arrival at Gibraltar. His appearance was remarkable: he was low of stature, and exceedingly slightly made; his features were pale but well formed; he had a magnificent head of crispy black hair, and as superb a pair of whiskers of the same colour as I ever beheld. He wore a white hat, with broad brim and particularly shallow crown, and was dressed in a light yellow gingham frock striped with black, and ample trousers of calico: in a word, his appearance was altogether queer and singular. On my return from my ramble to the cave, I found that he had himself just descended from the mountain, having since a very early hour been absent exploring its wonders.

A man of the rock asked him how he liked the excavations? "Liked them," said he; "you might just as well ask a person who has just seen the Niagara Falls how he liked them—like is not the word, mister." The heat was suffocating, as it almost invariably is in the town of Gibraltar, where rarely a breath of air is to be felt, as it is sheltered from all winds. This led another individual to inquire of him whether he did not think it exceedingly hot? "Hot, sir," he replied, "not at all: fine cotton gathering weather as a man could wish for. We couldn't beat it in South Carolina, sir." "You live in South Carolina, sir—I hope, sir, you are not a slave proprietor," said the short fat Jewish personage in the snuff-coloured coat, who had offered me the bitters on a previous occasion; "it is a terrible thing to make slaves of poor people, simply because they happen to be black; don't you think so, sir?" "Think so, sir—no, sir, I don't think so—I glory in being a slave proprietor; have four hundred black niggers on my estate—own estate, sir, near Charleston—flog half a dozen of them before breakfast, merely for exercise. Niggers only made to be flogged, sir: try to escape sometimes; set the blood-hounds in their trail, catch them in a twinkling: used to hang themselves formerly: the niggers thought that a sure way to return to their own country and get clear of me: soon put a stop to that: told them that if any more hanged themselves I'd hang myself too, follow close behind them, and flog them in their own country ten times worse than in mine. What do you think of that, friend?" It was easy to perceive that there was more of fun than malice in this eccentric little fellow, for his large grey eyes were sparkling with good humour whilst he poured out these wild things. He was exceedingly free of his money; and a dirty Irish woman, a soldier's wife, having entered with a basketful of small boxes and trinkets, made of portions of the rock of Gibraltar, he purchased the greatest part of her wares, giving her for every article the price (by no means inconsiderable) which she demanded. He had glanced at me several times, and at last I saw him stoop down and whisper something to the Jew, who replied in an under tone, though with considerable earnestness, "O dear no, sir; perfectly mistaken, sir: is no American, sir:—from Salamanca, sir; the gentleman is a Salamancan Spaniard." The waiter at length informed us that he had laid the table, and that perhaps it would be agreeable to us to dine together: we instantly assented. I found my new acquaintance in many respects a most agreeable companion: he soon told me his history. He was a planter, and, from what he hinted, just come to his property. He was part owner of a large vessel which traded between Charleston and Gibraltar, and the yellow fever having just broken out at the former place, he had determined to take a trip [his first] to Europe in this ship; having, as he said, already visited every state in the Union, and seen all that was to be seen there. He described to me, in a very naïve and original manner, his sensations on passing by Tarifa, which was the first walled town he had ever seen. I related to him the history of that place, to which he listened with great attention. He made divers attempts to learn from me who I was; all of which I evaded, though he seemed fully convinced that I was an American; and amongst other things asked me whether my father had not been American consul at Seville. What, however, most perplexed him was my understanding Moorish and Gaelic; which he had heard me speak respectively to the hamálos and the Irish woman, the latter of whom, as he said, had told him that I was a fairy man. At last he introduced the subject of religion, and spoke with much contempt of revelation, avowing himself a deist: he was evidently very anxious to hear my opinion, but here again I evaded him, and contented myself with asking him, whether he had ever read the Bible. He said he had not; but that he was well acquainted with the writings of Volney and Mirabeau. I made no answer; whereupon he added, that it was by no means his habit to introduce such subjects, and that there were, very few persons to whom he would speak so unreservedly, but that I had very much interested him, though our acquaintance had been short. I replied, that he would scarcely have spoken at Boston in the manner that I had just heard him, and that it was easy to perceive that he was not a New Englander. "I assure you," said he, "I should as little have thought of speaking so at Charleston, for if I held such conversation there, I should soon have had to speak to myself."

Had I known less of deists than it has been my fortune to know, I should perhaps have endeavoured to convince this young man of the erroneousness of the ideas which he had adopted; but I was aware of all that he would have urged in reply, and as the believer has no carnal arguments to address to carnal reason upon this subject, I thought it best to avoid disputation, which I felt sure would lead to no profitable result. Faith is the free gift of God, and I do not believe that ever yet was an infidel converted by means of after-dinner polemics. This was the last evening of my sojourn in Gibraltar.

CHAPTER LIV.

Again on Board—The Strange Visage—The Hadji—Setting Sail—The Two Jews—American Vessel—Tangier—Adun Oulem—The Struggle—The Forbidden Thing.

On Thursday, the 8th of August, I was again on board the Genoese bark, at as early an hour as on the previous morning. After waiting, however, two or three hours without any preparation being made for departing, I was about to return to the shore once more, but the old Genoese mate advised me to stay, assuring me that he had no doubt of our sailing speedily, as all the cargo was on board, and we had nothing further to detain us. I was reposing myself in the little cabin, when I heard a boat strike against the side of the vessel, and some people come on board. Presently a face peered in at the opening, strange and wild. I was half asleep, and at first imagined I was dreaming, for the face seemed more like that of a goat or an ogre than of a human being; its long beard almost touching my face as I lay extended in a kind of berth. Starting up, however, I recognised the singular looking Jew whom I had seen in the company of Judah Lib. He recognised me also, and nodding, bent his huge features into a smile. I arose and went upon deck, where I found him in company with another Jew, a young man in the dress of Barbary. They had just arrived in the boat. I asked my friend of the beard who he was, from whence he came, and where he was going? He answered, in broken Portuguese, that he was returning from Lisbon, where he had been on business, to Mogadore, of which place he was a native. He then looked me in the face and smiled, and taking out a book from his pocket, in Hebrew characters, fell to reading it; whereupon a Spanish sailor on board observed, that with such a beard and book he must needs be a sabio, or sage. His companion was from Mequinez, and spoke only Arabic.

A large boat now drew nigh, the stern of which was filled with Moors; there might be about twelve, and the greater part evidently consisted of persons of distinction, as they were dressed in all the pomp and gallantry of the East, with snow white turbans, jabadores of green silk or scarlet cloth, and bedeyas rich with gold galloon. Some of them were exceedingly fine men, and two amongst them, youths, were strikingly handsome, and so far from exhibiting the dark swarthy countenance of Moors in general, their complexions were of a delicate red and white. The principal personage, and to whom all the rest paid much deference, was a tall athletic man of about forty. He wore a vest of white quilted cotton, and white kandrisa, whilst, gracefully wound round his body, and swathing the upper part of his head, was the haik, or white flannel wrapping plaid, always held in so much estimation by the Moors from the earliest period of their history. His legs were bare, and his feet only protected from the ground by yellow slippers. He displayed no farther ornament than one large gold ear-ring, from which depended a pearl, evidently of great price. A noble black beard, about a foot in length, touched his muscular breast. His features were good, with the exception of the eyes, which were somewhat small; their expression, however, was evil; their glances were sullen; and malignity and ill-nature were painted in every lineament of his countenance, which seemed never to have been brightened with a smile. The Spanish sailor, of whom I have already had occasion to speak, informed me, in a whisper, that he was a santurun, or big saint, and was so far back on his way from Mecca; adding, that he was a merchant of immense wealth. It soon appeared that the other Moors had merely attended him on board through friendly politeness, as they all successively came to bid him adieu, with the exception of two blacks, who were his attendants. I observed that these blacks, when the Moors presented them their hands at departing, invariably made an effort to press them to their lips, which effort was as uniformly foiled, the Moors in every instance, by a speedy and graceful movement, drawing back their hand locked in that of the black, which they pressed against their own heart; as much as to say, "though a negro and a slave you are a Moslem, and being so, you are our brother—Allah knows no distinctions." The boatman now went up to the hadji, demanding payment, stating, at the same time, that he had been on board three times on his account, conveying his luggage. The sum which he demanded appeared exorbitant to the hadji, who, forgetting that he was a saint, and fresh from Mecca, fumed outrageously, and in broken Spanish called the boatman thief. If there be any term of reproach which stings a Spaniard (and such was the boatman) more than another, it is that one; and the fellow no sooner heard it applied to himself, than with eyes sparkling with fury, he put his fist to the hadji's nose, and repaid the one opprobrious name by at least ten others equally bad or worse. He would perhaps have proceeded

to acts of violence had he not been pulled away by the other Moors, who led him aside, and I suppose either said or gave him something which pacified him, as he soon got into his boat, and returned with them on shore. The captain now arrived with his Jewish secretary, and orders were given for setting sail.

At a little past twelve we were steering out of the bay of Gibraltar; the wind was in the right quarter, but for some time we did not make much progress, lying almost becalmed beneath the lee of the hill; by degrees, however, our progress became brisker, and in about an hour we found ourselves careering smartly towards Tarifa.

The Jew secretary stood at the helm, and indeed appeared to be the person who commanded the vessel, and who issued out all the necessary orders, which were executed under the superintendence of the old Genoese mate. I now put some questions to the hadji, but he looked at me askance with his sullen eye, pouted with his lip, and remained silent; as much as to say, "speak not to me, I am holier than thou." I found his negroes, however, far more conversable. One of them was old and ugly, the other about twenty, and as well-looking as it is possible for a negro to be. His colour was perfect ebony, his features exceedingly well formed and delicate, with the exception of the lips, which were too full. The shape of his eyes was peculiar; they were rather oblong than round, like those of an Egyptian figure. Their expression was thoughtful and meditative. In every respect he differed from his companion, even in colour, (though both were negroes,) and was evidently a scion of some little known and superior race. As he sat beneath the mast gazing at the sea, I thought he was misplaced, and that he would have appeared to more advantage amidst boundless sands, and beneath a date tree, and then he might have well represented a Jhin. I asked him from whence he came, he replied that he was a native of Fez, but that he had never known his parents. He had been brought up he added, in the family of his present master, whom he had followed in the greater part of his travels, and with whom he had thrice visited Mecca. I asked him if he liked being a slave? Whereupon he replied, that he was a slave no longer, having been made free for some time past, on account of his faithful services, as had likewise his companion. He would have told me much more, but the hadji called him away, and otherwise employed him, probably to prevent his being contaminated by me.

Thus avoided by the Moslems, I betook myself to the Jews, whom I found nowise backward in cultivating an intimacy. The sage of the beard told me his history, which in some respects reminded me of that of Judah Lib, as it seemed that, a year or two previous, he had quitted Mogadore in pursuit of his son, who had betaken himself to Portugal. On the arrival, however, of the father at Lisbon, he discovered that the fugitive had, a few days before, shipped himself for the Brazils. Unlike Judah in quest of his father, he now became weary, and discontinued the pursuit. The younger Jew from Mequinez was exceedingly gay and lively as soon as he perceived that I was capable of understanding him, and made me smile by his humorous account of Christian life, as he had observed it at Gibraltar, where he had made a stay of about a month. He then spoke of Mequinez, which, he said, was a Jennut, or paradise, compared with which Gibraltar was a sty of hogs. So great, so universal is the love of country. I soon saw that both these people believed me to be of their own nation: indeed, the young one, who was much the most familiar, taxed me with being so, and spoke of the infamy of denying my own blood. Shortly before our arrival off Tarifa, universal hunger seemed to prevail amongst us. The hadji and his negroes produced their store, and feasted on roast fowls, the Jews ate grapes and bread, myself bread and cheese, whilst the crew prepared a mess of anchovies. Two of them speedily came with a large portion, which they presented to me with the kindness of brothers: I made no hesitation in accepting their present, and found the anchovies delicious. As I sat between the Jews, I offered them some, but they turned away their heads with disgust, and cried *haloof* (hogsflesh.) They at the same time, however, shook me by the hand, and, uninvited, took a small portion of my bread. I had a bottle of Cognac, which I had brought with me as a preventative to sea sickness, and I presented it to them; but this they also refused, exclaiming, *Harám*, (it is forbidden.) I said nothing.

We were now close to the lighthouse of Tarifa, and turning the head of the bark towards the west, we made directly for the coast of Africa. The wind was now blowing very fresh, and as we had it almost in our poop, we sprang along at a tremendous rate, the huge latine sails threatening every moment to drive us beneath the billows, which an adverse tide raised up against us. Whilst scudding along in this manner, we passed close under the stern of a large vessel bearing American colours; she was tacking up the straits, and slowly winning her way against the impetuous Levant. As we passed under her, I observed the poop crowded with people gazing at us; indeed, we must have offered a singular spectacle to those on board, who, like my young American friend at Gibraltar, were visiting the Old World for the first time. At the helm stood the Jew; his whole figure enveloped in a gabardine, the cowl of which, raised above his head, gave him almost the appearance of a spectre in its shroud; whilst upon the deck, mixed with Europeans in various kinds of dresses, all of them picturesque with the exception of my own, trod the turbaned Moors, the haik of the hadji flapping loosely in the wind. The view they obtained of us, however, could have been but momentary, as we bounded past them literally with the speed of a racehorse, so that in about an hour's time we were not more than a mile's distance

from the foreland on which stands the fortress Alminar, and which constitutes the boundary point of the bay of Tangier towards the east. There the wind dropped and our progress was again slow.

For a considerable time Tangier had appeared in sight. Shortly after standing away from Tarifa, we had descried it in the far distance, when it showed like a white dove brooding on its nest. The sun was setting behind the town when we dropped anchor in its harbour, amidst half a dozen barks and felouks about the size of our own, the only vessels which we saw. There stood Tangier before us, and a picturesque town it was, occupying the sides and top of two hills, one of which, bold and bluff, projects into the sea where the coast takes a sudden and abrupt turn. Frowning and battlemented were its walls, either perched on the top of precipitous rocks, whose base was washed by the salt billows, or rising from the narrow strand which separates the hill from the ocean.

Yonder are two or three tiers of batteries, displaying heavy guns, which command the harbour; above them you see the terraces of the town rising in succession like steps for giants. But all is white, perfectly white, so that the whole seems cut out of an immense chalk rock, though true it is that you behold here and there tall green trees springing up from amidst the whiteness : perhaps they belong to Moorish gardens, and beneath them even now peradventure is reclining many a dark-eyed Leila, akin to the houries. Right before you is a high tower or minaret, not white but curiously painted, which belongs to the principal mosque of Tangier; a black banner waves upon it, for it is the feast of Ashor. A noble beach of white sand fringes the bay from the town to the foreland of Alminar. To the east rise prodigious hills and mountains; they are Gibil Muza and his chain; and yon tall fellow is the peak of Tetuan; the gray mists of evening are enveloping their sides. Such was Tangier, such its vicinity, as it appeared to me whilst gazing from the Genoese bark.

A boat was now lowered from the vessel, in which the captain, who was charged with the mail from Gibraltar, the Jew secretary, and the hadji and his attendant negroes departed for the shore. I would have gone with them, but I was told that I could not land that night, as ere my passport and bill of health could be examined, the gates would be closed; so I remained on board with the crew and the two Jews. The former prepared their supper, which consisted simply of pickled tomates, the other provisions having been consumed. The old Genoese brought me a portion, apologizing at the same time for the plainness of the fare. I accepted it with thanks, and told him that a million better men than myself had a worse supper. I never ate with more appetite. As the night advanced, the Jews sang Hebrew hymns, and when they had concluded, demanded of me why I was silent, so I lifted up my voice and chanted Aden Oulem :—

"Reigned the universe's Master, ere were earthly
  things begun ;
When his mandate all created Ruler was the
  name he won ;
And alone He 'll rule tremendous when all
  things are past and gone,
He no equal has, nor consort, He, the singular
  and lone,
Has no end and no beginning ; His the sceptre,
  might and throne.
He 's my God and living Saviour, rock to whom
  in need I run ;
He 's my banner and my refuge, fount of weal
  when call'd upon ;
In His hand I place my spirit at nightfall and
  rise of sun,
And therewith my body also ; God's my God
  —I fear no one."

Darkness had now fallen over land and sea;
not a sound was heard save occasionally the
distant barking of a dog from the shore, or
some plaintive Genoese ditty, which arose
from a neighbouring bark. The town seemed
buried in silence and gloom, no light, not even
that of a taper, could be descried. Turning
our eyes in the direction of Spain, however,
we perceived a magnificent conflagration,
seemingly enveloping the side and head of
one of the lofty mountains northward of Tarifa ; the blaze was redly reflected in the waters of the strait: either the brushwood was
burning or the Carboneros were plying their
dusky toil. The Jews now complained of
weariness, and the younger, unearthing a small
mattress, spread it on the deck and sought
repose. The sage descended into the cabin,
but he had scarcely time to lie down ere the
old mate, darting forward, dived in after him,
and pulled him out by the heels, for it was very
shallow, and the descent was effected by not
more than two or three steps. After accom-
plishing this, he called him many opprobrious
names, and threatened him with his foot, as he
lay sprawling on the deck. "Think you,"
said he, " who are a dog and a Jew, and pay
as a dog and a Jew ; think you to sleep in the
cabin ? Undeceive yourself, beast : that cabin
shall be slept in by none to-night but this
Christian Cavaliero." The sage made no
reply, but arose from the deck and stroked his
beard, whilst the old Genoese proceeded in his
philippic. Had the Jew been disposed, he
could have strangled the insulter in a moment,
or crushed him to death in his brawny arms, as I
never remember to have seen a figure so powerful and muscular ; but he was evidently slow to
anger, and long-suffering ; not a resentful word
escaped him, and his features retained their
usual expression of benignant placidity.

I now assured the mate that I had not the
slightest objection to the Jew's sharing the
cabin with me, but rather wished it, as there
was room for us both and for more. "Excuse
me, Sir Cavalier," replied the Genoese, "but
I swear to permit no such thing ; you are
young and do not know this canaille as I do,
who have been backward and forward to this
coast for twenty years ; if the beast is cold, let
him sleep below the hatches as I and the rest
shall, but that cabin he shall not enter." Observing that he was obstinate, I retired, and in

a few minutes was in a sound sleep, which
lasted till daybreak. Twice or thrice indeed
I thought that a struggle was taking place near
me, but I was so overpowered with weariness,
or "sleep drunken," as the Germans call it,
that I was unable to arouse myself sufficiently
to discover what was going on : the truth is,
that three times during the night, the sage,
feeling himself uncomfortable in the open air by
the side of his companion, penetrated into the
cabin, and was as many times dragged out by
his relentless old enemy, who, suspecting his
intentions, kept his eye upon him throughout
the night.

About five I arose : the sun was shining
brightly and gloriously upon town, bay, and
mountain ; the crew were already employed
upon deck repairing a sail which had been
shivered in the wind of the preceding day.
The Jews sat disconsolate on the poop ; they
complained much of the cold they had suffered
in their exposed situation. Over the left eye
of the sage I observed a bloody cut, which he
informed me he had received from the old Genoese after he had dragged him out of the cabin
for the last time. I now produced my bottle
of Cognac, begging that the crew would partake of it as a slight return for their hospitality. They thanked me, and the bottle went
its round ; it was last in the hands of the old
mate, who, after looking for a moment at the
sage, raised it to his mouth, where he kept it
a considerable time longer than any of his
companions, after which he returned it to me
with a low bow. The sage now inquired what
the bottle contained : I told him Cognac or
aguardiente, whereupon with some eagerness
he begged that I would allow him to take a
draught. "How is this ?" said I ; "yesterday you told me that it was a forbidden thing,
an abomination." "Yesterday," said he, "I
was not aware that it was brandy ; I thought
it wine, which assuredly is an abomination,
and a forbidden thing." "Is it forbidden in
the Torah ?" I enquired. "Is it forbidden in
the law of God ?" "I know not," said he,
"but one thing I know, that the sages have
forbidden it !" "Sages like yourself," cried I
with warmth ; "sages like yourself, with long
beards and short understandings : the use of
both drinks is permitted, but more danger lurks
in this bottle than in a tun of wine. Well said
my Lord the Nazarene, 'ye strain at a gnat,
and swallow a camel ;' but as you are cold
and shivering, take the bottle and revive yourself with a small portion of its contents." He
put it to his lips and found not a single drop.
The old Genoese grinned.

"Bestia," said he : "I saw by your looks
that you wished to drink of that bottle, and I
said within me, even though I suffocate, yet
will I not leave one drop of the aguardiente
of the Christian Cavalier to be wasted on that
Jew, on whose head may evil lightnings fall."

"Now, Sir Cavalier," he continued, "you
can go ashore : these two sailors shall row
you to the Mole, and convey your baggage
where you think proper ; may the Virgin bless
you wherever you go."

CHAPTER LVI.

The Mole—The Two Moors—Djmah of Tangier—House of God—The British Consul—Curious Spectacle—The Moorish House—Joanna Correa—Ave Maria.

So we rowed to the Mole and landed. This Mole consists at present of nothing more than an immense number of large loose stones, which run about five hundred yards into the bay; they are part of the ruins of a magnificent pier which the English, who were the last foreign nation which held Tangier, destroyed when they evacuated the place. The Moors have never attempted to repair it; the surf at high water breaks over it with great fury. I found it a difficult task to pick my way over the slippery stones, and should once or twice have fallen, but for the kindness of the Genoese mariners. At last we reached the beach, and were proceeding towards the gate of the town, when two persons, Moors, came up to us. I almost started at sight of the first: he was a huge old barbarian with a white uncombed beard, dirty turban, haik, and trousers, naked legs, and immense splay feet, the heels of which stood out a couple of inches at least behind his rusty black slippers.

"That is the captain of the port," said one of the Genoese; "pay him respect." I accordingly doffed my hat and cried, "Sba alkheir a sidi," (Good morning my lord.) "Are you Englishmans?" shouted the old grisly giant. "Englishmans, my lord," I replied, and, advancing, presented him my hand, which he nearly wrung off with his tremendous gripe. The other Moor now addressed me in a jargon composed of English, Spanish, and Arabic. A queer looking personage was he also, but very different in most respects from his companion, being shorter by a head at least, and less complete by one eye, for the left orb of vision was closed, leaving him, as the Spaniards style it, tuerto; he, however, far outshone the other in cleanliness of turban, haik, and trousers. From what he jabbered to me, I collected that he was the English consul's mahasni or soldier; that the consul, being aware of my arrival, had despatched him to conduct me to his house. He then motioned me to follow him, which I did, the old port captain attending us to the gate, when he turned aside into a building, which I judged to be a kind of custom-house from the bales and boxes of every description piled up before it. We passed the gate and proceeded up a steep and winding ascent; on our left was a battery full of guns, pointing to the sea, and on our right a massive wall, seemingly in part cut out of the hill: a little higher up we arrived at an opening where stood the mosque which I have already mentioned. As I gazed upon the tower I said to myself, "Surely we have here a younger sister of the Giralda of Seville."

I know not whether the resemblance between the two edifices has been observed by any other individual; and perhaps there are those who would assert that no resemblance exists, especially if, in forming an opinion, they were much swayed by size and colour: the hue of the Giralda is red, or rather vermilion, whilst that which predominates in the Djmah of Tangier is green, the bricks of which it is built being of that colour; though between them, at certain intervals, are placed others of a light red tinge, so that the tower is beautifully variegated. With respect to size, standing beside the giant witch of Seville, the Tangerine Djmah would show like a ten year sapling in the vicinity of the cedar of Lebanon, whose trunk the tempests of five hundred years have worn. And yet I will assert that the towers in other respects are one and the same, and that the same mind and the same design are manifested in both; the same shape do they exhibit, and the same marks have they on their walls, even those mysterious arches graven on the superfice of the bricks, emblematic of I know not what. The two structures may, without any violence, be said to stand in the same relation to each other as the ancient and modern Moors. The Giralda is the world's wonder, and the old Moor was all but the world's conqueror. The modern Moor is scarcely known, and who ever heard of the tower of Tangier? Yet examine it attentively, and you will find in that tower much, very much to admire, and certainly if opportunity enable you to consider the modern Moor as minutely, you will discover in him, and in his actions, amongst much that is wild, uncouth, and barbarous, not a little capable of amply rewarding laborious investigation.

As we passed the mosque I stopped for a moment before the door, and looked in upon the interior: I saw nothing but a quadrangular court paved with painted tiles and exposed to the sky; on all sides were arched piazzas, and in the middle was a fountain, at which several Moors were performing their ablutions. I looked around for the abominable thing and found it not; no scarlet strumpet with a crown of false gold sat nursing an ugly changeling in a niche. "Come here," said I, "papist, and take a lesson; here is a house of God, in externals at least, such as a house of God should be: four walls, a fountain, and the eternal firmament above, which mirrors his glory. Dost thou build such houses to the God who has said, 'Thou shalt make to thyself no graven image'? Fool, thy walls are stuck with idols; thou callest a stone thy Father, and a piece of rotting wood the Queen of Heaven. Fool, thou knowest not even the Ancient of Days, and the very Moor can in struct thee. He at least knows the Ancient of Days who has said, 'Thou shalt have no other Gods but me.' "

And as I said these words, I heard a cry like the roaring of a lion, and an awful voice in the distance exclaim, "*Kapul Udbagh*" (there is no God but one).

We now turned to the left through a passage which passed under the tower, and had scarcely proceeded a few steps, when I heard a prodigious hubbub of infantine voices: I listened for a moment, and distinguished verses of the Koran; it was a school. Another lesson for thee, papist. Thou callest thyself a Christian, yet the book of Christ thou persecutest; thou huntest it even to the sea-shore, compelling it to seek refuge upon the billows of the sea. Fool, learn a lesson from the Moor, who teaches his child to repeat with its first accents the most important portions of the book of his law, and considers himself wise or foolish, according as he is versed in or ignorant of that book; whilst thou, blind slave, knowest not what the book of thy own law contains, nor wishest to know: yet art thou not to be judged by thy own law? Idolmonger, learn consistency from the Moor; he says that he shall be judged after his own law, and therefore he prizes and gets by heart the entire book of his law.

We were now at the consul's house, a large roomy habitation, built in the English style. The soldier led me through a court into a large hall hung with the skins of all kinds of ferocious animals, from the kingly lion to the snarling jackall. Here I was received by a Jew domestic, who conducted me at once to the consul, who was in his library. He received me with the utmost frankness and genuine kindness, and informed me that, having received a letter from his excellent friend Mr. B., in which I was strongly recommended, he had already engaged me a lodging in the house of a Spanish woman, who was, however, a British subject, and with whom he believed that I should find myself as comfortable as it was possible to be in such a place as Tangier. He then enquired if I had any particular motive for visiting the place, and I informed him without hesitation that I came with the intention of distributing a certain number of copies of the New Testament in the Spanish language amongst the Christian residents of the place. He smiled, and advised me to proceed with considerable caution, which I promised to do. We then discoursed on other subjects, and it was not long before I perceived that I was in the company of a most accomplished scholar, especially in the Greek and Latin classics; he appeared likewise to be thoroughly acquainted with the Barbary empire and with the Moorish character.

After half an hour's conversation, exceedingly agreeable and instructive to myself, I expressed a wish to proceed to my lodging; whereupon he rung the bell, and the same Jewish domestic entering who had introduced me, he said to him, in the English language, "Take this gentleman to the house of Joanna Correa, the Mahonese widow, and enjoin her, in my name, to take care of him and attend to his comforts; by doing which she will confirm me in the good opinion which I at present entertain of her, and will increase my disposition to befriend her."

So, attended by the Jew, I now bent my steps to the lodging prepared for me. Having ascended the street in which the house of the consul was situated, we entered a small square which stands about half way up the hill. This, my companion informed me, was the *soc*, or market-place. A curious spectacle here presented itself. All round the square were small wooden booths, which very much resembled large boxes turned on their sides, the lid being supported above by a string. Before each of these boxes was a species of counter, or rather one long counter ran in front of the whole line, upon which were raisins, dates, and small barrels of sugar, soap, and butter, and various other articles. Within each box, in front of the counter, and about three feet from the ground, sat a human being, with a blanket on its shoulders, a dirty turban on its head, and ragged trousers, which descended as far as the knee, though in some instances I believe these were entirely dispensed with. In its hand it held a stick, to the end of which was affixed a bunch of palm leaves, which it waved incessantly as a fan, for the purpose of scaring from its goods the million flies which, engendered by the Barbary sun, endeavoured to settle upon them. Behind it, and on either side, were piles of the same kind of goods. *Shrit hinai, shrit hinai*, (buy here, buy here,) was continually proceeding from its mouth. Such are the grocers of Tangier, such their shops.

In the middle of the soc, upon the stones, were pyramids of melons and sandias, (the water species,) and also baskets filled with other kinds of fruit, exposed for sale, whilst round cakes of bread were lying here and there upon the stones, beside which sat on their hams the wildest looking beings that the most extravagant imagination ever conceived, the head covered with an enormous straw hat, at least two yards in circumference, the eaves of which, flapping down, completely concealed the face, whilst the form was swathed in a blanket, from which occasionally were thrust skinny arms and fingers. These were Moorish women, who were, I believe, in all instances, old and ugly, judging from the countenances of which I caught a glimpse as they lifted the eaves of their hats to gaze on me as I passed, or to curse me for stamping on their bread. The whole soc was full of people, and there was abundance of bustle, screaming, and vociferation, and as the sun, though the hour was still early, was shining with the greatest brilliancy, I thought that I had scarcely ever witnessed a livelier scene.

Crossing the soc, we entered a narrow street with the same kind of box-shops on each side, some of which, however, were either unoccupied or not yet opened, the lid being closed. We almost immediately turned to the left, up a street somewhat similar, and my guide presently entered the door of a low house, which stood at the corner of a little alley, and which he informed me was the abode of Joanna Correa. We soon stood in the midst of this habitation. I say the midst, as all the Moorish houses are built with a small court in the middle. This one was not more than ten feet square. It was open at the top, and around it on three sides were apartments; on the fourth a small staircase, which communicated with the upper story, half of which consisted of a terrace looking down into the court, over the low walls of which you enjoyed a prospect of the sea and a considerable part of the town. The rest of the story was taken up by a long room, destined for myself, and which opened upon the terrace by a pair of folding-doors. At either end of this apartment stood a bed, extending transversely from wall to wall, the canopy touching the ceiling. A table and two or three chairs completed the furniture.

I was so occupied in inspecting the house of Joanna Correa, that at first I paid little attention to the lady herself. She now, however, came up upon the terrace where my guide and myself were standing. She was a woman about five and forty, with regular features, which had once been handsome, but had received considerable injury from time, and perhaps more from trouble. Two of her front teeth had disappeared, but she still had fine black hair. As I looked upon her countenance, I said within myself, if there be truth in physiognomy, thou art good and gentle, O Joanna; and, indeed, the kindness I experienced from her during the six weeks which I spent beneath her roof would have made me a convert to that science had I doubted it before. I believe no warmer and more affectionate heart ever beat in human bosom than in that of Joanna Correa, the Mahonese widow, and it was indexed by features beaming with benevolence and good nature, though somewhat clouded with melancholy.

She informed me that she had been married to a Genoese, the master of a felouk which passed between Gibraltar and Tangier, who had been dead about four years, leaving her with a family of four children, the eldest of which was a lad of thirteen; that she had experienced great difficulty in providing for her family and herself since the death of her husband, but that Providence had raised her up a few excellent friends, especially the British consul; that besides letting lodgings to such travellers as myself, she made bread which was in high esteem with the Moors, and that

she was likewise in partnership in the sale of liquors with an old Genoese. She added, that this last person lived below in one of the apartments; that he was a man of great ability and much learning, but that she believed he was occasionally somewhat touched here, pointing with her finger to her forehead, and she therefore hoped that I would not be offended at any thing extraordinary in his language or behaviour. She then left me, as she said, to give orders for my breakfast; whereupon the Jewish domestic, who had accompanied me from the consul, finding that I was established in the house, departed.

I speedily sat down to breakfast in an apartment on the left side of the little wustuddur; the fare was excellent: tea, fried fish, eggs, and grapes, not forgetting the celebrated bread of Joanna Correa. I was waited upon by a tall Jewish youth of about twenty years, who informed me that his name was Haim Ben Atar, that he was a native of Fez, from whence his parents brought him at a very early age to Tangier, where he had passed the greater part of his life principally in the service of Joanna Correa, waiting upon those who, like myself, lodged in the house. I had completed my meal, and was seated in the little court, when I heard in the apartment opposite to that in which I had breakfasted several sighs, which were succeeded by as many groans, and then came "Ave Maria, gratia plena, ora pro me," and finally a croaking voice chanted:—

"Gentem auferte perfidam
Credentium de finibus,
Ut Christo laudes debitas
Persolvamus alacriter."

"That is the old Genoese," whispered Haim Ben Atar, "praying to his God, which he always does with particular devotion when he happens to have gone to bed the preceding evening rather in liquor. He has in his room a picture of Maria Buckra, before which he generally burns a taper, and on her account he will never permit me to enter his apartment. He once caught me looking at her, and I thought he would have killed me, and since then he always keeps his chamber locked, and carries the key in his pocket when he goes out. He hates both Jew and Moor, and says that he is now living amongst them for his sins."

"They do not place tapers before pictures," said I, and strolled forth to see the wonders of the land.

29

CHAPTER LVI.

The Mahasni—Sin Samani—The Bazaar—Moorish Saints—See the Ayana!—The Prickly Fig—Jewish Graves—The place of Carcases—The Stable Boy—Horses of the Moslem—Dar Dwag.

I WAS standing in the market-place, a spectator of much the same scene as I have already described, when a Moor came up to me and attempted to utter a few words in Spanish. He was a tall elderly man, with sharp but rather whimsical features, and might have been called good looking, had he not been one-eyed, a very common deformity in this country. His body was swathed in an immense haik. Finding that I could understand Moorish, he instantly began talking with immense volubility, and I soon learnt that he was a Mahasni. He expatiated diffusely on the beauties of Tangier, of which he said he was a native, and at last exclaimed, " Come, my sultan, come, my lord, and I will show you many things which will gladden your eyes, and fill your heart with sunshine; it were a shame in me to have the advantage of being a son of Tangier, to permit a stranger, who comes from an island in the great sea, as you tell me you do, for the purpose of seeing this blessed land, to stand here in the soc with no one to guide him. By Allah, it shall not be so. Make room for my sultan, make room for my lord," he continued, pushing his way through a crowd of men and children who had gathered round us; " it is his highness' pleasure to go with me. This way, my lord, this way ;" and he led the way up the hill, walking at a tremendous rate and talking still faster. " This street," said he, " is the Siarrin, and its like is not to be found in Tangier ; observe how broad it is, even half the breadth of the soc itself; here are the shops of the most considerable merchants, where are sold precious articles of all kinds. Observe those two men, they are Algerines and good Moslems ; they fled from Zair (*Algiers*) when the Nazarenes conquered it, not by force of fighting, not by valour, as you may well suppose, but by gold; the Nazarenes only conquer by gold. The Moor is good, the Moor is strong, who so good and strong? but he fights not with gold, and therefore he lost Zair.

" Observe you those men seated on the benches by those portals ; they are Mahasnish, they are my brethren. See their haiks how white, see their turbans how white. O that you could see their swords in the day of war, for bright, bright are their swords. Now they bear no swords. Wherefore should they? is there not peace in the land? See you him in the shop opposite? That is the Pasha of Tangier, that is the Hamed Sin Samani, the under Pasha of Tangier; the elder Pasha, my lord, is away on a journey; may Allah send him a safe return. Yes, that is Hamed ; he sits in his hanutz as were he nought more than a merchant, yet life and death are in his hands. There he dispenses justice, even as he dispenses the essence of the rose and cochi-

neal, and powder of cannon and sulphur; and those two last he sells on the account of Abderahman, my lord and sultan, for none can sell powder and the sulphur dust in his land but the sultan. Should you wish to purchase atar del nuar, should you wish to purchase the essence of the rose, you must go to the hanutz of Sin Samani, for there only you will get it pure ; you must receive it from no common Moor, but only from Hamed. May Allah bless Hamed. The Mahasniah, my brethren, wait to do his orders, for wherever sits the Pasha, there is a hall of judgment.— See, now we are opposite the bazaar; beneath yon gate is the court of the bazaar; what will you not find in that bazaar? Silks from Fez you will find there ; and if you wish for sibat, if you wish for slippers for your feet, you must seek them there, and there also are sold curious things from the towns of the Nazarenes. Those large houses on our left are habitations of Nazarene consuls; you have seen many such in your own land, therefore why should you stay to look at them? Do you not admire this street of the Siarrin? Whatever enters or goes out of Tangier by the land passes through this street. Oh, the riches that pass through this street! Behold those camels, what a long train; twenty, thirty, a whole cafila descending the street. Wullah! I know those camels, I know the driver. Good day, O Sidi Hassim, in how many days from Fez? And now we are arrived at the wall, and we must pass under this gate. This gate is called Bab del Faz; we are now in the Soc de Barra."

The Soc de Barra is an open place beyond the upper wall of Tangier, on the side of the hill. The ground is irregular and steep ; there are, however, some tolerably level spots. In this place, every Thursday and Sunday morning, a species of mart is held, on which account it is called Soc de Barra, or the outward market-place. Here and there, near the town ditch, are subterranean pits with small orifices, about the circumference of a chimney, which are generally covered with a large stone, or stuffed with straw. These pits are granaries, in which wheat, barley, and other species of grain intended for sale are stored. On one side are two or three rude huts, or rather sheds, beneath which keep watch the guardians of the corn. It is very dangerous to pass over this hill at night, after the town gates are closed, as at that time numerous large and ferocious dogs are let loose, who would to a certainty pull down, and perhaps destroy, any stranger who should draw nigh. Half way up the hill are seen four white walls, inclosing a spot about ten feet square, where rest the bones of Sidi Mokhfidh, a saint of celebrity, who died some fifteen years ago.

Here terminates the soc; the remainder of the hill is called El Kawar, or the place of graves, being the common burying ground of Tangier; the resting places of the dead are severally distinguished by a few stones arranged so as to form an oblong circle. Near Mokhfidh sleeps Sidi Gali; but the principal saint of Tangier lies interred on the top of the hill, in the centre of a small plain. A beautiful chapel or mosque, with vaulted roof, is erected there in his honour, which is in general adorned with banners of various dyes. The name of this saint is Mohammed el Hadge, and his memory is held in the utmost veneration in Tangier and its vicinity. His death occurred at the commencement of the present century.

These details I either gathered at the time or on subsequent occasions. On the north side of the soc, close by the town, is a wall with a gate. "Come," said the old Mahasni, giving a flourish with his hand; "come, and I will show you the garden of a Nazarene consul." I followed him through the gate, and found myself in a spacious garden, laid out in the European taste, and planted with lemon and pear trees, and various kinds of aromatic shrubs. It was, however, evident that the owner chiefly prided himself on his flowers, of which there were numerous beds. There was a handsome summer-house, and art seemed to have exhausted itself in making the place complete.

One thing was wanting, and its absence was strangely remarkable in a garden at this time of the year; scarcely a leaf was to be seen. The direst of all the plagues which devastated Egypt was now busy in this part of Africa—the locust was at work, and in no place more fiercely than in the particular spot where I was now standing. All around looked blasted. The trees were brown and bald as in winter. Nothing was green save the fruits, especially the grapes, huge clusters of which were depending from the "parras;" for the locust touches not the fruit whilst a single leaf remains to be devoured. As we passed along the walks these horrible insects flew against us in every direction, and perished by hundreds beneath our feet. "See the ayanas," said the old Mahasni, "and hear them eating. Powerful is the ayana, more powerful than the sultan or the consul. Should the sultan send all his mahasniah against the ayana, should he send me with them, the ayana would say, 'Ha! ha!' Powerful is the ayana! He fears not the consul. A few weeks ago the consul said, 'I am stronger than the ayana, and I will extirpate him from the land.' So he shouted through the city, 'O Tangerines! speed forth to fight the ayana,—destroy him in the egg; for know, that whosoever shall bring me one pound weight of the eggs of the ayana, unto him will I give five reals of Spain; there shall be no ayanas this year.' So all Tangier rushed forth to fight the ayana, and to collect the eggs which the ayana had laid to hatch beneath the sand on the sides of the hills, and in the roads, and in the plains. And my

own child, who is seven years old, went forth to fight the ayana, and he alone collected eggs to the weight of five pounds, eggs which the ayana had placed beneath the sand, and he carried them to the consul, and the consul paid the price. And hundreds carried eggs to the consul, more or less, and the consul paid them the price, and in less than three days the treasure chest of the consul was exhausted. And then he cried, 'Desist, O Tangerines! perhaps we have destroyed the ayana, perhaps we have destroyed them all.' Ha! ha! Look around you, and beneath you, and above you, and tell me whether the consul has destroyed the ayana. Oh, powerful is the ayana! More powerful than the consul, more powerful than the sultan and all his armies."

It will be as well to observe here, that within a week from this time all the locusts had disappeared, no one knew how, only a few stragglers remained. But for this providential deliverance, the fields and gardens in the vicinity of Tangier would have been totally devastated. These insects were of an immense size, and of a loathly aspect.

We now passed over the soc to the opposite side, where stand the huts of the guardians. Here a species of lane presents itself, which descends to the sea-shore; it is deep and precipitous, and resembles a gully or ravine. The banks on either side are covered with the tree which bears the prickly fig, called in Moorish, *Kermous del Inde*. There is something wild and grotesque in the appearance of this tree or plant, for I know not which to call it. Its stem, though frequently of the thickness of a man's body, has no head, but divides itself, at a short distance from the ground, into many crooked branches, which shoot in all directions, and bear green and uncouth leaves, about half an inch in thickness, and which, if they resemble any thing, present the appearance of the fore fins of a seal, and consist of multitudinous fibres. The fruit, which somewhat resembles a pear, has a rough tegument covered with minute prickles, which instantly enter the hand which touches them, however slightly, and are very difficult to extract. I never remember to have seen vegetation in ranker luxuriance than that which these fig-trees exhibited, nor upon the whole a more singular spot. "Follow me," said the Mahasni, "and I will show you something which you will like to see." So he turned to the left, leading the way by a narrow path up the steep bank, till we reached the summit of a hillock, separated by a deep ditch from the wall of Tangier. The ground was thickly covered with the trees already described, which spread their strange arms along the surface, and whose thick leaves crushed beneath our feet as we walked along. Amongst them I observed a large number of stone slabs lying horizontally; they were rudely scrawled over with odd characters, which I stooped down to inspect. "Are you Talib enough to read those signs?" exclaimed the old Moor. "They are letters of the accursed Jews; this is their mearrah as they call it, and here they inter their dead. Fools, they trust in Muza, when they might believe in Mohammed, and therefore their dead shall burn everlastingly in Jehinnum. See, my sultan, how fat is the soil of this mearrah of the Jews; see what kermous grow here. When I was a boy I often came to the mearrah of the Jews to eat kermous in the season of their ripeness. The Moslem boys of Tangier love the kermous of the mearrah of the Jews; but the Jews will not gather them. They say that the waters of the springs which nourish the roots of these trees pass among the bodies of their dead, and for that reason it is an abomination to taste of these fruits. Be this true, or be it not, one thing is certain, in whatever manner nourished, good are the kermous which grow in the mearrah of the Jews."

We returned to the lane by the same path by which we had come: as we were descending it he said, "Know, my sultan, that the name of the place where we now are, and which you say you like much, is Dar Sinah *(the house of the trades.)* You will ask me why it bears that name, as you see neither house nor man, neither Moslem, Nazarene, nor Jew, only our two selves; I will tell you, my sultan, for who can tell you better than myself? Learn, I pray you, that Tangier was not always what it is now, nor did it occupy always the place which it does now. It stood yonder (pointing to the east) on those hills above the shore, and ruins of houses are still to be seen there, and the spot is called Old Tangier. So in the old time, as I have heard say, this Dar Sinah was a street, whether without or within the wall matters not, and there resided men of all trades; smiths of gold, and silver, and iron, and tin, and artificers of all kinds: you had only to go to the Dar Sinah if you wished for any thing wrought, and there instantly you would find a master of the particular craft. My sultan tells me he likes the look of Dar Sinah at the present day, truly I know not why, especially as the kermous are not yet in their ripeness, nor fit to eat. If he likes Dar Sinah now, how would my sultan have liked it in the old time, when it was filled with gold and silver, and iron and tin, and was noisy with the hammers, and the masters and the cunning men! We are now arrived at the Chali del Bahar *(sea-shore.)* Take care, my sultan, we tread upon bones."

We had emerged from the Dar Sinah, and the sea-shore was before us; on a sudden we found ourselves amongst a multitude of bones of all kinds of animals, and seemingly of all dates; some being blanched with time and exposure to sun and wind, whilst to others the flesh still partly clung; whole carcases were here, horses, asses, and even the uncouth remains of a camel. Gaunt dogs were busy here, growling, tearing, and gnawing; amongst whom, unintimidated, stalked the carrion vulture, fiercely battening and even disputing with the brutes the garbage; whilst the crow hovered overhead, and croaked wistfully, or occasionally perched upon some upturned rib bone. "See," said the Mahasni, "the kawar

of the animals. My sultan has seen the kawar of the Moslems and the mearrah of the Jews; and he sees here the kawar of the animals. All the animals which die in Tangier by the hand of God, horse, dog, or camel, are brought to this spot, and here they putrefy or are devoured by the birds of the heaven or the wild creatures that prowl on the chali. Come, my sultan, it is not good to remain long in this place."

We were preparing to leave the spot, when we heard a galloping down the Dar Sinah, and presently a horse and rider darted at full speed from the mouth of the lane and appeared upon the strand: the horseman, when he saw us, pulled up his steed with much difficulty, and joined us. The horse was small, but beautiful, a sorrel with long mane and tail; had he been hoodwinked he might perhaps have been mistaken for a Cordovese jaca; he was broad-chested, and rotund in his hind quarters, and possessed much of the plumpness and sleekness which distinguish that breed, but looking in his eyes you would have been undeceived in a moment; a wild savage fire darted from the restless orbs, and so far from exhibiting the docility of the other noble and loyal animal, he occasionally plunged desperately, and could scarcely be restrained by a strong curb and powerful arm from resuming his former headlong course. The rider was a youth, apparently about eighteen, dressed as a European, with a Montero cap on his head; he was athletically built, but with lengthy limbs, his feet, for he rode without stirrups or saddle, reached almost to the ground; his complexion was almost as dark as that of a Mulatto; his features very handsome, the eyes particularly so, but filled with an expression that was bold and bad; and there was a disgusting look of sensuality about the mouth. He addressed a few words to the Mahasni, with whom he seemed to be well acquainted, inquiring who I was. The old man answered, "O Jew, my sultan understands our speech, thou hadst better address thyself to him." The lad then spoke to me in Arabic, but almost instantly dropping that language, proceeded to discourse in tolerable French. "I suppose you are French," said he with much familiarity; "shall you stay long in Tangier?" Having received an answer, he proceeded, "As you are an Englishman, you are doubtless fond of horses, know, therefore, whenever you are disposed for a ride, I will accompany you and procure you horses. My name is Ephraim Fragey: I am stable-boy to the Neapolitan consul, who prizes himself upon possessing the best horses in Tangier; you shall mount any you please. Would you like to try this little aoud *(stallion?")* I thanked him, but declined his offer for the present, asking him at the same time how he had acquired the French language, and why he, a Jew, did not appear in the dress of his brethren? "I am in the service of a consul," said he, "and my master obtained permission that I might dress myself in this manner; and as to speaking French, I have been to Marseilles and Naples, to which last place I conveyed horses, presents from the Sultan. Besides French, I can speak Italian. He then dismounted, and holding the horse firmly by the bridle with one hand, proceeded to undress himself, which having accomplished, he mounted the animal and rode into the water. The skin of his body was much akin in colour to that of a frog or toad, but the frame was that of a young Titan. The horse took to the water with great unwillingness, and at a small distance from the shore commenced struggling with his rider, whom he twice dashed from his back, the lad, however, clung to the bridle, and detained the animal. All his efforts, however, being unavailing to ride him deeper in, he fell to washing him strenuously with his hands, then leading him out, he dressed himself and returned by the way he came.

"Good are the horses of the Moslems," said my old friend, where will you find such? They will descend rocky mountains at full speed and neither trip nor fall; but you must be cautious with the horses of the Moslems, and treat them with kindness, for the horses of the Moslems are proud, and they like not being slaves. When they are young and first mounted, jerk not their mouths with your bit, for be sure if you do they will kill you; sooner or later you will perish beneath their feet. Good are our horses, and good our riders, yea, very good are the Moslems at mounting the horse; who are like them? I once saw a Frank rider compete with a Moslem on this beach, and at first the Frank rider had it all his own way, and he passed the Moslem, but the course was long, very long, and the horse of the Frank rider, which was a Frank also, panted; but the horse of the Moslem panted not, for he was a Moslem also, and the Moslem rider at last gave a cry and the horse sprang forward and he overtook the Frank horse, and then the Moslem rider stood up in his saddle. How did he stand? Truly he stood on his head, and these eyes saw him; he stood on his head in the saddle as he passed the Frank rider; and he cried ha! ha! as he passed the Frank rider; and the Moslem horse cried ha! ha! as he passed the Frank breed, and the Frank lost by a far distance. Good are the Franks; good their horses; but better are the Moslems, and better the horses of the Moslems."

We now directed our steps towards the town, but not by the path we came: turning to the left under the hill of the mearrah, and along the strand, we soon came to a rudely paved way with a steep ascent, which wound beneath the wall of the town to a gate, before which, on one side, were various little pits like graves, filled with water or lime. "This is Dar Dwag," said the Mahasni; "this is the house of the bark, and to this house are brought the hides; all those which are prepared for use in Tangier are brought to this house, and here they are cured with lime, and bran, and bark, and herbs. And in this Dar Dwag there are one hundred and forty pits; I have counted them myself; and there were more which have now ceased to be, for the place is very ancient. And these pits are hired not by one, nor by two, but by many people, and whosoever list can rent one of these pits and cure the hides which he may need; but the owner of all is one man, and his name is Cado Ableque. And now my sultan has seen the house of the bark, and I will shew him nothing more this day; for to-day is Youm al Jumal (Friday), and the gates will be presently shut whilst the moslems perform their devotions. So I will accompany my sultan to the guest house, and there I will leave him for the present."

We accordingly passed through a gate, and ascending a street found ourselves before the mosque where I had stood in the morning; in another minute or two we were at the door of Joanna Correa. I now offered my kind guide a piece of silver as a remuneration for his trouble, whereupon he drew himself up and said:—

"The silver of my sultan I will not take, for I consider that I have done nothing to deserve it. We have not yet visited all the wonderful things of this blessed town. On a future day I will conduct my sultan to the castle of the governor, and to other places which my sultan will be glad to see; and when we have seen all we can, and my sultan is content with me, if at any time he see me in the soc of a morning, with my basket in my hand, and he see nothing in that basket, then is my sultan at liberty as a friend to put grapes in my basket, or bread in my basket, or fish or meat in my basket. That will I not refuse of my sultan, when I shall have done more for him than I have now. But the silver of my sultan will I not take now nor at any time." He then waved his hand gently and departed.

CHAPTER LVII.

Strange Trio—The Mulatto—The Peace-Offering—Moors of Granada—Vive la Guadeloupe—The Moors—Pascual Fava—Blind Algerine—The Retreat.

THREE men were seated in the wustuddur of Joanna Correa, when I entered; singular looking men they all were, though perhaps three were never gathered together more unlike to each other in all points. The first on whom I cast my eye was a man about sixty, dressed in a grey kerseymere coat with short lappets, yellow waistcoat, and wide coarse canvass trousers; upon his head was a very broad dirty straw hat, and in his hand he held a thick cane with ivory handle; his eyes were bleared and squinting, his face rubicund, and his nose much carbuncled. Beside him sat a good looking black, who perhaps appeared more negro than he really was, from the circumstance of his being dressed in spotless white jean—jerkin, waistcoat, and pantaloons being all of that material: his head gear consisted of a blue Montero cap. His eyes sparkled like diamonds, and there was an indescribable expression of good humour and fun upon his countenance. The third man was a Mulatto, and by far the most remarkable personage of the group: he might be between thirty and forty; his body was very long, and though uncouthly put together, exhibited every mark of strength and vigour; it was cased in a ferioul of red wool, a kind of garment which descends below the hips. His long muscular and hairy arms were naked from the elbow, where the sleeves of the ferioul terminate; his under limbs were short in comparison with his body and arms; his legs were bare, but he wore blue kandrisa as far as the knee; every feature of his face was ugly, exceedingly and bitterly ugly, and one of his eyes was sightless, being covered with a white film. By his side on the ground was a large barrel, seemingly a water-cask, which he occasionally seized with a finger and thumb, and waved over his head as if it had been a quart pot. Such was the trio who now occupied the wustuddur of Joanna Correa; and I had scarcely time to remark what I have just recorded, when that good lady entered from a back court with her handmaid Johár, or the pearl, an ugly fat Jewish girl, with an immense mole on her cheek.

"*Que Dios remate tu nombre,*" exclaimed the Mulatto; "may Allah blot out your name, Joanna, and may he likewise blot out that of your maid Johár. It is more than fifteen minutes that I have been seated here, after having poured out into the tinaja the water which I brought from the fountain, and during all that time I have waited in vain for one single word of civility from yourself or from Johár. *Usted no tiene modo,* you have no manner with you, nor more has Johár.— This is the only house in Tangier where I am not received with fitting love and respect, and yet I have done more for you than for any other person. Have I not filled your tinaja with water when other people have gone without a drop? When even the consul and the interpreter of the consul had no water to slake their thirst, have you not had enough to wash your wustuddur? And what is my return? When I arrive in the heat of the day, I have not one kind word spoken to me, nor so much as a glass of makhiah offered to me; must I tell you all that I do for you, Joanna? Truly I must, for you have no manner with you.— Do I not come every morning just at the third hour; and do I not knock at your door; and do you not arise and let me in, and then do I not knead your bread in your presence, whilst you lie in bed, and because I knead it, is not yours the best bread in Tangier? For am I

not the strongest man in Tangier, and the most noble also?" Here he brandished his barrel over his head and his face looked almost demoniacal. "Hear me, Joanna," he continued, "you know that I am the strongest man in Tangier, and I tell you again, for the thousandth time, that I am the most noble.— Who are the consuls? Who is the pasha? They are pashas and consuls now, but who were their fathers? I know not nor do they. But do I not know who *my* fathers were?— Were they not Moors of Garnata (*Granada*), and is it not on that account that I am the strongest man in Tangier? Yes, I am of the old Moors of Garnata, and my family has lived here, as is well known, since Garnata was lost to the Nazarenes, and now I am the only one of my family of the blood of the old Moors in all this land, and on that account I am of nobler blood than the sultan, for the sultan is not of the blood of the Moors of Garnata. Do you laugh, Joanna? Does your maid Johár laugh? Am I not Hammin Widder, *el hombre mas valido de Tanger?* And is it not true that I am of the blood of the Moors of Garnata? Deny it, and I will kill you both, you and your maid Johár."

"You have been eating hsheesh and majoon, Hammin," said Joanna Correa, "and the Shaitan has entered into you, as he but too frequently does. I have been busy, and so has Johár, or we should have spoken to you before; however, mai doorshee (*it does not signify*), I know how to pacify you now and at all times; will you take some gin-bitters, or a glass of common makhiah?"

"May you burst, O Joanna," said the Mulatto, "and may Johár also burst; I mean, may you both live many years, and know neither pain nor sorrow. I will take the gin-bitters, O Joanna, because they are stronger than the makhiah, which always appears to me like water; and I like not water though I carry it. Many thanks to you, Joanna; here is health to you, Joanna, and to this good company."

She had handed him a large tumbler filled to the brim; he put it to his nostrils, snuffed in the flavour, and then applying it to his mouth, removed it not whilst one drop of the fluid remained. His features gradually relaxed from their former angry expression, and looking particularly amiable at Joanna, he at last said:

"I hope that within a little time, O Joanna, you will be persuaded that I am the strongest man in Tangier, and that I am sprung from the blood of the Moors of Garnata, as then you will no longer refuse to take me for a husband, you and your maid Johár, and to become Moors. What a glory to you, after having been married to a Genoui, and given birth to Genouillos, to receive for husband a Moor like me, and to bear him children of the blood of Garnata. What a glory too for Johár, how much better than to marry a vile Jew, even like Hayim Ben Atar, or your cook Sabia, both of whom I could strangle with two fingers, for am I not Hammin Widder Moro de Garnata, *el hombre mas valido de*

Tanger?" He then shouldered his barrel and departed.

"Is that Mulatto really what he pretends to be?" said I to Joanna; "is he a descendant of the Moors of Granada?"

"He always talks about the Moors of Granada when he is mad with majoon or aguardiente," interrupted, in bad French, the old man whom I have before described, and in the same croaking voice which I had heard chanting in the morning. "Nevertheless it may be true, and if he had not heard something of the kind from his parents, he would never have imagined such a thing, for he is too stupid. As I said before, it is by no means impossible: many of the families of Granada settled down here when their town was taken by the Christians, but the greater part went to Tunis. When I was there, I lodged in the house of a Moor who called himself Zegri, and was always talking of Granada and the things which his forefathers had done there. He would moreover sit for hours singing romances of which I understood not one word, praised be the Mother of God, but which he said all related to his family; there were hundreds of that name in Tunis, therefore why should not this Hammin, this drunken water-carrier, be a Moor of Granada also. He is ugly enough to be emperor of all the Moors. O the accursed canaille, I have lived amongst them for my sins these eight years, at Oran and here. Monsieur, do you not consider it to be a hard case for an old man like myself, who am a Christian, to live amongst a race who know not God, nor Christ, nor any thing holy?"

"What do you mean," said I, "by asserting that the Moors know not God? There is no people in the world who entertain sublimer notions of the uncreated eternal God than the Moors, and no people have ever shown themselves more zealous for his honour and glory: their very zeal for the glory of God has been and is the chief obstacle to their becoming Christians. They are afraid of compromising his dignity by supposing that he ever condescended to become man. And with respect to Christ, their ideas even of him are much more just than those of the Papists, they say he is a mighty prophet, whilst, according to the others, he is either a piece of bread or a helpless infant. In many points of religion the Moors are wrong, dreadfully wrong, but are the Papists less so? And one of their practices sets them immeasurably below the Moors in the eyes of any unprejudiced person: they bow down to idols, Christian idols if you like, but idols still, things graven of wood and stone and brass, and from these things which can neither hear, nor speak, nor feel, they ask and expect to obtain favours."

"*Vive la France, Vive la Guadeloupe,*" said the black, with a good French accent. "In France and in Guadaloupe there is no superstition, and they pay as much regard to the Bible as to the Koran; I am now learning to read in order that I may understand the writings of Voltaire, who, as I am told, has proved that both the one and the other were written with the sole intention of deceiving mankind. *O vive la France!* where will you find such an enlightened country as France: and where will you find such a plentiful country as France? Only one in the world, and that is Guadaloupe. Is it not so, Monsieur Pascual? Were you ever at Marseilles? *Ah quel bon pais est celui-là pour les vivres, pour les petits poulets, pour les poulardes, pour les perdrix, pour les perdreaux, pour les alouettes, pour les bécasses, pour les bécassines, enfin, pour tout.*"

"Pray sir, are you a cook?" demanded I.

"*Monsieur, je le suis pour vous rendre service, mon nom c'est Gerard, et j'ai l'honneur d'être chef de cuisine chez monsieur le consul Hollandois. A present je prie permission de vous saluer; il faut que j'aille à la maison pour faire le dîner de mon maître.*"

At four I went to dine with the British consul. Two other English gentlemen were present, who had arrived at Tangier from Gibraltar about ten days previously, for a short excursion, and were now detained longer than they wished by the Levant wind. They had already visited the principal towns in Spain, and proposed spending the winter either at Cadiz or Seville. One of them, Mr. * * * *, struck me as being one of the most remarkable men I had ever conversed with; he travelled not for diversion nor instigated by curiosity, but merely with the hope of doing spiritual good, chiefly by conversation. The consul soon asked me what I thought of the Moors and their country; I told him that what I had hitherto seen of both highly pleased me. He said that were I to live amongst them for ten years, as he had done, he believed I should entertain a very different opinion; that no people in the world were more false and cruel; that their government was one of the vilest description, with which it was next to an impossibility for any foreign power to hold amicable relations, as it invariably acted with bad faith, and set at nought the most solemn treaties. That British property and interests were every day subjected to ruin and spoliation, and British subjects exposed to unheard-of vexations, without the slighest hope of redress being afforded, save recourse was had to force, the only argument to which the Moors were accessible. He added, that towards the end of the preceding year an atrocious murder had been perpetrated in Tangier, a Genoese family of three individuals had perished, all of whom were British subjects, and entitled to the protection of the British flag. The murderers were known, and the principal one was even now in prison for the fact, yet all attempts to bring him to condign punishment had hitherto proved abortive, as he was a Moor, and his victims Christians. Finally, he cautioned me not to take walks beyond the wall unaccompanied by a soldier, whom he offered to provide for me should I desire it, as otherwise I incurred great risk of being ill treated by the Moors of the interior whom I might meet, or perhaps murdered, and he instanced the case of a British officer who not long since had been murdered on the beach for no other reason than being a Nazarene, and appearing in a Nazarene dress. He at length introduced the subject of the Gospel, and I was pleased to learn that, during his residence in Tangier, he had distributed a considerable quantity of Bibles amongst the natives in the Arabic language, and that many of the learned men, or Talibs, had read the holy volume with great interest, and that by this distribution, which, it is true, was effected with much caution, no angry or unpleasant feeling had been excited. He finally asked whether I had come with the intention of circulating the Scripture amongst the Moors.

I replied that I had no opportunity of doing so, as I had not one single copy either in the Arabic language or character. That the few Testaments which were in my possession were in the Spanish language and were intended for circulation amongst the Christians of Tangier, to whom they might be serviceable, as they all understood the language.

It was night, and I was seated in the wustuddur of Joanna Correa, in company with Pascual Fava the Genoese. The old man's favourite subject of discourse appeared to be religion, and he professed unbounded love for the Saviour, and the deepest sense of gratitude for his miraculous atonement for the sins of mankind. I should have listened to him with pleasure had he not smelt very strongly of liquor, and by certain incoherences of language and wildness of manner given indications of being in some degree the worse for it. Suddenly two figures appeared beneath the doorway; one was that of a bare-headed and bare-legged Moorish boy of about ten years of age, dressed in a gelaba; he guided by the hand an old man, whom I at once recognised as one of the Algerines, the good Moslems of whom the old Mahasni had spoken in terms of praise in the morning whilst we ascended the street of the Siarrin. He was very short of stature and dirty in his dress; the lower part of his face was covered with a stubbly white beard; before his eyes he wore a large pair of spectacles, from which he evidently received but little benefit, as he required the assistance of the guide at every step. The two advanced a little way into the wustuddur and there stopped. Pascual Fava no sooner beheld them, than assuming a jovial air he started nimbly up, and leaning on his stick, for he had a bent leg, limped to a cupboard, out of which he took a bottle and poured out a glass of wine, singing in the broken kind of Spanish used by the Moors of the coast:

> " Argelino,
> Moro fino,
> No beber vino,
> Ni comer tocino."

> (Algerine,
> Moor so keen,
> No drink wine,
> No taste swine.)

He then handed the wine to the old Moor who drank it off, and then, led by the boy, made for the door without saying a word.

" *Hade mushe halal*," (that is not lawful,) said I to him with a loud voice.

" *Cul shee halal*," (every thing is lawful,) said the old Moor, turning his sightless and spectacled eyes in the direction from which my voice reached him. "Of every thing which God has given, it is lawful for the children of God to partake."

" Who is that old man ? " said I to Pascual Fava, after the blind and the leader of the blind had departed. "Who is he ! " said Pascual; " who is he! He is a merchant now, and keeps a shop in the Siarrin, but there was a time when no bloodier pirate sailed out of Algier. That old blind wretch has cut more throats than he has hairs in his beard. Before the French took the place he was the rais or captain of a frigate, and many was the poor Sardinian vessel which fell into his hands.— After that affair he fled to Tangier, and it is said that he brought with him a great part of the booty which he had amassed in former times. Many other Algerines came hither also, or to Tetuan, but he is the strangest guest of them all. He keeps occasionally very extraordinary company for a Moor, and is rather over intimate with the Jews. Well, that's no business of mine; only let him look to himself. If the Moors should once suspect him, it were all over with him. Moors and Jews, Jews and Moors! Oh my poor sins, my poor sins, that brought me to live amongst them !—

> ' Ave Maris stella,
> Dei Mater alma,
> Atque semper virgo,
> Felix cœli porta ! ' "

He was proceeding in this manner when I was startled by the sound of a musket. " That is the retreat," said Pascual Fava. "It is fired every night in the soc at half-past eight, and it is the signal for suspending all business, and shutting up. I am now going to close the doors, and whosoever knocks, I shall not admit them till I know their voice. Since the murder of the poor Genoese last year, we have all been particularly cautious.

Thus had passed Friday, the sacred day of the Moslems, and the first which I had spent in Tangier. I observed that the Moors followed their occupations as if the day had nothing particular in it. Between twelve and one, the hour of prayer in the mosque, the gates of the town were closed, and no one permitted either to enter or go out. There is a tradition current amongst them, that on this day, and at this hour, their eternal enemies, the Nazarenes, will arrive to take possession of their country; on which account they hold themselves prepared against a surprisal.

THE END.

CPSIA information can be obtained at www.ICGtesting.com
Printed in the USA
BVOW09*0220110216

436351BV00007B/39/P